MANAGEMENT
An Introduction

MANAGEMENT
An Introduction

SECOND EDITION

David Boddy
University of Glasgow

FINANCIAL TIMES
Prentice Hall

An imprint of **Pearson Education**

Harlow, England · London · New York · Reading, Massachusetts · San Francisco
Toronto · Don Mills, Ontario · Sydney · Tokyo · Singapore · Hong Kong · Seoul
Taipei · Cape Town · Madrid · Mexico City · Amsterdam · Munich · Paris · Milan

Pearson Education Limited

Edinburgh Gate
Harlow
Essex CM20 2JE

and Associated Companies throughout the world

Visit us on the World Wide Web at:
www.pearsoneduc.com

———————————

First published 1998 under the Prentice Hall Europe imprint
Second edition published 2002

© Prentice Hall Europe 1998
© Pearson Education Limited 2002

ISBN 0273 655183

British Library Cataloguing-in-Publication Data
A catalogue record for this book can be obtained from the British Library

Library of Congress Cataloging-in-Publication Data
Boddy, David.
    Management : an introduction / David Boddy. -- 2nd ed.
        p. cm.
    Originally published: New York : Prentice Hall, 1998.
    Includes bibliographical references and index.
    ISBN 0-273-65518-3
        1. Management. I. Title.

    HD31 .B583 2002
    658--dc21

                                          2001051381

10 9 8 7 6 5 4 3 2 1
06 05 04 03 02

Typeset in 10.5/12pt Minion Roman by 30
Printed and bound by Ashford Colour Press, Gosport, UK

Brief contents

Contents

Part 1   AN INTRODUCTION TO MANAGEMENT

Part 2 THE ENVIRONMENT OF MANAGEMENT

Part **5** **LEADING**

This book is intended for readers who are undertaking their first systematic exposure to the study of management. Most will be first-year undergraduates following courses leading to a qualification in management or business. Some will also be taking an introductory course in management as part of other qualifications (these may be in engineering, accountancy, law, information technology, science, nursing or social work) and others will be following a course in management as an element in their respective examination schemes. The book should also be useful to readers with a first degree or equivalent qualification in a non-management subject who are taking further studies leading to Certificate, Diploma or MBA qualifications.

The book has the following three main objectives:

- to provide newcomers to the formal study of management with an introduction to the topic;
- to show that ideas on management apply to most areas of human activity, not just to commercial enterprises; and
- to make the topic attractive to students from many backgrounds and with diverse career intentions.

Most research and reflection on management has focused on commercial organisations. However there are now many people working in the public sector and in not-for-profit organisations (charities, pressure groups, voluntary organisations and so on) who have begun to adapt management ideas to their own areas of work. The text reflects this wider interest in the topic. It should be as useful to those who plan to enter public or not-for-profit work as to those entering the commercial sector.

European perspective

The book presents the ideas from a European perspective. While many management concepts have developed in the United States, the text encourages readers to consider how their particular context shapes management practice. There are significant cultural differences that influence this practice, and the text alerts the reader to these – not only as part of an increasingly integrated Europe but as part of a wider international management community. So the text recognises European experience and research in management. The case studies and other material build an awareness of cultural diversity and the implications of this for working in organisations with different managerial styles and backgrounds.

Integrated perspective

To help the reader see management as a coherent whole, the material is presented within an integrative model of management and demonstrates the relationships between the many academic perspectives. The intention is to help the reader to see management as an integrating activity relating to the organisation as a whole, rather than as something confined to any one disciplinary or functional perspective.

While the text aims to introduce readers to the traditional mainstream perspectives on management which form the basis of each chapter, it also recognises that there is a newer body of ideas which looks at developments such as the weakening of national boundaries and the spread of information technology. Since they will affect the organisations in which readers will spend their working lives, these newer perspectives are introduced where appropriate. The text also recognises the more critical perspectives that some writers now take towards management and organisational activities. These are part of the intellectual world in which management takes place and have important practical implications for the way people interpret their role within organisations. The text introduces these perspectives at several points.

Relating to personal experience

The text assumes that many readers will have little if any experience of managing in conventional organisations, and equally little prior knowledge of relevant evidence and theory. However, all will have experience of being managed and all will have managed activities in their domestic and social lives. Wherever possible the book encourages readers to use and share such experiences from everyday life in order to explore the ideas presented. In this way the book tries to show that management is not a remote activity performed by others, but a process in which all are engaged in some way.

Most readers' careers are likely to be more fragmented and uncertain than was once the case and many will be working for medium-sized and smaller enterprises. They will probably be working close to customers and in organisations that incorporate diverse cultures, values and interests. The text therefore provides many opportunities for readers to develop skills of gathering data, comparing evidence, reflecting and generally enhancing self-awareness. It not only transmits knowledge but also aims to support the development of transferable skills through individual activities in the text and through linked tutorial work. The many cases and data collection activities are designed to develop generic skills such as communication, teamwork, problem solving and organising – while at the same time acquiring relevant knowledge.

Preface to the second edition

This second edition takes account of helpful comments from staff and students who used the first edition, and the suggestions of five anonymous reviewers. The book now has a much clearer and more logical structure of six parts, the first of which is introductory. The most obvious change has been to introduce a new part on the Environment of Management, bringing together three previously separate chapters. The other four parts now explicitly reflect the generic management functions of planning, organising, leading and controlling.

Three of the six Part Cases are new – BP Amoco, The Virgin Group and The Royal Bank of Scotland. There are also eight completely new chapter cases – Chem-Tec, Nokia, Marks & Spencer, the Millennium Dome, ABB, the Environment Agency, Quintiles and Boeing. There are many more specific examples of current management practice in each chapter, and there are over 100 new references.

The book encourages an active approach to learning, introducing many real-world case examples illustrating how real people have tackled the issues under discussion. The cases are widely representative – European and international as well as UK; private, public and not for profit; manufacturing and service. As well as adding interest to individual study they are also suitable for group work in tutorials. All the cases are original in this form (though some draw on other published material) and describe real situations – some of which were unresolved at the time of writing. Some have to be anonymous but most are clearly identified so that readers can follow later developments in the company.

The book has a clear structure and is divided into six parts. A *Part Case* begins each part, illustrating aspects of management that will be covered in the part. Relevant aspects of the case are referred to throughout. *Part Case Questions* end each chapter by relating one or more of the issues in the chapter to the larger case.

Each chapter begins with a two-page spread highlighting the *Aims* and *Learning Objectives* of the chapter, and a one-page chapter *Case Study*. The objectives are reflected in the *Review Questions* at the end, which are intended to help readers to check their understanding of the material. *Case Questions* are included throughout the chapter to encourage the practical application of the concepts and issues being discussed and to allow comparisons between cases.

A short *Summary* section relates the material of the chapter to the integrative framework described. There is also a short guide to *Further Reading* at the end of each chapter for those who want to study aspects of the topic more deeply.

The book includes short *Management in Practice* features, usually drawn from current business events. Active learning is also encouraged by two features in each chapter. *Key Ideas* contain summaries of major theories, contributions or empirical studies. *Activity* features pose questions, encourage data collection and prompt reflection and comparison between the topic and the reader's interests and experience. Teachers can develop many of these into group and tutorial activities.

The chapters are self-contained and do not have to be read in a particular order. There are obviously links between them, but teachers can use the material in the order that best suits their teaching plan, supporting their lectures and tutorials with the case and Activity material.

Key terms have been highlighted throughout the book and are defined in a comprehensive *Glossary* on page 576.

Lecturer support

An integrated Instructor's Manual has been prepared to accompany the text. This provides additional material to support the case and Activity features (see page xxii).

Guided tour

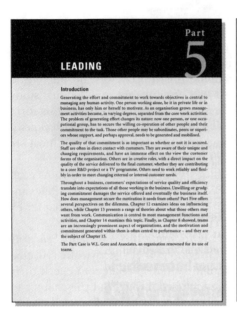

Part cases follow each part opening page and illustrate aspects of management that will be covered in the part. Relevant aspects of the case are referred to throughout the following part chapters

Case studies open each chapter and challenge students to apply management principles to real life situations

Case questions are included throughout the chapter to encourage the practical application of the concepts and to allow comparisons between cases

Learning objectives at the start of each chapter highlight the core coverage in terms of the learning outcomes students should acquire after studying each chapter, helping them evaluate their progress

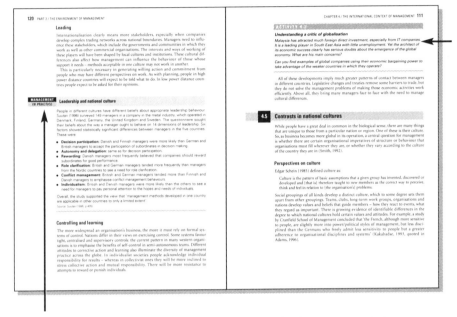

Activities pose questions, encourage data collection and prompt reflection and comparison between the topic and the student's interests and experience, and can be used independently or as part of group or tutorial activity

Management in Practice feature is drawn from current business events to help underpin the concepts and issues with real business examples

Key ideas contain summaries of major theories, contributions or empirical studies, encouraging students to familiarise themselves with and critically evaluate the key management ideas

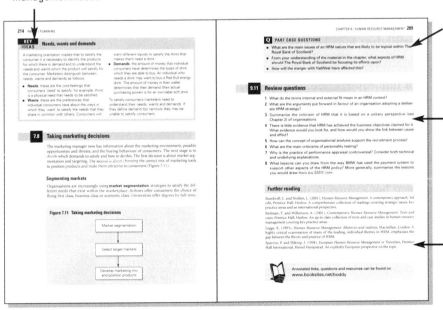

Part case questions appear at the end of each chapter and relate one or more of the issues in the chapter to the larger case featured in the relevant part opener

Review questions at the end of each chapter help the student review their understanding and/or critically assess what they have learnt, either individually or in a group

Annotated further reading encourages students to read more widely around the subject to promote criticality of thought

Companion Website

A Companion Website accompanies
MANAGEMENT: AN INTRODUCTION, 2nd edition
by David Boddy

Visit the *Management: An Introduction* Companion Website at
www.booksites.net/boddy to find valuable teaching and learning material including:

For Students:
- Study material designed to help you improve your results
- Multiple-choice questions to test your learning
- Weblinks to sites of interest
- Additional articles with associated questions

For Lecturers:
- A secure, password-protected site with teaching material
- A downloadable version of the full Instructor's Manual
- PowerPoint slides to use in your lectures
- A syllabus manager that will build and host your very own course web page

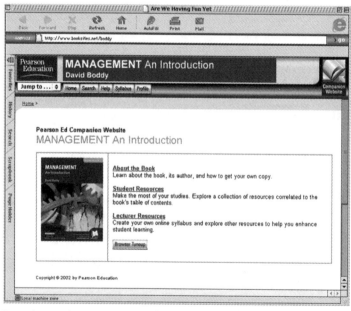

Screenshot reproduced by permission from Microsoft Corporation

Acknowledgements

This book has benefited from the comments, criticisms and suggestions of many colleagues and reviewers of the earlier edition. It also reflects the reactions and comments of students who have used sections of the material and earlier versions of some of the case material. Their advice and feedback have been of immense help.

Most of the chapters were written by the author, who has also edited the text throughout. I am grateful to these colleagues who contributed specific chapters: Alison More, Chapters 3 and 6; Dr Eleanor Shaw, Chapter 7; Iain Fraser and Dr Alison Price, Chapter 5; Professor Phil Beaumont and Dr Carol Boyd, Chapter 9; Douglas Briggs, Chapter 16; Professor Douglas Macbeth, Chapter 17; and Dr Albert Boonstra, Chapter 18. I am also grateful to Linda Dempster for The Benefits Agency case. Janie Ferguson, the Business School librarian, has willingly and efficiently searched for appropriate and unusual European sources. The errors and omissions in the text are my responsibility alone.

I also gratefully acknowledge the support and help that my wife, Cynthia, has provided throughout this project.

David Boddy
University of Glasgow, August 2001

Publisher's acknowledgements

We are grateful to the following for permission to reproduce copyright material:

Figure 2.2 from *Master Manager, 2nd Edition* by R.E. Quinn, S.R. Faerman. M.P. Thompson and M.R. McGrath. Copyright © 1996, John Wiley & Sons, Inc., New York. This material is used by permission of John Wiley & Sons, Inc; Figure 2.6 from Parker, D. and Stacey, R. (1994) *Chaos, Management and Economics*, Hobart Paper 125 reprinted by permission of the Institute of Economic Affairs; Figure 3.3 reprinted with the Permission of The Free Press, a Division of Simon & Schuster, Inc., from *Competitive Strategy: Techniques for Analyzing Industries and Competitors* by Michael E. Porter. Copyright © 1980, 1998 by The Free Press; Figures 3.5 and 6.3 from Johnson, G. and Scholes, K. (1999), *Exploring Corporate Strategy*, 5th Edition, Prentice Hall, Figure 6.6 from Mintzberg, H. (1994), *The Rise and Fall of Strategic Planning*, Prentice Hall, Figure 10.9 from Boddy, D. Boonstra, A. and Kennedy, G. (2002), *Information Systems: An organisational perspective*, Financial Times Prentice Hall and Table 11.4 from Boddy, D, (2001), *Managing Projects*, Financial Times Prentice Hall, reprinted by permission of Pearson Education Limited; Table 4.1 from *The Management of a Multicultural Workforce* by M.H. Tayeb. Copyright 1996, © John Wiley & Sons Limited. Reproduced with permission; Figures 6.2, 6.4 and 18.6 reprinted and/or adapted with the Permission of The Free Press, a Division of Simon & Schuster, Inc., from *Competitive Advantage: Creating and Sustaining Superior Performance* by Michael E. Porter. Copyright © 1985, 1998 by Michael E. Porter; Figure 8.8 from *Organizational Behaviour: Managerial Strategies for*

Performance, 1 Edition by Middlemist and Hitt, © 1998. Reprinted with permission of South-Western College Publishing, a division of Thomson Learning. Fax 800 730 2215; Table 9.1 from Guest, D. (1998) *The Occupational Psychologist*, February 1998 reprinted by permission of the British Psychological Society; Figure 10.4 from Woodward, *Management and Technology* reprinted by permission of Her Majesty's Stationery Office, Crown Copyright © 1958; Figure 12.5 reprinted from *Leadership and Decision Making* by Victor H. Vroom and Philip W. Yetton, by permission of the University of Pittsburgh Press. © 1973 by University of Pittsburgh Press; Table 13.3 reprinted from *European Management Journal*, 1995, Vol. 13, No. 3, J.M. Hiltrop, 'The changing psychological contract: the human resources challenge of the 1990s', pp.288–94. Copyright 1995, with permission from Elsevier Science; Fig. 13.8 from 'The empowerment of service workers: what, why, how and when?' by D.E. Bowen and E.E.Lawler, *Sloan Management Review*, Spring 1992, Vol. 33, No. 3, by permission of Los Angeles Times Syndicate International; Table 15.1 reprinted by permission of Harvard Business School Press from *The Wisdom of Teams* by J.R. Katzenbach and D.K. Smith. Boston, MA. Copyright © 1993 by the Harvard Business School Publishing Corporation, all rights reserved; Tables 15.2, 15.3, and 15.4 from *Groups That Work (And Those That Don't)* by J.R. Hackman. Copyright © 1990, Jossey-Bass, San Francisco. This material is used by permission of John Wiley & Sons, Inc. The Association of MBAs for an extract from 'Negotiating with other Europeans' by Balle and Gottschalk published in *Management Extra*; The Body Shop International plc for extracts from *The Body Shop: A Case Study*; and *The Economist* Newspaper Limited for an extract from The Economist 27th February 1993.

We are grateful to the Financial Times Limited for permission to reprint the following material:

Coping with economic pressures at Compaq, © *Financial Times*, 26 June, 2001; Is Brazil a worthwhile place for another car plant?, © *Financial Times*, 4 April, 2001; The legal side of business in Russia, © *Financial Times*, 12 July, 2001; Psion, © *Financial Times*, 12 July, 2001; ABB – the case continues – the company changes to a divisional structure, © *Financial Times*, 12 January, 2001; Changing structures as Internet firms mature, © *Financial Times*, 25 February, 2001; Two leaders' styles, © *Financial Times*, 8 December, 2000; Two leaders' styles, © *Financial Times*, 15 February, 2001; Two leaders' styles, © *Financial Times*, 24 February, 2001; Dell Computing, © *Financial Times*, 20 June, 2001; Figure 16.1 Pre-tax profits compared: Halifax/Bank of Scotland, © *Financial Times*, 5–6 May, 2001; Table 3.1 Forecast of online grocery sales, 2005, © *Financial Times*, July 2001; Table 12.4 Traits of those leading some of the world's most respected companies, 2000, © *Financial Times*, 15 December, 2000.

In some instances we have been unable to trace the owners of copyright material, and we would appreciate any information that would enable us to do so.

Part 1

AN INTRODUCTION TO MANAGEMENT

Introduction

This part considers why management exists and what it contributes to human wealth and well-being. Management as a universal human activity is distinguished from management as a distinct occupation. All of us manage in the first sense, as we organise our lives and deal with family and other relationships. We are all affected by the activities of those who manage in the second sense, as employees and customers. As business becomes more international so does the work of those managing businesses. The geographical scope changes, and in some respects so does the nature of the work as it is influenced by different national cultures and institutions.

Chapter 1, then, clarifies the nature and emergence of management and the different ways in which the role has been described. It argues that management is not a neutral, technical activity: it inevitably involves some degree of controversy as the manager balances the expectations of stakeholders and interest groups. They have different views about what counts as success. The chapter concludes with some discussion and ideas about managing your study of the topic. You are likely to benefit most by actively linking your work on this book to events in real organisations, and the chapter includes some ideas on that.

Chapter 2 sets out the main theoretical perspectives on management and shows how these can complement each other despite apparently competing underlying values about the nature of the management task. You are again encouraged to be active in relating these theoretical perspectives to real events to understand and test the theory.

The Part Case is The Body Shop, a leading retailer with extensive international operations. It is an organisation with two missions: to produce personal care products for a profit, and to create a vehicle for environmental education and practical social activism. It has also developed a controversial approach to management which contrasts sharply with that of conventional businesses.

The Body Shop International

Anita Roddick opened the first Body Shop in 1976:

My main motivation for going into the cosmetics business was irritation: I was annoyed that you couldn't buy small sizes of everyday cosmetics ... I also recognised that a lot of the money I was paying for a product was being spent on fancy packaging which I didn't want. So I opened a small shop to sell a small range of cosmetics made from natural ingredients in ... the cheapest possible plastic containers. (Roddick, 1991, p.19)

The company has grown rapidly and in 1997 had over 1,500 outlets around the world and in Europe.

What is wonderful about The Body Shop is that we still don't know the rules. Instead we have a basic understanding that to run this business you don't have to know anything. Skill is not the answer, neither is money. What you need is optimism, humanism, enthusiasm, intuition, curiosity, love, humour, magic and fun and that secret ingredient – euphoria. The status quo says that the business of business is to make profits. We have always challenged that. For us the business of business is to keep the company alive and breathlessly excited, to protect the workforce, to be a force for good in society and then, after all that, to think of the speculators. I have never kow-towed to the speculators or considered them to be my first responsibility. They play the market without much concern for the company or its values.

Social and environmental issues are woven into the fabric of the company itself. They are neither first or last among our objectives, but an ongoing part of what we do. Not a single decision is ever taken in Body Shop without considering environmental and social issues. We have an Environmental Projects Department which monitors the company's practices and products to ensure they are environmentally sound and up to date. We have a simple credo. You can run a business differently from the way most businesses are run: you can share your prosperity with your employees and empower them without being in fear of them: you can rewrite the book of how a company interacts with the community: you can rewrite the book on third world trade and on global responsibility and on the role of educating the company, customers and shareholders. You can do all this and still play the game according to the City, still raise money, delight the institutions and give shareholders a wondrous return on their money. (p.24)

The Body Shop's mission – 'Our reason for being' – is 'To dedicate our business to the pursuit of social and environmental change'. The mission statement is followed by five objectives intended to support it:

- To creatively balance the financial and human needs of our stakeholders: employees, customers, franchisees, suppliers and shareholders.
- To courageously ensure that our business is ecologically sustainable, meeting the needs of the present without compromising the future.
- To meaningfully contribute to local, national and international communities in which we trade, by adopting a code of conduct which ensures care, honesty, fairness and respect.
- To passionately campaign for the protection of the environment and human and civil rights, and against animal testing within the cosmetics and toiletries industry.
- To tirelessly work to narrow the gap between principle and practice, while making fun, passion and care part of our daily lives.

These values clearly stem from Anita Roddick's personal principles that have guided her in building up The Body Shop. She and her husband Gordon believe fervently that business must be a force for social and environmental change. Business organisations are not just for profit – their resources can be used to promote wider purposes. This inspiration and the set of values associated guide the trading principles of Body Shop management, which are:

- We aim to ensure that human and civil rights, as set out in the Universal Declaration of Human Rights, are respected throughout our business activities.
- We will support long term, sustainable relationships with communities in need.
- We will use environmentally sustainable resources wherever technically and economically viable.
- We will promote animal protection throughout our business activities and in many ways.

● We will institute appropriate monitoring, auditing and disclosure mechanisms to ensure our accountability and demonstrate our compliance with these principles.

The products are sold in refillable containers as part of the company's commitment to reducing packaging and waste. Environmental campaigns are promoted through the shops, with posters and information sheets designed to promote customer awareness of current threats and campaigns. Customers are encouraged to use the recycling service which entitles them to a discount. To help balance the energy used on the company's properties, management has invested in a wind-power development in Wales. The project had the support of the local community and was done in association with National Power, an electricity generating company.

In the past, the cosmetics industry routinely tested new products on animals. The Body Shop campaigned vigorously against this. It raised public awareness of the issue through its campaigns, and its Ethical Audit Department monitors the ingredients used to ensure that the suppliers have not tested them on animals.

Many of its ingredients come from suppliers in poor countries. The company uses its resources not just to buy the products but also to help the communities from whom it buys to achieve sustainable economic independence. It buys directly from the small producers (rather than through intermediate trading companies). It also supplies technical assistance to them to ensure sustainable and good quality supplies, as well as supporting the wider aspects of a community's development. Dismayed by the economic conditions in a deprived part of Glasgow, the company set up a plant in the area to make most of its soap.

The structure of the company is shown in Figure 1. About three-quarters of the shops are owned by franchisees. These are business people who provide the capital for a shop and the stock, and then run the shop. They do this under strict Body Shop guidelines which ensure that the brand image is projected consistently. The Body Shop provides advice and support in setting up and running the outlet but the franchisee is responsible for recruiting and managing staff and for making the shop a success.

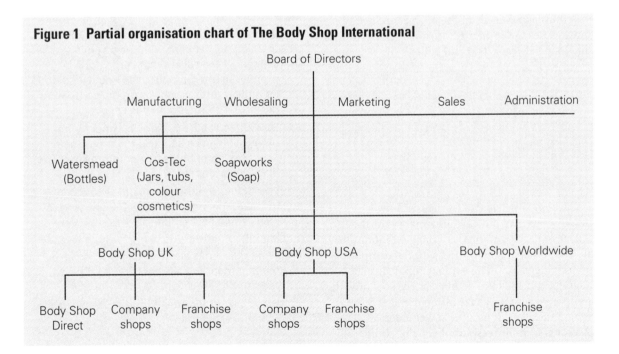

Figure 1 Partial organisation chart of The Body Shop International

Franchisees are carefully selected to ensure that they are fully committed to Anita Roddick's vision of the business. The company's culture values people who are able to work enthusiastically as a team to promote the mission. Specific financial or retailing experience is less important as this can be learned. The values are maintained and spread by many personal visits to the stores by the Roddicks. They also send a weekly video to all stores keeping staff up to date with developments elsewhere in the business and with news of the company's current environmental campaigns.

The mission statement itself is an attempt to institutionalise and systematise these values. The Roddicks hope that this will help to keep the values at the front of staff's minds even though the growth in the company means that staff are increasingly remote from the personal energy and charisma of the founder.

This charisma helped to hold the company together in the early days. As it grew and prepared to issue shares to the public in 1984 (to finance further expansion), more systematic ways of managing the business were needed. More professional managers were recruited at that time. There is a constant need to balance the values and the commercial needs of the business. The table summarises the company's turnover and profit for the financial years 2000 and 2001.

	2001 (53 weeks) £m	2000 (52 weeks) £m
Retail sales	691.4	596.6
Profit attributable to shareholders	9.5	18.4
Earnings per share (p)	5.0	9.6

The company has also formalised how it monitors its own ethical performance. As the business has grown there is a danger that decisions are taken that are out of line with the company's underlying values. The Annual Report for 2001 includes (pp.14–15) a detailed analysis of how the company's activities have affected 'stakeholder value indicators'. It lists the stakeholders as customers, employees, suppliers, shareholders, local communities, franchisees and the environment. It also records how it has developed formal mechanisms for consulting these stakeholder groups since 1994. For example, it records that in 2000–1 it held 4,000 customer interviews in nine countries, as well as focus groups with employees and suppliers. The growing 'social audit' process was verified by an independent foundation and a panel of independent experts on social issues.

Another issue for the company is to develop managers who can become future leaders of The Body Shop. Anita Roddick has said:

[We must] make sure that we don't suppress the leadership of our staff. By their nature big organizations always suppress leadership. They always do. It's their nature, their bigness. Our young people are born into a society that is very huge and impersonal going to large schools and large cities. I want to find ways of mentoring to encourage more moral leadership in our company.

Sources: extracts from Roddick (1991); 'The Body Shop: a case study', Kellogg School, North Western University, Case No. 495-019-8; Company Annual Reports; website: www.thebodyshop.com

Q PART CASE QUESTIONS

- If you have not done so, visit a Body Shop so that you are familiar with the physical aspects of the case. What campaigns is it running at the moment? You could also build up a file of press cuttings on the company's performance to update this account.

- How does The Body Shop compare with other companies selling similar products? Are other companies beginning to copy The Body Shop approach?

- What clues are there in the case about ways in which the individual founder is trying to institutionalise her ideas in this now very large company?

- What dilemmas are there likely to be for management in an organisation with two missions?

There will be other questions about the case in the chapters that follow.

CHAPTER 1

Managing in organisations

> **AIM** *To introduce the functions, processes and context of managerial work in organisations.*

OBJECTIVES

By the end of your work on this chapter you should be able to outline the ideas below in your own terms and:

1 Summarise the functions of organisations and how management affects their performance

2 Describe how management is both a universal activity and a distinct occupational role

3 Distinguish between the roles of functional, general, line, staff and project managers

4 Summarise the functions that make up the content of managerial work

5 Compare a functional view with research into the processes of managerial work

6 Identify the elements of the organisational context in which managers work

7 Give examples of how gender affects management

8 Explain the meaning of a critical perspective on management

9 Begin your active study of the topic by identifying sources of ideas

Chem-Tec

Chem-Tec is a small company created in 1990 to provide high quality chemicals for the semiconductor industry. It has a head office and a manufacturing site in the United States and in 1996 opened a site in the United Kingdom (Chem-Tec Ltd). In 2001 Chem-Tec Ltd. employed about 40 staff, and the the senior management team consisted of a chief executive, a commercial manager and a manufacturing manager. The latter, Bill Johnson, describes recent events:

> As manufacturing manager I am responsible for purchasing and receiving raw materials, production planning, production systems, packaging, inventory and shipment. About a year ago the parent company decided to implement a new information system which would allow us to receive consistent information about all aspects of the business. It's an Enterprise Resource Planning (ERP) system which combines all the separate company information systems.
>
> My role meant that I was heavily involved in designing the systems with the supplier and I became the manufacturing lead in implementing the project not just at Chem-Tec Ltd but also at head office and the Chem-Tec Inc. manufacturing site.
>
> The initial aim was to improve financial control across the whole company. But as we learned more about the potential of the system I realised that there were further possible benefits such as more consistent reporting across both manufacturing sites. This was agreed, but I became aware that there were differences of approach between the United States and UK sites. In the United States they intended the new system should match current practice to minimise the training effort. At Chem-Tec Ltd I wanted to use ERP to challenge all the current business systems, and where necessary change them. Several other critical changes were being implemented simultaneously, and they all required significant input from myself.
>
> The working environment at Chem-Tec Ltd is vibrant, dynamic, where change is welcomed rather than feared. There is only one employee over 45 and the average age of the management team is 35. Within the Chem-Tec Group we see ourselves as separate and view our decisions as autonomous because 'Europe is very different from the United States or Asia'.

Source: Personal communication.

Q Case questions

- Who is the manufacturing manager managing?
- How would you describe his relationship with corporate HQ?
- What are the main demands in his job?

1.1 Introduction

This chapter introduces the following ideas:

- Organisations
- Value
- Manager
- Management as a general human activity
- Management as a specialist occupation
- Role
- Functional, general, line and staff managers
- Management functions
- Management roles
- Critical perspective

The Chem-Tec case illustrates several aspects of management. A group of entrepreneurs created an organisation to make a product that customers in a high-technology, growing area of the economy are willing to buy. The company does this by bringing resources together and transforming them into something with greater value – which they sell to the customers. To be closer to their European customers the US-based company opened a UK plant, so that the activities of the enterprise take place at plants in different countries, which nevertheless need to work together. The parent company introduces a new system, which the manager in the United Kingdom sees can do much more than those at head office realise. He is under pressure to meet current manufacturing requirments, but at the same time wants to influence head office to make more radical changes.

Some managers are always looking for opportunities to innovate and make the most of new opportunities such as the Internet. Publishing companies such as Associated Newspapers (publishers of the *Daily Mail*, a leading UK title) have responded by creating a new division, Associated New Media (ANM), whose managers focus on building a new business on the Internet. Other managers face a different challenge – to meet growing demand with fewer resources. In almost every public health care organisation managers face a growing demand for treatment, but find it difficult to secure the resources they require to meet that demand. A new management team at British Airways is working to turn the airline from loss to profit by concentrating on a different, and more profitable, group of pasengers. This will mean managing substantial internal changes.

Organisations of all kinds – from relatively small operations such as Chem-Tec to large, established businesses such as Associated Newspapers or British Airways – depend on people who can manage stable, continuing activities and who can also drive change. They need people at all levels who can keep things running efficiently now, and at the same time anticipate changes in the external world. This book is about the knowledge and skills that enable managers to deal with these internal and external expectations. Both need to be satisfied if an organisation is to survive and prosper.

Figure 1.1 illustrates the themes of this chapter. It represents the fact that people draw inputs such as other people, finance and materials from the external environment and manage their transformation into an output that they hope is of greater value than the inputs. They pass the outputs back to the environment. The value they obtain for their outputs (money, reputation, goodwill etc.) enables them to continue attracting resources to continue in business (shown by the feedback arrow from output to input). If the outputs fail to generate sufficient new resources the enterprise fails – its performance has not been good enough to generate the support it needs.

Figure 1.1 Managing organisation and environment

The chapter begins by examining the significance of managed organisations in our world. It then outlines what management means and introduces theories about the nature of managerial work. Finally it shows how managerial work interacts with the organisation and the external environment.

ACTIVITY 1.1

What is management?

Write a few notes summarising what you think 'management' means. You might find it helpful to think of instances in which you have encountered 'management' – when you have been managed, or when you have managed something. Keep the notes where you can refer to them later.

1.2 Management and organisation

Organisations affect most aspects of our lives. We live in communities, families, households, groups of friends, all of which help to shape our lives. Those communities are part of the wider societies that also contain economic and political organisations. We live in a world of managed **organisations**. In a normal day we experience many organisations – domestic arrangements of various kinds (family or flatmates), large public organisations (the postal service), small businesses (the newsagent), well-known private companies (which made the jar of coffee), or a voluntary group (the club where we attended a meeting). They have an effect on us and we make some judgement about the encounter. Did the transaction work smoothly or was it surrounded by chaos? Was the service good, reasonable, poor? Will you go there again?

If you feel good about an organisation it probably means that people are managing it well, and so creating wealth or human well-being. Most resources – people, equipment, land, finance – are fundamentally scarce, and so people have to choose what to use them for, and how to use them. Nothing happens without some human intervention. People create wealth or well-being when they manage resources in a way that adds **value** to them. Gerard Egan (1993) wrote:

> Well-run businesses create wealth for the societies in which they operate. While for-profit businesses create material wealth, not-for-profit and human service institutions create human capital or wealth. Counselling the troubled and helping them manage problems in living more effectively, creating learning opportunities for young and old alike, helping children grow and develop, healing the sick ... all these activities create human capital, human wealth. Furthermore since the best for-profit companies tend to develop [the skills and abilities of their staff] in the pursuit of financial goals, they benefit society by creating both material and human wealth. (p.9)

Some organisations work inefficiently, use resources to do things that people do not value, or create excessive pollution and waste. Management is then reducing value and destroying wealth – as many investors in failed dot.com companies have found. Thousands of the new companies founded during the late 1990s to exploit the Internet have failed, as they were unable to convince enough customers of the value of what they were offering. Companies can also waste material things and destroy socially valued assets. If the management of a motorway construction site fails to plan deliveries properly staff will be paid for doing nothing while they await materials. So the road will be late, and cost more than if its construction had been well managed. This will be a problem for the contracting company, perhaps for the users, but for no one else.

Some will take a more critical view. If they oppose a motorway being built through an area of woodland rich in wildlife, or because it will add to pollution, they will not regard the activities of the construction company as adding wealth to society. They will see it as using resources in a way that destroys some of our natural wealth. Even if the construction has been managed efficiently it would still have destroyed valuable assets and placed long-term costs on society. From this perspective management will be reducing, not creating, value. The idea of wealth creation is a subjective and relative matter.

Organisations perform other functions as well as economic ones. They enable people to share common causes and interests. Charities such as Oxfam or Greenpeace were created by a few like-minded individuals. They have become worldwide organisations with significant resources and operations for raising funds and managing their charitable activities. Other organisations serve particular interests – such as Unison, a trade union that represents workers in the UK public sector, or the Law Society, which defends the interests of lawyers. Firms in most industries create trade organisations to protect their interests by lobbying or public relations work. Organisations of all kinds can provide psychological support for members and non-members. Table 1.1 summarises these organisational functions.

Whatever its function, how well an organisation performs depends on those who work within it. Luck plays a part, but most of the time it is the quality of management which makes the difference between an organisation that fails and one that succeeds.

ACTIVITY 1.2

Managing in voluntary organisations

Voluntary bodies are organisations too. Charities and other kinds of voluntary group are big business. A recent estimate is that UK charities have an annual income of £16 billion and employ 250,000 people – and have perhaps another 1.5 million volunteer staff. All that needs managing. If you are connected with a voluntary group of any kind, reflect on how it is managed. How is it different from a business?

Table 1.1 Some functions of organisations

Functions	Description	Examples
Create wealth or human well-being	By providing goods and services that people value	Commercial and public organisations
Articulating and implementing ideals	Individuals with an interest in a topic, or a passion to change something, usually need the tangible or moral support of others	Charities, protest groups or political parties
Gaining power to protect sectional interests	Large organisations have access to political and economic resources beyond those of individuals	Trade unions, professional associations and industry groups
Give people work, status and social contact	A source of careers and training as well as immediate jobs, of contact with others, of a wider outlook, a source of structure in life	Any long-lasting and respected organisation

1.3 Meanings of management

Management as a general human activity

The skills required to run an organisation well are not confined to people called managers. As individuals we run our own lives, and in this respect we are managing. Management is both a **general human activity** and a distinct occupation. In the first sense, people manage an infinite range of activities as well as economic ones:

> When human beings 'manage' their work, they take responsibility for its purpose, progress and outcome by exercising the quintessentially human capacity to stand back from experience and to regard it prospectively, in terms of what will happen; reflectively, in terms of what is happening; and retrospectively, in terms of what has happened. Thus management is an expression of human agency, the capacity actively to shape and direct the world, rather than simply react to it. (Hales, 1993, p.2)

Rosemary Stewart (1967) expressed this idea of the universality of management when she described a **manager** as someone who gets things done with the aid of other people. So described, the activity takes place in a great variety of human circumstances – domestic, social and political, as well as in formally established organisations.

In pre-industrial societies work is typically done by people on their own or in family units. They retain control of their time and other resources used in producing goods or delivering services. They decide what to make, how to make it and how or when to sell it. Management and work are intertwined in the process of creating goods and services. Self-employed craftworkers, many professionals in small practices or individuals running a one-person business combine both activities. We all do it when we work on household tasks or take part in voluntary activities in which we do the work (planting trees or rattling a can) and the management activities (planning the winter programme).

ACTIVITY 1.3

An accurate definition?

- *Does Rosemary Stewart's definition accurately describe 'management'? Test it by choosing some domestic, community or business activity you have undertaken.*
- *Does it capture, very broadly, what you did?*
- *What more specific things did you do to 'get things done with the aid of other people'?*

Management as a specialist occupation

Human action can also separate these activities so that the 'management' element becomes distinct from the 'work' element. This separation creates 'managers' who are in some degree separated from those doing the core work.

Management as a specialist occupation emerges when external agents, such as a private owner of capital, or the state, gain some control of a work process that a person used to complete in its entirety. They then decide what to make, how to make it and where to sell it. They take responsibility for some elements of management previously integrated with the work itself – even if their job titles do not include the term 'management'. Previously independent workers become employees, selling their labour rather than the results of their labour. During the process of industrialisation in western economies factory owners took control of the physical and financial means of production. They also tried to take control of the time, behaviour and skills of those who were now employees rather than autonomous workers.

The same evolution takes place when an individual or a partnership starts an enterprise. While it is a one- or two-person operation management and ownership functions are combined. The owner or the partners perform all the management functions involved in the work as well as the work itself. If the business grows and employees are engaged the owners or partners take over certain management activities, leaving employees with more limited responsibilities. This creates the distinct occupational role of management – a **role** being the expectations that others have of the person occupying it.

KEY IDEAS   **Tony Watson (1994) on separating roles**

All humans are managers in some way. But some of them also take on the formal occupational work of being managers. They take on a role of shaping .... work organisations. But these managers are not supermen and women. They have all the human anxieties, inadequacies and needs for meaning to be found in those whom they are meant to 'manage'. Managers' work thus involves a double ... task: managing others at the same time as managing themselves. But the very notion of 'managers' being separate people from the 'managed', a notion at the heart of traditional management thinking, undermines a capacity to handle this. Managers are pressured to be technical experts, devising rational and emotionally neutral systems and corporate structures to 'solve problems', 'make decisions', 'run the business'. These 'scientific' and rational-analytic practices give reassurance but can leave managers so distanced from the 'managed' that their capacity to control events is undermined. And they also tend to leave managers isolated from the essentially human community which the organisation might be. This can mean that their own emotional and security needs are not handled, with the effect that they retreat into all kinds of defensive, backbiting and ritualistic behaviour which further undermines their effectiveness. (pp.12–13)

This separation of management and non-management work is not inevitable or permanent. People have deliberately separated the roles, and on other occasions have brought them together. Chester Barnard (1938) in the United States and Henri Fayol (1949) in France both pointed out the fluidity of the division. Barnard observed that while what he called executive work was distinct, executives themselves would often undertake the technical work of the organisation. Fayol wrote that:

> Management ... is neither an exclusive privilege nor a particular responsibility of the head or senior members of a business; it is an activity spread, like all other activities, between head and members of the body corporate. (p.6)

> ### CASE STUDY   Chem-Tec – changing boundaries – the case continues

Bill Johnson has used the opportunity of the ERP system to pass many of his responsibilities to the operators:

> The operators are making decisions, whereas before they looked to me. Before they knew about the operations, but didn't have the information. Now they have the information, and understand the significance of what they are doing. As a process finishes they key in what's happened (such as the materials used) and they realise that is going to inform management activities. I've asked them to structure the reports, investigate any problems and talk to me about them. They can now plan production and raise purchase orders – which is a big change. Before it was left to me to check how much raw material we had and decide if we needed to order some. Now they know what they've used, decide if they need to order more, and manage the offsite warehouse. I'm no longer part of that process – it's great.

Source: Personal communication.

> ### Q Case questions 1.1
>
> - What specialised management functions have been created at Chem-Tec?
> - What is Bill Johnson doing to break the established boundaries?
> - How are others reacting?

Someone in charge of part of an organisation, say a production department, will usually be treated as a manager, and referred to as one. The people who operate the machines will be called something else. Managers such as Bill Johnson at Chem-Tec Ltd are changing the boundaries, so that 'non-managers' perform significant management tasks irrespective of their title.

1.4   Specialisation between areas of management

As organisations become larger management itself becomes divided. Senior managers create separate management functions, and a management hierarchy develops.

Functional specialisation

Functional managers are those responsible for a single common activity within the organisation, such as personnel, research, marketing or production. Most of their staff will be specialists in those areas, and typically the manager will have worked in that area. At Safeway, a UK supermarket group, there are managers in charge of functions such as marketing, supply, trading and stores.

General managers typically head a complete unit of the organisation, such as a division or a subsidiary, within which there will be several functions. The general manager is responsible for the overall performance of the unit, and therefore relies on the managers in charge of particular functions. A small organisation will have just one or two general managers, who will also manage specific functions. At Safeway the most senior general manager in 2001 was Carlos Criado-Perez, the chief executive.

Line managers are those in charge of a function that is directly involved in making or supplying products or services to customers. Depending on their level they will be in charge of a retail store, a group of nurses, a social work department or a manufacturing area. Their performance has a significant impact on the performance and image of the organisation, as they and their staff are in direct contact with the customers or clients. Mike Street is the director of Customer Services and Operations at British Airways, and leads the 25,000 staff in the company who are in direct contact with passengers – on the ground and in the air.

Staff managers are in charge of support functions such as finance, personnel, purchasing or legal affairs. These functions do not earn income directly for the organisation, and their staff are not usually in direct contact with external customers. Their customers are the line departments of their own organisation, so although their impact on outside customers may not be direct it will affect the performance of the line departments. In managing their own staff, heads of such departments operate as line managers. At Safeway managers in charge of support areas such as finance or human resources advise line managers in charge of the stores.

Project managers are reponsible for a temporary team that has been created to plan and implement a change – a new product or system, for example. Mike Buckingham, an engineer, was responsible for managing a project to invest milllions of pounds in new manufacturing plants at a truck plant owned by Leyland Vehicles. He still had line responsibilities for some aspects of manufacturing, but worked for most of the time on the project. To help him he had a team of technical specialists from around the organisation. When the project was complete he went back to his line job for a few months and then took on another change project.

Management hierarchies

As organisations grow, senior managers usually create a hierarchy of positions. The amount of 'management' and 'non-management' work within these positions varies.

Performing direct operations

People who who perform direct operations do the manual and mental work to produce and deliver products or services. These range from low-skilled ancillary activities, through skilled or technical work, to highly paid professionals such as lawyers and doctors. The activity is likely to contain some aspects of management work, though in lower-level jobs this will be limited.

Managing staff on direct operations

Sometimes called supervisors or first-line managers, these managers ensure that staff perform the daily operations of the organisation. They also help to overcome any difficulties that arise. Examples would include the supervisor of a production team, the head chef in a hotel, a nurse in charge of other nurses in a hospital ward or the manager of a bank branch. They will probably spend less time on direct operations than their subordinates except in small companies. The example of Barings illustrates a case in which senior management failed to control a member of staff, with disastrous consequences for the bank.

Whatever happened at Barings?

On 27 February 1995 Barings, one of the UK's oldest merchant banks, collapsed following the revelation that one of its Singapore traders, Nick Leeson, had accumulated losses of over £800 million in trading financial products. The initial response by the senior management of the bank was to place all the blame for the disaster on the individual trader – who had clearly acted in an unauthorised and fraudulent way. Inquiries into the incident told a different story:

> While it is true that Leeson traded in an unauthorised fashion ... it is astonishing that the layers of controls and supervision ... failed to detect the fiasco, or to pick up warning signals ... Both official inquiries conclude that the failure at Barings was not due to the complexity of the business undertaken. The UK report states that: 'The failings ... were primarily a failure on the part of a number of individuals to do their job properly'.
>
> First, the organisation structure was ill-defined ... Leeson had confused reporting lines locally and to head office. He was left in the astonishing position of being in charge of both the front office [trading] and back office [settlements] which allowed him ... to cover up ...
>
> Second, Barings internal audit failed to act upon warnings ... that the concentration of power in Leeson's hands was a potentially explosive situation ...
>
> Third, although Barings managed risk through an Asset and Liability Committee ... vast funds were remitted to Leeson from within the group [which] were never subject to credit check.

Source: extracts from Stonham (1996).

Managing managers

Usually referred to as middle managers (a very numerous group), these managers – such as Bill Johnson at Chem-Tec – are expected to ensure that the supervisors work in line with broader company policies. They check whether performance targets are being met, keep in touch with what is happening and provide support or pressure as required. They also form a communication link, ensuring that information flows up and down the organisation. They tell first-line managers what they expect, and brief senior management about developments deep down in the business. They spend time managing other managers at the same level and those above them in the hierarchy. Some have close and frequent links with managers in other organisations on whom they depend in some way. The performance of middle managers is evaluated largely on how well they manage other managers.

Managing the business

Managing the business is the work of a relatively small group of people who are responsible for the overall direction and performance of the organisation. These managers establish policy and have a particular responsibility for managing relations with people and institutions in the world outside, such as shareholders, media, elected representatives. They need to be aware of the internal detail, and able to comprehend it, but spend most of their time looking to the future or dealing with external affairs. They will spend little, if any, of their time on direct operations – though in small companies they will usually remain directly involved. At Safeway the Operations Board deals with this, and is made up of the chief executive and the directors responsible for supply, trading, marketing, stores, finance, and human resources. This Board also includes several non-executive directors. These are senior managers from other companies who are intended to bring a wider, more independent view to the discussions, supplementing the internal view of the executive directors.

**MANAGEMENT
IN PRACTICE**   **The Board of Directors of The Body Shop**

The Board of Directors, which currently consists of six Executive and three Non-executive Directors, determines the strategic direction of the Group, and is responsible for the Group's system of corporate governance. The Board meets regularly throughout the year to review the operating and financial performance of the group ... The Non-executive Directors are independent with wide business experience.

Source: The Body Shop PLC 2001 Annual Report and Accounts, p. 28.

1.5   The content of management work

This section presents some ideas on what people do to manage the transformation of resources into more valuable outputs. Building on Figure 1.1, **management** is the task of planning, organising, leading and controlling the use of resources in order to achieve some performance objectives. Whatever their level, people who perform these tasks are managing. The amount of each varies with the job and the person, and they do not perform them in any particular sequence. They do so more or less simultaneously, switching rapidly between them as the situation requires – but these functions make up the substance or content of management work.

Figure 1.2 illustrates the elements of this definition. It expands the central 'transforming' circle of Figure 1.1 to allow it to show the activities that together make up the transformation process. People draw inputs (resources) from the environment and transform them through the management activities of planning, organising, leading and control. This results in goods and services that they pass back as output into the external environment. The feedback loop indicates that this output is the source of future resources.

Environment

Organisations depend on the external environment for the resources to sustain them. These are most clearly those of finance, people, ideas, materials or information. They could also include more intangible resources such as goodwill, licences, permissions and authorisations to undertake certain activities. Equally an organisation depends on players in the external environment being willing to buy or recognise what it produces. It depends on this cash, recognition or reputation to secure the resources to survive. Commercial firms sell goods and services and use the receipts to buy future resources. Public or not-for-profit organisations depend on relevant authorities being sufficiently satisfied that they are willing to provide future budgets or donations. Part Two of the book deals with aspects of the external environment.

Planning

This deals with the overall direction of the work to be done. It includes forecasting future trends, assessing actual and potential resources and developing objectives and tar-

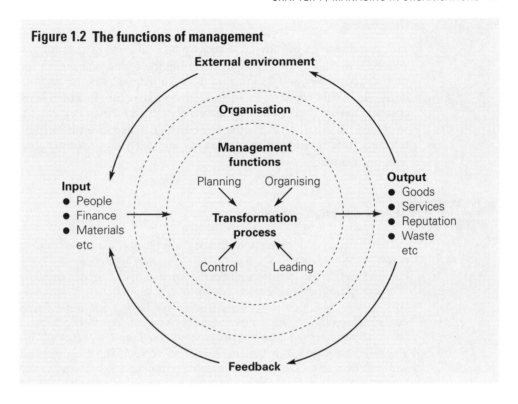

Figure 1.2 The functions of management

gets for future performance. Any work activity raises choices about where to concentrate effort and resources.

As more people and interests become involved and the cost of resources increases, setting objectives, targets and plans becomes more essential than ever. Managers therefore invest time and effort in developing a sense of direction for the organisation, or their part of it, and express this in a set of objectives for the activity. Part Three of the book deals with planning.

<table>
<tr><td>**MANAGEMENT IN PRACTICE**</td><td>**David Simon – planning targets at BP**</td></tr>
</table>

David Simon was chairman and chief executive of BP from 1992 to 1995. He believes that setting simple goals is an important part of developing a culture of continual performance improvement. He made it clear to BP employees that they should be cost and profit conscious. He has a golden rule for attaining goals: 'Targeting is fundamental to achieving. If you do not target, you do not measure and you do not achieve.' He believes that:

> Picking the right targets is a skill in itself. The difficulty of leadership is picking the targets and having a dialogue as you progress towards that goal so that, when it is achieved, it seems the easiest thing in the world. Then you can pick another target.

One top executive described Simon's accomplishment: 'What he has done so well is pull the company together in a very calming way, setting clear targets and telling people how they can achieve them.

Source: See Part Three case.

Organising

This is the activity of moving abstract plans closer to realisation, by deciding how to allocate time and effort. It includes defining the primary business processes required to meet the objectives, and deciding on the technologies and other facilities that people will need. The whole needs to be organised into a structure in which work is allocated and co-ordinated. Who is to be responsible for which business process? How should their work be linked with that of others? At more detailed levels it includes matters such as selecting staff, revising payment systems, or which supplier to choose. Part Four deals with organising.

MANAGEMENT IN PRACTICE **Reshaping strategy at Safeway**

In 1999 Safeway appointed Carlos Criado-Perez as chief executive, in an effort to rebuild the business after several years of poor performance. The company's Annual Report to share-holders for 2001 summarised some of the management practices he had introduced.

Planning activities had included developing a new strategy to focus on deep-cut promotions, a wider range of fresh products and a portfolio of four distinct types of store. At the operating level it has meant greater effort at forecasting, ordering and managing the supply chain. *Organising* had included rearranging management responsibilities at head office, employing more people in the stores in direct contact with customers and working closely with suppliers to ensure greater availability of products (especially in support of the promotions). *Leading* had included giving store managers more authority to run their stores as individual businesses. The company has also changed the payment system to give enhanced rewards for good performance. *Control*, especially in the critical area of stock replenishment, had been enhanced by devolving more of this from the centre to the store manager (closer to local trading patterns) and by a new 'shelf-edge' computer system that gives staff immediate information on stocks at any time of day.

Source: Based on information in the Annual Report and Accounts, 2001.

Leading

This is the activity of generating effort and commitment towards meeting objectives. It includes influencing and motivating other people to work in support of the plans.

The more complex an organisation becomes, and subdivided into horizontal and vertical specialisms, the more the task of securing the required commitment and action from others becomes problematic. People exercise choice over what they do at work, and managers cannot assume that others will act as they would like them to. For David Simon at BP, setting targets was itself a vital part of his leadership. And Bill Johnson at Chem-Tec is also working to generate commitment amongst his staff, using a different aproach. Part Five deals with this topic.

Controlling and learning

Control is the process of monitoring events so that they can be compared to the plan. This may lead to some corrective action. Managers set a budget for a housing department, an outpatients clinic or for travel. They then ensure that a system is in place to collect information regularly of expenditure or performance so that they can check that they are keeping to budget. If not, they can decide how they bring actual costs back into line with budgeted costs. Are outcomes consistent with objectives? If so, they can leave things alone. But if by Wednesday the week's production schedule is clearly not going to be met, or if the level of customer complaints in March is well above the monthly average, then managers need to do something. It may require a very short-term response – such as to authorise some immediate overtime to catch up. Other deviations are so severe that the board decides to leave a business altogether – such as when Philips decided to stop making mobile phones in 2001, as it was losing so much money from the activity.

MANAGEMENT IN PRACTICE **Control at Global Instruments**

The company supplied a unique component to leading makers of mobile phones. A new design of phone threatened to destroy demand for this component, and the company was urgently seeking to sell new products. The finance director commented:

> A critical factor will be getting totally focused on costs – because we will be bringing new products right through from design to manufacture and then on to distribution. We won't have made them before, so we'll have to be very closely focused on the costs. We've put out quotations for new business based on estimates of what we think it will take – so it's going to be absolutely critical to know if we're as good as we think we are at doing the new satellite products. So we've got a new costing group to focus on monitoring what everything costs, against what we said it was going to cost. We knew the assembly costs on the old business very well, but now we're taking a new product from a new customer, we're into the unknown. The costing group includes engineering people, product design and finance people, and will monitor exactly what we do.

Source: Private communication.

Control also provides an opportunity to learn from past events. The ability of managers to learn from their experience is critical to the long-term performance of their organisation. This does not mean sending people on external courses, but creating and using opportunities for staff to learn from what they are doing. Part Six of the book deals with control.

MANAGEMENT IN PRACTICE **Encouraging learning**

The organisation is a national charity that runs residential homes for people with severe learning disabilities. It has a high reputation not only for the quality of the care it gives to users, but also for the attention it gives to developing the carers it employs. Managers throughout the organisation take whatever opportunities they can to help staff gain confidence in the difficult and often stressful work. Research into how they do this indicates examples such as:

> Staff in one area described how their manager supported their studies by creating a file for them containing information on relevant policies and legislation. The same manager recognised that a night shift worker doing a qualification was not getting the full range of experience necessary to complete college assessments: 'So she took me to a review last week and also took me to a referral for a service user. That was new for me because I'd never seen that side before – but now I can relate to the stuff that will come up at college. It's about giving you the fuller picture, because sometimes the night shift can be quite isolating.'

Source: Unpublished research.

The functions in practice

Managers typically switch between activities many times a day. They deal with them in an intermittent and often parallel fashion, touching on many different parts of the job at once. However, they can usually identify these elements in their job, as this manager in a housing association explains:

> 'My role involves each of these functions to some extent. Planning is an important element in that I am part of a team which is allocated a budget of £8 million to spend in pursuit of specific objectives, and to promote particular forms of housing. So planning or "profiling" where we will spend the money is very important. Organising and leading are important too, as staff have to be clear on which projects to take forward, clear on objectives and clear on deadlines. Controlling also forms part of my role, as I have to compare the actual money spent with the planned budget and take corrective action as necessary.'

And a manager in a legal firm:

> 'As a manager in a professional firm, I find that each assignment involves all the elements in the list, to ensure that we carry it out properly. For example, I have to set clear objectives for the assignment, organise the necessary staff and information to perform the work, supervise staff and counsel them if necessary, and evaluate the results. However, all the roles interrelate with each other and there are no clear stages for each one.'

Q Case questions 1.2

● Which of these four management functions are evident at Chem-Tec?

1.6 The process of management work

Management functions make up the content of management work – *what* managers do. It is also useful to be aware of the process perspective – *how* managers work. Research by Rosemary Stewart, Henry Mintzberg and Fred Luthans gives some insights.

Rosemary Stewart – how managers spend their time

What are managers' jobs like? Do they resemble an orderly, methodical process – or a constant rush from one problem to the next? One of the best-known studies was that conducted in the 1960s by Rosemary Stewart (1967), an academic at Oxford University. She persuaded 160 senior and middle managers to keep a diary for four weeks, and it remains the largest study of its kind. The managers (from different functions and from large and small organisations) completed the diary in a way that allowed the researchers to establish how the managers spent their time.

The results showed that managers worked in a fragmented, interrupted fashion. This was measured by the number of times the manager was alone long enough to concentrate on a problem. The study also measured the number of brief contacts the manager had, and the number of separate diary entries, each signifying the start of a new activity or a continuation after an interruption. Over the four weeks, the managers had, on average, only 9 periods of 30 minutes or more alone, 12 brief contacts each day, and 13 diary entries each day. They spent 36 per cent of their time on paperwork (writing, dictating, reading, calculating) and 43 per cent in informal discussion. They spent the remainder on formal meetings, telephoning and social activities.

Stewart also found great variety between managers. For example, the proportion of time they spent on paperwork ranged from 7 to 84 per cent. The research team also analysed the data to show different profiles of management work, based not on level or function but on how they spent their time.

KEY IDEAS

Rosemary Stewart's management profiles

- **The Emissaries** spent much of their time out of the organisation, meeting customers, suppliers or contractors.
- **The Writers** spent most of their time alone reading and writing, and had the fewest contacts with other managers. If they had meetings they were usually with just one other person.
- **The Discussers** spent most of their time with other people and with their colleagues.

- **The Troubleshooters** had the most fragmented work pattern of all, with many diary entries and many fleeting contacts, especially with their subordinates.
- **The Committee Members** had a wide range of internal contacts, and spent much time in formal meetings. They spent half their working day in discussions with more than one other person.

Source: Stewart (1967).

Fragmentation and diversity are the key messages of Rosemary Stewart's research. While some find the fragmented pattern of work stressful others accept it as the only way to keep in touch with events. Her conclusions about fragmentation and variety have been broadly supported in later work by Mintzberg and Luthans.

Henry Mintzberg – ten management roles

Mintzberg (1973) developed the most widely quoted challenge to the traditional perceptions of management functions. His research built on earlier empirical studies by Carlson (1951) and Stewart (1967) and used structured observation to gather the data – albeit from only five chief executives. Despite this limitation other studies (such as that by Martinko and Gardner (1990) of 41 school managers) have generally supported his conclusions. He concluded, as did Stewart, that managers' work was varied, brief, fragmented and involved much time being spent on interpersonal activities. He found he could categorise management work into ten roles, grouped into three categories: informational, interpersonal and decisional as shown in Table 1.2.

Informational roles

Through the leader and liaison roles the manager gains access to valued information – external and internal – and so becomes a nerve centre of the organisation. The *monitor role* involves seeking out, receiving and screening information to understand the organisation and its environment. It comes from papers and reports, but equally usefully from chance conversations with customers or new contacts at conferences and exhibitions. Much of the information received is oral (from hearsay as well as formal meetings), building on personal contacts. Other information comes from formal measurement systems such as that which Bill Johnson installed at Chem-Tec – and where he is using that to encourage operators to learn new skills and develop larger roles for themselves. In the *disseminator role* the manager shares information with subordinates and other members

Table 1.2 Mintzberg's ten management roles

Category	Role	Activity
Informational	Monitor	Seek and receive information, scan papers and reports, maintain interpersonal contacts
	Disseminator	Forward information to others, send memos, make phone calls
	Spokesperson	Represent the unit to outsiders in speeches and reports
Interpersonal	Figurehead	Perform ceremonial and symbolic duties, receive visitors
	Leader	Direct and motivate subordinates, train, advise and influence others
	Liaison	Maintain information links in and beyond the organisation
Decisional	Entrepreneur	Initiate new projects, spot opportunities, identify areas of business development
	Disturbance handler	Take corrective action during crises, resolve conflicts amongst staff, adapt to external changes
	Resource allocator	Decide who gets resources, schedule, budget, set priorities
	Negotiator	Represent department during negotiations with unions, suppliers, and generally defend interests

Source: Based on Mintzberg (1973).

of the team or organisation. By forwarding reports and papers, telephoning to pass on gossip or briefing staff about impending changes the manager ensures others are aware of relevant events. As a *spokesperson* the manager transmits information to people outside the organisation. This happens when the manager gives information at a conference on behalf of the organisation, speaks to the media or gives his or her department's view at a company meeting.

Interpersonal roles

Interpersonal roles arise directly from a manager's formal authority and status, and involve relationships with other people both in and out of the organisation. In the *figurehead role* the manager is a symbol, representing the unit in legal and ceremonial duties such as greeting a visitor, signing legal documents, presenting retirement gifts or receiving a quality award. The *leader role* defines the manager's relationship with subordinates, including motivating, communicating and guiding their training and career development (such as at the charity quoted on page 19). The *liaison role* focuses on a manager's contacts with people outside the immediate organisational unit. Managers maintain a network in which they trade information and favours for mutual benefit with clients, government officials, customers, suppliers. For some managers, particularly chief executives or sales managers, the liaison role is paramount, taking a high proportion of their time and energy.

MANAGEMENT IN PRACTICE   **Strengthening interpersonal roles**

A company restructured its regional operations, closed a sales office in Bordeaux and transferred the work to Paris. The sales manager responsible for south-west France was now geographically distant from her immediate boss and the rest of the team. This caused severe problems of communication and loss of teamwork. She concluded that the interpersonal aspects of the role were vital as a basis for the informational and decisional roles. The decision to close the office had broken these links.

She and her boss agreed to try the following solutions:

- a 'one-to-one' session of quality time to discuss key issues during monthly visits to head office;
- daily telephone contact to ensure speed of response and that respective communication needs were met;
- use of fax at home to speed up communications.

These overcame the break in interpersonal roles caused by the location change.

Decisional roles

In the *entrepreneurial role* the manager initiates change within the organisation. They see opportunities or problems and create projects to deal with them. Managers play this role when they introduce a new product or create a major change programme – as Bob Horton did at BP when he became chief executive, determined to change what he saw as a very established and inflexible culture, unsuited to the newly competitive oil business. Managers play the *disturbance-handler role* when they deal with problems and changes that are unexpected.

MANAGEMENT IN PRACTICE   **Two examples of handling disturbance**

In early 2001 Ericsson (the Swedish-based telecoms equipment supplier) had to react to a sudden collapse in demand for telecoms equipment. The chief executive Kurt Hellstrom called it 'the fastest dive in our industry that we have ever seen' and took rapid action to conserve cash and save the business – including making thousands of staff redundant.

In June of the same year Anne Mulcahy, president and CEO of Xerox, decided to kill the company's entire line of desktop ink-jet printers – 'a one-year-old business that employed 1,500 people worldwide, and had been championed by Mulcahy herself. The division would not turn a profit for at least two years, though, and Xerox needed cash now. "In a year of tough decisions, this one was toughest," Mulcahy says.'

Source: *Business Week*, 6 August 2001, p.56.

The *resource-allocator role* involves choosing among competing demands for money, equipment, personnel and other demands on a manager's time. How much of her budget should the housing manager quoted on page 20 spend on different types of project? What proportion of the budget should a company spend on advertising and what on improving an existing product line? The manager of an ambulance service regularly has to decide whether to pay overtime to other staff to replace an absent team member, or let the speed of the service decline until a new shift starts. Closely linked to the resource-allocator role is the *negotiator role*, in which managers seeks to reach agreement with other parties on whom they depend. When managers at Sun Microsytems want to change the prices at which they buy a component they negotiate the new deal with their suppliers.

Mintzberg proposed that every manager's job consisted of some combination of these roles, with their relative importance varying between the manager's level and the type of business in which they work. Managers can usually identify with many of the roles, and see them as complementing rather than contradicting the traditional framework. They view the roles as describing how they perform the functions of management.

Managers often highlight two roles that are missing from Mintzberg's list – manager as subordinate and manager as worker. Most managers have subordinates but, except for those at the very top, they are subordinates themselves. Part of their role is to advise, assist and influence their boss. This is the role of 'managing up'. Much management work involves such attempts to influence people over whom the manager has no formal authority. In today's fluid and fast-moving organisation managers often cannot wait to go through the 'right' channels: in order to get things done they need to persuade people higher up the organisation that their ideas will work, or that they need a larger budget. A project manager recalled:

> 'This is the second time we have been back to the management team, to pose how we wish to move forward, and to try and get the resources that are required. It is, however, worth taking the time up front to get all members fully supportive of what we are trying to do. Although it takes a bit longer we should, by pressure and by other individuals demonstrating the benefits of the system we are proposing, eventually move the [top team] forward.'

Many managers, especially those in small organisations or those in junior positions in large ones, spend some of their time doing the work of the organisation. A director of a small property company helps with sales visits, or an engineering director helps with difficult technical problems. A lawyer running a small practice performs both professional and managerial roles. A final point is that changes in the context will affect managers' ability to perform their role, as the Management in Practice feature on page 26 shows.

Fred Luthans – managers as networkers and politicians

Does the way in which managers interpret their role affect their performance? There was no evidence on this point in Mintzberg's study. He did not suggest that spending time on all the roles he identified would improve performance. However, work by Luthans (1988) showed a link between how managers divide their time between different roles and their performance. The team studied 292 managers at different levels in four organisations. Trained staff observed each manager over a two-week period, and recorded their behaviours in agreed categories. The research team also developed measures to distinguish between levels of 'success' (relatively rapid promotion) and 'effectiveness' (work-unit performance and subordinates' satisfaction). The behavioural groups and categories were:

Communicating	Exchanging information and paperwork
Traditional management	Planning, decision making, controlling
Networking	Interacting with outsiders, socialising/politicking
Human resource management	Motivating, managing conflict, staffing, training

The conclusion was that *successful* managers spent considerably more time networking (socialising, politicking, interacting with outsiders) than the less successful managers. Human resource management took least time. In contrast, *effective* managers spent most time on communication and human resource management activities. They spent little time networking. These results implied that managers who want to rise to more senior positions should spend relatively large amounts of time and effort on networking and on the political skills of management.

1.7   Managers work within a context

Organisational context

Figures 1.1 and 1.2 showed the links between managers, their organisation and the external environment. Figure 1.3, a development of Leavitt's (1965) model, enlarges the 'organisation' circle of the earlier diagrams to allow it to show more fully the elements that make up the organisational context within which managers work. Any organisation contains these elements – they represent the immediate organisational environment that shapes the manager's work. For example, Railtrack managers have been severely criticised for the company's safety record. While individual managers bear some responsibility the report into the 1999 crash at Ladbroke Grove in London traced the problem to cultures and structures that encouraged complacency towards safety matters. As Jorme Ollilia has built Nokia into a major business, he and his management team have made significant changes to technology, business processes – and indeed to all the organisational elements shown in the figure (Steinbock, 2001).

The elements in the model are described here briefly – each is examined in later chapters:

- **Objectives** – sometimes called purposes or goals, these represent some future desired state of the organisation, or a part of it.
- **Business processes** – the activities that people and technologies perform on materials and information to meet the objectives. They include processes for designing products, receiving orders, making the product, delivering, receiving payment and many more.
- **Technology** – the type and location of physical facilities, machinery, and information systems that people use to transform inputs into useful outputs.

Figure 1.3 Elements of the organisational context of management

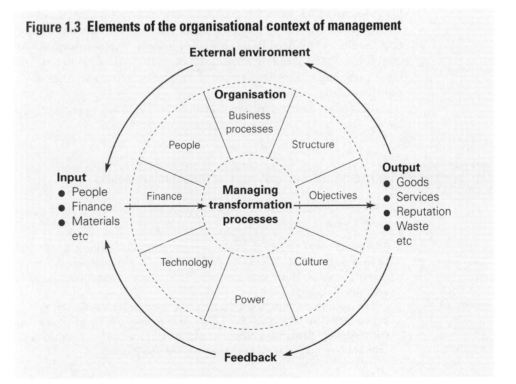

- **Finance** – the financial resources available to the organisation.
- **Structure** – the way tasks are divided and co-ordinated; this includes formal and informal structures, which can have equally important effects on meeting objectives.
- **People** – their knowledge, skills, attitudes and goals; it is sometimes useful to include here people from outside the organisation as well as regular employees, if they influence performance.
- **Culture** – norms, beliefs and underlying values that characterise the unit.
- **Power** – the amount and distribution of identifiable sources of power.

Models like this bring out the fact that there are limits to what the individual manager can do – they can be constrained, or helped, by any of the elements in Figure 1.3. Managers do not necessarily accept their context passively. They can try to shape aspects of it as they work to meet personal and organisational objectives, as discussed in Chapter 11. For example, one of the aims of the chief executive at Safeway has been to bring about a radical change in the culture of that organisation in the belief that this will help him meet the performance targets set by the board.

The historical context

Management also takes place within a flow of historical events. What people do now reflects the influence of past events and future uncertainties. Managers naturally focus on dealing with the tangible details of current operations – the urgency of present issues. They work to bring resources together to achieve some performance target. They try to ensure that things run properly, sense trouble, make the organisation work. At the same time, history exerts an influence through the structure and culture of the organisation. People remember successes and failures, and this affects how they respond to current proposals.

Management also means looking to the future. However good the present situation, or the present operation, effective managers must look outwards, and to the future. This means questioning present systems and seeking improvements, and this involves observing how the environment is changing and considering the implications for the current activity. Does work need to be redirected towards another purpose? Are resources being used too wastefully, requiring some changes in method? What are others doing? All of these pose issues for most kinds of human activity, and they are resolved through processes of management.

Managers experience endless conflict between dealing with the day-to-day and the longer term.

| MANAGEMENT IN PRACTICE | **Balancing present and future at Global Instruments** |

Lisa Scott, European account manager at Global Instruments, on the dilemma she faced in working for the plant's survival:

> There had never been a marketing function as such in the UK, so I was brought in to try to look at that. I set up the marketing function, and especially to look after our three major accounts. There was a marketing function at headquarters, but it didn't pay much attention to Europe.
>
> We need to be able to anticipate what the customers require, and come up with innovative ideas, be proactive. But I also have to spend a lot of time at the moment dealing with existing customers. We are renegotiating a contract with one of them, so a lot of time is taken on that, and not enough on marketing.

I am still having to deal with current issues, with current customers, rather than being able to concentrate on the strategy bit. That's a big tension, because it's two different people: analysing inventory and costings, negotiating pricing; and then turning the mind to what we need to be producing in 1998. That's my biggest problem, because the short term always takes priority. Yet people are asking a lot of questions of me, about what we are going to do.

1.8 Gender in organisations

If organisations are mainly coalitions of interest groups, depending on a range of stake-holders for their survival, then this has implications both for assessing their performance in relation to their goals and for the meaning of the activity of management.

One particular way in which organisations can be used to protect established interests is through their effects on gender inequality. There are several perspectives on the gendered nature of work.

ACTIVITY 1.4

Researching women and work

The female share of economic activity has increased in every member state of the European Union throughout the 1990s. Despite this growth and the debates and campaigns about equal opportunities, women are much less likely than men to be economically active. Why do you think this is? Arrange a discussion with a woman of working age who is not in paid employment. Try to establish which, if any, of the following factors have influenced her situation: insufficient childcare arrangements; lack of flexible working hours; inequalities of access to training and education; prejudices such as 'women's place is at home'; and stereotypes such as 'men are the breadwinners' and 'women are less career minded'.

Compare your answers with those of other students to see what conclusions you can draw.

Gendered segregation

Many tasks are predominantly male or female occupations. For example, women are much more likely than men to work as teachers, nurses or librarians than as doctors, judges or chartered accountants. They often do routine office work and shop work, but rarely do what is defined as skilled manual work. The reverse is true for men.

Gender segregation is both horizontal and vertical. Horizontal segregation occurs where men and women are associated with different types of jobs. For example, a survey on women in broadcasting occupations across the European Union found that females were overrepresented in the administrative category (which includes secretarial and clerical posts), while men were overrepresented in craft and technical occupations (Gallagher, 1992).

Even when male and female employees have the same job title and formal role in their organisation they are likely to undertake different tasks and responsibilities. Podmore and Spencer (1986) studied male and female solicitors and concluded that the profession was not homogeneous:

> Men solicitors were more likely than women to be engaged in company and commercial work, one of the most prestigious areas of legal practice, and in criminal and litigation work which often involves frequent court appearances. Women solicitors … were more heavily involved than men in matrimonial work and such 'desk-bound' work as wills and estate duty. (p.40)

Sonnentag (1994) studied female and male team leaders in software development in Swiss and German organisations. Women leading teams experienced less complex work situations than did their male colleagues. When a man was promoted to team leader he was more likely to deal with an increased amount of complexity in his work and to spend more time communicating with other people. When a woman was promoted the complexity of the work and the pattern of communication remained much the same. Clearly the same job title does not imply equivalent responsibilities, challenge and opportunity for further advancement.

Similarly an exploratory study in the United Kingdom by Grundy (1996) showed that men get intensively involved with the 'pure', abstract computing work that is challenging and prestigious. They leave the 'messy' type of work to their female colleagues. This latter involves tasks such as merging and tidying databases and writing summary report programs. These are important tasks but are considered monotonous and unglamorous.

If women are confined to lower occupational positions and to less responsible work they will have fewer opportunities for professional growth and promotion. This in turn distances them from positions of power and the exercise of formal authority. This results in vertical segregation – men in the higher ranks of an organisation and women in the lower. To return to broadcasting, few senior management posts are held by women. Data from 43 organisations in 12 European states in 1990 showed that women constituted at most 11 per cent of those in the top three levels of management (Gallagher, 1992). Vertical segregation occurs even in the so-called traditional women's occupations: 9 per cent of nurses are men but they occupy 45 per cent of the nurse-manager jobs (Stamp and Robarts, 1986).

Gendered work and organisational processes

How are these horizontal and vertical divisions created? A major influence has been the simplification and standardisation of work, often as a result of automation. Historians on the evolution of computerisation identified that feminisation and automation of work are highly interrelated. Steiger and Reskin (1990) carried out a historical analysis of feminisation in the baking industry over the period 1950 to 1980, concluding that:

> what has changed is not the traditional sexual division of labour in baking but the baking process itself … Technological innovation that permitted freezing and preserving dough so it could be shipped long distances ushered in bake-off bakeries and allowed schools, hospitals and restaurants to purchase ready-made or ready-to-bake products instead of baking them from scratch … Rather than significantly altering the entrenched social roles of men and women in the baking industry, technical innovations gave rise to a less-skilled variant, bake-off baking, that was quickly defined as women's work. (p.269)

The supposedly masculine nature of organisational work is also identified as a barrier to the entry and advancement of women (Knights and Murray, 1994). Managers who emphasise the value of hard analytical skills above soft interpersonal skills support, perhaps unwittingly, the progression of men and discourage that of women. Stressing competitiveness, tension and long unsocial working hours has a similar effect. It drives some women away from senior positions owing to domestic responsibilities that continue to be primarily theirs.

Gendered organisational studies

A third perspective that gives insight into gender inequality at work is the attention that researchers give to women. Research on management has focused on the male side of organisations, and remained largely blind and deaf to gender (Wilson, 1996). Studies have treated the workforce as unisex or only involved male participants in the research. See, for example, Acker and Van Houton's (1992) critique in Chapter 2 of one influential piece of research.

Even some comparative male/female studies and analyses obstruct understanding of male and female experience in organisations. Men and male behaviour become the standard against which women's experiences are evaluated (Marshall, 1984). Similarly, the idea of male as a norm may be implicitly accepted (Wilson, 1995). For instance, in a university course on management it is common to have a lecture on 'women in management' but rare to have one on 'men in management'. The presence of men is always taken for granted and their progression in organisations is not only not constrained but is encouraged by organisational and wider social factors.

Put together, the three perspectives show that the dynamics of gender inequality at work are complex. Even research on the topic is often shaped from a male perspective, while the efforts that women themselves make to gain occupational identity and/or to change organisational practices are overlooked.

1.9 Current challenges

Most considerations of the nature of management stress the dilemmas that managers face. The theme is that there are no easy prescriptions and managers are inevitably having to balance different interests and moral dilemmas. A study sponsored by the Institute of Management (1995b) drew attention to what it called the emerging paradoxes and contradictions of management. The research team held discussions with a representative group of managers about the nature of the management job that is emerging. They identified the following paradoxes and contradictions within the role:

- balancing short term and long term;
- internationalisation vs local performance;
- process skills vs technical skills;
- higher quality with fewer resources;
- teamwork vs individual performance;
- reflection vs action;
- thinking strategically while acting operationally.

The emphasis here is on ambiguity, which contrasts with some of the earlier certainties about the job of managing.

1.10 Conventional and critical perspectives

Management takes place in a social setting in which people and institutions hold and express many different values, priorities and interests. These reflect deeper divisions in wealth, power and opportunity. Alvesson and Wilmott (1996) argue that, in capitalist societies, the development of management as an occupational group limits the risks of ownership and protects established positions. Managers act as agents of the owners and represent their interests. They are accountable to the owners of the business, not to employees, consumers or wider communities.

> The rise of management has institutionalised the lack of democratic control over the allocation of resources within, and by, work organisations. This lack of accountability increases the social and ecological risks for employees, customers and citizens. Once management becomes a separate social group the idea of a community of interest becomes problematical, especially when there is little or no accountability of managers to the managed. (Alvesson and Wilmott, 1996, p.12)

In consequence, management is not a neutral, professional process. It reflects existing unequal divisions within societies and within organisations. Writers such as Alvesson and Wilmott use a **critical perspective** to challenge institutions and practices that obstruct the search for alternative ways to manage co-operative activity. They do not see 'best practice' in terms of how best to achieve current ends (such as profitable growth or market share). Instead they ask what a practice contributes to objectives such as autonomy, responsibility, democracy and ecologically sustainable development.

They argue that a critical perspective is not 'anti-management'. Rather, their aim is to raise a broader set of questions not only about ways of accomplishing existing ends, but about whether the '*existing ends routinely generate needless waste and divisiveness*' (p.3, emphasis in original). The technical and other skills of management remain highly relevant – solving technical problems is an essential activity in complex organisations. Their argument is that society will benefit more from such technical skills within a less socially divisive practice of management.

Managing in the hope of adding value and creating wealth is not just a logical or rational process – it cannot be so when it takes place within a human institution. Organisations have a history that shapes how people respond to events, and the political as well as rational choices they make. It is also taking place within a social and political context, where other values and influences shape what happens. Organisations do not exist in a vacuum, but in a wider economic and social structure, made up of many interest groups. It is therefore about managing both internally and externally in order to create wealth or well-being in a way that is acceptable to a wide range of stakeholders.

1.11 Studying management

Courses in management have been a rapidly growing area of European higher education in recent years as students seek courses with greater perceived relevance to their future. Do not confuse relevance in such a complex topic as management with easy examples or simple prescriptions. Managers often disagree about ends and means, especially over the strategic issues that determine the future direction and shape of the business. Simple prescriptions and ready solutions rarely work in the complex and ambiguous reality of a particular organisation.

Taking a critical perspective will deepen your understanding of management. Thomas (1993) cites the following four components of critical thinking, namely, a readiness to:

- challenge assumptions;
- understand management in its wider context;
- be aware of alternative ways of doing things;
- be generally sceptical towards what is presented.

This in no way implies a do-nothing cynicism that leads nowhere. A critical perspective lays the foundation for a successful management career, as it helps to ensure well-founded proposals and arguments.

KEY IDEAS   ## Ways of thinking critically

1 Identifying and challenging assumptions about:
- the nature of management, its tasks, skills and purposes;
- the nature of people and why they behave as they do;
- the nature of organisations;
- learning, knowing and acting;
- values, goals and ends.

2 Creating contextual awareness by understanding:
- how management practices have developed historically;
- how people in other societies see management;
- the implications of different contexts for management;
- the interrelationship between organisations and society.

3 Identifying alternatives by:
- becoming aware of the variety of ways in which managing and organising can be undertaken;
- inventing and imagining new ways of managing;
- specifying new goals and priorities.

4 Developing reflective scepticism by:
- adopting a questioning, quizzical attitude;
- recognising the limitations of much that passes for knowledge in the management field;
- knowing how to evaluate knowledge claims;
- developing a resistance to dogma and propaganda;
- being able to distinguish systematic argument and reasoned judgement from sloppy thinking and simplistic formulae.

Source: Thomas (1993).

Studying management is itself a task to be managed – and so an opportunity to gain some practice in the subject. You can go through the processes of planning what you want to achieve and of organising the resources you will need. You will also experience various controls as you go through the course – such as your examinations. Studying management will also develop mental and personal skills, and as you work on this book you will have opportunities to improve your skills of literacy, understanding arguments, numeracy, communicating, problem solving and teamwork.

The most accessible sources of ideas and theory about management that you will have are this book, and your lectures and tutorials. There are many other ways in which you can supplement this material that should add to your interest and enrich your understanding. Such resources include media, the World Wide Web, and films or novels (such as *The Goal* (Goldratt and Cox, 1989) or *Nice Work* (Lodge, 1989), which give unusual insights into the work of managing. You can also draw on the experience of friends and relatives to help with some of the activities and discussion points in the book. These help you to gather information about current practices, which you can compare with that of other members of your tutorial group and with the theories in the book. Remember too that as you go about your educational and social lives you are experiencing organisations, and in some cases helping to manage them. Actively reflecting on these experiences will support your study of management.

1.12 Summary

This chapter has outlined perspectives on the management job and its contribution to organisational performance. Management is an activity that everyone undertakes to some extent as they manage their daily lives. In another sense management is an activity within organisations – which is conducted in varying degrees by a wide variety of people. It is not exclusive to managers – non-managers may engage in parts of the activity. The title of 'manager', or its close relatives, is often attached to jobs with rather limited management responsibilities – branch manager, executive consultant. Conversely, many people with significant management responsibilities have titles that do not include the word – director of television, chief actuary, principal, senior partner.

A functional perspective identifies the management tasks of planning, organising, leading, controlling and learning – making up the *content* of the management task. This is complemented by a *process* perspective that examines how people perform the functions of management in a highly fragmented way, but containing identifiable interpersonal, informational and decisional roles. While both the content and process dimensions include a monitoring and control element, the significance of this is such that it is useful to recognise a *control* perspective on management. This emphasises the scope in both the other perspectives to monitor and learn from the way they are performed, to identify a need for immediate corrective action or to identify opportunities for longer-term learning and development. Each chapter will conclude with a short summary relating the topic of the chapter to these three perspectives on the management role.

Content

Management involves developing objectives and dealing with both short-term and long-term issues. A primary aim is to create wealth and well-being for society – though views will differ on whether they do that, and some see organisational objectives as destroying rather than adding value. The range of organisational objectives extends far beyond providing goods and services. Planning involves securing and allocating resources of many kinds to support the prevailing objectives. It is the primary role of management to add value to those resources.

Process

Process refers to the way in which people perform the content (or functions) of management. Studies have shown the fragmented nature of the task, and also significant variations in the way managers choose to get things done. Within the organisation they need to get things done with the support of others, which support cannot be taken for granted. Studies of the process help illuminate how managers approach that aspect of the role. They also need to manage their processes in ways that maintain an acceptable degree of external support, using both personal and formal methods. Since management is not a neutral, technical activity, managers are more likely to support the interests of powerful stakeholders than those of disadvantaged or weak ones.

Control

Managing an activity effectively also depends on periodically monitoring what is happening and taking corrective action. Separate activities inevitably need co-ordination and control or they fail to achieve what is expected of them. The external environment changes after the task has begun – only through some monitoring and control process can people see that, and take it into account in changing direction. Monitoring and reflection is also the basis for learning. The measures used will need to reflect the interests of stakeholders, and leads to corrective action and learning. That information leads to a further set of content and process actions.

This features largely in Bill Johnson's work at Chem-Tec. The ERP system is a sophisticated way of monitoring the production process and providing information to allow people to decide on the next step. Moreover Bill has used the opportunity of the technical change to also change the way he manages. He is encouraging subordinates to use the control data and decide the next actions, rather than refer the issue to him to decide. This develops the skills of all concerned, and indicates the fluidity of the boundaries between management and non-management work.

Q PART CASE QUESTIONS

- What organisational functions does The Body Shop perform?
- In what ways are managers in The Body Shop adding value to the resources they use?
- What aspects of the content and process perspectives of management can you observe in the case?
- What tensions may there be between the organisation's objectives that managers have to reconcile?

1.13 Review questions

1 Apart from delivering goods and services, what other functions do organisations perform?

2 What is the difference between management as a general human activity and management as a specialised occupation? How has this division happened, and what are some of its effects?

3 What examples are there in the chapter of this boundary being changed, and what were the effects?

4 Describe, with examples, the differences between general, functional, staff, line and project managers.

5 Summarise the four functions of management.

6 How does Mintzberg's theory of management roles complement the functional approach?

7 What is the significance of Luthan's theory to management practice?

8 Give an example of the way in which an organisation has been managed in order to maintain or increase gender inequality. What are the consequences of such practices likely to be?

9   How can a critical perspective help managers do their job?

10   Review and revise the definition of management that you gave in Activity 1.1.

Further reading

Thompson, P. and McHugh, D. (1995), *Work Organisations: A critical introduction*, Macmillan, Basingstoke.

Alvesson, M. and Wilmott, H. (1996), *Making Sense of Management*, Sage, London.

Both provide very detailed discussion of management from a critical perspective, with numerous further references.

Handy, C. (1988), *Understanding Voluntary Organizations*, Penguin, Harmondsworth. This chapter has stressed that management is not confined to commercial organisations, and Handy's book offers a valuable perspective for anyone wanting to consider management in the voluntary sector more fully.

Roddick, A. (2000), *Business as Unusual*, Thorsons, London. More background from the founder of The Body Shop.

Drucker, P. (1999), *Management Challenges for the 21st Century*, Butterworth/Heinemann, London. The publisher has exaggerated the newness of the ideas in Drucker's latest book, and the thesis is not coherently developed. It is nevertheless worth reading as a collection of insightful observations from the enquiring mind of this great management theorist.

Annotated links, questions and resources can be found on
www.booksites.net/boddy

CHAPTER 2

Models of management

AIM *To present the major theoretical perspectives on management and to show how they relate to each other.*

OBJECTIVES

By the end of your work on this chapter you should be able to outline the concepts below in your own terms and:

1 Explain why models are useful in studying management

2 Compare unitary, pluralist and critical perspectives

3 Outline Morgan's 'images of organisation' and show your understanding by giving your own examples

4 Outline the structure of the competing values framework

5 Outline the main elements of the following approaches:
   - rational goal (Taylor, the Gilbreths and operational research);
   - internal process (Weber, Fayol);
   - human relations (Follett, Mayo);
   - open systems (sociotechnical, contingency and chaos)

   and explain their contribution to understanding management

6 Illustrate how each of the earlier theories has contributed to some aspect of the management agendas

7 Compare the approaches in terms of their contribution to specific management situations

8 Explain the influence of uncertain conditions on management

9 Compare the assumptions of linear and non-linear models of management

10 Evaluate how well these models represent reality in an organisation

Robert Owen – an early management innovator

Robert Owen (1771–1856) was a successful manufacturer of textiles, who ran mills in England and at New Lanark in Scotland, which he bought in 1801. New Lanark was an unusually large business unit for the time, requiring a range of management and production control techniques beyond the needs of the owner of a smaller enterprise. The mills were in poor shape when Owen took them over, and he quickly tried to improve the quality of the labour force. Most employees, at this stage of the Industrial Revolution, had little or no experience of factory work. He found 'the great majority of them were idle, intemperate, dishonest [and] devoid of truth' (quoted in Butt, 1971). He also had 'to deal with slack managers who had tolerated widespread theft and embezzlement, immorality and drunkenness ' (Butt, 1971).

Owen quickly introduced new management practices. These included daily and weekly measurements of stocks, output and productivity; a system of labour costing and measures of work-in-progress. He used a novel technique to control employees. A small, four-sided piece of wood, with a different colour on each side, hung beside every worker. The colour set to the front indicated the previous day's standard of work – black indicating bad. Everyone could see this measure of the worker's performance. Overseers recorded this to check any trends in a person's work. Owen was keen on discipline, and introduced community singing 'to counteract incipient lawlessness'. The workers are reported to have been less than enthusiastic.

Owen actively managed the links between his business and the wider world. On buying the mills he quickly became part of the Glasgow business establishment, and was closely involved in the activities of the Chamber of Commerce. He took a prominent role in the social and political life of the city. He used these links in particular to argue the case for reforms in the educational and economic systems, and was critical of the effect that industrialisation was having upon working-class life. Owen believed that education in useful skills would help to release working-class children from poverty. He provided a nursery for workers' children over one year old, allowing both parents to continue working, and promoted the case for wider educational provision. He also developed several experiments in co-operation and community building, though with only limited success. More broadly, he sought new ways of organising the economic system in a way that would raise wages and increase security of employment, at a time of severe business fluctuations. For example, in 1815 he persuaded allies in Parliament to propose a bill on child labour. This would have made it illegal for children under 10 to work in mills. It would also have limited their working hours to 10 a day. The measure met strong opposition from mill owners and a much weaker measure became law in 1819, to Owen's disappointment.

Q Case questions

- What management issues was Owen dealing with at New Lanark?
- How did the wider context affect Owen's management activities, and how did Owen try to change that context?
- What parallels can you see between Owen's approach to management and that of Anita Roddick at The Body Shop?

2.1 Introduction

This chapter introduces the following ideas:

- Model
- Feedback
- Metaphor
- Scientific management
- Operational research
- Bureaucracy
- Administrative management
- Human relations
- System
- Subsystem
- Open systems
- System boundary
- Sociotechnical systems
- Non-linear systems
- Contingency

The brief historical sketch of Robert Owen illustrates three themes that run through this book. First, he was active in devising management systems of all kinds to improve the performance of his mills, and paid particular attention to ways of controlling the workforce to ensure productive activity. Second, Owen engaged with the wider social environment in which he lived – especially with a workforce unused to the factory system and with different values from his own. He criticised the effects of industrialisation on that social system and tried to influence local and national policy – advocating the end of child labour, for example. His practice of providing nurseries for employees' children from the age of one year would be rare even today. Third, he was managing at a time of transition from an agricultural to an industrial economy, and many of the practices he invented were attempts to resolve the conflicts between these two systems.

Managers today cope with similar issues. They too need to recruit willing and capable staff, and control them to ensure that their work contributes to organisational performance. Many managers today also share Owen's concerns with the social context of work. They see that family circumstances affect staff performance, and take steps to balance the two. Littlewoods, the UK retail chain, offers 'family-friendly' policies such as subsidised child care and flexible working hours to make it easier for people with family responsibilities to continue working if they wish.

Managers operate in a world that is going through changes equal to those facing Owen. In the newer industrial countries of eastern Europe and Asia the transition is again from agriculture to industry. All are coping with the transition from a world conducted largely within national business systems to one in which ever more business is done on a global scale. The Internet is enabling great changes in the organisation of economic activity, equivalent to the Industrial Revolution of which Owen was part. It has encouraged the growth of 'pure' Internet companies such as lastminute.com, and transformed the way established companies use information internally. It is also changing the way companies work with suppliers and customers. And many businesses will be affected in unknown, yet almost certainly substantial ways, by the consequences of sustained climate change.

In coping with such changes managers, like Owen before them, have searched for ways to manage the enterprises they have created and to overcome the pressing issues they faced in their times. Through trial and error they developed practices that are now part of the historical context of management. Understanding this context helps present and future managers shape their practice to suit current circumstances.

This chapter traces the evolution of ideas about management. The next section introduces the idea of management models, and how they can illuminate the activity of managing. Later sections present four such models. The final section indicates some of the issues that managers face today – and the new models that may represent these conditions.

2.2 Why study models of management?

A **model** represents a more complex reality. Focusing on the essential elements and their relationship helps us understand that complexity, and how a change may affect it. Most management problems require several perspectives, so no model offers a complete solution. Those managing a globally competitive business such as motor vehicle production require flexibility, quality *and* low-cost production. Managers at Ford or DaimlerChrysler want models of the production process that help them organise it efficiently from a technical perspective. They also want models of human behaviour that will encourage high performance from their staff. Those models will show how best to organise a production process from a human perspective. The management task is to reconcile both approaches into an acceptable solution.

Managers act in accordance with their theory or perspective about the task in hand. To understand management action we need to know the range of perspectives available and how they guide practice.

Models help to understand complexity

Models identify the key variables, suggest possible relationships and predict the possible outcomes of change. The more accurately the model represents the reality it is describing, the more useful it will be. Models represent a toolkit managers choose from to cope with complexity, rather than ignore it. Charles Handy (1993) has pointed out that theories can:

Help to *explain* the past, which
in turn
helps one to *understand* the present
and thus
to *predict* the future, which leads
to
more *influence* over future events
and
less *disturbance* from the unexpected.

Many people find models and theories of management vague and imprecise, especially if they have previously studied in the physical or natural sciences. The fixed laws governing those scientific phenomena allow people to predict relationships accurately. Management has few such certainties. One reason is the number of variables that affect the situation. Figure 2.1 develops Figure 1.3 to show just some of the range of factors in

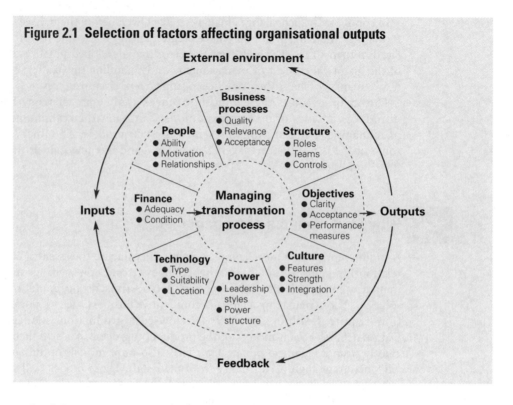

Figure 2.1 Selection of factors affecting organisational outputs

each of the organisational elements that affect organisational outputs, and hence performance. In addition, these elements interact: the quality and motivation of *people* will evidently affect output. Their motivation will be affected, amongst other things, by what the organisation can pay (*finance*) – but the staff budget will reflect the *objectives*, which in turn will reflect the *power* of different interests. All will be affected by factors in the external environment that are the subject of Chapter 3.

Scientific phenomena also embody numerous variables. The difference in developing theories of management is that data about many of the variables in Figure 2.1 is difficult to collect, and its meaning often depends on the unique context and circumstances. This means that relationships between the variables are often subjective and open to different interpretations – especially amongst those who have provided the data. There is an example in Chapter 10 of a study of the organisational culture within a retail business, in which senior managers, store managers and shop-floor staff attached different meanings to the culture in which they worked. This implies they would have equally diverse views on the causes and consequences for performance of that factor in Figure 2.1.

Q **Case questions 2.1**

● Which of the variables in Figure 2.1 was Robert Owen attempting to influence?
● Which of the variables were influencing the performance of his mill?

Models offer a range of perspectives

Models represent different ways of thinking about phenomena, so they broaden perspectives. Being aware of several models enables people to see more aspects of a problem, and so they are more likely to identify an acceptable way forward. In practice, people rarely approach an issue within an open mind. They are more likely to do so from the perspective they prefer and have become used to taking – whether unitary, pluralist or critical.

Unitary

Someone who takes a unitary perspective tends to emphasise the common purpose of the organisation, and to believe that members share and accept this purpose. They expect members to subordinate individual interests to the good of the whole. They see disagreement or dissent as a sign of disloyalty or failure, and expect all the parts to work together for the common good. They often use analogies of sporting teams ('let's play to win') or ships ('we're all in the same boat'), and stress the importance of loyalty to the leader.

Pluralist

People who take a pluralist view see the organisations as a coalition of interest groups. Each group has its own objectives that will sometimes coincide and at other times conflict with those of other groups. They see that members have personal goals and competing loyalties – to colleagues, their profession, business unit, family or local community – as well as to the organisation as a whole. Pluralists expect that people will reflect these loyalties in debate within the organisation about both ends and means. Within reason, they see disagreement as a sign of strength not of weakness. Pluralists compare organisations to nation states, in which different and equally legitimate views are resolved through political systems and processes.

Critical

Those who take a critical perspective believe organisations reflect deeper divisions and inequalities in society. They believe that organisations are not just vehicles for the efficient delivery of services but are also tools for achieving personal or group interests. Some stakeholders are more powerful than others, so that apparently democratic debate will always favour those in more powerful positions. Those with a critical perspective stress the underlying differences of power in organisations and society, and believe that 'rational' methods attempt to disguise underlying sectional interests.

Models reflect their context

People develop models and theories in response to circumstances, in this case to the most pressing issues facing managers at the time. In the late nineteenth century skilled labour was scarce, unskilled labour plentiful, and management was keen to increase its control of both. The pressing problem was how to control vast numbers of people with limited experience whom factory owners had recruited to work for them. Managements wanting to increase production to meet growing demand were receptive to theories about methods of production. They sought ways of simplifying tasks so that they could make more use of less-skilled employees. Early management theories gave priority to these issues.

Gareth Morgan's images of organisation

Since organisations are complex and contradictory creations, no single perspective or theory can explain them adequately. We need to see them from several viewpoints, each of which will illuminate one aspect or feature – while at the same time obscuring others. Gareth Morgan (1997) shows how alternative mental images and **metaphors** can represent organisations. Metaphors are a way of thinking about a phenomenon, attaching labels to it, which vividly indicate the image being used. We express alternative images in different theoretical constructions, focusing on different ways of looking at the problem. Images help understanding – but also obscure or distort understanding if we use the wrong image. Morgan explores eight images, which represent organisations as:

- **Machines** – mechanical thinking and the rise of the bureaucratic organisation.
- **Organisms** – recognising organisational needs, and how organisations' health is affected by the environment.
- **Brains** – an information-processing, learning and self-organising perspective.
- **Cultures** – a perspective focusing on the underlying assumptions, beliefs and values.
- **Political systems** – the role of interests, conflicts and power in shaping organisations.
- **Psychic prisons** – how people can become imprisoned or confined by modes of thinking and acting that become habitual.
- **Flux and transformation** – a focus on change and renewal, and the logic behind them.
- **Instruments of domination** – the exploitation of members, nations, environments.

Today a key issue for many managements is how to organise to meet a rapidly changing market. They are interested in models that suggest ways of organising work for maximum flexibility. Current theories reflect this interest by offering ways of coping with a turbulent and competitive world where flexibility, quality and low cost are often essential for survival. The value of studying management does not lie in the immediate detail of current trends and boardroom conflicts – however exciting these are. It lies in knowing that people will see any situation from different points of view. This awareness enables you to examine a problem more comprehensively – looking for patterns and connections – and therefore more surely.

2.3 The competing values framework

The range of models of management appears confusing and contradictory. Researchers study different variables, in different contexts and with different aims. It is not immediately obvious how the different approaches relate to each other. The Quinn *et al.* (1996) 'competing values' model attempts to relate models to each other by highlighting the values that lie behind them. Figure 2.2 shows the framework.

Quinn and his colleagues (Quinn *et al.*, 1996) argue that while each model adds to our knowledge of management none is sufficient. They are complementary elements in a larger whole. The vertical axis represents control and flexibility. Control is a pervasive concern of management as they try to ensure that activities are in line with expectations. Others emphasise ways of enhancing flexibility – apparently the opposite of control. The horizontal axis distinguishes an internal focus from an external one. Some theories are primarily inward looking, while others focus on the links between an organisation and its external environment.

Figure 2.2 Competing values framework

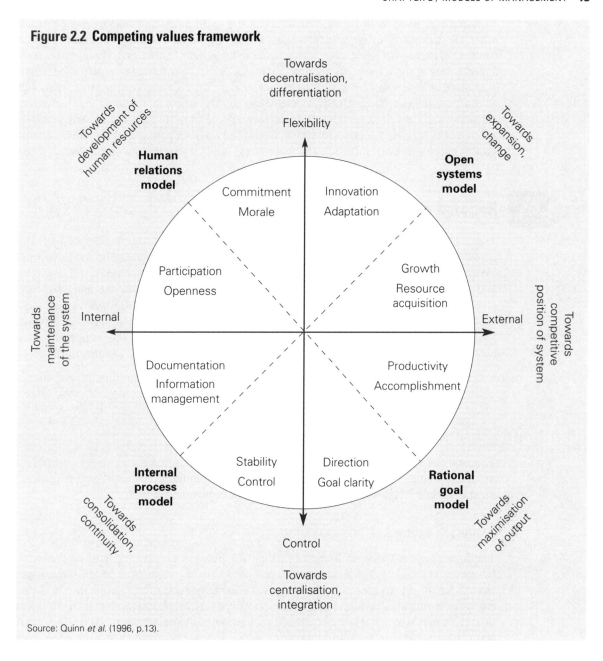

Source: Quinn *et al.* (1996, p.13).

The labels within the circle indicate the primary concerns of theories in that segment. The four broad models that have sought to address those concerns appear around the outside. The human relations model, upper left in the figure, stresses the human-centred criteria of commitment, participation, openness. The open systems model, upper right in the figure, stresses criteria of innovation, adaptation, resource acquisition. The rational goal model in the lower right focuses on productivity, direction, goal clarity. Finally, the internal process model stresses administrative efficiency, documentation, control.

Lastly, the outer ring indicates general values associated with each of the models. For example, it shows that the value associated with the rational goal model is that of maximising output, while the human relations model emphasises developing personnel.

Quinn uses the overall framework to relate the main models of management to each other. He uses the term 'competing' values, as each of the models seems at first to carry a competing message. They may however be complementary, in that each illuminates a different aspect of the same phenomenon. Each model has a perceptual opposite: the human relations model, defined by flexibility and internal focus, is a sharp contrast to the rational goal model, defined by control and external focus. The first values people for themselves while the second values them as contributors to goals. Quinn stresses that the parallels amongst the models are also important. Both the human relations and the open systems models emphasise flexibility: internal process and rational goal models emphasise control.

2.4 Rational goal models

The availability of powered machinery during the Industrial Revolution enabled the transformation of manufacturing and mining processes. These technological innovations were not the only reason for the growth of the factory system. The earlier 'putting-out' system of manufacture, in which people worked at home on materials supplied and collected by entrepreneurs, allowed great freedom over hours, pace and methods of work. It was difficult to control the quantity and quality of output. Emerging capitalist entrepreneurs concluded that they could secure more control if they brought workers together in a factory. Having all workers on a single site meant that:

> coercive authority could be more easily applied, including systems of fines, supervision ... the paraphernalia of bells and clocks, and incentive payments. The employer could dictate the general conditions of work, time and space; including the division of labour, overall organisational layout and design, rules governing movement, shouting, singing and other forms of disobedience. (Thompson and McHugh, 1995, p.25)

This still left entrepreneurs across Europe and later the United States with the problem of how to manage these new factories profitably. Although domestic and export demand for manufactured goods was high, so was the risk of business failure.

Frederick Taylor

The fullest answer to the problems of factory organisation came in the work of Frederick W. Taylor (1856–1915), who is always associated with the ideas of '**scientific management**'. An American mechanical engineer, Taylor focused on the relationship between the worker and the machine-based production systems that by then were in widespread use. He wrote that 'the principal object of management should be to secure the maximum prosperity for the employer, coupled with the maximum prosperity for each employee. The words 'maximum prosperity are used ... to mean the development of every branch of the business to its highest state of excellence, so that the prosperity may be permanent' (Taylor, 1917, p.9). He believed the way to achieve this was to ensure that each worker reached their state of maximum efficiency, so that each was doing 'the highest grade of work for which his natural abilities fit him' (p.9). This would follow from detailed control of the process, which would become the primary responsibility of management, not of the worker. Management should concentrate on understanding the production systems, and use this knowledge to specify every aspect of the operation. Taylor advocated five basic principles designed to help managers achieve this greater control and predictability:

Adam Smith and Charles Babbage

Adam Smith, the Scottish economist, had written enthusiastically in 1776 of the way in which pin manufacturers in Glasgow had broken a job previously done by one man into several small steps. A single worker now performed each of these steps repetitively. This greatly reduced the discretion that workers had over their work but, because each was able to specialise, output increased dramatically. Smith believed that this was one of the key ways in which the new industrial system was increasing the wealth of the country.

Charles Babbage supported and developed Smith's observations. He was an English mathematician better known as the inventor of the first calculating engine. During his work on that project he visited many workshops and factories in England and on the Continent. He then published his reflections on 'the many curious processes and interesting facts' that had come to his attention (Babbage, 1835). He believed that 'perhaps the most important principle on which the economy of

a manufacture depends is the division of labour amongst the persons who perform the work' (p.169). There were several reasons why this method – in which 'each process by which any article is produced is the sole occupation of one individual' – had become so widespread. It reduced training costs, saved the time of moving between jobs and increased the skill that people working at one task would acquire. This in turn meant that workers were able to suggest improvements to the process (pp.169–76).

Babbage also observed that employers in the mining industry had applied the idea to what he called 'mental labour'. 'Great improvements have resulted … from the judicious distribution of duties … amongst those responsible for the whole system of the mine and its government' (p.202). He also recommended that managers should know the precise expense of every stage in production. Factories should also be large enough to secure the economies made possible by the division of labour and the new machinery.

- Use scientific methods to determine the one best way of doing a particular task, rather than rely on the older 'rule of thumb' methods.
- Select the best person to do the job so defined, ensuring that both physical and mental qualities were the most appropriate for the task.
- Train, teach and develop the worker to follow the defined procedures precisely.
- Provide financial incentives to ensure that all the work is done in accordance with the prescribed method.
- Shift all responsibility for planning and organising work from the worker to the manager.

Taylor's underlying philosophy was that scientific analysis and fact, not guesswork, should inform management. Like Smith and Babbage before him, he believed that efficiency rose if tasks were as routine and predictable as possible. He therefore advocated the use of techniques such as time and motion studies, standardised tools and individual incentives. Control would be increased if work was broken down into small, specific tasks. Specialist managerial staff would design these, and generally plan and organise the work of manual staff:

> The work of every workman is fully planned out by the management at least one day in advance, and each man receives in most cases complete written instructions, describing in detail the task which he is to accomplish, as well as the means to be used in doing the work … This task specifies not only what is to be done but how it is to be done and the exact time allowed for doing it. (Taylor, 1917, p.39)

Managers in the industrialised economies adopted Taylor's ideas widely, if selectively, during the 1920s and 1930s (Thompson and McHugh, 1995). His methods allowed productivity to rise many times, and led to the replacement of skilled artisans by semi-skilled workers following set routines of work. Taylor also encouraged managers to employ separate planning and administrative staffs. Henry Ford was an enthusiastic advocate of Taylor's ideas. When he introduced the assembly line in 1914 he was able to reduce the time taken to assemble a car from over 700 hours to 93 minutes. Taylor also influenced the development of administrative systems to support the core operation in areas such as record keeping and stock control. Ford also developed his systems of materials flow and plant layout, making a significant contribution to the development of scientific management (Biggs, 1996; Williams *et al.*, 1992).

MANAGEMENT IN PRACTICE   **Ford's Highland Park plant**

Ford's plant at Highland Park, completed in 1914, was deliberately designed on rationalised lines, in that it introduced predictability and order 'that eliminates all questions of how work is to be done, who will do it, and when it will be done. The rational factory, then, is a factory that runs like a machine' (Biggs, 1996, p.6). Biggs provides abundant evidence of the effects of the wide application of rational production methods in the plant:

> The advances made in Ford's New Shop allowed the engineers to control work better. The most obvious and startling change in the entire factory was, of course, the constant movement, and the speed of that movement, not only the speed of the assembly line, but the speed of every moving person or object in the plant. When workers moved from one place to another, they were instructed to move fast. Laborers who moved parts were ordered to go faster. And everyone on a moving line worked as fast as the line dictated. Not only were workers expected to produce at a certain rate in order to earn a day's wages but they also had no choice but to work at the pace dictated by the machine. By 1914 the company employed supervisors called pushers (not the materials handlers) to 'push' the men to work faster.

The 1914 jobs of most Ford workers bore little resemblance to what they had been just four years earlier, and few liked the transformation of their work. Even as early as 1912, job restructuring sought an 'exceptionally specialized division of labor [to bring] the human element into condition of performing automatically with machine-like regularity and speed' (Biggs, 1996, p.132).

However, the gains in worker productivity were often achieved at great human cost. The trade unions in the United States believed Taylor's methods increased unemployment, and vigorously opposed them. For many people, work on an assembly line or similarly routine operation is boring and alienating, devoid of much human meaning. In extreme cases the time taken to complete an operation before starting to repeat it – the cycle-time – is less than a minute, and uses few human abilities.

Frank and Lillian Gilbreth

Frank and Lillian Gilbreth (1868–1924 and 1878–1972) worked as a husband and wife team, and enthusiastically promoted the development of scientific management. Frank Gilbreth had originally been a bricklayer, and observed a variety of practices that made the pace of work slow and output unpredictable. He studied the movements involved with the help of film, and used this to find the most economical motions for each task. He also specified exactly what the employer should provide. This included equipment such as trestles at the right height and materials at the right time. Supplies of mortar and bricks (arranged the right way up) should arrive at the right time so as not to interrupt the work. In an influential work (Gilbreth, 1911) he laid down very precise guides on the process of laying the bricks. These were intended to reduce unnecessary actions, and hence fatigue. He claimed that his methods would reduce the number of movements needed to lay a brick from 18 to 5. He gave equally precise guidance on how to train apprentices, to ensure that they followed the correct systems: 'These rules and charts will enable the apprentice to earn large wages immediately, because he has here a series of instructions that show each and every motion in the proper sequence. They eliminate the 'wrong' way [and] all experimenting' (quoted in Spriegel and Myers, 1953, p.57).

Lillian Gilbreth focused on the psychological aspects of management, and on promoting the welfare of the individual worker. She too promoted the ideas of scientific management, believing that, properly applied, they would enable individuals to reach their full human potential. Through careful development of systems, careful selection, clearly planned training and proper equipment workers would build their self-respect and pride. *In The Psychology of Management* (1914) she argued that if workers did something well, and that was made public, they would develop pride in their work and in themselves. She recognised that workers had inquiring minds, and that management should take time to explain the reasons for work processes: 'Unless the man knows why he is doing the thing, his judgment will never reinforce his work … His work will not enlist his zeal unless he knows exactly why he is made to work in the particular manner prescribed' (quoted in Spriegel and Myers, 1953, p.431).

ACTIVITY 2.1

What assumptions did they make?

What assumptions did Frederick Taylor and Lillian Gilbreth make about the interests and abilities of industrial workers?

Operational research

Another perspective that is included within the rational goal model is that of operational research (OR). This originated during the early 1940s, when the UK War Department faced severe management problems. To solve these it formed what were called operational research teams, which pooled the expertise of various scientific disciplines such as mathematics and physics. The teams produced significant results, especially when their intellectual expertise was supported by the earliest computers, which were developed in the same period.

After the war, management in both industrial and governmental organisations saw that they could apply OR to the problems of managing complex civil organisations as well as military ones. The scale and complexity of business were increasing, and required new techniques to analyse the many interrelated variables involved. Mathematical models could help and computing developments supported the increasing sophistication of the models the scientists produced. This led to the continuing growth of the 'management science approach'.

The management science approach to a problem usually begins by putting together a team from relevant disciplines to analyse the issue and propose a solution to management. The team constructs a mathematical model showing the links between all the relevant factors. By changing the values of variables in the model (such as increasing transport costs) and comparing different forms of the equations, the team can establish the quantitative effects of each change. The team can present management with apparently objective analyses of alternatives, as a guide to their decisions.

Large organisations in both the public and private sectors use the techniques of management science. The model supports the planning function in areas such as production scheduling, cash flow management and estimating the inventory required for different levels of production. It also contributes to the control function by helping to specify and measure appropriate performance levels.

One difficulty with management science is that some managers find the mathematical basis forbidding and inaccessible. A second difficulty is that it cannot take into account the human and social uncertainties of modern organisations. The assumptions built into the models may in practice be invalid, especially if they involve political interests. The technique can clearly contribute to the analysis of management problems, and probably does so best when recognised as only one, relatively technical, part of the total solution.

Current status

Table 2.1 summarises principles common to the rational goal models of management and indicates their modern application.

Table 2.1 Modern applications of the rational goal model

Principle of the rational model	Current applications
Systematic work methods	Work study and process engineering departments develop precise specifications for processes and job descriptions for staff
Detailed division of labour	Where staff focus on one type of work or customer in manufacturing or service operations
Centralised planning and control	Modern information systems increase the scope for central control of worldwide operations – for example in the electronics industry
'Low-involvement' employment relationship	Using temporary staff called in as required, rather than permanent employees

Examples of rational goal approaches are common in manufacturing and service organisations. Watch the staff in a bank or a travel agency dealing with a routine transaction with a customer. The chances are that they will follow a set of prompts on their computer screen, key in the answer, and the system then prompts the next question. This limits the scope for error and deviation from the prescribed route (Gabrial, 1988; Ritzer, 1993).

Using technology to control staff

A successful travel company introduced a networked computer system linking all of its branches to head office. Many benefits were expected and achieved. One of these was that, having sold a holiday, staff should work in a more disciplined routine to complete the administrative details. The information technology director commented:

> We are finding that paper is never a standard system – there are always different ways you can handle paper. You can always choose to fill in a form or not fill it in, choose to complete a box or not. We expect that automation will finally provide the disciplined system that people must adhere to.

Source: Boddy and Gunson (1996).

Q Case questions 2.2

- Which of the ideas in the rational model of management was Owen experimenting with at New Lanark?
- Would you describe Owen's approach to management as low involvement?
- What assumptions did he make about the motivation of workers?

ACTIVITY 2.2

Finding current examples

Try to find an original example of work that has been designed on rational goal principles. There are examples in office and service areas as well as in factories. Compare your examples with those of colleagues.

2.5 Internal process models

Max Weber

A major contribution to the search for ways of managing organisations efficiently came from Max Weber (1947). Weber (1864–1920) was a German social historian who drew attention to the growing significance of large organisations. As societies became more complex, responsibility for core activities became concentrated in specialised units. They could only operate with systems that institutionalised the management process by creating organisations that relied heavily on rules and regulations, hierarchy, precise division of labour and detailed procedures. Weber was one of the first to write extensively about the problems of organisations and to observe that the process of **bureaucracy** was bringing routine to office operations just as machines had to production.

Bureaucratic management is usually associated with the six characteristics shown in Key Ideas below.

KEY IDEAS The characteristics of bureaucratic management

Rules and regulations The formal guidelines that define and control the behaviour of all employees while they are working. This formal system helps to provide the discipline that an organisation needs to exercise control and reach its goals. Adherence to rules and regulations ensures uniformity of procedures and operations, regardless of an individual manager's or employee's personal desires. Rules and regulations also enable top management to direct and co-ordinate the efforts of the middle managers and, through them, the efforts of first-line managers and employees. Managers may come and go, but rules and regulations help to maintain organisational stability.

Impersonality Reliance on rules and regulations leads to impersonality, which protects employees from the personal whims of managers. Although the term often has negative connotations, Weber believed that impersonality ensured fairness for employees. An impersonal superior evaluates subordinates objectively on performance and expertise rather than subjectively on personal or emotional considerations. In other words, impersonality heightens a manager's objectivity and minimises discretion (or favouritism).

Division of labour Managers and employees perform officially prescribed and assigned duties based on specialisation and expertise, with the benefits originally noted by Adam Smith. This enables management to set people to work on jobs that are relatively easy to learn and control.

Hierarchical structure Weber advocated the use of a clear hierarchical structure in which jobs were ranked vertically by the amount of authority the holder had to make decisions. Typically, power and authority increase through each level up to the top of the hierarchy. Each lower position is under the control and direction of a higher position.

Authority structure A system based on rules, regulations, impersonality, division of labour and hierarchical structure is tied together by an authority structure – the right to make decisions of varying importance at different levels within the organisation.

Rationality The last characteristic of bureaucratic management, rationality, refers to using the most efficient means to achieve the organisation's objectives. Hence managers should run their organisations logically and 'scientifically'. All decisions should lead directly to achieving the organisation's objectives.

ACTIVITY 2.3

Bureaucratic management in education?

Reflect on your role as a student and how rules have affected the experience. Try to identify one example of your own to add to those below or that illustrates the point specifically within your institution:

- *Rules and regulations – the number of courses you need to pass for a degree.*
- *Impersonality – admission criteria, emphasising previous exam performance, not friendship.*
- *Division of labour – chemists not teaching management, and vice versa.*
- *Hierarchical structure – to whom your lecturer reports, whom they in turn report to.*
- *Authority structure – who decides whether to recruit an additional lecturer.*
- *Rationality – appointing new staff to departments that have the highest ratio of students to staff.*

Compare your examples with those of other students and consider the effects of these features of bureaucracy on the institution and its students.

Weber was aware that, as well as creating bureaucratic management structures, organisations were applying scientific management techniques to the control of production systems. He approved of this development, seeing it as the ideal vehicle for imposing discipline on factory work. The two systems complemented each other. Formal structures of management enhance the centralisation of power, and hierarchical organisation aids functional specialisation. Fragmenting tasks, imposing close discipline on employees and minimising their discretion ensures controlled, predictable performance (Thompson and McHugh, 1995). Job descriptions that define the work expected and performance measures which assess each employee have the same effect.

While the work organisation aspects of Weber are therefore consistent with those of scientific management, his ideas on the employment relationship were new. He stressed the importance of a career structure clearly linked to the position a person held in the hierarchy. This would allow them to move up the hierarchy in a predictable, defined and open way, which would increase their commitment to the organisation.

He also believed that officials should work within a framework of rules. The right to give instructions was based on a person's authority derived from impersonal rules set by those higher in the organisation. This in turn reflected a rational analysis of how staff should do the work. This approach worked well in large public and private organisations, such as government departments and banks.

The systems had both positive and negative aspects for staff. They may have objected to rules that overspecified how they should do their job, but they are likely to have welcomed those to do with selection and promotion. Rules brought some fairness to these processes at a time when nepotism and favouritism were common.

Is bureaucracy always bad?

Rules and regulations often get a bad press, and we have all been frustrated at times by rules that got in the way of what we wanted to do. Are they always bad news? Think back to a job that you or a friend has held.

- *Did the supervisors appear to operate within a framework of rules, or did they do as they wished? What were the effects?*
- *Did clear rules guide selection and promotion procedures? What were the effects?*
- *As a customer of an organisation, how have rules and regulations affected your experience?*

Henri Fayol

Managers were also able to draw on the ideas of **administrative management** developed by Henri Fayol (1841–1925), whose work carries echoes of both Taylor and Weber. While Taylor's scientific management focused on the production systems, Fayol devised management principles that would apply to the organisation as a whole. Fayol was a distinguished French mining engineer who from 1860 to 1918 worked for a major coal mining company. From 1888 until his retirement he was managing director of the Commentry–Fourchambault–Decazeville combine, turning it from an almost bankrupt business into one of the success stories of French industry. Throughout his career he maintained close contacts with French business and government. From 1918 until his death in 1925 he worked to publicise his ideas on business administration. His book *Administration, industrielle et générale* only became widely available in English in 1949 (Fayol, 1949).

Fayol credited his success as a manager to the methods he used, not to his personal qualities. He believed that managers should use certain principles in performing their functions, and these are listed in Key Ideas. The term 'principles' did not imply they were rigid or absolute:

> It is all a question of proportion … allowance must be made for different changing circumstances … the principles are flexible and capable of adaptation to every need; it is a matter of knowing how to make use of them, which is a difficult art requiring intelligence, experience, decision and proportion. (Fayol, 1949, p.14)

KEY IDEAS Fayol's principles of management

1. **Division of work** If people specialise, the more can they concentrate on the same matters and so acquire an ability and accuracy, which increases their output. However, 'it has its limits which experience teaches us may not be exceeded.'

2. **Authority and responsibility** The right to give orders and to exact obedience, derived from either a manager's official authority or his or her personal authority. 'Wherever authority is exercised, responsibility arises.'

3. **Discipline** 'Essential for the smooth running of business … without discipline no enterprise could prosper.'

4. **Unity of command** 'For any action whatsoever, an employee should receive orders from one superior only' – to avoid conflicting instructions and resulting confusion.

5. **Unity of direction** 'One head and one plan for a group of activities having the same objective … essential to unity of action, co-ordination of strength and focusing of effort.'

6. **Subordination of individual interest to general interest** 'The interests of one employee or group of employees should not prevail over that of the concern.'

7. **Remuneration of personnel** 'Should be fair and, as far as possible, afford satisfaction both to personnel and firm.'

8. **Centralisation** 'The question of centralisation or decentralisation is a simple question of proportion … of finding the optimum degree for the particular concern … [the] share of initiative to be left to [subordinates] depends on the character of the manager, the reliability of the subordinates and the condition of the business. The degree of centralisation must vary according to different cases.'

9. **Scalar chain** 'The chain of superiors from the ultimate authority to the lowest ranks – the route followed by all communications which start from or go to the ultimate authority … is at times disastrously lengthy in large concerns, especially governmental ones.' Fayol pointed out that many activities depend on speedy action. Then it was appropriate for people at the same level of the chain to communicate directly, as long as their immediate superiors approved of the contact. 'It provides for the usual exercise of some measure of initiative at all levels of authority.'

10. **Order** Materials should be in the right place to avoid loss, and the posts essential for the smooth running of the business filled by capable people.

11. **Equity** Managers should be both friendly and fair to their subordinates – 'equity requires much good sense, experience and good nature'.

12. **Stability of tenure of personnel** A high employee turnover is not efficient – 'Instability of tenure is at one and the same time cause and effect of bad running.'

13. **Initiative** 'The initiative of all represents a great source of strength for businesses. This is particularly apparent at difficult times; hence it is essential to encourage and develop this capacity to the full. The manager must be able to sacrifice some personal vanity in order to grant this satisfaction to subordinates … a manager able to do so is infinitely superior to one who cannot.'

14. **Esprit de corps** 'Harmony, union among the personnel of a concern is a great strength in that concern. Effort, then, should be made to establish it.' Fayol went on to suggest two ways of doing so: avoid sowing dissension amongst subordinates, and use verbal rather than written communication when it is simpler and quicker.

Source: Fayol (1949).

Current status

Table 2.2 summarises some principles common to the internal process models of management and indicates their modern application.

Table 2.2 Modern applications of the internal process model

Some principles of the internal process model	Current applications
Rules and regulations	All organisations have these, covering areas such as expenditure, safety, recruitment or confidentiality
Impersonality	Appraisal processes based on objective criteria or team assessments, not personal preference
Division of labour	Setting narrow limits to employees' areas of responsibility – found in many organisations
Hierarchical structure	Most company organisation charts show managers in a hierarchy – with subordinates below them
Authority structure	Holders of a particular post in the hierarchy have authority over matters relating to that post, and not to matters which are the responsibility of others
Centralisation	Organisations balance central control of (say) finance or online services with local control of (say) pricing or recruitment
Initiative	Current practice in some firms to increase the power and responsibility of operating staff
Rationality	Managers expected to focus on things that support the organisation's objectives, and assess issues on the basis of fact, not preference

Some organisations have been spectacularly successful with these methods, especially when they have many geographically dispersed outlets. Hotel groups, estate agents, retail chains and banks are usually like this – customers expect them to deliver a common and predictable service in each location. So they centralise design and development activities to ensure a standard product. Manuals set out precisely how to deliver the service. They also set out standards and procedures that managers should follow in running the operation. These include how staff are to be recruited and trained and what the premises must look like. The manuals explain how to treat customers, how to conduct the transaction and the accounting procedures to follow. As Fayol advised, these procedures must be applied 'in proportion', allowing for unusual circumstances. Applied incorrectly they dehumanise work and annoy customers.

The main danger stems from the fact that the principles were designed to support management in relatively predictable and routine situations. Many parts of business life are still like that, and in those circumstances the internal process models are valuable. They are less suitable for those aspects of organisation that deal with change and innovation.

2.6 Human relations models

In the early twentieth century several writers such as Follett and Mayo recognised the limitations of the scientific management perspective as a complete answer.

Mary Parker Follett

Mary Parker Follett (1868–1933) graduated with distinction from Radcliffe College (now part of Harvard University) in 1898, having studied economics, law and philosophy. She took up social work and quickly acquired a reputation as an imaginative and effective professional, both in creating innovative policies and in putting them into practice. Local and national government sought her advice. As well as being a practical manager she was a keen observer of events. She was learning at first hand about the dynamics of group process – how people work together to develop and implement plans and tasks. She became impressed by the creativity of the group process and realised the potential it offered for truly democratic government – which people themselves would have to create.

KEY IDEAS **Mary Parker Follett on teams**

Follett saw the group as an intermediate institution between the solitary individual and the abstract society, and argued that it was through the institution of the group that people organised co-operative action. In 1926 she wrote:

Early psychology was based on the study of the individual; early sociology was based on the study of society. But there is no such thing as the 'individual ', there is no such thing as 'society '; there is only the group and the group-unit – the social individual. Social psychology must begin with an intensive study of the group, of the selective processes which go on within it, the differentiated reactions, the likenesses and the unlikenesses, and the spiritual energy which unites them.

Source: Quoted in Graham (1995, p.230).

Follett advocated replacing bureaucratic institutions by group networks in which people themselves analysed their problems and then produced and implemented their solutions. True democracy depended on tapping the potential of all members of society by enabling individuals to take part in groups organised to solve particular problems and accepting personal responsibility for the result. If the essence of democracy is creating, the technique of democracy is group life. Such ideas are finding renewed relevance today in the work of institutions such as community action and tenants' groups.

In the 1920s Follett became involved in the business world, investigating problems at the invitation of management. She again advocated the application of the self-governing principle that would facilitate the growth both of individuals and of the group to which they belonged. Conflict was essential if people brought valuable differences of view to bear on a problem. The group then had to solve the conflict in a way that helped to create what she called an integrative unity amongst the people concerned. The essential point about a common belief or policy was not that people shared it, but that they had *produced* it in common, through processes aimed at integrating the differences.

She agreed that organisations had to optimise production, but did not accept that the strict division of labour advocated by scientific management was the right way to achieve this (Follett, 1920). The notion of individual workers performing endless repetitive tasks under close supervision devalued human creativity. The human side should not be separated from the mechanical side, as the two are bound up together. She believed that people, whether managers or workers, behave as they do because of the reciprocal response that occurs in any relationship. If managers tell people to behave as if they are extensions of the assembly line they will do so. This implied that, to achieve effective results, managers should not manipulate their subordinates but train them in the use of responsible power – 'managers should give workers a chance to grow capacity or power for themselves'.

Follett also wrote about leadership, pointing out that leadership shifts from one person to another, depending on the situation. The situation determines what needs to be done, but not who should do it. The person who discovers how best to deal with the situation should take over the leadership. An excellent review of Follett's contribution is provided by Graham (1995).

Mayo's perspective

Elton Mayo was a professor at the Harvard Business School who drew attention to aspects of human behaviour that practitioners of scientific management had neglected. In terms of Morgan's images, the appropriate metaphor should not be that of the machine but of the living organism. This organism has needs that it can satisfy in inter-action with the environment. Mayo's insight grew out of attempts to discover the social and psychological factors that affected performance. His team conducted a series of studies at the Hawthorne plant, owned by the Western Electric Company. The work began in 1924 as a series of experiments to discover the effect on output of changing defined environmental factors. With the emphasis on the physical working conditions, and how they might affect productivity, the questions were similar to ones Taylor might have asked.

The first group of experiments was into the effect of lighting. The researchers estab-lished a control and an experimental group, then gradually varied the level of illumination and measured the output. As light rose, so did output. More surprisingly, as lighting fell, making it harder to see the components being assembled, output continued to rise. Even stranger was the fact that output in the control group also rose, even though there had been no change in their lighting. Clearly the physical conditions had only a small effect on the results. The team set up a more comprehensive set of experiments to identify the other factors.

They assembled a small group of workers in a separate room and altered several vari-ables in turn. These included the working hours, the length of breaks and the provision of refreshments. The experienced workers were assembling small components into tele-phone equipment. A supervisor was in charge of them. There was also an observer to record the experiments and how the workers reacted. Great care was taken to prevent external factors disrupting the effects of the variables under investigation. The researchers were careful to explain what was happening and to ensure that the workers understood what they were expected to do. They also took into account the workers' views on aspects of the working situation.

The experiment began, with conditions being varied every two or three weeks and output measured regularly by the supervisor. The trend in output showed a gradual, if erratic, increase – even when the researchers returned conditions to those prevailing at an earlier stage. Figure 2.3 shows the trend.

ACTIVITY 2.5

Explaining the trend

Describe in your own terms the pattern shown in Figure 2.3. Compare in particular the output in periods 7, 10 and 13. Before reading on, what explanations would you put forward for this trend?

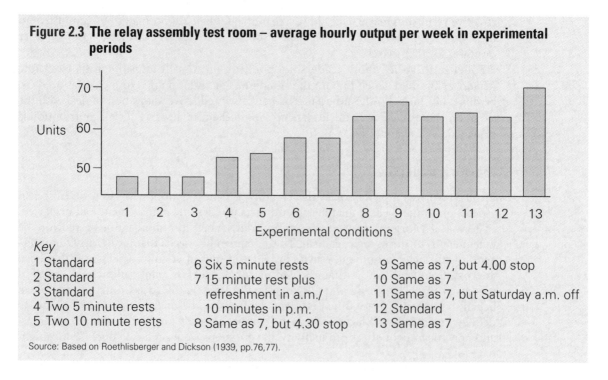

Figure 2.3 The relay assembly test room – average hourly output per week in experimental periods

Key

1 Standard
2 Standard
3 Standard
4 Two 5 minute rests
5 Two 10 minute rests

6 Six 5 minute rests
7 15 minute rest plus refreshment in a.m./ 10 minutes in p.m.
8 Same as 7, but 4.30 stop

9 Same as 7, but 4.00 stop
10 Same as 7
11 Same as 7, but Saturday a.m. off
12 Standard
13 Same as 7

Source: Based on Roethlisberger and Dickson (1939, pp.76,77).

During the experiments, Mayo and some associates from Harvard tried to interpret the results (Roethlisberger and Dickson, 1939; Mayo, 1949). They concluded that the increase in productivity was not related to the physical changes, but to a change in the social situation in which the group was working:

> the major experimental change was introduced when those in charge sought to hold the situation humanly steady (in the interests of critical changes to be introduced) by getting the co-operation of the workers. What actually happened was that 6 individuals became a team and the team gave itself wholeheartedly and spontaneously to co-operation in the environment. (Mayo, 1949, p.64)

The group felt they were special: managers asked for their views, were involved with them, paid attention to them and they had the chance to influence some aspects of the work.

The research team also observed another part of the factory, the bank wiring room. This revealed a different aspect of group working. Workers in this area received their wages according to a piece-rate system. This is a system in which management pays workers a set amount for each item, or piece, that they produce. Such schemes reflect the theory that financial incentives will encourage staff to work.

Mayo's researchers were surprised to observe that employees regularly produced much less than they could have done. The reason was that the group had developed their own sense of what a normal rate of output should be, and ensured that all members of the team adhered to this rate. The workers believed that if they produced, and earned, too much, management would reduce the piece-rate, so that employees would have to work harder for the same pay. Group members therefore exercised informal sanctions against colleagues who worked too hard (or too slowly), until they came into line. Members who did too much were known as 'rate-busters' while those who did too little were 'chisellers'. Anyone who told the supervisor about the norms was a 'squealer'. Sanctions included being 'binged' – tapped on the shoulder to let them know that what they were doing was wrong. Managers had little or no control over these groups, who appointed an informal leader.

Finally, the research team conducted an extensive interviewing programme of employees. The team began by asking fairly direct questions about the working environment, how employees felt about their job, and then moved on to questions about the employees' life in general. The responses showed that there were often close links between work and domestic life. Work experiences went much more deeply into people's wider life than had been expected. Conversely, events in their domestic life affected their feelings about work. The implication was that supervisors needed to pay attention to emotional needs of subordinates.

ACTIVITY 2.6

A comparison with Taylor

How does this evidence compare with Frederick Taylor's belief that piece-rates would be an incentive to individuals to raise their performance?

Overall, these and similar observations led Mayo to introduce the idea of 'social man', in contrast to the 'economic man' who was at the centre of the earlier theories. While financial rewards would influence the latter, work group relationships and loyalties would influence the former. These would outweigh management pressure.

> *Mayo on financial incentives:*
>
> 'Man's desire to be continuously associated in work with his fellows is a strong, if not the strongest, human characteristic. Any disregard of it by management or any ill-advised attempt to defeat this human impulse leads instantly to some form of defeat for management itself. In [a study] the efficiency experts had assumed the primacy of financial incentive; in this they were wrong; not until the conditions of working group formation were satisfied did the financial incentives come into operation.'
>
> (Mayo, 1949, p.99)

People had social needs that they sought to satisfy – and how they did so may be either in line with management interests or in opposition to them. Mayo's study also drew attention to the informal groups existing alongside the formal organisation designed by management.

Latter analysis of the experimental data by Greenwood *et al.* (1983) suggested that the research team had underestimated the influence of financial incentives on performance. For example, becoming a member of the experimental group in itself increased the worker's income. Despite the possibly inaccurate interpretation of the data, the findings stimulated interest in the influence of social factors in the workplace. The research therefore added another dimension to knowledge of the management process. Scientific management stressed the technical aspects of work, and the importance of designing that correctly. The Hawthorne studies implied that management should give at least as much attention to human factors. Employees would work more effectively if management showed some interest in their well-being through more humane supervisory practices.

Q Case questions 2.3

- In what ways did Robert Owen anticipate the conclusions of the Hawthorne experiments?
- Which of the practices that he used took account of workers' social needs?

Current status

The Hawthorne studies themselves have been controversial, and the interpretations questioned. Also, the idea of social man is itself now seen as an incomplete picture of people at work. Providing good supervision and decent working environments may increase satisfaction, but not necessarily productivity. The influences on performance are certainly more complex than Taylor assumed – but are also more complex than Mayo assumed.

Other writers have followed and developed Mayo's emphasis on the human side of organisations. McGregor (1960), Maslow (1970) and Alderfer (1972) have suggested ways of integrating human needs with those of the organisation as expressed by management. Some of this reflected a human relations concern for employees' own well-being. A much stronger influence was the changing external environments of organisations, which have become much less predictable since the time of Frederick Taylor and Elton Mayo. The theoretical roots of these ideas are contained in open systems models.

KEY IDEAS   **Women and research**

The Hawthorne studies are often quoted as an example of theorists' failure to pay attention to the significance of gender (Acker and Van Houton, 1992; Wilson, 1996). Despite the striking differences between the findings of the relay assembly test female group and the male group in the bank wiring observation room, generalisations made were equally applicable to workers of both genders. The female group increased their output and showed increasingly co-operative attitudes towards management. The male group restricted their output, contrary to management's efforts. These observations rightly led the researchers to acknowledge the significance of group dynamics.

However, when Acker and Van Houton (1992) re-examined the Hawthorne studies they found that the researchers failed to pay attention to the possible effect of the different sex of the subjects in the two rooms. They 'also seem to have taken no notice of the possible effects of variation in research procedures and the interaction of those variations with the sex of the subjects' (p.21). The analysis of the experiments ignored the fact that the women in the relay assembly test room were individually and informally selected by the plant manager to make sure that they really wanted to participate. Further to this, when two of these women were unco-operative to managers' strenuous efforts to control, they were replaced. In contrast to the female group, in the male-based experiment the pressure to participate in the research was on the group rather than on the individuals. During this experiment no one was replaced, even though 'there was slowing down, laughing and talking'.

2.7   **Open systems models**

The open systems approach builds on earlier work in general systems theory, and has been widely used to help understand management and organisational issues. The basic idea is to think of the organisation not just as a **system**, but as an **open system**.

The open systems approach draws attention to the links between the internal parts of a system, and to the links between the whole system and the outside world. The system is separated from its environment by the **system boundary**. It is sustained by flows of energy and materials, which enter it from the environment across this boundary, undergo some transformation process within the system, and leave the system as goods and services. The central theme in open systems views of management is that organisations depend on the wider environment for different kinds of sustenance if they are to survive and prosper. Figure 2.4 is a simple model of the organisation as an open system.

The figure shows input and output processes, conversion processes and feedback loops. The message in emphasising the relationship between the organisation and the wider environment is that the organisation must satisfy the environment well enough to receive sustaining resources from it. The management task is to sustain those links if the organisation is to thrive. **Feedback** refers to information about the performance of the system. It may be deliberate through customer surveys or unplanned, such as the loss of business to a competitor. Feedback enables those managing the system to take remedial action.

Q Case questions 2.4

A systems diagram of Owen's mill

Draw a systems diagram detailing the main inputs, transformation and outputs of Robert Owen's mill. Which aspects of the environment probably had most influence on his management practices?

Another key idea is that of **subsystems**. A course is a subsystem within a department or faculty, the faculty is a subsystem of a university, the university a subsystem of the higher education system. This in turn is part of the whole education system. A course itself will consist of several systems – one for quality assurance, one for enrolling students, one for teaching, another for assessment, and so on. In terms of Figure 2.1, each of the organisational elements is itself a subsystem – there is a technical subsystem, a people subsystem, a finance subsytem and so on, as Figure 2.5 shows.

These subsystems interact with each other, and how well people manage these links affect the functioning of the whole system: when universities move their teaching from three terms to two semesters this has implications across the system – such as accommodation (*technology*), costs (*finance*), arrangements for admission and examinations (*business processes*).

Figure 2.4 The systems model

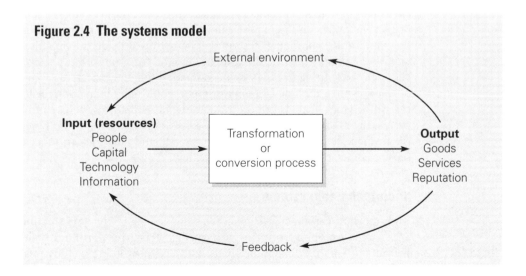

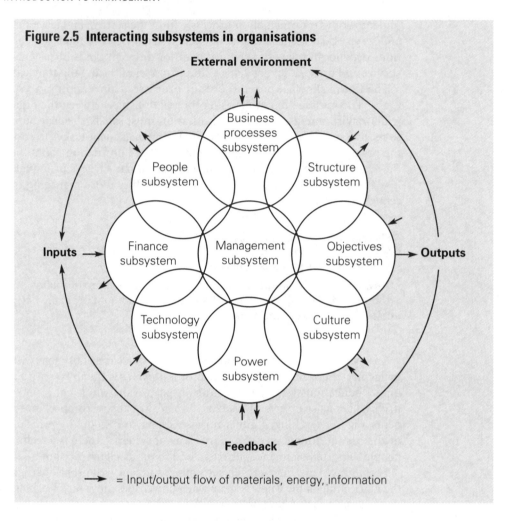

Figure 2.5 Interacting subsystems in organisations

⟶ = Input/output flow of materials, energy, information

A systems approach emphasises the links between systems, and alerts management to the likelihood that a change in one will have consequences for others. What counts as the environment depends on the level at which the analysis is being conducted. If a team at British Airways is discussing their new strategy of concentrating on business passengers, the relevant environmental factors will be mainly outside the organisation – the strategies of competing airlines, the level of demand for the more expensive service, whether better-timed landing slots can be negotiated. If the discussion was about the reservations procedures then the relevant environment would mainly include related systems within the airline (such as their call centres and the information systems) and the links to travel agents. In either case the principle is the same: take account of the systems that surround the immediate one. That implies being ready and able to scan those environments, to sense changes in them, and to act accordingly.

Sociotechnical systems

An important variant of systems theory is the idea of the **sociotechnical system**. The approach developed from the work of Eric Trist and Ken Bamforth at the Tavistock Institute in London during the 1950s. Their most prominent study was of an attempt by the coal industry to mechanise the mining system. Introducing what were in essence assembly line technologies and methods at the coalface had severe consequences for the social system that the older pattern of working had encouraged. The technological system destroyed the fabric of the social system, and the solution lay in reconciling the needs of both systems.

This and similar studies in many different countries showed the benefits of seeing a work system as a combination of a material technology (tools, machinery, techniques) and a social organisation (people, relationships, constitutional arrangements). In other words, an organisation has technical and social subsystems. Each affects the other, so people need to manage them together for them to work in harmony.

The general message of systems theory is that in designing any kind of system it is necessary to take account of the interdependencies between the various elements of the system. The sociotechnical view, in particular, argues that organisations are best understood as interdependent systems. Analysis should deal with both the social and technical components. The aim is to integrate them rather than to optimise one without regard to the other. The experience of applying the approach in many practical management situations is reflected in a set of principles to be used in designing organisations (Cherns, 1987), a topic discussed in Chapter 10.

Those advocating the approach acknowledge that it will enable people to articulate different objectives for a system, if it is to satisfy social as well as technical criteria. They recommended open discussion to resolve these conflicts, in the belief that this process is not creating the conflict, but merely bringing it out into the open. Resolving it early in the process will be more productive than ignoring it.

Contingency management

A further development of the open systems view of organisations is what has become known as the contingency model (discussed in Chapter 10). The model began with the work of Woodward (1958) and Burns and Stalker (1961) in the United Kingdom, and of Lawrence and Lorsch (1967) in the United States. The main theme of such models is that organisations must adapt their internal structures and processes to match the conditions in the outside world if they are to survive and prosper. The **contingency approach** looks for those aspects of the environment that management should take into account in deciding how to structure the organisation. As the environment becomes more complex managers can use contingency perspectives to examine what structure will meet the needs of the business. For example, contingency theorists place a particular emphasis on creating organisations that can cope with uncertainty and change. At the same time they recognise that some functions within such organisations may need to be handled in a highly stable and predictable way, using the values of the internal process model.

A further group of ideas has developed since the publication by Peters and Waterman of their best-selling book *In Search of Excellence* (1982). As management consultants with McKinsey & Co. Peters and Waterman set out to discover the reasons for the success of what they regarded as 43 excellently managed US companies.

One of their conclusions was that the excellent companies had a distinctive set of philosophies about human nature and the way that people interact in organisations. They did not see people as rational beings, motivated by fear and willing to accept a low-involvement employment relationship. Instead, the excellent companies regarded people as emotional, intuitive and creative social creatures who like to celebrate victories, however small, who value self-control, but who also need and want the security and meaning of achieving goals through organisations. From this, Peters and Waterman deduced some general rules for treating workers with dignity and respect. This was not out of a sense of philanthropy, but to ensure that people did quality work in an increasingly uncertain environment. In his later work, Peters (1987) continued to stress that people were not components in a rational machine but were the main source of ideas and creativity. Only by tapping the full ingenuity of its staff could management succeed in the current business world.

In Search of Excellence had a significant influence on management thinking and practice. It reflected a move away from rational goal approaches that emphasised complex and usually quantitative analytical techniques as the route to effective management. Peters and Waterman criticised management for having become overreliant on analytical techniques at the expense of the more intuitive and human aspects of business. This, they believed, led to inflexibility and an inability to innovate through experimentation, especially through encouraging attention to the culture and values of organisations. In this they developed the ideas associated with the human relations school, such as those of Douglas McGregor.

The excellent companies appeared to have succeeded by developing strong cultures. As Watson (1994) suggested:

> people do not wander away from serving the key purposes of the organisation's founders or leaders. The tightness of control comes from people *choosing* to do what is required of them because they wish to serve the *values* which they share with those in charge. These values, typically focusing on quality of service to customers, are transmitted and manifested in the organisations' culture. This culture uses stories, myths and legends to keep these values alive and people tend to be happy to share these values and subscribe to the corporate legends because to do so is to find meaning in their lives. (p.16)

Despite some criticism of the empirical basis of their work, Watson went on to observe that these shortcomings in themselves should not obscure the importance of Peters and Waterman's underlying message. He notes with approval Thompson and McHugh's (1995) comment that:

> Creating a culture resonant with the overall goals is relevant to any organisation, whether it be trade unions, voluntary groups or producer co-operatives. Indeed, it is more important in such consensual groupings. Co-operatives, for example, can degenerate organisationally because they fail to develop adequate mechanisms for transmitting the original ideals from founders to new members and sustaining them through new shared experiences. (pp.18–19)

Current status

Those writing about management in the late nineteenth and early twentieth centuries were not unaware of the external world. They could observe the massive shift from an agricultural to an industrial economy and the often severe economic fluctuations and political changes that periodically affected organisations. Yet there were also significant sources of stability. Communication systems were such that most organisations were able to operate in a local market with relatively little risk of new competition. Scientific discoveries opened up new possibilities, and threatened old businesses, but more slowly than today. There was widespread conflict between management and labour, but the fundamental power of capitalist enterprises remained intact.

These may explain why the emphasis in the early theorists' work was on ways of perfecting the internal arrangements of business so that it could cope with, to modern eyes, a relatively stable business environment. Hence they appear to have viewed organisations as if they were closed systems, and paid relatively little attention to the external world.

An open systems perspective is different, emphasising that people need to plan with the environment of the system in mind. This not only affects the need to adjust objectives and plans more rapidly to external change but also raises the need to find new ways of motivating people to act appropriately in these new conditions.

Yet identifying successful management practice in such conditions is hazardous. The subsequent history of the 'excellent' companies identified by Peters and Waterman demonstrates this. Richard Pascale (1990) found that within five years of publication only 14 of the original 43 companies were still regarded as excellent, and some were in serious trouble. He argued that the pursuit of excellence should not be seen as an end in itself but as a never-ending task. What produced excellence at one time may not do so later.

It is important to recall that organisations in themselves achieve nothing: any change in policy depends on the initiative and action of individuals. Open systems models draw attention to the wide, theoretically infinite, range of issues that potentially have implications for an organisation. They only affect internal affairs when a person notes an issue and chooses to do something that places it on the management agenda. Whether issues are noticed, how they are interpreted, and what action is taken on them depends on the goals, interests and power of individuals. Factors such as these shape an organisation's response to uncertain conditions.

2.8 Management theories for uncertain conditions

Although theories of management develop at particular times in response to current problems this does not mean that newer is better. While new concerns bring out new theories, old concerns usually remain. Hence, while current theories are heavily weighted towards ways of encouraging flexibility and change, management still seeks control. Rather than thinking of theoretical development as a linear process it may be better to think of it as a circular or iterative process in which certain themes recur in addition to new concerns arising.

The competing values approach is useful in that way, in that it captures the main theoretical developments in one framework and shows the relationships between them. Table 2.3 summarises the model and the earlier discussion in a comparative way.

Table 2.3 Summary of the models within the competing values framework

Features/model	Rational goal	Internal process	Human relations	Open systems
Main exponents	Taylor Gilbreths	Fayol Weber	Mayo Follett Barnard	Trist and Bamforth Woodward Burns and Stalker Lawrence and Lorsch Peters and Waterman
Criteria of effectiveness	Productivity, profit	Stability, continuity	Commitment, morale, cohesion	Adaptability, external support
Means/ends theory	Clear direction leads to productive outcomes	Routinisation leads to stability	Involvement leads to commitment	Continual innovation secures external support
Emphasis	Rational analysis, measurement	Defining responsibility, documentation	Participation, consensus building	Creative problem solving, innovation
Role of manager	Director and planner	Monitor and co-ordinator	Mentor and facilitator	Innovator and broker

The emerging management challenges that theorists are beginning to deal with come from many sources. One is the increasingly global nature of the economic system (electronics, branded consumer products such as tobacco). Another is the deregulation of many areas of activity allowing new competitors to enter previously protected markets (airlines, financial services). Still another is the closer integration between many previously separate areas of business (telecommunications, consumer electronics and entertainment). Consumer expectations are increasing and networked computer systems are developing rapidly. Some radical solutions are being sought by management thinkers – just as was done at the start of the Industrial Revolution.

Some argue that traditional notions of efficiency and asset management may not be adequate to meet the new tasks. They talk instead of *resource leverage*, signifying a search for ways of exploiting more fully the physical and especially the invisible intellectual resources of the company. They talk also of the speed with which this has to be done, as intellectual or performance assets can be short-lived. Assets need to be fully exploited to achieve the greatest return from investment. This leads to an emphasis not on size to achieve economies of scale, but on speed and flexibility; on integration, not specialisation and on management that encourages innovation, not control.

Another new theme in management thinking in such volatile conditions is to consider the implications of feedback. People in organisations, both as individuals and as members of a web of working relationships, can choose how they react to an event or to an attempt to influence their behaviour. That reaction in turn leads to a further response – setting off a complex feedback process. Figure 2.6 illustrates this for three individuals, X, Y and Z.

If we look at the situation in Figure 2.6 from the perspective of X, then X is in an environment made up of Y and Z. X discovers what Y and Z are doing, chooses how to respond and then acts. That action has consequences for Y and Z, which they discover. This leads them to choose a response, which has consequences that X then discovers, and acts on. This continues indefinitely. Every act X takes feeds back to have an impact on Y and Z's next action – and the same is true of Y and Z. Hence, as they interact, they make up a feedback system – and what is true of individuals as depicted in the diagram can also be used to indicate the interactions of three groups or three organisations. It can then extend to large numbers of organisations operating in their economic and social environment.

A key element in this way of thinking about organisations is to understand the difference between what are called 'linear' and **'non-linear' systems**. 'Linear' describes systems in which an action leads to a predictable reaction. If you light a fire in a room, the thermostat will turn the central heating down. 'Non-linear' systems are those in which outcomes are less predictable. If a company reduces the price of a product it will be surprised if sales in the following period accord exactly with expectations – the company cannot predict with certainty the reactions of competitors, of changes in taste or the appearance of completely different products that attract customer spending away from their industry.

Events happen and circumstances in the outside world change in ways that management cannot anticipate in their plans. For these reasons it is impossible to trace with certainty any clear links between actions and their long-term effects. While short-run consequences may be clear, long-run ones are not. Hence managers cannot predict accurately the long-term outcomes of what they do.

Figure 2.6 Feedback in non-linear systems

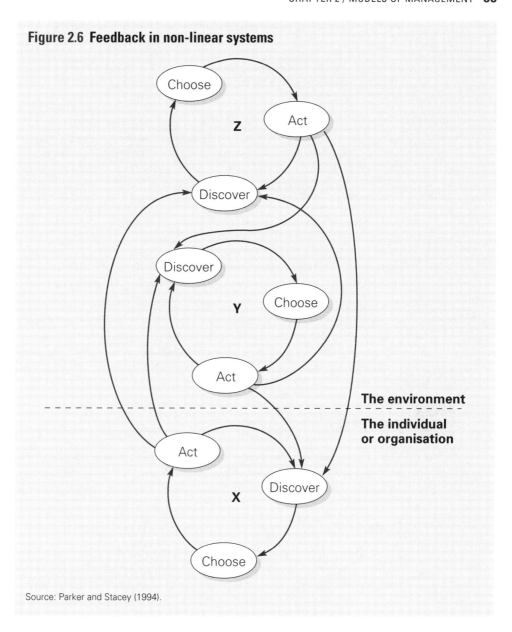

Source: Parker and Stacey (1994).

Glass (1996) argues that the modern business world corresponds much more closely to this non-linear world than to a linear one. Table 2.4 summarises the contrasts between the linear and non-linear models.

In linear systems, negative or damping feedback brings the system back to the original or preferred condition. People used to such systems think in terms of 'what actions can we take to return to the desired equilibrium?' (Glass, 1996, p.102). In non-linear systems, the complexities of the feedback loops mean that outcomes are highly sensitive to small differences in initial conditions. Small actions can be amplified through a series of actions and reactions so that the eventual effect is out of all proportion to the initial action or change. Glass argues that sudden changes in technology, taste or regulation can

Table 2.4 Contrasting assumptions in linear and non-linear systems

Linear	Non-linear
The organisation is a closed system. Generally, what it decides to do will take place without too much disruption from outside events.	The organisation is a complex open system, constantly influenced by, and influencing, other systems. Intended actions will often be diverted by external events or by the internal political and cultural processes.
The environment is stable enough for management to understand it sufficiently well to develop a relevant detailed strategy. That strategy will still be relevant when implemented.	The environment is changing too rapidly for management to understand it and to develop a detailed strategy. By the time a strategy is implemented the environment will have changed.
There are defined levers within an organisation that cause a known response when applied (cut staff numbers, increase profits).	Actions lead to unexpected consequences, which can be either positive or negative.

amplify small actions. Many of the growth industries of today have come from scientific breakthroughs that have been aggressively exploited. He goes on:

> A manager's way of thinking and acting are quite different if they see the world as being in something near stable equilibrium, than if they believe they are operating in chaos ... In stable equilibrium the manager is constantly trying to bring a situation back to a pre-planned state. In chaos, managers have goals but are also looking for the kind of positive amplification that can give extraordinary, rather than just ordinary, results. (p.102)

2.9 Summary

This chapter has reviewed four main approaches to understanding management within the competing values model. It has also indicated some of the attempts to develop new models to deal with the profound uncertainty that many managers now face.

Content

Many of the approaches help us to understand the issues that arise in the content agenda. The rational goal models outlined ways in which management could meet its objectives by separating management from work activities. The internal process model also stressed the need for carefully planned organisations, through which management could control activities. The open systems models pay particular attention to the external environment in which management is operating. They stress the need for management to satisfy key stakeholders.

Process

The human relations approaches introduced ideas relevant to the process agenda – *how* management goes about its task. Mary Parker Follett and Elton Mayo drew attention to the weaknesses of rational approaches to management. They showed the importance to individuals of social contact and argued that groups could be powerful creative forces in organisations. Members should be trained to deal with conflicts openly and constructively. These writers also emphasise trying to understand the internal processes of organisations. Follett, in particular, drew attention to the benefits of involving people in groups in decision making, given their capacity for creative problem solving. She, Mayo and those who followed in the human relations school emphasised the importance of establishing effective communication systems to keep staff informed. This is all the more important in a turbulent environment.

Control

A recurring theme since the earliest days of management has been management's search for a better way to control people. Some theories have sought to solve this by focusing on the individual worker, with a battery of fairly direct techniques of measurement and control. Others focused on broader organisational systems that would help to institutionalise and depersonalise this aspect of management. The techniques range from Owen's bits of coloured wood to the very tight controls that can be exercised by modern computer-based work systems. The Hawthorne studies also drew attention to the way in which cohesive groups can themselves exert control over people, irrespective of management wishes. Control is not just a prerogative of management.

The increasing turbulence and unpredictably of a system as complex as that of the world economy is leading to a search for theories that help to capture at least some of that complexity. Rational goal models advocated that control should lie with management. Current models argue that greater complexity makes it impossible for distant management to exercise control. Hence the emphasis is on the scope for self-control that reintegrates this aspect of management with the work itself.

Despite the gap of 200 years since Owen purchased New Lanark, there are similarities in the issues that occupied his managers and which occupy those of today. He was dealing with the internal affairs of the mill, and was aware of external forces that he also wanted to manage. He had a strong interest in control – and developed a battery of fairly direct techniques of measurement and control. These have echoes today in situations where managers use computer-based work systems to exercise very tight controls over what staff do. Owen's attempts to introduce community singing did not get very far – but many organisations today use similar principles to create a strong internal bond amongst employees.

Q PART CASE QUESTIONS

- In what ways, if at all, are the models in the competing values framework supported by the evidence of The Body Shop case?
- How does the management approach of Anita Roddick compare with that of Robert Owen?
- How do you imagine (on the evidence) that Body Shop managers view uncertainty?

2.10 Review questions

1 Name three ways in which theoretical models help the study of management.
2 What are the different assumptions of the unitary, pluralist and critical perspectives on organisations.

3 Name at least four of Morgan's organisational images.

4 Draw the two axes of the competing values framework, and then place the theories outlined in this chapter in the most appropriate sector.

5 List the five principles of scientific management and evaluate their use in examples of your choice.

6 What was the particular contribution that Lillian Gilbreth made concerning how workers' mental capacities should be treated?

7 What did Follett consider to be the value of groups?

8 Compare Taylor's assumptions about people with those of Mayo. Evaluate the accuracy of these views by reference to an organisation of your choice.

9 Compare the conclusions reached by the Hawthorne experimenters in the relay assembly test room with those in the bank wiring room.

10 Compare examples of open and closed systems.

11 Outline an organisational system of your choice, paying particular attention to the feedback loops.

12 How does uncertainty affect organisations and how do non-linear perspectives help to understand this?

Further reading

Taylor, F.W. (1917), *The Principles of Scientific Management*, Harper, New York.

Fayol, H. (1949), *General and Industrial Management*, Pitman, London.

The original works of these writers are short and quite readable. Taylor (1917) contains illuminating detail that brings the ideas to life, and Fayol's (1949) surviving ideas came from only two short chapters, which again are worth reading in the original.

Biggs, L. (1996), *The Rational Factory*, The Johns Hopkins University Press, Baltimore, MD. A short and clear overview of the development of production systems from the eighteenth to the early twentieth centuries, in a range of industries, including much detail on Ford's Highland Park plant.

Graham, P. (1995), *Mary Parker Follett: Prophet of management*, Harvard Business School Press, Boston, MA. The contribution of Mary Parker Follett has been relatively unrecognised, perhaps overshadowed by Mayo's Hawthorne studies. Or perhaps it was because she was a woman. This book gives a full appreciation of her work.

Gillespie, R. (1991), *Manufacturing Knowledge: A history of the Hawthorne experiments*, Cambridge University Press, Cambridge.

Alvesson, M. and Wilmott, H. (1996), *Making Sense of Management*, Sage, London.

Thompson, P. and McHugh, D. (1995), *Work Organisations: A critical introduction* Macmillan, Basingstoke.

Morgan, G. (1997), *Images of Organization*, Sage, London.

These last four books discuss the ideas in this chapter from a critical perspective.

 Annotated links, questions and resources can be found on
www.booksites.net/boddy

THE ENVIRONMENT OF MANAGEMENT

Introduction

Management takes place within a context, and this part examines several aspects of the external context of organisations. A key management task is to be familiar with that external environment. People do not need to accept it passively – they can try to influence it by lobbying key players, by reaching agreement with competitors or by trying to influence public opinion. Nevertheless, since the organisation draws its resources from the external world, it needs to deliver goods or services well enough to persuade decision makers in that environment to continue their support. This is most obvious in commercial organisations. It is equally relevant in the public service: if a department set up to deliver care is managed badly it will not deliver. Taxpayers or clients will bring pressure on their elected representatives to improve performance, and they in turn are likely to demand improved performance from management and staff. All those involved with the organisation have some expectations of it. How satisfied they are will affect whether or not they are willing to continue their support. If they do not, the enterprise will fail.

Chapter 3 offers some tools for analysing systematically the relevant forces in the general environment, and what the most influential players in that environment expect of the organisation. Chapter 4 reflects the growing international aspects of business, by examining specifically international features of the general environment – political developments such as the European Union or the World Trade Organization, international economic factors and differences in national cultures.

Organisations can no longer act as if their shareholders were the only legitimate external interests. Pressure from interest groups and many consumers has encouraged some companies to take a positive approach to issues of corporate social responsibility and ethical behaviour. There are conflicting interests here and difficult dilemmas: Chapter 5 presents some concepts and tools that help to consider these issues in a coherent and well-informed way.

The Part Case is BP Amoco – a leading player in the world oil business. The business itself is inherently international, being affected by political and economic developments around the world. It also raises issues of social responsibility in environmental as well as political terms.

PART CASE

BP Amoco

In 2001 BP Amoco was the world's second biggest oil company, which had recently announced the largest earnings ever reported by a British company. It had grown rapidly in the last three years, mainly from buying other oil businesses, notably Amoco in 1998. It was now the world's second biggest oil and gas producer. The chief executive John Browne believed that the period of rationalisation and cost cutting associated with those mergers was now almost complete, so that attention would now turn to profitable growth.

BP is a British registered company, but 40 per cent of its assets are in the United States, and it is that country's largest gas producer. It does 80 per cent of its business outside the UK, and is inevitably involved with political considerations. Browne suggests that Britain must encourage companies such as his to remain there, by introducing acceptable taxation and related policies. With so much business in the United States, the company is also sensitive to policy there – such as US policy on the Middle East. While BP would be perfectly entitled to follow Royal Dutch Shell and make production agreements with Iran, he believes it would be 'inappropriate' for the company to ignore US sanctions on Iran.

It also faced problems in Colombia when anti-government guerillas increased their attacks against oil exploration and production sites. In August 1996 the company signed an agreement with the Colombian Defence Ministry by which the Colombian army would protect the company's Colombian production sites. Some human rights activists in Europe attacked the company for reaching this deal with a government that had been criticised for its poor record on human rights.

Though Browne has been in charge since 1995, the strong position of the company (recognised in a *Financial Times* survey as one of the world's best-managed companies) is the culmination of a period of radical change in line with the changing environment. This began when Robert Horton was chairman and CEO between 1990 and 1992 and continued under both David Simon and John Browne.

When Horton took over he faced a market environment that had become more competitive. There was strong competition for markets throughout Europe, with too many refineries producing too much fuel. Demand was also declining due to better fuel efficiency of new vehicles and rising fuel taxes. BP, like other major oil companies, had tried to maintain profitability by diversifying into other activities – such as minerals, coal production, consumer products (such as detergents) and information systems. A matrix organisation had been created, with 10 business streams and 40 local companies throughout the world. This was supposed to have been a move towards decentralisation, but in fact it had only encouraged more centralisation and bureaucracy. Most observers thought that BP would benefit from Horton's ability to take charge rapidly and from his experience in instituting change.

One of Horton's first actions as CEO was to create Project 1990. Its goals were to transform the prevailing 'civil service' mentality and to create a new culture based on OPEN – 'Open thinking, Personal impact, Empowering and Networking'. BP's hierarchical, bureaucratic structure would be replaced with a flatter organisation, leading to reductions in head office staff. But Horton also realised that the corporate culture would have to change to make the new structure work. He wanted to get rid of the stuffiness, power hoarding and atmosphere of distrust.

In 1992 BP's financial situation worsened. In response, Horton began another round of cost cutting, which in turn exacerbated the severe morale problem at BP. Robert Horton resigned in 1992.

When David Simon took over it was clear the organisation needed to revise its strategy to reverse losses, and to repay billions of dollars debt. Simon moved fast to implement a three-year plan with a simple name: '1-2-5' – cut debt by $1 billion per year, build profits to $2 billion per year and keep capital spending below $5 billion per year. Over the following two years he sold many peripheral businesses and reduced staff by almost 50 per cent, with a large reduction in middle management. He narrowed BP's core interest to petroleum only –

'finding it, extracting it, shipping it, refining it, converting it and selling it', as he put it – through three main divisions: exploration, oil and chemicals.

He is described as 'wily, subtle, diplomatic, and knowledgeable about the undercurrents of the British establishment' – an area in which Horton showed little sensitivity. And despite his mild demeanour, he has a mind like a steel trap. 'He knows the figures like the night sky,' says a colleague, 'and that allows [him] to navigate [his] way through a group as complex as BP.' He is good at anticipating issues that no one else has focused on.

In August 1994 Simon declared that BP's recovery programme was nearly complete – the 1-2-5 strategy had been achieved a year ahead of schedule. By early 1996 BP's share price was more than double that in 1992.

David Simon has said that setting simple goals is an important part of developing a culture of continual performance improvement. He tells the symbolic story of his visit to a multi-million dollar oil-drilling platform:

'I asked the workers, "What are you doing?" "Drilling oil," they replied. "How much money are you making?" I asked them. The workers had no idea. I wanted to know how much money they were making there, and they said they could tell me how much oil they produced. I told them I wasn't interested in how much oil they produced. The platform is a factory, for me. Where's the money? That oil is relevant only in terms of money for the shareholders, not in terms of barrels.'

Since then, Simon has made it clear to BP employees that they should be cost and profit conscious. He has a golden rule for attaining goals: 'Targeting is fundamental to achieving. If you do not target, you do not measure and you do not achieve.' He believes that:

'Picking the right targets is a skill in itself. The difficulty of leadership is picking the targets and having a dialogue as you progress towards that goal so that, when it is achieved, it seems the easiest thing in the world. Then you can pick another target.'

One top executive described Simon's accomplishment during his first three years as CEO as follows: 'What he has done so well is pull the company together in a very calming way, setting clear targets and telling people how they can achieve them.' An outside analyst commented: 'I think you have to put an awful lot of BP's recovery down to him. A complete cultural change has been put into place.'

John Browne took over from Simon in 1995, and continued to persuade the board and managers that BP must keep changing. He has stated that:

'To achieve distinctive performance from a portfolio of first-class assets requires continuous development of our organisation and management processes. We are further decentralising the organisation in order to encourage personal initiative and creativity. Simultaneously, we are strengthening the sharing of experience and best practice so that BP's total competitive strength is greater than the sum of its parts.'

Yet the firm prides itself on its collegiate management style, with large amounts of power passed to senior managers below CEO level. So bosses have to rule with a bit of medieval cunning, using strength of personality to chivvy along this potentially fractious group of mini-potentates.

Browne is said to lead by power of intellect. Everything pivots around his ability to absorb vast amounts of information, keeping on top of what is happening anywhere in the company. He carries a heavy workload, even by the standards of multinational bosses.

'He is extremely bright, extremely well-organised and is a very good lateral thinker. Very strong on the numbers side, financially extremely astute, but the same also goes for the technological side. He understands geopolitics and has got the nose for a deal.'

Dealing head on with the industry's impact on the environment has become one of the keynote principles of his leadership.

'These are issues of tremendous complexity. Do you want a clean environment or do you want hydrocarbons? False trade-off. You have to ask if you want both, and in the service of gaining both usually comes technology and better ways of doing things.

PART CASE continued

The industry hasn't handled it well. Consumers want to consume more, they recognise the consequences of consumption, they don't want to shoulder the burden of that themselves, so they transfer it on to the shoulders of the oil and gas companies ... The reality is it's a shared responsibility. We can do a lot but so must consumers.'

Browne has impressed green campaigners, who see him as the first oil leader to take the issues seriously. This stance on green issues is dictated by BP staff. Browne asked how they felt about it and the answer was that they worry about global warming, their children talk to them about it, they think the company ought to get on the front foot about it. When Browne asked for suggestions internally on how the company might hit new, greener targets he was deluged with email: 'People believe that this is a principal value of this company: green.'

On the controversial issues of drilling in the Alaskan National Wildlife Refuge, Browne believes that it should be opened for drilling. Although he reckons that new technology would allow this to be done with minuscule damage, he recognises that

this would bring BP into conflict with some environmental lobby groups: 'While this would dent Sir John's carefully cultivated "green" image, he claims to have always been in the business of pragmatic trade-offs between nature and the world's insatiable thirst for oil.'

Sources: European Case Clearing House Case No. 497 -013-1, 'British Petroleum: transformational leadership in a transnational organisation', by Elizabeth Florent-Treacy and Manfred Kets de Vries, 1997; Buchan, D. 'Mergers over, now primed for organic growth', *Financial Times*, 18 February 2001, p.18; The Davidson Interview, *Management Today*, December 1999, pp. 60–5; and other sources.

Q PART CASE QUESTIONS

- What are the main aspects of the external environment that affect BP?

- In what ways will managing in BP Amoco, with such an international exposure, be different from managing in a national company with no international business? List the three most significant.

- What issues of ethics and social responsibility are indicated in the case?

CHAPTER 3

The business environment

> **AIM** *To identify major external influences on organisations and outline tools with which to analyse any business environment.*

OBJECTIVES

By the end of your work on this chapter you should be able to outline the concepts below in your own terms and:

1 Identify the main sets of forces exerting influence on organisations

2 Conduct a PEST analysis for an organisation with which you are familiar

3 Use Porter's five forces model to analyse competitive environments

4 Give examples of stakeholders seeking to influence organisations and explain a model for assessing stakeholder power

Nokia is the world's leading manufacturer of mobile phones. With a market share of 35 per cent, its sales in 2000 were three times that of second-placed Motorola and far ahead of other rivals such as Ericsson of Sweden and Siemens of Germany. A Finnish company, founded in 1895 as a paper manufacturer, Nokia grew into a conglomerate with interests including electronics, cable manufacture, rubber, chemicals, electricity generation and, by the 1960s, telephone equipment. In the early 1990s the company decided to focus on the mobile phone industry, then still in its infancy.

A number of factors favoured this move. First, the Finnish government had taken an early lead in telecoms deregulation and Nokia was already competing vigorously with other manufacturers supplying equipment to the national phone company. Second, the EU adopted a single standard – the Global System for Mobile Telephony (GSM) – for Europe's second generation (digital) phones. Not only did this create an opportunity to build economy of scale, but it also coincided with Finnish entry into the EU. The GSM standard is now used by two-thirds of the world's mobile phone subscribers. Finland's links with its Nordic neighbours also helped. In these remote and sparsely populated countries mobile communications were enthusiastically adopted.

Nokia's success is also attributed to strong design skills and to its early recognition that mobile phones were not just a commodity but a fashion accessory. By acknowledging the importance of individuality, different ring tones and coloured covers allowed Nokia to establish itself as the 'cool' mobile brand and gave it a lead that its competitors were forced to follow. Nokia has also mastered the logistics of getting millions of phones to customers around the world.

While many competitors subcontract the manufacture of their handsets, Nokia assembles most of its own, with factories in countries including Brazil, Finland and China. The company believes that this gives it an understanding of the market and the manufacturing process that it would not otherwise have. Nokia does buy in components (some 80 billion a year) but has developed close working relationships – through 'virtual companies' that comprise representatives from both sides – with the most important of its 150 suppliers.

While all of these factors lie behind Nokia's success, Matti Alahuhta, head of mobile phones at Nokia, believes there was a further reason. Although competitors such as Motorola and Ericsson already had advantages of scale, experience and distribution networks, the arrival of the new digital technology changed the rules of the game, forcing all players to start from scratch. Mr Alahuhta acknowledges that some factors favoured Nokia's development but has also argued that 'good luck favours the prepared mind'.

Source: Based on *Financial Times*, 29 June 2001; *The Economist*, 16 June 2001.

Q **Case questions**

- How has the environment favoured the development of Nokia?
- How could the same factors turn to the disadvantage of the company?
- What are the implications of your conclusions for management in any organisation?

3.1 Introduction

This chapter introduces the following ideas:

- The general environment
- The competitive environment
- PEST analysis
- Five forces analysis
- Stakeholders
- Stakeholder mapping
- Strategic business unit
- Scenario planning

The organisational environment comprises a wide range of forces that can affect organisational performance. These forces differ between organisations according to the geographical location, industry and market served. Multinational firms face a different situation from that of a small local business. The forces affecting the electronics industry are different from those influencing the food industry. Even within the same industry forces will vary. Rolls-Royce and Renault, for example, both produce cars, but their products appeal to different types of consumer. Organisations need to understand the forces that affect them so that they can plan for the future.

Figure 3.1 shows that the various environmental forces exist at different levels. At the outer level is the organisation's external environment. This comprises first the **general environment**, sometimes known as the macro-environment. At this level there are a range of economic, political, social and technological factors that generally affect all organisations. Then there is the organisation's more immediate **competitive environment**, that is the industry-specific environment comprising the organisation's customers, suppliers and competitors.

For most organisations the external environment is constantly changing. Change gives rise to uncertainty and can pose threats to an organisation's future, but it can also open up opportunities. Business development, success and survival depend on how well organisations cope with change and uncertainty in the external environment. Management must therefore scan the environment for potential opportunities and warning signs, anticipate change and assess the potential impact of change on the organisation.

Responding to change in the external environment requires, in turn, an assessment of the organisation's internal environment, shown at the centre of Figure 3.1. This comprises the elements shown in Figure 1.3 – its structure, financial resources, culture and so on. Management's task is to assess how well positioned the organisation is, in terms of the strengths and weaknesses of these elements, to take advantage of the opportunities and overcome the threats in the outside world.

Spanning both internal and external environments is a third set of forces exerted by various stakeholders. These are individuals, groups or organisations with an interest in what the organisation does. These **stakeholders** might be inside the organisation, such as employees, managers, owners and shareholders or outside, such as customers, bankers, pressure groups and government. Management must try to satisfy the sometimes conflicting demands of stakeholders while responding to other environmental changes. Generally speaking, those forces closer to the centre of the diagram have a more direct impact on the organisation and are more likely to be controllable or at least influenced by the organisation than those in the wider macro-environment (Dobson and Starkey, 1993).

But all environmental forces can affect many areas of the organisation, such as its strategy (for example its choice of geographical or product markets), its structure, its

Figure 3.1 Environmental influences on the organisation

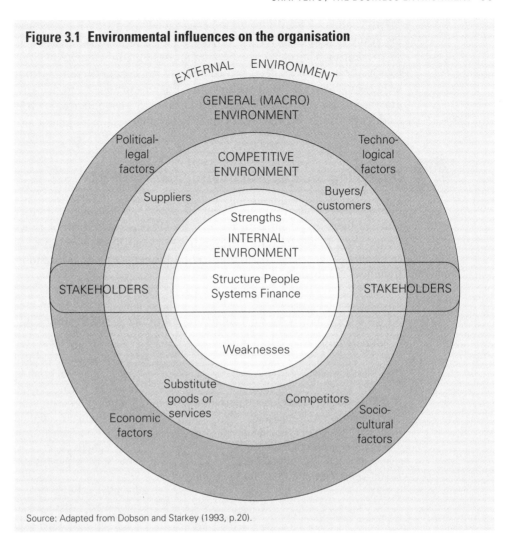

Source: Adapted from Dobson and Starkey (1993, p.20).

production methods or distribution systems. For this reason it is vital for management to undertake environmental analysis to assess:

● how the environment has changed;
● how it is likely to change;
● what impacts these changes are likely to have on the organisation, its customers and markets.

Corresponding to the four levels identified in Figure 3.1, analysis entails an assessment of the following:

● the general environmental factors that might affect the business;
● the immediate competitive environment in order to identify the key forces at work in this arena;
● the expectations of stakeholders;
● the internal operation of the organisation to see how well placed it is to respond to changes in the external environment, such as new market opportunities or the threat from new competitors.

This chapter concentrates on the external environment. It examines the forces operating at the first three levels and introduces tools to facilitate analysis. The chapter begins by presenting a model for analysing an organisation's general environment. It then focuses on how management can analyse the competitive environment facing their unique business. The chapter shows the different forms of external environment and the practical issues that management must deal with in conducting such an analysis. It concludes by introducing the idea of stakeholder analysis.

3.2 Analysing the general environment – PEST

Management's objective in analysing the general environment is to identify those factors that are likely to be most important for their organisation. A useful approach is to undertake a PEST analysis, comprising political-legal, economic, socio-cultural and technological factors – the main external influences on organisations. Figure 3.2 illustrates these influences.

Figure 3.2 Identifying environmental influences – PEST analysis

Political/legal
- Employment law
- Taxation policy
- Company law
- Privatisation/deregulation policies
- Environmental legislation
- Health & safety regulations
- Public expenditure controls
- European Union directives
- Government stability

Economic
- Interest and inflation rates
- Consumer confidence
- The business cycle
- Economic growth prospects
- Unemployment rates
- Disposable incomes
- Labour costs
- Energy availability and cost

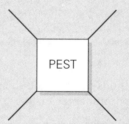

Socio-cultural
- Demographics (population and household numbers)
- Values in society
- Changing lifestyles (e.g. changing failmy composition, changing attitudes to work and leisure)
- Changes in consumer tastes and preferences (e.g. attitudes to green issues)
- Levels of education

Technological
- New product potential, creating new competition
- Alternative means of providing services
- New discoveries
- Rates of government and industry expenditure on research and development
- Changing communications technology
- New production technology
- Rate of technology transfer

Source: Adapted from Johnson and Scholes (1999, p.105) and Smith (1994, p.54).

Political-legal factors

Political and legal systems vary between countries and often have a direct impact on organisations by placing boundaries on what they can and cannot do. Governments tend to regulate industries such as power supply, telecommunications, postal services and transport – and these regulations differ between countries (as illustrated in Management in Practice by Deutsche Post). Merger activity is increasingly subject to the approval of competition authorities. In July 2001, despite approval by US authorities, a proposed merger between two US companies, General Electric and Honeywell, was blocked by the European Union competition commission. It did so on the grounds that the enlarged company could dominate parts of the aerospace market.

Other factors, such as the stability of political systems and legislation governing employment rights, are also critical in firms' location and policy decisions. When Motorola responded to the global downturn in sales of mobile phones in 2001 it decided to close a manufacturing plant in the United Kingdom rather than in Germany as redundancy terms are less costly in the former. Environmental and safety legislation is also a factor of increasing importance in many industries. Intergovernmental agreements to control toxic emissions are forcing oil companies to produce cleaner fuels and car manufacturers to fit catalytic convertors and improve fuel efficiency.

MANAGEMENT IN PRACTICE **Deutsche Post**

European governments are gradually liberalising postal services. In 2000 the German government sold a 25 per cent interest in Deutsche Post, Germany's postal operator. Some years before, a US parcels and logistics group, UPS, had complained to the European Commission (EC) in Brussels that Deutsche Post was using its monopoly profits on domestic letters to unfairly subsidise acquisitions and expansion into the international logistics market. In March 2001, following a long inquiry, the EC found Deutsche Post guilty of predatory pricing and anti-competitive practices. The company was fined 24 million euros and required to split its operations, creating a separate entity to run its business parcel services.

The postal operator faces a second EC investigation into whether its use of cash from state-owned property sales effectively constitutes illegal state aid. A finding against the operator in this case could mean receipts having to be repaid with serious financial consequences for the company. It is lobbying hard to avoid this situation.

Source: *The Economist*, 24 March 2001.

Economic factors

Economic factors such as wage levels, inflation and interest rates are critical in driving an organisation's cost base. Globalisation of some markets is being driven by increasing competition and the search for cost advantages. Electronics companies such as National Semiconductor or Seagate have switched many production facilities to low wage economies in Asia to cut costs. Similarly, Marks & Spencer chose to sever long-standing relationships with British clothing manufacturers in order to source clothing supplies from lower cost countries such as Turkey and India.

The business cycle or general state of the economy is also a major influence on organisational well-being and changes in one of the major economies have far-reaching effects. The global economic downturn in 2001, stemming from slowing demand in the United

States, had repercussions for many organisations in different industries across the world – as the Compaq experience shows. The economies of eastern Europe, still struggling to catch up with the west, found the US downturn hit their exports, investment plans and economic growth.

Specific factors can stimulate growth or decline at the level of a local economy. Establishing the Scottish Parliament in Edinburgh triggered economic and business growth in the city, with increases in population, incomes and commercial rents. Rising incomes lead to increased demand for luxury goods and services, larger homes and foreign travel. It is worth noting that economic factors are often shaped by government policy, illustrating the interrelationships that can exist between different environmental factors.

MANAGEMENT IN PRACTICE | **Coping with economic pressures at Compaq**

The computer industry was badly affected by the 2001 global economic downturn. Texas-based Compaq Computer was the world's leading maker of personal computers (PCs). In June 2001, faced with falling revenues because of a rapid deterioration in demand and prices for its main product areas, particularly PCs, the company announced plans to improve its position. First, it will make a radical change in strategy, to focus on sales of software and services rather than hardware (a move which rival IBM made several years ago). Second, it will cut costs. One way is to reduce annual operating costs by $800 million (on top of 5,000 job losses already announced in March), reduce the cost of supplies by $1 billion, and replace its own microprocessors with ones bought from Intel (saving several hundred million dollars a year).

Source: *Financial Times*, 26 June 2001.

FT

Socio-cultural factors

A key force for most organisations is demographic change, since changes in the number and age of the population will directly affect the demand for particular products and services. An ageing population increases the demand for healthcare and pharmaceuticals. Demographics also play an important role in an organisation's approach to marketing and advertising.

Education and skill levels affect firms' location decisions. India, for example, has a highly skilled workforce but a low wage economy – this is attracting many western companies to arrange for software development work to be done in India, at about half the cost of doing it in their own base. As Chapter 4 shows, differences in national culture have significant implications for management.

Consumer tastes and preferences change. The growing demand for organic foods is encouraging retailers to stock a larger range of organic produce, which in turn opens up new opportunities for producers/suppliers. European consumers' appetite for out-of-season vegetables and flowers has driven supermarkets to source supplies from Africa, which has a year-round growing cycle and low labour costs. However it has limited water supplies, and there have been serious disputes where farmers supplying European markets have extracted water from rivers at the expense of those downstream.

Technological factors

Technology is an increasingly important environmental influence and is leading many managements to reconsider fundamentally the way they operate. Advances in information technology in particular can affect all aspects of a business, from its overall strategic position through to how it manages marketing, design, production and distribution. The growing use of the Internet makes it possible to use new distribution channels for many products and services, such as retailing, travel and financial services. This enables new competitors to enter an industry (such as Virgin Financial Services and Kwik-Fit Insurance Services), often with lower costs that the established players. Equally the established players have responded to the new environment by setting up online distribution networks (such as Egg.com, owned by the Prudential and IF, owned by the Halifax Group) alongside their existing businesses.

MANAGEMENT IN PRACTICE **Online shopping at Tesco**

Tesco, the leading British supermarket, has become the world's second biggest online retailer. Started in 2000, the business covers 90 per cent of the UK population. By mid-2001 it was taking 70,000 weekly orders, worth £6 million, and already turning in a profit. Tesco's success is based on its 'store-picking' system, under which orders are made up by specially employed pickers selecting items from the shelves of existing stores, using a computer-based system. This contrasts with the system of dedicated warehouses used by other e-tailers that demand a high throughput to be viable and have so far struggled to cover costs.

The success of Tesco's model attracted the attention of California's biggest food retailer, Safeway (no relation to the UK Safeway). The two have struck a deal under which Tesco is to export its technology in return for a 35 per cent stake in Safeway's online business, GroceryWorks. With plans to build GroceryWorks into the biggest online grocer in the United States, Tesco is poised to benefit from a potentially sizeable earnings stream. Analysts have been quick to note the irony of a British invention driving deliveries in California, the birthplace of e-commerce.

Source: *Financial Times*, 26 June 2001; *The Economist* 30 June 2001. **FT**

Technological advances have reduced the time taken to bring new products to market and introduced marked improvements in quality control. Technology is also changing the nature of work, for instance by enabling employees to work at remote locations. Chapters 10 and 18 have more on the influence of developments in information technology for organisations.

Q Case questions 3.1

- Gather some information from current newspapers about developments in the telecommunications industry. What are the main factors that are affecting it?
- Also collect information on Nokia and the part of the market (mobile phones) in which it is operating.
- Use the PEST framework to identify the general environmental factors that:
  (a) were important in Nokia's development in the 1990s;
  (b) are posing threats for Nokia and the mobile telecoms industry in 2001.
- What are the specific PEST factors that management needs to take into account?

The PEST analysis is just as relevant to public and voluntary sector organisations as it is to profit-making companies, although there may be some differences of emphasis. Given their central concern with profitability, companies are likely to focus on forces that will impact upon revenue income and costs. Many public service organisations are in business to meet needs or to solve problems that are not catered for by market systems (although these organisations are increasingly subject to a range of market forces). In their case, PEST analysis serves to identify the problems that society may wish to solve and the ways in which such problems or needs are changing. A clear example is the changing age structure of the population, with growing numbers of elderly people that will impact upon several services such as care in the community, the welfare benefits system and hospitals. Public sector organisations are often unable to expand their operations where new problems or needs are identified, but the results can be used to lobby for increased funding or to better target their existing budgets.

By providing a checklist of possible environmental influences, the PEST framework is a useful starting point for analysis. However, the aim is not just to produce a list of factors that might affect organisational performance. Its aim is to help managers identify those forces that seem to be the most relevant and critical to the organisation's business both now and in the future, and provide the stimulus for considering the possible effects of change in these key forces on the organisation.

ACTIVITY 3.1

Anticipating the future of Tesco online

How might continuing environmental change affect Tesco's online business?

You could also consult the forecast for online grocery sales in Section 3.5.

3.3 The competitive environment – Porter's five forces

The PEST framework provides the first step in environmental analysis. Management is most concerned with the forces at work in their immediate competitive environment since they will survive only if they can cope with the competition. According to Porter (1980a, 1985) the state of competition in an industry is determined not only by the existence of competitors but also by the strength of buyers (customers) and suppliers, by the existence of substitute products or services and by the ability of new competitors to enter the industry. Figure 3.3 sets out Porter's **five forces analysis**.

Porter argues that it is the *collective* strength of the five forces that determine industry profitability. The stronger the forces, collectively, the less likely the industry is to be profitable in the long term; conversely, the weaker the forces the greater the opportunity for high levels of profit. It is therefore in a company's interest to examine these forces in detail to establish the industry strengths and weaknesses. Knowing these forces, and how they are likely to affect their industry, enables management to decide on future direction.

New entrants

The threat of new competitors to an industry depends on the ease with which they can enter a market. Amongst the major barriers to entry are:

Figure 3.3 The five forces of industry competition

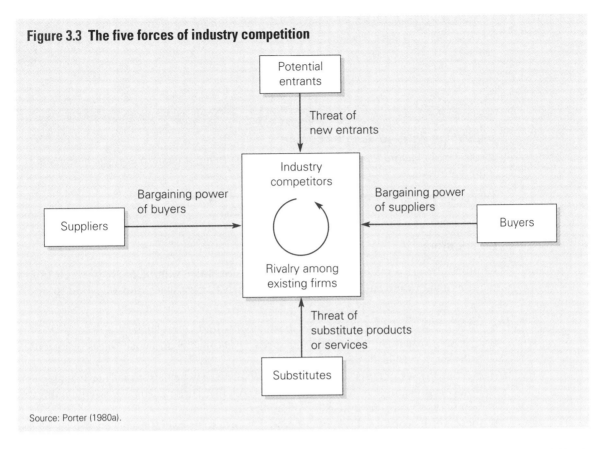

Source: Porter (1980a).

- the need for economies of scale (to compete on the basis of cost), which are difficult to achieve in the short run;
- high entry costs, where significant capital investment is required (for example in plant and machinery);
- lack of distribution channels;
- legislation or other government policy, such as selective subsidies, which benefit the organisation relative to its competitors;
- cost advantages held by existing firms, such as access to raw materials or technological know-how;
- strong product or service differentiation stemming from existing customer loyalties.

<table>
<tr><td>MANAGEMENT
IN PRACTICE</td><td>**Multinationals in eastern Europe**</td></tr>
</table>

The economic liberalisation that followed the fall of communism created big opportunities for multinational groups. With their superior access to capital, technology and managerial know-how, they captured whole industries for themselves. Local governments usually encouraged the process, using privatisation to attract major international corporate buyers in preference to local bidders. Foreign companies have done particularly well in sectors where size is a big advantage, as in banking, telecoms and integrated manufacturing such as car making. They are also strong in large-scale retailing and food processing. While many small local companies have been created, most remain very small. They dominate sectors such as small-scale retailing, construction, road haulage and tourism, where economies of scale are less significant and local knowledge is important.

Source: *Financial Times*, 2 July 2001.

ACTIVITY 3.2

Explaining entry to eastern Europe

List the main factors that allowed multinationals to enter eastern European markets with relative ease.

What barriers to entry were local firms able to put up?

Competitors

Competitors are a major environmental force. Strong rivalry is likely to result in low margins and low industry profitability and is likely to exist where the following apply:

- there are many firms, but none is dominant;
- there is slow market growth, precipitating fights for market share;
- fixed costs are high; this creates pressure to use capacity and encourages overproduction that in turn leads to lower prices;
- there are high exit costs; specialised assets (which may be hard to sell) or management loyalty (for example in long-established family firms) can create exit barriers; this can lead to excess capacity and low profitability;
- there is little scope for differentiation, so that customers switch easily between suppliers.

A highly competitive market will also be one in which the threats of new entrants and of substitution are high and supplier and buyer power strong.

Buyers

Buyers (customers) tend to seek lower prices or higher quality at constant prices, thus forcing down prices and industry profitability. Buyer power is likely to be high when these criteria apply:

- the buyer purchases a large part of a supplier's total output, as in the relationship between major supermarkets and food producers;
- there are plenty of substitute products or services; this allows switching between suppliers, as in the electricity market;
- the product or service represents a major proportion of the buyer's total costs, creating the incentive to shop around for lower prices;
- there is a threat of backward integration by the buyer (bringing the source of supply within the company) if they cannot obtain satisfactory prices or suppliers;
- buyers have influence over consumers' purchasing decisions, as seen in audio equipment and sporting goods, for example.

Not all of these sources of power apply to retail consumers to the same extent as industrial and commercial buyers. Consumers tend to be more price sensitive where products are undifferentiated, are costly relative to their incomes or where quality is unimportant.

Suppliers

Conditions that increase the bargaining power of suppliers tend to be the converse of those applying to buyers. Their power is high when the following is the case:

- there are relatively few suppliers, allowing them to raise prices or reduce quality without loss of sales;
- their product or service is unique or at least differentiated;
- the costs of switching from one supplier to another are high (for example where a buyer has invested heavily in a particular supplier's product, for instance computing software, it would be costly to change to another);
- where there is the possibility of the supplier integrating forward if it does not obtain the prices it seeks;
- they are not important customers to the supplier (for example in terms of volume purchases).

Substitute products or services

In Porter's model substitute products refer to products in other industries that can perform the same *function* as the product of the industry, for example using aluminium cans instead of plastic bottles for soft drinks. Close substitutes constrain the ability of firms in an industry to raise prices and this can undermine industry attractiveness. The threat of substitutes typically impacts an industry through price competition, and is high when buyers are able and willing to change their buying habits. Technological change and the risk of obsolescence poses a further threat of substitution. Examples include using fax or email instead of the postal service, or watching cable TV instead of traditional transmission.

Q Case questions 3.2

- Conduct a five forces analysis for Nokia.
- How do these compare with the competitive forces facing BP Amoco?

ACTIVITY 3.3

Conducting a five forces analysis

Conduct a five forces analysis for an organisation with which you are familiar. Discuss with a manager of the organisation how useful he or she finds the technique. Does it capture the main competitive variables in his or her industry? Are any variables missing?

Analysing the key forces in the competitive environment enables managers to seize opportunities, counter threats and generally improve their position relative to competitors. They can consider how to improve their position by building barriers to entry or by increasing their power over suppliers or buyers. The analysis of the industry in this way also enables them to judge the likely profitability of different industries. Porter considered this to be a major determinant of company profitability, so the knowledge can influence choices about which markets to serve. Chapter 6 examines the steps organisations can take to improve their position within the competitive environment.

3.4 The nature of the external environment

The five forces vary between industries, organisations and over time. Managers need both to identify the forces in their environment and anticipate future trends. How they do this depends on the nature of their environment. In broad terms there is a distinction between (a) static and dynamic environments and (b) simple and complex environments.

A static environment changes relatively slowly. Competitors offer the same products and services at much the same prices, there are rarely new entrants to the market and no technological breakthroughs by current competitors. The business is affected by relatively few key forces and their course is relatively predictable. Some aspects of health and education, where demand is driven largely by demographic change, may fit this pattern. The capacity needed in primary and secondary schools is easy to predict several years ahead.

Conversely, in dynamic environments change occurs rapidly and usually affects many key forces. These might be characterised by changing government regulations, continually changing preferences amongst consumers, new competitors in the market, constant product innovation, difficulties in obtaining supplies and so on.

Simple environments are relatively straightforward in terms of their business processes and technology. This type of environment might apply to professions such as legal conveyancing and executry work and traditional trades such as joinery. In static/simple environments people can use past trends to predict the future with a reasonable degree of confidence. But there are very few static environments nowadays, and changing technology in particular is affecting previously stable businesses.

Environmental complexity arises in part from diversity as experienced, for example, by multinational firms operating across diverse political, legal and cultural systems. Local government, as a multifunctional service provider, also faces complexity, although some services may operate in less dynamic environments than others. Complexity also arises because of the sheer diversity of environmental influences on an organisation or industry. Not only are there many influences to consider, and more analysis required, but there are often complex interconnections between forces that hamper efforts to isolate cause and effect and thus make prediction of the future harder.

CASE STUDY Nokia – the case continues

By 2001, fortunes in the global telecoms sector began to change. Traditional telecoms companies, mobile manufacturers and mobile network operators reported declining sales and profits, manufacturing plant closed, jobs were cut and share prices fell. Even Nokia was forced to lower its sales projections.

While many of the problems are attributed to the economic downturn, which started in the United States and is spreading to Europe, there are also clear signs that the market for mobile handsets is saturated. Consumers are neither buying new phones nor upgrading their old ones and average selling prices have fallen. The industry's hopes are pinned on the introduction of third generation (3G) systems that will deliver text and images to mobile handsets.

Nokia is hoping that 3G will arrive soon, that the company will win a substantial share of the market and, above all, that 3G content – access to the Internet, transmission of pictures, etc. – will appeal to consumers. But none of this is certain. The technology is taking longer than anticipated to develop. Network operators (such as Vodafone and BT) borrowed heavily to secure 3G licences. They are already cutting back on subsidising consumers' handsets and may have insufficient resources to market the new services. Moreover, there are concerns that demand has been overestimated so that it will take longer for the 3G business to become profitable.

Meantime Nokia is trying to increase its share of the handset market to 40 per cent, taking advantage of the problems being experienced by rivals Ericsson and Motorola. But some mobile operators are concerned at their dependence on Nokia; with an even larger market share customers might want to differentiate themselves by *not* buying the Nokia brand. Nokia itself is also planning to increase sales of mobile phone infrastructure to reduce its dependence on handsets, which currently account for 70 per cent of its sales.

Even if 3G does work out as Nokia hopes the company is likely to face new competitors, with the possibility of Asian handset manufacturers entering the European and US markets in a big way. Nokia's rival, Ericsson, whose phones are widely regarded as unfashionable, has formed a joint venture with Sony of Japan whose reputation for design is as good as Nokia's. As technology leads to a convergence between mobile phones and handheld computers competition could also come from companies that have previously specialised in personal digital assistants. There are many more competitors now than in the early 1990s and this time around players are not starting from scratch. Nokia's management remains positive about the company's future but its outlook is more uncertain than it has been for years.

Source: *Financial Times*, 20–22 and 29 June 2001; *The Economist*, 16 June 2001.

Most managers claim to work in dynamic and complex situations. This implies they face great uncertainty over how the future will unfold. In these circumstances historic analysis is likely to be a less useful guide to the future and managers need to develop different ways of anticipating what may lie ahead.

KEY IDEAS   Does planning affect performance?

A number of empirical studies have examined industries in different types of environment to see whether the use of strategic planning tools (such as PEST and five forces analysis) affect company performance. Andersen (2000) investigated the position in three industry groups for which he calculated indices of environmental complexity and dynamism as shown below. In a review of recent studies, he also concluded that there was a positive association between planning and performance, particularly in dynamic and complex environmental settings.

Industry group	Dynamism index	Complexity index
Food and household products	1.5	8.3
Computer products	7.6	24.5
Banking	4.4	12.1

Source: Andersen (2000).

ACTIVITY 3.4

Considering environmental factors

Consider the environmental factors that might explain the different levels of complexity and dynamism in Andersen's industry groups.

Q Case questions 3.3

● How would you classify the form of environment in which Nokia operates?

3.5 Organising environmental analysis

As well as deciding what type of analysis to conduct, management also has to organise the activity. It has to allocate responsibility, and decide on sources of data, frequency of analysis and the techniques to use.

Responsibility

De Wit and Meyer (1998) report that analysis is most frequently carried out by corporate planning departments, product or market divisions or strategic business units. These groups often share responsibility. Corporate planning departments are more likely to focus on issues in the general macro-environment while divisions or strategic business units are likely to analyse the competitive environment that they face. The organisation of the process also varies according to organisational complexity and diversity. Multinationals devolve many aspects of the analysis to local level. In small firms senior staff do whatever analysis they have time for alongside their other duties.

Data sources

Analysis of both the general and competitive environments usually involves collecting, analysing and interpreting information from many internal and external sources. External sources include government economic and demographic statistics, industry surveys and general business intelligence services. Managers also commission market research on, for example, individual shopping patterns, attitudes towards particular firms or brand names, or satisfaction with existing products or services. Many firms use focus groups to test consumer reaction to new products (for more on this see Chapter 7). Companies are also aware of many valuable sources of information they already have, especially about actual and potential customers. They can use this to predict likely future demand, especially for new products.

Given the diversity and complexity of organisational environments it is easy to have too much information. Management needs to focus on the few trends and events that are likely to be of greatest significance. De Wit and Meyer (1998) report that in relation to the general environment Royal Dutch/Shell focus on critical factors such as oil demand (economic), refining capacity (political and economic), the likelihood of government intervention (political) and alternative sources of fuel (technological).

The frequency of analysis

Medium and large organisations operate according to a regular routine, such as annual, three-yearly or five-yearly planning cycles. Analysis, involving forecasting and scenario planning (see below), might therefore be concentrated in periods to coincide with these timetables. Analysis may also occur at irregular points, often triggered by an unexpected event, such as the interruption of supplies. At some levels, however, analysis should be continuous. Especially in conditions of change and uncertainty, management should ensure that both the general and competitive environments are scanned continually to ensure that potential threats and opportunities are spotted at the earliest opportunity.

Forecasting and scenario planning

Forecasts or predictions of the future are often based on an analysis of past trends in factors such as input prices (wages, components, etc.), sales patterns (see Management in

Practice on page 90), or demographic characteristics. All forecasts are based on assumptions. In relatively simple environments it might be assumed that past trends will continue in future. However, in conditions of uncertainty it is prudent to introduce alternative assumptions. For example, in a new market it might be assumed that sales will grow more rapidly than in the past, whereas in a saturated market (e.g. mobile phones) it might be more realistic to assume a lower or nil growth rate. Table 3.1 shows a recent forecast of the likely growth of online shopping in several countries.

Table 3.1 Forecast of online grocery sales, 2005

Country	% online		Market value ($m)		5-year growth (%)
	2000	2005	2000	2005	2000-05
France	0.21	3.15	369.0	6277.8	76.3
Germany	0.10	1.04	202.7	2399.7	63.9
Italy	0.02	0.95	18.6	1029.1	123.2
Netherlands	0.36	5.53	165.0	1845.8	77.2
Spain	0.05	1.55	37.8	1370.2	105.0
Sweden	0.27	3.34	49.1	701.8	70.2
UK	0.40	5.37	580.0	9167.2	73.7
US	0.33	4.83	1792.8	32322.3	78.3
Overall	0.24	3.62	3155.6	55114.0	77.2

Source: Datamonitor in www.news.ft.com/news/industries/retailing (July 2001).

Forecasting is a big business, with several organisations specialising in the sale of general or industry analyses to business and government. The planning model of strategy (discussed in Chapter 6) places considerable emphasis on forecasting with the use of techniques such as time-series analysis, econometric modelling and simulation. However, because forecasts rely heavily on extrapolations of past trends users must take care to establish the nature of these trends and the other assumptions on which forecasts are based and to ensure that the results are interpreted accordingly.

The Scottish Executive (2000), for example, draws attention to the assumptions underpinning its household projections. These are calculated by applying trends in household formation observed between the two most recent population censuses (conducted every 10 years) to population projections. The Executive cautions that 'it is important to note that the projections should not be treated as forecasts but as an indication of what might happen if past trends were to continue'.

Forecasting is not irrelevant in more dynamic and complex situations but cannot be relied on as uncertainty increases and where the rate of environmental change shows signs of discontinuity (marked and often rapid changes from trend). In these sorts of situation, a common approach is to build up a number of possible scenarios of what the future may look like. Johnson and Scholes (1999, p.111) note that:

> **scenario planning** is not just based on a hunch, but builds plausible views of different possible futures for an organisation based on groupings of key environmental influences and drivers of change about which there is a high level of uncertainty. The result is a limited number of logically consistent, but different scenarios which can be considered alongside each other.

Scenarios would typically be developed for the best, worst and most likely cases. No one can predict the future, but there are two main benefits of scenario planning. The first is that it discourages reliance on what is sometimes referred to as 'single-point forecasting', that is a single view of the future, and the second is that it encourages organisations to develop contingency plans or strategies to cope with outcomes that depart from the most likely case scenario.

MANAGEMENT IN PRACTICE   **Scenario planning at Shell**

In today's global and fast-changing environment, extrapolating from historical performance using medium and long-term forecasting techniques has not proved very reliable, and a number of companies now prefer scenarios as a means of testing their plans for the future. Royal Dutch/Shell was one of the earliest to adopt this approach. Traditionally, Shell planners would forecast refining plant requirements for several years ahead by extrapolating from current demand. However, the volatility in the oil market makes accurate prediction difficult. Shell underestimated oil demand in the 1950s and 1960s and overestimated it in the 1970s. Rather than rely on a single projection, Shell now develops a range of possible scenarios for managers to explore and imagine how they might act in differing conditions, so that when the future comes it 'feels' familiar. Forecasting is still used, but only to suggest possible scenarios. Shell finds scenarios very important as they 'alert you to what was previously invisible' and offer a means of keeping ahead of competitors. The method proved particularly useful in the months around the Gulf War when the market was exceptionally volatile. Although Shell had not considered such a specific and violent event, they had considered a situation in which there was a serious disruption to oil supplies in the Gulf. So that when the war came there was little effect on Shell's business.

Source: Dobson and Starkey (1993, pp.24–5).

A combination of PEST and five forces analysis should ensure that managers recognise all the major influences in the external environment. Forecasting and scenario planning then enable them to consider the possible implications for the business.

3.6   Stakeholder analysis

All organisations have a wide range of internal and external stakeholders. Often their interests will conflict because, as groups or as individuals, stakeholders are themselves subject to a wide range of influences that condition or shape their views and what they expect of organisations. External stakeholders include suppliers, financiers, central and local government, shareholders and customers. They have expectations of organisations and will seek to influence them in various ways. They may be able to influence staff or board members directly through personal contact, or they may seek to exert influence indirectly, for instance by the use of the press and other media to raise issues of concern.

MANAGEMENT IN PRACTICE   **Shell and Brent-Spar**

Shell's reaction to pressure from various external groups illustrates the influence stakeholders can exert. Shell acknowledged that 'externally the Group was challenged over the proposed deep-water disposal of Brent-Spar as well as environmental and human rights concerns elsewhere … [and] we learned that we need to have greater external focus if we are to create a better acceptance of the Group's business among varied audiences'.

Source: Shell Annual Report (1995).

Figure 3.4 indicates the different expectations that stakeholders may have.

Much of the literature on this subject conveys the impression that organisations should aim to *balance* the interests of stakeholders, but opinion on what this means is divided. Campbell (1997) argues that the achievement of purpose and, ultimately, survival, requires companies to win 'the loyalty of all the "active" stakeholders – shareholders, customers, employees and suppliers' because companies compete in each of the relevant markets, for capital, labour and goods.

Argenti (1997), on the other hand, assumes 'balance' to mean 'equality' and argues that 'some stakeholders are vastly more equal than others'. He considers, for example, that a retailer contemplating longer opening hours will '*not* attempt to balance the convenience of his employees with that of his customers', but will instead 'ask himself what effect each decision might have on his profits. That is how all legitimate decisions are made in companies – they are, by definition, profit-making organisations.' Since profit is the objective criterion by which 'the capitalist company' will act, shareholders are, in Argenti's view, the stakeholders whose interests should come first. While he recognises that performance would suffer were companies to fail to engage everyone affected by their operations, he maintains that 'an organisation designed to serve more than one set of people will fail to satisfy any'.

Both Campbell and Argenti make valid points. The overall message is that it *is* important to the long-run success of organisations to embrace stakeholder expectations, but that the degree of priority they give to each is unequal and changing.

Figure 3.4 Examples of possible stakeholder expectations

Shareholders
- Growth in dividend payments
- Growth in share price
- Consistent dividend payments
- Growth in net asset value

Customers
- Price always competitive
- Emphasis on product/service quality
- Return and replacement policies
- Warranty/guarantee provisions
- Product reliability

Suppliers
- Timely payment of debt by company
- Adequate liquidity
- Integrity and public standing of directors
- Negotiating ability of the purchasing manager

Employees
- Good compensation and benefits
- Job security
- Sense of meaning or purpose in the job
- Opportunities for personal development
- Amount of interesting work

Government
- Efficient user of energy and natural resources
- Adhering to the country's laws
- Paying taxes
- Provision of employment
- Value for money in the use of public funds

Lenders
- Liquidity of the company
- Character and standing of company management
- Quality of assets available for security
- Potential to repay interest and capital on due date

Stakeholder power

The inequality to which Argenti refers is a reflection of the extent to which different stakeholder groups exert power over organisations. As described in Chapter 12, there are several sources of power within and outside organisations. Some examples of the way in which power can be used by external stakeholders are given below:

- **Formal power** This may be exercised by stakeholders who are members of influential outside bodies or committees such as those concerned with legislative or regulatory matters.
- **Resource power** Many small companies are dependent on large manufacturers, such as those in the car and electronics industries. These large buyers often dictate product quality and prices. Some suppliers may exercise control over strategic assets: an example is the collective power of oil-producing countries to control world oil prices. Resource dependence is also a key feature of public services: those that control access to resources (usually government or its agents) are in a strong position to shape the objectives and strategies of organisations dependent on them for funding.
- **Expert power** Superior knowledge of customers held, for example, by distribution companies may enable them to dictate terms (say on design, quality or price) to manufacturers.

An analysis of stakeholders must therefore assess how much their expectations matter to the business. A structured approach to this task is **stakeholder mapping**. According to Johnson and Scholes (1999), this aims to assess:

- how interested each stakeholder group is in influencing the organisation, and therefore how likely it is that it will seek to do so;
- whether each group has the means, or the power, to do so, as this will determine its ability to influence the organisation.

Stakeholders can be categorised in a power-interest matrix, according to the degree of interest and power they are perceived to hold, as shown in Figure 3.5. Those who have both a high interest and high power may be regarded as the 'key players' and those whom the organisation must seek, in particular, to satisfy. Conversely those groups with low levels of both interest and power may require only minimal attention from the organisation. As a tool, stakeholder mapping helps to determine which stakeholders are the most important to keep on board when major decisions are being taken. It also suggests that communication strategies, ranging from simple provision of information to direct involvement, are likely to differ for each group.

Q Case questions 3.4

- Who are the main stakeholders in Nokia?
- What are their interests in the success of the company?
- How could management ensure it maintained the support of the most important stakeholders?

A final point is that the exercise of power works in both directions. Just as external stakeholders seek to influence the people inside the organisation, the organisation can itself take steps to change the perceptions and expectations of its external stakeholders.

Figure 3.5 Stakeholder mapping – the power/interest matrix

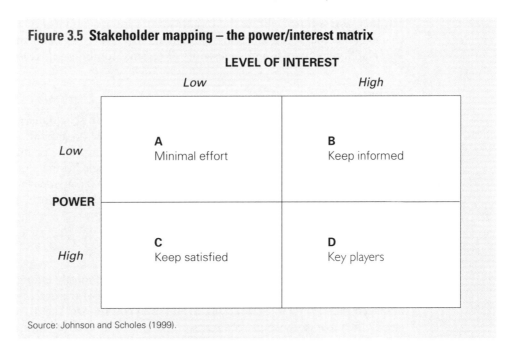

Source: Johnson and Scholes (1999).

In some organisations this extends to the active involvement of major external players. The growth in various forms of strategic alliances and partnerships (see Chapter 6, pages 175–7) demonstrates this type of collaboration between stakeholders.

3.7 Summary

This chapter has shown how external events influence the management of organisations, and vice versa. It focused on two widely used techniques that people can use to analyse and anticipate key elements in their environment – the PEST analysis and the five forces analysis. These forces are typically transmitted to organisations through the actions of stakeholders, so it is essential that management identifies and actively manages those with relatively high levels of power over the organisation.

Content

The external environment has a major impact on what organisations do, affecting decisions on strategy, production, distribution, marketing, organisation and so on. An understanding of the organisational environment is therefore crucial in planning for the future.

The general environment, sometimes known as the macro-environment, comprises a range of economic, political, social and technological factors that generally affect all organisations. The competitive environment encompasses the organisation's existing and new competitors, customers, suppliers and substitute products and services. The expectations of stakeholders can also be influential in determining what organisations do. Forecasting and scenario planning techniques help in predicting their future course.

Management therefore needs to scan the environment, identify forces that are the most critical for the organisation, and consider how these will develop in future. They can then assess how well the the organisation's internal environment will cope with changing external conditions. Environmental analysis becomes ever more important as the volatility, complexity and uncertainty of external conditions increase.

Process

The processes of environmental analysis need to be organised. Management has to consider where intelligence gathering and analysis are located organisationally. Commonly these functions are undertaken by central strategic or corporate planning units in conjunction with separate divisions, departments or strategic business units that focus on particular product, service or geographical markets. Management must also address information needs but avoid 'paralysis by analysis' by carefully identifying the key factors of relevance to the future.

Control

Many factors, especially in the general environment, are mostly outwith the direct control of organisations. The closer forces are to the centre of the organisation, the greater management's ability to exert influence and even control over them. Internal factors are clearly the most easily controlled but some steps can be taken to influence external factors. In the competitive environment companies can seek to gain advantage over competitors by building relationships with suppliers or customers or by making it harder for other firms to enter their territory. As far as stakeholders are concerned management will probably aim to satisfy the more powerful rather than the weaker interests. But it does not always act passively and can try to influence both the power and the behaviours of some external stakeholders if it so chooses.

Nokia has been highly successful by sensing the way the environment was changing, and being able to position itself accordingly. Some of that environmental change was good fortune – such as the actions of government to encourage mobile telephony. But other companies were in the same environment, and were not able to move as rapidly. It was Nokia's management skills that enabled it to secure an early lead. The environment is now changing again, and it may be that a new set of skills is needed to cope equally well with these changed conditions, especially from new competitors.

> ### Q PART CASE QUESTIONS
>
> - Construct a PEST analysis for BP Amoco.
> - Analyse the five forces acting on BP Amoco. Which of them appear to bring the greatest threat to the company?
> - Make a list of stakeholders for BP Amoco. Assess their sources of power, and rank them according to the likely degree of influence they hold.

3.8 Review questions

1 How should managers decide which of the many factors easily identified in a PEST analysis they should attend to? If they have to be selective, what is the value of the PEST method?

2 Identify the relative influence of Porter's five forces on an organisation of your choice and compare your results with a colleague's. What can you learn from that comparison?

3 Illustrate the stakeholder idea with an example of your own, focusing on what affects the relative power of the stakeholders to influence an organisation's policy.

4 Evaluate Argenti's comment on stakeholder power in view of your answer to question 1.

Further reading

Johnson, G. and Scholes, K. (2001), *Exploring Corporate Strategy*, Financial Times Prentice Hall, Harlow.

Dobson, P. and Starkey, K. (1993), *The Strategic Management Blueprint*, Blackwell, Oxford.

Both texts cover PEST analysis, scenarios, five forces analysis and stakeholder analysis.

Smith, R.J. (1994), *Strategic Management and Planning in the Public Sector*, Longman/Civil Service College, Harlow. Approaches the topics from a public sector perspective, in Chapters 4, 5 and 7, and includes a summary of forecasting and market research techniques.

Steinbock, D. (2001), *The Nokia Revolution*, American Management Association, New York, NY. Authoritative account of the development of the company, and its interaction with the external environment.

The weekly publication *The Economist* often contains useful articles in its leader pages or business section that highlight the impact of environmental factors on particular industries or companies – see, for example, the 31 March 2001 issue on the car industry and the 30 June 2001 issue on the steel industry.

Annotated links, questions and resources can be found on

www.booksites.net/boddy

CHAPTER 4

The international context of management

AIM	*To outline how managing internationally changes the context in which managers work, and so affects their functions and roles.*

OBJECTIVES

By the end of your work on this chapter you should be able to outline the concepts below in your own terms and:

1 Describe the forces driving the growth of international business activity

2 Assess the extent to which managers need to deal with international issues

3 Distinguish between low- and high-context cultures

4 Outline Hofstede's research on cultural differences between nations

5 Compare differences in management roles and practices amongst different countries

6 Compare the main features of Japanese, US and European management systems

7 Describe and illustrate how greater internationalisation of business affects how managers perform their functions

8 Compare the arguments for and against greater globalisation of business, and the dilemmas these create for management

Lufthansa and globalisation

Senior management at the German airline Lufthansa decided in 1995 to turn the airline into a truly global company. It could see that competition from other airlines was going to increase because of new EU regulations enabling free competition in Europe. Internationally, the barriers to entry are low and many governments subsidise national airlines. Lufthansa wishes to be one of the few big players and has embarked on a strategy of globalisation. Its plans include creating a global network of services by developing alliances with carriers in other regions; internationalising its costs to balance the increasing proportion of non-German revenues; developing managers willing to operate in a variety of markets and cultures; and developing a service culture that meets the expectations of increasingly diverse customers.

Lufthansa has alliances with Thai Airways in South East Asia, United Airlines in the United States and the Scandinavian airline SAS in Europe. The carriers remain financially independent but merge many of their operations. They can then offer customers similar service from ground and flight staff throughout a trip. These alliances have since been formalised within the Star Alliance.

In 1996 about 50 per cent of the company's revenue came from Germany, compared with 65 per cent of costs and 80 per cent of staff. Employing German staff is expensive because of German statutory requirements, and management believes that if it is to compete internationally it needs to reduce costs. One way is to transfer some administrative and support functions to cheaper overseas locations. For example, it sends aircraft to be maintained in the Republic of Ireland.

Senior management acknowledges that to implement a strategy of globalisation more of the company's managers must become 'global'. Some feel that the company should train managers to understand and respect other cultures; others that they should spend part of their career outside Germany. A further view is that a proportion of the company's managers will need to be non-German.

One of the few ways that airlines can compete is through the quality of the interaction between customers and staff, both on the ground and in the air. Now that Lufthansa is in partnership with other airlines such as Thai it must meet the service expectations of Thai's customers as well. By 1996 the need to develop a more customer-focused service culture had become a major issue for Lufthansa. On some Asian routes over half the passengers are non-German, raising the question of whether the company should recruit more cabin staff locally.

Source: Based on Ghoshal *et al.* (1996), with permission.

Q Case questions

- What external pressures are persuading management to build a global airline?
- What issues do you think it will need to manage to achieve this?

4.1 Introduction

This chapter introduces the following ideas:

- Internationalisation
- Globalisation
- International management
- National culture
- High-context and low-context cultures
- Power distance
- Uncertainty avoidance
- Individualism/collectivism
- Masculinity/femininity
- National institutional features
- Japanese, US and European management models

Lufthansa is facing problems similar to those of many other businesses wanting to move towards a global operation – yet at the same time they experience forces pressing them to remain a distinctively German airline. If it decides to go down the globalisation route, that will raise new management questions about staffing, management development and a host of other aspects of managing the airline. It could rely on growing the Star Alliance network to extend the global reach rapidly – but such collaborative arrangements are themselves difficult to manage. It may also raise the expectations of customers beyond what the company, or the alliance, can deliver. Airlines such as Lufthansa or British Airways that want to be seen as global players have to decide whether to match the cultural diversity of their customers with an equally diverse cabin crew: or do customers prefer the 'different' experience of a distinctly European airline?

Companies in other industries face dilemmas of similar kinds. Microsoft needs to decide how far to go in 'localising' software to suit each country. Ireland has become a leading player in this business, with all the world's leading software companies, including Microsoft, having facilities to adapt products to suit the tastes of local markets. How can Ford best manage the joint venture it has established with the ChongQing Automobile Group in China to manufacture a compact family car? Companies considering a move into a new market face legal dilemmas, such as whether the institutions in countries where they plan to make long-term investments will give adequate protection. The growth in global brands such as Microsoft, IBM, Intel or McDonald's symbolise a much wider trend.

This international aspect of business raises new issues for managers, and indeed for the wider community. The basic stages of the value-adding process such as design, manufacture or distribution remain much the same across the world. So do the management functions of planning, organising, leading and controlling. Yet performing these on an international or global scale brings additional complexities that managers need to overcome if they are to gain the benefits of doing business internationally. The economic resources possessed by the major multinational corporations is greater than that of many of the countries in which they conduct their operations.

These developments have considerable implications. So this chapter introduces some models and perspectives that help understand the hazards which companies face in managing internationally. The chapter begins by outlining the factors driving the growth of international business. These forces affect organisations in different ways, and so managers differ in the degree to which their work changes. Where this is significant, they need to understand how the PEST factors described in Chapter 3 affect them as they work internationally. Further sections therefore examine the influence of economic, political and cultural factors. The chapter then presents some views on contrasting national management systems, and concludes by relating the themes presented to the generic functions of management. How management adapts these functions to meet the conditions of managing internationally will affect the outcomes of such activities. Figure 4.1 indicates the main issues that managers operating on a global scale look for as they work across national boundaries.

4.2 The growth of international business

Driving forces

There has been international trade since the earliest times. The founding of the East India Company in London in 1599, to develop trade with the spice islands in South East Asia (in close and violent competition with the Dutch East India Company, founded in 1602), signify the practice being put on a more formal basis. By the nineteenth century many great trading businesses were operating across the world. What is new today is the much greater proportion of production that crosses national boundaries. Much of this trade is organised by businesses operating not on a national but on a regional or global scale.

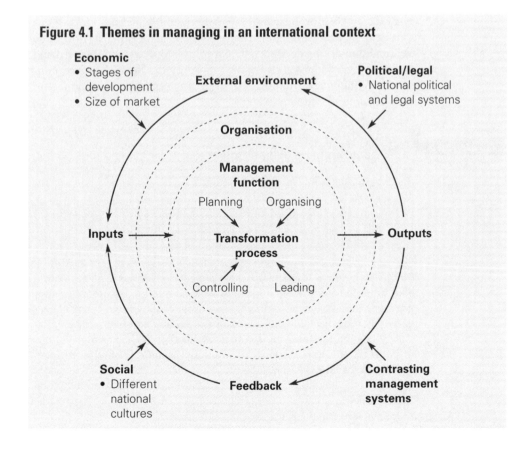

Figure 4.1 Themes in managing in an international context

In some areas of business global operations are inevitable. Logistics companies such as Federal Express or Maas operate services on a global scale and develop practices and structures accordingly. Oil companies such as BP Amoco or Esso and mining companies such as Lonrho necessarily secure resources in some parts of the world and sell them in others. A newer development is the way many financial businesses such as ABN-AMRO (a Dutch bank), telecommunications businesses such as Nortel or BT or retailers such as Tesco or Carrefour have ambitions to operate on a global scale.

Two market forces have an especially strong influence on this growth – capital and information technology (IT). The availability of capital makes it possible for companies to finance direct investment in a foreign country – as when Ford decided to build an engine plant in Spain. Instead of investing capital in a US plant and then exporting the product Ford invested in Spain and made vehicles there. Capital is mobile and almost all countries compete with each other for investment. This is most visible in the publicity surrounding attempts to attract major manufacturing investments to less prosperous regions, whether of Europe, Asia or South America. Investment in services – financial, legal, design and other forms of intellectual capital – also increase world trade. One estimate is that one-third of all trade takes place within transnational companies, quite apart from external sales of foreign subsidiaries.

Developments in IT also stimulate trade. It does this both as a product and as a way of supporting dispersed production systems. Electronic products are assembled from many small components. These have a high value-to-weight ratio, so they are cheap to transport long distances. Companies choose to do this if it gives them access to a cheap source of components. Much of the growth in international trade is due to the emergence of countries in Asia as suppliers of electronic components. These flow in vast numbers every day to US, European and Japanese assembly plants.

Information technology also helps to manage the efficient flow of data on which international operations depend. The complex supply and manufacturing networks depend on computer systems to track and monitor the flow of orders, components and payments. Without information systems of the kind now common, world trade could not have grown to the present scale.

MANAGEMENT IN PRACTICE   **IBM becomes more globally integrated**

IBM has long been a major, and at one time a dominant, player in the world electronics industry. Yet until quite recently the separate business units and manufacturing operations operated with a high degree of independence from each other. Each manufacturing unit made their supply arrangements independently.

In 1996 management centralised the function into 17 Global Commodity Councils. Each manages the supply of a group of parts (such as drives or monitors) for the whole company. Global Commodity Managers handle strategic relations with suppliers, regularly agreeing prices and forecast volumes for the following quarter, based on the requirements of all the the company's divisions. The suppliers, most of whom are themselves global players, then deliver as required to any of the company's manufacturing facilities around the world. Each facility has some staff who are part of the Global Procurement Organisation, helping to manage the strategic aspects of the supply chain. Each site also has buyers who work within the manufacturing function to deal with the day-to-day execution of requirements to meet current needs from the overall schedule agreed between the Global team and a particular supplier.

Source: Information provided by the company.

Other firms find they can gain competitive advantage by extending their brand on to a global scale. The larger consulting companies, for example, have found that they are better able to meet the needs of global clients by themselves organising as a global business. This requires them to give a unified shape to geographically dispersed businesses – a move that requires significant internal change.

Dicken (1992) distinguished between internationalisation and globalisation. **Internationalisation** includes activities such as joint ventures with partners in other countries to co-operate in some aspects of a business. Coca-Cola has distribution arrangements with many local companies that promote and distribute the product. The European Airbus is produced by a consortium made up of companies from six countries that make different parts, for assembly at the Aerospatiale factory in Toulouse.

Globalisation is an extension of this process, in the sense that most aspects of the production or service process are performed, and integrated, across many global locations. To continue the IBM story, the company has many manufacturing sites dispersed around the world, which bring components from many other companies – that also have sites around the world. Customer orders trigger a flow of components through the transport networks that links these sites – making this closer to Dicken's definition of a global, rather than an international business. The difference is one of degree, and the only significance is that one implies a more complex process of international management.

Q Case questions 4.1

Consider Dicken's two definitions in relation to Lufthansa.

● From what you know about airline operations, how would a global airline differ from an international one?

● What are the additional management issues raised by globalisation, compared with internationalisation?

One effect of both processes is that transactions across national borders increase in importance relative to those within them. National boundaries become less significant barriers to the movement of goods and services – most clearly seen in the growing trade in electronically transmitted information products. Globalisation marks a new phase in business activity with, as Dent (1997) notes, the following characteristics:

● the accelerated growth of foreign direct investment;
● the growth of intra-firm trade in which companies buy or make components in one country and export them to their own assembly plants in another (Digital Europe, the Case Study in Chapter 12, is an example of this);
● the growth of complex supply arrangements amongst multinational firms as a result of mergers, joint ventures and other forms of supply-chain relationships.

MANAGEMENT IN PRACTICE   Building a global consultancy

In 1998 Price Waterhouse (now part of PricewaterhouseCoopers) was one of the world's leading accountancy and consulting organisations, with over 50,000 staff in 100 countries. The company had traditionally operated as a collection of national or regional groups, further divided into functions. These worked in relative isolation from colleagues, especially those in other countries. In 1990 the company had realised that clients (especially large multinationals) required them to handle bigger and more complex consultancy assignments. Staff would have to offer a wider range of experience – which was largely available in the collective but unorganised experience of the consultants. The company moved initially to a European rather than national organisation. In 1998 a senior manager recalled:

> In the consulting group we have for several years had a single European organisation with one management structure and therefore able to move resources to where they are needed. A year ago that developed into a global practise, when we integrated our American, European and Japanese practises. So we now manage it on a global basis across those territories.
>
> The pace at which this has happened is remarkable. Only five years ago we managed our consulting practice in the UK regionally. We could either be duplicating or having omissions in terms of skills. Only five years ago we were a UK business, and since then we have moved to the global organisation. That's because our business focus has narrowed – we aim to service the 500 largest global organisations. That is our strategy, and you cannot do that with an organisation that is geographically based.

Source: Information provided by the company.

Variations in the scale of international management

The extent to which managers need to be aware of the factors in Figure 4.1 depends on their situation. At one extreme organisations deliver a service to a local community and manage the whole process from within that country, so international involvement will not arise. Others engage in a limited amount of export business, or may franchise the provision of services in other countries. Here there is rather more need for awareness of cultural differences. A very limited awareness will probably be sufficient. At the other extreme are those global businesses that deliberately operate in many countries around the world, have major foreign subsidiaries or significant joint ventures with companies based in another country. Here the issues are much greater, and the penalties for misunderstanding other systems more severe. Table 4.1 sums up the options.

Where the significance of foreign cultures is high Tayeb (1996) suggests that management needs to deal with a range of interface and internal activities.

Table 4.1 Company strategies and relevance of national culture

Character of the firm	Relevance of national culture	
	Home culture	Foreign culture
Domestic, single-nation firm with no foreign interests	high	nil
Single-nation firm with import/export activities	high	low to moderate
Multinational firm with franchising and licensing activities	high	moderate to high
Multinational firm with units abroad	high	high
Global firm active in most parts of the world	high	high

Source: Tayeb (1996).

From a career point of view, international management means several things: working as an *expatriate manager* in another country, joining or managing an *international team* with members from several countries, or managing a *multicultural organisation* whose employees, systems and structures are truly international in that they no longer reflect its original, national base (Adams, 1996). ABB is an example. Formed by the merger of a Swiss and a Swedish business it retains only a small head office in Zurich, and the board deliberately contains people of different nationalities.

Activities most affected in managing internationally

Some aspects of a firm's operations are more likely to be affected when it manages internationally than others.

Advertising

A company's advertising is its most visible aspect in many countries, and is particularly susceptible to differences about what is acceptable. Many advertising tactics that companies use widely in Europe are unacceptable in the Middle East. However, it is through advertising that companies which want to establish a global position do so. One of Lou Gerstner's first moves when he became chairman of IBM was to raise the profile of marketing within the business. The company reasserted the primacy of the IBM brand across the globe by, for example, consolidating all advertising work at a single advertising agency. The goal was to bring a consistent global message across all of IBM's products, services and geographic markets (*Business Week*, 6 August 2001).

Negotiating

Severe difficulties arise when people from different countries engage in direct interpersonal contact towards an agreement. The way they approach the interaction will reflect their respective cultures. Some will aim to get straight to the point; others will expect to spend hours, perhaps even several meetings, establishing a relationship with the other.

MANAGEMENT IN PRACTICE **A British negotiator in Paris**

Mrs Brown is a senior executive of a British design company that is trying to break into the French market. She flies to France to meet a potential client, makes a snappy, clever and witty presentation, shows how much money there is to be gained by using her agency, and has a very satisfactory lunch with several French top executives of the target company. The French promise to get in touch soon and they part on the best of terms. Two months later our executive still has not heard anything and picks up the telephone to chase the lead. She is told that other senior people must be involved in the decision.

Consequently she flies to Paris once more, goes through the whole thing again, and has another excellent lunch. Time passes and nothing happens. She spends time on the telephone with her contacts and pushes for a trial but they explain to her that 'things are difficult' and that they will see what they can do. A year – and several more trips to Paris – down the line, nothing has happened. Our executive has more or less given up the whole thing when she gets a telephone call from Paris. Another manager would like to see her. She agrees, and is introduced to a very senior French manager – who finally discusses price for work. Taken by surprise, the executive negotiates a fairly good fee for a trial, but feels that something is 'not quite right'. Nevertheless, the trial goes well and the company is asked to do another job, then another one.

However, in the mean time a major British retailer contacts the British firm and proposes a major redesign effort that will take up all the resources of the company. Considering the size and the importance of the contract, they hastily finish all other jobs to concentrate on this unexpected opportunity. Our executive wraps up her business with France but soon starts being bothered by her French client. The job has not been well finished, things have to be redone, tempers run high, misunderstandings follow, and finally both parties break contact feeling disgruntled; no more contracts will ever come from that French company.

What happened? The French were surprised that the British executive only proposed rather small contracts to them, although they gave her to understand that some rather major jobs needed doing. They felt betrayed and let down when she broke the relationship, particularly since they were counting on her for all this extra work. They felt they had invested their time in somebody who just wanted a 'quick kill'.

Both sides had widely different expectations of their obligations towards each other. The British executive assumed a relationship built on a continuation of specific one-shot deals; you start with a trial, if it works you do another, then another and so on. It was natural for her to choose to pursue a much more profitable opportunity. On the other side, the French managers expected to build a relationship with the executive before they would give her a large amount of work. They had to know her, be able to trust her. Once she had been accepted they expected her to remain within the relationship for as long as possible, regardless of outside circumstances.

Fundamentally, both parties had widely different understandings of the deal and the relationship, and as a result failed to develop a mutually beneficial partnership.

Source: Ballé and Gottschalk (1994), reproduced with permission.

Internal organisational activities

An organisation with significant international activities will need to develop a management style to reflect these differences. Even the geographical spread of the activities introduces a new dimension. People have to spend more time arranging meetings and securing the agreement of different interests. There are also technical issues to do with the conditions of people working for the same company in different countries. Is pay to be common across the company, or varied to suit local conditions? Of greatest interest here is the extent to which national differences affect management processes such as the exercise of power and influence, team-building, managing change and managing between different cultures.

Implications for managing

While the story of Mrs Brown is instructive, it signals only some of the issues that those managing internationally have to deal with. As companies choose to respond to apparent international opportunities they need to deal with structural issues such as:

- managing matrix structures where products are made and sold in several countries;
- improving the links between research, marketing and production to speed the introduction of new products;
- facilitating knowledge transfer between the national components of the business;
- encouraging tactical and local flexibility while maintaining strategic coherence.

They also deal with a range of process issues – the way managers work. The range of stakeholders is greater, with correspondingly more competing interests to satisfy. At the political level, governments are aware that they need multinational business to support their economies – but want also to protect domestic interests. This can lead to tense relations that have to be managed at the highest level. Reaching decisions and communicating them become more difficult when the players are physically distant. Distance usually means different ways of controlling distant ventures.

In varying degrees these trends mean that employees will work with colleagues from countries, organisations, institutions and cultures widely different from their own. To handle this well means more than learning foreign languages, though that clearly helps. It means being aware of the main factors in the international context – economic, political/institutional and cultural factors.

> **Q Case questions 4.2**
>
> - What criteria would you use to decide if Lufthansa had succeeded in the aim of becoming a truly global airline?
> - Which stakeholders is management having to satisfy while moving in that direction?
> - What practical issues do you expect to arise if more managers and cabin staff are non-German?

4.3 Economic context

The economic context of a country includes such factors as its state of economic development, the quality of its communications and other infrastructure, its systems of markets. It also includes aspects of the current economic situation such as inflation, exchange rates and levels of debt.

Stage of economic development

The wide difference between countries in their stage of economic development is a major factor in international management. The measure usually used is income per head of population – a measure of a country's total production, adjusted for size of population. Lower-income countries are concentrated in the southern hemisphere, and include many in Asia, Africa and South America. The richer, developed countries tend to be in the northern hemisphere, which is where most international business firms are located.

Companies from the wealthier countries are attracted to those in less-developed areas by their large potential markets. Consumer products companies (especially those in the tobacco business such as British American Tobacco or Phillip Morris) are reaching the limits of their markets in the developed countries. They are attracted by countries in the developing world, whose high birth rates mean a growing number of young and adult consumers. Companies with strong brand names are attracted to the more prosperous of these countries, such as China, Malaysia or South Africa, by the prospect of large and growing markets. Others see them as sources of cheap labour from which to obtain supplies of products and components.

Infrastructure

Infrastructure includes all of the physical facilities that support economic activities – ports, airports, surface transport and, increasingly, telecommunications facilities. Companies operating abroad, especially in less-developed countries, are closely interested in the quality of this aspect of a country as it has a huge effect on the cost and convenience of conducting business in the area.

MANAGEMENT IN PRACTICE | **Is Brazil a worthwhile place for another car plant?**

At the Fiat car plant on the outskirts of Belo Horizonte, part of the test track has been left broken and rutted to mimic a typical Brazilian road.

Throughout the day, cars rolling off the production line at Betim factory – Fiat's largest outside Italy – are driven over the crumpled surface to test durability ... Speaking at the factory Gianni Coda, Latin American president of Fiat Auto, says the Brazilian car-making business is now generating an operating margin of about 4.5 per cent (implying a profit of $132m for 2000). He admits, however, that Fiat's ability to make money in its largest overseas market will be harder in years to come.

When the company first began assembling cars in Brazil in 1976, it was facing competition only from Ford, General Motors and Volkswagen. Now Toyota, Daimler-Chrysler, Mitsubishi, Renault and most recently Peugot Citroën have arrived.

Given that only 150,000km of the 1.6m km of roads in Brazil are paved – less than 10 per cent – and cars remain out of reach for large sections of the population, doubts remain over whether the market can sustain so many manufacturers.

Source: *Financial Times*, 4 April 2001, p. 32.

FT

Conversely a poor infrastructure is an opportunity for those supplying such facilities. European water companies have contracts to apply their expertise to providing water and sanitation services to many less-developed countries – as have many construction companies such as Balfour Beatty and John Laing.

Markets

A major choice for a company deciding to sell in a foreign country is whether to export goods to the country or to make them locally. The greater the size of the market the more likely they are to aim for the latter option. That in turn raises questions about the local availability of raw materials and other production requirements. Ensuring these may be a condition of being allowed to do business in the country, yet raises further issues of developing sources of supply to an acceptable quality.

4.4　Political/institutional context

Whitley (1996) shows how differences in national institutional features lead to different forms of organisation. These include things such as the extent of state involvement in business, or the features of the financial systems that shape a country's practices for overseeing the management of enterprises. In some countries such as Japan, Germany or France firms are typically part of a network of mutual relations with banks, state agencies, suppliers and unions. In others these links are much weaker or do not exist at all, so that organisations work in relative isolation. Management is then able to act much more autonomously.

At one extreme are the Japanese networks of interdependent relations. Here the tradition is of mutual ownership between different but friendly business units. Companies have close financial and obligational links with companies in other sectors. The Ministry of Industry actively supports and guides the strategic direction of major areas of business. The firms create a network of mutually dependent organisations with interlocking obligations. They decide strategy by negotiation with independent stakeholders, which are mainly other companies and financial institutions.

In contrast, firms in the United Kingdom and the United States work in a more isolated way. They receive less direct support from banks, which have traditionally avoided long-term investments. Their boards rarely contain representatives of companies with common interests.

KEY IDEAS — Whitley's elements of national institutional features

Cultural conventions
- Strength of institutions governing trust relations and collective loyalties

State structure and policies
- Extent to which state dominates economic system
- Level of risk sharing with private economic actors
- State support for co-operation between firms
- Formal regulation of entry to and exit from markets

Financial system
- Credit-based financial system

Labour system
- Significance of labour in strategic decision making
- Centralisation of bargaining
- Collaboration in training

Source: Whitley (1996, p.51).

The level of dependence affects companies' attitudes towards growth and profitability. Whitley suggests that a high level of dependence on the state encourages growth but discourages concern over profit, and he cites France as an example of this. In Japan firms seek market share and growth within their sector, but not beyond it. The network of relations between Japanese firms and their customers and suppliers restricts unrelated diversification, but there is a strong collective interest in expansion. In contrast the more isolated UK and US firms, where owners operate as portfolio holders, find growth goals limited by the need to meet profit targets and expectations of the capital market. Dividend pay-outs and growth in share price are more significant measures of corporate performance than growth as such. In addition, family-owned businesses may experience limited growth because of a reluctance to share control and a desire to increase family wealth rather than the size of the firm.

MANAGEMENT IN PRACTICE — Elf Aquitaine

Elf, the largest company in France, was privatised in 1994. Before that the state owned the company and ran it as an instrument of industrial policy. It supported the interests of the Mitterand presidency, and profit was a secondary consideration.

At the beginning of the 1980s the independent Atochem branch had been at the centre of the socialists' restructuring of the French chemical industry, while a decade later the investment policies served to create a set of interlocking shareholdings, securing crucial parts of French industry from hostile takeover. The stake in the textile company Biderman was taken to help rescue a major employer and the largest French company in the sector. The absence of any significant industrial logic behind these participations was confirmed by the reversal of the investment strategy by privatisation.

Source: Mayer and Whittington (1996, p.102).

Ownership and control have traditionally been closely connected in Continental Europe. For example in France at the end of the 1980s 44 per cent of top industrial and commercial organisations were under family control and 13 per cent state owned (Mayer and Whittington, 1996). In Germany and France the banks are much more closely involved in providing long-term finance for business through extended credit-based systems, and they are represented on company boards of directors.

> ### Q Case questions 4.3
>
> ● How would you expect these institutional arrangements to have influenced the management of Lufthansa?

Doing business internationally inevitably involves unfamiliar political and legal risks. Foreign companies are often seen as intruders in a country, threatening the political or economic sovereignty of the host nation. Political activists sometimes attack or damage the property of foreign companies. Unstable governments increase the risk that the terms on which a company is permitted to enter a country may be revoked if there is a change in power. The process of reaching agreement with some governments can itself open a company to criticism in its home country, as when BP reached a deal with the government of Colombia.

Each jurisdiction has its own regulations affecting all aspects of business practice, which they expect companies operating in the country to meet. Ensuring that the company complies with this often implies working with a local partner, able to negotiate in the local context. Companies also query the legal system of a country in which they plan to work, and whether it will give sufficient protection in the event of legal disputes arising.

MANAGEMENT IN PRACTICE The legal side of business in Russia

To judge from Moscow's news media, earlier this year, it is hardly a golden period for the rule of law in Russia.

The country's former justice minister was on trial for corruption in Moscow, while the former head of the Kremlin property department was sitting in a New York jail waiting extradition to Switzerland. The Government grudgingly agreed to stop using teams of heavily armed, masked agents to raid companies accused of tax evasion ...

Yet more than 50 international law firms have established offices in Moscow. And that raises the question of how they can operate in such a lawless environment. The answer is: astonishingly well ...

Setting up a company can take three months and involves registering with several local and national government bodies in a prescribed sequence. Many foreign lawyers privately admit that they leave the bureaucratic details to their local contacts – following a policy of 'don't ask, don't tell'.

This is probably just as well. A partner with one of Russia's biggest law firms, who declines to be named, smiles at the Western connotations of the word 'corruption'. 'We give gifts to almost everyone,' he says. 'Maybe it's not money – maybe just a box of chocolates – but you always need to do something or else your application will only be considered when they have nothing else to do. It's the mentality here.'

Yet international lawyers argue that most people's perceptions are dangerously one-sided. Most insiders believe that operating in Russia is no worse than it is in other developing countries.

Source: Extracts from an article by Richard Marsland, *Financial Times*, 4 April 2001, p.18.

The most significant developments in the political-legal environment are those associated with international trade agreements and regional economic alliances.

Trade agreements

The General Agreement on Tariffs and Trade (GATT) reduces the propensity of national governments to put tariffs on physical goods to protect domestic companies, and other institutions are furthering this opening process. Thus the Uruguay trade agreement was reached by 68 countries committing themselves to liberalising markets in telecommunications. The World Trade Organization (WTO) is negotiating for the removal of tariffs and other barriers on a wide range of goods and services. It is also seeking a world agreement on rules governing foreign investment – both to encourage it and, where thought necessary, to control it.

European Union

The EU is credited with being the model for many other regional trade groupings (Dent, 1997). Since the Treaty of Rome was signed in 1959 the aim has been to gradually eliminate tariffs and other restrictions that national governments use to protect domestic industries. This was broadly achieved by 1968, and led to further efforts to bring about closer economic integration between the member states. This culminated in the Single European Act of 1986 that aimed to create a single internal market by 1993. This further extended the scope for companies to operate in an integrated way across Europe. Companies were able to offer their goods and services much more widely within the EU, leading to a rapid growth in trade within the region. Much of this growth has been of trade within the same industry. Car companies such as Ford and DaimlerChrysler have plants in several countries, specialising in particular components or models. They then simultaneously import and export their products between the countries as part of a region-wide production system, leading to growth in intra-industry trade.

The EU is both widening its membership and deepening the scope of the issues with which it deals. Current applicants for membership include countries as diverse as Turkey, Hungary and Lithuania, which need to meet six political and economic conditions before admission. The deepening process is intended to extend the EU from the customs union with which it started. The intention is gradually to establish common European policy on a range of matters affecting business and competitiveness. These include policies on industry (such as subsidies for local businesses and/or foreign investment), mergers, employment rights, transport and environmental protection.

ACTIVITY 4.1

Access the European Union website

Access the European Union website at http://europa.eu.int/comm

Go to the page for the internal market and then to the scorecard that the Commission regularly publishes on progress towards the single market. What is the latest score, and what is the recent trend?

Check further and try to establish how the scorecard is compiled, and what it means.

The globalisation controversy

Supporters of more liberal world trade argue that it brings benefits of wider access to markets and cheaper goods and services. The growth in trade that follows benefits both consumers and workers by encouraging innovation and investment. Others take a much more critical view, pointing out that moves towards liberalisation through bodies such as the WTO are driven by the rich countries. They believe the agreements reached serve the interests of multinational businesses and richer economies rather than indigenous producers in local economies.

MANAGEMENT IN PRACTICE   **Globalisation: what it means to small nations**

In July 1996 the prime minister of Malaysia, Dr Mahathir, gave a lecture in which he questioned whether globalisation would bring benefits to poorer countries. Some extracts from his speech were reported as follows.

A globalised world is not going to be a very democratic world but will belong to powerful, dominant countries. Those countries would impose their will on the rest who will be no better off than when they were colonies of the rich. Fifty years ago, the process of decolonisation began and in about twenty years was virtually completed. But before any had become truly and fully independent, recolonisation has begun. This is what globalisation may be about. It does not contain much hope for the weak and poor. But unfortunately it is entirely possible.

He said that globalisation might bring about a utopia but nothing that had happened so far seemed to justify this dream. As interpreted by developed countries, it meant breaking down boundaries so that every country had access to others.

The poor countries will have access to the markets of the rich, unrestricted. In return, or rather by right, the rich will have access to the markets of the poor. This sounds absolutely fair. The playing field will be level, not tilted to favour anyone. It will be a borderless world. But if there is only one global entity there cannot be nations. Everyone would be equal citizens of the globe. But will they be truly equal?

Dr Mahathir said that, after thirty years or more of 'independence', the former colonies of the West have found out the emptiness of the independence they had won. They have found that their politics, their economy, their social and behavioural systems are all under the control, directly or indirectly, of the old colonial masters and the great powers. He added that it was clear that the developed countries wished to use the World Trade Organization to impose conditions on the developing countries. This will result not in improving human rights or labour practices or greater care for the environment but in stunting their growth and, consequently, in suffering for their people. If the developing countries were competing with the West in any way then their records were scrutinised and threats issued. The net effect is to prevent the development of these newly industrialising economies.

Dr Mahathir said globalisation would leave these countries totally exposed and unable to protect themselves, adding that true globalisation might result in increasing foreign investment in these countries. The effect would be the demise of the small companies based in the developing countries: 'Large international corporations, originating in the developed countries will take over everything.'

He said globalisation would result in all societies being exposed to the global culture, adding that this was going to become more universal because of the development of information technology. 'The unfortunate things is that the IT industry, and all that will be disseminated through it, will again be dominated by the big players – the huge corporations owned by the developed countries.'

Source: *New Straits Times*, July 1996.

ACTIVITY 4.2

Understanding a critic of globalisation

Malaysia has attracted much foreign direct investment, especially from IT companies. It is a leading player in South East Asia with little unemployment. Yet the architect of its economic success clearly has serious doubts about the emergence of the global economy. What are his main concerns?

Can you find examples of global companies using their economic bargaining power to take advantage of the weaker countries in which they operate?

All of these developments imply much greater patterns of contact between managers in different countries. Legislative changes and treaties remove some barriers to trade, but they do not solve the management problems of making those economic activities work efficiently. Above all, they bring many managers face to face with the need to manage cultural differences.

4.5   Contrasts in national cultures

While people have a great deal in common in the biological sense, there are many things that are unique to those from a particular nation or region. One of these is their culture. So, as business becomes more global in its operation, a central question for management is whether there are certain organisational imperatives of structure or behaviour that organisations must fill wherever they are, or whether they vary according to the culture of the country they are in (Smith, 1992).

Perspectives on culture

Edgar Schein (1985) defined culture as:

> Culture is the pattern of basic assumptions that a given group has invented, discovered or developed and [that is] therefore taught to new members as the correct way to perceive, think and feel in relation to [the organisation's] problems.

Social groupings of all kinds develop a distinct culture, which to some degree sets them apart from other groupings. Teams, clubs, long-term work groups, organisations and nations develop values and beliefs that guide members – how they react to events, what they regard as important. There is growing evidence of identifiable differences in the degree to which national cultures hold certain values and attitudes. For example, a study by Cranfield School of Management concluded that 'the French, although more sensitive to people, are slightly more into power/political styles of management, but less disciplined than the Germans who freely admit less sensitivity to people but a greater adherence to organisational disciplines and systems' (Kakabadse, 1993, quoted in Adams, 1996).

MANAGEMENT IN PRACTICE | **Cultural variety in the European Commission**

Marcello Burattini is the head of protocol for the European Commission. On the 40th anniversary of the Treaty of Rome he recalled the early days of the Commission:

> At the beginning of the 1960s the rules, based on the principles of Franco-Prussian administration, were strict, formal modes of address, and ties were *de rigeur* ... Then certain political leaders decided to enlarge [the Community]. Thus the British and the Irish arrived, bringing with them the English language, humour, simplicity in human relations, many original ideas – for example, pragmatism – somewhat softening the rigorous orthodoxy. The Danes taught us to be less formal, and were astonished by our way of doing things – and by the fact that secretaries made coffee for their bosses.

Source: The European, 27 March 1997.

Social beliefs affect what managers expect from their job, how work relates to family life and what reward they expect. Tayeb (1996) contrasts US and Japanese managers. She suggests the former typically give priority to things that are of personal importance to them. These include their long-term professional career, their individual personal development and the quality of family relationships. They come from:

> an individualistic culture in which 'self' takes precedence over group. For the Japanese manager the company's performance and victory ... comes first. And if this means sacrificing private leisure time so be it. [They] come from a collectivist culture, where group takes precedence over self. (p.37)

Tayeb goes on to argue that people learn their culture in the family, from religious influences and through the history of the nation, illustrating this last point with Australia:

> Australia is another example of the influence of history on people's values and attitudes. The origins of modern Australia go back to the eighteenth century, when Britain used to send her convicted political and social offenders there. The convicts carried with them their lack of respect for authority. On the ships that took them there everyone was on an equal footing with their fellow passengers. This combination of low respect for authority and a belief in equality has over time evolved into a democratic political system which (with New Zealand) is more or less unique within their immediate neighbouring region.
>
> Today, Australians are as law abiding as the citizens of any other nation, but they are sceptical about people in positions of power, such as politicians, police and judges. Their federal system of government reflects their belief in decentralisation and delegation of authority. (p.41)

ACTIVITY 4.3

Comparing cultures

Form a group amongst your student colleagues made up of people from different countries and cultures. Identify some of the main characteristics of the respective cultures that affect management. Note them down and compare your evidence with that from Hofstede's research (see pages 114–16).

Organisations and their management operate within this cultural context. Employees, including managers, bring their prevailing values, attitudes and beliefs into the workplace as part of their cultural heritage. Tayeb identifies further aspects of culture relevant to the work situation, namely high- and low-context cultures and attitudes to conflict.

High-context and low-context cultures

In a **low-context culture** information is explicit and clear. A **high-context culture** is one in which information is implicit, and can only be fully understood in conjunction with shared experience, assumptions and various forms of verbal codes. High-context cultures occur when people live closely with each other, where deep mutual understandings develop, and that then provide a rich context within which specific communication takes place. Low-context cultures occur where people are typically distant from each other so that information needs to be very explicit:

> Japanese, Arabs and Mediterranean people, who have extensive information networks among family, friends, colleagues and clients and who are involved in close personal relationships, are examples of high context cultures. Low context peoples include Americans, Germans, Swiss, Scandinavians and other northern Europeans; they compartmentalise their personal relationships, their work and many aspects of day-to-day life. (Tayeb, 1996, pp.55–6)

Attitude to conflict and harmony

Disagreements and conflict arise in all societies. The management interest is in how different societies have developed different ways of handling conflict. Individualistic cultures such as those of the United States or the Netherlands see conflict as healthy, on the basis that everyone has a right to express their views. People are encouraged to bring contentious issues into the open and to discuss conflicts rather than suppress them. Other cultures place greater value on social harmony and on not disturbing the way things are:

> The notion of harmony is central in almost all East Asian cultures, such as Korea, Taiwan, Singapore and Hong Kong, through their common Confucian heritage. In the context of Korea, for instance, Meek and Song argue that the traditional implicit rules of proper behaviour provide appropriate role behaviour for individuals in the junior and subordinate roles of an interpersonal relationship. (Tayeb, 1996, p.60)

Other clear differences between nations include their view of change and their time orientation.

View of change

This varies greatly between cultures. In the west, many take a relatively proactive view of change. People believe that they can shape what happens, things do not have to be as they are, and that change is part of the nature of the world. Other cultures see change as something that is slow, inevitable and not greatly influenced by human beings. The notion that events will take their natural course and that human intervention will probably be fruitless is difficult for a western manager in a non-western culture to accept.

Time orientation

Managers in western organisations typically view time as a scarce commodity. They take courses on how to manage it better. They expect others to meet deadlines and to arrive for meetings at the appointed time. Not all cultures see time this way. Some view it as a limitless resource, unbounded by death. Time is inexhaustible, so that the widespread western concern about saving time is seen as curious.

Are we overemphasising diversity?

So far only the diversity of national cultures has been emphasised. There is another view that the underlying fundamentals of management may outweigh cultural variations in detailed processes. One powerful constraint on diversity is the economic context of an essentially capitalist economic system. This places similar requirements on managers wherever they are. They have to provide acceptable returns, create a coherent organisational structure, maintain relations with stakeholders and try to keep control.

Further, if managers work in multinational organisations that have often developed their own strong and distinctive corporate culture, will corporate culture exercise more influence on behaviour than the local national culture?

Another constraint is the dramatic spread of integrated information systems across companies (and their suppliers) operating internationally. Some companies use such systems to place new and common reporting requirements on managers irrespective of their location. Such integration is often of competitive significance, and serves to tie units more closely together. This is also likely to bring convergence in the work of management.

These are unresolved questions to remember throughout this chapter. Look for evidence as you read that supports or contradicts either point of view.

4.6 Hofstede's comparison of national cultures

Geert Hofstede (1980), a Dutch academic, provides a widely quoted insight into national cultural differences. He had the opportunity to survey the attitudes of employees of IBM, one of the earliest global companies. He defines culture as a collective programming of people's minds, which influences how they react to events in the workplace. He defined four dimensions of culture (described below), and was able to establish how this varied amongst people in the different countries in which IBM operated.

Power distance

Hofstede defined **power distance** (PD) as 'the extent to which the less powerful members of ... organisations within a country expect and accept that power is distributed unevenly' (1991, p.28). One of the ways in which countries differ is the way that power and authority are distributed. A related difference is the way they view any resultant inequality. In some the existence of inequality in boss/subordinate relationships is seen as problematic. Others see it as part of the natural order of things. The questionnaire allowed the researchers to calculate scores for PD, countries with a high PD being those where people accepted inequality. Those with high scores included Belgium, France, Argentina, Brazil and Spain. Those with low PD scores included Sweden, Britain and Germany.

Uncertainty avoidance

Uncertainty avoidance is 'the extent to which the members of a culture feel threatened by uncertain or unknown situations' (Hofstede, 1991, p.113). People in some cultures tolerate ambiguity and uncertainty quite readily – if things are not clear they will improvise or use their initiative. Others are reluctant to move without clear rules or instructions. High scores, indicating low tolerance of uncertainty, were obtained in the Latin American, Latin European and Mediterranean countries, and for Japan and Korea.

Low scores were recorded in the Asian countries other than Japan and Korea, and in most of the Anglo and Nordic countries. The United Kingdom was 47th in the list – similar to the United States, Canada and Australia. Germany ranked 29th, indicating a lower tolerance of uncertainty than Anglo-American countries.

Individualism/collectivism

Hofstede distinguishes between **individualism** and **collectivism** as follows:

> Individualism pertains to societies in which the ties between individuals are loose: everyone is expected to look after himself or herself and his or her immediate family. Collectivism as its opposite pertains to societies in which people, from birth onwards, are integrated into strong, cohesive in-groups which throughout people's lifetime continue to protect them in exchange for unquestioning loyalty. (1991, p.51)

Some people live in societies in which the power of the group prevails: there is an emphasis on collective action and mutual responsibility, and on helping each other through difficulties. Other societies emphasise the individual, and his or her responsibility for their position in life. High scores on the individualism dimension occurred in wealthy countries such as the United States, Australia, United Kingdom and Canada. Low scores occurred in poor countries such as the less developed South American and Asian countries. Germany, the Netherlands, the Nordic countries and Japan showed medium individualism.

ACTIVITY 4.4

Implications of cultural differences

Consider the implications of differences on Hofstede's first two dimensions of culture for management in the countries concerned. For example, what would Hofstede's conclusions lead you to predict about the method that a French or Argentinian manager would use if he or she wanted a subordinate to perform a task, and what method would the subordinate expect his or her manager to use?

How would your answers differ if the manager and subordinates were Swedish?

Masculinity/femininity

Hofstede defines the two characteristics, as they pertain to society, as follows:

> **masculinity** pertains to societies in which social gender roles are clearly distinct (i.e. men are supposed to be assertive, tough and focused on material success, whereas women are supposed to be more modest, tender and concerned with the quality of life); **femininity** pertains to societies in which social gender roles overlap (i.e. both men and women are supposed to be modest, tender and concerned with the quality of life). (1991, pp.82–3, emphasis added)

Hofstede argues that societies differ in the desirability of assertive behaviour (which he labels as masculinity) and of modest behaviour (femininity). He sees a common trend in many societies that expect men to seek achievements outside the home while women care for things within the home. Masculinity scores were not related to economic wealth: 'we find both rich and poor masculine countries, and rich and poor feminine countries' (p.84). The most feminine countries were Sweden, Norway, the Netherlands and Denmark. Masculine countries included Japan, Austria, Germany, Italy and the United States.

The results obtained from Hofstede's work indicate the attitudes typically held by people in different national cultures to four dimensions. They have implications for understanding how people in the different areas in which a global company operates may react to particular management and organisational practices. An implication is that people operating internationally need to develop an ability to deal with the cultural contexts in which they will work. Adams (1996) examined several models attempting to identify the competences required to manage internationally. For example, Barham and Wills (1992) found that one of several competences that successful international managers possessed was the ability to act as 'intercultural mediator and change agent'. They defined this as:

> switching one's frame of reference rapidly between different cultures; being aware of one's own cultural underpinnings and of the need to be sensitive to cultural differences; managing change in different contexts and pushing the boundaries of different cultures; and balancing the need for speed and the need for sensitivity. (p. 49)

Hofstede collected information on the values and attitudes of respondents. These are different from observable behaviour, which we can only infer from the attitudes expressed. It is also worth distinguishing between the details and minutiae of interpersonal behaviour across cultures and those behaviours with significant effects on business performance. Again we can only infer that there is a link. There are visible and illuminating examples (such as the visitor to France quoted in Management in Practice), but there are dangers in overgeneralising from good anecdotes.

4.7   Contrasting management systems

Management takes place in a social context that influences its character, so we would expect that different national or continental cultures would produce different views on how management is, or should be, conducted. Keith Thurley and Hans Wirdenius (academics working in the United Kingdom and Sweden respectively) noted the apparent domination of management writing and teaching by the North American experience. They believed that while many of the ideas were powerful, they jarred with the distinctive and varied cultural experience within Europe. Was there such a thing as a European approach to management, as distinct from the prevailing US and emerging Japanese styles? Thurley and Wirdenius (1989, pp.19–20) summarised the distinctive features of the US and Japanese styles as set out below.

US style

US management theory is built on seven crucial ideas:

1 *Scientific management* Using a systematic approach to improve task performance.
2 *Classical management theory* Defining roles with specific job/role responsibilities and authority.
3 *Individualism* Assuming that managers are primarily individuals with their own personalities and interests and their own idea of individual self-interest.
4 *Human relations* Concern for fostering work group norms and relationships to serve organisational goals.

KEY IDEAS

National culture or corporate culture?

A study by Laurent (1983) surveying successive groups of managers participating in executive development programmes at INSEAD (a leading European centre for management education and development) provides support for the view that differences in national cultures override the influence of corporate cultures.

The managers came from many different companies and many different organisations. When their responses were analysed, it appeared that the most powerful determinant of their assumptions about the role of management was their nationality. Across 56 different items of inquiry, it was found that nationality had three times more influence on the shaping of managerial assumptions than any of the respondents' other characteristics such as age, education, function or type of company.

One of the most illustrative examples of national differences in management assumptions was reflected in the respondents' reaction to the following statement: 'It is important for a manager to have at hand precise answers to most of the questions that his subordinates may raise about their work' (p.86).

While only a minority of Northern American and Northern European managers agreed with this statement, a majority of Southern Europeans and South East Asians did. The research results indicated that managers from different national cultures vary widely as to their basic conception of what management is all about.

Laurent found that conceptions of organisations varied widely across national cultures, as managers from Latin cultures (French and Italian) consistently perceived organisations as social systems of relationships monitored by power, authority and hierarchy to a much greater extent than their northern counterparts did. US managers held an 'instrumental' view of the organisation as a set of tasks to be achieved through a problem-solving hierarchy where positions are defined in terms of tasks and functions and where authority is functionally based. French managers held a 'social' view of the organisation as a collective of people to be managed through a formal hierarchy, where positions are defined in terms of levels of authority and status and where authority is more attached to individuals than it is to their offices or functions.

The research led to the conclusion that deep-seated managerial assumptions are strongly shaped by national cultures and appear quite insensitive to the more transient culture of organisations.

Source: Laurent (1983).

5 *Contingency theory* All organisations need to develop structures and policies that are relevant to their particular context. All organisations therefore should be different.

6 *Planned organisational change* Change requires a systematic approach to alter organisational structures and culture.

7 *Strategic choice management* Organisations should try to define the basic business strategies required to achieve a satisfactory market position. This then leads to designing structures that fit this strategy.

Japanese style

Japanese management emphasises equality as the basis of competition and co-operation. This rejects the implicit technocratic approach of US scientific management. There are also seven crucial ideas that summarise the approach:

1 *Collective responsibility* All members of an organisation should feel responsibility for the success of that organisation.

2 *Generalist roles and job rotation* All employees work for the organisation and should be trained to perform a wide variety of roles. They do not own their jobs – they may have to do anything and need training for this.

3 *Trust of subordinates* Subordinates need to be allowed to get on with their work. They have potential that should be stimulated.

4 *Protection of all employees* All employees are vulnerable and need protection while working for the organisation.

5 *Life careers should be planned* Individuals need to perceive their whole potential career as an opportunity that offers a challenge for them to develop their skills and knowledge.

6 *Pragmatic adaptation and rationalism* Everything changes, so management must be flexible enough to adapt to new circumstances.

7 *Identity with the* michi *('the way') and personal work colleagues* The work ethic is seen as a daily personal experience and is essentially derived from constant interactions with others in the work group. Employees therefore need to have a clear identity with the way they live in the organisation and to show affection and loyalty to their co-workers. (Thurley and Wirdenius, 1989, pp.19–20)

Such models are highly generalised summaries of diverse populations. Their value is to give some clues about broad differences in approach to management. Above all, they show the variety of ways in which management is practised and encourage people to be ready to adapt the way they work to local circumstances.

European style

Thurley and Wirdenius acknowledged the great diversity within Europe, but also put forward a *European management model*. They noted six needs or values that were the starting points for managerial action:

1 *Base decisions on scientific, rational thinking.*

2 *Evolve specific pragmatic strategies* suited to the situation, rather than following universal theories or solutions based on ideologies.

3 *Build emotional commitment to making a change initiative work.* This implies inspiring employees to take future possibilities seriously.

4 *Use managerial and technical experience* – and the judgements based on this – to the fullest degree. Social capital is composed of such learnt behaviour, skills and knowledge.

5 *Take a 'pluralist' view of the enterprise,* which combines the necessity of achieving commitment to organisational goals and a democratic process for arriving at broadly consensual decisions.

6 *Creative learning, through and with colleagues,* together with self-development, as a continuous process within organisational work life.

Q Case questions 4.4

- Which of Thurley and Wirdenius's management models would you expect to shape management practice at Lufthansa?
- What examples of each approach can you find in the case study?

Arab style

Other cultures are now challenging the western and Japanese models, for example Islamic beliefs influence management in the Arab world. Arab executives are more person oriented than work oriented, and more susceptible to pressures from families, friends and the wider community. These pressures influence their decisions and behaviour practices. Al-Faleh (1987) found that Arab management had the following characteristics, stemming from the prevailing value system:

- Organisation members are motivated by friendship and power needs rather than by performance objectives.
- Social formalities are extremely important.
- Managers rely heavily on kinship ties to get things done.
- Nepotism is regarded as natural and acceptable.
- Punctuality and time constraints are of much less concern than in western cultures.
- Subordinates act with deference and obedience to those above them in the hierarchy.

4.8 Managing in an international context

Managing internationally brings managers into direct contact with diverse cultures and institutions, requiring a new level of awareness of and sensitivity to these differences. These are likely to affect each of the management functions. People perform management functions in ways that are compatible with the prevailing economic, institutional and cultural context of their country. As business spreads management makes contact with ever more diverse cultures, and meets different ways of interpreting the roles of management. While recognising the huge dangers of overgeneralisation, the following points are offered for discussion.

Planning

Increased opportunities for regional and global trade mean that the environment is bringing in new forms of competition to businesses – others can now compete in their home market. By the same token, businesses can develop their objectives towards extending their market into a wider area. Planning to achieve those objectives on a global scale raises new workflow and logistical challenges. People in countries with high power distance scores will expect managers to make plans and subordinates to implement them without complaint or disagreement. Attempts to involve subordinates in discussing the alternatives would be greeted with puzzlement.

Organising

Major challenges arise in developing the appropriate structural forms for international business. New organisational structures are created to manage internationally, which are usually supported by developments in information technology. In shaping these changes management and staff need to take account of the diversity of national cultures. People in high power distance countries will tend to expect structures to be centralised, formal and with strict job descriptions. People in low power distance countries will prefer more fluid structures that allow them to use their initiative.

Leading

Internationalisation clearly means more stakeholders, especially when companies develop complex trading networks across national boundaries. Managers need to influence these stakeholders, which include the governments and communities in which they work as well as other commercial organisations. The interests and ways of working of these players will have been shaped by local cultures and institutions. These cultural differences also affect how management can influence the behaviour of those whose support it needs – methods acceptable in one culture may not work in another.

This is particularly necessary in generating willing action and commitment from people who may have different perspectives on work. As with planning, people in high power distance countries will expect to be told what to do. In low power distance countries people expect to be asked for their opinions.

| MANAGEMENT IN PRACTICE | Leadership and national culture |

People in different cultures have different beliefs about appropriate leadership behaviour. Suutari (1996) surveyed 149 managers in a company in the metal industry, which operated in Denmark, Finland, Germany, the United Kingdom and Sweden. The questionnaire sought their beliefs about the way a manager ought to behave on 14 dimensions of leadership. Six factors showed statistically significant differences between managers in the five countries. These were:

- **Decision participation:** Danish and Finnish managers were more likely than German and British managers to accept the participation of subordinates in decision making.
- **Autonomy and delegation:** same as for decision participation.
- **Rewarding:** Danish managers most frequently believed that companies should reward subordinates for good performance.
- **Role clarification:** British and German managers tended more frequently than managers from the Nordic countries to see a need for role clarification.
- **Conflict management:** British and German managers tended more than Finnish and Danish managers to emphasise conflict management behaviours.
- **Individualism:** British and Danish managers were more likely than the others to see a need for managers to pay personal attention to the hopes and needs of individuals.

Overall, the study supported the view that 'management methods developed in one country are applicable in other countries to only a limited extent'.

Source: Suutari (1996, p.405).

Controlling and learning

The more widespread an organisation's business, the more it must rely on formal systems of control. Nations differ in their views on exercising control. Some systems favour tight, centralised and supervisory controls: the current pattern in many western organisations is to emphasise the benefits of self-control in semi-autonomous teams. Different attitudes to corrective action and learning also illuminate the diversity of management practice across the globe. In individualist societies people acknowledge individual responsibility for results – whereas in collectivist ones they will be more inclined to stress collective action and mutual responsibility. There will be more resistance to attempts to reward or punish individuals.

The primary lesson is that managing internationally will involve significant learning and reflection. How the ideas and models outlined in this chapter affect management practice in a particular location is essentially unpredictable, being a combination of so many individual, corporate, cultural and national influences. Entering a situation with at least an awareness of the differences outlined in this chapter is a start: reflecting on the experience of working in different cultures will add greatly to their value.

4.9 Summary

This chapter illustrates the interaction between the international environment and the management of organisations. Political, economic, social and technological factors encourage the regionalisation and globalisation of business activity. This has affected the pattern of international contacts that many managers have, with diverse cultures and institutions requiring a new level of awareness of and sensitivity to differences. This chapter has introduced models and perspectives that help managers be conscious of the hazards, and so be better able to secure the benefits of managing internationally. It began by recalling the rapid growth in the amount of business conducted across national boundaries and outlined the factors driving the growth of international business. The chapter focused on the influence of three contextual factors – economic development, political/institutional factors and cultural factors. These combine to shape contrasting national management systems – ways of describing the unique context of management in different geographical areas of the world. They shape the way people in different management systems interpret generic functions of management. How management adapts these functions to meet the conditions of managing internationally will affect how well they and their organisations perform in the international economy.

Content

Increased opportunities for regional and global trade mean that the environment is bringing in new forms of competition to businesses – others can now compete in their home market. By the same token, businesses can develop their objectives towards extending their market into a wider area. Planning to achieve those objectives on a global scale raises new workflow and logistical challenges. New organisational structures are created to manage internationally, which are usually supported by developments in information technology. In shaping these changes management and staff need to take account of the diversity of national cultures. This is particularly necessary in generating willing action and commitment from people who may have different perspectives on work.

Process

Internationalisation clearly means more stakeholders, especially when companies develop complex trading networks across national boundaries. These stakeholders include the governments and communities in which they work as well as other commercial organisations. The interests and ways of working of these players will have been shaped by local cultures and institutions. These cultural differences also affect how management can influence the behaviour of those whose support it needs – methods acceptable in one culture may not work in another. A probable consequence of globalisation is that it reduces the shared knowledge within the organisation. Communication internally assumes greater importance if the organisation is to be able to co-ordinate effectively over great distances.

Control

A strategy of internationalisation or globalisation may be a way to reduce dependency on any single source. If so, it affects the relative power of stakeholders. A similar issue from a critical perspective is the way in which the power of management in multinational companies is increasing at the expense of national states. It can also be observed that national governments are keen to encourage foreign direct investment by such companies in their country on account of the access to economic power they bring. Management can use the threat (real or imagined) of increased global competition to encourage their own staff to accept change that they might otherwise have opposed.

As businesses come to operate over ever wider grographic areas managers tend to rely on more formal methods of control. Yet attitudes to control vary between cultures, and managers need to take account of this as they construct systems to support the internationalisation of their organisations.

Lufthansa has continued to be part of the Star Alliance, which by 2001 included 15 airlines, including British Midland International and Singapore Airlines. It sees its route network as the counterpart to the developing networks in other businesses that spread their production around the world in the new global economy. Deregulation of air travel (an example of the political/legal changes outlined in Chapter 3) has meant more competition in its core business of flying passengers and cargo. Lufthansa has therefore diversified into other aviation-related services such as maintenance, catering and travel-related IT services.

Q PART CASE QUESTIONS

- In what ways is The Body Shop operating internationally?
- What issues does the Lufthansa case suggest might also be on the agenda of management at The Body Shop? And vice versa?
- How does The Body Shop culture relate to the local cultures in which it has retail operations? Does national or company culture prevail?

4.10 Review questions

1 What factors are stimulating the growth in world trade?

2 Compare internationalisation and globalisation. Give a specific example of a company of each type about which you have obtained some information.

3 Outline the difference between a high- and a low-context culture and give an example of each from direct observation or discussion.

4 Explain accurately to another person Hofstede's four dimensions of national cultures. Evaluate his conclusions on the basis of discussions with your colleagues from any of the countries in his study.

5 Give some illustrations of your own about the way in which the history of a country has affected its culture, and how that in turn affects the management of organisations there.

6 What are the distinctive features of Japanese, European and US management systems?

7 How is the growth of international business likely to affect management functions?

8 Compare the implications of globalisation for (a) national governments, (b) their citizens, (c) the management of global companies, (d) the environment.

Further reading

Nugent, N. and O'Donnell, R. (1994), *The European Business Environment*, Macmillan, Basingstoke. A detailed account of the European context of business, including chapters on the political, economic, legal, labour market, financial, marketing and technological environments within which European managements are operating.

Ghauri, P.N. and Prasad, S.B. (eds) (1995), *International Management: A reader*, Dryden Press, London. A set of readings on the themes of global strategy, understanding non-western structures and ways of developing global managers

Harris, N. (1999), *European Business* (2nd edn), Macmillan Business, Basingstoke;

Dent, C.M. (1997), *The European Economy: The global context*, Routledge, London.

Both trace the development of a more integrated European economy and its place within wider global trends.

Bennett, R. (1997), *European Business*, Pitman, London. Contains useful summaries of relevant institutions such as the World Trade Organization.

Monbiot, G. (2000), *The Captive State*, Macmillan, Basingstoke. A critique of multinational corporations and the way they seek to subvert democratic institutions.

Daniels, J.D. and Radebaugh, L.H. (1998), *International Business* (8th edn), Reading, MA. Provides a comprehensive exposure to many aspects of international business, combining a strong theoretical base with many current examples.

European Management Journal regularly publishes case studies and accessible research with an international perspective.

Annotated links, questions and resources can be found on

www.booksites.net/boddy

5

Corporate social responsibility

AIM *To introduce the ethical and social responsibility dilemmas that managers in all organisations face, and some tools to consider them coherently.*

In the late 1960s the US automobile industry's home market was under threat from overseas competitors. Lee Iacocca, then president of Ford, was determined to face the competition head-on, by having a new car, the Ford Pinto, on the market by the 1971 model year. This meant reducing the standard 'concept to production' time of a year and a half, and making changes on the production line rather than the drawing board.

In testing its new design Ford used current and proposed legislation. Crash tests indicated that the petrol tank tended to rupture when it was struck from behind at 20 mph, posing a significant risk to those inside. This contravened proposed national legislation which required that cars be able to withstand an impact at 30 mph without fuel loss. No one informed Iacocca of these findings, for fear of being fired. He was fond of saying 'safety doesn't sell'.

Management had to decide between production deadlines to meet competitive requirements and passenger safety. The engineers costed the design improvements at $11 per car, and turned to cost/benefit analysis to help quantify the dilemma. Using government figures that estimated the loss to society for every traffic accident at $200,000, Ford's calculations were:

Benefits of altering design
Savings: 180 deaths; 180 serious injuries; 2,100 vehicles
Unit cost: $200,000 per death; $67,000 per serious injury; $700 per vehicle
Total benefit: $49.5 million

Costs of altering the design
Sales: 11 million cars; 1.5 million light trucks
Unit cost: $11 per car; $11 per truck
Total cost: $137.5 million

From this calculation Ford determined that the costs of altering the design outweighed the benefits, so they would produce the Pinto in its original form. They reasoned that the current design met all the applicable federal regulatory safety standards. While it did not meet proposed future legislation it was as safe as current competing models.

Ford therefore launched the Pinto in 1971. Observers estimate that from 1971 to 1978 between 1,700 and 2,500 people died in fires involving Pintos. In 1977 the proposed fuel tank legislation was adopted. Ford recalled all 1971–6 Pintos to modify their fuel tanks. Civil action was brought against Ford and resulted in a pay-out of $250 million in damage awards. Many courts concluded that the Pinto's design was legally defective. However, when charged with criminal homicide, Ford was found not guilty in 1980.

Source: based on Shaw (1991) and Birsh and Fielder (1994)

Q **Case questions**

● As a marketing or production manager at Ford at the time, what dilemmas would you face?

● How would you express these dilemmas within the company?

5.1   Introduction

This chapter introduces the following ideas:

- Philanthropy
- Enlightened self-interest
- Ethical investors
- Social contract
- Deontology
- Teleology
- Utilitarianism
- Egoism
- Applied ethics
- Ethical relativism
- Corporate social responsibility
- Ethical consumers
- Ethical audit

Ford managers dealing with the Pinto problem chose to put short-term profit before safety. As things turned out they also failed to achieve their profit targets when they had to meet the cost of the legal claims against the company. So perhaps they made a poor business decision as well as an ethically questionable one. Yet they did not act illegally, and customers were not as interested in safety features then as they are today. A manager who tried to delay the model launch would probably have damaged his career, and his family's economic well-being. A delay may have harmed the company – and the livelihood of other Ford workers. But about 2,000 people died because of those managers' decisions.

Most people only become conscious of business ethics when there is a problem. Events such as the collapse of the Maxwell Group, the Bank of Credit and Commerce International or Barings Bank increase consumer distrust of corporate bodies. Successive waves of alarm about food safety in the United Kingdom have affected many consumers, and led to public concern about the responsibility of individual producers, supermarkets and government departments. The ensuing media debate invariably raises public awareness and displeasure, and ends in calls for legislation or court action. The stories of Persil Power, when clothes were said to have been slightly damaged when washed (German, 1995), and the British Airways 'dirty tricks' campaign against Virgin Atlantic, when BA used unusual tactics against a competitor (Glaister, 1991), make good reading. They also raise public questions about the ethics of such companies and their sense of corporate social responsibility.

While such situations seem clear-cut in hindsight many issues in the corporate response to social and ethical problems are ambiguous and complex. There are complexities and trade-offs in corporate decision making and responsibility, and there are usually several ways of seeing the ethical dimensions in a business issue. Each party will claim that their position is the most ethical or responsible in the circumstances. There are few rules to guide the manager, and no universally acceptable solution to balancing the needs of all the parties. Yet the issues arise throughout business activities, from human resource issues to environmental degradation. Managers look for some tools that help them approach the issues in a structured way.

The chapter begins by charting aspects of the history of responsible business practice, and then contrasts two views of the role of business in society. The topic of business ethics is considered, including four philosophical approaches to the solution of ethical dilemmas. Finally the chapter shows how some managers try to apply these ethical ideas by encouraging their organisations to develop socially responsible practices.

MANAGEMENT IN PRACTICE **Ford v Firestone Tyres**

In 2001 Firestone Tyres and the Ford Motor Company were in a dispute regarding the safety of their products. Having severed links, which stem from the first involvement of Harvey Firestone with Henry Ford over a century ago, both companies claim that the concerns over the safety of the four-by-four Explorer arise from the other's products. Ford has recalled 6.5 million Firestone tyres in response to consumer concerns, while Firestone believes that Ford is covering up problems with one of its models, the Explorer.

Q Case questions 5.1

- Did Ford act unethically at that time? Should the law be the only influence on a corporation's actions? What responsibilities do you think a major company has?
- Ford used cost-benefit analysis to decide what to do – could this have been improved? Was it a useful decision tool in this case?
- Imagine you were a Ford manager at this time. What would you have done, and why? List the social costs and benefits to the company and society of the alternatives to help you determine your answer.
- Imagine you worked for Ford as an engineer and were aware of this potential design fault. What would you do? What, if any, are your responsibilities to the customer and/or your employer?

5.2 The history of responsible business practice

While current newspaper headlines imply that business ethics has only just become an important issue the Pinto case shows it has been around for years. Indeed the history of economic development shows the scope for unethical business behaviour – not least in the employment of children as young as 8 in the mines and mills of nineteenth century Britain (a practice still common in some parts of the world).

Paradoxically, there is an equally long tradition of ethical behaviour in business. From the very start of the Industrial Revolution some entrepreneurs acted with philanthropy:

1803–76	Titus Salt	Textiles	Employee welfare; Saltaire Village
1830–98	Jeremiah Coleman	Mustard	Charities; Salvation Army; YMCA
1839–1922	George Cadbury	Chocolate	Employee welfare; Bournville Village
1836–1925	Joseph Rowntree	Chocolate	Employee welfare; New Earswick Village
1851–1925	William Lever	Soap	Employee welfare; Port Sunlight Village

Their approach to business recognised the social impact of industry and its potential to improve social conditions. By fostering an ethos of care, these industrialists developed the traditional notion of individual charity and redefined the responsibilities of business. They offered a different business model and showed society what was possible. Their **philanthropy** helped define **enlightened self-interest** as a viable approach to business. They were committed Quakers who believed it was morally unacceptable to exploit their workers to make money. They were also owner-managers and so free to give their own money to charitable aims if they desired. Managers of today's public companies are responsible to the shareholders and the communities in which they exist.

As business grew during the Industrial Revolution the original owner-managers required additional capital to finance expansion. The method chosen in most western economies was to issue shares in the business to wealthy individuals. If growth continued the number of separate shareholders grew and were often not individuals but financial institutions such as insurance companies and pension funds. This diverse group of shareholders rarely take an active part in managing the business – they appoint directors to manage the business on their behalf. The separation of management from ownership has a significant effect on the conduct of business. If owner-managers chose to be philanthropic, they could do so – they combined the two roles.

Separation of the roles reduced this possibility. The ownership role was spread amongst many individual or institutional shareholders, who were unlikely to have a coherent view of philanthropy. Moreover, the institutional holders have responsibilities to their policyholders or pensioners. Their interests may be damaged by overgenerous donations to another group of people. So the responsibility for the philanthropy or otherwise of the modern company is more diverse and policy is harder to set. The charitable ideals of the early philanthropists are rarely put into practice by modern corporations.

Another obstacle is that the problems identified within this area of **applied ethics** are complex, variable and constantly evolving. It is usually impossible to determine the definitively correct response to ethical issues in the workplace. It is often easier to ignore the problem by invoking the economic imperative rather than struggle to apply ethical theories to business decisions.

The economic imperative argues that in business financial priorities rank far above social or environmental ones. It leads to the view that overt and significant philanthropy ought to be a responsibility of charity rather than of business. Those of this view maintain that the 'business of business is business', and many managers and directors affirm that their primary duty is to increase shareholder wealth.

Others believe that this does not inevitably preclude a strategy of enlightened self-interest, and do not accept that acting responsibly damages business interests. However, they do accept that returns will be in the long run rather than the short. These benefits could include increased employee motivation, customer loyalty, verbal recommendations, repeat purchases, improved public and/or media relations, and increased customer awareness of the product or company. All of these can support the long-term success of a business.

MANAGEMENT IN PRACTICE   **Examples of ethical behaviour**

Some examples of prominent companies that have developed a clear policy of ethical behaviour are:

- Ford has an environmental manufacturing policy and a corporate citizenship programme.
- Tengelmann, one of the largest department store chains in Germany, is committed to offering products that are environmentally harmless and contain recycled materials as far as practicable.

- B&Q, a leading UK retail chain, actively employs people who are often discriminated against because of their age. It also avoids stocking products whose production is environmentally damaging (such as peat).
- The Body Shop, Camelot (which runs the UK Lottery) and British Telecom produce audited social statements.
- Ciba-Geigy, a Swiss-based chemicals company, sets environmental protection as an equal goal along with product innovation and profitability.
- BP has a formal policy on business conduct with a code of practice.

Ethical issues arise in all stages of the 'value chain' – from marketing, design, sourcing raw materials, manufacturing, through to distribution.

ACTIVITY 5.1

Looking for responsible business activity

- *Collect at least two new examples of organisations that seem to be taking the matter seriously by introducing explicit policies on environmental, social or ethical matters.*
- *What aspects of the company's operations does the policy cover?*
- *How did management develop the policy (for example, which people or groups took part in forming the policy)?*
- *How does management ensure that people follow the policy and that it has the expected effects?*

5.3 The role of business in society

There are two major schools of thought on the role of business in society. One follows Milton Friedman, a US economist who believes that the role of business is to create wealth by providing goods, services and employment. The other is based on the idea of corporate social responsibility, where the emphasis is on public good rather than private gain.

The Friedmanite position

Milton Friedman was clear:

> There is only one social responsibility of business – to use its resources and engage in activities designed to increase profits so long as it stays within the rules of the game, and engages in open and free competition without deception or fraud. (Friedman, 1970, p.126)

As an economist, Friedman believed that operating business 'without deception or fraud' provided sufficient social benefit through the creation of wealth or employment. For a business to give money away to charitable purposes was equivalent to self-imposed taxation. He argued that those who had been put in charge of a business (the managers/board of directors) had no right to give away the owners' (the shareholders) money. They were employed to generate wealth for shareholders, not to give it away.

This stance sees the role of business in society as being solely concerned with operating in a competitive market economy. For an individual business to undertake any additional roles is to operate beyond the remit of business.

Others disagree with Friedman's argument that management should focus solely on profit considerations. They argue that business does not have an unquestioned right to operate in society and do as it wishes. They see business as one of many subsystems in the wider social system. Just as society depends on business organisations for goods and services, so business depends on society. It cannot operate without inputs from that society in the form of employees, capital, physical resources. It also depends on some explicit or implicit legal right to operate and a framework of institutions that allow it to do so – courts, banking systems, educational systems and so on. To be accepted business needs to respond to society's demands and expectations, which will not be confined to generating wealth.

It is here that many thinkers on business ethics have sought to gain 'parity of esteem' between ethics and the other factors that companies routinely consider in deciding what to do. For example, they argue that when using Porter's five forces model managers should also consider the ethical dimension as a further force affecting competitive rivalry. If an ethically minded board of directors is considering entering a new line of business, members would pay attention to the ethical issues associated with the sector, as well as the other forces in the model. Similarly, in conducting a PEST analysis, they would want to add an 'ethics' element to prompt people to consider how issues arising under that heading may affect the business. In such circumstances ethical issues are not treated as separate concerns but as one element, of equal standing to all the others, in the context of management action.

This is where the ethical company (and **ethical investors**) will test the integrity of an industry before entering it. It will not enter that industry unless it believes that (a) it can compete in that industry without abandoning the company's ethical drivers, and (b) it can influence the ethical behaviour of the entire industry for the better.

MANAGEMENT IN PRACTICE   **Ethical investors**

Ethical investors will not invest their money in business activities that they consider unethical, such as those in countries with oppressive regimes or that produce nuclear power, tobacco, alcohol, armaments or pharmaceuticals.

Unit trusts are a form of collective investment, in which private individuals buy units in a trust managed by professional investment managers. They pool these individual sums and invest them in a range of companies on the unit-holders' behalf. During the 1980s many investment managers launched trusts that invested in 'ethical' companies. At first the investment policies of these 'ethical funds' consisted mainly of negative criteria – companies were excluded if they sold tobacco or traded with repressive regimes. Later they developed their policy to seek out, and invest in, companies with a positive record on issues such as animal testing, the environment, trade relations, working conditions and community or social involvement. However, since the mid-1990s, many policies use a 'best of sector' approach to ensure reasonable returns for investors.

Source: Pridham (2001).

ACTIVITY 5.2

Checking ethical unit trusts

● *Find out how the performance of ethical funds compares with equivalent funds which do not have that policy. Do so by consulting any full list of unit trust performance tables in the financial pages of a newspaper, where there is usually a separate section for ethical trusts.*

● *Can the growth in ethical investment be explained in the light of Friedman's assertions?*

Corporate social responsibility

The idea of corporate social responsibility reflects this interdependency: society and business depend on each other and have mutual obligations within a **social contract**. However, the social environment changes over time and, as society changes, so do its expectations of corporations. The Pinto case indicated that producers were not overly interested in safety in the late 1960s. Most motorists of that era were just as oblivious to the finer points of car safety. Today many companies advertise their safety features such as anti-lock brakes or airbags as major selling points. Governments legislate to protect consumers from undesirable selling practices or faulty goods and services. Society has become more sophisticated and demanding. Public demand for recycled or more environmentally friendly goods has prompted changes in corporate behaviour and in company product portfolios. Many now recognise the appalling working conditions in poor countries that produce the raw materials for western goods. This has developed into the notion of 'fair trade' and the recognised Fair Trade Mark – and corporate responses such as:

● Typhoo Tea changing its practices and being awarded the Fair Trade Mark.
● Café Direct successfully competing with the coffee giants.
● Smaller fair trade brands such as Green and Black, Divine and Dubble being able to enter the chocolate market.

Q Case questions 5.2

● Did Ford make the right decision *for that time*?
● Would it be the right decision *now*?
If you have given different answers, why is that?

Consumer and public expectations change. It appears that more European consumers expect ethical commitment or social responsibility to be demonstrated by large corporations. Management may damage rather than promote shareholder interests by ignoring its wider responsibilities to society. This raises numerous practical dilemmas about business ethics.

Consumers, environment and ethics

- 60 per cent of consumers consider environmental issues in their shopping.
- 40 per cent of those believe themselves to be 'dark green' (very committed to environmental issues).
- The percentage prepared to pay more for eco-products increased from 53 per cent to 60 per cent during 1990–5. There has been an increase since 1994 in the proportion of respondents in the strongly ethical category, who actively seek out ethical goods; one in four are now in this category, compared with one in five in 1994.
- Environmental concern is now found across all socioeconomic groups and a 1999 survey showed a marginal growth in interest in animal rights and ethical issues.
- A 1999 survey showed that issues of conscience were less widespread than 10 years ago, particularly in the teenage market. The percentages of both 'pale green' consumers (who buy environmentally friendly goods only when they see them) and 'armchair greens' (who pay lip service to the environment while not changing their spending habits) have decreased slightly. There has been an increase in the 'unconcerned' and 'no opinion' categories – though these two latter groups still account for only 14 per cent of all consumers.

Source: Mintel (1999).

5.4 What is business ethics?

Before looking at some tools for exploring the ethical dilemmas facing management, use Activity 5.3 to locate your own ethical positions.

ACTIVITY 5.3

Reflecting on your ethics

- *You are walking down the street. There is no one nearby and you see: (a) a 50 pence piece, (b) a £5 note, (c) a £50 note, (d) a £100 note, (e) £1,000. Do you keep it? Yes or no?*
- *The money you find was actually in a wallet with the owner's name and address in it. Does this make a difference?*
- *That name indicates to you that it belongs to: (a) a wealthy person, (b) a pensioner of modest means, (c) a single parent. Does this make a difference?*
- *Suppose there were some people nearby. Does this make a difference?*

Explore your reasons for each of your decisions.

Peter Drucker (1981) posed the question: What precisely is business ethics, and what could, or should it be? The challenge is not as strange as it may at first seem. There are two alternative positions, on whether business ethics refers to:

- **applied ethics** – applying ethical theory to business – or
- creating a separate set of rules about ethical behaviour in business that are distinct from those of society.

Some authors argue that business has its own ethics, describing it as 'the game of business' (Carr, 1968), and that, like any game, business has its own rules. Using the analogy of the game of poker (where bluffing is a central part of the game itself), Carr suggests that 'no one should think any the worse of the game of business because its standards of right and wrong differ from the prevailing tradition of morality in our society' (p.139). He believes that all the bluffing and hyperbole that surround business dealings are central to its operation and that all parties expect it: 'Violations of ethical ideals of society are common in business, but they are not necessarily violations of business principles' (Carr, 1968, p.147).

> ### Q Case questions 5.3
>
> - Do you agree with Carr's comments?
> - Does this help you take a different view towards Ford's action in the 1970s?
> - Is the following quote from Nash (1990) the logical conclusion to Carr's view?
>
>   'Suppose you are a business (wo)man. Now suppose you are of ruthless and greedy character ... But I repeat myself.'

Conversely, others (see, for example, Drucker, 1981; Frederick *et al.*, 1992) believe that management should not make up their own definitions of what is right and wrong. They believe that, as part of society, managers are subject to the rules of that society and should run their organisations accordingly. This implies that business ethics 'requires that the organisation or individual behave in accordance with the carefully thought-out rules of moral philosophy' (Robin and Reidenbach, 1987, p.45). What are these rules?

There are four main schools of thought in moral philosophy, offering different approaches to solving ethical dilemmas:

- **Deontology** This is the 'ethics of principle', equating any decision with a moral law. This means that any act is right if it is consistent with an accepted moral principle or law. Societies have developed certain rules that members generally accept (e.g. that people do not rob or deliberately injure each other) which are valid in many situations, including organisational ones (Honderich, 1995, pp.887–8).
- **Utilitarianism** This follows the logic of the 'ethics of consequence'. It looks at who gains from a decision and deems it right if the majority benefit. In examining the probable results or outcome of a decision utilitarianism suggests that what is good for most people is right (Honderich, 1995, pp.890–2).
- **Teleology** This is the 'ethics of purpose'. It considers whether the outcome of an action accomplishes the original goal. This uses the agent's vision as the criterion to judge the action. If an act (within the law) ensures the continuation of the corporation then it is right.
- **Egoism** This is the 'ethics of self-interest', claiming that personal or corporate benefit is the only rational criterion for judging economic actions. The argument (first developed in the teachings of Adam Smith, 1776) is that if people follow this principle it will, perhaps paradoxically, result in the general good. The assumption is that people will only be able to maximise their personal self-interest if they do things that others value and are willing to pay for.

Justifying decisions

Think about times when you have justified a decision you have made on the grounds that it was: (a) for the good of the group/family/friends, (b) the right thing to do, (c) the best option for yourself, (d) the best way to get the job done. Which of the ethical philosophies outlined above matches each reason?

These tools from moral philosophy enable a more informed and analytical insight into management dilemmas. They may however lead to more questions than answers. Table 5.1 identifies some questions under each philosophical approach.

Table 5.1 Dilemmas within each philosophy

Philosophy	Dilemma
Deontology	Who determines that a moral principle is 'generally accepted'? What if others claim that a principle leading to a different decision is equally 'accepted'?
Utilitarianism	Who determines the majority, and the population of which it is the greatest number? Is the benefit to them assessed over the short term or long term?
Teleology	Actions usually have many outcomes – how are they weighed and compared? If agents make conflicting decisions (justifying them by their different purposes) how should they resolve the conflict?
Egoism	Whose self-interest is central to the debate? What if the action of one damages the self-interest of another?

Management is likely to decide that the rationale of economic reasoning, while harsh, reduces the dilemma to a clearly understandable problem to which an apparently objective answer can be found. Other members of society may prefer a different logic that is equally legitimate.

Visualising a management dilemma

Consider the situation facing the European car manufacturers. The industry has built too much capacity in Europe so that there is a gap of 7 million units between production capacity and forecast demand. Many manufacturers are considering the closure of one entire manufacturing plant.

Imagine you are the chair of a global motor company. While as a global company you are profitable, in Europe you are losing money. Your shareholders expect profits. You need to reduce costs across the group, and you are aware that this high level of overcapacity in Europe suggests closing a plant. You know that other car manufacturers are also considering this, and that union and government opposition to that approach is growing.

Your company has several plants in Europe. What criteria should you use to select the one to close? Do you have enough information to make this decision? What other options are available? Do you ask for further information on the social impact that any closure might have? Might it be better to reduce the size of several plants rather than close one? Should you take social concerns into account in your decision?

Can you determine the solution provided by each of the ethical philosophies?

In this chapter, as in much of management, there are no right or wrong answers. These philosophical tools enable people to recognise the arguments that others use to support an action. They can then evaluate that argument critically, and suggest an alternative philosophy that could lead to a different decision. This makes the process for reaching an answer more transparent, and shows the complexities of business ethics and of major management decisions. Activity 5.6 introduces another level of complexity.

ACTIVITY 5.6

Working on a bigger dilemma

What if the problem is not that of reducing capacity but of relocating it? Demand in the developing world is potentially immense, especially for more basic models. So the major companies are tempted to reallocate capacity to these areas. Should a plant be relocated from an economically dependent and deprived European region to a country in South East Asia whose government is offering favourable incentives? The plant itself is currently not losing money but in the long term the financial returns will be higher in Indonesia or China. It could operate with a cheaper workforce, less demanding health and safety regulations, weak trade unions and few environmental conditions. It would also be contributing to the economic development and modernisation of the area.

What are the ethics of moving your production from your home country – and to whose standards should you operate when abroad? You could also consider the role of textiles across Europe as a relocating industry, moving to the developing countries. Or you could discuss companies such as Nike and their labour record.

Look for companies that have created policies stating how they will operate across the world – which international standards do they adhere to?

There are no easy answers. As Robin and Reidenbach (1981) observe: 'The study of business ethics is not without problems of interpretation. Major ethical philosophies are sometimes in conflict with one another as to how a single issue may be resolved' (p.45). This elusiveness leads some to argue that business ethics has not come to terms with business practice. They criticise it for being too general, theoretical and impractical for a manager to apply (Stark, 1993), especially when compared with the apparent clarity of data on financial performance (though see Chapter 16). There is an additional philosophy called **ethical relativism** that managers, especially those in corporations operating in many countries, use to justify what they do.

Ethical relativism

> Fire burns in Hellas and in Persia; but men's ideas of right and wrong vary from place to place. (Herodotus, *c.* 350 BC)

Ethical relativism argues that morality depends on a particular society. There is no absolute ethical standard independent of cultural context. What is right is determined by what a culture or society says is right, so that what is right in one place may be wrong in another.

This view allows management to operate to different standards depending on the culture or country in which they are conducting business. In some countries bribes are an expected part of business. For companies that operate internationally ethical relativism is a convenient philosophy. It is especially so when they are competing internationally against companies based in countries with different moral codes. What might be the views of the individual managers who have their own personal ethical views, which may perhaps be more absolute than relative? What constitutes a bribe in business? This issue arises in dramatic ways when major deals for armaments or construction projects are offered to competitive tender from international companies.

Think again about some of the ethical decisions you have already looked at in this chapter. Does ethical relativism help? Would it depend on what country you were in? It has been suggested that 'a bribe is only a bribe when it is taken as such'. Does ethical relativism help us think about the validity of corporate gift giving? Some firms consider that it is standard industry practice to exchange gifts and therefore this creates a level playing field – so it cannot be an incentive. Others have a policy that no gift to employees from any other company is acceptable as it may affect employees' judgement.

ACTIVITY 5.7

Accepting a gift?

In your job as a buyer for a multinational company you receive a gift from one of your minor suppliers at Christmas. It is: (a) a calendar with their brand name on it, (b) a pen set with their brand name on it, (c) chocolates, (d) a bottle of wine, (e) a bottle of whisky, (f) a case of whisky.

- *Which offer can you accept? If any, what should you do with it? What would stop you accepting these gifts?*
- *Should your employer have a policy that outlines solutions to such ethical problems so as to avoid the variety of approaches which may otherwise develop?*
- *Research a chosen company to find out if they have an ethics policy. What areas of concern are highlighted? Do you think all companies should state their ethical expectations? Can they be the same across the world, in all countries?*

Ethical decision making is a question of trade-offs, and it is necessary to have a clear idea of who will be affected. While some businesses declare themselves to be ethical many find it easier to think of the responsibilities they have, and to whom they are accountable. This idea of corporate social responsibility (CSR) makes abstract dilemmas more real, and helps managers reach decisions.

5.5 Corporate social responsibility

Social responsibility – it means something, but not always the same thing to everybody. To some it conveys the idea of legal responsibility or liability; to others it means socially responsible behaviour in an ethical sense; to others the meaning transmitted is of 'responsible for' in a causal mode; many simply take it to mean socially conscious or aware; many of those who embrace it most fervently see it as a synonym for legitimacy, in the context of belonging or being 'proper' or 'valid'; a few see it as a sort of fiduciary duty, imposing a higher standard of behaviour on business at large. (Votaw, 1973, p.12)

Corporate social responsibility is a way of gaining some grip on these ethical issues by considering to whom a company is responsible. The central point is that corporate decisions have social implications. In order to understand these social implications managers need to identify those affected and consider the problem from their point of view. So corporate responsibility continues the stakeholder theme that Chapter 3 introduced.

Stakeholder theory

Stakeholder theory suggests that it is possible to improve decision making by identifying and considering all individuals or groups who have some significant personal stake or interest in the organisation. This may be too narrow a definition and it may be more useful to think of those who are affected by corporate decision making:

● shareholders;
● customers;
● employees;
● suppliers/business associates;
● community;
● society;
● environment.

Shareholders

Traditionally management has assumed that the main concern of shareholders lies in maximising their wealth. This assumption is largely accurate, though with two qualifications. Shareholders will vary in their time horizon. If they judge performance over the short term they will have no time for considerations of social responsibility. If they take a longer view they may be willing to consider evidence that managing in a socially responsible way helps long-term profits. The second point is that there is clear evidence (from the growth of ethical unit trusts) that there are some 'ethical investors'. They place social priorities higher than maximising their own personal wealth and are willing to invest in companies that follow clear socially responsible policies.

Customers

Customers expect organisations to provide them with goods and services. Within the specific relationship that is established between individual customers and the organisation there are many implicit, unstated conditions. There is often an implied assumption about quality, durability, performance, safety and other factors. The Mintel research cited earlier suggests that consumers are nowadays more aware of issues of corporate responsibility.

> **Q Case questions 5.4**
>
> ● What did customers of Ford expect of the Pinto at that time?
> ● Would customers today have different expectations?
> ● Does that affect your view of the company's actions?

Employees

As well as gaining employment from an organisation, employees also have a range of implicit work needs such as job security, safe working conditions, the creation of rewarding work, fair treatment and reward as well as esteem and personal development. The area of human resource management has developed to explore the legal as well as ethical implications of a range of issues in the workplace: equal opportunities, promotion practices, employment continuity, remuneration, trade unions, working conditions, training, job enrichment, drug/alcohol abuse, positive discrimination.

Suppliers/business associates

Suppliers have expectations of organisations with whom they trade. They expect to be paid in full by the agreed date. Many are now developing much closer long-term relationships with customers (see Chapter 17) and so the range of mutual expectations between the parties is wider and more complex.

The community

The immediate area plays a central part in the creation of the corporation, its reputation and its continued operation. It was recognised earlier that with the creation of large multinational companies the direct link between manufacturers and their local community is not so distinct as in the past. However, the communities in which corporations operate are where their customers and workers live and so remain important.

Society

Society is the broader place in which business operates. The quality of all our lives will depend on how well business accommodates the often conflicting notions of 'profit' and the 'environment'. Under the social responsibility approach society has the right to sanction business operations, and will voice its concerns if a corporation is not recognising its global responsibilities.

The environment

The environment has, over the past 15 years, become increasingly common within the corporate agenda, prompted by a consumer interest in the environmental impact of corporate actions, which is now apparent even in the supermarket. However, the level at which recognition and respect for the environment is demonstrated by a corporation varies considerably. The Body Shop International has led the way for many consumers in allowing them to indicate their preference for environmentally friendly goods. Such companies recognise the wisdom not only of considering the environment of the organisation but also the impact of the organisation on its environment.

Hoechst, the German chemicals company's guidelines on environmental protection:

> We strive to improve our international competitiveness. Alongside the goal of profitability stand, equally, responsibility for our staff and social acceptance of our business, sparing use of our resources and care of the environment. Our company goals are at one with the ethical values of our culture and society ... At Hoechst, the demands of environmental protection lead to the following principles:
>
> - The environment should be polluted as little as possible by our activities.
> - We adopt preventive measures: the research department gives due consideration to the environment in the early stages of product development.
> - Raw materials are used economically. (Hopfenbeck, 1993, p.256)

Management comes to pay more attention to environmental and other issues as it recognises the links between corporate action and wider implications. This stakeholder approach to business is providing a competitive advantage for companies, as it can enhance corporate reputation, customer loyalty and goodwill, as well as media coverage.

ACTIVITY 5.8

Revising activity 5.5

Using the stakeholders listed above, try again to solve the dilemma of closing the factory in Activity 5.5. Whose 'stake' within the company should be given priority above the others? What did you decide?

Do you think that, as a global company, you have specific local responsibilities or a major responsibility to maintain a profitable company for the good of shareholders, customers and workers worldwide?

KEY IDEAS — Planet Earth

Planet Earth is 4,600 million years old. If we condense this to an understandable concept, the Earth is a 46-year-old person.

Not until the age of 42 did the Earth begin to flower.
Dinosaurs appeared when the planet was 45.
Mammals arrived only 8 months ago.
Modern man has been around for FOUR HOURS.
The Industrial Revolution began ONE MINUTE AGO
… and during those 60 seconds of biological time, man has made a rubbish tip of paradise.

Source: Adapted from *Paradise Lost – Countdown to Destruction*, Greenpeace.

The problem in such decision making is not determining who is affected, but whose interests should have priority. Considering the community as one group quickly shows that this itself contains many interests – workers, customers, neighbours, the local government agencies and so on. There may be divisions within these groups, and Figure 3.5 (page 93) shows how to assess their respective power and interest. This approach can focus corporate thinking upon the impact of decisions and help managers recognise the social fallout from corporate activities. It alerts them to potential problems and helps them formulate suitable strategies to address current responsibility issues.

As the issues from which corporate responsibilities stem are driven by society, this means that they are constantly changing, just as legislation and public opinion continue to change. Social disapproval of some forms of corporate activity is prompting firms to accept a broader view of their responsibilities. This contributes to the evolving nature of corporate responsibilities. For example, while the area of equal opportunities was until recently an ethical concern it has gained a critical mass, which has resulted in an improved legal reality for many groups that had previously suffered discrimination in the workplace.

While corporate social responsibility is difficult to isolate, the stakeholder approach to corporate decision making helps identify a central tenet within responsible business practice. Nonetheless a question still remains: why would, or why should, a company respond to the recognition of its stakeholders and their concerns?

5.6 Why be socially responsible?

While there are an increasing number of high-profile responsible and ethical companies, many still believe that these concerns are outside the role of management. This 'Friedmanite' view was discussed earlier in the chapter and it remains an unresolved debate. Table 5.2 identifies three sets of arguments why companies should act in a socially responsible way and three why they should not. They are grouped around the words 'should', 'can' and 'will', and are drawn from many arguments within the literature.

Table 5.2 Why companies should or should not act in a socially responsible way

Should	Should not
● Enlightened self-interest (Mintzberg, 1983)	● Dilution of business's primary purpose (Davis, 1960)
● Sound investment theory (Bowman, 1973)	● Subversive, a voluntary tax (Friedman, 1970)
● Long-term self-interest (Davis, 1960)	● 'Dangerous, alien and impermissible' (Levitt, 1958)
● Viability of business (Davis, 1960)	● Hand of government (Shaw, 1991)
● Public image (Davis, 1971)	● Profit maximisers (Davis, 1971; Friedman, 1970)
● Avoidance of government regulation (Davis, 1960; Mintzberg, 1983)	● Beyond their role (Stone, 1990)
● Prevention is better than cure (Davis, 1960)	● Against the 'rules of the game' (Carr, 1968)
	● Weakened competitiveness (Davis, 1960)
Can	**Cannot**
● Shareholder interest (Davis, 1960)	● Inept custodian, lack ability (Mintzberg, 1983; Shaw, 1991)
● Business has the resources (Davis, 1960)	● Lack of broad support (Davis, 1960)
	● Only people have responsibilities (Friedman, 1970)
Will	**Will not**
● Socio-cultural norms (Davis, 1960)	● Cost of social involvement (Davis, 1960)
● Let business try (Davis, 1960)	● Lack of social skills (Davis, 1960)

On one side are those who argue that corporate social responsibility is good for business. It enhances the public image of the company and may avoid government intervention. For these and several other reasons this group argues that positive policies on social responsibility are in a company's long-term interests. They also point out that business has the resources to pursue such policies and in many cases the shareholders will support some action in this area.

On the opposite side are those who argue that it is not management's job to extend its role into this area. Its role is to do the best for its shareholders, which will be reduced if competitiveness is lost by following wider considerations. They argue that such activities lack broad support, and that business is not democratically accountable to the wider public. Moreover, business may not have the skills to deal with these issues so that there may be more rhetoric than action.

Against that background management today faces sources of pressure towards a more socially responsible stance. These pressures can be expressed through consumer boycotts, ethical consumers and the costs of being irresponsible.

Consumer boycotts

Boycotts reflect the active disapproval of society and can generate media interest that then spreads the news of corporate misdemeanour across the globe. They register the displeasure of consumers with the corporation. In 1996 French products were (briefly) boycotted because of the decision of the French government to resume nuclear testing in the South Pacific.

There are examples of boycotts achieving their objectives (such as when Barclays Bank was persuaded during the 1980s that its involvement in South Africa supported apartheid), but they are rare. However, they are no longer the actions of extremists, and consumers are increasingly recognising new outlets for expressing their disappointment with corporate activities, for example via street protests and road blocks.

Ethical consumers

Until legislatory improvements match social concerns **ethical consumers** can act on their initiative. With increased access to information relating to the full range of corporate activities, consumer decision making is altering to include ethical issues. While individual consumers feel strongly about specific issues, *The Ethical Consumer Journal* identifies 10 specific areas where customers tend to require specific information:

- operating within oppressive regimes;
- trade union relations;
- wages and conditions;
- environment;
- irresponsible marketing;
- nuclear power;
- armaments;
- animal rights;
- political donations;
- boycott calls.

Such consumer action is not solely a negative response to corporate activities. There are many shoppers who use their 'ethical purchase votes' (Smith, 1990) to support the actions of companies that are conducting their business responsibly. Café Direct and Green and Black Chocolate have been the biggest successes of 'fairly traded' products. Many other companies are seeing the advantage in being responsible in areas of social concern and are responding to society's demands. For example Reebok and Nike are introducing codes of practice to eliminate child labour in the production of their products, in the face of increasing concerns about the exploitation of children in the clothing industry in the developing world. Also the major supermarkets (such as Sainsbury's in the United Kingdom) seek to reassure consumers with an increasing stock of organic and fair trade products.

Many organisations (Greenpeace, The New Consumer, The Ethical Consumer) are monitoring corporate actions and reporting adverse information widely. The Brent Spar, while a complex scenario, shows why business needs to recognise that society itself is constantly changing. It expects more of business. There is a multitude of stakeholders who now demand information and expect high standards of corporate behaviour. The major oil companies have realised that their contract with society has changed. For example, Shell suffered (briefly) from a consumer boycott across Europe in the summer of 1995. It also experienced some violent acts of 'eco-terrorism'. Irrespective of the merits of this debate the media has regularly spotlighted the activities of the major oil companies. To address this increased level of negative press many have responded to these changing social demands and are now developing ethical positions.

Cost of being irresponsible

The cost of being irresponsible is now counted in terms of its effect on corporate reputation. Table 5.3 summarises earlier research on the cost to corporations and society of irresponsible corporate activity.

Table 5.3 The costs of corporate failing

Year	Corporate failing	Cost: human/financial	Penalty/effectiveness
1970s	Production of Ford Pinto	Loss of life $250m	Loss of brand (BT)
1982	Tylenol – product tamper	$50m	Recall (B)
1984	Bhopal Union Carbide	2,500 deaths $4,700m	Loss of Indian operation only (P)
1988	*Exxon Valdez* Esso	Environment $7,250m	Loss of consumer accounts (P)
1988	Piper Alpha Occidental	167 deaths $1,400m	Loss of legitimacy in UK alone (P)
1989	King's Cross	Death $400m	No market substitution
1990	Perrier contamination	$200m	Recall Re-establish (B)
1992	The Guinness Affair	Fraud $295m	Chairman imprisoned – now runs another company
1994	Maxwell pension fraud	$1,650m	Collapse (T)
1995	Barings Bank	Financial viability	Collapse (T) and takeover

Key: T=termination   P=partial impact   B=impact on brand

Sources: Based on Hartley (1993); SAUS (1993); Cannon (1994); Harvey (1994).

Competitive advantage

Many companies have gained by stating very clearly specific values and following a responsible approach to business. Their activities can prove extremely newsworthy and increase customer awareness and loyalty with little advertising. Such companies have a strategic approach to responsible business practice.

MANAGEMENT IN PRACTICE   **The Body Shop campaigns**

The Body Shop has used a range of awareness-raising campaigns to spread a social message in response to its recognition of the concerns of stakeholders and the development of social issues within society. These have, over the past twenty years, included: Greenpeace – Save the Whale; Friends of the Earth – Acid Rain; Friends of the Earth – Think Globally, Act Locally; Green Consumer Week; Amnesty International; Friends of the Earth – Ozone or No Zone; Shelter; Aids; Friends of the Earth – Vanishing Countryside; Friends of the Earth –

Tropical Rain Forest; Start; Stop the Burning; Ken Saro-wiwa, The Ogoni and Shell Oil; Women's Rights are Human Rights; Domestic Violence; Would they do it in Paris – nuclear testing; Against Animal Testing.

These campaigns have been issue based and relate to the vision that The Body Shop has of its role in society. While many people feel that a company should not be so political or outspoken, such campaigns have established The Body Shop as a major player in the high street, without the need for traditional advertising.

This approach worked well for The Body Shop, and helped it become a major retailing group (see Part One Case). However, what was once a unique position has been eroded – partly by The Body Shop's success. Animal testing of cosmetics (one of the firm's early campaigns) has been stopped, and more people are aware of environmental issues. So what was a strategically valuable position, bringing great benefits to those it aimed to help, is itself under competitive threat. The financial performance of The Body Shop has been poor in recent years.

Another example of a company taking a strategic approach to responsible business practice is the Co-operative Bank, which was founded upon co-operative principles in the 1870s. It launched its present ethical policy in May 1992, under the philosophy:

> At the Co-operative Bank, we always remember that it's your money in your account. Our role is simply to take good care of it for you – and not do things with it that you wouldn't do yourself.

Ten years after this first initiative the Co-operative Bank not only retained its stance within the financial marketplace, but has decided to poll more than 2 million customers to ensure the stated concerns in its ethical policy reflect current issues (Treanor 2001).

ACTIVITY 5.9

Visit the Co-operative Bank website

- *Why do you think ethical concerns change?*

- *Make a list of your ethical worries and compare it with the Co-operative Bank's current list on their website (www.co-operativebank.co.uk.).*

It is possible to see the debate as simply whether a company should, or should not, accept its social and ethical responsibilities. It is clear that it can, and will, where there is an advantage in doing so. The Friedmanite/corporate social responsibility debate will run, but it is clear that some companies have been able to balance responsibility and corporate success. As Freeman and Gilbert argue: 'The search for excellence and the search for ethics are the same thing ... We must learn to build corporate strategy on a foundation of ethical reasoning, rather than pretending that strategy and ethics are separate' (Freeman and Gilbert, 1988, p.47).

From this recognition of the strategic implications of corporate decision making, and ultimately corporate practice, it has proved possible to articulate their interpretation of corporate responsibility. Having established that some companies have benefited from their responsible approach to business, it is equally necessary to recognise that some have attempted to incorporate a high degree of ethical behaviour into their corporate actions and failed. Companies accept or incorporate notions of ethical and responsible business in a multitude of different levels. In order to represent this reality of corporate behaviour Alison Price created a device that can be used as an **ethical audit** or profile of current practice, and so highlight a 'pathway' to improved corporate activity. By first recognising five core areas for corporate activity and thus potential ethical concern (product, the business process itself, employees, the community in which the company operates and the external environment) a company can be assessed. Each element shown in Figure 5.1 can then be broadly classified according to the corporation's record in this area – as either irresponsible, meeting the laws of the land (meeting the obligations of conducting business) or responsible. By making these five broad judgements it is possible to determine the ethical profile of the organisation and indicate a pathway to improved corporate behaviour. While this analysis can be very generalised, it helps identify key areas and potentially move a company towards improved corporate performance.

Such a profiling device can be used to start a dialogue with companies, which is increasingly important to all companies. Since July 2000 pension funds in the United Kingdom have been obliged to give members a 'statement of investment practice' providing insights into the responsibility stance of companies (Hagman 2000). While this tool would not form a complete record of corporate activity it might help with the development of dialogue between investment houses (pension and insurance companies) and companies in which they might invest (Levene 2001).

ACTIVITY 5.10

Assessing a company's profile

- *Can you research a company and determine its CSR profile using the data you have collected?*
- *By shading the blocks, can you identify a pathway for improved corporate behaviour? (Exclude areas if not enough information is available or if the area does not apply.)*
- *What recommendations would you make to the board relating to their public profile?*
- *What are the difficulties of using this device to make strategic decisions?*
- *Do you have enough information to make these judgements?*

Figure 5.1 A pathway to corporate responsibility

Product
Process
Employees
Community
Environment

| Irresponsible | Obligation | Responsible |

Having used the CSR profile to analyse a strategy, as with all decision making, it is necessary for any company to monitor and measure the outcomes of major actions to see if they are having the effects intended. Corporate actions have wide implications. Those with corporate power will decide how fully those implications are considered. They may choose to follow the Friedmanite philosophy, or they may choose to take account of wider interests, acknowledging the point made by Davis (1975): 'In the long run, those who do not use power in a manner which society considers responsible will tend to lose it.'

<table>
<tr><td>**MANAGEMENT IN PRACTICE**</td><td>**FTSE4GOOD**</td></tr>
</table>

FTSE4GOOD Index, launched in July 2002, will allow investors in the United Kingdom to see a share index made up of companies that are socially responsible investments. This benchmark is expected in Europe and the United States. But there are no plans for a FTSE4BAD index.

Source: Levene (2001).

5.7 Summary

The chapter has shown that both sides of the argument about ethics in business have a long and continuing history. Most early industrialists acted in their self-interest without much regard for other considerations – yet there were also those such as Titus Salt and William Lever who brought wider principles to bear on the way they conducted their businesses – a twin approach that continues today. After outlining the contrasting positions of the Friedmanite and social responsibility positions the chapter presented four perspectives from moral philosophy on justifying an action. These themselves inevitably raise further questions, rather than provide a simple answer, but are valuable in bringing structure to discussion in this area.

The chapter then outlined the social responsibility approach, in which organisations recognise the legitimate claims of a range of stakeholders and seek an acceptable balance between them. There is evidence that more consumers, albeit a minority, do take issues of the environment and aspects of corporate behaviour seriously. Companies where management has shown that it takes such concerns seriously have benefited commercially. However, a reputation for social responsibility has not in itself guaranteed success as this is only one of many factors that managers have to deal with. Perhaps there is a paradox that as more members of the public expect socially responsible behaviour from companies (at the expense of short-term financial gain), they also expect good returns from their investments and pension funds. Those managing such funds are one source of the pressure that managers experience to meet demanding financial targets.

Content

Choices about the objectives of the organisation are ethical decisions whether or not the managers taking them think of them that way. Deciding objectives and planning how to achieve them inevitably requires trade-offs between different interests. The conventional practice is to emphasise the economic imperative. Stakeholder analysis suggests that other perspectives are equally legitimate. The difficulty is that they are less easy to measure, and so can be diminished in a culture in which powerful players choose to adopt the convention of short-term quantitative performance measures.

Some managers now recognise that they have wider social responsibilities, and that these are not necessarily incompatible with securing an acceptable return for shareholders. A few have shown that staff can be highly motivated by association with a business that has wider aims than just delivering value to shareholders. In that way they may be able to do both. They may gain competitive advantage from responsible corporate behaviour, as well as pay penalties for irresponsible action.

Process

Stakeholder analysis identifies those who will be affected by corporate action. They will have different interests, and will interpret ethical and corporate social responsibility issues in different ways. Many traders and other local businesses have supported construction companies building by-passes and airport companies building extensions against environmental protestors. Devising and implementing policies that are accepted as more socially responsible will require developing processes and decision-making institutions that can take account of interests not usually included in such debates.

Control

At the macro level the issue of corporate social responsibility is linked to the degree of control that society has over business institutions. The Friedmanite position limits this to some essential legal and financial ground rules within which managers should be able to act as they see fit. The social responsibility position argues that these boundaries are negotiable and that society may want to protect a wider set of interests by setting more precise standards of business behaviour.

Some companies that have introduced environmental or social policies have also developed appropriate ways of auditing the results of these policies. These check the effectiveness of the policy and open the policy to external scrutiny – in the same way as financial performance is visible. Such audits also help organisations and the wider interest groups to learn from these experiences.

Ford overcame the negative publicity surrounding the Pinto, and is the world's second largest manufacturer of motor vehicles. It has developed a range of community and social programmes and is in discussions about the environmental impact of motor vehicles. Yet controversy still follows the company. The battle with Firestone over responsibility for the Ford Explorer crashes continues, and it recently faced law suits in the United States over a performance appraisal plan that the plaintiffs alleged discriminated against older workers. The company acknowledged these criticisms and withdrew the plan in July 2001.

Q **PART CASE QUESTIONS**

● What has BP Amoco done to indicate that it is acting in a socially responsible manner?

● A major issue for the company is to balance different stakeholder groups. What argument, from an ethical standpoint, could BP use to support the case for opening new oil fields in the Alaskan Wildlife Reserve?

● Is BP Amoco a socially responsible enterprise?

5.8 Review questions

1 Identify two recent examples of corporate philanthropy. What are the benefits to the donor and the recipient?

2 List the reasons why you think 'business ethics' is important to the success of firms.

3 Summarise the Friedman and social contract positions on social responsibility with an example of each being applied.

4 List three major ethical issues facing management at the present time, and give reasons for your choices.

5 Describe in your own terms each of the four schools of ethical thought and illustrate each with an example of how it has been used to justify a decision.

6 Outline the ways in which the consumer can affect business practice, and decide whether this is effective or not.

7 List the stakeholders in the Pinto case and prioritise them in order to justify the decision to manufacture.

8 What could Ford staff have done to promote the communication of these difficult issues to higher management?

9 Who should determine a company's level of acceptance of social responsibilities?

10 Are The Body Shop International and the Co-operative Bank responsible companies or are they operating a form of enlightened self-interest?

Further reading

Davies, P.W.F. (ed.) (1997), *Current Issues in Business Ethics*, Routledge, London. Identifies the 'current issues in business ethics' and provides a core understanding to these developing issues.

Jackall, R.(1998), *Moral Mazes: The world of corporate managers*, Oxford University Press, Oxford. Focuses on the managerial role in tackling the complexity of ethical issues.

Ackroyd, S. and Thompson, P. (1999) *Organizational Misbehaviour*, Sage, London. Looks at the larger corporate view of 'organisational misbehaviour'.

Chrysalides, G.A.D. and Kale, J.H. (1993), *An Introduction to Business Ethics*, Chapman & Hall, London. Good introductions to the main issues in business ethics.

Hopfenbeck, W. (1993), *The Green Management Revolution*, Prentice Hall International, Hemel Hempstead. Focuses on environmental issues and includes many examples and cases (though a little uncritically).

Annotated links, questions and resources can be found on
www.booksites.net/boddy

PLANNING

Introduction

This part examines the issues of strategy and marketing. Both depend on understanding the environment of the business and the stakeholders within it. They also both depend on building an internal capability to deliver whatever direction management decides upon.

Chapter 6 outlines the strategy process, and then outlines some commonly used techniques that managers use to analyse the options facing businesses of all kinds. This analysis can then lead to clearer choices about future direction.

A critical aspect of that is the markets which the organisation chooses to serve. Chapter 7 argues that marketing is not just a functional area within the organisation, but is closely allied to the core strategy process. Like strategy, it uses external and internal analysis to establish a way forward, and like strategy depends on other functions if the organisation is to meet the customer expectations profitably.

The Part Case is The Virgin Group, illustrating the interaction of the external environment with the developing corporate and marketing strategies.

The Virgin Group

Virgin is known all over Europe and is seen by the public as fun, daring and successful. The first record shop was opened in 1971 and the record label launched in 1973. Virgin Atlantic Airways began operating in 1984, quickly followed by Virgin Holidays. In 1995 the company entered a joint venture offering financial services. By 1997 it was an established global corporation with airline, retailing and travel operations. The original record business was launched shortly after the UK government had abolished retail price maintenance, a practice that had limited competition and kept prices high. Richard Branson saw the opportunity and began a mail order business offering popular records at prices about 15 per cent below those charged by shops.

The business prospered until there was a postal strike. Branson's response was to open a retail outlet, which was an immediate success, and the start of Virgin Retail. These retail interests were later consolidated around the Megastore concept in a joint venture with a major retailer. In prestige locations in major cities Megastores began to sell home entertainment products – music, videos, and books – on a large scale. They replaced the string of small secondary retail outlets for which Virgin had become known. The success of the Megastore concept was exported to major cities throughout the world, frequently through joint ventures.

In 1973 Virgin released the hugely successful album *Tubular Bells*. The ensuing inflow of funds enabled the record business to expand but by 1990 the high annual growth was ending. This affected Virgin, which was still a relatively small player, so the record business was sold to EMI in 1992.

In the early 1980s Branson was approached by Randolph Fields, who was seeking additional finance for a cut-price airline he had founded. The airline business then was tightly regulated, with routes, landing rights, prices and service levels established and maintained by intergovernmental arrangements. Decisions on these and other regulations were mainly used to protect inefficient, often state-owned, national 'flag carriers'. This had kept most air fares high. After three months of intense activity Branson and Fields had gained permission to fly, arranged to lease an aircraft and recruited staff. The first flight was in June 1984. To grow, he needed more landing rights, and would need to persuade government ministers in order to get them (at both ends of each route). Those ministers would also be being lobbied by the established airlines, which could try to persuade them not to approve the low fares that Branson was proposing. Alternatively, they could undercut his fares and subsidise the losses from profits on other routes.

Virgin Atlantic grew successfully and by 1990, although still a relatively small player, it competed with the major carriers on the main routes from London, winning awards for innovation and service, as well as plaudits from vital business travellers. The airline was now the focus of Branson's interests and was becoming a serious threat to the established airlines, shown by an acrimonious relationship with British Airways (the UK's national carrier).

Research on the Virgin brand name in the early 1990s demonstrated the impact over time of quirky advertising and publicity stunts. The brand was recognised by 96 per cent of UK consumers, and Richard Branson was correctly identified by 95 per cent as the company's founder. The Virgin name was associated by respondents with words such as fun, innovation, success and trust, and identified with a range of businesses, confirming what Branson and others had believed: in principle there were no product or service boundaries limiting a brand name, provided it was associated with a quality offering.

Encouraged by the research Virgin began entering new sectors outside its core activities of travel and retail. Virgin businesses as diverse as radio broadcasting, book publishing and computer games found a home in the same stable as hotels, railways, personal computers, cola drinks, cinemas and financial services. Branson continued to work at the centre, supported by a small business development group, a press office, and key senior advisers in the areas of strategy and finance. The early Virgin style of informality and openness remains. There is not the feel of a traditional corporate head office: neckties are rarely worn, denim jeans are common, and everybody is on first name terms.

Having a centre did not mean a centralised operation, a notion that Branson resisted until recently. Each operating unit was expected to stand alone, having little interaction with either head office or other units. Unit managers networked informally (usually at parties or similar events), but were not obliged to follow prescriptive corporate policies; these were 'understood' rather than codified. For example, there was no common human resource policy. Managers knew that employees must be treated 'fairly' since 'that is what Richard would want', and they complied in their own way. Similarly there was no group information technology strategist or central purchasing function, because Branson believed that those roles would constitute interference and discourage managerial creativity. Nor was there any systematic seeking out of synergy, either at the centre or by unit managers.

In 1999 a chance remark from one of his senior executives made Branson rethink his approach. The executive mentioned that the head of a rival organisation had commented that if Virgin enterprises ever decided to collaborate they would be unstoppable. To test whether this was true Branson immediately – and for the first time – brought together all his managing directors (some 30 in all) for a retreat at his hotel in Mallorca. The agenda was open, but two themes dominated – e-commerce and a proposed unifying document, the Virgin Charter.

Participants realised that, more by chance than planning, Virgin was in businesses 'that were ideally suited to e-commerce and in which growth is expected to occur – travel, financial services, publishing, music, entertainment'. To exploit this potential the participants decided to streamline their online services with a single Virgin web address: Virgin.com.

By early 2001 the Virgin.com site was attracting 1.9 million visitors a month, and was the 12th most popular web destination in Britain. Branson believes that the Virgin name, known for its consumer-friendly image and good service, would translate well across a range of businesses – 'Virgin isn't a company, its a brand' commented one senior manager in the company. This is attractive to partners, who provide the expertise and capital for a joint venture in their area of business (such as insurance or share trading), while Virgin provides the brand image. By putting all Virgin's business on one easily accessible site Branson hopes to cross-promote a wide range of offerings – tickets, wine, entertainment listings, financial services and many more.

Virgin is also using the web to streamline internal operations. The airline and the stores now order inventory electronically as they need it, rather than having to keep it in physical form. Airline mechanics can use the Internet to source local suppliers of a required part and have it available in hours – an impossible task with earlier technologies. The Megastores only stock the most popular products. The rest are held at a fulfilment house – ready to send to customers who order them, enabling the stores to offer a wide range of products. Advertising staff in each company use the Internet to co-ordinate their advertising spending and strategy before booking the business with a central agency.

During the meeting in Mallorca the group also endorsed Branson's proposed Virgin Charter. Running to some 60 pages, the charter is an agreement between Virgin Management Ltd (in effect the holding company) and all the subsidiaries. It defines the role of the centre vis-à-vis the subsidiaries in such matters as taxation, legal affairs, intellectual property and real estate. It also outlines closer links in areas previously left to individual units: IT, people, purchasing. Thus the Charter sets out ways for the many Virgin companies to tackle common activities with a common approach. Nearly all are private and owned entirely by the Virgin Group or Richard Branson's family trusts. Business should be 'shaped around people' Branson believes, citing his experience of subdividing the record company as it grew. Each new record label was given to up-and-coming managers, creating in-house entrepreneurs who were 'far more motivated to build a business' with which they and the staff identified. A natural extension of this is the notion of building a business organically, rather than by acquisition.

He believes this approach to expansion by creating discrete legal entities gives people a sense of involvement with, and loyalty to, the small unit to which they belong. This is particularly the case if he trusts the managers of subsidiaries with full authority and offers them minority share options. He is proud of the fact that Virgin has produced a considerable number of millionaires. He has said that he does not want his best people to leave the company to start a venture outside; he prefers to make millionaires within. He has created a structure of numerous small companies around the world operated quasi-independently. Both systems embody the maxims 'small is beautiful' and 'people matter'.

Source: Based on material from INSEAD Case 400-002-1, *The House that Branson Built: Virgin's entry into the new millennium*; 'Branson's brash new gambit', *Business Week*, 22 January 2001; and other published material.

Q PART CASE QUESTIONS

- What examples does the case give of links between Branson's strategy for Virgin and the environment in which it operates?

- What common themes link the different businesses in the group?

- Why does Branson use joint ventures with other companies to realise the Virgin strategy? Are there any disadvantages in this method of working?

- Do you share his optimism about the effects of the Internet on the business?

Planning and strategy

> **AIM** *To describe and illustrate the main elements of strategic planning and to show the flexible nature of the process.*

OBJECTIVES

By the end of your work on this chapter you should be able to outline the concepts below in your own terms and:

1 Explain how strategic planning contributes to the management of organisations

2 Explain the concepts of competitive and institutional advantage and give examples of how organisations achieve it

3 Describe the main stages and elements in the strategy process

4 Evaluate the usefulness of mission statements

5 Evaluate the contribution of value chain analysis in identifying the sources of a firm's competitive advantage

6 Conduct a SWOT analysis for an organisation

7 Identify examples of companies following different generic competitive strategies

8 Use the product/market matrix to identify alternative strategic directions

9 Identify examples to illustrate alternative methods of delivering a strategy

10 Discuss the role of benchmarking in comparing and improving organisational performance

11 Contrast the 'planning', 'learning' and 'political' perspectives on the strategy process

12 Debate the 'fit' versus 'stretch' views of strategy

Marks & Spencer

Originating in 1884 as a market stall, Marks & Spencer (M&S) has become the United Kingdom's largest clothing retailer, also selling food, home furnishings, gifts, beauty products and financial services. It began expanding overseas in the 1970s, developing stores in continental Europe and Asia (some under franchise), and in the United States through the acquisition of Brooks Brothers clothing retailers and the Kings Super Market chain. By 1997 the company's mission was 'to become the world's leading volume retailer' and it embarked upon an unprecedented programme of expansion at home and abroad. The M&S Direct catalogue, already selling homeware, flowers, hampers and wine, was extended to include clothing. In 1997–8 M&S became the first British retailer to earn annual profits in excess of £1 billion.

However, in the following year profits halved and the company's dividend was cut for the first time in its history. Despite efforts to revamp its style profits continued to slide, and in 2001 the company announced major changes to its strategy. It planned to keep its successful overseas franchises but to close its loss-making mainland European and Direct catalogue operations and sell its two US businesses in order to focus on its UK retail market and 'restore the trust and confidence of our core customers'.

While food sales continue to grow, the main weakness is in clothing (which represents 60 per cent of the business) especially womenswear. The company is operating in mature markets in which there is intense rivalry. It faces competition from fashion retailers such as Next, discounters such as Matalan and from grocery stores such as Tesco, which now carry clothes as well as food. Once the store of first resort for clothing, the company's reputation for 'value', which it defines as 'selling excellent products at competitive prices', has suffered, partly as a result of its decision to source more goods abroad. Perceptions of poorer quality have led to reducing brand loyalty and a falling market share.

The market is also segmenting and the company needs to develop a better understanding of its customers. It has appointed a former Next executive to produce a new collection for fashionable younger women and, for its core customers, it plans a return to classic styling. Stores are being modernised, new cafés, beauty shops and financial services centres introduced and more sales floor staff employed. Whether these steps will be enough to restore its reputation to full strength remains to be seen. As John Kay observed, 'M&S is right to go back to basics but it will learn that competitive advantage is more easily run down than built up'.

Q Case questions

Visit an M&S store, and also visit their website (www.marksandspencer.com).

- What have been the main additions to M&S business?
- Visit the *Financial Times* discussion forum about M&S (FT.com, then 'Discussion Forums'). Identify two comments which you agree with, and two with which you disagree.

6.1 Introduction

This chapter introduces the following concepts:

- Strategy
- Corporate strategy
- Operational strategy
- Competitive advantage
- Competitive or business strategy
- Value for money
- Institutional advantage
- Critical success factors
- Organisational capability
- Core competences
- The value chain
- Benchmarking
- SWOT analysis
- Differentiation
- Strategic planning
- Strategic management
- Bounded rationality
- Emergent strategy

In a time when the business environment is changing rapidly all managements, not just those in trouble, are paying more attention to strategy. Established organisations such as BT are in a growing and diversifying telecommunications market – and face new competition that threatens their core business. Should the company try to compete in all areas, or concentrate on one sector, as Vodafone has done? Should Virgin continue to extend the brand into ever more diverse areas of activity, or would it gain more by building profits in the existing areas, and achieving more synergies across the group? Some charities face declining income – should their managers just continue as they are now, or will they serve their cause better by initiating a radical review of their strategy? These are just a few examples of the strategic part of the management task.

Strategy links the organisation to the external world, and Chapter 3 showed how the external environment influences management practice within any organisation. The PEST framework summarises factors common to all organisations, while Porter's model identifies five forces specific to a particular industry's competitive environment. Changes in these external forces create both opportunities and threats to an organisation's position – but above all they create uncertainty. Planning offers a systematic means of coping with uncertainty and adapting to change. It enables management to consider how to grasp opportunities and avoid problems, to establish and co-ordinate appropriate courses of action, and to set targets for achievement.

The chapter begins by outlining different types of plans and strategies. It then describes the elements and stages of the strategy process, before examining the main stages in more detail. These include developing objectives, analysing the value chain, conducting a SWOT analysis, deciding on strategic direction, and finally a process of implementing and review. The chapter concludes with a review of different perspectives on the strategy process.

6.2 Types of planning and strategy

While people use different terms, the activity of planning and **strategy** essentially involves a generic planning process of setting objectives (or goals), identifying and implementing appropriate courses of action and monitoring achievements against the goals originally set. Strategy deals with both ends (*what* is to be achieved) and means (*how* it is to be achieved).

Robbins (2000) points out that plans can be classified by their breadth (strategic or operational) and their time frame (from short to long term). Strategic plans apply to the whole organisation. They set out the overall direction for the business, are broad in scope and cover all the major activities. Chandler (1962) defined this strategic planning as 'the determination of the basic long-term goals and objectives of an enterprise and the adoption of courses of action and the allocation of resources necessary for carrying out these goals'. Strategy is concerned with deciding what business an organisation should be in, where it wants to be and how it is going to get there. These decisions have long-term effects, involve major resource commitments and usually require a series of consequential operational decisions. So strategic plans usually look three to five years ahead.

Operational plans detail how the overall objectives are to be achieved. They are narrower in scope, relating usually to individual departments or functions and cover a period of up to a year. In contrast to strategic plans, operational plans are more action centred and routine in nature. Some organisations develop separate plans for autonomous divisions and strategic business units.

So plans can exist at different levels within an organisation, with a 'family' of interrelated plans forming a hierarchy. There will be a **corporate strategy** for the organisation as a whole, and perhaps several **operational strategies** dealing with constituent parts. Each will contain linked objectives and plans that become more specific as they move down the organisation. Management hopes that those at lower levels, or for separate divisions, are consistent with the overall corporate strategy. Table 6.1 shows this hierarchical arrangement, and how the character of plans changes at each level.

Table 6.1 The planning and strategy hierarchy

Plan/Strategy type	Strategic or corporate plans	Divisional/Business unit plans	Operational plans
Level	Organisation wide	Particular market	Functions/Departments
Focus	Scope, direction and strategy for organisation as a whole	Scope, direction and strategies for particular market	Operational strategies: resources and actions needed to deliver corporate objectives
Nature of decisions	Complex	Complex	More routine; action oriented
Timescale	Long term	Long term	Shorter term

For most organisations the underlying purpose in developing strategy is to perform well against competitors. This raises a concept of central importance in discussion of strategy, that of **competitive advantage**. Introduced by Porter (1980b, 1985), the concept is concerned with the factors that give an organisation an edge over its competitors and enable it to achieve higher levels of profitability. Section 6.5 discusses these factors. Strategy defined in this competitive sense, and that seeks to identify and sustain sources of competitive advantage, is called **competitive strategy.** It is concerned with how the organisation responds to the five forces in the competitive environment.

Because competitive advantage assumes competitors and a profit goal the concept does not always apply directly to not-for-profit organisations (Goold, 1997). Although some non-profits do have direct competitors (charities such as Oxfam, for example, compete with each other for the public's donations and for customers through shop and mail order networks) others, such as the Benefits Agency and local councils, do not. For these types of organisation the nature of competition differs: while they do not compete for customers they often compete for funding. Governments introduce many initiatives, often in the fields of social and economic regeneration, that invite local authorities and other non-profit organisations to compete for a share of public resources.

An important concept in the allocation of public funds is **value for money,** that is the provision of a project or service as economically, efficiently and effectively as possible. Non-profits try to maximise value for money (rather than profit) as a means of securing resources. Viewed in this way the concept of competitive advantage is relevant to not-for-profit organisations. Goold (1997) suggest a better term is **institutional advantage,** which 'is held when a not-for-profit body performs its tasks more effectively than other comparable organizations'.

Porter (1990) has also written about competition between nations. Nation states and, within them, individual cities compete with each other, vying to secure inward investment by multinational companies, the right to host events such as the Olympic Games, or to hold titles such as 'European City of Culture'. Such events can bring major employment and income benefits. Competing in this way countries and cities seek to identify sources of competitive advantage, which might include the levels of education and skill amongst the workforce and the attractiveness of the physical environment.

CASE STUDY Marks & Spencer – the case continues

The M&S brand is strongly associated with the company's values of quality, value, service and trust. These were severely tested during the difficulties in 2001, but Marks & Spencer believes it has a number of 'unique fundamental strengths' that will help its recovery. It has a good record of new product development. In food it has a leading share in fast-growing markets, such as ready meals; it has strong food development capabilities, changing a quarter of its food range every year, and has started introducing in-store bakeries, butcher's shops and hot food counters. Of the company's lines 40 per cent are suitable for vegetarians and M&S was the first retailer in the world to respond to customers' health and nutrition concerns by appointing teams of food technologists and animal welfare specialists.

In clothing, product ranges are constantly upgraded and the company is proud of its innovative 'magic fabrics' such as non-iron cotton, machine-washable wool and non-polish shoes. The company's scale facilitates innovation and also gives it buying power, although the close supplier relationships for which M&S is renowned were damaged by its decision to increase overseas sourcing in search of cost advantage.

Across the business the company stresses its high ethical trading standards and strong sense of environmental and social responsibility.

Sources: M&S *Annual Reports* 1997–2001; M&S website; *Financial Times* (various, 2001); TimeEurope.com; *The Economist,* 14 April 2001.

- What are the main factors that M&S believes give it an edge over its competitors?
- Do you agree with them?
- What does the company do in respect of its commitment to society? (See the website.)
- Do you think these commitments give M&S competitive advantage? Are they likely to encourage people to shop in M&S stores?

6.3 Elements and purpose of strategy

Figure 6.1 shows that developing an organisational strategy involves three main elements – strategic analysis, strategic choice and strategy implementation. Each of these contains further steps, corresponding to a series of questions that form the basis of strategic decision taking.

Strategic analysis

The foundation of strategy is a definition of organisational purpose. This defines the business of an organisation and what type of organisation it wants to be. Many organisations develop broad statements of purpose, aims or mission and these form the springboard for the development of more specific objectives and the choice of strategies to achieve them.

Environmental analysis – assessing both the external and internal environments – is the next element in the strategy process. Chapter 3 explained how the external environment presents both opportunities and threats and managers need to assess these in the light of the organisation's strengths (or 'capabilities') and weaknesses, and of what stakeholders expect.

Strategic choice

The initial analysis stage provides the basis for strategic choice. It allows management to consider what the organisation could do, given its mission, environment and capabilities. Choice will also reflect the values of management and other stakeholders (Dobson and Starkey, 1993). Management makes choices about overall scope and direction – what products to offer, and in what markets. These decisions allow it to set more specific objectives. These might specify where the organisation needs to change in order to improve its performance.

MANAGEMENT IN PRACTICE **Examples of objectives**

The Kingfisher Group has three core objectives for its home improvement division – major growth at B&Q and Costorama, driving best practice and scale benefits throughout the sector and building an international store network beyond the United Kingdom and France.

The Higher Education Council for England plans, amongst other things, to promote high standards of education and research and to enable its staff to provide a high quality service.

Figure 6.1 Elements in the strategy process

Elements in strategy process	Questions	Description
STRATEGY FORMULATION		
Strategic analysis		
Defining organisational purpose	What is our purpose? What kind of organisation do we want to be?	A clarification of the purpose of the business, sometime expressed in a mission statement. Some organisations also determine the values to which they wish to subscribe
Environmental analysis	Where are we now?	Environmental analysis involves the gathering and analysis of 'intelligence' on the business environment. This encompasses the external environment (general and competitive forces), the internal environment (resources, competences, performance relative to competitors), and stakeholder expectations
Strategic choice		
Objectives	Where do we want to be?	Objectives provide a more detailed articulation of purpose and a basis for monitoring performance
Strategies	How are we going to get there?	Strategies describe how the objectives are to be achieved
Options analysis	Are there alternative routes?	Alternative strategic options may be identified; options require to be appraised in order that the best can be selected
STRATEGY IMPLEMENTATION		
Actions	How do we turn plans into reality?	A specification of the operational activities and tasks required to enable strategies to be implemented
Monitoring and control	How will we know if we are getting there?	Monitoring performance and progress in meeting objectives, taking corrective action as necessary and reviewing strategy

Source: Adapted from Catterick (1995, p.14) and Johnson and Scholes (1999).

Objectives specify what the organisation plans to do or where it wants to be. With a more specific set of objectives to hand management can then formulate how it plans to achieve its goals. Kingfisher, for example, might expand internationally by building new stores or by taking over existing overseas companies. Firms also need to decide how they are going to compete with rivals – by offering standard products and competing through price, or by differentiating their products or services in some other way.

Since organisations are usually faced with alternative options for pursuing a particular strategy there may be a need to undertake an options analysis, so that alternatives can be assessed in terms of their feasibility, suitability and acceptability before a final decision is taken.

Strategy implementation

Once strategies are chosen management must put them into action. It has to ensure that the organisation has a suitable structure, the right resources (skills, finance, technology, etc.) and culture. Strategy depends on operational factors being put into place. Finally management must initiate monitoring and control systems. It must develop standards and targets to judge progress and performance, so that if necessary it can revise the strategy. Planning processes of this sort are common in larger organisations.

MANAGEMENT IN PRACTICE — **Scottish Homes, the national housing agency in Scotland**

Scottish Homes is an agency that assists in meeting government housing objectives. Its main purpose is 'to help provide good housing and contribute to the regeneration of local communities'. It achieves this by allocating government funds mainly to non-profit housing associations for the provision of affordable homes. To guide its funding allocations and activities throughout Scotland, Scottish Homes has a corporate planning framework comprising the following elements:

● A *national context statement* provides an analysis of social, demographic and economic trends at a national scale, highlights the nature of housing problems that need to be tackled and underpins the agency's strategy.
● A *strategic plan* sets out the agency's overall purpose and strategic objectives.
● *Statements of activities* describe the actions that will be taken in pursuit of strategic objectives.
● *Regional plans* translate national objectives into more detailed local strategies. Important inputs to these plans are:
  – *Local housing system analysis*: this identifies trends in the external environment (for example changes in population, households, employment levels and housing stock quality) and establishes the main housing needs in different parts of the region.
  – *Partners' plans*: these include the plans prepared by local authorities, housing associations, local enterprise companies (which have responsibilities for employment and economic development) and Community Care plans.
● *Strategic option analysis* may be used to assess and compare alternative local investment opportunities.
● *Impact assessment* takes a number of forms. A research programme includes evaluation studies to assess whether particular housing initiatives or projects have met their objectives. Performance in meeting corporate investment and output targets is also monitored annually.
● *Business plans* set out objectives and planned activities for the agency's support functions (which include Finance and Regulation, Organisation Development and Communications).

Source: Scottish Homes Planning Framework.

Comparing practice with the model

- *How does Scottish Homes' planning framework compare with the model in Figure 6.1?*
- *Which of the different stages in the strategy process can you identify?*
- *Can you identify the relationships between different plans?*

Figure 6.1 shows that the seven steps in the strategy process fall into two broad phases – formulation and implementation – though in practice the two interact closely. Implementation rarely proceeds according to plan, partly because the constantly changing environment brings new opportunities or threats. Since this may lead management to change the plan, there will be frequent interaction between the activities of formulating and implementing strategy. Management may also find that implementation fails because of a 'fault' in some of the organisational factors on which the plan depended – so it may need to return and reformulate the plan.

A structured approach to planning of this kind brings several benefits (Smith, 1994; Robbins, 2000) in that it:

- Reduces uncertainty: planning forces managers to look ahead, anticipate change and develop appropriate responses. It also encourages managers to consider the risks associated with alternative responses or options.
- Provides a link between long and short terms: planning establishes a means of co-ordination between strategic objectives and the operational activities that support the objectives.
- Provides clarity and unity of purpose: by setting out the organisation's overall strategic objectives and ensuring that these are reflected at operational level, planning helps departments to move in the same direction towards the same set of goals.
- Facilitates control: by setting out objectives or standards planning provides a basis for measuring actual performance.

However, the changing environment means that the strategy process is continuous. Although physical planning documents might be produced periodically, the strategy will usually require regular review and adjustment to changing circumstances.

6.4 Defining organisational purpose

The basis of a clear strategy depends on defining organisational purpose. This may seem obvious, but many managers find it useful to debate periodically what their organisation is about, what they want it to become, and what differentiates it from others. Such clarity can provide focus and direction for all the members. Even in public sector organisations, whose basic business is generally prescribed by government, the exercise can be valuable.

A fashionable medium for expressing purpose is the mission statement. Some use the term 'vision' to express what management would like the future to be like. According to Dobson and Starkey (1993) good mission statements should clarify:

- the principal business or activities of an organisation;
- its key aims or objectives;

- the beliefs or values of the company – defining what the organisation represents such as the balance between profit and other values such as reputation and community involvement;
- the organisation's main stakeholders.

Statements should also be short, clear and easy to understand. Some examples of mission statements are set out below.

MANAGEMENT IN PRACTICE **Examples of mission and vision**

Alliance & Leicester plc
Alliance & Leicester's vision is to deliver value to our shareholders by becoming the UK's most customer focused financial services organisation – bar none. We believe that speed beats size; Alliance & Leicester is big enough to be powerful, yet small enough to be fast. We will use this advantage to be responsive to the changing needs of our customers, delivering the services they want in the way they want them.

Link Housing Group (a non-profit housing provider)
Working Together – Providing Houses – Building Communities.

Royal Dutch/Shell Group
The objectives of Shell companies are to engage efficiently, responsibly and profitably in the oil, gas, chemicals and other selected businesses and to participate in the research and development of other sources of energy. Shell companies are committed to contribute to sustainable development.

Higher Education Funding Council for England
Mission: Working in partnership, we promote and fund high-quality, cost-effective teaching and research, meeting the diverse needs of students, the economy and society.

Marks & Spencer
Vision: To be the standard against which all others are measured.

Mission: To make aspirational quality available to all.

Values: Quality, value, service, innovation and trust.

ACTIVITY 6.2

Evaluating mission statements
- *Do you think that the examples above satisfy all of the requirements of a good mission statement (as defined by Dobson and Starkey)?*
- *Does the M&S statement of vision, mission and values meet those requirements?*
- *Give examples of the ways in which the company's values are reflected in its business activities.*

The dangers of mission statements

Although many organisations have mission statements, their value has sometimes been questioned. Kay (1996) asserts that visions or missions are indicative of a 'wish-driven strategy' that fails to recognise the limits to what might be possible, given finite organisational resources. He cites the case of Groupe Bull, a French computer company, which for many years sought to challenge the supremacy of IBM, particularly in the large US market. After several attempts, including entering into partnerships with two US companies, Bull finally conceded, entering into an alliance with IBM in 1992. Kay's analysis was that for 30 years Groupe Bull was:

> driven not by an assessment of what it was, but by a vision of what it would like to be. Throughout, it lacked the distinctive capabilities that would enable it to realise that vision. Bull – and other attempts at European clones of IBM – epitomises wish-driven strategy, based on aspiration, not capability. (Kay, 1996, pp.41–3)

In a study of local government in Britain Leach (1996) found that mission statements and strategic visions had also become fashionable. While in some authorities mission statements had made a real impact in clarifying organisational values and culture, others regarded them only as symbolic public relations documents that had little effect as a management tool.

The dangers are not just that missions are unrealistic and fail to recognise an organisation's capabilities (as in the case of Groupe Bull), but also that management fails to develop a belief in the mission statement throughout the organisation. People only become to believe in, and act on, the mission statement as they see others doing so, especially senior management and other influential players. The ideas of the mission statement need to be cascaded through the structure to ensure a link between mission and day-to-day actions.

6.5 Environmental analysis

With the organisation's general purpose clearly defined, management needs to address the question 'where are we now?' This involves assessing the organisation's environments.

The external environment

Chapter 3 established that the external environment comprises forces operating at two levels: the general and competitive environments. At the macro-level, the PEST framework helps to identify the forces that are the major drivers of change for the organisation. At the micro-level, Porter's five forces analysis helps management to assess the state of competition within the industry. The chapter also showed that external stakeholders, such as government and pressure groups, also influence organisations. It used the power-interest matrix to identify which of those interests are likely to have most influence. If you are unsure about any of these terms, refer back to Chapter 3.

Q Case questions 6.2

Referring to the analytical frameworks in Chapter 3:

- What are the main external factors affecting M&S at present?
- Are there any differences between the food and clothing businesses?

Kay (1996) defined strategy as the match between the organisation's internal capabilities and its external relationships, describing 'how it responds to its suppliers, its customers, its competitors, and the social and economic environment within which it operates' (Kay, 1996). So before devising future courses of action management needs to look inside the organisation to establish how well placed it is to cope with changes in the external environment.

The internal environment: resources and capabilities

Managers analyse the internal environment to identify the organisation's strengths and weaknesses. This means identifying what the organisation does well, where it might do better and whether it has the necessary skills and resources to deliver the chosen strategy. Those that are considered more than usually essential to outperforming the competition constitute **critical success factors**.

A competence is essentially an ability to undertake a particular task or perform a particular function but it can be hard to define. At a personal level, competence derives from a mix of skills, knowledge, behaviours and attitudes (Hellriegel *et al.*, 2002). Hamel and Prahalad (1994) describe an organisational competence as a 'bundle of skills and technologies', stressing the integration of people skills and business processes. Thus an organisational competence is unlikely to be held in its entirety by one individual or even a small team. **Organisational capability** extends this notion to include the organisation's resources.

Management's task in internal analysis is to identify those particular strengths (competences and capabilities) that distinguish the organisation from its competitors and underpin its competitive (or institutional) advantage. These are the organisation's core competencies (or *distinctive capabilities*), which stem from three factors (Johnson and Scholes, 1999). These are at the corporate level, as follows:

- the overall balance of activities carried out by the different business units, that is, the organisation's product/service portfolio. Does it have sufficient interests in growing rather than declining markets? Does it have too many new products (which tend to be a drain on resources) relative to longer established and more profitable ones?

At the divisional or strategic business unit level, the ability to compete effectively depends on:

- The resource base: includes physical resources (buildings and production facilities), human resources (employees' skills, knowledge, attitudes, etc), financial resources (growth prospects, debt-equity mix, liquidity position, financial control systems, etc.) and intangibles (such as 'goodwill', or good relationships with suppliers). Each can be assessed for their adequacy in supporting a strategy.
- How the organisation performs its separate activities – such as designing, producing, marketing, delivering and supporting its products or services – and manages the linkages between them. These, Johnson and Scholes argue, are the most important factors, since the key to performance often lies in the competence with which these processes are carried out rather than in the quantity or quality of resources at the organisation's disposal. A technique that is useful in assessing activities and linkages is value chain analysis.

Value chain analysis

The concept of the **value chain**, introduced by Porter (1985), is derived from an established accounting practice that calculates the value added to a product by individual stages in a manufacturing processes. Porter applied this idea to the activities of an organisation as a whole, arguing that it is necessary to examine activities separately in order to identify sources of competitive advantage.

Figure 6.2 shows two categories of activity. Primary activities relate directly to production or service delivery. These are:

- 'inbound logistics': focused on inputs, such as materials delivery, warehousing;
- 'operations': creating the product, such as machining and packaging;
- 'outbound logistics': moving the product to the buyer – storing, distribution;
- 'marketing and sales': creating consumer awareness of the product;
- 'service': enhancing or maintaining the product – installation, training, repairs.

The primary activities are supported by the actions of:

- 'firm infrastructure' (including organisational structure, strategic planning and financial and quality control systems);
- human resource management: recruitment, training, rewards, etc.;
- technology development: relate to inputs, operational processes or outputs;
- procurement: acquiring materials and other resources.

> **Q Case questions 6.3**
>
> Using the concept of the value chain, give some examples of activities and linkages likely to be important to M&S in securing its commitment to 'value'. Consider businesses, such as clothing (womenswear or menswear), foods and financial services, separately.

Figure 6.2 The value chain

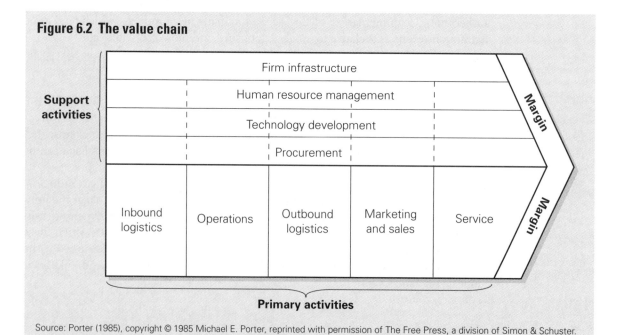

Source: Porter (1985), copyright © 1985 Michael E. Porter, reprinted with permission of The Free Press, a division of Simon & Schuster.

Johnson and Scholes (1999) observe that few organisations undertake all activities from product or service inception through distribution to point-of-sale themselves, but that the value chain exercise must incorporate the whole process, that is the entire *value system*. This means, for instance, that even if an organisation does not produce its own raw materials it must nevertheless seek to identify the role and impact of its supply sources on the final product. Even if it is not responsible for after-sales service it must consider how the performance of those who deliver the service contributes to overall product/service quality.

The usefulness of value chain analysis is that it recognises that individual activities in the overall production process play a part in determining the cost, quality, image and so on of the end-product or service. That is, 'each … can contribute to a firm's relative cost position and create a basis for differentiation' (Porter, 1985), the two main sources of competitive advantage. While a basic level of competence is necessary in all value chain activities management needs to identify the core competences that the organisation has (or needs) to compete effectively. Analysing the separate activities in the value chain helps management do this by addressing the following issues:

- Which activities are the most critical in reducing cost or adding value? If quality is a key consumer value then ensuring quality of supplies would be a critical success factor.
- What are the key cost or value drivers in the value chain?
- What linkages do most to reduce cost, enhance value or discourage imitation? How do these linkages relate to the cost and value drivers?

Porter identified the most important cost drivers as being:

- economy of scale;
- the pattern of capacity utilisation (including the efficiency of production processes and labour productivity);
- linkages between activities (for example, arrangements governing the frequency and timing of deliveries affect storage costs; the 'just-in-time' system, which aims to minimise inventory costs, relies on close liaison between supplier and buyer);
- interrelationships (for example, joint purchasing by different business units to achieve lower input costs);
- geographical location (for example, location can affect an organisation's labour and other input costs; proximity to suppliers may also be an important inbound logistical cost);
- policy choices (such as the choices on the mix and variety of products offered, the number of suppliers used, wages costs, skill requirements and other human resource policies);
- institutional factors (which include the political-legal factors considered as part of the PEST analysis, each of which can have a significant impact on costs).

Value drivers are analogous to cost drivers, but relate to features, other than low price, valued by buyers. Identifying value drivers comes from understanding customer requirements (see Chapter 7), but typically include:

- policy choices (on matters such as product features and performance levels, the quality of input materials, the provision of buyer services and the skills and experience of staff);
- linkages between activities (for example between suppliers and buyers where meeting delivery times is important to the buyer, or the links between sales and after-sales staff).

The value chain idea shows that companies can gain competitive advantage by controlling cost or value drivers and/or by reconfiguring the value chain – that is, by finding a better way of designing, producing, distributing or marketing a product or service. The cost and value drivers vary between industries, and change. The fluidity of the external environment means that organisations must also address the question of 'sustainability', by finding ways of ensuring that their competitive advantages are 'difficult for competitors to replicate or imitate' (Porter, 1985, p.97).

MANAGEMENT IN PRACTICE **Sun Microsystems refines the value chain**

Sun Microsystems, a leading player in the world electronics industry, has focused its resources on product development and final assembly. With limited capital and management resources, it relies on a worldwide network of suppliers to perform most of the manufacturing operations, with components being delivered to the company's two plants for final assembly and test. It has gradually reconfigured its value chain in many ways including the following:

● ensuring that component suppliers add more value to components before delivering them to Sun (so enabling their staff to focus on higher value work);
● having packaging suppliers deliver products directly to the Sun production line (to match the product currently being assembled);
● arranging with a worldwide logistics company to manage all incoming and outgoing freight movements, working directly from Sun's production schedules.

Source: Research by the author

Comparative analysis

Assessing organisational capability is only meaningful if contrasted with the position of competitors. Strengths and weaknesses are relative.

Competitive intelligence

Managers can begin to assess and develop their relative position by finding out about their competitors. Who are they? What are they doing? What are their plans and strategies? What assumptions are they making about changes in the market and the wider environment? What are their strengths and weaknesses? The answers to these questions can help organisations anticipate competitors' actions rather than merely react to them (Robbins, 2000).

Although one might think this information would be confidential, much is in the public domain. Press releases, newspaper reports, annual reports and company websites all reveal information. Research businesses provide analyses of industries and companies.

ACTIVITY 6.3

Explore some information websites

The Internet is now a major resource for collecting intelligence on competitors.

Look up www.hoovers.com/uk or www.business.com to see what type of information is held on industries, companies and products.

Industry norm analysis

A comparative analysis will usually involve comparing performance with industry norms. These are standard sets of performance measures that allow people to compare competitors in the same industry. In the private sector, these typically take the form of measures of financial performance and market share, while in the public sector measures are often published in the form of 'league tables' – such as those used to compare local authority performance.

MANAGEMENT IN PRACTICE

Performance of London Borough Councils in selected services

Borough Council	Education		Housing		Recycling	Taxation and expenditure	
	3–4 year olds with a school place (%)	Expenditure per primary school pupil (£)	Average time taken to relet dwellings (weeks)	Housing benefit claims processed in 14 days (%)	Household waste recycled (%)	Cost of council tax collection (£/dwelling)	Total expenditure by authority (£/head of population)
Inner							
Camden	49	2,435	6.9	25	15.4	21	1,338
Ken. & Chelsea	39	2,800	6.3	47	7.6	22	848
Tower Hamlets	84	3,080	5.5	35	n/a	29	1,684
Westminster	43	2,811	4.0	87	n/a	24	939
Outer							
Brent	61	2,330	5.0	40	5.8	23	1,040
Ealing	73	2,459	6.9	98	10.7	23	919
Richmond-upon-Thames	44	2,135	11.0	27	18.7	14	688

Source: www.Audit-Commission.gov.uk (indicators for 1999–2000).

League tables have limitations. They report on outputs or outcomes but do not adjust for differences in context or degrees of operational difficulty experienced by the different organisations. Nevertheless, many see their use in public services as a spur to efficiency in the absence of market forces.

Johnson and Scholes note that a danger – in both private and public sectors – in relying solely on industry-norm analysis is that 'the whole industry may be performing badly and losing out competitively to other industries that can satisfy customers' needs in different ways, or to different countries' (1999, p.181). It can, therefore, be valuable to draw comparisons with organisations in quite different businesses.

Benchmarking

A method that allows more in-depth analysis and came into fashionable use in the 1990s is **benchmarking**. It extends the idea of industry norm analysis by doing the following:

- encompassing not just quantitative measures of performance but also more qualitative or 'soft' dimensions, such as attitudes towards customers;
- focusing on industry leaders or the 'best in class' rather than the industry as a whole;
- emphasising operations or business processes rather than outputs; like Porter's value chain, this recognises the importance of the way things are done.

This form of 'process-' rather than 'output-'benchmarking is increasingly used as a means of improving organisational performance, often as part of a total quality management programme. Section 6.7 shows how firms can begin to benchmark their performance.

SWOT analysis

Strategy follows from finding a 'fit' between external environment and internal capabilities. Management therefore needs to identify the key issues from each analysis and draw out the strategic implications. It often uses a **SWOT analysis** – standing for strengths, weaknesses, opportunities and threats – to summarise the key internal and external issues. The value chain and comparative analysis usually identify internal strengths and weaknesses. The PEST and five forces analyses usually identify the opportunities and threats in the external environment. Thus a strength might be a highly skilled workforce and a weakness out-of-date plant and machinery. A new line of business directed at a customer might constitute an opportunity, but competition from cheaper imports could pose a threat.

Managers are usually advised to focus on identifying strengths that appear to give the company an edge over its competitors and constitute its core competences. They want to know if these can be sustained in the long term. If there is a threat from specific external factors that could erode them, can they be enhanced or protected from imitation (e.g. patenting of innovation)? If erosion is inevitable then a new strategy may be required. Management also needs to assess the critical success factors to ensure the organisation has the resources and competences needed to achieve a particular strategy. Management can therefore use SWOT to identify weaknesses that they need to strengthen.

> **Q Case questions 6.4**
>
> Drawing on your answers to previous questions:
>
> - make a summary SWOT analysis for Marks & Spencer's clothing business;
> - in your opinion as a consumer, does the company now appear to be following the right strategies for restoring its reputation in this market?

MANAGEMENT IN PRACTICE **Critical success factors in Glasgow City Council**

Glasgow City Council uses its corporate and departmental strategies to address major areas of concern. One of these has been the loss of population in the city, as people migrate to the suburbs. Through surveys and analysis the Council has established that one reason is a shortage of suitable housing within the city. Like many cities, Glasgow's manufacturing industry has declined, leaving behind large areas of vacant and unsightly land and an above-average unemployment level. Much of the city's existing housing also needs repair. The derelict land, although a weakness for the city's appearance, is an opportunity for housing and economic regeneration. Indeed, one of Glasgow City Council's key objectives is 'to promote the regeneration of the city'.

In relation to this corporate aim, the strategic housing plan identifies the following objectives:

- to retain population by ensuring that a full range of house types, sizes and tenure options is provided within the city;

- to pursue sustainable development in a comprehensive way within the Glasgow Alliance (a city-wide partnership group), relating housing to economic, environmental and social improvement;
- through both investment and management, to make Glasgow an attractive city in which to work, live and play.

The plan notes that achieving these objectives depends on other factors falling into place. These are the Critical Success Factors, and include:

- smooth delivery of land and grants to enable private housing development (requires assembly of suitable sites and government subsidies to cover the difference between building costs and selling prices);
- the creation of 'new neighbourhoods' (requires clearance and preparation of large land areas suitable for the building of new suburbs within city boundaries);
- delivery of 9,400 new private houses on brownfield (vacant) land between 1998 and 2003 (dependent on market demand and the willingness of house builders to produce);
- increased investment in land reclamation, industrial property and transport infrastructure (some depend on Scottish Executive approval; others also depend on funding from the Scottish Executive or the economic development agency).

The case shows that in Glasgow, as in other cities, achieving the city's objectives depends not just on the council's own resources and competences but also on those of others working in the city. It shows the extent to which regeneration objectives depend on a joint approach between the different players, which can itself be a competence (see also Section 6.6 – joint developments and alliances).

Source: Glasgow City Council, Strategic Housing Plans 1998 and 2001.

MANAGEMENT IN PRACTICE | **Using tools of strategic analysis**

In a survey of 113 UK PLCs in both manufacturing and service sectors Glaister and Falshaw investigated the use of a range of tools and techniques in strategic planning. The following were among the top 10 most often used:

Tool/technique	Mean
Analysis of critical success factors	3.86
Financial analysis of competitors	3.7
SWOT analysis	3.61
Core capabilities analysis	2.9
Value chain analysis	2.29

The mean is an average on a scale of 1= not used, to 5 = regular use

Source: Glaister and Falshaw (1999).

6.6 Strategic choice

Analysing the factors in the previous section provides the basis for choices about strategy. These choices decide the organisation's future (Johnson and Scholes, 1999), yet are often uncertain and open to different interpretations. At the corporate level, there are fundamental questions about which business(es) the company is, or could be, in. Should it remain focused on a small range of activities or diversify? Should it remain a local or national business, or seek to operate internationally? These decisions establish the direction of the organisation. There are then choices between the alternative ways of delivering the chosen strategy. And in developing competitive strategy for individual markets a key question is what generic (or positioning) strategy to adopt – whether to compete on the basis of differentiation or cost.

Strategic directions

Figure 6.3 shows the main options in the product/market matrix. The majority (with the exception of market withdrawal) assume growth. In some parts of the public sector dependence on public resources means that growth is not an option. Instead, decisions may be about altering the service mix to use existing resources more efficiently and effectively. Similarly, for private companies, periods of economic downturn and fierce competition can precipitate contraction or restructuring.

Existing markets, same product/service

Choice within this segment will depend on factors such as whether the market is growing, in decline or has reached maturity. Each box contains several possible strategies:

- Market penetration is a strategy designed to increase market share. This is likely to be easier in a growing than a mature market. Strategies may involve reducing price, increasing advertising expenditure, or improving distribution.
- Consolidation is concerned with protecting or maintaining market share in existing markets. In a growing market this means increasing the volume of business. In more mature markets firms might focus on improving cost efficiency and customer service in order to retain custom. In declining markets management might consolidate through the acquisition of other companies.
- Withdrawal from a market is a wise option in circumstances where, for instance, competition is intense and the organisation is unable to match the competence of rivals. Alternatively, changing priorities might require the redeployment of organisational resources. Health boards have withdrawn accident and emergency services from some hospitals to use limited resources more effectively.

Figure 6.3 Strategic directions – the product/market matrix

	Existing products/services	New products/services
Existing markets	Market penetration Consolidation Withdrawal	Product/service development
New markets	Market development ● new territories ● new segments ● new uses	Diversification: ● horizontal ● vertical ● unrelated

Source: Adapted from Johnson and Scholes (1993 and 1999).

Psion

In July 2001 Psion, the UK creator and manufacturer of handheld electronic organisers, announced its decision to withdraw from the market. The pocket-sized organiser was first launched in 1984 and soon replaced the Filofax as a must-have accessory amongst business professionals. In the early 1990s Psion fought off Japanese rivals but new competitors such as Palm and Handspring of the United States later entered the market. By 2001 the market was suffering from overcapacity and a price war had broken out. The organiser, like the PC, was now 'commoditised'. Psion lacked the scale to compete with global rivals in cheaper organisers and the top-of-range market was being invaded by smartphones with built-in organiser capability. David Levin, Psion's chief executive, believed the company's strengths lay in development and innovation, not mass manufacture, and said: 'it would have been commercially naive to press on'. Psion had previously withdrawn from the computer games market for the same reason. The company planned to focus on the market for corporate wireless data networks but would also provide maintenance and repair services to existing organiser owners.

Source: *Finanical Times*, 12 July 2001.

FT

Existing market, new product

A strategy of product (or service) development allows a company to retain the relative security of its present markets while altering products or developing new ones. In many retail sectors, such as fashion, consumer electronics and financial services, companies are continually changing products, usually in response to changing consumer needs and preferences. Similarly, car manufacturers compete by adding new features, improving technology and updating or extending their model range. Some new products, such as 'stakeholder pensions' in the United Kingdom, can arise out of changes in government policy. Because many new ideas do not come to fruition new product development is a risky as well as a costly process.

New market, present product/service

Market development requires seeking new markets for existing products or services. The three main ways of doing this are by entering new geographic markets (many companies do this by internationalising their operations), targeting new market segments (new groups of customers, by age, profession, lifestyle or interests) or by developing new uses for a product. New uses can often be found for manufactured materials. For example, a type of lightweight carbon originally developed for use in spacecraft is now used in the manufacture of golf clubs.

Q **Case questions 6.5**

- Use the product-market matrix to classify the various directions of Marks & Spencer's business both before and after 2000.
- Note down the methods M&S has used to deliver changes in strategic direction. Consider why these methods might have been selected.
- In the light of your reading and answers to previous questions, what kind of competitive strategy do you think M&S is following in respect of clothing and foods? Provide examples to support your answer.

New markets for retailers

Retailers such as Metro of Germany, Casino of France and Tesco of the United Kingdom are expanding into central and eastern Europe. Tesco first entered Hungary in 1996 before spreading into Poland, the Czech Republic and Slovakia. Consumer demand for low prices has favoured the development of hypermarkets. In 2001 Tesco had 70 hypermarkets in the region and was planning to open a further 18 within a year. These emerging markets offer growth opportunities for western European retailers. Many domestic markets are reaching maturity, characterised by limited growth and declining margins. Many retailers also face restricted planning controls, a barrier to further large store development.

For the same reasons, Tesco, Metro and Carrefour of France are developing in Asia. In this region development has been mainly through joint ventures with local partners, which enable them to cut supply costs through bulk purchasing, give them local knowledge (crucial to inventories and store locations) and help relations with local suppliers.

Source: *Financial Times*, 2 and 12 July 2001.

FT

Diversification

Diversification takes three basic forms:

- **Vertical integration**: moving either backwards or forwards into activities related to the organisation's products and services. A manufacturer might decide to make its own components rather than buy them from elsewhere. Equally, it could develop forward, for instance into distribution, such as when Ford acquired Kwik-Fit.
- **Horizontal integration**: developing competing or complementary activities, such as when mortgage lenders move into the insurance business. With both vertical and horizontal integration there is some link between existing and new activities. Advantages include the ability to control the quality of inputs and the opportunity to expand by using existing skills. Kwik-Fit has used its database of depot customers to create a motor insurance business.
- **Unrelated diversification**: developing into new markets outside the present industry. This is a strategy illustrated by the operations of conglomerate companies. The shift by some major supermarkets into banking or other types of financial service is another example. Amongst other reasons, unrelated diversification may be undertaken as a means of spreading risk or to achieve further growth where existing markets have reached saturation.

Alternative development directions are often not mutually exclusive and in practice most companies develop in a number of directions at the same time. Since several of the options are likely to require new organisational skills and competences, management needs to consider alternative methods for achieving a change in direction.

Alternative methods for delivering strategy

Any strategy can be delivered in one of three ways – internal development, acquisition, or through some form of alliance.

Internal development

The organisation delivers the strategy by expanding or redeploying relevant resources that it has or can employ. This enables the organisation to retain control of all aspects of the development of new products or services. This is often considered important where the product is highly technical in the design and manufacturing processes. Internal development was favoured by public service organisations. Many local authorities in the United Kingdom created in-house direct service organisations (DSOs) to repair and maintain council buildings. Nowadays, DSOs are usually required to compete with outside contractors. Similarly, many parts of local government and the Civil Service – for example legal services and the Stationery Office – have been privatised. The present climate for public services is not conducive to internal development. It is much more likely that attempts to meet new or growing demands will involve some form of joint venture or alliance (see below).

Acquisition (and merger)

Acquisition is where one firm takes over another. This allows rapid entry into new product or market areas and is a quick way of building market share. It is also used where the acquiring company lacks the necessary in-house skills, technology or other resources. For example, a company might be taken over for its expertise in research and development, its competences in relation to a specific production system or business process or its knowledge of a local market. Financial motives are often strong, particularly where there are opportunities to increase cost efficiency. Mergers are often undertaken for similar reasons but are more likely to come about by voluntary agreements than through contested takeover bids.

Starting in the 1990s, there have been many mergers and acquisitions in the financial services sector in the United Kingdom. Some have taken place between smaller high street institutions (e.g. the merger of the Alliance and Leicester building societies, now a PLC) in order to strengthen their position in a particular market, such as mortgages. They also achieve economies by closing branches and removing duplication in 'backroom operations'. Others have been undertaken to extend the range of activities. Some clearing banks have added specialist areas such as wealth management to their porfolio – such as when, some years ago, National Westminster took over Coutts. Most merger and acquisition activity in the banking sector has so far been on the domestic scale. However, in other industries such as telecommunications the forces of globalisation have seen a wave of international acquisitions and mergers. For example, Vodafone of the United Kingdom has made several acquisitions, including the takeover of Germany's Mannesmann, in its quest to become the world's largest mobile phone company.

One of the main problems with acquisition and merger is the difficulty in merging two different organisations with different cultures and ways of doing things. Combined organisations often face a long period of disruption as a common set of procedures and operations are put in place.

MANAGEMENT IN PRACTICE **The DaimlerChrysler merger**

In 1998 Daimler-Benz, the German auto company renowned for the powerful Mercedes-Benz range of luxury cars, bought Chrysler Corporation, the third largest, but most efficient US car maker. It was the biggest industrial merger ever, and many saw it as symbolising that German companies were prepared to play on the world stage. Jurgen Schremp, chief executive of Daimler, made the move as part of an aggressive expansion strategy to widen the company's product range. Investors supported the move, as they expected synergies between the two companies to follow from the merger.

Since then, Schremp has developed a grand vision for the group to compete in every segment of every major car market. This has included developing further links with Mitsubishi in Japan and Hyundai in Korea.

Yet the core merger has had difficulty in delivering on the promises. Chrysler has suffered from a shortage of new models, so that sales of its older models have been falling rapidly. It has had to reduce its engineering and design staffs to meet a directive from Germany to cut overhead costs by 25 per cent over three years. Many senior US managers at Chryslet left the company at the time of the merger. One major investor commented: 'Of course we're unhappy. The merger has not worked out as well as had been originally contemplated.'

Source: *Business Week*, 31 July and 7 August 2000.

Some form of joint venture or alliance might therefore be preferable, especially where cost efficiency is not the main motive.

Joint developments and alliances

Organisations sometimes turn to partners to co-operate in developing products or services. Arrangements vary from highly formal contractual relationships to looser forms of co-operation but there are usually advantages to be gained by both parties. One attraction of this method is that it limits risk. Pilkington, the UK glass manufacturer, has joint ventures in Brazil with one of its main rivals, Saint-Gobain of France. Each takes it in turn to build glass-making plants (which are expensive). Each then manages its own plants but they share the profits. By operating in this way they reduce the risk of having too much capacity for the local market. A second reason is to learn about new technologies or markets. Alliances also arise where governments want to keep sensitive sectors, such as aerospace, defence and aviation, under national control. Airbus, which competes with Boeing in aircraft manufacture, was originally a joint venture between French, German, British and Spanish manufacturers. Alliances – such as the Star Alliance led by United Airlines of the United States and Lufthansa of Germany – are also common in the airline industry, where companies share revenues and costs over certain routes. As governments often prevent foreign ownership of airlines such alliances are often an alternative to takeover or acquisition.

Other forms of joint development include franchising (common in many retailing activities – see the case on The Body Shop), licensing (for example building under licence) and long-term collaboration between manufacturers and their suppliers.

Alliances and partnership working have also become commonplace in the public sector. In many UK cities alliances or partnerships have been created between major public bodies, business and community interests. Their main purpose is to foster a 'joined-up' approach to the planning and delivery of public services in an attempt to tackle social and economic problems more effectively. Public bodies also increasingly act as enablers or commissioners rather than as direct providers and have therefore developed contractual partnership arrangements with other organisations to deliver services on their behalf.

MANAGEMENT IN PRACTICE   **PSA Peugeot-Citroën-Toyota joint venture**

In July 2001, Toyota and PSA Peugeot Citroën announced a joint venture to develop and assemble a new family of small cars for the European market. By splitting the investment costs and pooling their expertise in engine and transmission technology the two firms hope to generate a better return on their investments. Moreover, selling the vehicles under two brands will make it easier to run the new plant at full capacity. For Toyota the project is seen as a cost-effective way to increase sales volumes and market share in Europe. As Europe's second largest car maker PSA has superior knowledge of the market and a strong brand profile. For PSA the deal is the latest in a long-running partnership policy. PSA already has technical and assembly alliances with, among others, Ford, Fiat and Mitsubishi Motors. PSA believes that a network of alliances helps the company preserve its independence (guarding against takeover bids) and allows technology transfer from one alliance to another. Diesel engines developed through PSA's joint venture with Ford, for example, could be used in the small car venture with Toyota.

Source: *Financial Times*, 9 July 2001.

FT

Generic competitive strategies

At the business unit level firms face choice about how to compete with rivals. Porter (1980b, 1985) identified two basic types of competitive advantage: low cost or differentiation. From this he developed the idea that there are three generic strategies that a firm can use to develop and maintain competitive advantage: cost leadership, **differentiation** and focus. Figure 6.4 shows these strategies. The horizontal axis at the top shows the two bases of competitive advantage. Competitive scope, on the vertical axis, indicates whether the company competes industry-wide or within a smaller segment.

Cost leadership

Cost leadership is a strategy whereby a firm aims to deliver its product or service at a price lower than its competitors. This strategy requires economies of scale in production

Figure 6.4 Generic competitive strategies

	Competitive advantage	
	Lower cost	Differentiation
Broad target	1 Cost leadership	2 Differentiation
Narrow target	3A Cost focus	3B Differentiation focus

Competitive scope

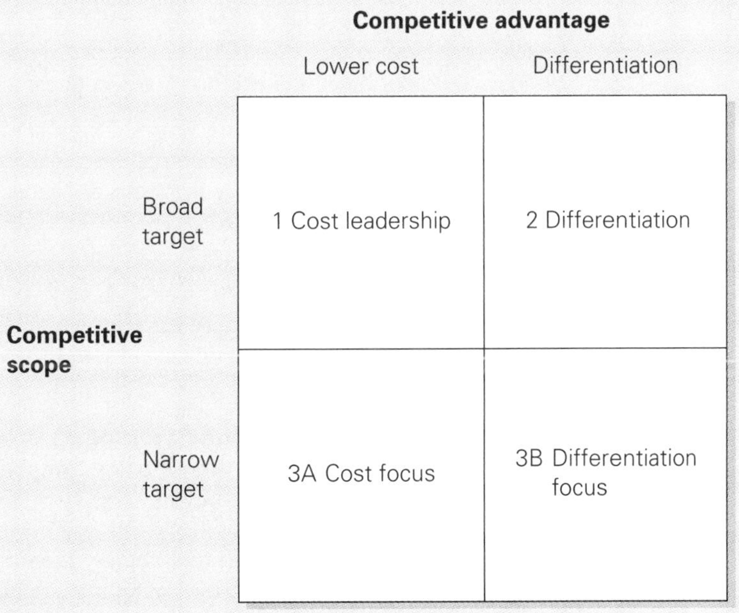

Source: Porter (1985).

and close attention to efficiency and operating costs, although other sources of cost advantage, such as preferential access to raw materials, also help. Low cost producers typically sell a standard no-frills product and place a lot of emphasis on minimising direct input and overhead costs. A cost leadership strategy is likely to work better where industry produce is standardised, competition is based mainly on price and consumers can switch easily between different suppliers. However, a low cost base will not in itself bring competitive advantage – the product must be perceived as comparable or acceptable by consumers. Firms that have used this strategy include Costco, Somerfield, Argos and Superdrug.

MANAGEMENT IN PRACTICE   **Low cost strategy at Ryanair**

Dublin-based Ryanair began operations in 1985 and is now Europe's largest low cost airline, operating (in mid-2001) 55 routes between 12 European countries. In 2000–1 its passenger numbers rose by 35 per cent to 7.4 million and pre-tax profits increased by 37 per cent. In contrast to the difficulties experienced by most of Europe's national flag carriers this was an impressive performance. Ryanair's success, based on offering a low-priced, no-frills service, is modelled on Southwest Airlines of the USA. Under this model costs are driven down in a variety of ways:

● No in-flight meals are served.
● Cabin crews do the cleaning, speeding up turnaround times and allowing aircraft to fly more hours every day.
● The fleet comprises one type of aircraft, the Boeing 737, reducing costs such as parts and maintenance.
● Using secondary airports at which landing charges are low (and sometimes zero). Airports such as Paris-Beauvais and Glasgow-Prestwick are some 50 and 20 miles respectively from the city centres.
● By keeping out of the market for connecting flights, aircraft are not delayed waiting for passengers.
● Emphasis is on direct sales: in 2000–1 70 per cent of Ryanair's tickets were booked over the Internet, 22 per cent by phone and just 8 per cent through travel agents; this saved the company 62% in selling costs.

Although difficult economic conditions and competitive pressures were affecting the industry in 2001, Ryanair believed its strategy was more 'recession-proof', with increasing numbers of business travellers 'trading down' from its more expensive rivals such as BA and Lufthansa.

Source: *The Economist*, 26 May 2001; *The Herald*, June 2001; *Financial Times*, 26 June 2001; www.ryanair.com

---

Differentiation

Differentiation exists when a company offers a product or service that is distinctive – and valued as such by customers – from those of its competitors. Porter (1985) argued that differentiation is 'something unique beyond simply offering a low price' that allows firms to command a premium price or to retain buyer loyalty. Because customers will pay more for what they regard as a better product, a differentiation strategy can be more profitable than a cost leadership strategy. Nokia achieves differentiation through the individual design of its product, while Sony in consumer electronics achieves it by offering superior reliability, service and technology. BMW differentiates by stressing a distinctive product/service image, while Coca-Cola differentiates by building a widely recognised brand. This strategy is often supported by high spending on advertising and promotion.

Differentiation strategy at British Airways

After several years of poor performance British Airways announced a new strategy in 2000. It would now seek to differentiate itself from other airlines by focusing on business travellers rather than those travelling in economy class. Business passengers pay the full fare for their ticket, and expect a high quality service before, during and after the flight. BA will gradually reduce the number of seats available in economy class, and take fewer low cost passengers travelling on connecting flights with other airlines. It sold GO, its low cost airline, in early 2001, as this was not consistent with the new strategy. However, the decision to restart Concorde flights in September of that year was consistent with the image of an airline focused on high fare, business travellers.

The form of differentiation varies. In construction equipment durability, spare parts availability and service will feature in a differentiation strategy, while in cosmetics differentiation is based on images of sophistication, exclusivity and eternal youth. Cities compete by stressing differentiation in areas such as a skilled workforce, good quality housing, available land, good transport links and recreational facilities.

Focus

A focus strategy involves competing in a particular market segment, such as targeting a specific consumer group (e.g. teenagers, the over-60s, the medical professions) or a specific geographic market. The two variants – cost focus and differentiation focus – are simply narrower applications of the cost leadership and differentiation strategies. There are many examples of firms pursuing focus strategies. Saga offers travel services for the over 60s, many insurance companies tailor policies to the needs of particular groups (e.g. NFU Mutual caters for farmers, Female Direct offers motor insurance for women) and The Body Shop's green credentials appeal to particular consumer groups.

Moore (2001) notes that each generic strategy gives a company some kind of defence against each of the five competitive forces. For example, cost leadership, achieved through economies of scale or other cost advantage, can raise barriers to entry, and a low cost base can provide a cushion to cope with cost increases from suppliers. Differentiation, based on strong brand loyalty, can amongst other things create an entry barrier and also insulate the firm from rivalry. But firms' relative positions can always change. For instance, consumer loyalty can falter if the price premium, relative to low cost competitors, is perceived as too great, and differentiation can be lost through imitation of a product by competitors.

Identifying generic strategies

- *Select three companies you are familiar with, and in each case gather evidence that indicates the generic strategy they are following.*
- *Then consider what features you would expect to see if the company decided to follow the opposite strategy.*

Porter's initial argument was that a firm had to choose between the two basic strategies of cost leadership and differentiation. Many people disputed this, given that companies often appeared to follow both strategies simultaneously. By controlling costs better than competitors companies can reinvest the savings in features that differentiate the product or service. Porter (1994) later offered some clarification: 'Every strategy must consider both relative cost and relative differentiation ... a company cannot completely ignore quality and differentiation in the pursuit of cost advantage, and vice versa ... Progress can be made against both types of advantage simultaneously' (p.271). However, he notes there are trade-offs between the two and that companies should 'maintain a clear commitment to superiority in one of them'.

Options analysis

As well as identifying options, management is also faced with evaluating them. Many tools and techniques are available to aid decision making. Some, including ranking, decision trees and scenarios, assist in an initial screening process. This narrows down the number of options to a more manageable list that would be subject to a more detailed appraisal. Others, such as profitability and cost/benefit analysis, assess the feasibility of options as well as their acceptability in terms of likely risks and rates of return. Each option would be scored against the criteria set, to produce an overall rating of the attractiveness of individual options. In practice each option usually has pros and cons, and no single option emerges as a clear 'winner'. Ultimately, strategic choice is a matter of judgement about which option is most likely to best meet organisational goals.

6.7 Implementation: actions, monitoring and control

Implementing strategy

Implementation is intended to turn strategy into action, moving from the corporate to the operational levels. Many strategies fail to be implemented, or fail to achieve as much as management expected. A common mistake is to assume that strategy formulation will lead to painless implementation. Sometimes there is an 'implementation deficit', which means either that strategies are not implemented at all or they are only partially successful. The reasons for this are numerous but usually include external constraints, inadequate time, too few resources or poor communication. A common reason is also that while strategy formulation has the appearance of rationality, strategy implementation will often be a political process. Those who were content with the earlier strategy may strongly oppose the new strategy if it affects their status, power or career prospects. Implementing a major change is a complex, often conflicting process (Boddy, 2001). Chapter 11 presents many ideas on the topic.

In essence, the task changes from strategic planning to that of **strategic management**. This includes all the aspects of strategic planning discussed earlier, *plus* all that is involved in managing implementation and control. In consequence, 'strategic management is characterised by its complexity ... arising out of ambiguous and non-routine situations with organisation-wide rather than operational-specific implications' (Johnson and Scholes, 1997, p.35).

Monitoring progress

The final stage in the strategy process, as depicted in Figure 6.2, is to monitor the implementation of strategy. In order to do this satisfactorily management needs to set standards and targets in respect of key objectives, at both strategic and operational levels. It also needs to ensure that information systems are in place.

Shareholders, analysts, management and others with an interest in the organisation's business will wish to compare performance results over time in order to reveal trends in business performance. It is only by tracking trends that a view can be taken on whether performance is in line with expectations or whether there is a need for corrective action. Many targets focus on financial and other quantitative aspects of performance, such as sales turnover, operating costs, profit margins and productivity. Some of these are the 'headline' profit and loss indicators, found in annual reports, which are of particular interest to shareholders and to industry analysts. For example, in its 2001 annual report Great Universal Stores plc (owners of Argos and Burberry) records the following 'highlights':

Indicator	2001	2000
Turnover	£6,041m	£5,658m
Profit before tax	£487m	£448m
Earnings per share	37.2p	34.5p
Annual dividend per share	21.0p	20.6p

Given the wide-ranging interests of stakeholders companies do not restrict their reporting to this type of information. In the public services, measures of quality and fairness of service outcomes may be more important to consumers and service users, but financial performance of greater interest to government and other funders.

Although monitoring is shown as the last stage in the strategy model, it is not the end of the strategy process. Strategy making is continuous as organisations adapt and adjust to the changes in their business environment. Regular monitoring of performance alerts management to the possibility that targets might not be achieved and that operational adjustments are needed. Equally, and in conjunction with continuous scanning of the external environment, performance monitoring can prompt wider changes to the organisation's corporate and competitive strategies.

Q Case questions 6.6

Review one of Marks & Spencer's annual reports (the most recent is on the website), including the summary financial statements (not the detailed version).

- What are the main ways in which the company measures its performance in different parts of the business?
- What measures does it use (or is it planning) in respect of its 'commitment to society' (see relevant web pages)?
- Is the emphasis on hard (quantitative) or soft (qualitative) measures?
- To whom are the measures you find likely to be of most interest?

Improving performance through benchmarking

Where performance is falling short of expectations, management sometimes undertakes a benchmarking exercise. The basic idea of benchmarking is that by looking at the performance of industry leaders the organisation can learn how to do things better. Figure 6.5 shows that this involves seven steps typical of any planning process.

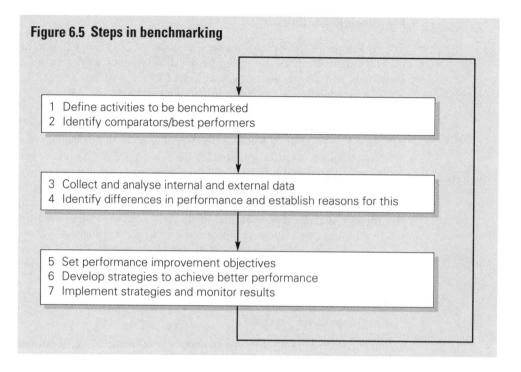

Figure 6.5 Steps in benchmarking

1 Define activities to be benchmarked
2 Identify comparators/best performers

3 Collect and analyse internal and external data
4 Identify differences in performance and establish reasons for this

5 Set performance improvement objectives
6 Develop strategies to achieve better performance
7 Implement strategies and monitor results

The first two decisions concern the choice of functions or activities to be benchmarked and comparator organisations. Because benchmarking can be a time-consuming process it is best to focus on those processes or activities that are central to competitive advantage, e.g. quality control systems. Comparators might be drawn from both inside and outside the industry.

The next stage involves collecting comparable data, which should help show why the two organisations have different levels of performance. Data on comparator organisations may be obtained from the sources described in Section 6.5 and these could be supplemented by information obtained from suppliers, customers and trade publications. Some organisations form benchmarking clubs that enable the sharing of much more detailed information on how particular activities or functions are carried out. The practice has become popular within UK local government as it strives to achieve 'best value' in service delivery.

Steps 5–7 ensure that changes designed to raise performance are clearly specified, implemented and evaluated. Like strategy, benchmarking is a continuous process. As markets, technology and other external factors change, fresh comparisons will be needed, with the focus perhaps shifting to different functions or processes.

Q Case questions 6.7

- Which functions or activities might M&S benchmark (be specific about which business unit)?
- Which comparators might it choose for this purpose?

Bendell *et al.* (1993) point out that in order to gain the most from benchmarking it should be 'a team-based activity, integrated with other quality improvement activities within the organisation and closely connected to the planning activities going on at the top' (p.12).

Investigating benchmarking

To find out more about benchmarking, the industries and companies that are involved, and the processes that are commonly benchmarked, have a look at the following websites: The Benchmarking Exchange at www.benchnet.com and the Benchmarking Network at www.benchmarkingnetwork.com

6.8 Alternative perspectives on strategy

The nature of the strategy process

The framework at Figure 6.1 is widely accepted as representing the basic content of strategy, but there are differing views on how the *process* of strategy making actually works in practice. Some views are *prescriptive* in that they seek to explain how management *should* make strategy, while others are *descriptive* in that they try to set out how management *does* make strategy. Table 6.2 shows three perspectives.

Table 6.2 Alternative perspectives on the strategy process

	Planning	*Learning*	*Political*
Approach	Prescriptive; assumes pure rationality	Descriptive; based on bounded rationality	Descriptive; based on bounded rationality
Content	Extensive use of analytical tools and techniques; emphasis on forecasting; extensive search for alternative options, each evaluated in detail	More limited use of tools and techniques and more limited search for options: time and resources don't permit	As learning view, but also some objectives and options disregarded as politically unacceptable
Nature of process	Formalised, systematic, analytical; top down – centralised planning teams	Adaptive, learning by doing; bottom up and top down	Characterised by bargaining and negotiation; use of power to impose objectives and strategies; top down and bottom up
Outcomes	Everything planned in advance; plans assumed to be achieved as set out	Plans are made but not all are 'realised'; some strategies are not planned but emerge in course of 'doing'	Plans are made but often couched in ambiguous terms to secure agreement; need interpretation in course of implementation; outcomes reflect compromises
Context/ environment	Stable environment; assumption that future can be predicted; if complex, use of more sophisticated tools	Complex, dynamic, future unpredictable	Stable or dynamic, but complex; stakeholders have diverging values, objectives and solutions

Planning view

The 'planning view' is prescriptive and based on a belief that the complexity of strategic decisions requires an explicit and formalised approach to guide management through the process. In the 1960s and 1970s a wide literature, most notably the work of Ansoff (1965), espoused this structured approach. At this time, strategy was seen as a highly systematised process, following a prescribed sequence of steps and making extensive use of analytical tools and techniques. This was the 'one best way' to develop strategy that, if followed, was believed almost to guarantee corporate success. Implicit in this view are assumptions that human beings always behave rationally and that events, facts and the world in general can be viewed and interpreted in purely objective terms. However, pure rationality and objectivity rarely pertain in the real world and two alternative perspectives – the learning and the political – highlight the weaknesses of the planning view.

Learning view

The message of the learning view is that strategy is an *emergent* or adaptive process. The idea can be illustrated by summarising Mintzberg's (1994a,b) critique of the formalised approach to strategy. In his opinion, strategic planning – which he refers to as the planning school – suffers from what he terms three 'fundamental fallacies', shown in Table 6.3.

Table 6.3 Mintzberg's views on the fallacies of strategic planning

Fallacy	Description	Counter-view
Predetermination	'The prediction of ... the unfolding of the strategy formation process on schedule ... and the imposition of the resulting strategies on an acquiescent environment, again on schedule'	Internal and external environments are dynamic, so that plans rarely unfold as intended
Detachment	'The prescription is that organizations should complete their thinking before they begin to act'	'effective strategists are not people who abstract themselves from the daily detail but quite the opposite: they immerse themselves in it [and] abstract the strategic messages from it'
Formalisation	Analytical, scientific approach to strategy, with a prescribed series of steps, boxes and checklists	Strategy requires insight, creativity and synthesis, all the things that formalisation discourages. It needs to function beyond boxes

Mintzberg's criticisms are deliberately pointed in order to emphasise his argument that, in contrast to the structured analytical approach advocated by Ansoff and others, there is no one best way to develop strategy. He regards strategic planning as 'strategic programming', a system developed during a period of stability (in contrast to the rapidly changing environment of the late twentieth and early twenty-first centuries) and designed primarily for what he calls 'the machine organisation' – the classic formalised, specialised and centralised bureaucracy typically found in manufacturing industry. This style of planning, he argues, may be appropriate for certain types of organisation but not for others. Thus, what is required is a flexible approach to strategy.

In a similar vein, Kay (1996) notes that there are 'no recipes and generic strategies for corporate success ... there cannot be, because if there were, their general adoption would eliminate any competitive advantage ... the foundations of corporate success are unique to each successful company' (p.37). The success of Honda in the US motorcycle market has become a classic case in corporate strategy. Kay (1996) notes that there are two perspectives on the company's achievement. The first, an assessment by the Boston Consulting Group, was that the success was simply another example of Japanese penetration of western markets. Richard Pascale's account was very different.

Kay's (1996) perspective is that 'we shall never know the extent to which Honda's success was truly the result of chance or rational calculation [but] like all successful

The Honda Motor Company

Richard T. Pascale of Stanford University (1984) has described the entry of Honda into the US motorcycle market. When Honda executives arrived in Los Angeles from Japan in 1959 to establish a US subsidiary, their intended strategy was to focus on selling 250cc and 350cc machines rather than the 50cc Honda Cubs that were a big hit in Japan. Their instinct told them that the Honda 50s were not suitable for the US market, where everything was bigger and more luxurious.

However, sales of the 250cc and 350cc bikes were sluggish and the bikes themselves were plagued by mechanical failure. It looked as though Honda's strategy was going to fail. At the same time, the Japanese executives were using the Honda 50s to run errands around Los Angeles,

attracting a lot of attention. One day they got a call from a Sears Roebuck buyer who wanted to sell them to a broad market of Americans who were not necessarily already motorcycle enthusiasts. The Honda executives hesitated over selling the 50cc bikes, for fear of alienating serious bikers, who might then associate Honda with 'wimp' machines. In the end they were pushed into doing so by the failure of the 250cc and 350cc machines. The rest is history. Honda had stumbled on a previously untouched market segment that was to prove huge. It had also found a previously untried channel of distribution: general retailers rather than speciality motorbike stores. By 1964, nearly one in two motorcycles sold in the United States was a Honda.

Source: Pascale (1984).

strategies, it was based on a mixture of calculation and opportunism, of vision and experiment' (p. 40). The important point is that strategists and managers should not expect rigid adherence to 'the plan', but should anticipate that some departure from it is inevitable, owing to unanticipated events and the emergence of new opportunities.

To underline this point, Mintzberg makes a distinction between intended and emergent strategies (see Figure 6.6 over). He acknowledges the validity of strategy as a plan, setting out intended courses of action, and recognises that some deliberate intentions may in fact be realised. But he challenges managers to review just how closely their realised strategies mirror their original intentions. As well as the realisation of deliberate strategies, it is also likely that some plans failed to be implemented at all (unrealised strategies) and that others which he describes as 'emergent strategies' were not expressly intended but resulted from 'actions taken one by one, which converged in time in some sort of consistency or pattern'. A flexible approach to strategy is one which recognises that 'the real word inevitably involves some thinking ahead of time as well as some adaptation en route'. The essence of the learning view is this process of adaptation, the ability to react to unexpected events, to exploit or experiment with new ideas 'on the ground'. Mintzberg gives the example of a salesperson coming up with the idea of selling an existing product to some new customers. Soon all the other salespeople begin to do the same, and 'one day, months later, management discovers that the company has entered a new market'. This was not planned but learned, in a collective process. People learn in the process of implementation.

Political view

The view of strategy as an emergent process has much in common with political perspectives on strategy. Both are based on the concept of 'bounded rationality'. This argues that limits on the intellectual capacity of humans, sources of information and resources are such that comprehensive rational planning, involving extensive analysis and detailed evaluation of alternative strategies, is impossible. Instead, strategists and policy makers,

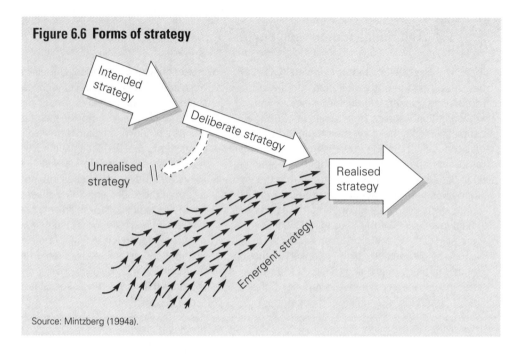

Figure 6.6 Forms of strategy

Source: Mintzberg (1994a).

while seeking to be rational, are constrained into 'satisficing' behaviour – performance that is considered acceptable rather than exceptional – because of psychological, organisational and cost limitations. While the learning view tends to be based on the logic that 'prior thought can never specify all subsequent action' (Majone and Wildavsky in Mintzberg, 1994a, p.289), the political view adds the further dimensions of power, conflict and ambiguity.

Drawing on his experiences in the public policy sphere, Lindblom (1959) was an early proponent of the political view. His arguments go beyond identifying the limits of perfect rationality (Hogwood and Gunn, 1984). He draws attention to the ways in which value judgements pervade and influence the planning process and points to the sectionalism or conflicting interests among stakeholders so characteristic of public policy, which frustrate attempts to reach agreement on objectives or on particular strategies to be pursued. He argued that the identification of values or objectives (ends) prior to the analysis of alternative strategies (means) to achieve them was an artificial construct because all strategies encompass implicit value judgements.

On the basis of these observations, Lindblom concluded that policy or strategy making was not a scientific, comprehensive or rational process, but an iterative, incremental process, characterised by restricted analysis and bargaining between the players or stakeholders involved. Lindblom labelled this the method of 'successive limited comparisons' whereby 'new' strategy is made simply by marginal adjustments to existing strategy: 'Policy is not made once and for all; it is made and remade endlessly...[through]... a process of successive approximation to some desired objectives.' Strategic choice is not a comprehensive and objective process but takes the form of a limited comparison of options, restricted to those that are considered politically acceptable and possible to implement. Lindblom's account is close to the *logical incrementalism* described by Quinn whereby 'strategy is seen to be worked through in action.'

ACTIVITY 6.6

Reviewing mission statements

Refer back to the examples of mission statements earlier in the chapter. Do you consider any of these stated intentions to be unclear or vague? If so, consider why they might have been expressed in this way.

Both the learning and the political views of strategy oppose the rigid planning view of strategy, but ultimately accept that a structured approach to strategy has its place. 'Too much planning may lead us to chaos, but so too would too little, more directly' (Mintzberg, 1994a). This view is reflected in several recent contributions to the literature on strategy that have mused upon the rise and fall, or death and reincarnation of 1960s-style 'strategic planning'. Just as organisations adapt to the changing environment, so too do approaches to strategy. Moncrieff and Smallwood (1996) note that different planning styles emerge in response to different economic and social conditions. The planning style of the 1960s seemed to suit the relative stability that characterised the period. The highly competitive, increasingly global and fast-moving markets that characterise the present time may be better matched by a learning, adaptive or even 'real time strategy' (Taylor, 1997).

In practice, the different styles are not mutually exclusive. Empirical studies have found that many organisations do adopt an explicit and deliberate approach to strategy formulation and most agree that 'strategic planning' is important (Glaister and Falshaw, 1999). But resource constraints, political processes and an ever-changing environment mean that for most organisations strategy develops through a mix of the planned and emergent styles.

MANAGEMENT IN PRACTICE **Changes in planning style at PowerGen**

PowerGen was formed in 1991 from the assets of the Central Electricity Generating Board. By 2001 it was a leading multi-utility supplying electricity, gas and telephone services in domestic and overseas markets. As a private and diversifying company, PowerGen moved into a more complex and uncertain environment with new competition and changing regulations, and the company's corporate planning process had to evolve. The company has retained a formal process with a five-year planning horizon, but there have been some significant changes.

Planning is a more devolved process: a much smaller central team focuses on overall corporate strategy while business units have a greater role in developing business strategy and more freedom to consider a wider range of options to cope with their particular competitive situations.

The previous emphasis on long-range demand forecasting, often found to be unreliable and inappropriate for anticipating changes in regulatory requirements, has given way to a greater use of scenario planning with participation by both planning and operational staff across the business. To stimulate strategic thinking, staff are encouraged to use a variety of techniques in the analysis of competitive forces, core competences and resources and in the development and appraisal of strategic options. Business unit plans have become shorter and are no longer required to follow a prescribed format. The overall planning cycle is completed in a shorter period of time. All of these developments have created a more adaptive style of planning that is consistent with the increased uncertainty of the company's business environment.

Source: Jennings (2000).

Strategy as 'fit' or 'stretch': the resource-based theory

Much of the literature on strategy takes the view that management's role is to 'fit' the organisation into the environmental context in which it operates, by adapting resources and competences to take advantage of the opportunities that arise through external change. Strategy is then about finding the right 'niche' and defending it. However, some writers contend that too much emphasis has been placed on the impact of external environmental factors in influencing strategy. They argue that strategy is about identifying the firm's distinctive resources and competences, and using (or 'stretching') these to create new opportunities. The idea of strategy development by 'stretch' is encapsulated in the resource-based theory which Kay (1996) outlines as follows:

- Firms are in essence collections of capabilities.
- The effectiveness of a firm depends on the match between these capabilities and the market it serves.
- The growth, and appropriate boundaries, of a firm are limited by its capabilities.
- Some of these capabilities can be purchased or created and are available to all firms.
- Others are irreproducible, or reproducible only with substantial difficulty, by other firms, and it is on these that competitive advantage depends.
- Such capabilities are generally irreproducible because they are a product of the history of the firm or by virtue of uncertainty (even within the firm itself) about their nature.

From his studies of successful companies Kay has identified only three largely irreproducible, and thus distinctive, capabilities: innovation, reputation and 'architecture', which he describes as 'the system of relationships within the firm or between the firm and its suppliers and customers, or both'. All are products of organisational resources. Through the use of examples, Kay demonstrates how the success of many well-known firms is based on one or more of such distinctive capabilities.

MANAGEMENT IN PRACTICE   **Competitive advantage: the importance of 'architecture'**

Observers of the rise of Toyota from second-line manufacturer of sewing machines to dominance of the world automobile industry in a period of 40 years have emphasised the role Toyota's *keiretsu* – the integrated but nevertheless independent group of suppliers that underpins Toyota's exceptional reputation for reliability – their pioneering of just-in-time inventory management, and their shortening of the traditional model cycle ... The *keiretsu* involves a complex structure of implicit contracts – long-lasting understandings whose context is not, and cannot be, written down. The nature of these relationships enables Toyota to be confident in the quality of its suppliers' parts, unconcerned about its potential vulnerability to component shortages, and ready to share proprietary knowledge in order to accelerate design and retooling ... Despite the internationalisation of markets ... there are still things that are done best by people who find themselves frequently in the same room. The most important of these are the transfer of skills and knowledge and the development of trust between individuals. It is on success in creating networks which facilitate these exchanges that many competitive advantages in today's world depend.

Source: Kay (1996, p.73–4).

Clearly internal capabilities can create powerful competitive advantages, but Porter (1994) argues that the resource-based view of the firm and other recent theories based on competences and capabilities have merely shifted the focus from the external to the internal environment, and he remains convinced that industry structure and the competitive environment are important influences on strategy.

> Any company can identify some positive qualities and skills – but the real question is how these qualities result in competitive advantage. Industry structure and competitive position define the value of competencies, capabilities and resources [so that] … identifying [them] in the abstract, decoupled from particular markets, is meaningless. (Porter, 1994, p.281)

There can be little doubt that the context provided by the external environment in which organisations operate is important. As a supporter of the resource-based view Kay is also clear on this when he refers to the match between capabilities and markets. But by turning the focus towards internal resources there can also be little doubt that the resource-based theory of strategy has added new perspectives to the study of what gives organisations competitive advantage.

6.9 Summary

This chapter has shown how management can take account of the forces in its external environment to develop a systematic plan to its strategy – establishing where it wants to go, where it is now, and how it is going to get there. It began by describing the different types of strategy, showing how corporate level and operational level need to be closely linked throughout the stages of analysis, choice and implementation. Having understood external developments through their PEST and five forces analyses, management can then analyse internal capabilities through the techniques of value chain and comparative analysis. A SWOT diagram can bring together the most significant factors shaping the choice of strategy. The process of choice can be focused by the product/market matrix and by the choices of internal development, acquisition or alliance. The chapter also introduced the strategic choices of cost leader, differentiation or focus. It concluded with a consideration of alternative perspectives on the strategy process, comparing the planning approach with the learning, political and resource-based approaches.

Content

Management needs to make plans for its organisation's future direction to help the enterprise survive. A strategy, sometimes expressed in a formal strategic plan, sets an overall direction. Drawing on information about the external environment and internal capabilities helps to shape the long-term direction and scope of the organisation. This provides a basis for consistent action throughout the organisation and a framework within which operational decisions can be made. Management chooses whether to follow low cost or differentiation strategies or one that delivers both. It also guides the overall strategic direction to follow in terms of the balance to strike between existing or new markets and products.

Developing a strategy also involves planning how the organisation is to achieve the objectives set. Management needs to set out how internal resources and capabilities will be deployed or changed so that they support the strategy. It also needs to decide whether other organisations are to be part of the plan – such as through mergers or joint ventures of some form. One of the benefits of a clear, if flexible, strategic plan is that it helps management to generate commitment and effort towards achieving the goals set out in it.

Process

The strategy developed usually reflects the interests of powerful individuals or groups. Strategy making is not an objectively rational activity. Strategy models depicting the key stages in the process should not be regarded as prescriptive but as frameworks that serve both as a guide to managers and as an analytical tool. Strategy rarely unfolds as intended. Rather it is an emergent process, which must be capable of adapting in complex, changing and ambiguous situations. As well as the traditional approaches to strategic planning, learning and political models are offered as more accurate ways to represent the process.

Control

As well as scanning the external environment for opportunities to build advantage, managers seek to identify those internal resources and competences that yield advantage. These must be assessed in relative terms. Numerous methods of performance measurement and assessment are available to both public and private sector managers. Internal trend analysis helps to see whether their area of responsibility is meeting its objectives or how it stands in comparison with other units. To measure their performance against other organisations managers can access published statistical data and/or league tables, or undertake benchmarking to gather comparable performance data on a range of inputs, processes and outcomes.

Strategy does not end when plans have been drawn up. Progress needs to be constantly monitored as the plans are implemented. Activities and achievements need to be checked against plans and against competitors' activities. Managers also need to exercise control in the sense of monitoring the plans against market and other developments to ensure that the direction chosen is still appropriate.

Q PART CASE QUESTIONS

- What environmental influences have particularly affected The Virgin Group?
- Which of these are similar to, and which are different from, those facing Marks & Spencer?
- Which generic strategy has Virgin followed at different periods in its history?
- What factors would you suggest Virgin Atlantic should include in a benchmarking exercise?
- What other business would it need to work with to benchmark its performance?
- On balance, does the Virgin story support the planned or the emergent view of strategy?

6.10 Review questions

1 What are four benefits that an organisation can gain from planning?

2 Distinguish between a corporate and an operating strategy.

3 In what ways does the concept of competitive advantage apply to for-profit organisations, non-profits, cities and countries?

4 Describe the main elements in the strategy process in your own terms.

5 Discuss with a manager from an organisation how his or her organisation developed its present strategy. Compare this practice with that set out in the model. What conclusions do you draw from that comparison?

6 Compare the strategies of Marks & Spencer and The Body Shop, and list any similarities and differences.

7 What are the main steps to take in analysing the organisation's environment? Why is it necessary to do this?

8 Can you describe clearly each of the stages in value chain analysis and illustrate them with an example? Why is the model useful to management?

9 Why do firms conduct benchmarking exercises? What difficulties can arise in external benchmarking?

10 The chapter described three generic strategies that organisations can follow. Give examples of three companies each following one of these strategies.

11 Give examples of company strategies corresponding to each box in the product/market matrix.

12 Compare the main ideas of the learning and political approaches to strategy with the traditional planning model.

13 Compare the 'fit' and 'stretch' perspectives on strategy. Evaluate the strengths and weaknesses of each approach.

Further reading

Johnson, G. and Scholes, K. (2001), *Exploring Corporate Strategy*, Financial Times Prentice Hall, Harlow. The best-selling European text on corporate strategy. Although more detailed than required at introductory level, a number of sections usefully build on this chapter.

Dobson, P. and Starkey, K. (1993), *The Strategic Management Blueprint*, Blackwell, Oxford.

Smith, R.J. (1994), *Strategic Management and Planning in the Public Sector*, Longman/Civil Service College, Harlow.

Both cover the main elements in the strategic planning process and explain, with the use of examples, some tools of strategic analysis in addition to those covered in this chapter. Smith's book also contains useful chapters on definitions and terminology and options analysis.

Kay, J. (1996), *The Business of Economics*, Oxford University Press, Oxford. Presents a readable account of competitive strategy written from an economic perspective, illustrated by a wide range of European and other international examples.

Hamel, G. and Prahalad, C.K. (1994), *Competing for the Future*, Harvard Business School Press, Boston, MA. Focuses on the importance of internal resources and competences in building strategic capability.

Wisniewski, M. (2001), 'Measuring up to the best: a manager's guide to benchmarking', in G. Johnson and K. Scholes (eds) *Exploring Public Sector Strategy*, Financial Times Prentice Hall, Harlow. A comprehensive account of benchmarking

Moore, J.I. (2001), *Writers on Strategy and Strategic Management* (2nd edn), Penguin, London. Summarises the work of the major contributors to the fields of strategy and strategic management – Part One contains a useful overview of the work of the 'movers and shakers', including Ansoff, Porter and Mintzberg.

Long Range Planning often contains useful articles. Examples include a review of the use of strategic planning tools in UK companies by Glaister and Falshaw (1999).

Annotated links, questions and resources can be found on
www.booksites.net/boddy

CHAPTER 7

Managing marketing

AIM *To explain the benefits that all organisations gain if they give a prominent role to marketing, and how they can organise the activity.*

OBJECTIVES

By the end of your work on this chapter you should be able to:

1 Compare and contrast marketing with alternative organisational orientations

2 Describe the benefits to any organisation of adopting a marketing orientation

3 Explain why marketing is an information intensive activity

4 Identify the roles and responsibilities of the marketing manager

5 Explain market segmentation and the practice of selecting a target market

6 Describe the components of the marketing mix

7 Explain what is meant by product positioning

8 Consider whether marketing enhances consumer choice or encourages materialism and the manipulation of consumers

The Millennium Dome

The Millennium Dome at Greenwich opened to the public on 31 December 1999. Following a public consultation exercise the Millennium Commission had announced in February 1996 that it favoured an exhibition sited at Greenwich, and by July of that year had developed the Dome concept. In June 1997 the newly elected government approved the project.

The exhibition featured 14 zones representing different aspects of life – and were intended to combine fun, education and participation. Each 'combined multimedia exhibits and games, film and art displayed in striking architectural structures'. There was also a Millennium Show in the Central Arena. The original business plan set the target of attracting 12 million visitors: an ambitious target that crucially depended upon a successful opening night and first month to attract the support of the media and interest of the general public.

The Dome opening night was marred by poor organisation – 10,000 guests including politicians, sponsors and members of the public were invited. To address security problems the then chief executive, Jenny Page, arranged for politicians to arrive by underground from Westminster. Other guests also had to arrive by underground. Due to an administrative error hundreds of tickets were not sent out in time and guests had to queue at underground stations to collect their tickets before making their way to the Dome. By the time they arrived the opening ceremonies had finished and the champagne had run out. This debacle was widely reported in the media (many of whose senior staff had been caught in the queues).

The next two days were more successful: both days were sold out and by day three 1 million tickets had been sold. At this stage other problems arose. Many of the exhibits, including the Body Zone sponsored by Boots, had only just been completed. Many did not work properly and queues for the popular Body Zone lasted more than two hours. By the second week ticket sales were not as expected and the problem of an empty Dome was then presented – leading to more negative publicity.

At the end of January it was announced that visitor figures were half what had been expected. By the end of 1999 the Dome had attracted 5.5 million paying visitors. Revenue was £187 million against a forecast of £344 million. It was, however, the most popular pay-to-visit attraction in Britain. Surveys of visitors to the Dome consistently showed that over 80 per cent expressed satisfaction with the experience. Nevertheless the low visitor numbers meant that the organisers of the Dome had to seek additional funds from the Millennium Commission.

Q Case questions

- What were the marketing implications of the events on the opening night?
- What might explain the visitor numbers for the year being below expectations?
- How might better marketing have helped the whole project?

7.1 Introduction

This chapter introduces the following ideas:

- Marketing
- Marketing orientation
- Consumers
- Consumer-centred organisation
- Transactional marketing
- Relationship marketing
- Marketing environment
- Marketing information system
- Market segmentation
- Target market
- Product
- Product position
- Marketing mix
- Product life cycle

ACTIVITY 7.1

Describing marketing

Before reading this chapter, write a few notes that capture your description of marketing. You might find it helpful to think of some recent purchases you have made and consider the different ways in which you came across marketing before, during or after your purchase. Keep your definition safe as you will use it again at the end of the chapter.

The Millennium Dome clearly got off to a bad start – and one explanation is that those responsible for the project paid too little attention to marketing. The project was conceived by the government as a publicity event related to the millennium: there was little indication of public demand for the attraction. As the opening day drew near there was evidence that the management was unclear about the customers they were targeting or the benefits they would provide. Was it to be an undemanding entertainment similar to a fairground, or was it to be intellectually stimulating, similar to the highly successful Tate Modern Art Gallery a few miles away? How should they promote the event and distribute tickets – bearing in mind that as it was only to last for a year there would be little chance for major changes once it had opened? How should they ensure that when visitors arrived they felt well-looked after? Perhaps most fundamental of all, what management structure would best ensure an effective marketing effort?

All organisations face the challenge of understanding what customers want, and ensuring that they can meet those expectations. Managers of profitable firms of any size will usually attribute much of their success to marketing. Just as marketing was a source of failure at the Dome, so it is a source of success in many organisations. IKEA, the Swedish furniture retailer, has clearly found and refined a formula that appeals to its target market. In 40 years it has grown from a single store to a business with over 150 outlets in over 30 countries. Virgin Direct, the financial services business founded in 1995 as a joint venture with Norwich Union, has become a major player in that sector, partly by using the telephone as its method of distributing the service to customers.

Successful not-for-profit organisations such as Oxfam or the Royal Society for the Protection of Birds also demonstrate the effective use of marketing principles.

All organisations need to deliver services that their users require in order to generate revenue or to retain the confidence of those who provide their budgets. To do so they need to be aware of their customers, sensitive to changing needs and organised to be able to deliver those needs to a level people find acceptable. Successful organisations adopt a marketing orientation that encourages a commitment to identifying and responding to the needs, wants and demands of their consumers. Managers in such organisations have had to develop a greater focus on marketing and create systems that meet those needs of the customer.

This chapter opens by considering marketing as an organisational orientation and identifying the benefits of the approach. It explains why all organisations can embrace marketing and how managers can build marketing into the structure. The chapter goes on to discuss the management of marketing information and the roles and responsibilities of marketing management – in both goods and services. It concludes with some critical reflections.

7.2 What is marketing?

People often associate marketing with the latest promotional offer at their supermarket or the sponsorship of popular television programmes by branded products (such as Cadbury's relationship with *Coronation Street*). Others think of it as being the email messages they receive from Internet companies with travel offers or new books. These illustrate the variety of techniques that marketers use to sell a product – but there is more to marketing than innovative promotional techniques.

The (UK) Chartered Institute of Marketing defines **marketing** as a management process: 'which identifies, anticipates and supplies consumer requirements efficiently and effectively'.

Peter Drucker (1999) places the activity even more firmly at the centre of business:

> Because the purpose of business is to create and keep customers, it has only two central functions – marketing and innovation. The basic function of marketing is to attract and retain customers at a profit.

Marketing has most recently been described as an approach to managing all of the relationships shared between an organisation and its stakeholder groups. These definitions imply that marketing refers both to a marketing function within the organisation and to a more deeply embedded marketing orientation that shapes other activities of the organisation.

A marketing orientation

Most medium and large organisations have a marketing function – usually a department or group of people that focus on activities such as market research, competitor analysis, product strategy or promotion. Those that recognise most fully the significance of marketing incorporate marketing more deeply in the organisation, adopting not only a marketing function but a **marketing orientation**. This means that they concentrate their activities on the marketplace and the **consumer**. They are '**consumer centred**' or 'consumer driven'.

Financial services become consumer centred

Today's financial services industry provides an example of one of the most aggressive and competitive markets. Faced with intense competition, encouraged by deregulation and the demutualisation of a number of building societies, most high street retail banks have had to adopt a more consumer-centred approach to the development of new products and delivery of their banking services. By listening to the demands of their consumers, investing in new products and widening access to their services by investing in telephone and electronic banking, organisations such as The Royal Bank of Scotland have successfully responded to new competition.

Levi's have positioned themselves as a successful manufacturer of fashion clothing by making marketing a central organisational activity. They respond to the changing needs, wants and demands of consumers by investing in product development and marketing communications. Charities such as Oxfam, Shelter and The Woodland Trust pay attention to the interests of their supporters. As well as promoting established lines of work they survey their donors, to ensure an acceptable match between the charity's campaigns and the issues that matter to those who donate the funds. Adopting a marketing orientation enables them to continue achieving their goals.

Alternative orientations

The fact that an organisation undertakes public relations or advertising does not necessarily mean it has adopted a marketing orientation, except in the most superficial sense. It may in reality still have a focus on product, production or sales. Table 7.1 summarises these alternative orientations.

Table 7.1 Alternative organisational orientations

Organisational orientation	Focus	Benefit	Disadvantage
Product	Product features	High quality products	Research may not have identified demand for the product and it may not sell
Production	Production	Low costs	Costs determine price and production, not consumer demands. Production may not match consumer demand
Sales	Turnover and shifting product	Sales targets met; good for cash flow in the short term	Hard-pressure sales techniques may meet current targets but lose future ones if users find product unsatisfactory
Marketing	Continually on consumers and consumer demands	Product offering determined by consumer demands; organisational goals achieved	Initial investment in becoming consumer centred

Source: Based on Lancaster and Messingham, 1993; Dibb *et al.*, 1997; Jobber, 2001.

By identifying and understanding consumer demands organisations with a marketing orientation can anticipate changes in consumer tastes. Then they respond to them quickly. They do not develop and offer products that they assume consumers will buy. Instead they use information about consumer demands to develop and offer products that satisfy those demands. The sportswear industry provides many examples of the benefits of a marketing orientation. Aware that a wider selection of sportswear was available to men than women at a time when women's participation rates in sport were increasing, Nike responded in a variety of ways. As well as extending their range of products to widen the choice of sportswear available to women they sponsored the Imperial Cancer annual series of 'Race for Life' events.

Product orientation

Organisations operating with a product orientation focus on their technological strengths and expertise. They stress the products and product features that these strengths allow them to make. They pay less attention to the demands of the market and can often find themselves in a position similar to that of the De Lorean car:

> This stainless steel car was built in Northern Ireland with UK grant money and Lotus expertise. It was targeted for the American market. It received much free publicity from its appearance in the film *Back to the Future*. When the manufacturers introduced the car to the market they found that there was no demand. Nobody wanted to buy the car. (*Car Magazine*, supplement, April 1997)

While a product orientation is focused on products for which there may or may not be demand, a marketing orientation is focused on identifying consumer demands for particular products.

Production orientation

An organisation operating under the production orientation uses production efficiency and cost of materials to determine the quantity and price of goods to be produced. The production orientation focuses on efficiency and costs.

Sales orientation

An organisation operating under the sales orientation aims to shift as much of a product as it can as quickly as possible. Levitt (1960) provides a clear understanding of the differences between selling and marketing philosophies:

> Selling focuses on the needs of the seller; marketing on the needs of the buyer. Selling is a preoccupation with the seller's need to convert his product into cash; marketing with the idea of satisfying the needs of the consumer by means of the product and the whole cluster of things associated with creating, delivering and finally consuming it.

Marketing orientation

Baker (1991) argues that by adopting a marketing orientation, 'which puts the consumer at the beginning rather than the end of the production–consumption cycle', organisations discover what consumers want. They can then decide how best to use the strengths of the organisation to meet these demands. They then *return* to the marketplace with a product for which a demand exists. They use information from the market about demand and the price that consumers are prepared to pay to determine how much to produce and what the costs must be to offer a price that consumers will accept. While the sales orientation focuses on shifting products, the marketing orientation focuses on satisfying consumers and building long-term, mutually satisfying relationships with them. They focus on selling products that will satisfy consumer demands.

ACTIVITY 7.2

Identifying consumers

A marketing orientation suggests that organisational success is best achieved by focusing on the consumer. Identify each of the following organisations' consumers and suggest the benefits that a focus on their consumers will bring to each organisation: Microsoft, easyJet, Virgin Holidays, The Big Issue.

Benefits of a marketing orientation

As an organisational orientation, marketing asserts that the most effective way of achieving organisational objectives is through consumer satisfaction. It is an orientation that uses the demands of consumers to determine products, levels of production, prices charged and sales techniques used. This means that organisations selecting marketing over alternative philosophies still assess product features, efficient levels of production and sales targets – but they do not make decisions about these matters the focus of organisational activities. Instead, consumer demands determine product development, levels of production and sales targets. Meeting these demands brings consumer satisfaction and organisational success.

The adoption of a marketing orientation ensures that the whole organisation commits to achieving organisational goals by *continually* satisfying consumer demands. Aware of this objective and of their contribution towards it, different areas within the organisation are able to co-operate and co-ordinate their activities. Organisations like Linn Products, Sony and the Halifax, which appreciate that consumer demands are continually changing, anticipate these changes and are more open and flexible in their approach to developing new products.

MANAGEMENT IN PRACTICE **Kodak**

For many years Kodak has maintained a strong position in the film and photo development industry, fending off aggressive competition presented by Fuji and own-brand labels such as Boots. By listening to consumers' demands and investing in research and product development Kodak have defended their market leader position by introducing products such as their Advanced Photo System (APS). This has enabled them to keep ahead of the competition, with a reputation for innovation (sometimes referred to as 'first mover advantage') and quality.

By identifying and monitoring consumer demands marketing-oriented organisations are able to respond to these demands and ensure that the products they offer satisfy consumers. Above all else the adoption of the marketing orientation offers stability in the marketplace (Figure 7.1).

Researchers such as Gronroos (2000) distinguish between **transactional marketing** and **relationship marketing**. They argue that in order to ensure a stable position in the marketplace many organisations have replaced their focus on transactions with one that seeks to develop mutually satisfying, long-term relationships with their consumers. This they argue is because a focus on one-off transactions encourages organisations to

Figure 7.1 Benefits of marketing as an organisational orientation

concentrate on the short-term maximisation of profit. They then pay less attention to their long-term position in the marketplace. Organisations that move towards a relational focus have a better understanding of consumer needs. They concentrate on developing a 'long-term, continuous series of transactions' that helps them maintain stability in the market and achieve their objectives in the long term.

By continuing to satisfy consumer demands marketing-oriented organisations are able to meet their performance goals. Many are replacing a focus on individual transactions with a focus on long-term relationships with their consumers.

MANAGEMENT IN PRACTICE **Supermarkets develop customer relations**

The idea of building relationships with consumers has historically been most evident in industrial markets in which organisations sell to other businesses and government. The supermarket industry has recently tried to develop similar relationships with individual consumers.

Loyalty cards aim to encourage the customer to buy from the same store by awarding points for every pound spent there. The cards also offer supermarkets a powerful tool with which to develop relationships with individual consumers. Passing a card through the electronic point-of-sale (EPOS) terminal at the checkout provides the companies with valuable information about the customer's shopping habits. It will show how often the person visits the shop, how much he or she spends and on what. The stores can then design messages and sales promotions to satisfy the shopping patterns and demands of individual consumers. So loyalty cards are used by retailers in many countries to build relationships with customers in two ways: they reward them for their repeat business and provide the stores with information to satisfy their precise demands more effectively.

While loyalty cards are widely used, can their value be overstated? For example, they can only supply data on goods that are offered by the store. They do not tell the store if the customer wanted a particular product that was not stocked or if any of the goods bought were second-choice alternatives. Either of these would imply that too much reliance on loyalty card data will lead to stores dictating what the consumer can buy, limiting the choice to the most frequently bought lines. These are not necessarily what they or other consumers actually wanted.

7.3 What types of organisation can use marketing?

The benefits offered by the marketing orientation apply to all types of organisations. Those managing not-for-profit organisations, charities, churches and sports teams can all benefit from a marketing orientation.

> The present day marketing concept views marketing as a social process ... [to identify] consumer needs and satisfy them through integrated marketing activities ... Marketing thinking will lead to a better understanding of the needs of different client segments; to a more careful shaping and launching of new services; to a pruning of weak services; to more flexible pricing approaches; and to higher levels of patient satisfaction.
>
> Some health care organizations are now beginning to apply marketing to a broader set of problems by trying to answer critical questions such as:
>
> ● Where should the hospital locate a clinic or an ambulatory care unit?
> ● How can the hospital estimate whether a new service will draw enough patients?
> ● What should the hospital do with a maternity wing that is only 20% occupied?
> ● How can the hospital attract more consumers to preventive care services such as annual medical check-ups and cancer-screening programmes?
>
> The acid test for the implementation of a marketing orientation in the health care sector is based on the existence of an orderly, systematic and complete strategic marketing plan. (Moutinho, 1995)

MANAGEMENT IN PRACTICE   Saint Honoré Hospital, Brussels

Saint Honoré Hospital is situated in a suburban area of Brussels. The administrator has for some time felt that he needs to pay closer attention to the marketing aspects of the operation. He feels this will ensure the successful use of facilities and will help the future development of the hospital. As a first step towards developing a comprehensive marketing strategy he arranged for some market research to be done. One of the questions he was particularly interested in was the factors that patients and doctors used in deciding which hospital to go to.

Amongst the data that the research produced was the following table:

Consumers' choice criteria in selecting a hospital

Aspect of the hospital	Very important (%)
Good doctors	95.7
Good nursing care	88.2
Good emergency room	86.5
Latest medical equipment	81.3
Keep patients informed about their care	71.4
Good reputation	68.7
Prices of services	59.1
Overall hospital management	56.3

Source: Moutinho (1995)

Evaluating market research

● *How might the information affect the decisions taken by the management of Saint Honoré Hospital? What other information would they be wise to take into account alongside this on the views of patients?*

● *Can you identify another social care organisation that could use market research to assist it?*

The marketing orientation has also been more recently adopted by organisations with social or charitable aims. These include raising awareness of the dangers of smoking, increasing charitable donations and promoting the benefits of an active lifestyle. Not-for-profit organisations focus on understanding the opinions, perceptions and attitudes of those individuals whose opinions and attitudes they want to change or whose support they seek.

MANAGEMENT IN PRACTICE **A marketing orientation helps the homeless**

The Big Issue was established to tackle the problem of homelessness in a progressive and entrepreneurial manner. Rather than campaigning to raise funding and donations that could be used to address homelessness, *The Big Issue* sought to challenge conventions. By adopting a marketing orientation *The Big Issue* has successfully approached the challenge of homelessness in a novel and unique manner. By developing a new product, a street magazine that homeless vendors can sell to the general public, *The Big Issue* has addressed several objectives. Vendors earn money from the magazines they sell, which highlights the extent of homelessness, the public purchase an informative magazine and also support a social cause.

Marketing activities such as product development can benefit social as well as commercial objectives.

7.4 Creating a marketing orientation

Michaels (1982) warned that: 'No one person, system, or technique will make a company marketing orientated' and stresses that a marketing orientation cannot be achieved overnight. Advising on the implementation of a marketing orientation, Michaels emphasises the following requirements:

● *Investment by top management*: before marketing can be instilled throughout the whole organisation senior managers must commit themselves to the marketing orientation. Without their support other managers will not implement the necessary changes.

● *Injection of outside talent*: Michaels notes that, in his experience, managements implementing a marketing orientation successfully have brought in new personnel. These have helped to educate other staff about the possible benefits of the new orientation.

● *A clear sense of direction*: as with any change, it is essential that management takes a planned approach to its implementation. It must set objectives and timescales to guide the introduction.

Kotler (1997) also stresses the importance of restructuring the organisation to focus on the consumer. Managers need to educate themselves and their staff about the idea and how it may support long-lasting success in the marketplace. This applies to all levels and functions who must share a common commitment if they are to work together in the interests of the consumers. Without the support of top management the focus on consumer satisfaction advocated by the marketing orientation will not become the guiding orientation for organisational decisions.

CASE STUDY   **The Millennium Dome – the case continues – a marketing structure?**

One of the reasons for the difficulties which management at the Dome experienced may have been the structure of the project. It was a vast project which had to be completed in a very short time. Moreover the specification of what the promoters expected appeared to change frequently. This would have been a difficult task for a professional development company with a team of experienced project staff. But many of those working on the Dome plans were temporary secondments from a range of Government Departments, combined with some external recruits. This may have prevented the creation of a team with sufficient management skill for a project of this complexity, working within a single reporting structure.

Several commentators noted that the design of the zones and their content was subject to many separate influences. They argued that the lack of a clear plan for the Dome at the outset meant that different and perhaps contradictory creative forces became involved, leading to duplication and confusion.

The pressure to complete the project on time may also have meant that the organisers ignored the need to develop and put in place a structure through which the Dome could be managed during its one year of operation. One solution could have been to have two teams – one concerned with creating the Dome, and another with the quite different task of operating it.

The structure of the organisation may have to change to allow all departments to become focused on and work together for the achievement of consumer satisfaction. Compare Figures 7.2 and 7.3. Figure 7.2 shows marketing as an important function within the organisation and Figure 7.3 is the structure required if an organisation is to become consumer centred. Such restructuring includes putting in place systems and procedures to collect, analyse and distribute data about the changing demands of consumers. It also requires that the achievement of organisational objectives through consumer satisfaction becomes the basis of decisions.

7.5   Managing the marketing function

The effective implementation of a marketing orientation requires that as a functional area within the organisation marketing has the central position displayed in Figure 7.3. The continual satisfaction of changing consumer demands relies upon information

Figure 7.2 Marketing as an important function

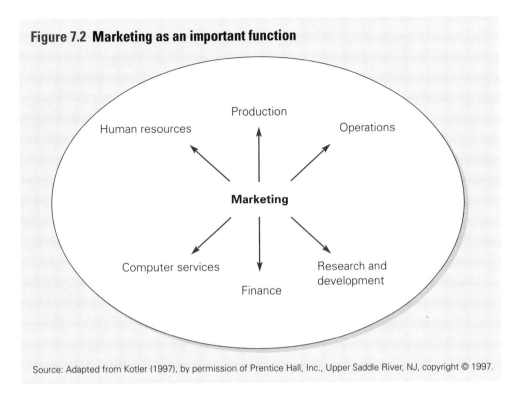

Production
Human resources
Operations
Marketing
Computer services
Finance
Research and development

Source: Adapted from Kotler (1997), by permission of Prentice Hall, Inc., Upper Saddle River, NJ, copyright © 1997.

Figure 7.3 Structure of a consumer-centred organisation

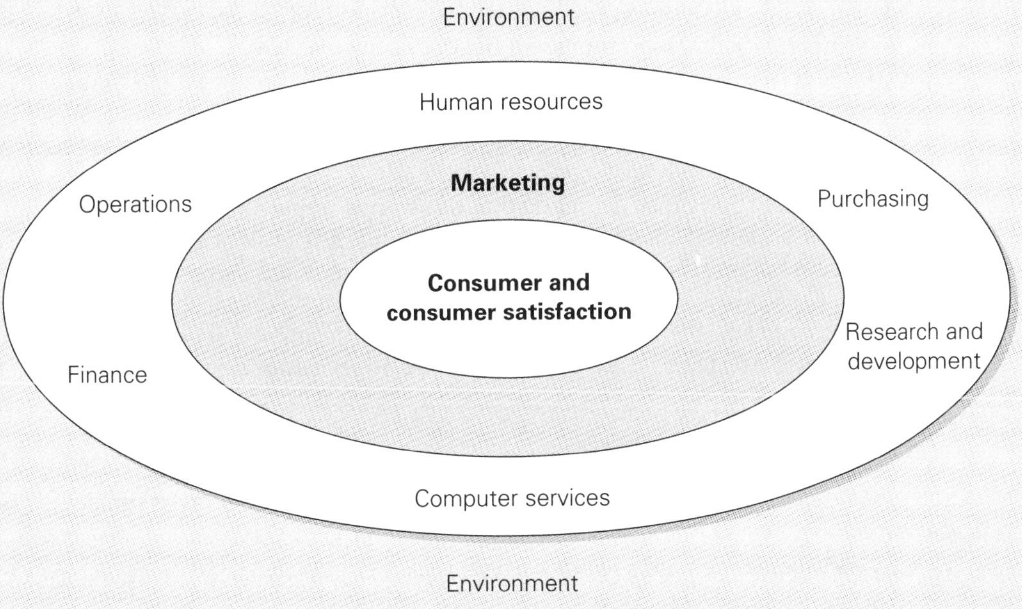

Environment
Human resources
Marketing
Operations
Purchasing
Consumer and consumer satisfaction
Research and development
Finance
Computer services
Environment

Source: Adapted from Kotler (1997), by permission of Prentice Hall, Inc., Upper Saddle River, NJ, copyright © 1997.

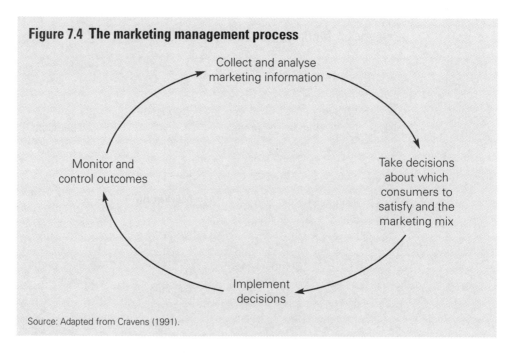

Figure 7.4 The marketing management process

Collect and analyse marketing information

Take decisions about which consumers to satisfy and the marketing mix

Implement decisions

Monitor and control outcomes

Source: Adapted from Cravens (1991).

about consumer demands distributed throughout the organisation. It is for this reason that marketing professionals claim that marketing requires a central position.

Within marketing-oriented organisations the marketing department links the consumer and the enterprise. It monitors changes in consumer demands and alerts other areas of the organisation to changes in the environment that may require a response. It is the responsibility of marketing to research the marketplace and decide which consumer demands the organisation can satisfy most effectively. That decision, and the marketing tools to use, are the responsibility of the marketing manager.

In common with other functional area managers, the marketing manager gathers information to plan direction, creates a marketing organisation, leads staff and other players and controls the activity by evaluating results and taking corrective action. Figure 7.4 outlines these activities.

The figure shows that the marketing function is responsible for (a) identifying those consumers whose demands the organisation can satisfy most effectively and (b) selecting the marketing mix that will satisfy consumer demands and succeed in achieving organisational objectives.

In order to take these decisions managers need information about consumer demands, competitor strategies and changes in the **marketing environment** (Kotler and

---

Q Case questions 7.1

- What customer demands was the Dome seeking to satisfy at the time of the case study?
- What other demands was the Dome seeking to satisfy?
- What marketing tools are mentioned in the case?
- How did the management structure prevent the creation of a marketing orientation?

Armstrong, 1997) that are likely to impact upon consumer demands. The marketing environment contains both micro and macro components. The micro-environment is that part of an organisation's marketing environment to which it is close and within which it directly operates. Each organisation will have a micro-environment unique and specific to it that, as shown in Figure 7.5, comprises those parts of the environment with which the organisation regularly interacts, including employees, suppliers, distributers, consumers, competitors and publics such as pressure groups and the general public. All organisations, including small and medium-sized enterprises, have some control over changes in their micro-environment and the likely impact these will have upon their marketing activities.

The macro component of an organisation's marketing environment is more remote and will be similar for all those in the same industry. Organisations have little direct influence over their macro-environment, which consists of the PEST factors outlined in Chapter 3 – repeated in Figure 7.6.

ACTIVITY 7.4

Identifying the marketing environment

- *Use Figures 7.5 and 7.6 to identify, for each of these organisations, those parts of their micro- and macro-environments that have most impact upon their marketing activities: British Airways, Abbey National, the Hilton Hotel group, Thomas Cook Holidays.*

- *How might they respond to these environmental influences?*

Such frameworks are useful in identifying whether changes in the environment will have a positive or negative impact on the marketing activities of an organisation. This is because they can be useful in identifying both the *opportunities present in the environment,* such as those presented to multimedia organisations by developments in e-commerce, as well as *threats,* such as the impact that foot and mouth disease has had upon Britain's farming and tourism industries.

Figure 7.5 The micro-environment

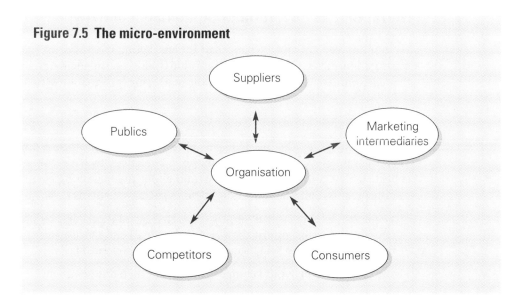

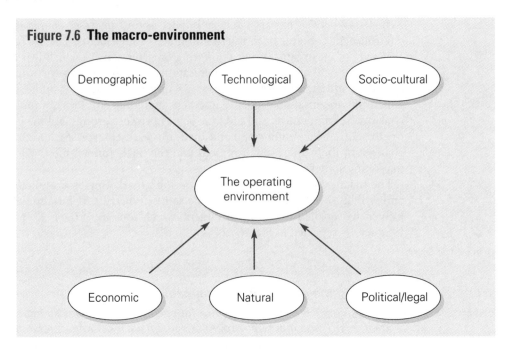

Figure 7.6 **The macro-environment**

It is marketing's responsibility to provide this type of information about the environment on a regular basis that makes it an *information intensive activity*. Information collected about the marketing environment is used to assist the marketing manager in taking decisions about products and the distribution outlets that consumers prefer to use. Other functional areas will also use marketing information. For example, manufacturing may use it to determine levels of production, or finance to estimate the capital required to purchase raw materials if marketing information suggests an increase in demand.

7.6 Marketing as an information intensive activity

To monitor and anticipate changes in the marketing environment marketing-oriented organisations use systematic procedures for collecting and analysing information about that environment. This is often called the marketing information system.

Marketing information systems

To keep in touch marketing managers need a **marketing information system** to provide accurate and up-to-date information. They need to have systematic processes to collect, analyse and distribute information about the marketing environment throughout the organisation. Cannon (1996) defines such a systems as:

> The organised arrangement of people, machines and procedures set up to ensure that all relevant and usable information required by marketing management reaches them at a time and in a form to help them with effective decision making.

Figure 7.7 details the typical component parts of such a system.

Figure 7.7 A marketing information system

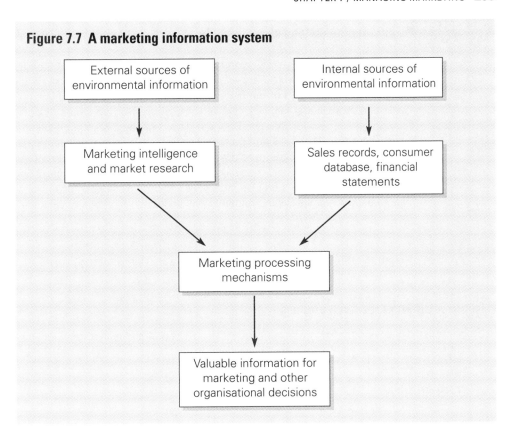

A marketing information system contains internal and external sources of data and mechanisms to analyse and interpret the data. As Chapter 18 explains, data is not the same as information. Data in itself has no meaning. A company may discover that in December 2000 59 per cent of a sample of people were aware of their product. In itself that has no value – but it does have value, becomes useful information, if it can be compared with similar data from earlier or later periods. Management may then see a trend, and be able to decide if it needs to act. Table 7.2 summarises the main sources of marketing information.

Table 7.2 Sources of marketing information

Source	Description and examples
Internal records	Size and regularity of orders, cost of each level of production, customer complaints, quality statistics
Marketing intelligence	Data on micro- and macro-environments. Usually secondary data from newspapers, trade associations and industry reports. Informal sources from staff or customers are also valuable guides to, for example, competitor plans
Market research	Involves five stages: 1 specifying information required (how many people with X income, living in place Y are aware of product Z?) 2 developing hypotheses (is awareness higher or lower in area B where the product has been advertised than in C?) 3 collecting quantitative or qualitative data to refute or confirm 4 analysing the data and 5 presenting the results

Information on food shopping habits

During the 1990s three UK supermarket chains introduced loyalty cards: Safeway's ABC Card, Sainsbury's Reward Card and Tesco's Club Card. The premise of such loyalty cards is that they keep a record of the frequency, value and type of food shopping bought by individuals and provide a small incentive of either money-off vouchers or additional products to reward customers for their store loyalty. They provide marketing departments with information about the address, income bracket, size of family, etc. of customers (gathered on the application form) and capture regular information about their buying patterns.

Such information has many uses. It can assist in sales forecasting and inventory management as well as provide information to inform marketing communications, in particular sales promotions. While Safeway has abandoned its loyalty card, Sainsbury and Tesco continue to use them.

Figure 7.8 shows the processes involved in a market research project.

Figure 7.8 Market research process

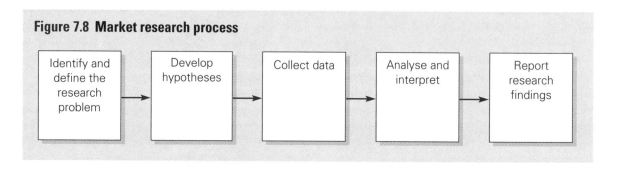

Q Case questions 7.2

- As part of the effort to understand how the opening night of the Dome impacted upon the public's perceptions of the Dome experience, what type of market research would you have recommended using?

7.7 Understanding the consumer – buyer behaviour

The marketing information system provides information on the marketing environment. The results of market research projects indicate solutions to precise marketing questions. Organisations with a marketing orientation also want to understand how customers decide to buy something.

ACTIVITY 7.5

Why did you buy that?

Pick a product that you buy regularly – such as a magazine, soft drink or chocolate bar. Think of the last time you bought that product and try to identify the factors which influenced your choice.

Research into buyer behaviour (Engel *et al.*, 1978; Howard and Sheth, 1969) has identified that consumers work through a series of decisions. Figure 7.9 presents a model of these decisions.

Awareness of unsatisfied need

Consumers become aware of a need that they want to satisfy in two ways. The first is self-discovery. When your stomach rumbles and your throat becomes dry these are physical signals that you are hungry and thirsty and need to satisfy these feelings. Consumers also become aware of an unsatisfied need by receiving some marketing communication from an organisation. For example, until 3M made you aware of 'Post-It pads' did you identify the need to have a small piece of paper on which you could write messages and stick to a surface?

Theories of human motivation described in Chapter 13 give marketing managers guidance on the needs of potential customers. They use this to ensure that the product or service is helping consumers satisfy a need – for status, recognition, a sense of achievement and so on.

Search for information

Aware of a need, consumers search for information that will help them decide which product to buy. Many sources provide this information – their experience is one powerful source, and that of family and friends is another. A third source of information is

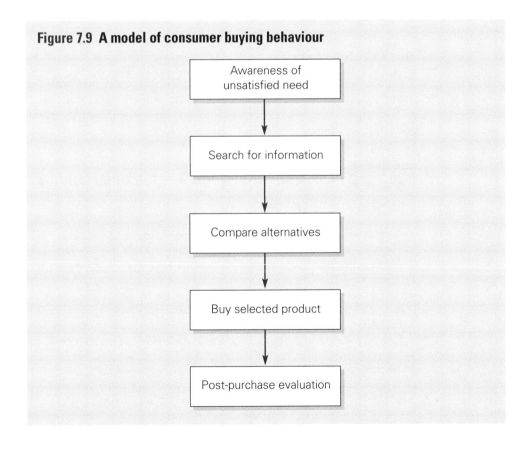

Figure 7.9 A model of consumer buying behaviour

Awareness of unsatisfied need

Search for information

Compare alternatives

Buy selected product

Post-purchase evaluation

from organisations providing products that may satisfy the need – by advertisements and other promotional activities. The source of the information provided at this stage in the buying process has great influence on the purchase decision. Passing on information about the poor service that a friend experienced at a restaurant will usually dissuade a potential customer.

ACTIVITY 7.6

Reflecting on consumer information

Select from one of the following expensive products: a DVD player, a mountain bike, a round-the-world air ticket. For your selected product describe the type of information you would want before deciding which brand to buy, and why.

The amount of time spent on this stage of the consumer buying process depends on the type of product that consumers believe will satisfy their identified need. Buying some products is more risky than others, and customers usually seek more information on them to reduce the risk. The degree of risk depends on factors such as expense, effect on self-image and knowledge of the product.

Compare alternatives

The more information a consumer has collected, the longer he or she will spend comparing different products against set criteria. For example, if a new television is to be purchased the main criteria may be brand name, surround sound, Internet access, wide screen and a reasonable price.

Buy selected product

Having compared the alternatives and decided which will best satisfy their need, the customer makes the purchase. Even at this stage of the process other factors may intrude – out-of-stock, a price-cut on one of the alternatives, or the advice of the salesperson may influence decisions.

CASE STUDY | **The Millennium Dome – the case continues – what kept people away?**

Although the Dome attracted 5.5 million paying visitors (and 1 million with free entry) management was disappointed that the number was so far below the target of 12 million. There was much speculation about why the expected number of 12 million visitors did not visit the Dome during 2000. Factors probably included the high degree of critical press coverage throughout the year, the decision not to allow car parking, and the strong competition from other new attractions in London. Another factor may have been ticketing strategy. The original intention was that all tickets would be sold in advance, using a variety of sales channels. In February 2000 the company began selling tickets at the gate for immediate entry, a move which probably contributed significantly to achieving the final number of visitors. Clearly the public valued being able to buy a ticket on the day of their visit.

Post-purchase evaluation

The final stage of the buying process is when the customer compares how they expected to feel after they had made the purchase with how they actually feel. If the expectation equates with reality then the consumer is more likely to buy in the future. At this stage the communications with consumers can affect future decisions. The quality of after-sales service might convince the car purchaser whether he or she made the right decision or not.

Internal and external influences shape the decisions consumers make at each stage. Table 7.3 describes these, and Figure 7.10 illustrates them.

Table 7.3 Internal and external influences on buying behaviour

Influence	Description	Example
Internal influences		
Perception	How people collect and interpret information	Affects reaction to advertisements – images, colours, words. See Chapter 14 on communication
Motivation	Internal forces that shape purchasing decisions to satisfy need	Marketers design products to meet needs. Insurance companies remind people of the dangers – which a policy will protect them against. See Chapter 13 on motivation
Attitudes	Opinions and points of view that people have of other people and institutions	Marketers design products to conform. Attitudes against testing cosmetics on animals led firms to stop this practice. Similarly for environmental issues
Learning	How people learn affects what they know about a product, and hence their purchasing decisions	Marketers help people to 'learn' to associate a product with unique colours or images – such as Coke with red and white, and Nike with its 'Swoosh' symbol
External influences		
Reference groups	Other people with whom the consumer identifies	Marketers establish the reference groups of their consumers, and allude to them in promotions – e.g. sponsoring athletes in return for product endorsement
Culture	The culture to which a consumer belongs affects their values and behaviour	Subcultures associated with punk and grunge influence buying behaviour – which marketers use in positioning products for those markets
Social class	People identify with a class based on income, education, where they live, etc.	Purchase decisions confirm and reaffirm the class to which people belong, or to which they aspire. Marketers use this information in promotional material

Figure 7.10 Influences on buyer behaviour

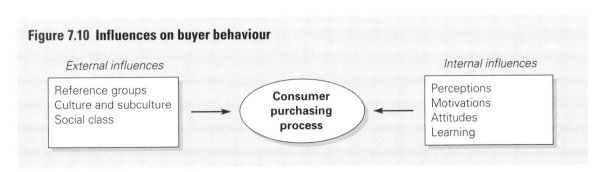

KEY IDEAS Needs, wants and demands

A marketing orientation implies that to satisfy the consumer it is necessary to identify the products for which there is *demand* and to understand the *needs* and *wants* which the product will satisfy for the consumer. Marketers distinguish between needs, wants and demands as follows:

- **Needs**: these are the *core* feelings that consumers 'need' to satisfy; for example, thirst is a physical need that needs to be satisfied.
- **Wants**: these are the preferences that individual consumers have about the ways in which they 'want' to satisfy the needs that they share in common with others. Consumers will

want different liquids to satisfy the thirst that makes them need a drink.

- **Demands**: the amount of money that individual consumers have determines the types of drink which they are able to buy. An individual who needs a drink may want to buy a Red Bull energy drink. The amount of money in their wallet determines that their demand (their actual purchasing power) is for an own-label soft drink.

To satisfy consumers marketers need to understand their needs, wants and demands. If they define demand too narrowly they may be unable to satisfy consumers.

7.8 Taking marketing decisions

The marketing manager now has information about the marketing environment, possible opportunities and threats, and the buying behaviour of consumers. The next stage is to decide which demands to satisfy and how to do this. The first decision is about market segmentation and targeting. The second is about choosing the correct mix of marketing tools to position products and make them attractive to consumers (Figure 7.11).

Segmenting markets

Organisations are increasingly using **market segmentation** strategies to satisfy the different needs that exist within the marketplace. Airlines offer consumers the choice of flying first class, business class or economy class. Universities offer degrees by full-time,

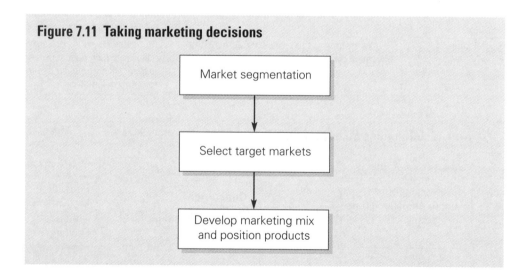

Figure 7.11 Taking marketing decisions

Market segmentation

↓

Select target markets

↓

Develop marketing mix and position products

part-time and distance learning study. Athletic shoe companies offer shoes specifically for running, aerobics, tennis and squash as well as 'cross' trainers for the needs of all these sports.

The logic behind segmentation strategies lies with the fact that consumers have different needs. The personal computer market consists of all the individuals who need a personal computer. Within that market people with similar needs can be grouped into distinct segments. Those who travel and need a laptop form one distinct segment; those who want to use a personal computer to help their children learn, and so need one with CD-ROM facilities, form another. Segmenting the personal computer market (and any other market) relies on identifying the variables that distinguish consumers with similar needs, as follows:

- *Demography* The easiest way to segment a consumer market is by using demographic variables such as age, gender and education level. Magazine companies use gender and age variables to ensure that within their portfolio they have magazine titles that will suit the needs of females as well as males and those of different ages.
- *Geography* This segmentation variable is commonly used by organisations competing in a global market. By segmenting markets on the basis of country, organisations such as McDonald's have been able to 'think global but act local'. This means that, while maintaining uniform global standards of service and hygiene, the company competes differently in each country by varying the menu available to suit local tastes.
- *Socioeconomic* Segmentation on the basis of socioeconomic variables – such as income, social class and lifestyle. Segmentation on the basis of lifestyle includes identifying groups of consumers who share similar values about the ways in which they wish to live their lives.

When segmenting consumer markets marketers commonly use a mixture of these variables to provide an accurate profile of distinct groups within a market. The magazine *Marie-Claire,* for example, uses age, gender, education, lifestyle and social class to attract a readership of educated, independently minded women between the ages of 25 and 35, in income brackets ABC1.

ACTIVITY 7.7

Identifying market segments

What market segments have the following identified: easyJet, Amazon.com, British Midland, Scream bars, Costa coffee houses, Borders book stores?

What benefits do you think their segmentation strategies offer?

Having segmented a market using the variables described above, marketers have to decide which of those segments to select as **target markets** – those it decides shall be the focus for its activities. Marketing managers usually select target markets that meet the following three criteria:

- contain demands that the resources of the organisation can satisfy;
- are large enough to provide a financial return;
- have growth potential.

Ultimately, segments selected as target markets are those that offer the greatest potential for achieving management goals.

Q **Case questions 7.3**

● What segmentation criteria would you have recommended the Dome using to target the visitors it was seeking to attract?

7.9 Using the marketing mix

The final decision facing the marketing manager is to select the mixture of price, **product**, promotion and place. This is known as the **marketing mix**. It positions products in the market in a way that makes them attractive to the target consumers. The **position** that a product has within a market reflects consumer opinions of that product and the comparisons that they make between it and competing products. The aim is to position products *within the minds of consumers* as more attractive, and better able to satisfy their demands, than competing products. To position products effectively the marketing manager is responsible for the development of a co-ordinated marketing mix. Kotler *et al.* (1996) define an organisation's marketing mix as 'a set of tools that work together to affect the marketplace'. The marketing mix consists of product, price, promotion and place.

Marketing mix – product

Decisions about which products to develop will establish the range of goods and services an organisation offers. Some are obviously physical products or intangible personal services. Most are a mixture of the two.

MANAGEMENT IN PRACTICE **Swatch**

The story of the development and introduction of Swatch is a classic example of marketing techniques being used by a traditional industry to launch a new product. Faced with competition from low cost producers SMH, an old established Swiss watchmaker (brands included Longines and Omega) urgently needed a new product line. Its engineers successfully developed a radically new product that was much cheaper to make than traditional models. The company

> worked closely with advertising agencies in the United States on product positioning and advertising strategy. In addition to the name 'Swatch', a snappy contraction of 'Swiss' and 'watch', this research generated the idea of downplaying the product's practical benefits and positioning it as a 'fashion accessory that happens to tell the time'. Swatch would be a second or third watch used to adapt to different situations without replacing the traditional 'status symbol' watch.

By 1996 it had sold over 200 million units and was the most successful wristwatch of all time. Its parent company, SMH, is the largest and most dynamic watch company in the world.

Source: Based on 'Swatch', Case No. 589-005-1, INSEAD-Cedep, Fontainebleau, and the Swatch web page at http://www.swatch.com

The extent to which goods are tangible or intangible affects how marketing staff deal with them. Services present marketing with particular challenges because of their characteristics. These include perishability, intangibility, heterogeneity and inseparability.

Perishability

This refers to the fact that services cannot be held in stock for even the shortest amount of time. If a plane flies with some empty seats these cannot be stored for another flight – empty seats are permanently lost sales.

Intangibility

This aspect of services presents the marketing manager with the greatest challenge. Services cannot usually be viewed, touched, tried on or sampled before their purchase. The marketing manager has to devise some way for consumers to try out services before buying them. One way is to produce leaflets with attractive information on the benefits of the service. The financial services industry, for example, relies on the use of information packs to inform consumers of the features and benefits of such products as mortgages, insurance policies and bank accounts. Consumers also have little information on which to assess the product benefits relative to their demands. A common source of product information on services is that which reference groups provide. For example, in moving to a new town, the selection of a new doctor, dentist, hairdresser or sports club is commonly influenced by the information provided by reference groups. Aware of this, organisations such as health clubs encourage existing members to invite friends and family to their fitness clubs for trial memberships.

Heterogeneity and inseparability

These terms reflect the fact that services are labour intensive. They rely on the skills, competences and experiences of the people who provide them, and this creates particular challenges for the marketing manager. It is inevitable that service providers and consumers will meet, for some amount of time. When attending a doctor's appointment, for example, it is necessary to meet with the doctor to discuss your health. Organisations operating through branch systems such as banks or fast-food restaurants have to overcome the hazards of inseparability and heterogeneity to ensure consistent delivery standards. Both service providers and consumers have personalities, opinions and values that make them unique. This can create differences in the levels of service and standards that consumers experience when buying services. Organisations such as Pizza Hut and UCI cinemas try to minimise differences by providing staff with company uniforms, decorating premises in a similar way and setting firm guidelines for the way staff deliver the service.

Consumer products (both goods and services) can by classified as convenience, shopping, speciality or unsought products. Each poses a different marketing challenge, which Table 7.4 summarises.

In managing the organisation's product decisions marketing managers use a concept called the **product life cycle** (Figure 7.12). The central assumption upon which the product lifecycle rests is that all products have a limited life. Depending on the stage reached by a product in its life cycle, a known set of competitive and consumer conditions exists that helps the marketing manager to specify the marketing activities required at that stage. Mapping the sales and profit generated, the product life cycle suggests that products pass through the stages of introduction, growth, maturity and decline.

Table 7.4 Market challenges by type of product

Type of product	Examples	Marketing challenge
Convenience	Regular purchases, low price – bread, milk, magazines	Widely available, and easy to switch brands. Managers counter this by heavy advertising or distinct packaging of the brand
Shopping	Relatively expensive, infrequent purchase – washing machines, televisions, clothes	Brand name, product features, design and price are important and will spend time searching for best mix. Managers spend heavily on advertising and on training sales staff
Speciality	Less frequent, often luxury purchases – cars, diamond rings, houses	Consumers need much information. Sales staff vital to a sale – management invest heavily in them, and in protecting image of product by restricting outlets. Also focused advertising and distinctive packaging
Unsought	Consumers need to buy – but don't get much pleasure from – insurance, a new car exhaust pipe	Managers need to make customers aware that they supply this need, and distinct product features

Figure 7.12 The product life cycle

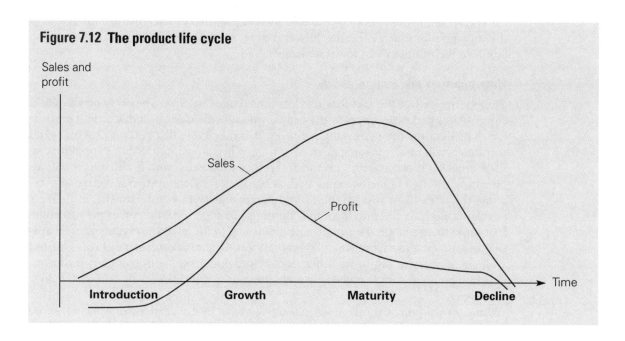

Introduction

This is the stage at which products enter the marketplace. Profits are negative because of the investment made in researching and developing the product. There are few consumers aware of and therefore interested in buying the product and few organisations involved in producing and distributing it. The aim of the marketing manager at this stage is to invest in marketing communication and make as many potential consumers as possible aware of the product's entry into the marketplace.

Growth

At this stage consumers have become aware of and started buying the product. It is during this stage that sales rise most quickly and profits peak. As people buy the product more consumers become aware of it and the high profit levels attract new competitors into the industry. The aim of the marketing manager at this stage is to fight off existing competitors and new entrants. This can be done by encouraging consumer loyalty and distributing the product as widely as is demanded by consumers.

Maturity

With profits peaking during the growth stage, profit and sales start to plateau and then decline towards the end of this stage. By this stage in a product's life cycle many consumers are aware of and have bought the product and there are many organisations competing for a decreasing amount of consumer demand for the product. The aim of the marketing manager is to fight competition by reducing the price of the product or differentiating it by, for example, altering its packaging and design. At this stage product differentiation can successfully reposition products to an earlier stage in their life cycle. It is also important that the marketing manager begins to consider ideas for replacement products and to select ideas for research and development.

Decline

There is now little consumer demand and all competing organisations are considering removing the product from the marketplace. In deciding when to remove products the marketing manager must assess the extent to which residual consumer demand exists in order to determine whether to remove the product at once or to phase it out gradually. It is important that, by this stage, the marketing manager has a new product ready to enter the marketplace and replace the product that is being removed.

An awareness of the stage at which a product is at in its life cycle can assist the marketing manager in deciding upon the course of marketing action to take. For example, aware that a product is at the maturity stage, the marketing manager might decide to reposition the product by changing the packaging or image created by the branding of the product. Consider the repositioning of Lucozade. Traditionally marketed as a health drink, product modifications together with new packaging and celebrity endorsement have been successful in repositioning Lucozade as a sports drink.

ACTIVITY 7.8

Using the product life cycle

State the stage that you believe each of the following products to be in and comment on how long, in years, you believe their life cycle to be: a drawing pin, mini-disks, umbrellas.

Activity 7.8 addresses two of the major criticisms of the product life cycle: that all products have a limited life and that all products follow each of the four stages of introduction, growth, maturity and decline. Clearly some products do not have a limited lifespan and other products can be repositioned to an earlier stage. Despite these criticisms, the product life cycle offers the marketing manager a useful aid to many product decisions.

Marketing mix – price

Price is the value placed upon the goods, services and ideas that are exchanged between organisations and consumers. For most products price is always measured with money, though consumers do not identify all the purchases they make as having a 'price'. The price, for example, of accessing BBC television programmes is the cost of a television license, and the price of street lighting and cleaning is the community charge that individual households are responsible for paying. A visit to the great public parks in Paris, Copenhagen and other European cities is free – but paid for by local taxpayers. In selecting the price of a product that will position it competitively within the minds of consumers, the marketing manager must be aware of the image which consumers have of the product. Consumers have price ranges that they expect to pay for certain types of product. In particular, for safety products, products for children, those associated with health or connected to their self-image, consumers have a minimum price they expect to pay. If the price is below this consumers will not purchase the product because they perceive such products as being of inferior quality or lower value.

Marketing managers need to be aware of the psychological effects that different prices have on consumer perceptions. They must also ensure that the price charged covers the costs of producing, distributing and promoting products. It must not only provide the organisation with an acceptable profit but also offer an acceptable margin to distributors and retailers.

Marketing mix – promotion

Properly referred to as marketing communications, this part of the marketing mix involves taking decisions about the type and amount of information that will encourage consumers to buy a product or, in the case of health promotion, change their attitudes and behaviours in some way. Decisions are also needed on how to present such information and where it should appear. Organisations can communicate with their target markets in many ways. Packaging can provide information, a company logo may transmit a particular message, and sponsoring a football team or a concert indicates an organisation's values and attitudes. The most common ways, however, of communicating with consumers for the purposes of encouraging them to buy products include advertising, sales promotion, personal selling and publicity.

Advertising is the form of communication commonly selected when an organisation wishes to transmit a message to a large audience. It is an impersonal form of communication as it does not involve direct communication between an organisation and a potential consumer. Advertising is effective in creating awareness of a good, service or idea but is less effective in persuading consumers to buy. It is the pervasive and impersonal characteristics of advertising that makes it a cost-effective method of communicating with potential consumers in a mass market.

Organisations typically use *sales promotions* to encourage consumers who are considering a product to take the next step and buy it. The fast-food industry provides good examples of sales promotion. Both McDonald's and Burger King frequently offer special promotions to encourage consumers to buy their brand. The unique characteristic of sales promotion is that it offers potential consumers an incentive to make a purchase within a certain time. Companies also use promotions to encourage repeat buys and to encourage consumers to try out new products of which advertising has made them aware.

Marketing departments use *personal selling* when consumers require first-hand information and advice before making a purchase. It is particularly useful for infrequently purchased products such as DVD players and cars. Personal selling is a direct transfer of product information to potential consumers. This form of communication has the advantage of being able to respond to any questions that consumers might have and to explain complicated or technical product features. To be effective, however, personal selling requires that managers train salespeople properly, especially on specific product features. The cost and characteristics of personal selling make it useful for more expensive products and for products that are technically sophisticated or difficult to understand.

Publicity is effective in supporting a positive image of the organisation and its use is not particular to any specific stage in consumers' buying decisions. Publicity involves building good working relationships with the media and using them to promote a positive image of the organisation. The aim is to ensure that positive incidents in which the media might have an interest, such as launching a new product, are fully reported, and that negative ones do as little damage as possible.

Marketing mix – place

Place refers to decisions about the ways in which products can be most effectively distributed to the final consumer. Decisions about marketing channels concentrate on whether the distribution of products should be owned and organised by the organisation producing products or whether products should be distributed by external parties. These decisions are determined by the products involved and the costs of distribution. If the quality of a product is vital to its positioning in the marketplace and it is important that the organisation maintains some control over the distribution of its products, organisations may decide to manage the distribution of their products in-house. Clearly the distribution of a product must be consistent with the image that consumers have of the product and the position that consumers regard it as holding in the marketplace, relative to competing products.

MANAGEMENT IN PRACTICE **Protecting the brand**

Paul Mitchell hair products maintain the quality image which consumers attach to the Paul Mitchell name by detailing on the product packaging that the authenticity of the product cannot be guaranteed unless it is purchased from an outlet approved by Paul Mitchell. Similarly brands such as Calvin Klein, Nike and Clarins have expressed concerns about the distribution of their products through such stores as Tesco and Superdrug, which they believe detract from rather than add to the value of their branded products.

A second consideration is the cost of using distributors. Having identified the price at which consumers demand to buy particular products, the costs involved in distributing products in-house relative to externally must be considered. So consumer-products companies distribute goods through retailers.

Related to this a third decision is whether to make the purchase of products available electronically through the Internet. This decision has been driven by advances in electronic technology and has been embraced by organisations such as amazon.com and lastminute.com. Such organisations have decided to use electronic channels of distribution as a differentiation tool. For most organisations the availability of their products electronically is regarded as a complementary distribution channel that is used, for example, to widen access to their products to geographically remote markets.

In describing the component parts of the marketing mix the interrelated nature of decisions about product, price, promotion and place has been mentioned. In developing a mix that will place products competitively within the minds of consumers the marketing manager must be aware that changes in one area will create changes in other areas. For example, if the price of a product is reduced, consumer perceptions of the product might change. Creating an effective marketing mix with which to position products relies upon integration and co-ordination of each tool used to position products.

MANAGEMENT IN PRACTICE   **Maintaining consistency**

In positioning their products as value for money, organisations such as easyJet and Aldi (a German retailer) ensure that each part of the marketing mix supports and reinforces this image. This means that products must not be highly differentiated, prices should be low, promotion should stress the low price and value for money. The stores in which products are distributed should be simple in design. This avoids sending a message that the costs of creating a smart place in which to buy products will be reflected in the prices.

7.10 A critical perspective on marketing

The adoption of a marketing orientation can clearly bring significant benefits to the commercial or other success of organisations. Commentators have also been critical of marketing. It has been argued that marketing manipulates consumer choices and encourages materialism and over-consumption. In 1996 several drinks companies introduced products that were known as Alcopops. These were fruit-flavoured carbonated drinks that taste like soft drinks but contain alcohol equivalent to a 330 ml bottle of beer. This sparked a lively debate over marketing's role in society. The manufacturers argued that they were responding to the tastes of adults who enjoy alcohol but prefer the flavour of soft rather than alcoholic drinks. Rather than encouraging youths and children to buy these drinks, they had widened the choice of alcoholic drinks available to those over the legal age. The charity Alcohol Concern argued that the fruity flavour of such drinks and the bright colours used in their packaging serve to manipulate the under-age drinker into making unwanted or possibly harmful purchases.

The debate on marketing's role within society will continue to run. Those concerned with environmental and public health issues will criticise organisations that they perceive to be damaging the environment or knowingly causing harm to people's health. Important, however, to this discussion is the consideration of whether organisations embracing the marketing orientation are criticised on the grounds of their morality or on the ethics of their approach to business. While the morality of an organisation in terms of its values, attitudes and belief systems can be difficult to define and therefore criticise or otherwise, the degree to which an organisation is ethical in its approach to the marketplace is more readily measured. The adoption of a marketing orientation, it can be argued, is not an issue of morality and, as long as it is used for its intended purposes of informing consumers and widening their choice, should not be regarded as an ethical consideration either. The adoption of a marketing orientation does not advocate that consumers should be 'tricked' into making purchases. Where, for example, incidences of product misinformation occur and it is clear that an organisation has engaged in unethical practices, the marketing orientation would advocate that a focus on consumer satisfaction has not been adhered to. Consequently marketing thinkers would argue that such an organisation had failed to conduct its activities under the guidance of a marketing orientation. Nevertheless it is a fact that some people use marketing concepts to sell pornography, traffick drugs and invade privacy.

ACTIVITY 7.9

Revising your definition

- *Having completed this chapter, how would you define marketing?*
- *Compare this definition with the one that you were asked to make in Activity 7.1 and comment on any changes.*

7.11 Summary

The chapter began by showing that marketing is much more than a promotional gimmick. A firm with a genuine consumer-centred marketing orientation focuses all activities on meeting consumer needs. It is organised with that in mind. To meet consumer needs effectively, especially in rapidly changing markets, means that marketing is inevitably an information-intensive activity. Greater understanding of consumers enables a company to segment the market in various ways, and to target certain of those segments in the hope of meeting their distinctive needs. Whether it can do so satisfactorily depends on its internal capabilities and the way management organises these. The chapter then outlined the components of the marketing mix – product, price, promotion and place – that a company can use to relate to consumers.

Content

Marketing represents an attempt by management to recognise explicitly the needs and interests of customers and other stakeholders in an organisation's environment. It does so in the belief that meeting these needs is likely to add more value to the organisation's activities than ignoring them. It places particular emphasis on keeping in touch with external (micro and macro) developments that affect customers' needs and the organisation's objectives. Adopting a marketing orientation wholeheartedly implies making the customer the centre of attention and is distinct from product, production and sales philosophies. It becomes a guiding orientation for the whole organisation, with all committed to meeting customer demands and thus meeting organisational objectives. Implementing the approach involves the increasingly precise targeting of defined segments of the whole market. It also implies restructuring to ensure that the whole organisation focuses on the customer and planning organisation-wide information systems to deal with marketing data.

Understanding buyer behaviour draws on motivational theories described in Chapter 13. Management uses this knowledge to design products that aim to satisfy one or more human need. This is believed to help generate consumer commitment to buy a product.

Process

The primacy of marketing advocated by its professionals needs to be seen in the light of the needs of other professional groups. Their relative status and position may be threatened by the primacy of the marketing group in organisations embracing the marketing emphasis. Other departments are expected to support and be committed to the central position of marketing. A marketing orientation implies that marketing is active in major business decisions to ensure that management hears a consumer perspective. This implies creating mechanisms for involving the relevant players.

A major element in marketing is the management of communications. They need to ensure that information about external developments and customer needs is gathered, processed and transferred around the organisation. They also require various external means of communication to inform consumers about the product and to influence them to buy it.

Control

If management wishes a marketing orientation to pervade the organisation, all activities are focused on meeting customer needs. This implies that activity is monitored and controlled to ensure that work is done in a way which meets their needs – and also that much effort is put into monitoring and controlling customer opinions and satisfaction levels. Only in that way can management be confident that decisions on segmenting and targeting the market, and the marketing mix that is delivered, have the intended effects on profitability.

Management at the Millennium Dome appears to have suffered from a lack of clear understanding about its target market, or what kind of marketing mix would satisfy it. One of its difficulties was that, being open for only a year, there was little chance to alter the major aspects of the product in the light of visitor comments (or to take account of the larger number who did not visit). Nor did the organisation have time to create a structure that ensured a marketing focus until well into the year, when the original management was changed. By then it increasingly appeared to be adopting a sales orientation – doing whatever it could to sell the product it had, rather than having the luxury of redesigning it into something the customers may have welcomed. It illustrates the point with which the chapter began, that marketing is more about organisation structures than it is about promotional gimmicks.

Q PART CASE QUESTIONS

- To what extent has Virgin implemented a marketing orientation?
- Visit the website (Virgin.com) and comment on how it has used this to support its marketing activities.
- Where do Richard Branson's publicity stunts fit into the company's marketing strategy?

7.12 Review questions

1 What advantages does the marketing orientation have over each of the following organisational philosophies: production, product and sales?

2 Outline the benefits that the marketing orientation can offer each of the following organisations: a global brand, a university, a charity, a small firm and a high street retailer.

3 What are the key responsibilities of the marketing manager?

4 In what way is an organisation's micro-environment different from its macro-environment? Comment on those areas of the following organisations' marketing environment that have the greatest impact upon their marketing activities: LivingWell health clubs, McDonald's, your local library.

5 Outline various sources of marketing information and compare and contrast alternative ways of collecting and analysing information about an organisation's market environment.

6 Describe the process of buying decisions involved and identify the factors that might influence the purchase of: a new car, a soft drink, a present for a friend's 30th birthday, a new outfit for work.

7 What are the advantages of market segmentation and what are the variables upon which consumer markets are commonly segmented?

8 How are target markets identified and what is meant by product positioning?

9 What position does each of the following have in the marketplace and what mix of marketing tools has each used to achieve this position? Carrefour, Tango soft drinks, Irn-Bru, Save the Children Fund, Surf washing powder.

Further reading

Jobber, D. (2001), *Principles and Practices of Marketing* (3rd edn), McGraw-Hill, London.

Kotler, P. and Armstrong, G. (1997), *Marketing: An introduction* (4th edn), Prentice Hall International, Hemel Hempstead.

Both texts provide detailed introductions to marketing, the former in particular having a strong European focus.

Zeithaml, V.A. and Bitner, M.J. (2000), *Services Marketing: Integrating customer focus across the firm*, Irwin/McGraw-Hill, Boston, MA. This is recommended to students wishing to read more about services marketing.

Baker, M. (1991), *The Marketing Book*, Butterworth/Heinemann, London.

Contains an excellent selection of classic marketing articles.

Annotated links, questions and resources can be found on
www.booksites.net/boddy

Access the Internet for company information

To find out how each of the following organisations have responded to the opportunities that have been made available to them by the Internet, log on to the World Wide Web and locate their web pages: Nike, lastminute.com, The Body Shop, Warner Brothers cinema.

Which pages did you think were the best? The worst? Why did you reach that conclusion?

ORGANISING

Introduction

Part Four examines how management creates the structure within which people work. Alongside planning the direction of the business, managers need to consider how they will achieve the direction chosen. A fundamental component of that is the form of the organisation within which people work. This is a highly uncertain area of management as there are conflicting views about the kind of structure to have and how much influence structure has on performance.

Chapter 8 describes the main elements of organisation structure and the contrasting forms they take. It also looks at the related idea of organisational culture – a less tangible but equally influential factor in organisational performance. Chapter 9 deals with one aspect of an organisation's structure: its human resource management policies. These are intended to ensure that employees work towards organisational objectives.

Management wants a structure that will best serve organisational goals. The main balance to strike is between tightly structured, formal arrangements, and looser ones that leave more scope for individual initiative. Chapter 10 examines these issues and describes some newer forms of organisation that developments in information technology make possible. Chapter 11 looks at some of the practical issues that management faces in implementing change. The Part Case is an account of structure and change at The Royal Bank of Scotland.

PART CASE   The Royal Bank of Scotland

The Royal Bank of Scotland Group, founded in 1727, is one of Europe's leading financial services groups. During the economic recession of the early 1990s the bank was in trouble. It had had to make heavy provisions for bad debts and was losing customers to the new building society banks. The share price of just over £1 in 1992 reflected investors' critical view of recent performance. The cost:income ratio (a key measure of bank performance) was over 70 per cent.

A little over five years later the share price had risen to over £10. Observers regarded The Royal as one of the most innovative and best performing banks in the United Kingdom. By 2001 it had (by market capitalisation) become the UK's seventh largest company, the second largest bank in the United Kingdom and in Europe, and it ranks seventh in the world. In March of the previous year it completed the acquisition of NatWest in a £21 billion deal that was the largest takeover in British banking history. The enlarged Royal Bank of Scotland Group has more than 15 million customers, more than 2,200 UK branches and total assets at 31 December 2000 of £320 billion. The Group employs over 88,000 staff. The enlarged group increased its profit by 31 per cent to £4,401 million in the year to 31 December 2000. Between 31 March 2000 and 31 March 2001 it had the best performing UK shares in the FTSE100 Index with a 96 per cent increase during that year.

What happened to bring about this change? Much of the credit is due to a programme of major change that management in the Retail Banking Division implemented between 1992 and 1997. They called it Project Columbus, after the Genoese explorer who set sail for unknown territory exactly 500 years earlier. They created Project Columbus to drive a series of radical changes throughout the retail division, including:

- segmenting customers into three new streams – retail, commercial and corporate;
- new management, roles and organisation structures;
- new human resource policies to base appointment and promotion on achievement and ability;

- each branch to have ready access to specialist centres and knowledge without having to house all the traditional back-office functions;
- over £100 million spent on new information systems to improve efficiency and customer service.

Such a range of initiatives, all starting around the same time and involving a huge investment of resources, required a structure of guidance and control above and beyond pure project management. Management believed that a Programme Management approach would ensure that individual projects worked together towards the overall aim – to Build the Best Retail Bank in Britain by 1997.

Project Columbus' simple mission statement was clear, and repeated in posters and mousemats throughout the Programme Offices. The phrase was used in countless proposal documents and stated regularly in project meetings – 'If we want to Build the Best Bank in Britain, then our staff have to have the best system in the market.' This created a shared vision amongst the many project teams. It helped to focus disparate staff on a common goal. No specific measures were ever stated for what 'Best' meant, but it gave staff something to strive for, and to guide them in their day-to-day activities.

The complex project required imaginative change management techniques, of which these are two examples:

Black Box As a high profile project, the bank's board was demanding constant reassurance of progress and control. Realising the need for rapid, accurate updates on the various projects, the Columbus Programme Office team devised a method of gathering regular information from each project area against a prior-agreed set of measures. They developed a system – nicknamed the 'Black Box' – for collating these reports and producing an overview of the current situation. The reports were in a simple, easy-to-understand format that focused on exceptions. These reports kept people adequately informed and 'surprises' were kept to a minimum. It helped the project to retain the support of the board and other vital stakeholders within and beyond the Bank.

Quick Wins These included:

(a) reducing the cost of cash stocks in branches through more frequent movements;
(b) removing charges which cost more to administer than they earned;
(c) adding charges for services whose costs were not covered;
(d) identifying and stopping inefficient work processes.

In an interview the Programme Director discussed Quick Wins:

'Like every other area of the Bank, Columbus has been set tough commercial targets. It must deliver radical improvements in the performance of Branch Banking Division (BBD) while being self-financing. The cost of the project has to be met from measurable improvements in BBD's bottom line. Quick Wins are initiatives that can be introduced rapidly and require limited investment in technology, people or buildings. Next year the Quick Wins programme is intended to meet the cost of Columbus and also to deliver benefits worth over £30 million. In fact over 60 per cent of the benefits from Quick Wins will come from increased revenue rather than cost reduction.'

The Bank has continued to evolve since the Columbus project, as external forces continue to drive it to change. Deregulation of financial services continues to encourage new players to enter the market, which is increasingly international. The capital markets are also demanding better returns on their shareholdings in banks. They have put pressures on all banks to reduce costs. This was a big part of Project Columbus and continues to drive change today – the cost:income ratio is now 50 per cent. It continues to segment the retail market by a lifecycle approach, namely that customers have different needs at different stages of life suggested as follows:

- Rainbow Savings Accounts for children (piggy banks);
- youth accounts for early teens ('Cool' image, CDs, Gameboys, Playstations);
- student accounts (low cost overdraft, drinks vouchers);
- early professionals, first job (cheque books, bank cards, car loans);
- first-time home owners (low-start mortgages)
- young married couples (home improvement loans, pensions, life assurance);
- parents of young children (child investment accounts, mortgage breaks);
- parents of older children (investment funds, pension checks, car loans);
- retirees (investments);
- older (advice on pensions and investment).

On the business side, the segmentation is by size of turnover – small trader (treated as retail customer) up to 100,000; up to £1 million; £1m–£5m; and over £5m. Structure reflects this, with Retail (personal and small trader customers); Commercial (up to £5 million) and Corporate (over £5 million). These divisions operate separately.

There have also been changes in centralisation. Initially banks operated as decentralised operations, as branch managers had considerable autonomy. With the first wave of IT in the 1960s many functions were centralised. Now the balance may be switching again, as customers complain they cannot get decisions from remote regional offices. Control brings more centralised decisions over products, margins, risk management, etc. Against that the customer relationship managers press for more local flexibility to override the system.

The Manufacturing Division, which deals with routine functions such as clearing cheques, account opening and various other paper processes, is a very mechanistic structure. The bank created the Manufacturing Division by transferring most administrative tasks from the branches to a central location. To select staff for the new division from those working in the branches they used psychometric tests to draw out those more comfortable with processes and systems. Those who were more interested in people remained in the branches.

The branches themselves had been mechanistic, with tellers having strictly defined tasks. Now the branches are much more organic, with tellers trying to interest customers in other products, and the physical layout is more open. The bank tries to be organic at the customer-facing areas, with customer relationship managers trying to improve service quality.

The bank was quick to exploit the opportunities that new technology offers. It was an early innovator when it launched Direct Line as one of the first examples of delivering financial services by telephone, and now one of the United Kingdom's largest private motor insurers. It has launched an online bank (www.rbsdigital.com), complementing the services offered by the traditional bank.

The formal structure in 2001 was that it had eight 'customer-facing' divisions:

- retail (Royal Bank of Scotland and NatWest);
- wealth management;
- retail direct;
- corporate banking and financial markets;
- Direct Line;
- Ulster Bank;
- Citizens Bank (United States)

These were supported by six Group divisions – Manufacturing, Legal, Strategy, Finance Risk and Internal Audit, Communication and Human Resources.

Amongst its alliances it includes a strategic alliance with BSCH of Spain, which provides scope to develop financial service activities across Europe. It also has a joint venture with Tesco – Tesco Personal Finance, one of the main supermarket banking brands in the United Kingdom.

Q PART CASE QUESTIONS

- What are the performance expectations that The Royal Bank of Scotland has to meet?
- What are the main features of the structure that it has in 2001?
- What management practices did it use to help manage the change?
- In what ways are its present policies helping to lay foundations for future moves?

CHAPTER 8

Organisation structure and culture

AIM *To introduce terms and practices that describe organisational structures and cultures.*

OBJECTIVES

By the end of your work on this chapter you should be able to outline the concepts below in your own terms and:

1 Outline why structure influences performance

2 Illustrate the links between the elements of an organisation

3 Describe five alternative forms of organisation structure

4 Describe the advantages and disadvantages of functional, divisional and matrix forms

5 Describe and illustrate the main forms of co-ordination

6 Compare unit or organisational structures using ideas from the chapter

7 Describe the main dimensions of organisational culture

8 Give examples of Quinn's or Handy's types of organisational culture

Asea Brown Boveri – a global business

ABB was formed in 1987 by the merger of two established companies to create a powerful world business in the market for electrical systems and equipment. It has continued to expand by internal growth and by acquiring other companies: its share price had increased steadily since the merger. In 2001 it employed about 160,000 people in 140 countries. Europe accounts for about 60 per cent of revenues, with a growing presence in eastern Europe where there is a huge capital investment programme.

The company has no geographical centre, and was seen by a former chairman, Percy Barnevik, as a federation of national companies with a global co-ordination centre. The head-quarters are in Zurich, but only 100 professionals work there. The company reports financial results in US dollars, and their official language is English.

The organising logic of ABB until 1998

Barnevik had developed a clear principle on which to organise this diverse global business. He chaired the 12-member executive committee that met every three weeks to plan and monitor ABB's global strategy and performance. Several members were based outside Zurich, and their meetings were held around the world.

The business was organised as a matrix structure. Along one dimension activities were organised into broad product groups – power generation; power transmission and distribution; and industrial and building systems. Each was the responsibility of one member of the executive committee. For example the industry group, which sold components and software to automate industrial processes, had five business areas, including metallurgy, drives and process engineering. The senior managers of these groups were expected to decide on product strategy and performance targets irrespective of national borders.

On the second dimension were three regions, each again the responsibility of one member of the executive committee. The traditionally organised national companies within each region were expected to serve their respective markets as well as they could. This system was intended to 'facilitate integrated systems thinking and to encourage teamwork'. However, there were drawbacks, as managers of a local business had two bosses, and strategic decisions often resulted in lengthy political debate.

The change in 1998

In 1998 Goran Lindahl took over as chief executive and made radical changes to the structure. He divided the organisation into eight core businesses, all of which will be directly represented on the new executive board. He also eliminated the regional matrix management structure, cutting 100 jobs. Mr Lindahl described the change as 'an aggressive move aimed at greater speed and efficiency by further focusing and flattening the organisation'. It would provide clear lines of leadership for the company's core businesses, though ABB would remain decentralised. Mr Lindahl said ABB 'was more than a power engineering company. By splitting the group into eight divisions, it should help focus investor attention on its role as a world leader in fast-growing businesses such as automation.'

Source: Based on Taylor (1991); *Financial Times*, 12 August 1998; and other sources.

Q Case questions

- What might be the advantages and disadvantages of the matrix structure that ABB used for many years?
- What issues may have prompted the new CEO to change the structure?

8.1 Introduction

This chapter introduces the following ideas:

- Structure
- Formal structure
- Informal structure
- Division of tasks – vertical and horizontal
- Horizontal specialisation
- Centralisation and decentralisation
- Functional, product, geographical and matrix structures
- Co-ordination of tasks
- Organisation chart
- Span of control
- Scalar chain
- Power culture
- Role culture
- Task culture
- Person culture

In 2000 the directors of ABB were concerned about the performance of the business. They have not met shareholder expectations, and the share price had fallen sharply. They wondered if part of the trouble lay with the structure of the organisation – and whether a change would improve matters. Operating around the world in a wide variety of businesses meant that the search for the right structure was continual. The structure would always represent a balance between the need for some degree of central oversight and control of the group to ensure returns to shareholders, and the need to encourage creativity in the widely different operating businesses.

All companies face this problem of how best to organise the business to suit changing conditions, new strategies or new products. In mid-2001 senior management at BT were under similar pressure to respond to two years of poor performance. The board responded by dividing the company into five separate business areas, with clearer reporting relationships to the board. David James, chairman of the New Millennium Experience Company, attributed many of the problems that the Dome experienced to a confused reporting structure. Nokia has announced the move of its manufacturing to SCI Systems in the United States – another form of structural change.

When an owner-manager is running a business he or she decides what tasks are to be done and co-ordinates them. If the enterprise grows the need to create some form of structure usually becomes apparent. The entrepreneur divides the overall task between people, even if the division is flexible and informal. They can also co-ordinate their activities informally as people can easily communicate directly with each other. As the business grows new structural questions arise. Expansion brings the possibility of confusion and misunderstanding, with more people, separate units and less direct contact. Staff need to understand their responsibilities, and structures clarify what others expect.

As they create such structures managers decide how to deploy the resources of the organisation to achieve their objectives. They decide how to divide the whole organisation into distinct units of activity, establish reporting relationships and ensure co-ordination between the units. What they decide reflects their theory about the best arrangement to support the current strategy.

Figure 8.1 Structural and cultural elements of organisations

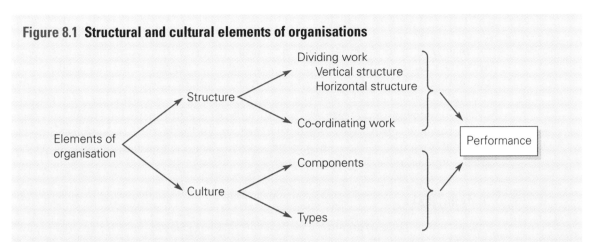

This chapter outlines the structural issues that managers in all organisations need to resolve, and which Figure 8.1 illustrates. Managers create a formal structure when they decide how to divide the work of the organisation. They create a vertical structure that shows the reporting relationships throughout the organisation, and a horizontal structure as they allocate work to departments. Having divided work they need to decide how best to co-ordinate the parts so that they work together. Finally the chapter introduces ideas about the components and types of organisational culture. Together with many informal arrangements, these decisions shape the distinctive nature of an organisation.

8.2   Dividing work – creating the vertical structure

Organisation structure describes the way tasks are divided, supervised and co-ordinated. The **organisation chart** shows this in picture form. When people join a department or take a job within the structure the organisation chart gives a fairly clear signal about what they should do. The director of marketing is expected to deal with issues in marketing, not finance. Various 'operating policies' reinforce the signal from the basic structure. These cover matters such as selection, development, appraisal and reward, which managers design to influence employee behaviour that supports their objectives. Operating policies shape the kind of people the company selects, what behaviour it rewards and what career moves it will encourage.

The organisation chart

This is a diagram showing the main departments and positions within the organisation. Lines link senior executives to the other departments or people for whose work they are responsible. It shows to whom each department or division reports, and clarifies four features of the **formal structure**:

● tasks – the major tasks or activities the organisation undertakes;
● subdivisions – how the major tasks are further divided;
● levels – the position of each post within the management hierarchy, and the reporting links;
● lines of authority – the lines linking the boxes show who has formal authority over whom.

Such charts are always changing, but provide a convenient summary of the current allocation of tasks and who is responsible for them. Figure 8.2 shows the organisation chart for an aircraft factory within what is now BAE Systems, a large UK manufacturing business. The factory has six main departments – design, production engineering, purchasing, inventory, production and human resources. The chart shows the chain of command within the plant and the tasks of the respective departments (only some of which are shown). In this case the chart includes direct staff such as operators and engineers, and shows the lines of authority throughout the factory. It does *not* show the **informal structure** – the many patterns of work and communication that are part of organisational life.

Dividing tasks

One person working as an independent owner-manager has no need for an organisation structure. He or she decides what to do, and how they will plan and co-ordinate the different activities. Growth increases the problems of co-ordination, though in small businesses staff usually handle these issues informally by mutual give-and-take. People usually (not always) begin to experience more difficulties with informal structures if the business starts to grow. The dangers of informality begin to outweigh the benefits.

Figure 8.2 The structure within a BAE aircraft factory

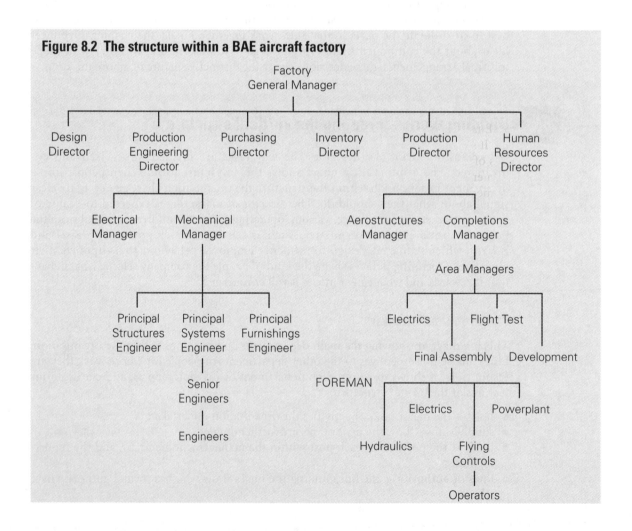

| MANAGEMENT IN PRACTICE | Multi-show Events |

Multi-show Events employs 11 people providing a variety of entertainment and promotional services to large businesses. When Brian Simpson created the business in 1990 with a full-time staff of two the company obviously had no formal structure. He reflected on the process of growth and structure:

> While the company was small thinking about a structure never occurred to me. It became a consideration as sales grew and the complexity of what we offered increased. There were also more people around and I believed that I should introduce a structure so that clear divisions of responsibility would be visible. It seemed natural to split sales and marketing from the actual delivery and production of events as these were two distinct areas. I felt that by creating 'specialised' departments we could give a better service to clients as each area of the company could focus more on their own roles. [Figure 8.3 shows the structure.]

> We had to redesign the office layout and introduce a more formalised communication process to ensure all relevant information is being passed on – and on the whole I think this structure will see us through the next stage of business growth and development.

Source: Private communication

'Job specialisation ... is an inherent part of every organisation, indeed every human activity' (Mintzberg, 1979, p.69). Management divides work into smaller tasks, with people or departments specialising in one or more of these. They become more expert in one task than they could be in several and save time by not moving between them. By concentrating on one, they are more likely to come up with improved ideas or methods. Taken too far specialisation leads to the negative effects noted in Chapter 13.

The principle applies at all levels. Figure 8.2 shows the specialisation of work in the BAE factory. At the top is specialisation between design, production, purchasing and so on. It shows a **vertical specialisation** in that people at different levels deal with distinct sets of activity. It also shows a **horizontal specialisation** throughout. Within production engineering the chart shows that some specialise in electrical problems and others in mechanical. Within the latter it shows that separate groups specialise in structures, systems and fittings.

Figure 8.3 The organisation structure at Multi-show Events

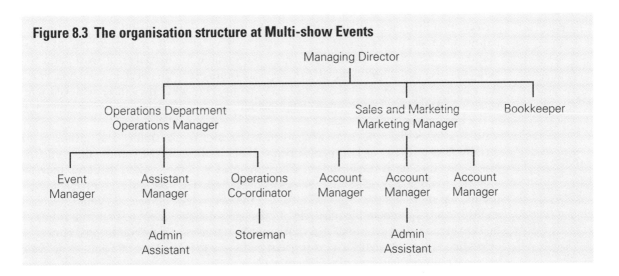

Lines of authority

The lines of **authority** show the links between people in the organisation, by showing everyone who they report to and who reports to them. It shows who they can ask to do a piece of work, who they can go to for support – and who will be expecting results from them. In Figure 8.2 the production director can give instructions to the aerostructures or completions manager, but not to the electrical manager in production engineering. The powerplant foreman reports to the final assembly manager, who in turn reports to the completions manager. Figure 8.3 shows the lines of authority in the comparatively tiny Multi-show Events. In both cases there are many informal contacts in the course of normal human activity. These bring extra life to the organisation and help it cope with unplanned events, which the formal system cannot deal with.

Authority, responsibility and delegation

The **lines of authority** show the allocation of formal power within the organisation. Formal authority is the right that a person has to make decisions, allocate resources or give instructions. It is based on the position, not the person. The production engineering director at BAE has formal authority over a defined range of matters – and anyone else taking over the job would have the same amount of formal authority.

Subordinates – those below someone else in the hierarchy – comply with instructions or requests because they accept the person has the formal (sometimes called legitimate) authority to make that request. An operator in the hydraulics area of final assembly would accept an instruction from the hydraulics foreman, but probably not from the powerplant foreman (he or she may do something as a personal favour for the latter, but that is different from accepting formal authority). If managers attempt to give instructions or do things that are beyond their area of formal authority, they are likely to meet resistance – they have no formal authority over those areas.

Responsibility is a person's duty to perform a task that has been assigned to them. The production director and the hydraulics foreman are responsible for the tasks that go with those positions. To fulfil those responsibilities they require the formal authority over the relevant resources, including the right to deploy them. A person who has been given responsibility for a task, but not the authority to match it, will be in a difficult position. He or she will need to rely on other sources of power (Chapter 12) to influence people to get things done.

Accountability means that people with authority and responsibility for an area are required to report on, and justify, their work to those above them in the chain of command. The principal systems engineer is responsible for that area of work, and has authority over certain resources. He or she is accountable to the mechanical manager for the way they have used those resources, by comparing what they have achieved with what was expected. The measures could include the cost, quantity, quality or timeliness of the work.

Delegation is the process by which people transfer responsibility and authority for certain parts of their work to people below them in the chain of command. While the production director is responsible and accountable for all the work in that area, they are only able to do this by delegating the work downwards. They are still accountable for the results, but they pass the responsibility, and the necessary authority, to subordinates – and this continues down the hierarchy. If managers delegate more to their subordinates this enables quicker decisions and more rapid responses to new conditions. However, delegation is not a straightforward process, and some managers are reluctant to delegate in case it reduces their power (see Chapter 12).

Line and staff authority

Chapter 1 distinguished between line managers and staff managers. Line departments are those that have direct responsibility for delivering the products or services of the organisation. People in those departments have line authority over their direct subordinates – as the production director in Figure 8.2 has line authority over the completions manager. Staff departments have an advisory relationship in support of the line departments, in matters such as human resources or finance. Their authority is more of an advisory one. The human resources director has no line authority to instruct the production director how to design an appraisal system – but can offer help and advice on how to do this.

The span of control

The **span of control** refers to the number of subordinates reporting to a supervisor. Where staff are closely supervised then there is a narrow span of control – as shown in the top half of Figure 8.4. Other organisations have wider spans of control, by introducing more autonomy and team working – producing broader spans of control and flatter organisation structures. Managers have more people reporting to them, implying that subordinates will have more freedom to use their initiative.

Centralisation and decentralisation

When an organisation grows beyond the smallest operation management divides work vertically, as those at the top delegate more of their work to those below them – and so

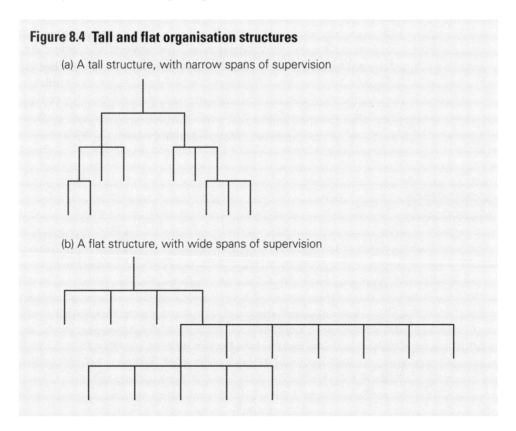

Figure 8.4 Tall and flat organisation structures

(a) A tall structure, with narrow spans of supervision

(b) A flat structure, with wide spans of supervision

KEY IDEAS **Joan Woodward's research**

Joan Woodward's study of 100 firms in Essex found great variety between them in the number of subordinates managers supervised (Woodward, 1965). The number of people reporting directly to the chief executive ranged from 2 to 18, with the median span of control being 6. The average span of control of the first line supervisors varied from 10 to 90, with a median of 37. Woodward explained the variation by the technological system used (discussed more fully in Chapter 11).

begin to create a hierarchy such as that shown in Figure 8.4. As the business grows the hierarchy becomes more complex, but behind the detail it is often possible to see three levels – corporate, divisional and operating.

- *Corporate* The most senior group, such as the ABB executive committee, and the small headquarters staff in Zurich. They are responsible for managing the overall direction of the organisation. This includes not only guiding and monitoring the performance of subordinate levels of the organisation but also maintaining links with significant external institutions such as banks and political bodies.
- *Divisional* Responsible for implementing broad areas of policy and for securing and allocating budgets and other resources. An example in ABB in 1999 would be the power transmission division responsible for meeting the targets set for the division by the executive committee. Divisional managers represent the division's interests to the committee and also monitor and control the performance of the operating units.
- *Operating* The level responsible for doing the technical work of the organisation – making products, catching thieves, caring for patients or delivering services,. In ABB the operating level would include a group of engineers working to develop a new seabed pumping system to separate oil from water and other debris before being pumped to the surface – or any of thousands of other operational activities within the group.

A key issue in designing the vertical hierarchy is what decisions are made at the different levels. Who has the right to make decisions? **Centralisation** is when those at the top make most of the decisions. The divisional level ensures that those at operating level follow the policy.

MANAGEMENT IN PRACTICE **Kwik-Fit**

The Part Six Case Study shows how the company balanced centralisation and decentralisation. The major reason for introducing the electronic point-of-sale system described in the case was to increase the amount of control the centre had over the business. The new information system allowed senior managers to monitor activities in the depots much more closely than with the manual system. They used this to reinforce uniform policies (on, say, pricing) across the group, and to centralise functions such as purchasing. At a later stage in the story they used the power of the new systems to decentralise various functions to divisional level. Divisional managers now had more scope to decide on matters such as investment and pricing: though functions such as finance and purchasing remained centralised.

Source: Boddy and Gunson (1996).

Decentralisation is when a relatively large number of decisions are taken in the divisions or operating units. People in the operating units work as they think best, provided they deliver the results expected by the corporate level and keep within some broad guidelines. Branch managers in ATMays, a chain of retail travel agents (since absorbed into Going Places) had considerable freedom over pricing and promotional activities, but were required to follow very tight financial reporting routines.

A political analogy

The same issue arises in the wider political world. European nations vary in how they divide power between central, regional and local government. France and the United Kingdom are relatively centralised, while the Netherlands and probably Spain are more decentralised, with strong provincial or regional governments. Much of the controversy over the UK's relationship with the European Union relates to the similar question of subsidiarity: what matters should those in Brussels decide, and what should individual member states decide? As in business, pressures for changes in the current balance are always present – and the solutions reflect both rational and political influences.

In practice, organisations display a mix of both – as in Kwik-Fit. Many companies have moved towards more decentralised structures in the belief that those who are closest to the action will be in a better position to make the right decisions. Others have moved in the opposite direction, limiting the power of divisions and operating units and taking more decisions at the centre. Hewlett-Packard had a tradition of local autonomy ('The HP Way'). The company founders believed that 'smart people will make the right choices if given the right tools and authority' – and so pushed strategic decisions down to the managers most involved in each business. The company appointed a new chief executive, Carleton Fiorina, in 1999. She created a Strategy Council that now advises her on strategy and allocates resources across the company – a big change from 'The HP Way'.

There is always a tension between centralising and decentralising (Table 8.1). The profile at any point reflects the shifting power of these forces, as managers weigh the benefits of a move in one direction or the other (including their personal career interests).

Table 8.1 Advantages and disadvantages of centralisation

Factor	Advantages	Disadvantages
Response to change	Can ensure thorough debate taking account of all issues	Slower response to local variations in conditions
Use of expertise	Concentration of expertise at the centre makes it easier to develop new services and promote best practice methods	Less likely to take account of local knowledge
Cost	Economies of scale in purchasing supplies and facilities, and less administrative cost if using common systems Retains control over major/costly decisions	Centralised systems may be wasteful when applied locally – local suppliers may be better value than corporate suppliers May lack relevant knowledge for good decisions
Policy implications	Less risk of local managers breaching legal requirements	More risk of local managers breaching legal requirements
Staff commitment	Backing of centre ensures wide support	Staff motivated by greater local responsibility
Consistency	Provides consistent image to the public – less variation in service standards Able to compare performance on common measures	Local staff discouraged from taking responsibility – problems can be blamed on the centre Common measures may not be appropriate locally

> **Q Case questions 8.1**
>
> ● What problems would ABB have experienced with a centralised structure?
> ● What advantages would they gain from such a structure?

Formalisation

Formalisation is the practice of using written or electronic documents to direct and control employees. Documents include rule books, procedures, instruction manuals, job descriptions – anything that sets out what people must do in designated circumstances. They include the scripts that operators in most call centres must use to guide their conversation with a customer. The intention of these formal methods (consistent with the ideas of Max Weber discussed in Chapter 2) is to bring more consistency and predictability to organisational work.

There is always tension between formality and informality. If people are to be more responsive to individual needs, and able to adapt to local conditions, they favour informal arrangements with few rules. The informal organisation appears to be the most responsive and effective approach. Yet many organisations introduce more formal methods in the shape of detailed procedures and guidelines to meet the requirements of industry regulators or consumer legislation. They need to protect customers against unsuitable selling methods or to protect staff against unfounded complaints. This often leads managers to introduce more formal systems and recording procedures.

ACTIVITY 8.1

Gathering information on structures

How is your college or university structured? Focus on the parts most directly involved in delivering your education. How have the various parts of the task been divided up? Are all the teaching staff you see in one department or in several? Do you have a separate management library or computing suite or share a wider facility? Answers to such questions reflect how the overall task has been divided.

8.3 Dividing work – creating the horizontal structure

A highly visible aspect of structure is the way an organisation's work is divided into smaller units or departments. There are five approaches to this aspect of structural design, which Figure 8.5 illustrates in summary form. The functional, divisional and matrix forms are widely used, each using the chain of command within whichever form is chosen. Two forms that are becoming more common use teams and networks as the basis of structure.

The five approaches to structure are:

1 *Functional* People work in departments made up of those with a common technical or professional expertise, such as purchasing or legal affairs.
2 *Divisional* People work in departments that are themselves part of a division delivering a product or service to a distinct group of customers. These are sometimes called strategic business units, and have their own profit and loss account.

Figure 8.5 Five types of structure

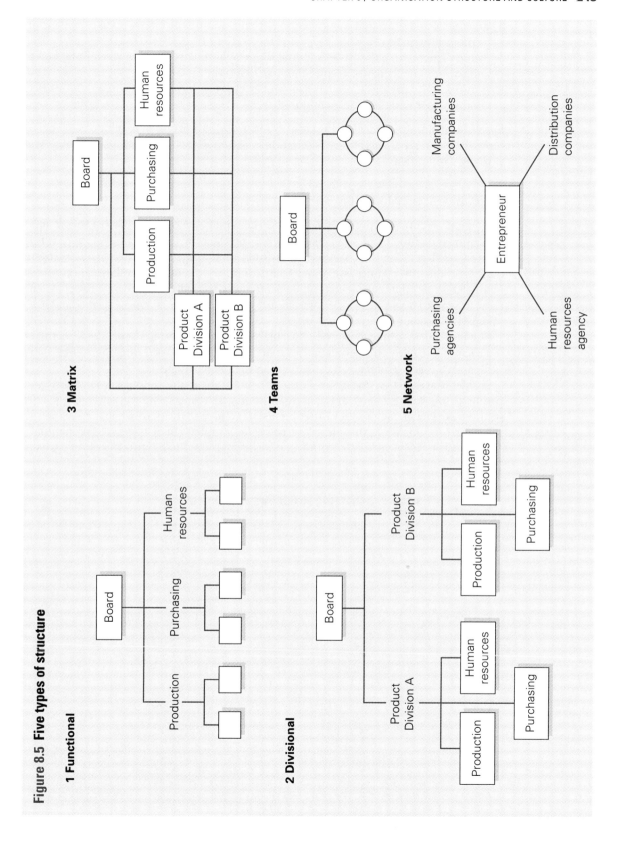

1 Functional

2 Divisional

3 Matrix

4 Teams

5 Network

3 *Matrix* People are based in a functional group, and then work for a divisional group or project on distinct tasks.

4 *Teams* The team is the basic building block, with teams forming to complete tasks and co-ordinate their work with others, at all levels.

5 *Networks* The organisation acts as a broker between independent organisations that contract to provide services as required.

Each has advantages and disadvantages – and organisations often combine elements of more than one type. Each form also has different implications for those managing and working within them.

Specialisation by function

In a functional organisation managers group activities and employees according to their professional or functional specialisms, such as production, finance, marketing or information services. The BAE factory has a functional approach, with staff working in design, production engineering, purchasing, inventory, production or human resources. Figure 8.6 shows the main structural division of a National Health Service hospital. The chart at senior levels shows a clear functional division into nursing and quality, medical, finance and human resources.

The functional approach can be efficient. Management creates a separate department for each major task, and people with expertise in that task work together. They share skills and can see a professional career path in their department.

Problems arise when an organisation grows and diversifies into a range of different products, markets or geographical areas. Managers responsible for achieving results in these areas will each expect functional staff to give priority to what they need. If a sales executive makes a commitment to a customer he or she will expect the manufacturing facility to meet that commitment. The manufacturing unit may have equally

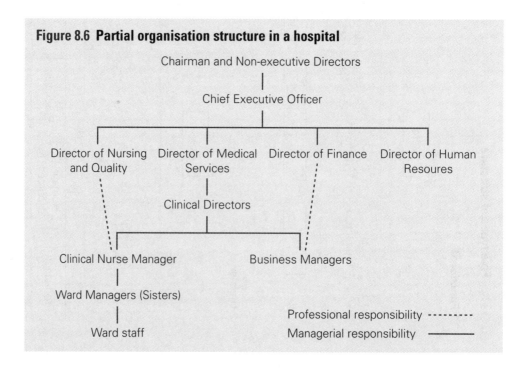

Figure 8.6 Partial organisation structure in a hospital

Chairman and Non-executive Directors

Chief Executive Officer

Director of Nursing and Quality · Director of Medical Services · Director of Finance · Director of Human Resoures

Clinical Directors

Clinical Nurse Manager · Business Managers

Ward Managers (Sisters)

Ward staff

Professional responsibility ---------
Managerial responsibility ————

Table 8.2 Advantages and disadvantages of functional specialisation

Factor	Advantages	Disadvantages
Staff careers	Clear career paths and professional development	Isolation from wider issues damages promotion prospects
Resources	Specialisation leads to high standards and efficiency	Conflict over priorities
Working relations	Common professional interests support good internal relations	Lack of wider awareness damages external relations

pressing orders from other sales staff. Units compete with each other for functional services such as information systems – which can never meet all the demands for systems development. The focus of staff tends to be inward, towards the interests of the function, rather than outward towards the whole business. Table 8.2 summarises the advantages and disadvantages.

Divisional approach

Managers create a divisional structure when they arrange the organisation around its main products, services or customer groups. They create separate units and make them responsible for all the functions necessary to deliver their services to the customer. The units focus on defined groups of customers who have significantly different requirements.

CASE STUDY

ABB – the case continues – the company changes to a divisional structure

The performance of ABB was less satisfactory than investors required, so in September 2000 the board decided to appoint a new chief executive. Goran Lindahl was replaced by Jorgen Centerman. In January 2001 Centerman announced that he would dismantle the structure he took over from his predecessor. In place of the four industrial divisions there would be four customer segments – process industries, utilities, manufacturing and consumer industries and oil, gas and petrochemicals. The company claimed to be the first in its industry to be fully organised around customers rather than technologies.

Source: *Financial Times*, 12 January 2001, p.29.

FT

Product or customer

Many divisional structures enable staff to specialise in a particular product or customer group. For example, the major banks have identified that wealthy private clients have different needs from other individuals – and have created separate divisions to focus solely on delivering services to those clients. Many hospitals are now introducing what they term the 'named-nurse' system, in which one nurse is responsible for several identified patients. That nurse is the patient's prime point of contact with the system, and their job is to manage the delivery of services to the patient from other (functional) departments. Figure 8.7 contrasts the task and named-nurse approaches.

In a divisional structure senior managers give each unit the authority to design, produce and deliver the product or service, using resources under its control or bought from outside suppliers. The advantages are that they can focus all resources on the one product. Separate areas of functional expertise are more likely to co-operate as they all

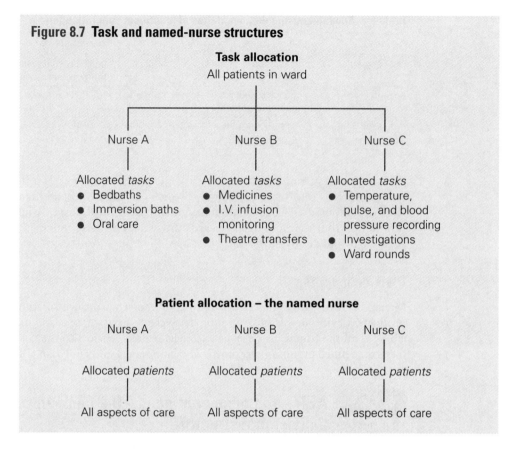

Figure 8.7 Task and named-nurse structures

depend on satisfying the same set of customers. It is probably more expensive, as each product group may have a wide range of specialisms duplicating provision. The problems of co-operation between departments that beset functional structures may still arise, though in different forms.

Geographic divisions

Here managers divide the organisation geographically, usually according to the location of customers. They group all the tasks required under the management of that geographic region rather than having them divided amongst functions at the centre. For example, large companies with many service outlets – supermarkets, hotels, breweries – often divide the business into regions. This allows management to focus on identifying and meeting different customer requirements in the region, or on meeting different environmental conditions. A geographical management structure also makes it easier for the centre to monitor and control the many relatively small outlets. Table 8.3 summarises these points.

Matrix organisation

This arrangement combines functional and divisional structures. On one axis of the matrix is a range of functional groups and on the other are the products or projects, with a manager responsible for each. Staff from the functional areas work on one or more projects. When a project no longer needs their expertise they are allocated by their

Table 8.3 Advantages and disadvantages of divisional structure (product or geographic)

Factor	Advantages	Disadvantages
Staff focus	Functional staff focus on product and customer needs	Isolation from wider professional and technical developments
Resources	Dedicated facilities meet customer needs quickly	Costs of duplication across the organisation (e.g. distribution networks, computer systems)
Working relations	Common customer focus supports good internal relations	Potential conflict with other divisions over priorities, and no incentive to support other divisions
Control	Regional divisions use autonomy to meet local needs	Develop policies independently of wider organisational interests

functional boss to work on another. Subordinates have two bosses – a long-term, functional head, and a temporary head of the project currently being worked upon. ABB was an example of this form until 1998. Table 8.4 shows that while the approach has advantages it can also raise some serious management problems.

Table 8.4 Advantages and disadvantages of a matrix structure

Factor	Advantages	Disadvantages
Staff focus	Staff gain variety of work experience, and develop understanding of customer needs Functions develop professional expertise	Isolation from wider professional developments in functional base Conflicting demands of project and functional boss
Resources	Dedicated facilities can be arranged to meet customer needs as required	Costs of duplication across the organisation as demands vary
Working relations	Project focus supports good internal relations	Potential conflict with functional divisions over priorities

MANAGEMENT IN PRACTICE   **Product development at Toyota**

Toyota used to organise its product development in a matrix form. The product planning division employed about 7,000 people working on 16 current projects. Each represented a new model and employed a chief engineer and several hundred staff. There were also 16 functional engineering divisions.

> A chief engineer had to co-ordinate people in 48 departments in 12 divisions to launch a new product ... In addition, relatively young chief engineers did not always get sufficient co-operation from senior functional managers ... For their part, functional managers found it difficult to spend the time on managing details on so many projects. Most of these managers had to oversee work for about 15 different projects at the same time.

Source: Cusumano and Nobeoka (1998, pp.22–4).

Mixed forms

Especially in large organisations, practice is more complex than these simple categories suggest. Such businesses typically use a variety of methods for dividing tasks – The Body Shop example shows functional, product and geographical structures within the same company – see Figure 1 in Part One, page 3.

The structure of Unilever, the Anglo-Dutch conglomerate that produces a vast range of household brands throughout the world, is a good example of the complexity such structures can reach.

MANAGEMENT IN PRACTICE **A summary of the management structure of Unilever**

During the year ended 31 December 2000 Unilever was organised, and its internal results were reported, on both a product and a regional basis.

On a product basis, Category Directors were responsible for developing category strategies for implementation across Unilever's operations and they worked closely with Business Groups to develop regional strategies. They were also responsible for directing and managing the allocation of corporate resources for research and development and the innovation network.

On a regional basis, Unilever's operations were organised into 12 (regionally based) Business Groups. Western Europe and North America were further subdivided by Foods and Home and Personal Care product categories.

The individual operating companies, which formed the core building blocks of the Unilever organisation, came within the Business Groups. The President of each Business Group was accountable for the performance of the companies in their group.

Source: Unilever Annual Report 2000.

Teams

In their search for more flexibility, lower costs and faster response more managements use teams as a way of organising work. This is particularly true in companies with high commitments to developing new technologies – such as ABB, with over 20,000 scientists and engineers working on new products and systems. The company uses an extensive system of teams, bringing together people from different parts of the business to work in multidisciplinary teams. This enables research scientists to collaborate closely with engineers who spend most of their time dealing with customers. Similar examples are at GlaxoSmithKline and W.L. Gore and Associates.

Management delegates significant responsibilities and authority not to individual workers but to an identifiable team, which is then mutually accountable for the results. The team may be from across functions or from within a single area – in which case it looks like a small department. The difference is that there is probably less hierarchical division amongst the members and more mutual accountability for results. They are sometimes called 'self-managing teams' to emphasise the relative absence of hierarchical relationships (Manz and Sims, 1993). The many potential advantages are balanced by disadvantages, such as a tendency to take on their own purpose and to spend time in debate rather than action (see Chapter 15).

Networks

Network structures are those where management breaks the functions, especially those it regards as not being core to the business, into separate companies. The remaining, relatively small organisation concentrates on setting the strategic direction of the firm, and on managing the core units. All other services are contracted in as required from the market – either from the former divisions or from other suppliers. MG Rover (sold in 1999 by BMW) has announced it will outsource the development of future new vehicle 'platforms' from leading component manufacturers. The company already buys the car bodies used in its MGF sports model from Mayflower, an engineering group (*Financial Times*, 2 November 2000, p.2). BP Amoco (see Part Two case) outsourced its global telecommunications network to MCI WorldCom. The arrangement is becoming common in personal services – such as when Care UK won a contract to manage seven homes for mentally ill elderly patients for Surrey County Council – a UK local authority (*Financial Times*, 30 November 2000) .

A similar structural form is when companies sell the function to another company, but still deliver the service to customers under their own name. Abbey National has sold its credit card business to MBNA as the cost of updating its systems to compete effectively in the card business was too high. However, the company will continue to offer cards – designed and operated by MBNA but showing the Abbey National logo (*Financial Times*, 20 March 2001, p.27).

This section has described five alternative ways of dividing tasks. Most enterprises adopt a mix of forms and continually adapt to changing circumstances. They seek to achieve a balance between the advantages and disadvantages of each type in their circumstances. Structures are transitional rather than permanent forms. Networks enable small firms to grow rapidly with limited capital expenditure, if they can secure services from suppliers, and the boundaries of organisations become harder to identify. Arrangements with suppliers to provide services that were available within the company raise new challenges of co-ordination.

> ### Q Case questions 8.2
>
> - What benefits was ABB expecting to gain from the new structure it announced in 2001?
> - What other issues will management need to deal with when implementing the change? This is a bigger task than it may sound, so you may want to make your own list, and then compare it with those of other students.
> - What disadvantages (such as those listed in Table 8.3) may it experience?

8.4 Co-ordinating work

The division of work must be co-ordinated to achieve the intended results – without it there will be confusion and poor performance. Effective co-ordination becomes more essential as customers expect higher quality and shareholders expect higher profits. Yet it is difficult to co-ordinate large, widely dispersed businesses, operating and changing at great speed.

Direct supervision

This is where a manager ensures co-ordination by directly supervising his or her staff to ensure they work together in line with company policy. The limitation lies in the idea of the span of control – the number of people whom a manager can effectively supervise directly. Chapter 10 shows that spans of control vary with circumstances.

Hierarchy

If disputes or problems arise between staff or departments, they can be reconciled by putting the arguments to their common boss in the hierarchy. It is the boss's responsibility to reach a solution. At the BAE aircraft factory (Figure 8.2), if the engineer responsible for structures has a disagreement over some work problem with the systems engineer, they can ask the mechanical manager to adjudicate. If that fails they can escalate the problem to a higher level – the production engineering director. The weakness of this method is that it takes time to get a response, and meantime the issue is unresolved. In rapidly changing circumstances the hierarchy cannot cope with the volume of issues requiring attention, and becomes slow at making decisions.

Standardising inputs and outputs

This involves making sure that what goes into the system, and what managers expect it to produce, are standardised. This makes co-ordination with other stages easier. If the purchaser of components specifies accurately what is required, and the supplier meets that specification, co-ordination between those who use the parts will be easier. Similarly, if staff work to precise specifications, co-ordinating with the next stage of the process becomes easier. If staff all receive the same training in how to do a task they will need less direct supervision, as their manager can be more confident that they will be working consistently.

Rules and procedures

Another way to co-ordinate the activities of people or departments is to prepare rules or guidelines on how they should perform.

MANAGEMENT IN PRACTICE **Safety procedures in a power station**

The following instructions govern the steps that staff must follow when they inspect control equipment in a nuclear power station:

1 Before commencing work you must read and understand the relevant Permit-to-Work and/or other safety documents as appropriate.
2 Obtain keys for relevant cubicles.
3 Visually inspect the interior of each bay for dirt, water and evidence of condensation.
4 Visually inspect the cabling, glands, terminal blocks and components for damage.
5 Visually check for loose connections at all terminals.
6 Lock all cubicles and return the keys.
7 Clear the safety document and return it to the Supervisor/Senior Authorised person.

Organisations have procedures for approving capital expenditure. To compare proposals on a common basis they give strict guidelines on the questions a bid should answer, how people should prepare a case, and to whom they should submit it. Companies developing new computer software have major problems in co-ordinating the work if several designers are working on different parts of the same project. People can easily duplicate work that others have done, or work on an older version, not realising that someone has produced a new version. To overcome this companies use strict change control procedures to ensure that the sub-projects fit together efficiently.

Information systems

Information systems help to ensure that people who need to work in a consistent way have common information about what is happening. Sharing information makes it easier to co-ordinate the different activities within a company. The Internet offers a radical solution to the problem of moving information and knowledge between organisations, which many companies now use.

MANAGEMENT IN PRACTICE

BT's Shared Workspace product

In 1998 BT created a service that enables companies to share common information with each other. Such 'Extranets' use standard web servers and browsers to enable authorised users to share information. They can be used by people outside a company, such as supplier or customer staff, as long as they have a password. Shared Workspace (SWS) is an Extranet product offered by British Telecom that enables businesses to conduct their trade with BT electronically. It contains collaborative software, shared document access and contact management. Customers access SWS via the BT home page, using a standard browser.

An early application was within BT itself, to manage the flow of information with a global customer. SWS provides a private and secure virtual meeting place for authorised users in the two companies, who create, distribute and access documents of all kinds electronically. Standard processes such as order transactions and report management are automated using forms within SWS. Users can gain direct access to some BT databases showing the status of faults or orders. Perhaps most significant of all from a human and organisational point of view, they can exchange current working information online amongst many linked users – in both customer and BT – wherever they are located.

Another example is IBM, which has changed its purchasing processes so that they are now conducted almost entirely over the Internet. This ensures that new instructions to hundreds of suppliers flow almost automatically as the manufacturing programme changes to match current orders. This was previously a laborious activity in which people easily made mistakes. Modern information systems have transformed it into a much more tightly co-ordinated activity.

Direct personal contact

This is the most human form of co-ordination: people talking to each other. Mintzberg (1979) found that people use this method in both the simplest and the most complex organisation. There is so much uncertainty in the latter that information systems cannot cope with all eventualities. Only direct contact can co-ordinate these.

Structure in a social service

The organisation cares for the elderly in a large city. Someone who had worked there for several years reflected on the structure:

> Within the centre there was a manager, 2 deputies, an assistant manager, 5 senior care officers (SCOs) and 30 officers. Each SCO is responsible for 6 care officers, allowing daily contact between the supervisor and the subordinates. While this defines job roles quite tightly, it allows a good communication structure to exist. Feedback is common as there are frequent meetings of the separate groups, and individual appraisals of the care officers by the SCOs. Staff value this opportunity for praise and comments on how they are doing.
>
> Contact at all levels is common between supervisor and care officers during meetings to assess the needs of clients – for whom the care officers have direct responsibility. Frequent social gatherings and functions within the department also serve to enhance relations and satisfy social needs. Controls placed on the behaviour of the care officers come from the highest positions in the hierarchy, especially those derived from legislation such as the Social Work Acts and the Health and Safety Executive. Performance measures also exist. For example outsiders regularly assess how the Quality of Practice code is working, along with those established in the department on absenteeism and lateness.
>
> Structure certainly plays a major role in the effectiveness of employees at work by encouraging and motivating them. However, in a department such as this the need to improve quality of service has to come from the desire of the individual to do better for clients.

ACTIVITY 8.2

Dividing and co-ordinating work

What broad division of work has been made in an organisation you are familiar with? How is the task divided at strategic or operational levels?

How are the separate activities typically co-ordinated? You may want to focus on co-ordination between one or two specific groups or departments. List the main methods that are used, taking the headings above as a point of reference.

How effectively does this structure support people's work towards the objectives?

8.5 Organisational cultures

The idea of organisational culture has been part of the management vocabulary since the early 1980s. Academics and managers frequently refer to it as one of the reasons for the success or failure of an organisation – the chief executive of ABB hopes that the changes he has introduced will 'change the culture' – implying that recent under-performance can by traced to an inadequate culture. In 2000 British Nuclear Fuels introduced a programme of culture change designed to win back the confidence of its customers after a series of damaging safety failures. The safety watchdog, the Nuclear Installations Inspectorate, concluded that the company was guilty of systematic management failure and had a serious safety culture problem. The company's response was a programme of cultural change designed to instil openness and self-discipline. The company has imposed, and is rigorously enforcing, practices designed to reduce vehicle speeds on internal roads, 'the mis-use of site passes, abuse of the e-mail system, sloppy time-keeping and eating in active areas' (*Financial Times*, 9 February 2001, p.13). Mergers sometimes experience difficulties over a clash of cultures.

**MANAGEMENT
IN PRACTICE**   **Cap Gemini and Ernst & Young**

When the French company Cap Gemini merged with the information technology consultancy of Ernst & Young (E&Y) they found significant cultural differences. Cap Gemini's chief operating officer commented that accurate statistics from E&Y were scarce: 'They changed their figures repeatedly. We said we needed audited accounts. They said: "Do you really need audited accounts from a third party?" For them that was somehow traumatic.'

Source: Based on an article by Caroline Daniel, *Financial Times*, 5 February 2001, p.15.   **FT**

Interest in **organisation culture** has grown as academics and managers have come to believe that it influences behaviour. Several claim that a strong and distinct culture helps to integrate individuals into the team or organisation (Deal and Kennedy, 1982; Peters and Waterman, 1982). They claim that creating the right culture is a key element in high performing organisations – provided the culture is the right one for the situation.

Others question the link between a strong culture and economic performance. Kotter and Heskett (1992) studied 207 companies and attempted to relate the strength of their culture to economic performance. Although the two variables were positively correlated the relationship was much weaker than the advocates of organisational culture as an influential variable have predicted. Some also doubt the ability of managers to change an organisation's culture.

Edgar Schein (1985) believed that as people work together they develop a distinctive culture, reflecting what they perceive to be the correct way to approach and deal with organisational problems. He believed that culture develops as group members share enough experiences to form a view of what works and what does not. This view then shapes how members expect each other to behave. Culture is less tangible than structure, but the common assumptions and beliefs can exert a profound influence on how a group performs.

**KEY
IDEAS**   **Edgar Schein on culture**

The main beliefs that Schein identified were those concerned with the following:

- *mission and strategy* – beliefs about the overall mission and its reason for being;
- *goals* – what the operational goals should be so as to meet the broader mission;
- *means* – how the group is to meet its goals;
- *criteria for measuring results* – consensus on how performance is to be measured;
- *remedial strategies* – the prevailing assumption about how to put things right.

Schein believed that cultures act as a filter for coping with information and provide members with a common set of guidelines that they use to work out how to make a contribution. The more clearly members work through these issues to develop a common understanding, the better the group will perform.

Source: Schein (1985).

Components of organisational cultures

Deal and Kennedy (1982) refer to culture as 'the way we do things around here' and Hofstede (1991) sees it as the 'collective programming of the mind', which distinguishes one group from another. While the idea of **culture** appears vague it reflects the identifiable components of practices, customs, beliefs and values.

- *Practices* These represent the surface level of a culture – the visible elements such as language, etiquette, form of greeting, clothing, and include also the artefacts of the business – the physical layout (open-plan or closed offices).
- *Customs* These are the accepted modes or norms of behaviour within the organisation, reflecting the values and beliefs, which provide guidelines for the way people and groups are expected to behave towards each other. These often shape aspects of the physical appearance of the organisation – the artefacts.
- *Beliefs* The assumptions that members hold about the organisation and the situation within it – about what practices work well in this business, for example how people make decisions, how teams work together and styles of problem solving.
- *Values* Deeply held ideas of members about what is right or wrong, fair or unfair – anything that has personal worth or meaning. These values are expressed in operating beliefs and norms of behaviour.

Figure 8.8 illustrates how cultures develop – as people come to share a set of beliefs they use these to establish norms about the way they should behave towards each other and to outsiders. If the outcomes are positive this reinforces their shared belief in the values underlying their behaviour. In this way organisations develop deep-seated values and beliefs about the way that staff should run things. What degree of direction should there be? Should people have job titles? How should they dress at work? What is the expected pattern of behaviour in meetings – confrontational and challenging, or co-operative and supportive? Do bosses expect staff to defer to them, or to challenge prevailing practices and attitudes? How important is time keeping, or meeting commitments to colleagues? Should they follow the rules or use their initiative?

You can sense and observe the distinctiveness of organisational cultures once you have been in a few different departments or organisations. They feel different; receive visitors differently; people work together differently; the pace is different – some buzz with life and

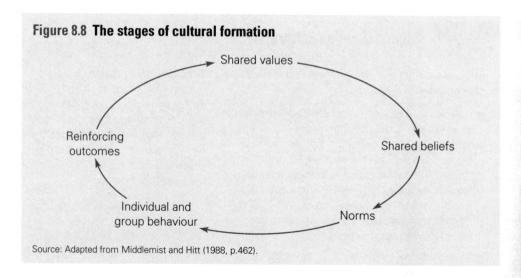

Figure 8.8 The stages of cultural formation

Shared values

Reinforcing outcomes

Shared beliefs

Individual and group behaviour

Norms

Source: Adapted from Middlemist and Hitt (1988, p.462).

activity, others seem asleep. Some feel as if rules guide behaviour while others use procedures as little as possible. The same is true of departments and groups within organisations. Some are welcoming and look after visitors and those from outside, while others seem inward looking. Some stick to the rules, others are entrepreneurial and risk taking. Some have regular social occasions while in others staff rarely meet except at work.

Types of organisational culture

The competing values model developed by Quinn *et al.* (1996) – introduced in Chapter 2 – offers a way of describing cultures and of comparing one with another. The model is based on two inherent tensions – flexibility/control and internal/external. The four cultural types shown in Figure 8.9 express competing views on how organisations should be managed, and staff motivated.

Open systems

This represents an open systems view, in which people recognise that the external environment plays a significant role, and is seen as a vital source of ideas, energy, resources, etc. They also see the environment as complex and turbulent, requiring entrepreneurial, visionary leadership and flexible, responsive behaviour. Key motivating factors are growth, stimulation, creativity and variety. Examples are start-up firms, new business units – organic, flexible operations.

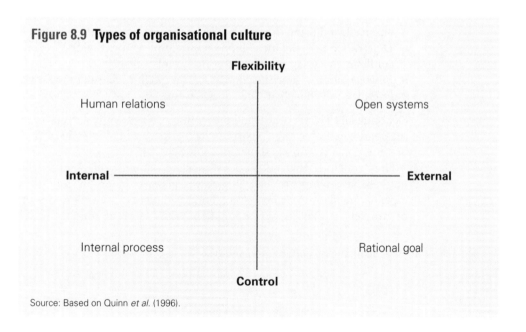

Figure 8.9 Types of organisational culture

Source: Based on Quinn *et al.* (1996).

Rational goal

Members see the organisation as a rational, efficiency-seeking unit. They define effectiveness in terms of production or economic goals that satisfy external requirements. Managers create structures to deal with the outside world. Leadership tends to be directive, goal-oriented and functional. Key motivating factors include competition and the achievement of pre-determined ends. Examples are large, established businesses – mechanistic.

Internal process

Here members pay little attention to the external world, having instead an inward focus. Their goal is to make the unit internally efficient, stable, controlled. Goals are known, tasks repetitive, and methods stress specialisation, rules, procedures. Leaders tend to be conservative and cautious, emphasising technical issues. Key motivating factors include security, stability and order. Examples include utilities, public authorities – suspicious of change

Human relations

People emphasise the value of informal interpersonal relations rather than formal structures. They place high value on maintaining the organisation and the well-being of its members, and define effectiveness in terms of developing people and their commitment. Leaders tend to be participative, considerate, supportive. Motivating factors tend to be attachment, cohesiveness and membership. Examples are found in professional service firms, some internal support functions.

Multiple cultures

Building on work by Martin (1992), Ogbonna and Harris (1998) provide a useful insight into the diversity of cultures within organisations. Much of the discussion of culture has been in terms of identifying the components and nature of a single, unified culture within an organisation. Martin suggested three perspectives:

- *Integration* – the emphasis here is on identifying consistencies in the data that is observed, and using those common patterns to explain the events.
- *Differentiation* – the focus is on conflict, and on identifying the different and possibly conflicting views of members towards events.
- *Fragmentation* – here the emphasis is on the fluid nature of organisations, and on the interplay and change of views about events.

Ogbonna and Harris conducted in-depth interviews with staff in three retailing companies and concluded that positions in the hierarchy determined their perspective on organisational culture, as shown in Table 8.5.

They conclude that cultural perspective depends on place in the hierarchy. This implies that attempts to introduce cultural change based on head office values and perceptions are likely to be ineffective. Since complete consensus across an organisation will be unlikely, it may be better for managers to pursue policies which recognise sub-

Table 8.5 Hierarchical position and cultural perspectives

Position in hierarchy	Cultural perspective	Description	Example
Head office managers	Integration	Cultural values should be shared across the organisation. Unified culture both desirable and attainable	'If we can get every ... part of the company doing what they should be doing, we'll beat everybody in the market.'
Store managers	Differentiation	Reconciling conflicting views of head office and shop floor. See cultural pluralism as inevitable	'People up at head office are all pushing us in different directions. Jill in Marketing wants customer focus, June in Finance wants lower costs.'
Store employees	Fragmented	Confused by contradictory nature of the espoused values. See organisation as complex and unpredictable	'One minute it's this, the next it's that You can't keep up with the flavour of the month.'

Source: Based on Ogbonna and Harris (1998).

cultural differences, and only seek to reconcile those differences that are essential to policy. They also observe that culture remains a highly subjective idea, which is largely in the eye of the beholder – 'and is radically different according to an individual's position in the hierarchy' (p.45). The Management in Practice feature on p.258 uses quantitative survey data from a different industrial setting to confirm this idea.

KEY IDEAS   ## Charles Handy's cultural types

Charles Handy, developing an idea of Roger Harrison, also distinguished four cultures, which he designated **power, role, task** and **person culture**.

- *Power* A dominant central figure holds power: others follow the centre's policy and interpret new situations in the way the leader would. Many entrepreneurial firms operate in this way, with few rules but with well-understood, implicit codes on how to behave and work. The firm relies on the individual rather than on seeking consensus through discussion. It can respond quickly as, once the centre approves, staff implement ideas. The main problem is size since, as it grows, it becomes harder for the person at the centre to maintain the required degree of close control. He or she may be unwilling to let go and remain involved in detail, slowing the response to new situations.

- *Role* Typical characteristics are the job description or the procedure. Managers define what they expect in clear, detailed job descriptions. They select people for a job if they meet the specified requirements. Procedures guide the way people and departments interact. If all the parts follow the rules co-ordination is straightforward. People's position in the hierarchy determines their power. A role culture works well in a stable predictable environment. Problems arise when things change. Then it becomes hard for the role culture to adapt, with problems as expectations mount.

- *Task* This focuses on completing the task or project rather than the formal roles that people occupy. People value each other for what they can contribute and expect everyone to help as needed. The emphasis is on getting the resources and people for the job and then relying on their commitment and enthusiasm. People will typically work in teams, to combine diverse skills into a common purpose. Expertise is typically the source of power – the person with the evident knowledge taking the lead for that part of the task. Groups can re-form quickly around new tasks, so task cultures are highly adaptable. They are hard to control and may waste resources. Staff may develop less professional or technical knowledge than they would in a role culture, as they are moving between different projects too quickly for full specialisation.

- *Person* Here the individual is at the centre and any structure or system is there to serve the individual. The form is unusual – places such as small professional or artistic organisations are probably closest to it. These organisations exist to meet the interests of the professional stars rather than some larger organisational goal. Various forms of experiment in communal or co-operative living may also take this form. People do things to satisfy the needs of the members rather than an external market. Handy also points out that while the full form of personal culture is rare, many technically specialised individuals in conventional organisations aspire towards that form of environment.

Source: Handy (1993).

Cultures and subcultures in an electronics plant

In 1999 staff in the UK plant of a major semiconductor company completed a well-established survey instrument, intended to measure the cultural pattern within an organisation. The instrument can be used to identify the dominant culture, and any subcultures, within an organisation. The study showed that there were significant differences between departments – a dominant culture, several subcultures and a counter-culture within the organisation. The latter was very security oriented and appeared to be misaligned with the objectives of the organisation.

The most obvious subcultures found were:

- **Dominant culture** The organisation is dominated by a competitive/oppositional style, indicating an organisation is a driven, task-oriented 'Theory X' place to work.
- **Process Development Group** The survey identified that this department was heavily weighted towards achievement, self-actualising, humanistic-encouraging and affiliation – essentially a 'Theory Y' group of staff.
- **The Fab 3 Management Team** Broadly competitive/oppositional, but expressed cautiously (low scores on the factors).
- **Manufacturing operators** A different and intense culture, focused on opposition, defensiveness, avoidance and dependence – very security conscious. Management believed this would reduce organisational effectiveness

The Process Development Group and the Fab 3 Management Team had subcultures that management concluded were broadly complementary to the dominant culture and aligned to the overall business objectives. However, management was deeply concerned to discover the existence of a strong counter-culture within the Manufacturing Operator group that made up 700 of the 1400 employees at the plant.

Source: Private information from a manager within the company.

8.6 Summary

This chapter has traced the ways in which people create structures to bring some degree of formality to the management activity. Some aspects of management are performed directly and personally by the people involved. Others are supported and reinforced by arrangements that are institutionalised in an organisation's structure. It has shown that structure is made up of vertical and horizontal dimensions, and that management combines these elements into a unique structure for their unit.

Content

Management creates a structure to help it achieve organisational objectives. Resources are acquired and arranged in some more or less stable pattern to encourage attitudes and behaviour in line with the current objectives. The vertical dimension creates a hierarchy of authority and influence, and so shapes the (unequal) distribution of power through defining access to organisational resources. The second creates a degree of functional or other specialisation – and again influences the distribution of influence around the organisation. The chapter examined a variety of structures that managements have evolved. Similarly, several different kinds of culture were observed. Although culture is a much more recent topic of study in management, many believe that it has significant effects on organisational performance. The choice of structure affects people's motivation and commitment, as discussed in Chapter 13.

Process

The form of structure adopted affects the position of stakeholders in the organisation. It determines such things as their status, their experience of work, their power, and their ability to be involved in or to influence decisions. Structures affect many of the processes of management such as decision making and communicating. Some make it possible to involve the appropriate people in decisions. Others obstruct that and can severely hinder the ability of the organisation to react to changing circumstances. Some forms of structure encourage horizontal communication among a wide network of people. Others limit communication within narrowly defined functions or departments. Structures also shape and influence the flow of information into and out of the organisation.

Control

Structures fundamentally affect the ability of management to control other organisational members. Centralised structures tend to work in favour of those at the top, while decentralised structures enhance the positions of those lower in the hierarchy. So the design of structure is not a technical matter. Different groups will try to influence structure to maintain or increase their access to institutional sources of power, such as knowledge and economic resources. Information technology is greatly increasing the ability of managers to monitor what is happening around the organisation, even if they are not personally present. Appropriate structures are also needed to support the learning opportunities identified in the control processes.

ABB appears to be moving towards a structure that gives more central control. The company is concerned to improve performance, and one way it hopes to do this is by making managers more directly accountable. So it is strengthening the vertical hierarchy. It sees this as being more important than the possible disadvantage, that of subduing local initiative in the operating companies. As a global business it will undoubtedly be making full use of information systems to help it co-ordinate its widespread activities – a further factor tending to encourage stronger vertical hierarchies.

Q PART CASE QUESTIONS

- Is The Royal Bank of Scotland becoming more centralised or more decentralised?
- Both RBS and ABB are geographically dispersed organisations. What do you expect would be the role of each of the methods of co-ordination within them?
- Which type of culture would best describe RBS?

8.7 Review questions

1 Describe what is meant by a model of an organisation, and compare two organisations using any model from the chapter.

2 Draw the organisation chart of a company or department that you know. From discussing it with people in one or more of the positions shown, compare their account of the structure with that shown on the chart.

3 What factors are encouraging companies to (a) centralise, (b) decentralise organisational functions?

4 Summarise the advantages and disadvantages of the various forms of horizontal specialisation outlined.

5 Several forms of co-ordination are described. Select two that you have seen in operation and describe in detail how they work – and how well they work.

6 Describe an educational or commercial organisation that you know in terms of the competing values model of cultures.

7 What is the significance of the idea of 'fragmented cultures' for those who wish to change a culture to support performance?

Further reading

Bainham, K. and Heimer, C. (1998), *ABB: The dancing giant*, Financial Times Management, London. Traces the long-term history of the company, paying particular attention to the philosophy and achievements of the legendary Percy Bainevik.

Hall, W. (1995), *Managing Cultures*, Wiley, Chichester. Gives a very clear and practical introduction to the topic of culture, based on extensive empirical work within major European companies.

Burnes, B. (2000), *Managing Change*, 3rd edn, Financial Times Prentice Hall, Harlow. While mainly on change, this includes chapters on the elements of organisational structure and culture.

Annotated links, questions and resources can be found on
www.booksites.net/boddy

CHAPTER 9

Human resource management

> **AIM** *To introduce the topic of human resource management and to examine some of the major practices.*

OBJECTIVES

By the end of your work on this chapter you should be able to outline the concepts below in your own terms and:

1 Understand the reasons for the increased interest in human resource management (HRM)

2 Recognise the potential importance for organisational performance of HRM

3 Be aware of the varying status, role and influence of HRM professionals

4 Understand the potential links between organisational strategy and HRM

5 Discuss how the wider context shapes the ability to change HRM practice

6 Understand the main difficulties of a longer-term approach to HRM

7 Describe and analyse the changing nature of job requirements

8 As a potential job seeker, recognise some of the important issues that will face you at the recruitment/selection stage

9 Understand the skills that are involved in a successful performance appraisal interview

10 Recognise that change in one area of HRM usually triggers change in other areas

BMW

This case study describes some of the human resource management changes BMW introduced in its German operations as part of its strategic response to competitive pressures.

BMW was established in 1916 and by 1964 was producing almost 150,000 cars each year; it has grown substantially since then. By the late 1980s it employed some 54,000 people, was the seventh largest automobile manufacturing company in the world, and had subsidiaries in many European countries, New Zealand, South Africa, the United States, Canada and Japan. In 2000 BMW employed almost 115,000 people – 69,000 in Germany alone. In May 2000 it sold the loss-making Rover Company, reducing employee numbers by 7,500, while in January 2001 growing demand for BMW premium vehicles led to the creation of more than 2,500 jobs in Germany. In 2000 BMW sold a record of over 800,000 cars, up 9.4 per cent on the previous year. Western Europe is the major market for the group, accounting for 59 per cent of all BMW cars sold. BMW also manufactures motorcycles and has a joint venture with Rolls-Royce to produce aircraft jet engines.

BMW needs to be placed in the larger context of growing concerns about the loss of competitiveness in the German motor industry. A 1996 report by the German Motor Industry Association identified increased wage costs, higher non-wage labour costs, shorter agreed working time than many competitor countries and the continuing strength of the Deutschmark as being major sources of concern in this regard. These concerns have lowered employment in the industry, stimulated investments abroad and resulted in a high priority being given to initiatives to improve productivity.

Diversification has been central to BMW's competitive strategy, while the HRM changes to be detailed in this chapter derive from, and are highly consistent with, the company's 'six inner values': communication, ethical behaviour to its staff, achievement and remuneration, independence, self-fulfilment and the pursuit of new goals. This value-oriented policy dates back to the early 1980s, arising out of a scenario-planning exercise among senior managers. This underlying philosophy is important in shaping the design of any new BMW plant ('an open design' that advances the visual management of the process) and the process of introducing any new or reformed HRM practices. In the latter case much emphasis is placed on extensive consultation, information sharing and seeking to establish positive interrelationships between individual changes.

Q Case questions

- What issues concerning the management of people are likely to be raised in a group such as BMW that has rapidly expanded its production and distribution facilities?
- How have these issues been affected by domestic developments in Germany?
- How is the increased competition likely to affect the people who work for BMW?

9.1 Introduction

This chapter introduces the following ideas:

- Human resource management
- External fit
- Internal fit
- Succession planning
- Job analysis
- Competences
- Selection tests
- Assessment centres
- Performance-related pay
- Performance appraisal

ACTIVITY 9.1

Defining HRM

Before reading on, note down how you would define human resource management. What topics and issues do you think it deals with, and how does it relate to management as a whole? Keep your notes by you and compare them with the topics covered in the chapter as you work through it.

BMW is a large and successful business in a growing area of the world economy – automobile production. Yet it faces competitive problems stemming in part from big employment costs in its German operations, and competition from new sources. Management is attempting to retain the company's position by diversifying the product range and the number of countries in which it manufactures. The company believes that its business strategy has to be matched by its HRM strategy – and is adapting this to bring about a better-trained and more flexible workforce suited to the new condition.

Such activities are part of a broader change taking place in many western companies, as managers try to align the way they deal with people with broader strategies. Management influences other people through both personal and institutionalised practices. It seeks to be less reactive, less focused on grievances and the routine aspects of personnel administration. Instead it wants to be more proactive in developing a labour force at all levels that will support the organisation's strategy. It also seeks greater coherence between the main aspects of HRM – especially in the areas of selection, development, appraisal and rewards.

This chapter focuses on some institutionalised practices intended to influence the attitudes and behaviour of employees. These practices are commonly referred to as **human resource management** (HRM). The chapter begins by discussing the basic purpose and objectives of HRM, and the reasons for its greater prominence in management discussions. HRM covers four main areas (Beer and Spector, 1985):

- employee influence (i.e. employee involvement in decision making);
- human resource flow (i.e. recruitment, selection, training, development and deployment);
- work systems (i.e. work design, supervisory style);
- reward systems (i.e. pay and other benefits).

Employee influence and work systems are discussed elsewhere, particularly in Chapters 12 and 13. Here, the focus is on policies and arrangements under human resource flow, which concerns the flow of individuals into and through the organisation – human resource planning, job analysis, employee recruitment and selection, and performance appraisal. Management designs these practices to help ensure that the organisation has the right people available to help it achieve its larger strategic objectives. Aspects of reward systems, particularly that of performance-related pay, are also examined. These issues illuminate some of the more general issues concerning HRM, especially the concepts of external and internal fit. They also constitute areas where some of the most notable contemporary changes are occurring in the way that organisations are seeking to manage people.

9.2 Emergence and meaning of human resource management

The term 'human resource management' is relatively new, gaining prominence in US companies and business schools since about 1980 (Brewster, 1994). It is now widely used in the business world, and Guest (1987) attributes this wider use to:

- The emergence of more globally integrated markets in which competition is more extensive and severe. Product life cycles are shorter, with innovation, flexibility and quality often replacing price as the basis of competitive advantage.
- The economic success during the 1980s of countries that had given employee management a relatively high priority, such as Japan and (West) Germany.
- The highly publicised 'companies of excellence' literature (Peters and Waterman, 1982) which suggested that high performance organisations were characterised by a strong commitment to human resource management.
- Changes in the composition of the workforce, particularly the growth of a more educated staff.
- The decline in trade union membership and collective bargaining in many advanced industrialised economies.

Traditionally, managers had tried to institutionalise the way they managed staff by creating separate personnel departments. Partly stimulated by the human relations model (see Chapter 2), management believed they could ensure a committed staff by paying attention to employee grievances and looking after their general welfare. Growing trade union power also led management to create departments that specialised in conducting negotiations and monitoring the agreements reached.

Such personnel management departments typically had limited power, and found it difficult to show that they contributed to financial or any other measures of organisational performance (Legge, 1978; Tyson and Fell, 1985). Senior management saw personnel as reactive, self-contained and obsessed with procedures. It was overwhelmingly concerned with managing employee grievances, discipline and relations with trade unions. The main aim was to minimise costs and avoid any disruption of production. The consequence was that personnel departments typically had little influence on the strategic decisions of organisations.

Greater competition, and changes in the nature of that competition, led to change. Management came to believe that HRM was too important to be left exclusively to personnel specialists with that image. They took the view that *line* management needed to be more actively involved in managing people. Only then would HRM issues receive senior management attention (Fombrun *et al.*, 1984). In particular, the early advocates of HRM argued that the approach would be very distinct from personnel management. The key themes of HRM would be 'integration', 'planning', a 'long-run' orientation, 'proactive' and 'strategic'.

Writers on HRM have argued that the more effective management of people will lead to improved organisational effectiveness and performance. This is based in theories of sustained competitive advantage that emphasise the importance of firm-specific, valuable resources which are difficult to imitate (Pfeffer, 1994). Table 9.1 shows the HRM policies that are likely to affect HRM outcomes and wider organisational outcomes.

Table 9.1 A human resource management model

HRM policies	HRM outcomes	Organisational outcomes
Organisation/job design		High job performance
Management of change	Strategic integration	High problem solving, change and innovation
Recruitment, selection and socialisation	Commitment	
Appraisal, training, development	Flexibility/adaptability	High cost effectiveness
Reward systems	Quality	Low turnover, absence, grievances

Source: Guest (1988).

Many managers and academics now stress the advantages of adopting what has been variously labelled a 'high commitment', 'best practice' or 'mutual gains' human resource management model. Recent evidence suggests that HRM practices have more influence on business performance than initiatives in areas such as quality, technology, competitive strategy or R&D (Patterson *et al.*, 1998). Proponents typically advocate a high quality competitive strategy, underpinned by a high wage/high productivity employment relationship. BMW is an example of this approach.

Q Case questions 9.1

- When did HRM policies begin to be seriously developed at BMW?
- What led management to take this initiative?

ACTIVITY 9.2

Assessing the changes needed

An organisation has decided to pursue a quality-enhancement strategy in which teamworking arrangements will be a central feature. It recognises the need to enhance its level of workforce training and to replace its individual performance-related pay arrangements. Are there any other changes in the HRM area that it needs to consider? (Use Table 9.1 to assist you.)

There are different emphases within the broad HRM approach. One distinction is between 'hard' and 'soft' approaches (Storey, 1992, pp.26–8; Legge, 1995, pp.66–7). The former takes a rational, planning, business-led perspective. The latter sees people as

KEY IDEAS

Features of an organisation committed to HRM

- The firm competes on the basis of quality and differentiation as well as price.
- Human resource considerations weigh heavily in corporate strategic decision making and governance processes. Employee interests are represented through the voice of human resource staff and/or senior executives consult with employee representatives on decisions that affect HRM policies and employee interests. In either case, employees are treated as legitimate stakeholders in the organisation.
- Investments in new hardware or physical technology are combined with the investments in human resources and changes in organisational practices required to realise the full potential benefits of these investments.
- The firm sustains a high level of investment in training, skill development and education, and

personnel practices are designed to use these skills fully.
- Compensation and reward systems are internally equitable, competitive and linked to the long-term performance of the firm.
- Employment continuity and security are important priorities and values to be considered in all corporate decisions and policies.
- Workplace relations encourage flexibility in the organisation of work, empowerment of employees to solve problems, and high levels of trust amongst workers, supervisors and managers.
- Workers' rights to representation are acknowledged and respected. Union or other employee representatives are treated as joint partners in designing and overseeing innovations in labour and human resource practices.

Source: Kochan (1992).

valuable assets whose motivation, involvement and development should have priority. Another theme is that if HRM is to support performance, management needs to balance external and internal fit (Beer and Spector, 1985).

External fit

External fit refers to the link between wider strategy and HRM strategy. Ideally management tries to establish a close and consistent link between the two so that HRM activities encourage people to act in ways that support the wider competitive strategy. Chapter 6 distinguished low cost and differentiation strategies. These require different employee attitudes and behaviours, which HRM policies can encourage. Extensive training, team-working and shop-floor problem-solving arrangements are likely in an organisation committed to a differentiation strategy.

Such HRM practices are unlikely in an organisation that follows a low cost strategy, paying low wages to a casual labour force. Indeed, a recent US review (Greer, 2001, p.292) suggested that in general there is a greater performance impact when HRM policies match particular comprehensive strategies. In addition, the study showed that some human resource practices appear to increase performance in almost any setting, including cognitive tests in selection, staffing selectivity and training.

Q Case questions 9.2

- What is your image of BMW cars? What words would you use to describe them?
- In order to meet the image you expect, what kind of behaviour would you expect of employees?
- What HRM practices will encourage/discourage that behaviour?

Comparing HRM policies

List the major differences in HRM policies that you would expect to observe between two organisations, one pursuing a low cost strategy and the other a quality enhancement strategy. (Use the Key Ideas on page 267 to assist you.)

Internal fit

Organisations also benefit if they have HRM policies that are internally consistent. The individual measures need to complement and reinforce each other by sending a *consistent* set of signals to the workforce. An organisation that encourages teamworking can support this through the payment system. It is likely to fail if this rewards people mainly for their individual contribution, encouraging people to compete rather than co-operate. Achieving **internal fit** may require particular competencies among HRM professionals, with knowledge not only of HRM issues but of business issues as well. Research at the University of Michigan highlighted five leading competency domains (Becker *et al.*, 2001, pp.158–61):

- knowledge of the business;
- delivery of HR practices;
- management of change;
- management of culture;
- personal credibility.

9.3 Human resource planning

In the 1960s and 1970s (at a time of labour shortage) researchers tried to develop techniques for forecasting the demand and supply of labour in organisations. They expected the demand for labour to follow from the organisation's business plan, as an estimate of the numbers and types of employees to meet financial and output objectives. There are various techniques for making these estimates:

- *Forecasting human resource demands* Two techniques are used here: judgemental forecasts or statistical projections. An example of the former is the *Delphi technique.* This approach involves obtaining independent estimates of future staffing needs by means of the successive distribution of questionnaires to various levels of management. The expectation is that some four or five iterations should produce a convergence in the estimates. An example of the latter is *simple linear regression*, in which projected future demand is based on a past relationship between the organisation's employment level and a variable such as the level of sales.
- *Forecasting human resource supplies* Again there are two techniques: judgemental and statistical. An example of the former is *replacement* or **succession planning**, which involves developing charts indicating present job holders and the names of possible replacements. An example of the latter is *Markov matrix analysis,* which can model or simulate human resource flows by examining the rates of movement between job categories over time.

The ability to meet forecast staffing needs (in terms of overall numbers and types of workers) depends on existing staffing levels in the various job categories at the beginning of the planning period, adjusted for (a) the outflow of staff over the planning period (e.g. retirements, dismissal, resignations), (b) the inflow of staff during the planning period (i.e. new recruits), and (c) the internal movement of staff between job categories (e.g. promotions).

A major limitation of human resource planning models is the uncertainty of the business environment. Uncertainty may, paradoxically, make comprehensive planning a waste of time. Operating in a highly volatile environment might seem like a strong incentive to engage in human resource planning. Yet these same circumstances make sophisticated planning extremely difficult. The forecasts are likely to be of limited accuracy and value because of rapidly changing circumstances. This has led to changes in the practice of human resource planning, namely reduced planning horizons, more line management involvement, more qualitative forecasting techniques and more attention to the process, as opposed to the outcomes, of planning.

MANAGEMENT IN PRACTICE   **Uncertainty and human resource planning**

This computer manufacturing plant operates in a very competitive product market, characterised by short product life cycles (i.e. six months) and strong, unpredictable shifts in product demand. It forecasts future sales and estimates a corresponding demand for labour each year. These figures are then adjusted each month. However, it solely 'produces to order' (i.e. holds virtually no stock) and has found that sales, output and hence its demand for labour vary a great deal each week. It has therefore established a pool of 40 people in the area (generally unemployed) upon which it can draw to meet sudden increases in demand. Currently some 15–20 per cent of its workforce are temporary staff, many on monthly contracts.

Source: Interview with manager.

9.4   Job analysis

Job analysis typically leads to a written job description that has important implications for employee selection, training and performance appraisal.

MANAGEMENT IN PRACTICE   **A job description**

The appointment

Title: Assistant General Manager, Mills
Reports to: General Manager, Mills

Main functional role

To provide a strategic focus and overview of production optimisation issues, constraints and development opportunities equally for both mills.

Responsibilities

To work with established mill management teams to proactively address matters of plant future developability and resolution of current problems through line management.

To improve the overall performance of the mill management teams through example and leadership.

To liaise with UK and International Sales in order to ensure the needs of the customer are met by anticipating and overcoming production challenges through research and comprehension of key issues.

To assist with all administrative tasks of the General Manager, in particular ensuring that all reports to head office of mill performance are completed accurately, on time and with such elaboration as required on trend deviations from budget, and plans to overcome.

To deputise for the General Manager in his absence and to attend senior managers' and other meetings as necessary on mills' performance.

The candidate

Experience and qualifications

A graduate of chemical/mechanical engineering or chemistry with subsequent experience in paper science. Should have 8–10 years in the paper (ideally, but not exclusively) or other process industry as a production manager or engineer. Strong production focus and proven ability to solve production problems that have a technical origin.

Skills

- Able to take a broad overview with the initiative and judgement to identify the optimum route for implementation.
- Able to maintain several activities without losing perspective or priority.
- Able to identify with and champion corporate focus and direction for the mills.
- Strong interpersonal and leadership skills in influencing mill management teams.
- Presentation skills.

Future prospects

Candidates must possess potential for further career development with the Group to General Manager or equivalent.

The literature on job analysis is largely concerned with the following steps:

- How is the data for the job description collected? Possibilities include interviewing the job incumbent, observing people doing the job, and distributing questionnaires.

KEY IDEAS   Some key terms in job analysis

Job analysis The process of describing and recording many aspects of jobs.
Job title Refers to a group of positions that are identical with regard to their significant duties.
Position description Refers to a collection of duties performed by a single person.
Work performed Identifies the duties and underlying tasks that make up a job.
Job requirements The experience, education, training, knowledge, skills and abilities needed to perform a job.

Job context The environment that surrounds the job.
Job elements The smallest identifiable components of a job.
Job descriptions Are generated from the information gathered through job analysis. On the basis of job descriptions performance appraisal forms can be developed and job classification systems established for job evaluation purposes.

- Who should collect this information or data? Should it be the job incumbent, the supervisor or a specialist from inside or outside the organisation?
- How should the job information be structured and put into a standardised format?

The job analysis process aims to describe the purpose of a job, its major duties and activities, the conditions under which it is performed and the necessary knowledge, skills and abilities. Jobs are broken into *elements*, such as information input, mental processes, work output, relationship with other people, and job context. These elements are rated along various dimensions such as extent of use, importance, amount of time involved, possibility of occurrence, etc.

| MANAGEMENT IN PRACTICE | Job analysis in an electronics plant |

This example outlines how management in an electronics plant produced a job analysis. In this plant teamworking operations (eventually without any supervisory personnel) are all important and a new job, of manufacturing team member, was created. To help identify the key competences of the job, a work profiling questionnaire was completed by people such as the managers of production, engineering and HR, as well as some production supervisors. This produced the key tasks for the position, and the participants then ranked these in order of importance. The skills identified were:

- hard skills: visual checking, technical understanding, fault-finding skills, and mechanical comprehension;
- soft skills: attention to detail, data rational, practical, and sociable/supportive in a team environment.

Source: Personal interview with manager.

Smaller workforces mean that management often broadens the job descriptions of the staff who remain. The move towards teamworking in many organisations, as discussed in Chapter 15, also has implications for the approach to job analysis:

Essentially, job analysis consists of methods and procedures that accurately describe the set of tasks that represent jobs. Inherent in the traditional approach to job analysis is the assumption that the work activities of individual employees can be objectively described … [In] a team situation individual tasks may be quite fluid. Further, team effectiveness often asks for team members to develop a wide variety of skills so that they are capable of providing an assortment of inputs. Thus cross-training is becoming more common and narrow job descriptions are giving way to individual contributions being driven by dynamic relationships within the team. The fluidity of tasks and the flux of individual inputs as a function of interdependency on the inputs of other team members means that a snapshot of the work activities for individual employees may be difficult to take and would likely soon be limiting and out of date in a team environment. Thus, the traditional job analysis assumption of continuing tasks for individuals appears to be incorrect when in team situations. (Academy of Management, 1996, p.11)

The continuation of the BMW case study below illustrates the teamworking arrangements introduced amongst production employees in the German operations of the group.

CASE STUDY   BMW – the case continues – new work structures

In response to increased competition, market over capacity and substantial reductions in collectively agreed working hours in Germany (a 35-hour week in the metal/electrical industries from October 1995), BMW sought greater efficiency through increased employee performance. Following a 1991 agreement on a 'pilot phase for future work structures', and with the agreement of the works council, the company introduced in 1995 new forms of work organisation. Employees were arranged into self-managing groups (each with 8–15 workers), with a high degree of autonomy but with clearly defined tasks. Members of the group decide upon each individual's responsibility and the rotation of jobs, as well as making on-the-spot suggestions and decisions about product improvement.

Each group elects a spokesperson as an activity co-ordinator and representative of the group, although they have no power to give orders or take disciplinary action. Supervisors remain as the group's immediate superior in technical and disciplinary matters, but play more of an advisory/facilitating role. The supervisor is responsible for proposing and agreeing objectives, presenting progress figures, helping progress continuous improvements and ensuring the improvement of qualifications of group members. The company has to ensure that adequate training is available, goals are agreed upon and results circulated. Improved product quality and job satisfaction are the aims, leading in turn to greater productivity. BMW was hoping for a 4 per cent annual increase in productivity, compared with 2 per cent previously.

Source: *European Industrial Relations Review*, issue 271 (1996), pp.23–4.

Q Case questions 9.3

- How will the introduction of teamworking help to improve the external fit between HRM and broader strategy?
- To achieve internal fit, what other changes will BMW need to make to support teamworking?

Finally, some mention needs to be made of the development of the 'competences' theme. The aim here has been to identify and develop the behavioural competences required for the satisfactory and/or high performance of individual jobs. Competence frameworks are used by organisations for job analysis purposes.

MANAGEMENT IN PRACTICE   Competences in an international business

This organisation, which has plants in five different countries, has a long-standing performance management system, centred around the notion of employee competences. However, these competences had not been updated for some 12 years which, in conjunction with other issues concerning the performance management systems, had resulted in some of the individual plants developing their own approaches. Such local initiatives were seen to put at risk the achievement of certain corporate-wide objectives, and made it difficult to compare performance appraisal information and results between plants. To address these problems the organisation in 2000 established a seven-person, multi-functional performance management team. The consultations and deliberations of this team resulted in the establishment of the following eight key competences for the organisation as a whole:

- results orientation (achievement and initiative);
- teamwork;
- leadership;
- quality and process focus;
- influence and interpersonal skills ;
- personal adaptability;
- technical and business skills;
- management and supervision.

Fuller definitions and associated metrics have been established for each of the competences.

Source: Personal interview with manager.

9.5 Employee recruitment and selection

A job analysis exercise is intended to produce a comprehensive and accurate job description. The next part of the HRM process is recruitment and selection. The aim here is to produce a good pool of applicants and select the best of these to fit the job. The selection process aims to minimise (a) *false positive errors*, whereby the selection process predicts success in the job for an applicant, who is therefore hired, but who fails and (b) *false negative errors*, whereby an applicant who would have succeeded in the job is rejected because the process predicted failure. As the costs of the latter are not directly experienced by the organisation managers are more concerned about the former.

Studies of the selection process have mainly centred on the **validity** of the process, in the sense of its ability to predict future performance. Additional criteria in the selection process include fairness and cost.

Interviews

Management traditionally relies on application forms, references and interviews for selecting employees. The interview remains popular (because of low direct costs and applicability to a wide range of jobs) despite research showing the low validity of the method (Robertson, 1996). Interviewer ratings correlate poorly with measures of subsequent on-the-job performance of the candidates hired (i.e. it generates far too many false positive errors). The reason for this is that many interviewers are not good at seeking, receiving and processing the amount and quality of information that is necessary to make an informed hiring decision. Problems with the interview as a selection device are:

- Decisions are made too quickly.
- Information in the early stage of the interview has a disproportionate influence on the decision.
- Interviewers compare applicants with an idealised stereotype.
- Appearance and non-verbal behaviour strongly shape decisions.
- Interviewers are poorly prepared and ask too many questions of limited value.
- 'Good' responses to certain questions are overly generalised.

Interviewing interviewees

Arrange to talk to some friends or colleagues who have recently been interviewed for jobs. Ask them to describe the overall process and to identify any features or aspects of the experience that they particularly liked or disliked. Ideally you should talk to at least one person who was offered the job and to one who was not.

As background work for this exercise, compile a checklist of the key features of 'good practice' interviews that should help inform the way you ask questions. A useful reference here is Rebecca Corfield's (1999) Successful Interview Skills. *As well as practising your own interviewing skills you should compare the experience of the interviewees with best practice techniques.*

Aware of these difficulties, more organisations are systematically training people in good interview techniques. Others use standard interview schedules in which all applicants are asked the same set of questions in roughly the same order. The membership of interview panels is also changing. Organisations using teamworking arrangements often include team members in the selection process as well as personnel staff and line management. There is evidence that structured interviews, such as 'situational' or 'behavioural' approaches, have a higher predictive validity than unstructured ones (Heffcutt and Arthur, 1994). Nevertheless the latter are widely used, possibly because of their perceived flexibility.

Selection tests

The weaknesses of the interview method and the changing nature of jobs has encouraged more managements to use formal methods such as ability tests and personality questionnaires (*People Management*, August 1996, p.22). Psychometric tests appear to be even more popular in Sweden and Portugal than in the United Kingdom, although they are less used in France, Switzerland and the Netherlands (Sparrow and Hiltrop, 1994, p.341).

MANAGEMENT IN PRACTICE **Slimming down the selection process**

This organisation's selection process originally involved applicants visiting the site on four separate occasions: for personality testing, for two separate interviews and then a medical examination. However, in a very tight labour market environment, and with a leading local competitor only requiring a single visit for interview/medical examination purposes, it has tried to streamline the process by combining the personality testing and the first interview on a single day. The number of individual tests has also been reduced. This was because the tests were resulting in the hiring of individuals who were 'overqualified' relative to the needs and demands of the job, which was leading to employee dissatisfaction and relatively high turnover rates.

Source: Personal interview with manager.

There are many long-established tests available, both for abilities and personality. In recent years it has been the growing use of personality tests that has been particularly noticeable, and at the same time controversial. The Management in Practice on page 271 described an electronics facility. Management had identified a set of key skills for the new position of manufacturing team member. It then established the following selection process for candidates:

- Three aptitude tests concerned with technical understanding, fault diagnosis, mechanical comprehension and/or visual checking.
- One personality test concerned with tolerance, attention to detail, data rational, initiative, sociable, supportive, willingness to take responsibility and critical. This test would only be scored for candidates who reach second interview.
- First interview covering work experience, health, suitability for shift working, and an eyesight test.
- Second interview – structured, using the results of the personality test.

Organisational psychologists hold varying opinions about the accuracy and value of personality tests. Some of the concerns and criticisms of this form of testing are:

- They should only be used and interpreted by qualified and approved experts.
- Candidates can fake the answers to some questions, to give the answers they think the organisation is looking for.
- An individual's personality may vary with their circumstances.
- Good performers in the same job may have different personalities.

The feature below shows the personality test score of a company director's secretary, based on the commonly used 16 PF test.

MANAGEMENT IN PRACTICE   **A personality profile (16 PF test)**

	(1	2	3	4	5	6	7	8	9	10)	
Reserved								8			Outgoing
Concrete thinking								8			Abstract thinking
Affected by feelings							7				Calm, unruffled
Not assertive								8			Assertive, dominant
Serious, reflective						6					Happy-go-lucky
Expedient						6					Conscientious
Shy					5						Venturesome
Tough minded							7				Tender minded
Trusting						6					Suspicious
Practical						6					Imaginative
Forthright					5						Shrewd
Self-assured										10	Apprehensive
Conservative						6					Experimenting
Group oriented								8			Self-sufficient
Undisciplined								8			Self-disciplined
Relaxed								8			Tense

There is a growing concern that the misuse of tests may run foul of equal opportunities legislation and regulations. A final point is the potential problem of managing employee expectations. One long-standing criticism of the employee selection process is that the organisation is 'over-sold' to those hired. If employees' expectations are then not met on the job they are likely to leave. There is a danger of creating a sense of an elite labour force that will be well looked after when 2,000 applicants are reduced to fewer than 300 who are offered a job. Extensive testing risks adding to the 'over-sell' problem.

Assessment centres

Assessment centres use many systematic tests and several assessors to arrive at a comprehensive picture of a candidate's abilities and potential. They have been used for many years to help select candidates for positions at senior levels, but their use is becoming more widespread. Industrial Relations Services (IRS 1997) reports that in the United Kingdom the use of assessment centres is increasing more rapidly than any other selection procedure, with 65 per cent of large firms (over 1,000 employees) using them. Evidence from across Europe suggests that using assessment centres is common in the Netherlands but much less in Portugal, Switzerland and France (Sparrow and Hiltrop, 1994, p.341).

Assessment centres appear to have much higher levels of validity for selection purposes than interviews and employee tests. To some this is a positive finding. That is, the package approach of assessment centres (with their multiple tests and multiple assessors) comes closest to being a reasonable simulation of what the actual job will involve. Other commentators offer a more critical explanation for the relatively high validity of the results from assessment centres – they involve a self-fulfilling prophecy. Knowing that someone has succeeded in an assessment centre, their managers and colleagues act in ways that ensure that the person subsequently does well. Other concerns about assessment centres include:

- their relatively high cost;
- their tendency to become a 'paper factory', with a huge amount of documentation being generated and analysed;
- the ethical and practical problems of providing feedback to individuals whose performance was not impressive;
- the possibility of producing 'clones' who are very similar to the present job incumbents, which may not be appropriate in rapidly changing circumstances.

E-recruitment is a more recent development in recruitment and selection processes. Technology can save huge amounts of time and money in the first stages of shortlisting and interviewing candidates. According to a recent Reed Executive report (2000), cost savings are reported as the biggest advantage of e-recruitment. The report notes that, on average, only 5–6 per cent of the recruitment budget is currently being spent on web recruiting, suggesting that traditional methods are still dominant. However, this may change in the near future. Research indicates that within five years up to 30 per cent of job adverts would be placed on the Internet. This finding is supported by Institute for Personnel and Development (IPD) research showing that the use of the Internet for recruitment in the United Kingdom had more than doubled in the past two years (*People Management*, 3 June 1999).

Evaluation

This essentially narrow, technical task of achieving an 'individual employee/individual job fit' has been called into question in recent years by some of the strategic human resource management literature. For instance, some of the literature on cultural change programmes has emphasised the need to recruit and select employees who fit well with the larger direction of change in the organisation. A specific instance of change along these lines is the attempt to identify individuals who will work well in teams. Research here has concentrated on identifying the competences necessary to contribute in, for example, multi-disciplinary teams (West and Allen, 1997).

Such an orientation will have important implications for job analysis. It is also likely to result in important changes in selection methods and in the individuals involved in selection processes. Indeed there is now a growing body of literature which argues that individuals should be hired for the organisation, not the job. As Bowen *et al.* (1996) write:

> Diverse firms … are using the approach to build cultures that rely heavily on self-motivated, committed people for corporate success. New, often expensive, hiring practices are changing the traditional selection model. An organisational analysis supplements a job analysis, and personality attributes are screened in addition to skills, knowledge and abilities. (p.139)

KEY IDEAS   **Hiring for the organisation rather than the job**

Potential benefits

- More favourable employee attitudes (e.g. greater organisational commitment).
- More desirable individual behaviours (e.g. lower absence and turnover).
- Reinforcement of organisational design (e.g. support for desired organisational culture).

Potential problems

- Greater investment of resources in the hiring process.
- Relatively undeveloped and unproven supporting selection technology.
- Individual stress.
- May be difficult to use the full model where pay-offs are greatest.
- Lack of organisational adaptation.

Source: Bowen *et al.* (1996, p.146).

The *organisational* analysis mentioned here is concerned with the leading components of the larger work *context*, such as the longer-term goals and values of the organisation, rather than simply the content of the individual job.

Q   **Case questions 9.4**

- In what ways are developments in BMW already encouraging a 'hire for the organisation, not for the job' approach?
- What implications will that have for achieving internal fit in the company's HRM policies?

9.6   Performance appraisal

The prime purpose of **performance appraisal** is to try to improve an individual's current on-the-job performance, although the process may also be important for pay purposes ('performance-related pay') and for longer-term training/development purposes. Appraisal is widespread throughout the United Kingdom. The Workplace Employee Relations Survey (Cully *et al.*, 1999), covering over 3,000 United Kingdom workplaces, finds that non-managerial employees are formally appraised in 56 per cent of United Kingdom workplaces. The last decade has seen its introduction in the public sector, in particular in schools, hospitals, universities, local authorities and the Civil Service. The growth in performance appraisal is underlined by IRS surveys (1994, 1999). In 1994, 39 per cent of organisations applied appraisal to every employee. By 1999 coverage had increased to 75 per cent.

Performance appraisal, at least on a formal basis, is not a widespread feature of all national systems. For instance, it is not a characteristic of even relatively large organisations in Finland, while in many well-known Japanese companies it is a much more informal, ongoing process than is the case in UK and US organisations. However, it is becoming more popular in China (Chow, 1994), Hong Kong (Snape *et al.*, 1998), and India (Lawler *et al.*, 1995).

Although performance appraisal has spread from private to public organisations, and to different groups of employees, personnel and human resource managers frequently cite it as the area of their responsibilities they would most like to improve. In consequence performance appraisal arrangements are frequently changing.

A recent development is 360 degree feedback. The term describes the comprehensive nature of the system, where feedback on any individual is derived from peers, subordinates, supervisors and, occasionally, customers. In what might be called phase one of 360 degree feedback the emphasis was on its use as a development tool. It was usually applied in the context of career development. More recently phase two has seen 360 degree feedback being used as part of the ongoing evaluation of employees, and in some cases organisations are linking it to pay. While many organisations have gained some advantages from using this form of feedback as a developmental tool, some commentators argue that it remains to be seen whether any benefits are outweighed by the considerable time, effort and costs involved in the process (Redman and Wilkinson, 2001). Advantages include a more objective picture of an individual's contribution, strengths and development needs, thus overcoming some of the limitations of top-down appraisals. The system should also promote higher levels of trust in the fairness of the process. Despite this, one US study found that half of the firms it surveyed which had implemented 360 degree appraisals had later dropped them (*People Management*, 1 October 1998). Problems included:

- Raters may fear adverse consequences if they give negative feedback.
- The risk of political game playing. For example, subordinates may ask for a pay rise just before they give their assessments, hoping to tempt the manager to court popularity.
- Assessments from peers or subordinates are no less biased than other methods.

KEY IDEAS — Making 360 degree appraisals work

1 Establishing trust is the first step in moving 360 degree feedback from developmental to appraisal tool. This entails genuine consultation with those receiving feedback and those giving it about how the process is to work, what the content of the feedback form is to be and how the output will be used.

2 Adequate and effective training of appraisers in evaluating feedback as interpreting data of this kind is complex.

3 Ensure the system is as economical as possible. Amongst other things, this means keeping the feedback forms reasonably short and focused.

4 Carry out regular evaluations to ensure the systems are working in the way intended.

Source: *People Management*, 1 October 1998.

Attempts to improve the appraisal process usually concentrate on four issues: the criteria used to appraise performance, the face-to-face appraisal interview, who does the appraisal and what happens afterwards.

The criteria

The criteria used in appraisal systems have changed. Early arrangements concentrated on employee traits, such as leadership or loyalty. These have generally given way to criteria that focus on the employee's *on-the-job behaviour*. More recently still the emphasis has been on job *outcomes* – what the person has achieved. As part of the general increase in performance management contemporary appraisal systems frequently consider whether employees have achieved their specified job performance goals over the appraisal period. There are important differences here in the length of the appraisal period and the extent to which the performance goals were jointly set.

The interview

For many appraisers and appraisees the interview is a particularly awkward moment. It surfaces tensions, conflicts and contradictions – summarised by Beer (1985):

> The most significant conflict is between the individual and the organisation. The individual desires to confirm a positive self-image and to obtain organisational rewards of promotion or pay. The organisation wants individuals to be open to negative information about themselves so they can improve their performance. It also wants individuals to be helpful in supplying this information. The conflict is over the exchange of valid information. As long as individuals see the appraisal process as having an important influence on their rewards (pay, recognition), their career (promotions and reputation), and their self-image, they will be reluctant to engage in the kind of open dialogue required for valid evaluation and personal development. (p.316)

KEY IDEAS
Common appraisal interview problems

The halo effect The appraiser gives a favourable rating to overall job performance in essence because the person being appraised has performed well in the particular aspect of the job the appraiser considers all important.

The pitchfork effect This is the exact opposite of the halo effect, whereby the appraiser gives an unfavourable rating to overall job performance in essence because the appraisee has performed poorly in the particular aspect of the job the appraiser considers all important.

Central tendency The appraiser deliberately avoids using the end points of the rating scale and rates all employees as average in virtually all aspects of job performance.

The recency error In rating an employee's job performance over, for example, a 12-month period, the appraiser makes disproportionate use of instances of performance that are relatively recent (i.e. close to the interview in time) to make an assessment.

Length of service bias The appraiser assumes that an experienced employee who has been rated well in the past has absorbed and responded well to any new aspects of his or her job, and hence does not closely monitor performance in this regard.

The loose rater In order to avoid any conflict with a subordinate, an appraiser does not discuss any weak areas of an individual's job performance.

The tight rater An appraiser has unrealistically high expectations for all subordinates, which means that no one receives an excellent or outstanding rating.

The competitive rater An appraiser links his or her own rating with that of subordinates, so that no one receives a rating higher than the appraiser's.

Source: Adapted from Lowe (1986, pp.60–2).

There are numerous ways that individual appraisers adjust to the potential dilemma of being both a judge and a helper. In some organisations the formally scheduled appraisals do not take place; in one organisation the human resource (HR) director estimated that one manager in three was not conducting the recommended quarterly appraisals. In other cases the appraiser avoids disrupting working relationships by giving the appraisee an easy time.

Aware of these problems, managers can try to improve the quality of face-to-face appraisal interviews. They have provided training to eliminate the problems listed by Lowe (see Key Ideas on page 279) and have developed processes with the following features:

- Regular informal monitoring of and feedback to the appraisee takes place before the appraisal interview. There are then no surprises during the formal interview.
- A completed self-appraisal form provides the basis for the interview.
- The content of the interview is largely shaped by the person being appraised. They do most of the talking, and are encouraged/coached to identify weaknesses, discuss these and suggest solutions.
- The appraiser should use open questions to encourage dialogue.
- Criticism must be constructive in nature, with positive comments substantially outweighing negative ones.
- Comments must be factually based and focused on specific job activities.

MANAGEMENT IN PRACTICE   **Different approaches to appraisal**

An appraisal interview training video (with a recommended approach along the above lines) was shown to an audience that included managers from UK and French companies. Comments by the French managers indicated many similarities in approach. They also highlighted the following differences:

- The appraisal interview lasted much longer in France (three hours compared with an hour or so in the United Kingdom).
- The interview involved three people (i.e. the appraisee, the boss and their boss), rather than two.
- The very detailed self-appraisal form (8–10 pages) was much more significant in the French than in the UK organisations represented.

The appraiser

Traditionally, appraisals have involved an individual being appraised by his or her immediate superior. However, Fletcher (1996) has observed:

> With fewer management layers and more direct reports to each manager, increased use of matrix or project management and greater geographical spread of staff, the old principle of the immediate boss carrying out the appraisal becomes unworkable in many instances. A manager may have too many appraisees to deal with, or see them too infrequently to know how they are doing. An appraisee may work for several bosses throughout the year. Who, then, should be the appraiser? (pp.235–6)

This topic is being actively discussed in many organisations. There seems considerable emphasis on encouraging more self-appraisal while some team-based organisations have introduced peer group appraisals. Some organisations have gone even further in this regard, using full circle (360 degree) appraisal arrangements. An HR manager made these comments about such arrangements:

● In theory, such arrangements have a great deal to recommend them.
● In practice they are extremely time consuming.
● Only a small, self-contained part of his organisation uses them. They appear to have been most successful at the top of the organisation where numbers are small.
● Such arrangements are probably most suitable for smaller organisations characterised by close, 'high trust' working relationships.
● It is difficult to maintain the momentum of such arrangements, particularly in the face of more immediate business pressures.

The importance of the 'high trust' working relationships point above cannot be emphasised too strongly.

The aftermath

What happens when the appraisal has been conducted and training needs identified? The issues here can be illustrated by the case of an organisation that annually appraised all its white-collar and professional staff to assess development needs. At the company's request a senior academic conducted focus group meetings with 40–50 of the staff to gain their perceptions of the value of the process. The major points made were:

● The overwhelming majority of the staff rated the interpersonal skills of the appraisers very highly. The interviews were well conducted.
● The development needs of individuals that were identified were rarely followed through.
● Training courses were promised but never delivered.

This arose from policy in the training section of the HR department. The content of the annual training plan was driven by budgetary concerns and the programmes offered by local training consultants. The results of the appraisals did not enter the plan in any significant way. One unexpected outcome of this exercise was the departure of the training manager.

The weak link demonstrated here between the appraisal system and the development/ training programme is by no means unique. Indeed this finding is highly consistent with the general view that training/development activities in many organisations are determined in a very piecemeal manner. In order to ensure a much better follow-up process to appraisal interviews it will be essential for organisations to involve the HR department more fully in the appraisal process. They will need to recognise that at least three parties, and not just two (the appraisee and appraiser) are involved. An example of this is the organisation that has recently changed its performance appraisal system with a view to encouraging more regular self-appraisal for personal development purposes. Its new documentation sets out the following areas of responsibility:

● *Appraiser*: sets the direction, coaches on a day-to-day basis, provides timely reviews on request, conducts final assessment of results.
● *Job holder*: interprets manager's direction, develops plans, arranges meetings and leads the system, tracks own development progress.
● *HR department*: issues the documentation, provides training where appropriate, audits the system, approves the outcome.

MANAGEMENT IN PRACTICE **Fox's Biscuits – using training to transform the business**

Fox's Biscuits has used training to revolutionise both the manufacturing process and the company's culture to make it the most cost-effective biscuit manufacturer in the industry. Over the past five years it has invested some £300,000 in training. This investment addressed the problem of a long-serving workforce with a low skills base. Despite earlier investment in new production technologies little had been spent on providing employees with commensurate skills. A tailor-made NVQ was developed for manufacturing employees, which was highly successful in raising skills levels and enhancing commitment to continuous quality improvement in the manufacturing process. Restructuring and retraining created multi-skilled production teams where workers are able to do each other's work while at the same time individuals have a 'principal job', allowing them to specialise. In management's view improving capability through developing employees has been the catalyst for success.

Source : *People Management*, 25 January 2001.

9.7 Performance-related pay

Changes in reward management have been at the heart of developments in HRM. While merit/performance pay have been highly visible in many countries, there has been a more recent shift towards more flexible and variable reward systems. This change has been driven by clear government support for greater employment flexibility. According to the Department of Trade and Industry (1996), 'Britain's deregulated labour market now allows employers considerable freedom to choose pay systems that meet their own needs and those of the workforce … flexible pay is an integral part of the pay agenda' (p.3). A Towers Perrin (1999) study of 460 European organisations found that, in the previous three years, 94 per cent had made significant changes to pay systems, while 96 per cent planned further changes. The key developments in UK remuneration policies appear to be:

- a shift away from collectively bargained pay towards more individual performance or skills-driven systems;
- an attempt to link pay systems more directly to business strategy and organisational goals;
- an emphasis on non-pay items, such as life assurance and childcare vouchers;
- the developments of more flexible pay components and individualised reward packages.

MANAGEMENT IN PRACTICE **The Royal Bank of Scotland – trading in options**

In 1997 The Royal Bank of Scotland set out to improve its reward system in a bid to strengthen its 'employer brand'. Facing tight labour market conditions in the financial services market, the bank needed to rethink how to reward staff, as well as how to get more value from the £100 million benefits spend. In 1998 the company launched 'RBSelect', the biggest flexible benefits plan of its kind in the United Kingdom, covering more than 18,000 employees in 170 locations. RBSelect is a 'total reward' benefits package giving employees a wide choice of benefits and almost complete flexibility in how they allocate the overall value of their remuneration package. The package is divided into six groups: private health cover; insurance, including life assurance for spouses and partners; savings such as voluntary contributions to pension schemes; 'lifestyle features', which include the manager's company car, childcare vouchers and retail vouchers; basic salary; and holiday. Innovative features include the facility to buy or sell up to three days' leave, the provision of a legal helpline and the availability of an additional car leasing scheme to all employees. Even the Christmas bonus can be traded in for a different benefit. Employees can change their benefits package once a year. The new 'total reward' system has been positively received and is expected to have a positive impact on recruitment and retention.

Source: *People Management*, 6 May 1999.

Developments in pay policies are also linked to changes in work organisation. The case study below shows the new bonus payment arrangements for production employees in the German operations of BMW and recent developments in BMW's UK operations. These team-based payment arrangements fit the new work structures outlined earlier.

CASE STUDY   BMW – the case continues – new work structures

The new work structures, with their emphasis on multi-skilled workers, quality objectives and the individual's contribution to group performance, were accompanied by new payment arrangements. A bonus system applied to all 36,000 production employees who operated with defined performance targets.

Basic remuneration consists of the minimum pay rate agreed in the metalworking industry collective agreement plus a 10 per cent BMW supplement. The previous six wage groups were expanded to nine. This allowed for finer gradations determined by the demands placed on the employee. These reflected the criteria of function, difficulty and variety of activities, and scope for decision making. If a worker regularly performed a higher value activity then movement up the groups was possible.

On top of the basic remuneration a fixed 25 per cent *additional bonus* was paid to all employees for meeting prearranged quotas. This quota involved producing a set number of units to the company's quality standards by a workforce of an agreed size. Employees in each group were consulted and invited to comment on whether the quotas were realistic and achievable.

Employees could also earn extra pay through a *personal supplement*, which was payable if an individual contributed to the group results. Expectations and specific goals were discussed and agreed in talks between the employee and the supervisor. An individual's contribution to the group was discussed every year and this assessment determined the personal supplement received.

More recent developments in BMW's UK operations further underline the linkage between pay and the drive for increased worker flexibility and efficiency. In early 2001 new pay agreements emphasising flexible working arrangements and performance-related pay were introduced. In the new Hams Hall plant the two-year pay deal contains a performance bonus that will deliver up to 5 per cent of production workers' annual pay. This will be calculated on an individual basis rather than on the site's performance. A similar deal was initially rejected by workers at the Cowley, Oxford plant, where pay was not the stumbling block. Instead, workers and unions were opposed to the new flexible working arrangements that included an extended working week. Further flexibility gains are expected at the Oxford plant following the recruitment of temporary workers, which will allow flexibility in production systems, including the abolition of traditional shutdown periods for holidays.

Source: *European Industrial Relations Review*, Issue 271 (1996), p.24; *Financial Times*, 26 January 2001; *The Times*, 8 February 2001.

> **Q Case questions 9.5**
>
> - What external business factors have prompted this review of the payment system at BMW?
> - How will it affect the management of the appraisal system?
> - How will it affect the demands on the management information system (see Chapter 18)?

Performance-related pay arrangements involve a linkage between a human resource flow activity (i.e. performance appraisal) and reward systems. To some observers this is an unfortunate linkage to make because it risks 'overloading' the appraisal process. That is, it is asking the appraisal process to achieve too many objectives, risks making awkward interviews even more difficult and will ultimately cause the training/development objectives of appraisal to take second place to money considerations.

That said, there are some positive points to be made about performance-related pay arrangements, in that (a) such arrangements do have some theoretical or conceptual underpinnings in expectancy theory (see Chapter 13) and (b) some organisations have used such arrangements for many years and report positive effects on both individual and organisational performance. However, there are many other organisations where the track record of performance-related pay has been much less impressive. Either there has been little positive impact on organisational performance or the arrangements have been counter-productive for other reasons. Research by Purcell (2000) finds that 'reward management does more harm than good in building trust, commitment and motivation'. A Towers Perrin (1999) survey found that 84 per cent of companies that linked pay and performance experienced operating difficulties including ineffective communication and inadequate support from senior management. Lawson (2000) notes, 'the amount of work being undertaken in organisations to modify, change and improve individual performance pay schemes indicates a trend of unhappiness with them. In short, the record of performance-related pay arrangements has been highly variable' (p.315). There are various possible reasons for this:

- The expectancy theory of employee motivation that underpins such arrangements does not apply universally or at all times.
- Performance-related pay arrangements have not been well received by employees because of inadequate prior discussion, consultation and explanation.
- Performance-related pay fits the circumstances of some organisations much better than others. For instance, introducing performance-related pay arrangements into an organisation characterised by 'low trust' relationships between employees and management is a certain recipe for creating further problems.
- Performance-related pay arrangements have multiple goals or objectives, but not all of these can be achieved by the one set of arrangements. For instance, individual performance-related pay is most successful in demonstrating to employees that performance affects their pay – but may inhibit co-operation within the workforce.
- There is an embedded assumption that companies are rationally directed organisations and that managers have the foresight to know what is needed for the forthcoming year. In reality, change is quicker and messier than that.

**MANAGEMENT
IN PRACTICE** **Performance-related pay in a not-for-profit organisation**

This not-for-profit organisation has 23 separate grades of employees, with annual salary increases being related to changes in the cost of living, and incremental payments occurring (within grades) every three years. In 1995 a new chairman (with a private sector background) was appointed, with some other individuals (also from the private sector) being appointed to the finance committee. The chairman and other new appointees were highly critical of the existing salary/grading arrangements. They viewed them as 'very old-fashioned, with little capacity to motivate staff'. In particular, the absence of performance-related pay was viewed as highly undesirable. Although the personnel manager could point to no employee dissatisfaction with the existing arrangements or give examples of tangible organisational difficulties, a senior working party was established to 'move things along' and a consultancy firm engaged to help introduce some changes.

ACTIVITY 9.5

Deciding when performance-related pay is appropriate

Identify some of the key features of an organisation where performance-related pay arrangements are likely to be appropriate.

One of the major growth areas of performance-related pay in recent years has been in the public sector of many advanced industrialised economies.

**KEY
IDEAS** **Common problems with performance-related pay in the public sector**

- A lack of differentiation in performance ratings.
- A clustering of managers at the top of the salary range in merit pay schemes where they are no longer eligible for merit increments.
- Dissatisfaction amongst staff who are rated fully satisfactory but who, under quotas and other restrictive guidelines for some schemes, either receive a smaller pay award than their colleagues or no award at all in a given year.

- Relatively low levels of funding that make schemes highly competitive and, in some countries, cut-backs in funds during times of economic restraint.
- A narrowing of the range and a reduction in the average size of bonuses paid.

Source: OECD (1993).

9.8 Critical perspectives on HRM

Although the philosophy and terminology of HRM has spread widely in the management literature there are questions about how widely management has applied it, whether it can show results when it has been applied, and its effects on power relations within organisations, involving a set of techniques and practices that are potentially contradictory (Blyton and Turnbull, 1994).

More rhetoric than reality?

One argument is that while many managers talk about human resource management a much smaller number use it in the fullest sense of the term. It may not suit the circumstances of all countries. For example, an economy that typically follows a low wage strategy, has a limited tradition of planning and works to short-run financial measures will not provide a suitable place in which to develop advanced HRM policies. Even within a more benign national system HRM is likely to be confined to a relatively small and atypical group of organisations. Foreign-owned, non-union, greenfield site operations have often been identified as the most natural homes for such an employment approach (Guest, 1987). Another point is that, while organisations may adopt certain HRM practices, few will do so in a comprehensive, strategic manner. In other words there will be little evidence of internal fit; rather, a more *ad hoc*, reactive, piecemeal approach will be apparent (Storey, 1992).

Does it work?

The second line of questioning in relation to HRM is the limited evidence that the use of the approach has enhanced organisational effectiveness and performance. That is, the quantity and quality of evidence supporting a strong, positive relationship between HRM and organisational performance is far from impressive (Legge, 1995). Certainly there are some individual studies that have demonstrated such a relationship. For example, an important study in the United States involving some 1,000 firms reported a strong relationship between a set of high performance work practices and certain measures of firm performance, such as employee turnover, productivity and financial performance (Huselick, 1995). This study has been followed up by others in the United States, and indeed such research has become more widespread in the United Kingdom. There are now some useful reviews of this body of research, which has been one of the most important in the HRM area in recent times (Ichniowski *et al.*, 1996; Wood 1999; Becker *et al.*, 2001). In general the findings emphasise that a bottom-line pay-off will only come about if a more strategic orientation is adopted towards the introduction and operation of HRM, i.e. the notions of external and internal fit are more strenuously observed.

Does it shift the power balance?

Finally there is a line of criticism that HRM can have negative effects on employees and unions. The underlying contention here is that HRM embodies a unitary view of organisations. This view (see Chapter 2) rejects the legitimacy of employees/management conflict in the employment relationship and seeks to align the aims and objectives of individual employees with those of owners and their agents (i.e. senior management). To some commentators HRM is simply the latest in a long line of attempts to shift the terms of the wage/effort bargain in favour of management. Others stress that HRM practices are designed to help organisations to be run on a non-union basis, or at least that they will have the effect of reducing the role, strength and presence of unions. However, in the United Kingdom, HRM practices seem to be more a feature of the union rather than the non-union sector, probably because there are more small firms in the non-union sector (Beaumont, 1996). This being said, the relevance of HRM practices to small firms should not be ignored, as one UK survey indicates:

> the larger the organization, the more chance there was that each of the new employment initiatives had been launched. The reasons are fairly obvious: the larger organizations had more expertise at their disposal, and the relevance of some of the initiatives was clearly tied to size. However, there was an interesting and important new finding. When we

looked at the degree to which certain initiatives had been sustained, we found that smaller organizations had enjoyed the greater success. The reason for this is presumably that once the head of a small enterprise decides to introduce a new approach, it is more likely to be followed through. (Storey, 1995, p.20)

9.9 Emerging themes

This chapter has described a range of strategies and policies associated with HRM that are intended to influence the attitudes and behaviour of employees. Selective recruitment, extensive training and focused appraisal systems are some of the mechanisms utilised in attempting to secure a loyal, committed and flexible workforce. However, different contexts will determine outcomes, such as the nature and focus of business strategy or the boundaries that management place, on employee autonomy and influence. This illustrates the complex nature of HRM outcomes and offers some explanation for the different accounts of HRM in the literature. Those of an unorthodox nature juxtapose the orthodox accounts of HRM, arguing that the reality of HRM is enhanced managerial control over work, work intensification, extensive monitoring and strict discipline. Providing some support for the unorthodox perspective is the UK call centre industry. Emerging trends in this burgeoning industry suggest a failure on management's part to secure employee commitment and consensus evidenced by high employee turnover and employee dissatisfaction. It is important to note, however, that call centres are not homogenous and a spectrum of working conditions is recorded in the wider literature (see, for example, IDS 1997; Reed 1999).

MANAGEMENT IN PRACTICE — A call for help?

This organisation operates in the global telecommunications industry. Technology provides opportunities for detailed monitoring and measuring illustrated by the complex range of performance measurements made on each call (e.g. call handling time, number of calls answered). Call taping is also a standard procedure that assesses formal adherence to scripts and allows judgements to be made on the quality of interaction with the customer (e.g. agent enthusiasm, agent helpfulness). Improvements to productivity are driven by the weekly publication of performance results, which include team and individual targets. These in effect lead to supervisory attempts to speed up, or intensify, work where under-performance is identified. Such attempts have in the past involved threats to bonuses. This organisation, along with many other call centres, has experienced high labour turnover and absence, as well as problems with motivation and commitment. Until recently there was no trade union presence in the organisation. However, following widespread employee dissatisfaction over pay and working conditions (e.g. oppressive shiftwork, unpaid breaks, health and safety concerns), around one-third of employees joined a trade union.

Source: Bain and Taylor (2000).

ACTIVITY 9.6

Putting the perspective to use

How could HRM be utilised to reverse the problems in the call centre industry?

9.10   Summary

Many companies in the United Kingdom and the United States have in recent years begun to give more prominence to HRM issues (a status they have long had in countries such as Japan and (West) Germany). These need to be evaluated in terms of their external and internal fit. If there is a good degree of fit it is more likely to have a lasting effect on business performance. There is some quantitative evidence that HRM practices contribute to wider organisational objectives.

Content

HRM practices represent an attempt to institutionalise those aspects of management concerned with employees. The approach is an attempt to support the achievement of broader business objectives and strategy. It does this by organising activities such as HR planning and job analysis to ensure that available resources fit the requirements of the external world. Organising and planning the approach also aims to ensure a degree of internal fit between the several components of HRM. It also seeks a fit with other organisational policies such as teamwork or the creation of autonomous business units. An underlying principle is that employees can be motivated to appropriate behaviours by HRM practices that accurately reflect their pattern of human needs. The approach is also criticised by some commentators for having other, more covert, objectives. It may be followed for primarily cost-cutting reasons or as a way of weakening the power of representative bodies such as trade unions.

Process

HRM initiatives are affected by the interests of other stakeholders around the organisation. They may or may not see their interests served by HRM. Other senior managers may be more powerful than the HRM specialists, and have other priorities. An organisational commitment to HRM initiatives is inevitably competing with other possible innovations such as business process re-engineering. HRM may also be opposed by trade unions if the latter see it as an attempt to shift the power balance against them or to remove some of the functions they have performed on behalf of their members. There is a discussion within management as to whether HRM policies are decided and managed by a central department or delegated to the line managers responsible for particular business units. The acceptance of the approach is likely to vary between countries, depending on wider institutional arrangements.

Control

HRM can be seen as one of the ways in which management seeks to exercise control over employees. Some accuse those promoting the approach of adopting a fundamentally unitary perspective to management and seeking to displace or weaken trade unions. It can also contribute to both individual and organisational learning. Practices such as performance appraisal attempt this at the individual level. However, commentators have noted that few companies regularly appraise the appraisal process to see if it is meeting whatever objectives were held for it. Not doing so prevents learning about the benefits or otherwise of the monitoring, correction and learning cycles embodied in appraisal systems.

Q **PART CASE QUESTIONS**

- What are the main issues of an HRM nature that are likely to be topical within The Royal Bank of Scotland?
- From your understanding of the material in the chapter, what aspects of HRM should The Royal Bank of Scotland be focusing its efforts upon?
- How will the merger with NatWest have affected this?

9.11 Review questions

1 What do the terms internal and external fit mean in an HRM context?

2 What are the arguments put forward in favour of an organisation adopting a deliberate HRM strategy?

3 Summarise the criticism of HRM that it is based on a unitary perspective (see Chapter 2) of organisations.

4 There is little evidence that HRM has achieved the business objectives claimed for it. What evidence would you look for, and how would you show the link between cause and effect?

5 How can the concept of organisational analysis support the recruitment process?

6 What are the main criticisms of personality testing?

7 Why is the practice of performance appraisal controversial? Consider both technical and underlying explanations.

8 What lessons can you draw from the way BMW has used the payment system to support other aspects of the HRM policy? More generally, summarise the lessons you would draw from the BMW case.

Further reading

Beardwell, L. and Holden, L. (2001), *Human Resource Management: A contemporary approach*, 3rd edn, Prentice Hall, Harlow. A comprehensive collection of readings covering strategic issues, key practice areas and an international perspective.

Redman, T. and Wilkinson, A. (2001), *Contemporary Human Resource Management: Texts and cases*, Prentice Hall, Harlow. An up-to-date collection of texts and case studies in human resource management covering key practice areas.

Legge, K. (1995), *Human Resource Management: Rhetorics and realities,* Macmillan, London. A highly critical examination of many of the leading, individual themes in HRM, emphasises the gap between the theory and practice of HRM.

Sparrow, P. and Hiltrop, J. (1994), *European Human Resource Management in Transition*, Prentice Hall International, Hemel Hempstead. An explicitly European perspective on the topic.

Annotated links, questions and resources can be found on
www.booksites.net/boddy

CHAPTER 10

The developing organisation

AIM *To contrast mechanistic and organic forms of organisation structure, and outline the factors that influence management choice.*

OBJECTIVES

By the end of your work on this chapter you should be able to outline the concepts below in your own terms and:

1 Explain why organisational structure is deliberately shaped by management

2 Compare the features of mechanistic and organic structures

3 Describe each of the factors that influence managers to choose one form rather than the other

4 Summarise the work of Woodward, and that of Burns and Stalker, and show how they contributed to this area of management theory

5 Contrast contingency and structural choice perspectives on structure

6 List the external factors prompting change in the form of organisations, especially developments in information technology

Oticon

This Danish company is one of the world's five largest producers of hearing aids, with about 1,200 staff. It has its own basic research and production facilities and stresses the high engineering and design quality of its products. Competition intensified during the 1980s and the company began to lose market share. Lars Kolind was appointed chief executive in 1988. In 1990 he concluded that a new approach was needed to counter the threats from larger competitors who were becoming stronger. Oticon's only hope for survival and prosperity was to be radical in all aspects of the business. The changes were intended to turn Oticon from an *industrial* organisation producing hearing aids into a *service* organisation with a physical product.

Work is organised around projects. The project leader is appointed by management and has to recruit a team. Employees choose whether or not to join – and can only do so if their current project leader agrees. Previously most people had a single skill; now all have several. Chip designers have skills in customer support, for example. Employees can work on several projects at once. These arrangements allow the company to respond quickly to unexpected events and to use skills fully. Different backgrounds mean more insights.

Previously Oticon had a conventional structure, now it has no departments, and no hierarchy. There is no formal structure, just teams. Kolind refers to this as 'managed chaos'. The company tries to overcome the dangers of this by developing a very strong and clear purpose and mission 'to help people with X problem to live better with X'; and a common set of written values. Examples include: 'an assumption that we only employ adults (who can be expected to act responsibly)', and 'an assumption that staff want to know what and why they are doing it', so all information is available to everyone (with a few legally excepted areas). There are no titles – people do whatever they think is right at the time. Again the potential for chaos is averted by building underneath the flexible organisation a set of clearly defined business processes, setting out how they are to be carried out. 'The better your processes are defined, the more flexible you can be.' The absence of departments avoids people protecting local interests and makes it easier to cope with fluctuations in workload.

Oticon has redesigned the workplace to maximise disturbance. It refers to this as the mobile office, in which each workstation consists of a desk without drawers (nowhere to file paper). There is no installed telephone – but everyone has a mobile. The workstations are equipped with powerful PCs through which all work is done. Staff have a small personal trolley, for personal belongings only, which they wheel to wherever they are working that day.

Source: Based on Bjorn-Andersen and Turner (1994).

Q Case questions

- What factors persuaded management to change the structure at Oticon?
- How would you expect staff to react to changes of this sort?

10.1 Introduction

This chapter introduces the following ideas:

- Mechanistic structure
- Organic structure
- Differentiation
- Integration
- Contingency approaches
- Determinism
- Structural choice
- Virtual organisation

Lars Kolind was taking a big risk with the changes he made at Oticon. Yet the previous organisation was not working, and he needed to change the way people worked together. Changing the structure towards a team-based operation was the way he chose to go, hoping that this would make better use of scarce resources and mean a faster response to customer needs. Chapter 8 showed the components of structure that are present in all kinds of businesses. This chapter shows how managers try to shape those structural components to achieve their objectives.

Companies regularly restructure their organisations in the hope of improving performance. Some try to centralise their activities, to ensure greater control over local operations – such as the changes that Hewlett-Packard introduced in 2000. In the same year Littlewoods, a large UK retail chain, merged its three businesses – Index stores, Littlewoods stores and its large home shopping division – into one operation. In 2001 Ford of Europe placed its transmissions operations in a joint venture with Getrag, a German transmissions group, to help reduce costs and improve its use of assets (*Financial Times*, 1 February 2001, p.35). Other companies go the other way. After mounting criticism of its performance, British Telecom announced in 2000 that it would divide its business into five separate units. GlaxoSmithKline has grouped its research activities into five autonomous divisions – for similar reasons to those that encouraged Oticon to make its changes. These are just a few of the many examples in which companies reshape the chain of command or the way departments are grouped together to help improve performance.

The reason for such activity is the view that an organisation's strategy is more likely to succeed if it has an appropriate structure – one that encourages people to act in ways that support the strategy. Conversely, the wrong structure defeats the intended strategy by encouraging inappropriate behaviour. The volatile business environment means new structures are appearing as a way of supporting new strategies. In shaping their department or organisation managers use the components examined in Chapter 8. They decide how to divide work vertically and horizontally, and how best to integrate those separated activities. They decide which decisions those at the centre should take, and how much formality there should be. They also decide whether to adjust these features as circumstances change.

This chapter reviews how managers have resolved these questions, and what theoretical ideas have developed from research on the topic. These are summarised in Figure 10.1. The chapter begins by comparing mechanistic and organic forms of organisation – two broad types that reflect the accumulation of decisions on particular components. It then reviews the factors that one line of research ('contingency' theory) suggests influence management choice. It goes on to contrast this approach with an alternative which

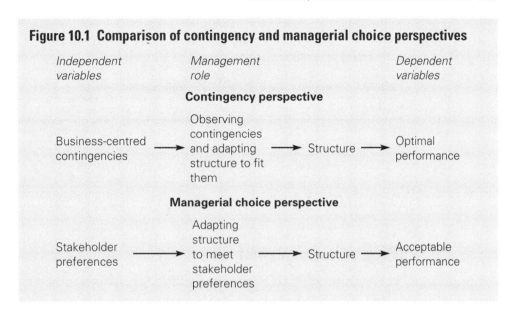

Figure 10.1 Comparison of contingency and managerial choice perspectives

emphasises the wider scope for 'managerial choice' of structure than contingency theorists imply. A final section shows how current developments in information technology are affecting the structural options available.

10.2 Mechanistic and organic approaches to structure

Chapter 8 indicated that the purpose of structure is to support organisational goals – the right structure is a powerful management tool, as it encourages people to behave in ways that management hopes will support its objectives. That chapter also outlined the elements of the structure – the vertical and horizontal division of work, and the co-ordination of that work – that combine to give an overall organisational structure.

Some companies have developed a structure that emphasises the vertical hierarchy to achieve co-ordination. They define responsibilities clearly, take most decisions at the centre, delegate tightly defined routine tasks and have rigorous reporting requirements. This enables the centre to know what is happening lower down the organisation. They ensure that policies are applied consistently, that a uniform image is presented to the outside world, that customers receive consistent treatment and that best practice passes rapidly around the organisation. Communication is likely to be mainly vertical, as the centre passes down instructions and staff send queries to those above them in the hierarchy. The vertical aspects of the structure dominate and control the organisation. This is very similar to what Burns and Stalker (1961) called a **mechanistic structure**.

In other organisations the horizontal aspect of structure is more influential. They make more use of broadly defined, flexible tasks, frequently set up cross-functional teams to work on problems (such as Oticon has done) and authority is based more on expertise than on position in the hierarchy. Management accepts that those at the centre cannot know all the answers, and must depend on those nearest the action to find the best solution to problems. Communication is likely to be horizontal amongst those familiar with the task. There may not even be an organisation chart, so fluid is the division of labour and departmentalisation. This approach corresponds to what Burns and Stalker (1961) called an **organic structure**. Table 10.1 compares the features of mechanistic and organic organisations.

Table 10.1 Characteristics of mechanistic and organic systems

Mechanistic	Organic
Specialised tasks	Contribute experience to common tasks
Hierarchical structure of control	Network structure of contacts
Knowledge located at top of hierarchy	Knowledge widely spread
Vertical communication	Horizontal communication
Loyalty and obedience stressed	Commitment to goals more important

Source: Based on Burrns and Stalker (1961).

Q **Case questions 10.1**

- What was the role of strategy and technology in encouraging the change at Oticon?
- What features of the present form correspond to the organic model?
- How does management hope that the new structure will support their strategy?

10.3 Contingencies shaping the choice of form

Why do managers favour one form of structure rather than another? A widely held (though disputed) view is that it depends on certain 'contingencies' – factors that encourage managers to adopt one form rather than another. Comparative research in many organisations in different circumstances has shown that managers create a structure that is consistent with certain factors – the 'contingencies'. These include its strategy, technology, size, life cycle stage and environmental uncertainty. Successful organisations appear to be those in which managers have maintained a good fit between these contingent factors and the structure through which people deploy and manage organisational resources. Figure 10.2 illustrates these contingent factors, which the following sections examine.

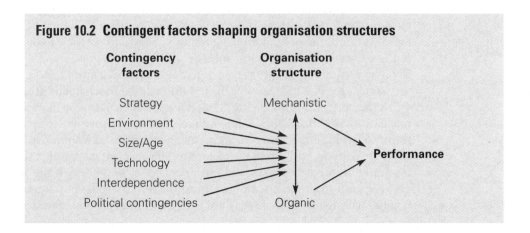

Figure 10.2 Contingent factors shaping organisation structures

An alternative perspective is that this is too rational a view of organisational life, and that managers develop structures that reflect other factors – such as fashion or personal ambition supported by political empire building. After outlining the contingency factors the chapter presents the managerial choice perspective.

Strategy

Chapter 6 outlined Porter's view that firms adopt one of a small number of alternative generic strategies – cost leadership, differentiation or focus. With a cost leadership strategy managers concentrate on increasing efficiency to bring their costs below those of competing firms. A differentiation strategy focuses on innovation – on developing new products or services more rapidly and imaginatively than competing firms. Contingency theory suggests that each strategy requires people to behave in a different way, and therefore a structure which supports that behaviour.

A cost leadership strategy is likely to be best supported by a clear functional structure. This uses task specialisation and a strict chain of command to ensure that the work is done as efficiently as possible. People have clear roles in which performance against set targets can be easily measured, and they can focus on their part of the task. Powergen, the privatised electricity utility, initially followed a cost-leadership strategy, aiming to keep costs low in the face of tougher competition in the electricity generating business. It adopted a tight functional structure, with detailed rules and performance measures governing power station operations. There is some evidence of more companies moving towards more centralised, tightly controlled structures – a move that often appears to be driven by a need to cut costs.

A differentiation strategy, on the other hand, requires innovation and flexibility – with ideas flowing easily between people with something to contribute, wherever they work. A matrix or team-based structure is most likely to work best, since they encourage the mixing of people from across functional boundaries to work together on projects to develop innovative solutions to customer problems. Oticon moved towards this team-based structure, as has ABB in its research organisation. As PowerGen diversified into many different businesses it tried to support this with a new structure – based on three autonomous product divisions.

The idea is that teams or autonomous divisions enable organisations to differentiate themselves by being able to respond more quickly than competitors to new demands. A study by Hill and Pickering (1986) of divisionalised companies supported this idea. It showed that companies which had passed more decision-making authority to business units performed more successfully than those which had not. The decentralised structure was a more appropriate structure in volatile conditions – as BT and its shareholders hope will be the result of its recent changes to structure.

MANAGEMENT IN PRACTICE **British Telecom**

In face of mounting criticism over its poor performance the then chairman of BT, Sir Iain Vallance, announced in July 2000 that the company would be restructured into separate divisions. These were:

● BT Wireless – an international mobile phone business;
● BT Ignite – providing European-based business customers with data communications services;

- BTopenworld – offering Internet services to consumers;
- Yell – an international directories and e-commerce business;
- BT Retail – the main means of delivering services to customers in the UK; and
- BT Wholesale – providing network services to other communications companies.

Management intentions were reflected in the comment of Sir Peter Bonfield, chief executive of BT: 'I think we can significantly change the style and culture of BT as a result of these changes.'

Source: *BT Annual Report* 2001, and *Financial Times*, 10 November 2000.

Figure 10.3 expresses the idea that different strategies require different structures, by showing on one axis the structural types described in Chapter 8, with the strategic goals on the other. The more strategic goals correspond to those of cost leadership, the more likely it is that managers will support their strategy with a functional structure. The more they approximate to differentiation, the more likely management will use a team or network structure. There are intermediate possibilities as well. A company using a cost-leadership strategy may see an opportunity to develop a new product that will help it differentiate – so creates cross-functional teams within a basic functional structure. The divisional structure promotes differentiation because each division can concentrate on a particular aspect of the market – though divisions will be larger and less flexible than small teams or networks.

Technology

Technology includes the knowledge tools and techniques used to transform organisational inputs into outputs. It includes buildings, machines, computer systems and the knowledge and procedures associated with them. Just as structure needs to fit the strategy of a firm, so it also needs to fit the technology of the firm – whether in manufacturing or services.

Woodward's manufacturing technology

Joan Woodward's study of organisations and their structure (Woodward, 1965) had a great influence on thinking about management. When she conducted the research the dominant view was that there were certain principles (see, for example, Brech, 1957) that managers should apply, irrespective of the business they were in. These principles were based on the work of writers in the scientific management and human relations

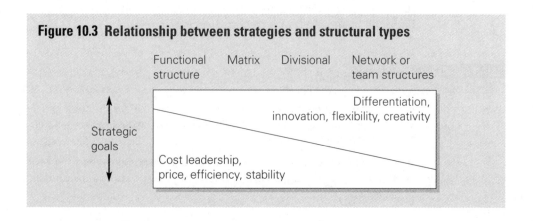

Figure 10.3 Relationship between strategies and structural types

traditions discussed in Chapter 2. In either case the emphasis was on identifying the 'one best way', which would apply universally. However, Woodward questioned this prescriptive approach, choosing instead to conduct empirical research into current organisational practice.

She gathered information from 100 British firms to establish whether basic structural features such as the span of control, the number of levels in the hierarchy or the degree of formalisation varied between them. The research team could see no pattern until they they analysed the companies by their manufacturing process, which they grouped into 11 categories, of 3 broad types. These formed a scale of increasing technical complexity. The researchers then observed a relationship between the degree of technical complexity and the structural arrangements in the company:

- *Unit and small batch production* Firms in this group produce goods in small numbers, often to a customer's unique order. It is similar to craft work, as people and their skills are deeply involved in the process. Examples of such products are custom-built cycles, designer furniture, Aston Martin sports cars or luxury yachts.
- *Large batch and mass production* This form is typified by the production of large quantities of standard products. All customers receive the same product, supplies of which are placed in stock until customers need them. Machines, typically a production line of some kind, do most of the physical work, with people complementing the machinery as they produce things such as computer discs, cigarettes, Ford cars or Electrolux washing machines.
- *Continuous process* Here the entire workflow is mechanised, in a sophisticated and complex form of production technology. The machinery does the production work, with operators in a supporting role – monitoring it, fixing faults and generally overseeing the process. Examples include the Guinness Brewery in Dublin, an Esso oil refinery or a Corus steel plant.

The difference between them is what Woodward called technical complexity – the degree to which machinery is involved to the exclusion of people. Figure 10.4 shows one of the structural characteristics associated with each type – the span of control of first-line supervisors. The span of control is greatest for mass production work, with the median span of control being lower in the other forms of technology.

ACTIVITY 10.1

Describing the pattern

In your own words, describe the patterns shown in Figure 10.4. What differences does the diagram show between the structures most commonly found in the different types of production system?

Woodward explained this by observing that different manufacturing techniques impose different demands on people and organisations. Unit production technology requires close supervision as this enables managers to ensure that staff meet the unique requirements. They can communicate directly with those working on different parts of the task and so manage the uncertainties and changes involved in designing and producing 'one-off' items. Firms with large batch or mass production systems face less uncertainty, and more of the necessary knowledge has been incorporated into the design of the plant and its procedures. On an assembly line the work is so routine that a supervisor can oversee many employees – a wider span of control.

Figure 10.4 Span of control of first-line supervision in three production systems

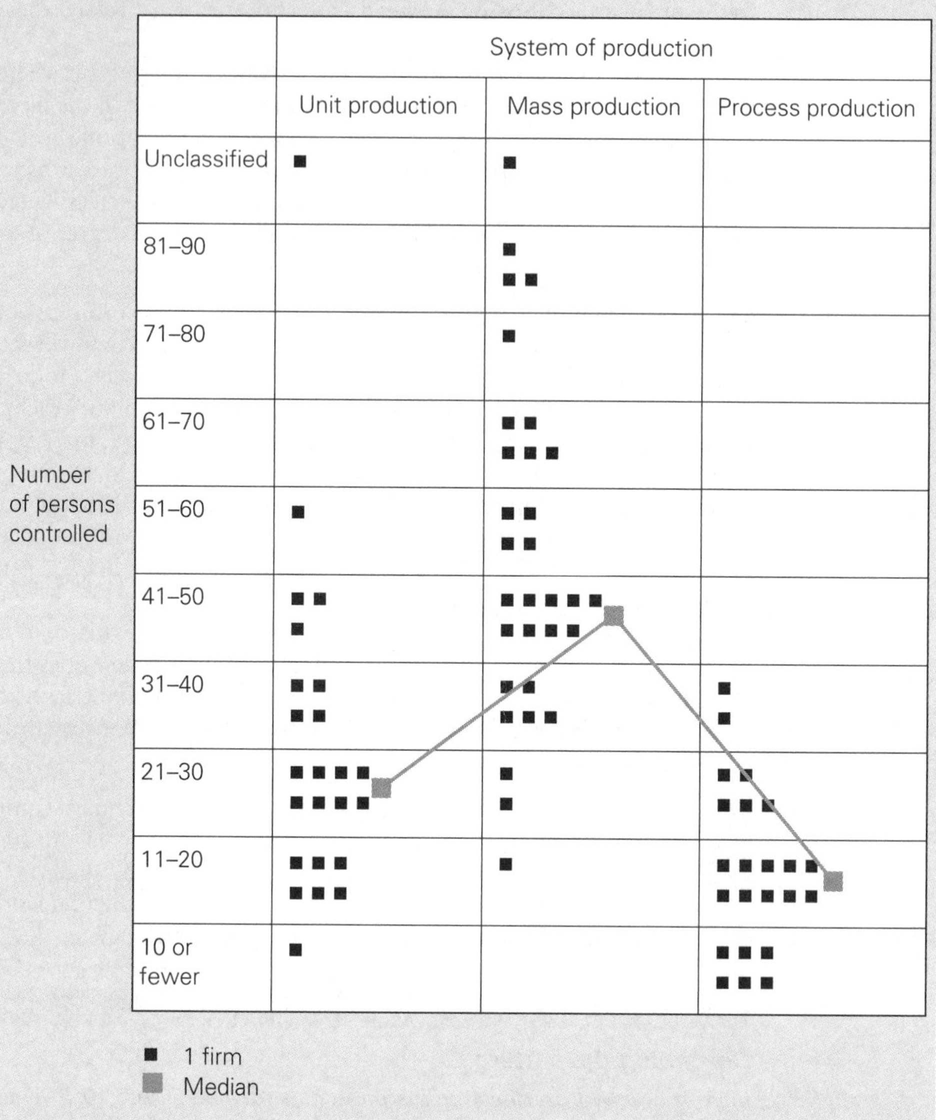

Number of persons controlled	System of production		
	Unit production	Mass production	Process production
Unclassified	■	■	
81–90		■ / ■ ■	
71–80		■	
61–70		■ ■ / ■ ■ ■	
51–60	■	■ ■ / ■ ■	
41–50	■ ■ / ■	■ ■ ■ ■ ■ ▦(Median) / ■ ■ ■ ■	
31–40	■ ■ / ■ ■	■ ■ / ■ ■ ■	■ / ■
21–30	■ ■ ■ ■ ▦(Median) / ■ ■ ■ ■	■ / ■	■ ■ ▦(Median) / ■ ■ ■
11–20	■ ■ ■ / ■ ■ ■	■	■ ■ ■ ■ ■ / ■ ■ ■ ■ ■ ▦(Median)
10 or fewer	■		■ ■ ■ / ■ ■ ■

■ 1 firm
▦ Median

Source: Woodward (1958, p.15), Crown copyright, reproduced with permission of the Controller of Her Majesty's Stationery Office.

The research team also asked whether a particular kind of structure ensured business success. They found that firms which conformed to the median organisational structure for their 'technology group' were more successful financially than those that deviated from it. Firms that had adopted the classic management principles, such as formal definitions of responsibility, were not always financially successful. These principles worked well in large batch and mass production, but not in unit or process production systems. These demands had to be met by an appropriate structure, and the commercially successful firms were those where the structure provided the right kind of support to the work of employees.

Flexible manufacturing

Manufacturing firms such as Rolls-Royce, British Aerospace and Leyland Vehicles now often use what is termed a flexible manufacturing system to produce small batches of components. Such systems depend on highly automated systems, in which the details of the parts to be manufactured are held in the computer system. This also plans the order in which different batches will be manufactured, and drives the computer-aided machine tools that physically transform metal into finished parts. Robotic vehicles move parts to and from the machines, in response to instructions from the computer. Operators usually work as a team, ensuring that supplies of material are available, that tools are maintained and ready for use, and that finished products are removed.

Service technologies

The companies that Woodward studied were engaged in manufacturing – activities which physically change materials. Service activities are different – they relate to the transaction of intangibles (hairdressing, theatre performances, holidays) or they support the production and delivery of physical products (the financial, human resources or advertising staff in a business manufacturing cars or compact discs).

More employees now work in service jobs than in manufacturing. Advances in production technologies mean that manufacturing companies employ fewer people to make the things they sell – and employ many more people on internal service activities such as marketing or human resources. At the same time there has been a steady growth in the number of people working in organisations that sell or provide intangible products – banks, bars, retailing, health care.

Technology plays as central a role in delivering services as it does in delivering manufactured goods. Managers can use technology to shape the way staff interact with customers. Staff at branches of Barclay's Bank (or any other retail bank) used to handle many cash transactions with customers, and for security reasons sat behind protective glass screens. These necessary precautions made banks seem remote and unwelcoming to customers. Technological developments in payment systems mean that much less cash is now handled in bank branches – which are now designed to bring staff and customers closer together.

More generally, service technology influences the structure of the organisation, though the effect is far from clear-cut. Information technology has great implications for the structuring of service activities.

MANAGEMENT IN PRACTICE   **Credit control at The Royal Bank of Scotland**

Until the early 1990s managers of local branches decided loans for personal and small business customers. This had some advantages, in that they made decisions quickly, face to face, using local customer knowledge. A disadvantage was that decisions lacked consistency across the organisation. It was also expensive to support since highly qualified, experienced credit managers had to be available at every branch.

Faced with damaging bad debts and a more competitive market the bank decided to centralise loan decisions in one location, and support staff with a new credit information system.

This was called Automated Product Set-up and would assess loan applications against a 'scorecard' of standard measures known to indicate whether the loan was likely to be repaid. It covered a range of credit 'products' such as personal loans, overdrafts, mortgages and cheque guarantee cards.

The terminals in each branch were connected to the central mainframe computer. This meant that any updates would only have to be made once, and the scorecard could be adjusted at any time according to recent information on loans performance. A further advantage of the centralised system was that it helped ensure consistent decisions for all customers, and managers consider the project a success.

Source: Adapted from Boddy *et al.* (2002).

Companies use information technology to rationalise processes and ensure consistent quality to the customer wherever he or she is receiving the service – as happened at The Royal Bank of Scotland. Another example is when service companies such as Airtours (the UK's second largest package holiday group) use information technology to change their distribution system. In 2001 the company announced it would close many of the shops through which it sells holidays. The decision was a response to the fact that now more people prefer to book their holidays by telephone. The company can take these calls at centralised, low cost call centres that use advanced communications and computing technologies to manage the way staff handle calls. Many companies have used information technology in this way to rationalise services and cut costs – consistent with the cost-leadership strategy described earlier (see Boddy *et al.*, 2002 for a fuller discussion) .

Other service companies, such as Oticon, use the technology in a different way, to support a more decentralised, organic structure. Consulting companies such as PricewaterhouseCoopers and Arthur Andersen have introduced information systems designed to encourage staff to share knowledge and expertise directly amongst themselves. These 'groupware' systems capture information from staff as they work on projects, and then store in a database information about the methods used and lessons learned. Other staff can search the database for other people with similar interests, and seek their advice on the consulting problems they face. This spreads good practice around the organisation and encourages people to form teams that can learn from each other.

The technology of the Internet further illustrates this. Some companies use it to cut costs very significantly. EasyJet, the low cost airline, only accepts reservations over the Internet, and the savings this brings help towards the company's low cost strategy. Others use it to offer a highly differentiated service. Amazon.com uses data about customers to build a profile of products likely to interest them, and then alerts them to new goods or services that are likely to be of interest to that individual customer. It is using the technology to support a differentiation strategy.

Size and life cycle

Size, as measured by the number of employees, affects the structure of organisations. Small organisations tend to be less formal with less division of labour – people take part in a wide range of tasks to get the work done. Weber (1947) noted that larger organisations tended to have more formal, bureaucratic structures. Research by the Aston group

(Pugh and Hickson, 1976) showed that size of organisation was positively related to increasingly formal structures. Blau (1970) argued that size leads to more levels in the hierarchy, and more separate specialised units. In small organisations the necessary co-ordination between the parts can be achieved informally by face-to-face contact or direct supervision. Like the head of Multi-show Events (see Chapter 8), as managers divide a growing business into separate units, perhaps over a wide geographical area, they need to install more formal controls. These include detailed job descriptions, formal reporting relationships and tighter control systems.

This implies that organisations go through distinct stages in their life, each of which has a structure suited to that stage.

Birth stage

The entrepreneur creates the business alone, or with a few partners or employees. They operate informally with little division of labour – tasks overlap. There are few rules or few formal systems for planning and co-ordination. Decisions are made by the owner – such as Pierre Levicky – so in that sense they are a centralised form.

MANAGEMENT IN PRACTICE **The growth of Pierre Victoire**

Pierre Levicky opened the first Pierre Victoire restaurant in 1988, with a small personal investment and a large bank loan. It was a restaurant designed to offer quality French food and wine at reasonable prices. The decor was simple and the furniture second-hand – the simple design becoming part of the group's brand image. The format proved popular and Levicky opened a second restaurant – and he was still cooking seven days a week. Despite this market success, management controls were weak, and by 1990 the company had debts of £350,000. The bank offered to help clear the debts, but in return insisted on Levicky appointing an experienced board of directors to provide advice. He had to produce a business plan, and provide weekly management accounts – but remained very much in control of the business.

In 1992 the recovery was complete, and expansion began by franchising the idea. This means that someone with the requisite capital invests in an outlet, which they operate under the Pierre Victoire name and using the same format. By 1994 about four franchises were opening each month and by 1996 it was one of the biggest independent restaurant chains in the United Kingdom.

There was a network of regional directors (successful franchisees) who actively managed the restaurants in their area (as well as their own) and ensured standardisation of operations. There was an executive chef at each director's restaurant who trained other chefs and monitored standards. As a further control, the company in 1996 supplied computer-based terminals to each franchisee, enabling management to get an accurate and timely picture of the previous day's business in each outlet. As others became more experienced, and as management controls developed, Levicky experienced a change in his role. As he observed: 'Once the company was Pierre, now it doesn't need me.' Figure 10.5 shows the structure at this stage.

Source: Based on European Case Clearing House Case No. 497-022-1 Pierre Victoire: An Organisation in Transition, prepared by Alison Morrison and Sandra Watson.

Figure 10.5 The structure at Pierre Victoire during the youth stage

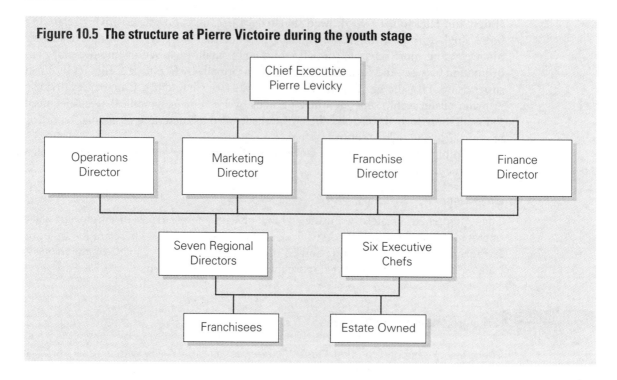

Youth stage

If the business survives and thrives it will probably need to raise more capital to finance growth. As at Pierre Victoire, the owner probably no longer has sole control, and decisions will be shared amongst a small group of senior colleagues. There is some division of labour (such as the creation of regional directors and executive chefs) as the work grows. Separate departments will be created, and controls will therefore become more formal to ensure co-ordination.

Mid-life

If growth continues, it begins to resemble a formal bureaucracy. There is extensive division of responsibility and many formal rules to ensure co-ordination among the parts. There are more professional and specialist staff, performing support functions in areas such as finance or human resources. There are common systems for budgeting, financial control and rewards. This leads to the growth of stronger functional departments, which take over responsibility for their areas from top management.

> **MANAGEMENT IN PRACTICE** **Changing structures as Internet firms mature**
>
> For an industry to lose four leading chief executives in a matter of weeks looks careless by any standards. But since the beginning of this month Terra Lycos, Tiscali, Yahoo! Europe and LibertySurf have joined the list of European Internet giants that have lost top executives ... Each individual departure was triggered by an individual tale of either power struggle, management frustration or changes of corporate control.
>
> However on a deeper level, the game of musical chairs at the top of the industry is a reflection of the profound changes that have taken place since the dot.com boom ended in

March .... Fabiola Arredondo – who built Yahoo! Europe from a 13-person start up in 1997 into a business with revenues of $114 million and 500 staff – is also understood to have quit just over a week ago because she felt that the important decisions were being taken in the US...

But the departures underline a more subtle change. Investors are now concentrating on profit over growth. This is leading to a transition from entrepreneurial managers – who thrived on building Internet businesses during the frantic growth phase of the late 1990s – towards managers focusing on more traditional management challenges of milking the maximum profit from the assets available.

Source: Extracts from an article by Thorold Barker, *Financial Times,* 25 February 2001, p.20.

Maturity

Here the organisation is large and mechanistic, with a strong vertical system and well-developed controls. There are rules and policies for most things, with large specialist staff carrying out defined tasks. More decisions are made at the centre – bringing the danger of slow response to new conditions. To overcome these barriers to innovation and to encourage cross-functional communication managers may change the structure. They may decentralise the organisation by creating separate divisions with profit responsibility – as BT has done. GlaxoSmithKline is another example of a mature company making radical changes to encourage innovation in research and development, and so increase the output of commercial products.

MANAGEMENT IN PRACTICE **GlaxoSmithKline**

In February 2001 Tachi Yamada, head of Research and Development at GlaxoSmithKline (GSK), set out the company's plan to split the company's research organisation ('the engine room of any pharmaceutical company') into six 'internal biotechnology companies'. These units will compete for resources. Divided along therapeutic lines, they will operate autonomously. The company is the world's second largest drugs company, and employs 15,000 scientists with an annual budget of £2.5 billion. Jean-Paul Garnier, chief executive, said that organising this research group required a radical new structure. Early research, where scarce skills and expensive equipment are applied across a range of diseases, needed to stay big. So did late-stage development where huge dossiers of clinical trial data were prepared for regulators. However, the section in the middle, where bright ideas were honed into drugs, would work best as competing, autonomous units, he said. 'We start big, we move to small and then back to big again. Nobody has ever attempted this before'.

The job of the six autonomous units is to deliver drugs with 'proof of concept' – after small-scale clinical tests on patients – to GSK's development organisation. There, drugs will be put through full-scale clinical trials, aimed at winning regulatory approval and maximising sales potential.

The business units, called Centres of Excellence for Drug Discovery, can deliver molecules invented at GSK or brought in from academia or external biotech groups. 'They have complete autonomy. They can have 100 chemists per project, or 5. It doesn't matter to me how they do it, so long as they produce drugs,' says Dr Yamada.

Clinical trials are undertaken on a massive scale, often across continents, and must comply with strict regulatory conditions. Thus corporate control, uniformity and economies of scale are pre-eminent. The other area where scale will be leveraged is early research, where hundreds of millions of pounds are spent on platform technology. Two divisions, Genetics Research and Discovery Research, will work on understanding basic biology and on producing leads to set drug discovery units on their way. Figure 10.6 illustrates the new structure.

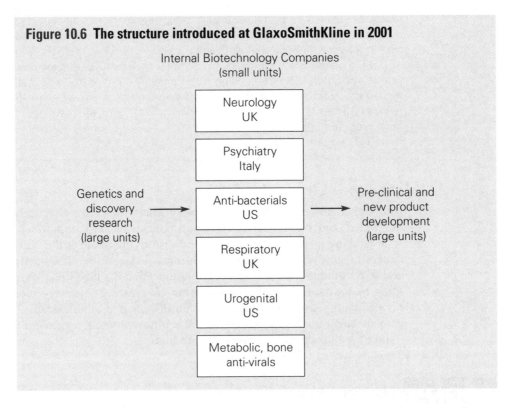

Figure 10.6 The structure introduced at GlaxoSmithKline in 2001

Internal Biotechnology Companies
(small units)

- Neurology UK
- Psychiatry Italy
- Anti-bacterials US
- Respiratory UK
- Urogenital US
- Metabolic, bone anti-virals

Genetics and discovery research (large units) →

→ Pre-clinical and new product development (large units)

'The merger provided us with huge scale, so I had to design something that would take advantage of that', says Dr Yamada. 'But we know that big can sometimes mean bad. So we had to design something that could maintain agility, entrepreneurial spirit and individual accountability.' Dr Yamada describes the hybrid structure as 'six biotech companies nested within a full array of platform technologies'. In an effort to attract talent and emulate biotech's entrepreneurial culture, GSK scientists will have incentives. Big share option packages will be reserved for teams that come up with drugs. More radically still, scientists will receive royalties on the sale of medicines they helped invent. 'If you can become a millionaire by joining a biotech company, why shouldn't you do that by joining GSK?' asks Dr Yamada. 'What we are aiming for is a step change in productivity. I believe we've been as productive as any other company. It's just that we need to do much, much better.'

Source: Based on an article by David Pilling, *Financial Times*, 23 February 2001, p. 26.

FT

Moving through the life cycle

Organisations do not go through these stages in an orderly fashion – they move at their own pace, and the transition stages are not necessarily clear at the time. Some do not progress beyond the early stages, while for others the attempt to move from one to the next is a source of tension and disagreement. People who have been comfortable with the earlier stages may resent the increasing distance and formality that size often brings. Organisations that prematurely impose a 'mature' structure on a 'young' organisation probably have the wrong structure, and their performance will suffer. Conversely those that grow without putting in place appropriate controls and systems are also likely to suffer economically (as the early disaster at Pierre Victoire showed). In times of rapid external change and uncertainty a major management challenge in large organisations is to create a structure that allows the organisation to recover the advantages of flexibility it once had, and which its younger competitors now have.

MANAGEMENT IN PRACTICE	Growth and structure in a housing association

A manager in a housing association, which was created to provide affordable housing for those on low incomes, describes how its structure changed as it grew.

Housing associations have to give tenants and their representatives the opportunity to influence policy. In the early days the association had few staff, no clear division of labour and few rules and procedures. It was successful in providing housing, which attracted more government funds, and the association grew. As more houses came into management this activity required an organisational structure to support it. The association no longer served a single community, but a number of separate geographical areas. Staff numbers grew significantly and specialised departments were created to provide specific and separate functions. The changes have led to concerns amongst both staff and committee that the organisation is no longer responsive to community needs and that it has become distant and bureaucratic.

Source: Private communication from the manager.

Environment

Classical organisation theories specified, broadly, that management should exercise control over employees through practices such as tight job descriptions, clear rules and a defined hierarchy. Research over many years such as that by Hage and Aiken (1967), Gerwin (1979) and Hill and Pickering (1986) showed that performance depends on having a structure that is suitable for the particular environment in which a firm is operating. Burns and Stalker (1961) from the University of Edinburgh compared the structure of a long-established rayon plant in Manchester with the structures of several new electronics companies then being created in the east of Scotland. Both types of organisation were successful – but had different structures.

The rayon plant had clearly set out rules, tight job descriptions, clear procedures, and co-ordination was primarily through the hierarchy. In this mechanistic form of organisation management creates a high degree of specialisation by dividing tasks into small parts. The boundaries of responsibility and authority are clearly defined, and people are discouraged from acting outside of their remit. Decision making is centralised, with information flowing up the hierarchy, and instructions down.

The small companies in the newly created electronics industry were completely different. They had very few job descriptions and their rules and procedures were ambiguous and imprecise. Staff were expected to use their initiative in deciding priorities. They worked together to solve problems. Communication was largely lateral, rather than through the hierarchy. They termed this an organic form of organisation. Table 10.1 summarised the contrasts between the mechanistic and organic forms.

CASE STUDY Oticon – the case continues – communication and technology

While the company uses advanced information systems for many functions it believes that dialogue is better than email, and has designed the building to support face-to-face dialogue between staff. When an issue arises (e.g. a customer complaint) staff are forbidden to write a memo. Instead the problem owner gets two or three people together and has a stand-up meeting. Decisions are noted in the computer (accessible by everyone). By 1994 the company had halved product development time and more than doubled sales. It employed half as many administrative staff as in 1990, but double the number on product development. Financial performance improved dramatically in the years following the change.

> Hardware companies have organisations that look like machines: a company that produces knowledge needs an organisation that looks like a brain, i.e. which looks chaotic and is un-hierarchical. (Lars Kolind)

Source: Based on Bjorn-Andersen and Turner (1994).

Q **Case questions 10.2**

- Oticon has had both mechanistic and organic structures: what prompted the change?
- Why has the new structure improved business performance?

Burns and Stalker (1961) concluded that both organisational forms were appropriate for their particular circumstances. The rayon plant was operating in a stable environment. It was the production unit of a larger business, and its sole purpose was to supply a steady flow of rayon to the company's spinning factories. Delivery schedules rarely changed, the technology of rayon manufacture was well known, and fully documented in printed manuals.

Figure 10.7 Relationship between environment and structure

		Structure	
		Mechanistic	*Organic*
Environment	*Uncertain (unstable)*	**Incorrect Fit:** Mechanistic structure in uncertain environment Structure too tight	**Correct Fit:** Organic structure in uncertain environment
	Certain (stable)	**Correct Fit:** Mechanistic structure in certain environment	**Incorrect Fit:** Organic structure in certain environment Structure too loose

The electronics companies were in direct contact with their customers, the largest of which was the Ministry of Defence. The demand for both commercial and military products was volatile, with frequent changes in delivery requirements. The technology was new, often applying a recent discovery from a research laboratory. Contracts were often taken in which neither the customer nor the company knew what the end product would be: it was likely to change during the course of the work.

Burns and Stalker (1961) concluded that neither mechanistic nor organic structures were appropriate in all situations. Stable, predictable environments were likely to encourage a mechanistic structure. Volatile, unpredictable environments were likely to encourage an organic structure. This recognition that environmental conditions place different demands upon organisations was a major step in understanding why companies adopt contrasting structures – an idea illustrated in Figure 10.7.

ACTIVITY 10.2

The structure where you study

Is your college or university a mechanistic or an organic organisation? What about the department in which you study? Look for evidence of the characteristics in Table 10.1 to help you assess whether it is closer to one form than the other.

Interview someone who works in an organisation to find out if his or her organisation is, on balance, mechanistic or organic. See if you can establish why it has developed the form it has. Compare your conclusions with those of other students and see if you can identify any common themes emerging from the data you have collected.

MANAGEMENT IN PRACTICE — Organic problem solving in a mechanistic structure

The organisation I work for has just come through a short-term cash-flow crisis. The problem arose because, while expenditures on contracts are relatively predictable and even, the income flow was disrupted by a series of contractual disputes.

The role culture permeates the head office, and at first the problem was pushed ever upwards. But faced with this crisis all departments were asked for ideas on how to improve performance. Some have been turned into new methods of working, and others are still being considered by the 'ideas team', drawn from all grades of personnel and departments. This was a totally new perspective, of a task culture operating within a role culture – that is, we developed an organic approach. What could be more simple than asking people who do the job how they could be more efficient?

To maintain the change in the long run is difficult, and some parts have now started to drift back to the role culture.

Source: Private communication.

Organisations do not face a single environment. Each department tries to meet the expectations of their particular part of the wider environment, and so their managers develop structures which suit that environment. So some departments take a mechanistic form and others an organic one.

An important implication of this is that co-ordination between such departments will be difficult, as they will work in different ways. Paul Lawrence and Jay Lorsch explored this issue, and their contribution is in the Key Ideas feature.

Lawrence and Lorsch: differentiation and integration

Two American scholars, Paul Lawrence and Jay Lorsch, developed Burns and Stalker's work. They observed that organisations typically contain distinct subunits (departments). If these subunits are doing different tasks each will face a separate segment of the total environment. These will place different demands on each subunit – some being relatively stable, others unstable. Lawrence and Lorsch predicted that in order to cope with this demand subunits will develop different structures and ways of working, appropriate to their respective environments. Those in stable environments would move towards mechanistic forms, while those in unstable environments would move towards organic forms.

How would that diversity affect the task of co-ordinating their efforts? They examined these issues through a study of six organisations facing stable, moderately stable and unstable

environments respectively. One firm in each was chosen as a successful operation, the other as an unsuccessful one.

Lawrence and Lorsch concluded that the subunits did indeed differ from each other, and in ways they had predicted. Those facing unstable environments (research and development) had less formal structures than those facing stable ones (production). The greater the **differentiation** between departments the more effort managers needed to devote to integrating their work. Successful firms achieved more **integration** between subunits than the unsuccessful ones. They used a variety of integrating devices such as task forces and project managers with the required interpersonal skills. The less effective companies in the uncertain environment used rules and procedures.

Source: Lawrence and Lorsch (1967).

Departmental interdependence

The final characteristic influencing structure is the degree of interdependence between the departments. Interdependence is the extent to which departments rely on each other for resources (including information) or materials to perform their tasks (Thompson, 1967). A low level means they can work independently with little need for contact – a high level implies constant exchanges while working on a task. These imply different structural forms, as shown in Figure 10.8.

Pooled interdependence

Departments work relatively independently because the work does not flow between units. The branches of Pret á Manger or Lloyds TSB Bank are examples of pooled inter-dependence. They draw on some common resources such as advertising and finance but have little need for day-to-day interaction with each other.

Sequential interdependence

The output of one department provides an input to the next. Departments depend on others to provide material or information of the right quality at the right time for them to begin working on their part of the task. The editorial departments of the *Financial Times* must complete their work before printing can begin; the drug development units at GlaxoSmithKline need to develop drugs before the clinical trial organisation can start work.

Reciprocal interdependence

The degree of interaction here is most intense. The output of activity A is the input to activity B, and the output of B is an input back into A – and possibly into several others

Figure 10.8 Tpes of co-ordination required for different forms of interdependence

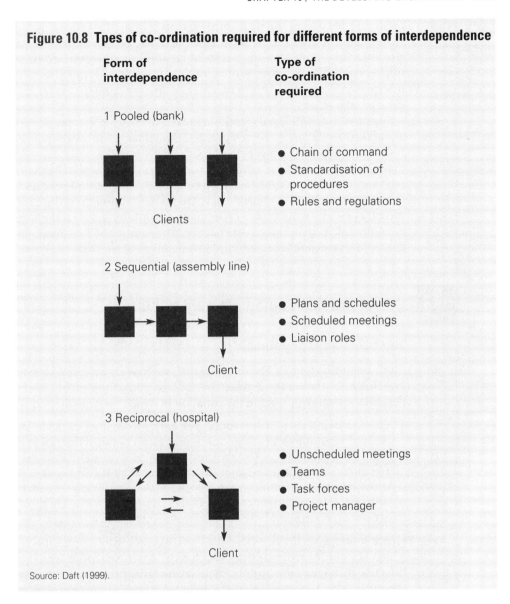

Source: Daft (1999).

as well. Acute services in hospitals are an example, where a dangerously ill patient requires treatment from a range of services such as X-ray, surgery and blood transfusion. The output of each activity is uncertain when it begins, but affects what the others then need to do. The structure that hospital management creates will affect how smoothly or otherwise these activities fit together.

Structural implications

Pooled interdependence requires little day-to-day co-ordination, and what is required can be handled by standard procedures and guidelines to ensure that each branch offers the same service. Sequential interdependence is more challenging, and management supports this interdependence by creating planning and scheduling structures. They intend these to ensure that material or information passes from one unit to the next at the right time and in the right form. Reciprocal interdependence is the most difficult to co-ordinate, as little can be planned in advance. People need to be able and willing to work flexibly, using their initiative to respond to whatever inputs they receive. This implies relatively high degrees of autonomy, possibly with much teamworking and direct interpersonal contact. This is made easier if management places the units physically close to each other.

Organisations will usually combine these approaches – some departmental activities are pooled while others are reciprocal. Departments can work independently on many tasks, but need to work more closely with others for other tasks. Suppliers and customers may also be part of this interdependence, so structures need to be such that they provide relevant information to them. At GlaxoSmithKline the three phases of basic research, drug development and clinical trials are pooled – though in the case of an individual drug they will be sequential. At the point of handover between the stages there may be a great deal of reciprocal interdependence. The Centres of Excellence operate with a high degree of interdependence amongst the members of a team.

10.4 Contingencies or management choice?

The contingency approach

The ideas discussed in Section 10.3 are collectively referred to as the **contingency approach** to organisation structure. This says that the most effective structure will depend (be contingent) upon the situation in which the organisation is operating:

> The organization is seen as existing in an environment that shapes its strategy, technology, size and innovation rate. These contingent factors in turn determine the required structure; that is, the structure that the organization needs to adopt if it is to operate effectively. The effectiveness of the organization is affected by the fit between the organizational structure and the contingencies. This leads the organization to adapt its organization structure so that it moves into fit with the contingency factors. In this way organizational structure is determined by the contingencies. (Donaldson, 1996, p.2)

Hence contingency theorists take the view that successful organisations adopt a structure which is right for their strategy and for the environment in which they are working. Effective management involves formulating an appropriate strategy and developing a structure which supports that strategy by encouraging appropriate behaviour. The emphasis is **determinist** (the form is determined by the environment) and functionalist (the form is intended to serve organisational effectiveness) (Donaldson, 1995).

The appropriate form develops incrementally as management observes some misfit in its present arrangements. It makes what it hopes will be appropriate adjustments in aspects of the structure – altering the degree of, say, formalisation by introducing some new procedures or rules such as Pierre Victoire did to cope with growth. Or they may increase the degree of centralisation – as Kwik-Fit did at one stage, before it then decentralised more decisions to local management.

Management choice

The contingency approach has become the mainstream theory attempting to explain the shape of organisations, and it has obvious practical implications. However, it has been criticised on several grounds by writers such as Child (1972, 1984). He argues that the determinism of contingency theory has been overstated. Contingency theorists ignore the degree of structural choice which management has over the form. The process of organisational choice and design is not only a technical, rational matter but one shaped by political processes. These political considerations (reflecting the values and interests of influential groups) are able to influence the structure that emerges for the following reasons:

- The standards of performance against which organisational performance is assessed are not always rigorous. Some degree of under-performance caused by an inappropriate structure may be tolerated if there is sufficient 'slack' within the system.
- There is evidence that a degree of choice is available between different modes of organisation without serious diseconomies being incurred. So managers can choose from the available range, in view of their own or their staff's preferences, rather than be required to adopt the form implied by contingency theory for their environment.
- To the extent that political interests are pursued in organisational life, structures will reflect the interests of politically powerful groups within the organisation. They will try to secure organisational structures that protect or advance their positions. This approach rejects the functionalism of contingency approaches.

Overall, writers of this view argue that contingency theory reduces managers almost to automatons, or puppets, able to exercise little influence on their own actions. In practice, they argue, managers do have choice over the structure they design. The contrasting ways in which leading grocery companies have used the Internet seems to support that view.

MANAGEMENT IN PRACTICE   ## Retailers' response to the Internet

The Internet makes it possible for supermarket chains to create a website on which customers can order their shopping, which the company then delivers to their home. Sainsbury has responded by creating a separate division to handle this business, with a separate management structure, warehouses and distribution system. Tesco has integrated its Internet shopping business with the existing stores – staff pick the customer's Internet order from the shelves of a conventional store. Other chains, such as Somerfeld and Safeway, have chosen (in 2001) not to offer an online service. So while the technology is available to all only some have chosen to use it, and those that have adopted it have chosen different structures to manage it.

Those favouring a contingency approach reject these criticisms. They concede that managers exercise choice, but argue that this choice is constrained by the need to adapt the structure to ensure acceptable performance:

As an organization grows it must bureaucratize and structurally differentiate. Similarly as an organisation diversifies it must adopt a more decentralized structure, shifting from functional to multi-divisional. Organizations are under pressure to perform from several sources: from competitors, from stakeholders such as owners and employees, and from the aspirations of their own managers. Therefore organizations will seek to avoid the performance loss that comes from retaining structures that are in misfit with the contingencies. [They] will move from misfit into fit by adopting the structure which fits. There will typically be one particular structure, or a narrow band of structural alternatives, out of all the various conceivable types of structure. Hence the discretion exercised will be severely limited. (Donaldson, 1996, p.51)

This implies that while managers go through the motions of choosing, the direction they can follow is substantially set. Nevertheless their role remains significant. It includes, for example, interpreting the contingencies correctly, selecting a form of structure appropriate for those contingencies, implementing it and continuing to adapt it. They add value by choosing and implementing a structure which will be effective in those circumstances.

ACTIVITY 10.3

Assessing an organisation's structure

Arrange an interview with someone who works in an organisation. Ask him or her to describe how their organisation or department is structured and to comment on whether that structure is right for the environment the business is working in.

Would you describe the organisation or department as relatively mechanistic or relatively organic? Does this fit the environment?

Have there been major changes in structure recently? If so, what prompted management to make them?

Q **Case questions 10.3**

- Does the Oticon example support contingency or management choice approaches?
- Does the role of management in the company support either of these approaches?

10.5 The Internet enables new structures

Many changes in the external environment (See Chapter 3) are stimulating managers to adapt the structure of their organisation. An external development that is bringing change to almost all businesses is the rapid development of information technologies, and especially of the Internet. This section outlines these trends, and the following section introduces some of the new forms of organisation that are emerging.

Advances in information and communications technologies are changing the goods and services that organisations offer, and how they organise to deliver them. Since organisations depend on information (see Chapter 18), they are deeply affected by developments in technologies for capturing, manipulating and transferring information. The potential of the Internet is high on the agenda of many management discussions.

Convergence

The three devices at the front of the information revolution – the telephone, the computer and the television, have been around for more than half a century. They are in widespread daily use throughout the developed world, and have developed independently of each other. They are familiar to us as separate devices.

Recent developments are eroding the boundaries between them. This brings powerful new tools that are revolutionising the way people and organisations communicate information. The primary development here is the new ability to process and transmit information in a common digital format. Computers have always handled information this way, while telephones and television used an analogue method. Now that they can use digital methods there is a common platform between the three communication devices. This greatly simplifies the exchange of information and functions between them. Personal computers can download television broadcasts over the Internet, while telephones can display information held on a company database, and send email. Televisions can allow users to interact with, say, a retailer to order goods and pay for them over a system linked to their bank or credit card company.

In short, the distinction between these three common devices is blurring and will soon disappear. People can send and receive information in ways that will enable radically new ways of working and living. Figure 10.9 shows how the convergence of telephones, computers and televisions creates overlaps between the once-segregated functions of these devices

Cheap and powerful networks

The world's main financial and business centres are now linked by optical fibres. This network is capable of carrying many times the world's present telecommunications traffic. Increasing capacity leads to rapidly reducing charges for transmitting data. This capacity is providing a level of communications infrastructure unimaginable less than 10 years ago. Developments in optical fibres and switching devices are bringing further vast increases in the capacity of communication networks. The cost of transporting voice and data is falling towards zero, so distance then becomes irrelevant to the cost of sharing information. People can connect to the network through both fixed and mobile devices at all times.

In summary, the development of digital technology is enabling the convergence of telephones, computers and televisions, while the use of optical fibre makes it possible to build more powerful networks to carry data. Cumulatively these changes are revolutionising the availability of information, and have major implications for organisations and their management.

Figure 10.9 The convergence of telephones, televisions and computers

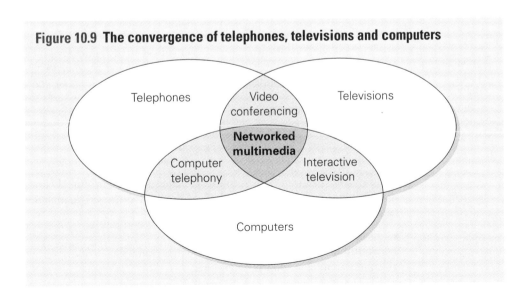

10.6 The balance between old and new forms

Warren Bennis predicted over three decades ago that, since most organisations now face turbulent environments, mechanistic, bureaucratic structures would soon disappear:

> The social structure of organisations of the future will have some unique characteristics. The byword will be 'temporary'. There will be adaptive, rapidly changing temporary systems. There will be task forces organised around problems to be solved by groups of relative strangers with diverse professional skills. The group will be arranged on an organic rather than mechanical model; it will evolve in response to a problem rather than to programmed role expectations. The executive thus becomes co-ordinator or 'linking pin' between various task forces. People will be evaluated not according to rank but according to skill and professional training.

> Adaptive, problem-solving, temporary systems of diverse specialists, linked together by co-ordinating and task evaluating executive specialists in an organic flux – this is the organisational form that will gradually replace bureaucracy as we know it. As no catchy phrase comes to mind, I call these new style organisations adaptive structures. (Bennis, 1969, p.34)

Developments in information technology such as those described in the previous section make that vision increasingly possible – yet the evidence to support Bennis's prediction is mixed. Many companies undoubtedly are responding to turbulent environments by using the technology partially to dismantle mechanistic structures – such as GlaxoSmithKline and BT quoted earlier, and Haliburton below. Henry Lucas has put forward some radical ideas in this area (see Key Ideas).

KEY IDEAS Lucas and electronic design variables

Henry Lucas coined the phrase 'electronic design variables' to reflect the opportunities for structural change that information technology provides. He proposed that managers can now consider basing much more of their organisation on electronic means. Rather than start with the structure and ask how technology can support this, they may consider how objectives can best be served by electronic means, and then build a structure to support that.

'Electronic design variables', as Lucas calls them, such as networked computing and telecommunications systems, can be used to change structures by:

- Restructuring work so that parts can be outsourced to other companies, easily linked by electronic means.
- Automating information processes in the vertical hierarchy removes layers of management and gives wider spans of control.
- Co-ordination of work can be improved by using electronic links of various kinds to ensure smoother flow within and between organisations.

Source: Lucas (1996).

Champy and Nohria (1996) prophesy that in the face of global competition, changing markets, and technological breakthroughs, the business organisation of the future is emerging with distinct characteristics. It will be:

- information-based
- decentralized, yet densely linked through technology
- rapidly adaptable and extremely agile

- creative and collaborative, with a team-based structure
- staffed by a wide variety of knowledge workers, and
- self-controlling, which is possible only in an environment of clear, strong, and shared operating principles and of real trust. (Champy and Nohria, 1996, pp. xv–xvi)

In cases such as these managers are using the power of information systems to redesign organisations in the way Bennis predicted. They are dividing large companies into smaller ones, as specialist service providers take over non-core functions. Large companies seek to improve their return on assets, and information systems allow them to split off businesses that are not central to their mission.

MANAGEMENT IN PRACTICE **Virtual oil companies?**

In 2000 Haliburton, an oil services and equipment company, formed a joint venture with Science Applications International, a research and engineering company, to launch a virtual workspace for oil and gas companies. It would source teams of professionals and provide the technical expertise and data management for exploration and development projects.

Bob Peebler, vice-president of e-business strategy and ventures at Haliburton, likened the approach to the movie business – the portfolio of projects is always changing and different teams of professionals are necessary to meet unique project criteria. Such an approach, he says, will meet the industry's long-standing need for more agile technical teams, access to the precise resources required for each venture and innovative partnerships. He predicts that oil companies could emerge as large-scale brands which are essentially marketing companies that have separated out their expertise and given up their oil fields and refining assets.

'At one point it made sense to have those assets tied together – but with the digitisation of the industry the role of the corporate body as facilitator becomes less important.' He pointed to Enron as an example of a company that understood the impact of the Internet and had been willing to transform itself (although late in 2001 Enron collapsed when it was unable to pay its debts).

Source: Based on an article by Hillary Durgin, *Financial Times*, 11 January 2001.

FT

The Internet offers a radical means of creating such networked organisations. Some predict that the work of temporary companies can be co-ordinated by the people who make up the organisation, with little or no central direction and control. Brokers, venture capital firms, suppliers, contractors could all play a role, with little apparent need for central supervision. For all the hyperbole, it is worth recalling that the term 'virtual organisation' is usually a new term for an old practice. Most organisations have some degree of physical separation within their value chain.

In contrast others are using the power of Internet technology to enhance the degree of central control. The technology that makes it possible for managers to decentralise their structures also enables them to centralise it. Mergers often lead to attempts to impose greater central control on the merged businesses, and modern information systems make such control possible. They can collect data as transactions occur in the most distant locations of the company, giving the centre greater insight into events and greater possibilities of tighter control.

KEY IDEAS   **The process of becoming virtual**

Venkatraman and Henderson (1998) offer a useful and practical perspective on the topic in proposing that the virtual organisation is not so much a state as a process. Organisations differ in the degree to which they are 'virtual', rather than either being so or not. Venkatraman and Henderson suggest that virtualness is a characteristic of any organisation, based on its position along three vectors – customer interaction, asset configuration and knowledge leverage. This idea allows us to consider how IT developments enable long-established organisations to introduce a greater degree of physical separation in their activities:

- **Customer interaction** Here consider how IT makes it easier for customers to experience

products and services remotely and perhaps engage in some dynamic customisation.
- **Asset configuration** Here the focus is on the extent to which a firm co-ordinates resources and activities within a network: it does not depend only on assets that it physically controls.
- **Knowledge leverage** This means gaining access to wider sources of expertise, including that in other organisations.

In all these respects organisations can be to a greater or lesser extent virtual, measured by the number and importance of cross-boundary transactions. The authors argue that moving along the spectrum needs a new set of management skills, as opposed to when most assets are within the organisation.

MANAGEMENT IN PRACTICE   **A trend to centralise?**

Recent research is showing that after years of decentralising control to individual business units and allowing them to operate almost as independent companies many organisations are changing direction. They are taking personnel, finance and other specialist functions away from their business units and national subsidiaries and are setting up shared service centres for the whole organisation. According to the survey (by the Institute for Personnel and Development) almost all organisations – 94 per cent – are responding to external pressures by creating a coherent product or service image. Based on telephone interviews with 153 chief executives from across UK industry, the survey also found that 85 per cent of organisations are providing more leadership direction from the centre, while a third are taking decision making away from divisional business units. The survey concluded that recentralisation is firmly on the agenda.

Source: *People Management*, 6 May 1999.

10.7   Summary

The chapter has shown the choices management faces in creating a structure. The underlying belief is that the right structure, like the right HRM policies, can support an organisation's strategy. It is management's task to establish what the right structure is for their chosen strategy, and then to implement it. While contingency approaches emphasise the rational or functional bases of such decisions, the management choice view places more emphasis on the possibility that management creates structures that support its personal preferences or political ambitions. The interaction can also work the other way, in that a structure can itself encourage the creation of new strategies that make use of that base.

Content

External changes in the business or political environment can lead to changes in the objectives that management is following. Such a change in strategy often prompts management to change other organisational elements so that they match the new strategy. A rational view of change management suggests that planning how to deal with the change involves paying attention to the relevant parts of the content agenda, and the interactions between them. Contingency approaches stress limited management choice in adapting structure to external events. Other views suggest that management has more scope to decide on structure with limited penalties.

Process

The form of structure adopted affects the processes of management and the way people work together in organisation. The patterns of interaction are very different between mechanistic and organic structures. There is evidence of a dilemma emerging between the widely held belief that changing markets need organisations to be flexible (and so decentralised and relatively organic) and the observation that many companies are using the power of modern information systems to centralise control. Political processes will also influence the process of change, as these are affected by decision processes that management creates. Signals about performance and external change compete for management attention. Information has to be accurately received before someone can attend to it, so communication skills also affect this aspect of management.

Control

Successful strategies will depend on ensuring the right balance between central control and local autonomy. Information systems make possible a more centralised, vertically focused business: competitive pressures may point towards relaxing central control and ensuring more local autonomy. Changing a structure may itself be seen as threatening to alter the pattern of control; some may resist these attempts to control them. Those pushing such change will need to build their power to overcome resistance, especially by creating institutional support mechanisms. Organisational development often begins as a result of signals from the organisational control systems that corrective action is needed. However, the perception and interpretation of these external signals are not technical but human processes, and the interpretations are not unique. The next chapter discusses the processes of organisational change.

Management at Oticon has clearly concluded that their new (differentiation) strategy needed a new structure, which would encourage more intense interaction and exchange of ideas. The new structure also, incidentally, helped to reduce costs – the two are not necessarily mutually exclusive. The strategy appeared to work – financial and other measures of performance were moving in the right direction. The company continues to prosper – and you can visit their website to find out some more about the company and its products.

> ### Q PART CASE QUESTIONS
>
> - Does The Royal Bank of Scotland have a mechanistic or an organic structure?
> - What contingency factors have probably shaped that structure?
> - Does the evidence seem to support, or not, the contingency approach?

10.8 Review questions

1 How does the structure of an organisation support or hinder its strategy?
2 Explain the difference between a mechanistic and an organic form of organisation.
3 Give an example to illustrate each of the factors that influence management's choice between mechanistic and organic structures.
4 What is meant by the term 'a contingency approach'?
5 If contingency approaches stress the influence of external factors on organisational structures, what is the role of management in designing organisational structures?
6 What is the main criticism of the contingency approaches to organisation structure?
7 What do you understand by the term 'virtual organisation', and what is the contribution of Venkatraman and Henderson to our understanding of the term?
8 Is the Internet fulfilling Bennis's prediction about the emergence of less bureaucratic organisations?

Further reading

Woodward, J. (1965), *Industrial Organization: Theory and practice*, Oxford University Press, Oxford. Second edn 1980.

Burns, T. and Stalker, G.M. (1961), *The Management of Innovation*, Tavistock, London.

Lawrence, P. and Lorsch, J.W. (1967), *Organization and Environment*, Harvard Business School Press, Boston, MA.

The research reports by these writers who initiated the contingency approaches to organisation were published over 30 years ago. They are short and accessible accounts of the research process, and it would add to your understanding to read at least one of them in the original. The second edition of Woodward's book (1980) is even more useful, as it includes a commentary on her work by two later scholars.

Ostroff, F. (1999), *The Horizontal Organisation: What the organisation of the future looks like*, Oxford University Press, Oxford.

Ashkenas, R. (1995), *The Boundaryless Organisation: Breaking the chains of organisation structure*, Jossey-Bass, San Francisco, CA.

These two books recount how some organisations (mainly GE in the Ashkenas book) have attempted radical new forms of structure.

Steinbock, D. (2001), *The Nokia Revolution: The story of an extraordinary company that transformed an industry*, McGraw-Hill, London. Excellent account of the evolution of Nokia, its evolving strategy, and how it has adapted the structure to support that.

Annotated links, questions and resources can be found on
www.booksites.net/boddy

CHAPTER 11

Managing change

> **AIM** *To outline theories of change in organisations and show how these relate to practice.*

OBJECTIVES

By the end of your work on this chapter you should be able to outline the concepts below in your own terms and:

1 Explain why managers need to be able to plan and implement change

2 Illustrate the types of organisational change

3 Explain how a change project interacts with its context

4 Outline a model of the steps in a change process

5 Compare life cycle, emergent, participative and political theories of change

6 Use a technique to diagnose the characteristics of a change

7 Recognise different forms of resistance, including counterimplementation

8 Evaluate management proposals to implement change by using these ideas

The Environment Agency

The board of the Agency announced in October 2000 that it would introduce a new management structure. It gave the chief executive, Catherine Hayes, the task of planning the transition from the present structure based on geographic regions to one based on functions. The senior team consisted of Ms Hayes and five other managers, each responsible for one geographic area.

The main aim of the change was to use resources more efficiently and effectively. The board wanted staff to deliver a consistent national service, based on unified professional practices. It believed that a national, functional structure would be more likely to achieve this than the regional structure. It also hoped to give staff a clearer set of priorities on which to focus their work, as staff had expressed concerns about this in a recent attitude survey.

The Agency employed about 900 staff, and one requirement was that the new structure should be introduced with as little impact on current operations as possible. For financial and performance measurement reasons the most appropriate time to introduce the new structure was the start of the new financial year and therefore the new structure was to be in place no later than 1 April 2001. This allowed five months for a planned implementation. To handle this transition, the chief executive appointed a Transition Planning Group (TPG), which was required to produce and manage a plan to implement the new structure within that time. The head of human resources led the TPG, which also included three senior staff from the Agency and a consultant.

The change would affect many staff, and the chief executive had been appointed within the last year. Some of the present senior team would have equivalent posts within the new structure. They had a keen interest in the new structure and associated sub-structures, but the board wanted to limit their role in planning the change. The board required the new structure to fit the business needs of the Agency, not individual preferences. The overall impact of the board-imposed top level restructure was to reduce the number of senior staff from 35 to 9, which meant that most of these staff could face redundancy.

Source: Private communication from the head of human resources.

Q Case questions

● What has prompted the board to go ahead with this project?
● What management issues is the head of human resources likely to face in implementing the change?

11.1 Introduction

This chapter introduces the following ideas:

- Project management models
- Life cycle model
- Emergent change model
- Participative model
- Political model
- Inner context
- Outer context
- Counterimplementation

The head of human resources at the Environment Agency faces a problem that is familiar to many managers. The chief executive has put her in charge of implementing a major change that the board has decided on. Many people will be affected, and most will be uneasy about how the change will affect them. The change from a regional to a functional structure will have major implications for budgeting processes, reporting relationships, and for links with other bodies, such as local authorities. And she has less than six months in which to do it.

Successive chief executives at companies such as BP have had to implement major changes. In BP the challenge had been to transform the business from a relatively small (in world terms), diversified business into the second largest oil company in the world. Mergers, such as that between the Commercial Union and General Accident companies (and then the merger between that combined business and the Norwich Union) usually bring major internal changes. Small businesses make radical change too – as when Hindle Power, an engineering company with 30 employees, faced the loss of a valuable distribution contract unless it changed the way it worked. It embarked on a radical programme of change that returned the company to profit, and to grow the business (*People Management*, 3 February 2000, p.52).

The external environment described in Chapter 3 is the main source of organisational change. Political, economic, social and technical developments change what people expect of organisations – which in varying degrees change the way they operate in an attempt to meet these new expectations. Research by the Institute of Personnel and Development of 151 multisite organisations found that the major reasons for recent organisational changes were a need to create closer customer relations, significant financial pressure to improve performance, or intensifying competition (IPD, 1999). A survey by the Institute of Management (1995a) showed that 70 per cent of respondents had experienced one or more corporate restructurings in the past two years. Anecdotal evidence is that while most managers accept the need for change many are critical of the way their organisations introduce it. Organisations still experience great difficulty in managing change successfully.

This chapter presents theories about the nature of change in organisations. It begins by explaining how a change project interacts with its context, and illustrates projects to change each of the elements in that context. The chapter then outlines four perspectives on organisational change with different management implications, followed by an empirically based diagnostic technique for identifying critical characteristics of a change. The chapter concludes by introducing the role of influence in change projects.

KEY IDEAS **TQM and BPR**

Though Total Quality Management [TQM] appears to be central to the success of Japanese companies, the experience of Western companies has been that it is difficult to introduce and sustain. Indeed, one of the founders of the TQM movement, Philip Crosby (1979), claimed that over 90 per cent of TQM initiatives fail. Though a 90 per cent failure rate seems incredibly high, studies of the adoption of TQM by companies in the UK and other European countries shows that they too have experienced a similarly high failure rate – perhaps as much as 80 per cent. (Kearney, 1992; Economist Intelligence Unit, 1992)

Business process re-engineering (BPR) has been hailed as 'the biggest business innovation in the 1990s' (Mill, 1994, p.26). Wastell *et al.* (1994, p.23) concluded from the available evidence that 'BPR initiatives have typically achieved much less than promised'. Other studies have come to similar conclusions (Coombs and Hull, 1994).

Therefore even well-established change initiatives, for which a great deal of information, advice and assistance is available, are no guarantee of success.

Source: Burnes (1996, pp.172–3)

ACTIVITY 11.1

Recording a major change

From discussion with colleagues or managers, identify a major attempt at change in an organisation. Make notes on the following questions and use them as a point of reference throughout the chapter.

What was the change?

Why did management introduce it?

What were the objectives?

How did management plan and implement it?

How well did it meet the objectives?

What lessons have those involved taken from the experience?

11.2 The context of change

Chapter 1 introduced the idea that managers work within a context that shapes what they do, and which they can also try to change. This chapter explains the processes by which managers try to make such changes, inevitably working within the influence of the context they are trying to change. Figure 11.1 illustrates five steps in the process of such change.

Influential players usually initiate change when they become conscious of a performance gap – some disparity between actual and desired performance. External or internal events are threatening their ability to deliver the performance that influential stakeholders expect. This awareness, and their implicit theory of change, encourages someone to propose an organisational change. If they secure agreement, someone with the authority to do so creates a project through which people plan the change, diagnose the implications, and influence people to do something differently. How well people manage the steps in this process determines the effect on the performance gap. This in turn feeds back to the **outer context** of the organisation.

Figure 11.1 A model of the change process

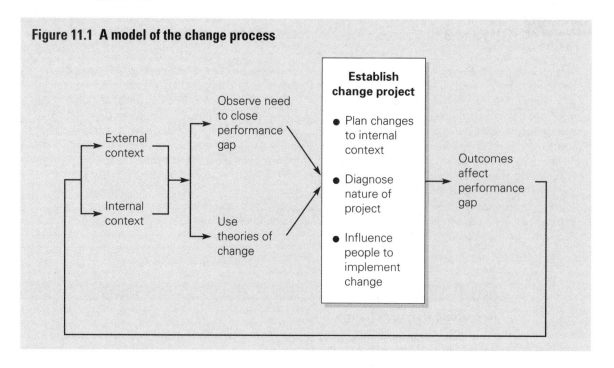

Chapter 3 described the external environment of business, and Chapter 10 some current changes that place new demands and changes on organisations. BP faced new competitive pressures throughout the 1980s, but it was only around 1990 that the pressures for change built up to initiate a period of rapid change. British Airways has responded to the pressure of new competition from low cost airlines such as Ryanair and easyJet by launching competing businesses, and then making wider changes in its strategy. The growth of the Internet has prompted most organisations to consider what changes they should make in the way they organise their activities.

Chapter 1 introduced the internal context (Figure 1.3, repeated here as Figure 11.2) as the set of elements within an organisation that shape behaviour. These in themselves can lead to change – if people believe, for example, that an unacceptable performance gap is due to a failure of technology or structure. Someone may decide that internal communication problems can be resolved by making a change in structure or in the design of a business process. Change also arises internally, when, say, a new director decides to raise the target level of profit for a division (so widening the performance gap). Employees or trade unions can propose changes in the way things are done to improve working conditions.

Change projects only occur when someone sees a threat or opportunity. They then have to persuade enough other people that the matter is serious enough to earn a place on the management agenda. Some organisations are open to proposals for change, others tend to ignore them (as BP did for many years). The need for change is a subjective matter – what some see as urgent others will leave until later. People can affect that process by managing external information – magnifying customer complaints to make the case for change, or minimising them if they wish to avoid change.

Figure 11.2 Elements of the organisational context of management

11.3   The interaction of context and change

How managers implement change depends on their theory about the nature of organisational change. This section presents an 'interaction' theory, describing the way a change interacts with its context. The next section outlines four complementary perspectives on managing that interaction.

Change is meant to alter the context

Management attempts to change elements of its context so as to encourage behaviours that support its objectives (this is, to close the performance gap). In the Environment Agency, the board is focusing on changing the structure and some of the people to encourage a more consistent and higher quality service. When Tesco introduced online shopping management needed (at least) to make decisions about changes to technology, structure, people and business processes to enable staff to deliver the new service. When people plan and implement a change they are creating new 'rules' (Walsham, 1993) that they hope will guide the behaviour of people involved in the activity.

People do not necessarily accept the new arrangements without question, or without adapting them in some way. They may themselves make further changes to the context. As people begin to work in new circumstances – with a new technology or a new structure – they make small adjustments to the original plan. As they use a new information system or website they decide which aspects to ignore, use or adapt.

As people become used to working with the new system their behaviours become routine and taken for granted. They become part of the context that staff have created informally. These new contextual elements may add to, or replace, the context that those formally responsible for planning the change created. These informally created aspects of the context may or may not support the original intentions of those who initiated the project. The interaction between people and context continues as the system evolves.

MANAGEMENT IN PRACTICE **Sun Microsystems and a supplier**

Boddy *et al.* (2000) studied Sun Microsystems and one of their suppliers as they moved towards a more co-operative supply chain relationship. Managers in both companies introduced changes to the context of work – technology, processes and roles. These were designed to create a context that encouraged more co-operation, and closer interpersonal links, between people in the two companies. For example, the supplier's sales co-ordinator:

> There is a close relationship with my opposite number in Sun. We speak several times a day, and he tries to give me as much information as he possibly can.

Sun staff echoed this:

> What makes them different is that you're talking to them daily … The relationships are a bit different – it is a bit closer than an ordinary supplier where you don't have that bond. Dealings are more direct. People are becoming more open with each other.

Both groups came to appreciate the other's requirements and tried to make things easier for them. Sun staff learned about the supplier, and vice versa. Both spoke of 'harmonising expectations'.

Source: Boddy *et al.* (2000).

The context affects the ability to change

While the project aims to change the context, elements in the context itself will help or hinder that attempt. All of the elements of Figure 11.2 will be present as the project begins, and some of these will influence how people react to the proposal. At the Environment Agency the managers who occupy places in the existing regional structure clearly had an interest in the change that the board had begun, and tried to shape its direction. At Tesco the existing technology (stores, distribution systems, information systems) and business processes would influence managers' decisions about how to implement the Internet shopping strategy.

The prevailing culture – the shared values, ideals and beliefs that hold a unit together – has a particularly strong influence on how people view a change. Cultures develop as members work together to deal with problems, and in so doing develop shared assumptions about the external world and their internal processes. As firms grow, subcultures develop within them. Members are likely to welcome a project that they believe fits the culture or subculture. They are likely to resist one that conflicts with or challenges the culture.

MANAGEMENT IN PRACTICE **Culture and change at a European bank**

While teaching a course to managers at a European bank, the author invited members to identify which of the four cultural types identified in Chapter 8 best described their unit within the bank. They were then asked to describe the reaction of these units to an Internet banking venture that the company was introducing.

Course members observed that colleagues in an internal process culture (typically performing routine back-office data-processing functions) were hostile to the Internet venture. They appeared to be 'stuck with their own systems', which were so large and interlinked that any change was threatening. Staff in new business areas of the company (open systems) were much more positive, seeing the Internet as a way towards new business opportunities.

Source: Data collected by the author.

The prevailing organisational culture is a powerful influence on the success or failure of innovation. Some cultures support and encourage change: a manager in Sun Microsystems commented on the culture within that successful and fast-moving business:

> A very dynamic organisation, it's incredibly fast and the change thing is just a constant that you live with. They really promote flexibility and adaptability in their employees. Change is just a constant, there's change happening all of the time and people have become very acclimatised to that, it's part of the job. The attitude to change, certainly within the organisation, is very positive at the moment.

At Sun (and many other companies) the culture encourages change. At other organisations the culture encourages people to resist change, or at least be cautious towards it. Such cultures, especially the deeper values and beliefs, have a force and momentum that reflects fundamental assumptions about the nature of people, the organisation and the environment. They are hard to change, and yet are a crucial factor in determining the organisation's response to attempts to change. Lorsch (1986) argued that culture could have a strong influence on how people respond to change. The norms, values and beliefs (about market expectations, competitors or internal organisation) that make up the culture have developed over years of successful operation: 'Managers learn to be guided by these beliefs because they have worked successfully in the past' (p.97).

The existing distribution of power also affects receptiveness to change. Change threatens the status quo, and is likely to be resisted by stakeholders who benefit from the prevailing arrangements. Innovation depends on those behind the change developing political will and expertise that they can only attempt within the prevailing pattern of power.

The context has a history, and several levels

The present context is the result of past decisions, and is usually focused on one of several 'levels' of context. Both features influence the process of change. Management seeks to implement change against a background of previous events. Past decisions shaped the organisation context as it is today, and its ability to change. As a manager introducing a change observed:

> There are so many changes taking place, they are more or less numb, and this is simply another change which they are just going to have to take on board. The result is that they are somewhat passive and neutral, and when I ask what their requirements might be, the response is usually 'you tell me.' (Boddy and Buchanan, 1992, p.33)

The promoter of a major project in a multinational also experienced the effects of history, as he tried to raise enthusiasm amongst his colleagues:

> They were a little sceptical and wary of whether it was actually going to enhance our processes. Major pan-European redesign work had been attempted in the past and had failed miserably. The solutions had not been appropriate and had not been accepted by the divisions. Europe-wide programmes therefore had a bad name. (Boddy and Buchanan, 1992, p.95)

Beliefs about the future also affect how people react to a proposal. Optimists are more receptive and open to change than those who feel threatened and vulnerable.

The context represented by Figure 11.2 occurs at several levels of the organisation – such as operating, divisional and corporate. People at any of these levels will be acting to make changes in their context – which may help or hinder the manager of a particular change. For example, a project at one level will often depend on decisions at other levels about the resources available. The manager leading a refinery team experienced this:

> One of the main drawbacks was that commissioning staff could have been supplemented by skilled professionals from within the company, but this was denied to me as project manager. This threw a heavy strain and responsibility on myself and my assistant. It put me in a position of high stress, as I knew that the future of the company rested upon the successful outcome of this project. One disappointment (and, I believe, a significant factor in the project) was that just before commissioning, the manager of the pilot plant development team was transferred to another job. He had been promised to me at the project inception, and I had designed him into the working operation. (Boddy and Buchanan, 1992, p.78)

Acting to change an element at one level will have effects at this and other levels. Any elements of the context may change independently. Part of the manager's job is to create a coherent context that encourages desired behaviour. They do so using their preferred model of change.

ACTIVITY 11.2

Assessing the effects of the context

What aspects of the contemporary context, shown in Figure 11.2, have had most effect on a project you are familiar with?

How have historical factors affected people's reactions?

Were the effects positive or negative for the project?

Did those managing the project take sufficient account of these contextual factors?

Q Case questions 11.1

- How may the existing context of the Environment Agency affect how staff react to the change?
- How may they affect the way that the head of HR has to manage the change?
- What three changes to the context is the change most likely to require, as well as the structure?

11.4 Four models of change

There are four complementary perspectives on change, each with different management implications. These are the life cycle, emergent, participative and political perspectives.

Life cycle perspective

Much of the advice given to those responsible for managing projects uses the idea of the project **life cycle**. Projects go through successive stages, and results depend on conduct-

Figure 11.3 Transition Planning Group timetable (see Chapter Case)

	Task Name	Duration	Start	Finish	Resource
	PHASE I	**85 days**	**Mon 20/11/00**	**Fri 30/03/01**	
	Develop structure options	25 days	Mon 20/11/00	Fri 22/12/00	TPG with
	Develop means to assess change effectiveness	10 days	Tue 21/11/00	Mon 04/12/00	TPG
	Identify potential benefits of proposed changes	20 days	Tue 21/11/00	Mon 18/12/00	TPG
	Identify implementation arrangements	10 days	Wed 22/11/00	Tue 05/12/00	TPG
	Consult with Directors	20 days	Fri 24/11/00	Thu 21/12/00	TPG with
	Consult with Unions	20 days	Mon 27/11/00	Fri 22/12/00	RS and TP
	Get information to staff	79 days	Tue 28/11/00	Fri 30/03/01	TPG + JNC
	Agree severance/retiral availability	1 day	Tue 05/12/00	Tue 05/12/00	CMT
	Report to CMT	73 days	Tue 05/12/00	Thu 29/03/01	TPG
	Early severance/retiral admin notice/process	10 days	Wed 06/12/00	Tue 19/12/00	RS
	Review accommodation for Directors/new starts	20 days	Wed 06/12/00	Tue 18/01/01	CMcD/AH
	Consult with staff on options/dev	20 days	Fri 08/12/00	Thu 18/01/01	TPG/JNC
	Evaluate and recommend option/substructure options	10 days	Mon 11/12/00	Fri 22/12/00	TPG for C
	CMT/TPG report to Board	0 days	Tue 12/12/00	Tue 12/12/00	TPG/CMT
	Develop recruitment/selection criteria and process	8 days	Tue 12/12/00	Thu 21/12/00	TPG/JNC
	PHASE II	**68 days**	**Wed 13/12/00**	**Fri 30/03/01**	

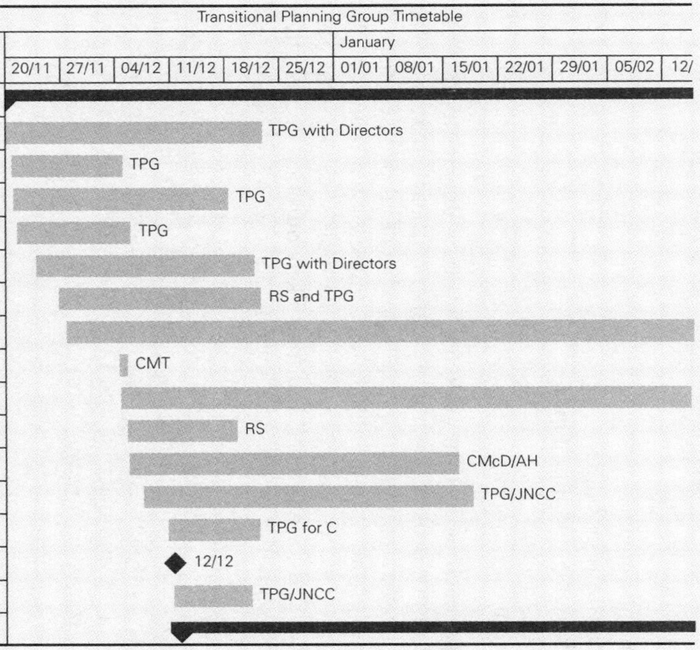

Transitional Planning Group Timetable — January

Timeline scale: 20/11 | 27/11 | 04/12 | 11/12 | 18/12 | 25/12 | 01/01 | 08/01 | 15/01 | 22/01 | 29/01 | 05/02 | 12/

Gantt bar labels: TPG with Directors; TPG; TPG; TPG; TPG with Directors; RS and TPG; TPG for C; TPG/JNCC; CMT; RS; CMcD/AH; TPG/JNCC; 12/12

ing the project through these stages in an orderly and controlled way. The labels vary, but major themes are:

1 define objectives;
2 allocate responsibilities;
3 fix deadlines and milestones;
4 set budgets; and
5 monitor and control.

This approach (sometimes called a 'rational–linear' approach) reflects the idea that a change can be broken down into smaller tasks, and that these can be done in some preferred, if overlapping, sequence. It predicts that people can make reasonably accurate estimates of the time it will take to complete each task and when it will be feasible to start work on later ones. People can use tools such as Gantt Charts, which show all the tasks required for a project, and their likely duration, to help them to visualise and plan the likely sequence of events. Figure 11.3 shows a section of the Gantt Chart developed for the Environment Agency change.

In this model successfully managing a project depends on specifying these elements at the start and then monitoring them tightly to ensure the project stays on target. Ineffective implementation is due to managers failing to do this. For example, Lock (1996), in his authoritative and highly regarded text on project management, identifies the 'key stages' of a manufacturing project, shown in Figure 11.4. He advises project

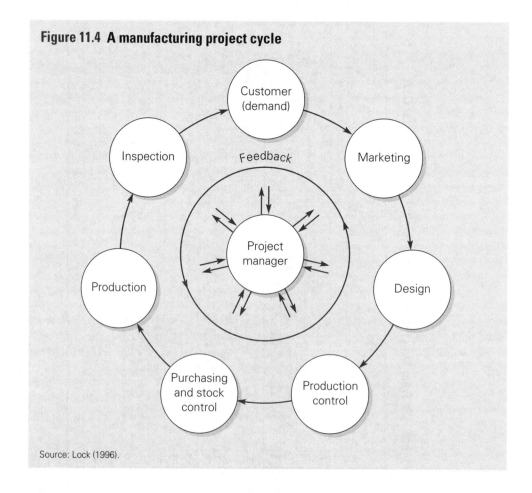

Figure 11.4 A manufacturing project cycle

Source: Lock (1996).

managers to ensure that the stages are passed through in turn, 'until the project arrives back to the customer as a completed work package'. Emphasising the iterative, cyclical nature of the method, he writes that 'Clockwise rotation around the cycle only reveals the main stream. Within this flow many small tributaries, cross-currents and even whirlpools are generated before the project is finished' (p.16).

Many books on project management (such as Lock, 1996; Woodward, 1997) present advice on tools and techniques for each stage of the life cycle. Those advising on changes to information systems usually take a similar approach, recommending a variety of 'system development life cycle' approaches (see for example Chaffee, 1999). For some projects, and for some parts of other projects, the project life cycle approach gives valuable guidance to those introducing change. It is not necessarily a sufficient approach in itself and those managing change may need to use additional methods. One difficulty is that people may not be able to specify the end point of the change at the start – or the sub-tasks that will lead to that result. Many changes have uncertain outcomes that cannot be planned in detail but which emerge as the change unfolds.

ACTIVITY 11.3

Using the project life cycle

If you are unfamiliar with this approach you can gain some insight into it by using it on a practical task. For example:

if you have a piece of work connected with your studies to do, such as an assignment or project, sketch out the steps to be followed, by adapting Figure 11.4;

alternatively do the same for some domestic or social project.

After doing the assignment or project, reflect on how the life cycle approach affected the way you worked.

Emergent perspective

Projects are the building blocks of organisational strategy, so they are likely to resemble the nature of that broader process. Early views of strategy saw it as a planning activity, based on assumptions that people behave rationally and interpret events and information objectively. However, as Chapter 6 showed, writers such as Quinn (1980), Mintzberg (1994a, 1994b) and Stacey (1994) believe these assumptions of rationality, objectivity and certainty rarely apply in the real world. They developed the view of strategy as an *emergent* or adaptive process. Mintzberg believed that strategic planning suffers from three 'fundamental fallacies', shown in Table 11.1.

Mintzberg's ideas apply to projects as much as they do to strategy. Projects are the means through which organisations deliver broad strategy. They take place in the same volatile, uncertain environment as does the organisation as a whole. People with different interests and priorities influence the ends and the means of a project. So while the planning techniques associated with the life cycle perspective can help, their value will be more limited if the change is closer to the **emergent** than the life cycle perspective.

Boddy *et al.* (2000) show how this happened when Sun Microsystems began the partnering project described earlier. Sun's initial intention from the partnership was to secure a UK source for the bulky plastic enclosures that contain their products, while the supplier was seeking ways to widen the customer base. There were few discussions about a long-term plan. As Sun became more confident of their supplier's ability the work

Table 11.1 Mintzberg's views on the fallacies of strategic planning

Fallacy	Description	Counter-view
Predetermination	'The prediction of ... the unfolding of the strategy formation process on schedule ... and the imposition of the resulting strategies on an acquiescent environment, again on schedule' (1994a, p.228)	Internal and external environments are dynamic, so that plans rarely unfold as intended
Detachment	'The prescription is that organizations should complete their thinking before they begin to act'	'...effective strategists are not people who abstract themselves from the daily detail but quite the opposite: they immerse themselves in it [and] abstract the strategic messages from it'
Formalisation	Analytical, scientific approach to strategy, with a prescribed series of steps, boxes and checklists	Strategy requires insight, creativity and synthesis, all the things that formalisation discourages. It needs to function beyond boxes

became more complex. Initially they only supplied the plastic enclosure, into which Sun fitted components such as cables and power supplies. The supplier later took on this work, delivering a more valuable product. They also began to supply Sun's US factory as well as that in the United Kingdom, and have taken more responsibility for managing inventory.

Both have gained from this emerging relationship. They acknowledge that in 1991 they did not foresee the amount and type of business they would eventually be undertaking. A sales co-ordinator:

> It's something we've learnt by being with Sun – we didn't imagine that at the time. Also at the time we wouldn't have imagined we would be dealing with America the way we do now – it was far beyond our thoughts.

Mintzberg's point is that managers should not expect rigid adherence to 'the plan'. Some departure from it is inevitable, due to unforeseeable changes in the external environment, the emergence of new opportunities, and other unanticipated events. A flexible approach to change is one which recognises that 'the real word inevitably involves some thinking ahead of time as well as some adaptation en route' (p.24).

Participative perspective

The **participative** approach to management has become a familiar theme in the management literature. The term indicates feelings of personal involvement in, and contribution to, events and outcomes. The underlying belief is that if people can say 'I helped to build this', they will be more willing to live and work with it, whatever it is. Many texts offer advice on how to involve employees in implementing change effectively. This applies to the 'quality of working life' movement of the 1960s and 1970s, to the 'quality circle' movement of the 1970s and 1980s and to 'high involvement management' practices (Lawler, 1986).

Enid Mumford's Ethics approach to participation

A well-known example of the participative approach in the field of systems design is Mumford and Weir's (1979) Ethics approach, summarised in Figure 18.7 (p.557). Here the key ingredients include user involvement in system development, recognising the social issues in implementation and using sociotechnical principles to redesign work. Several other methodologies are available for involving users in the system design process, for understanding users' needs more effectively and for giving them wider influence in design decisions that will affect their work.

Staff participation in planning the CGU merger

One of the UK's biggest mergers in 1998 was that of Commercial Union and General Accident to form CGU. The merger involved many changes throughout the merged organisation, and management decided to involve employees very widely in planning the change, mainly through three large meetings of hundreds of staff at all levels, nominated by their colleagues:

1 200 staff conducted a culture survey of the two companies. They were paired, one from each company, and escorted each other into the other's company, where they used a set format to build a culture map – how the firms were similar and how they were different.
2 500 managers and technical specialists attended a two-day conference to work in teams on the results of the Discovery programme and other survey data. Their task was to form a view about what would make CGU Insurance the best place to work for its employees. Video cameras captured the action and displayed it overhead on giant television screens around the hall, giving the two days the feel of a vibrant sporting event. Amongst the priorities the delegates agreed were: clear boundaries of authority; the freedom to take decisions within those boundaries; clear expectations; feedback; access to opportunity; and support for development.
3 80 people attended a four-day structured design workshop. Their task was to start designing a new organisation to meet the needs of shareholders, customers, employees and business partners. They produced a design that included principles of access (such as ensuring all brokers have easy entrance to our new offices), size of business units (30 to 50 people), and the size of teams (between 10 and 12).

Tony Clarry commented:

> 'The roll-out in the 51 locations so far has been smooth, which we attribute to the degree of commitment to the integration teams and to the conscientiousness of our people. Of course, there has been pain ... but involving people in decision making continues to be at the heart of what we do. We believe our approach has proved the value of real consultation.'

Source: Based on an article by Tony Clarry, who led the integration of the two companies, in *People Management*, 2 September 1999.

While the approach is consistent with democratic values, it is not free. It takes time and effort, and may raise unrealistic expectations. There are circumstances in which it may be inappropriate or unworkable, such as where any of the following apply:

● there is already full agreement on how to proceed;
● the scope for change is limited, because of decisions made elsewhere;

- those to take part in the exercise have little knowledge of the topic;
- decisions are needed urgently to meet deadlines set elsewhere;
- management has decided what to do and will do so whatever views people express;
- there is fundamental disagreement and inflexible opposition to a change.

CASE STUDY | **The Environment Agency – the case continues – problems with consultation**

'A significant hindrance was the timing of the project. The most active period was around Christmas, which the project plan had to accommodate by bringing forward some significant milestones. The result was less consultation than would normally be expected for such a high level restructure and less opportunity to discuss the perceived benefits of this structure with staff.

'Difficulties in communication with Central Management Team were aggravated by the exclusion of TPG from meetings at which directors were discussing the project. On at least 3 occasions, these meetings led to changes in the plan and the timetable, which at times placed the project in jeopardy.'

Source: Private communication from the head of human resources.

Participative approaches assume that a sensitive approach by reasonable people will result in the willing acceptance and implementation of change. For some changes that is the case, and a participative approach will help people to manage the change successfully. However, in other situations there will be issues to deal with that participation cannot solve.

ACTIVITY 11.4

Reflecting on participation

Have you been involved, or affected by, a change in your work or studies?

(a) If so:

    What evidence was there that those managing the change agreed with the participative approach?

    In what way, if any, were you able to participate?

    How did that affect your reaction to the change?

(b) If not:

    Identify three advantages and three disadvantages for the project manager in adopting a participative approach.

    Suggest how they should decide when to use the approach.

Political perspective

The perspectives described so far offer little guidance where a change challenges established interests, or where powerful players have opposing views. Whipp *et al.* (1988), for example, argue that change often involves several actors, representing different levels and sections of the organisation. They will probably be pulling in different directions, in the pursuit of personal as well as organisational goals:

Strategic processes of change are now more widely accepted as multi-level activities and not just as the province of a .... single general manager. Outcomes of decisions are no longer assumed to be a product of rational .... debates but are also shaped by the interests and commitments of individuals and groups, forces of bureaucratic momentum, and the manipulation of the structural context around decisions and changes. (p.51)

Several sociological analyses of organisational change emphasise a **political** model of the change process (Pettigrew, 1985 and 1987; Pfeffer, 1992a; Pinto, 1998; Buchanan and Badham, 1999). Pettigrew (1985) was an early advocate of the view that decisions on strategic change combine political as well as rational factors. In Pettigrew's view change is a complex and untidy cocktail of ostensibly rational assessment mixed with differential perceptions and quests for power. People who bring about successful change spend time creating a climate in which people accept the change as legitimate – often by manipulating apparently rational data about the business context to build support for their ideas.

Pfeffer (1992a) also argues that power is essential to get things done in organisations. His point is that decisions in themselves change nothing. It is only when someone implements them that anyone notices a difference. He proposes that projects require more than people able to solve technical problems. Projects frequently threaten

KEY IDEAS Tom Burns on politics and language

Tom Burns (1961) observed that political behaviour in the organisation is invariably concealed or made acceptable by subtle shifts in the language that people use:

'Normally, either side in any conflict called political by observers claims to speak in the interests of the corporation as a whole. In fact, the only recognised, indeed feasible, way of advancing political interests is to present them in terms of improved welfare or efficiency, as contributing to the organisation's capacity to meet its task and to prosper. In managerial and academic, as in other legislatures, both sides to any debate claim to speak in the interests of the community as a whole; this is the only permissible mode of expression.' (p.260)

the status quo: people who have done well in the past are likely to resist them. Innovators need to ensure the project is on the agenda, and that senior managers support and resource it. Innovators need to develop a political will, and to build and use their power.

Many observers now stress the importance of power and political behaviour for those

KEY IDEAS Henry Kissinger on politics in politics

In another work Pfeffer (1992b) quotes Henry Kissinger:

'Before I served as a consultant to Kennedy, I had believed, like most academics, that the process of decision-making was largely intellectual and all one had to do was to walk into the President's office and convince him of the correctness of one's view. This perspective I soon realised is as dangerously immature as it is widely held.' (p.31)

managing change. Buchanan and Badham (1999) consider why political behaviour occurs, and conclude that:

> Its roots lie in personal ambition, in organisation structures that create roles and departments which compete with each other, and in major decisions that cannot be resolved by reason and logic alone but which rely on the values and preferences of the key actors involved.

> ... Power politics and change are inextricably linked. Change creates uncertainty and ambiguity. People wonder how their jobs will change, how their workload will be affected, how their relationships with colleagues will be damaged or enhanced. Change in one organisational dimension can have knock-on or 'ripple' effects in other areas. As organisations become more complex, the ripple effects become harder to anticipate. (p.11)

Reasonable people are likely to disagree about means and ends, and to fight for what they believe to be the appropriate line of action.

MANAGEMENT IN PRACTICE   **Politics and change in the public sector**

These views of change as a fluid process find support in a contemporary account of project management in the public sector, based on research amongst a group of managers implementing major change projects:

> The powerful influence of the political process on organisational and cultural change is transparent for local authorities, but this may also be relevant in other non-elected organisations. Competing values and interests between different stakeholders are often less overt but none the less powerful factors championing or blocking processes of change.

Source: Hartley *et al.* (1997, p.71).

This implies that successful project managers will be those who understand that their job consists of more than being technically competent, and who are able and willing to engage in political actions.

MANAGEMENT IN PRACTICE   **Political action in hospital re-engineering**

A major hospital responded to a persistent performance gap (especially unacceptably long waiting times for certain treatments) by 're-engineering' the way patients moved through and between the different clinical areas. This included creating multi-functional teams responsible for all aspects of the flow of the patient through a clinic, rather than dealing with narrow functional tasks. The programme was successful, but was also controversial. One of those leading the change recalled:

> 'I don't like to use the word manipulate, but ... you do need to manipulate people. It's about playing the game. I remember being accosted by a very cross consultant who had heard something about one of the changes and he really wasn't very happy with it. And it was about how am I going to deal with this now? And it is about being able to think quickly. So I put it over to him in a way that he then accepted, and he was quite happy with. And it wasn't a lie and it wasn't totally the truth. But he was happy with it and it has gone on.'

Source: Buchanan (2001, p.13).

The political perspective recognises the messy realities of organisational life. Major changes will be technically complex and will often challenge established interests. These will pull in different directions and pursue personal as well as organisational goals. The practical implication of this is that political tensions are likely to arise in projects where people disagree about ends and means, and where resources are scarce. Managers will need political skills as well as those implied by rational or participative models of change.

MANAGEMENT IN PRACTICE **Pensco**

Pensco was a medium-sized life insurance business. Changes to pensions legislation brought new opportunities in the market for personal and group pensions, and also brought more competition. The industry changed and so did the company. A new general manager arrived, who immediately began to move the organisation vigorously in the direction of a market-led, sales-maximising approach. He recruited a colleague from his previous company as head of information systems (IS), who had a reputation as an autocratic and aggressive manager. The changes to the pensions products depended on changing the information systems to process the new business.

In response to new legislation managers began developing new pensions products. The initial proposals came from the Actuarial Department (AD). Staff in sales and marketing (S&M) were dismissive of the AD proposals and had a different interpretation of market requirements. They actively lobbied for their view. S&M also believed that the IS Department had:'too much power in the organisation ... We are working to change that. S&M should drive the organisation ... But I can't get away from the view that IS still dictate what the company can and can't do' (p.187).

For their part, IS had trouble finding out what the business requirements were – partly because of unresolved conflicts between AD and S&M over the product range. In part also the head of IS was seen to be keen to curry favour with the general manager. He did so by appearing to accept all requests for systems developments – which they were unable to deliver.

The company maintained the public position and despite the many difficulties the project was successful. The authors of the case reported different views from the clerical staff who were processing new proposals (without adequate IS support). As a team leader commented: 'They [the managers] don't have a grasp of what's going on. They just want the figures. They don't appreciate our problems. I wish they'd acknowledge there is one' (p.162).

Source: Based on Knights and Murray (1994).

In politically charged situations those managing change need to be sensitive to the power and influence of key individuals in the organisation, and to how the change will alter the pattern of influence. They will need to be able to negotiate and sell ideas to indifferent or sceptical colleagues. They may have to filter information to change perceptions, and do things that make the change seem legitimate within the organisation.

These perspectives (life cycle, emergent, participative and political) are complementary in that successful large-scale change, such as that at the Environment Agency, is likely to require elements of each. Each perspective can be linked to management practice, as illustrated in Table 11.2.

Table 11.2 Perspectives on change and examples of management practice

Perspective	Themes	Example of management practices
Life cycle	Rational, linear, single agreed aim, technical focus	Measurable objectives; planning and control devices such as Gantt Charts or critical path analysis
Emergent	Objectives change as learning occurs during the project, and new possibilities appear	Open to new ideas about scope and direction, and willing to add new resources if needed
Participative	Ownership, commitment, shared goals, people focus	Inviting ideas and comments on proposals, ensuring agreement before action, seeking consensus
Political	Oppositional, influence, conflicting goals, power focus	Building allies and coalitions, securing support from powerful players, managing information

11.5 Planning to change the internal context

Managers attempting to close a performance gap create a project that is intended to change one or more organisational elements. Figure 11.5 illustrates this with an example of a change in each element from elsewhere in the book.

Figure 11.5 Examples of projects to change organisational elements

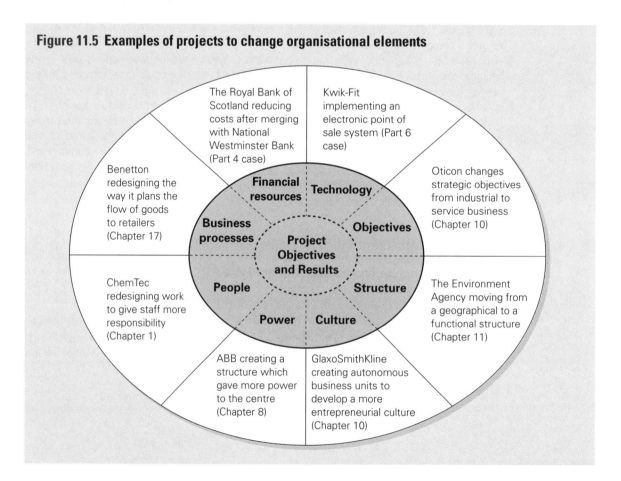

Table 11.3 illustrates some additional types of change that organisations initiate under each element.

Table 11.3 Examples of change in each element of the organisation

Element	Example of change to this element
Objectives	Developing a new product or service Changing the overall mission or direction Changing the emphasis given to a particular market
Technology	Installing new computer hardware or software Building a new factory Creating a website on the Internet
Business processes	Introducing a new process for dealing with customer orders Improving the way maintenance and repair services are delivered Redesigning systems to handle the flow of cash and funds
Financial resources	A set of changes, such as closing a facility, to reduce costs New financial reporting requirements to ensure consistency
Structure	Reallocating functions and responsibilities between departments Redesigning work to increase empowerment Centralising or decentralising decisions
People	Designing a training programme to enhance skills Changing the tasks of staff to offer a new service Deliberately encouraging staff to be more friendly to customers
Culture	Creating a more innovative or flexible culture Unifying the culture between two or more merged businesses Encouraging greater emphasis on quality and reliability
Power	An empowerment programme giving greater authority to junior staff Centralising decisions to increase the control of HQ over operations

It is rare for any significant change to be confined to only one of these elements. The systemic nature of organisations means that a change in any of these areas is likely to have implications for the others. When Tesco introduced its Internet shopping service alongside its established retail business it did not only create a website through which customers could place their orders. It needed to make decisions about structure and people (would it be part of the existing store business or a separate business unit with its own premises and staff?) and about business processes (how exactly would an order on the website be converted to a box of groceries delivered to the customer's door?). Tesco had to manage these ripple effects of the main decision. Managements that ignore these consequential changes achieve less than they expected. When ABB made a change in structure it also changed the roles of many senior managers to match talent with new responsibilities. It also made changes to the information systems (technology) to provide accurate performance information to those managing the new divisions.

Q Case questions 11.2

- Identify the possible ripple effects that may need to be managed in the Enterprise Agency, using the elements in Figure 11.2 as a guide. Start by entering the move to a national structure in the structure area. Then think of the possible implications that this change will have for other elements. These begin to form the management agenda for this project. Which of these are likely to cause most difficulty for the head of human resources and the TPG?

11.6 Diagnosing the characteristics of a change

When implementing a specific organisational change the management task depends on the unique features of that process. Research into a variety of changes has indicated the factors that make a change more or less difficult to manage, and this sections outlines these.

Driving and restraining forces

Lewin (1947) observed that any social system is in a state of temporary equilibrium. Driving forces are trying to change the situation in directions that they favour. Restraining forces push the other way to prevent change, or to move it in another direction. This equilibrium 'can be changed either by adding forces in the desired direction, or by diminishing the opposing forces' (p.26). Figure 11.6 illustrates the idea.

Driving forces encourage change from the present position. They encourage people and groups to give up past practice and to act in ways that support the change. They take many forms – such as a newly available technology, an inadequate business process or the support of a powerful player. Conversely factors such as the already-installed technology, shortage of finance, the opposition of powerful players or the company culture can be restraining forces. They encourage opposition, inertia and the maintenance of existing practice.

Those advocating a change can, in Lewin's terms, 'add forces in the desired direction' by stressing the advantages of the change, emphasising the threat from competitors or making the benefits seem more attractive. Alternatively they can seek to 'diminish the opposing forces' by showing that the problems will not be as great as people fear, or pointing out that difficulties will be temporary.

Lewin observed that while increasing the driving forces could produce change in the desired direction it could also increase tension amongst those 'forced' to change. The change may then be short-lived, or offset by the negative effects of the tension. Since these secondary effects may go against the interests of those promoting change, he suggested that trying to reduce the forces restraining change is usually the wiser route.

External events can trigger and drive change: new competition, a change in legislation, the activities of a pressure group, a chance conversation. Information from any of these sources can trigger change. People with sufficient power can use these and countless other external signs to justify a proposal.

Figure 11.6 Driving and restraining forces

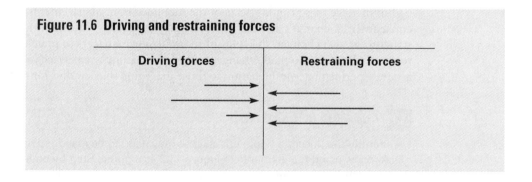

| MANAGEMENT IN PRACTICE | **An external driving force**

Boddy (2002) recounts the case of a proposed change to the Social Work Information System (SWIS) used by staff in a local authority. A manager initially proposed the system in 1996, and she made some progress. A reorganisation, budget cuts and limited enthusiasm for the project by the head of social work meant that enthusiasm waned, and the project was deferred. In 1999 the need for the system became more urgent. Legislative change required the authority to provide much more detailed information on clients, staff workloads and overall performance before they could receive extra funds. The old information system was unable to provide the management information to meet these requirements. This rapidly encouraged the authority to provide funds to re-establish the SWIS project – with the support of the head of social work.

Source: Boddy (2002, p.17).

In the same way forces within the organisation – changing management priorities, the availability of funds, opposition from groups who see their privileges threatened – can drive change, or restrain it. The degree and direction of change in an organisation reflects the shifting balance and direction of the driving and restraining forces.

Diagnosing the change

Change projects vary in the their difficulty, and Boddy and Buchanan (1992) identified those features that distinguished projects and which affected the change management challenge it represented. Later work by Boddy (2002) is the source of the following paragraphs.

Core/margin

Some changes aim to change an activity that is marginal to the business or which is in a background, supporting role – changing the way pensions are paid, or relocating administrative functions. Others are such that their success or failure is critical to the business. They are part of a broader strategy – such as a new online service for a bank or creating a website for an established retailer. They affect core operating processes, basic technologies or visible aspects of the business and its reputation. An example would be the series of projects that The Royal Bank of Scotland initiated to merge the operations of the National Westminster Bank with its own, or the doomed project to automate the settlement process at the London Stock Exchange (Drummond, 1996).

Novel/familiar

Some changes introduce novel, untried solutions and so depend on much learning and discovery during the project itself – both the problem and the solution are uncertain. The ideas floated are novel and highly uncertain – such as when Sainsbury or Tesco set up their Internet retailing operations. Other projects centre on systems that others have used in similar situations. People understand the setting and the likely solution at the start of the project – as when Sainsbury or Tesco refurbish a branch. They have done it many times before and both the problem and the solution are familiar.

Figure 11.7 shows these two critical dimensions of change projects. Those in quadrant 4 are likely to be most challenging to those responsible for implementing them. They are core to the business, and at the same time involve designing novel solutions.

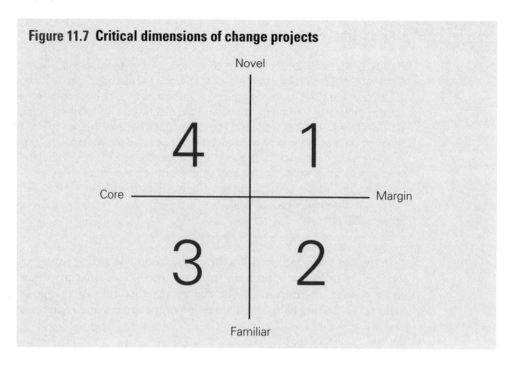

Figure 11.7 Critical dimensions of change projects

Rapid/gradual

Senior managers, such as the board of the Environment Agency, usually expect rapid change. They expect the project manager to achieve quick results and become impatient with requests for more time for design, testing, training or consultation. Pressure to implement a project rapidly inevitably leads to a search for short cuts. Others are able to make the change at a more leisurely pace, with adequate time for pilot schemes, revisions and training.

Controversial/uncontroversial

Some changes are vigorously opposed from the start by one or more parties, who seek to undermine the project by overt or covert means. Major production or administrative reorganizations threaten established interests, who may disagree fundamentally about the direction of the change. The Pensco change studied by Knights and Murray (1994) and described on page 337 is an example of this. Other changes arouse no such controversy as everyone concerned accepts the desirability of the change.

Changing goals

As the discussion on emergent projects implied, goals typically evolve in dialogue between senior management and project management. Sometimes these changes reflect poor initial planning – at other times they reflect the fact that the business environment has changed since the project began. Even if sponsors set clear goals at the outset, changing circumstances make it necessary to change them. This is a feature of the world that business operates in, and which shapes the job of the project manager. Projects in which the priorities and goals are frequently questioned will be harder to manage than ones in which they are stable.

Outside links

A feature of business life is the significant growth in co-operation between companies and public sector organisations. These broad policy trends shape tangible projects, many of which now involve working with people in other organisations or departments. These will contain the same elements shown in Figure 11.2 – but they will take a different form. Some differences may be of no consequence – others will cause severe difficulties, such as incompatible technologies or cultures. Some will have cultures that are receptive to change and keen to move ahead quickly; others need longer to adjust. They have different priorities, reflecting their part of the business, and other demands on them. Changes that are entangled with changes in other units are harder to manage than those that are self-contained.

Senior stance

The attitude of top managers towards the project is critical. They cannot give detailed guidelines, and may not even set out a clear blueprint for change. But their actions and words affect the ability of the project manager to influence other people. They shape part of the context in which the project manager works. Are they visibly behind the idea of change, willing to give it the resources it needs, and with reasonable expectations of what the project can achieve? How demanding are they, how tolerant of risk and delay? Will there be pressure for short cuts?

Other changes

Volatile environments mean that change is more frequent, and so comes in clusters. Most changes take place at the same time as other major changes. The turbulent environment of organisations prompts management to initiate simultaneous responses – and multi-project situations bring more uncertainty. There will be more competition for resources, and more scepticism as staff observe yet another change being launched. Table 11.4 summarises the features presented so far.

Table 11.4 Project profile tool

Significance:	Margin	1	2	3	4	5	Core
Solution:	Familiar	1	2	3	4	5	Novel
Pace:	Gradual	1	2	3	4	5	Rapid
Intentions:	Uncontroversial	1	2	3	4	5	Controversial
Changing goals:	Rare/minor	1	2	3	4	5	Often/major
Outside links:	Few	1	2	3	4	5	Many
Senior stance:	Supportive	1	2	3	4	5	Unsupportive
Other changes:	Few	1	2	3	4	5	Many

Source: Boddy (2002).

ACTIVITY 11.5

Identifying the pitfalls of change

Review a project against these features, by drawing a circle round the number on each of the scales that most accurately describes the project. High scores indicate where trouble is most likely to arise.

| 11.7 | **Influencing people to implement change** |

Like the head of human resources at the Environment Agency, most managers are expected to implement change in the context in which they work. In doing so they use their power to influence others to act in a particular way. Chapter 12 outlines theories of power and influence, so this section examines just three aspects of this activity – gaining commitment to change, using front-stage and back-stage tactics, and supporting individual activity with formal structures for managing change.

Resistance to change

Much of the management literature presents resistance to change in pejorative terms as something to be overcome. This discussion takes a more neutral stance. Some changes are clearly of general benefit to the organisation and all or most of its members. There is also much anecdotal evidence of managers who have introduced change mainly to further their local interests – to build a personal reputation or extend the influence of a department. Since organisations are made up of political and career systems as well as working systems (see Chapter 8), this is inevitable. Even when people intend to support organisational interests they sometimes misinterpret signals from the outside world and propose misguided changes.

For all these reasons people at all levels in an organisation will sometimes resist change. They may see it as a threat to their interests or status. Or they may believe that the change proposed will damage rather than benefit the organisation.

Forms of resistance

Overt and public resistance is often unnecessary. There are many other ways in which those opposed to a change can delay it, including the following:

- refusing to use new systems or procedures;
- making no effort to learn;
- using older systems whenever possible;
- not attending meetings to discuss the project;
- excessive fault finding and criticism;
- deliberate misuse;
- saying it has been tried before and did not work;
- protracted discussion and requests for more information;
- linking the issue with pay or other industrial relations matters;
- not releasing staff for training.

These delaying tactics come from anywhere in the organisation – they are as likely to come from managers who see a change as a threat to their interests as they are to come from more junior staff. Change creates winners and losers, and potential losers are apt to engage in what Keen (1981) termed the tactics of **counterimplementation**.

Sources of resistance

Johnston *et al.* (1967), in one of the earlier papers on the topic, distinguished between change that one can choose to accept or reject and change over which one has little influence or control. They propose that only the latter sort of change is resisted, for reasons such as a threat to economic security or job status (including symbolic factors),

Peter Keen on counterimplementation

Keen (1981) suggested that overt resistance to change is often risky, and may not in practice be necessary. He identified several ways in which those wanting to block a change can do so – even while appearing to support it. They include such tactics as:

- **Divert resources** Split the budget across other projects; have key staff given other priorities and allocate them to other assignments; arrange for equipment to be moved or shared.
- **Exploit inertia** Suggest that everyone wait until a key player has taken action or read the report or made an appropriate response; suggest that the results from some other project should be monitored and assessed first.
- **Keep goals vague and complex** It is harder to initiate appropriate action in pursuit of aims that are multidimensional and which are specified in generalised, grandiose or abstract terms.

- **Encourage and exploit lack of organisational awareness** Insist that 'we can deal with the people issues later', knowing that these will delay or kill the project.
- **'Great idea – let's do it properly'** And let's bring in representatives from this function and that section, until we have so many different views and conflicting interests that it will take for ever to sort them out.
- **Dissipate energies** Have people conduct surveys, collect data, prepare analyses, write reports, make overseas trips, hold special meetings ...
- **Reduce the champion's influence and credibility** Spread damaging rumours, particularly among the champion's friends and supporters.
- **Keep a low profile** It is not effective openly to declare resistance to change because that gives those driving change a clear target.

Source: Based on Keen (1981).

uncertainty and increased complexities. As well as the individual reaction in isolation, they also suggest that resistance may stem from changes in group relations, especially if the importance of these informal social relationships in the workplace is underestimated. If change means that the superior exercises closer control over the subordinate, the subordinate is likely to resist it.

ACTIVITY 11.6

Discussing resistance

Discuss with someone who has tried to introduce change in an organisation what evidence there was of resistance.

Which of the forms listed by Keen (in Key Ideas above) were in evidence?

Can they identify any other forms?

Have you ever resisted a proposed change?

What form did your resistance take?

Kotter and Schlesinger (1979) also identified individual sources of resistance, such as self-interest, misunderstanding and lack of trust: 'people also resist change when they do not understand its implications and perceive that it might cost them much more than they will gain'(p.108). Employees assess the situation differently from their managers and may see more costs than benefits for both themselves and the company. Recardo (1991) made similar points from a study of new manufacturing systems. Change requires learning and exposure to uncertainty, insecurity and new social interactions. It is often marked by poor communication and management of the change process.

Additional factors which he identified as engendering resistance were reward systems that did not reward the desired behaviour and a poor fit between the change and the existing corporate culture.

These views can be brought together by using the elements of the organisation shown in Figure 11.2. People can base their resistance on any of these contextual elements, as shown in Table 11.5.

Table 11.5 Reasons for resistance to change

Element	Source of resistance to change
Objectives	Lack of clarity or understanding of objectives, or disagreement with those proposed
People	Change may threaten important values, preferences, skills, needs and interests
Technology	May be poorly designed, hard to use, incompatible with existing equipment, or require more work than is worthwhile
Business processes	As for technology, and may require unwelcome changes to the way people deal with colleagues and customers
Financial resources	Scepticism about whether the change will be financially worthwhile, or less so than other competing changes; lack of money
Structure	New reporting relationships or means of control may disrupt working relationships and patterns of authority
Culture	People likely to resist a change that challenges core values and beliefs, especially if they have worked well before
Power	If change affects ownership of and access to information, those who see they will lose autonomy will resist

In addition to these substantive or content reasons for resisting change people may also resist because of the way the change is managed. They object to the process of change, irrespective of the specific change being made. Change is disturbing, and people are likely to resist if they do not feel they have been able to participate in discussions about the form it should take.

Managing front-stage and back-stage

Buchanan and Boddy (1992) suggest that two strategies are necessary to implement large-scale changes. Those promoting the change have to produce a 'public/front-stage performance' of logical and rationally planned change linked to widespread and convincing participative mechanisms. They also have to pursue 'back-stage activity'. They have to exercise power skills, influencing, negotiating, selling, searching out and neutralising resistance.

Front-stage performance

Change processes within organisations have to conform to organisational 'theatre' to be successful. People affected have to be convinced that they are genuinely involved in the change and have some influence over its outcome. Top management and expert staff have to be convinced that the change is technically rational, logical and also congruent with the strategic direction of the organisation. Established project management techniques such as network planning and control techniques, cost/benefit analysis and technological appraisals are useful in themselves (see, for example, Lock, 1996); so are bar and Gantt Charts, cumulative spending curves and scheduling tools. Such techniques are widely recognised as appropriate tools for managing change projects. They are also valuable in sustaining the image of the project manager. They reassure senior managers that the right things are being done in their name.

Back-stage activity

While the literature on participative management advises that manipulation and threats are counterproductive, management does use them in situations when there is a lack of time, resources and expertise as well as according to the scale and complexity of the project. Back-stage activities include establishing who can damage the project, co-opting likely opponents early, providing clear incentives to people to support the new system, and trying to create a 'bandwagon' effect. This is a 'back-stage' political strategy that depends heavily on the presence of a 'fixer' with prestige, visibility and legitimacy. Boddy and Gunson (1996) cite several examples of such moves based on mobilising coalitions. Some led from the front and put strong political pressure on sometimes reluctant managers to push a project through. While the front-stage activities of technical and strategic logic and user-participation strategies are important to provide organisational credibility at all levels, the back-stage activity is key to success or failure.

Individual skills and institutional support

Change depends on someone being able and willing to influence others to plan and implement. Yet as Hartley *et al.* (1997) observed, a 'recurring theme [amongst the internal change agents] was how best to mobilise programmes of organisational and cultural change … when they lack direct access to the traditional levers of line-management power … and the role influence rather than direct command' (p.67). Project managers usually have little formal authority – yet the key part of their job is to influence others to do certain things. Personal skills alone will often be insufficient. More formal structures and institutions need to support them.

Without some human agency, without someone putting personal effort into the problem, nothing will change. Kanter (1983) and Buchanan and Boddy (1992) identify the attitudes and skills that the change agent requires – and these include the skills required by the practices listed in Table 11.1. There are, however, limitations to what people acting on their own to manage change can achieve. As individuals they have limited power. This can to some extent be overcome by supporting individual action with appropriate structures, such as clearly establishing their role, establishing links to the board or senior managers, and creating project teams with the expertise and power to support the work of the individual manager. These all serve to enhance the power sources available to someone managing a change.

MANAGEMENT IN PRACTICE
Roles with and without formal authority

'A number of interesting things have happened. I personally have been legitimized by my division's management team as the Customer Service and Order Fulfilment Manager. I have also been legitimized as the European Programme Manager for order scheduling.' (p.46)

'My role was not properly set up, and clearly it was my mistake that I would be subordinate to the Board, and not a member of it. In hindsight I really needed to operate at the highest level to carry the necessary "clout", and to keep the Board itself properly informed.' (p.45)

Source: Boddy and Buchanan (1992).

11.8 Summary

This chapter has shown how management can respond to changes in the external world that require a change of strategy. That in turn will require them to manage some change to the context in which people work. The chapter outlined the sources of change and four main theories of the change process – which are complementary rather than competing.

Content

Management spends a great deal of time managing change. Its aim is usually to ensure that the organisation continues to add value to resources as the external world changes. Change can start in any of the elements of the organisation and will usually have indirect effects on other aspects of the organisation. Although change is widespread, the evidence suggests that it is often poorly managed. This affects business performance and staff commitment, and may be particularly damaging when the change is at the core of the business and has novel features – the quadrant 4 projects. A technique was described that those managing change can use to assess where particular planning and implementation problems are likely to arise.

Process

Change may challenge the interests of some stakeholders. While those promoting the change clearly see advantages, others have different goals – especially that of protecting their own or their department's interests. Four alternative and complementary models were presented of how management typically tries to generate the action it requires in change – life cycle, emergent, participative and political. Life cycle and participative approaches will be adequate in some combination if the change is uncontroversial and does not threaten valued interests. However, careful planning and involving people in decision making will not ensure they accept the outcome if they are going to be worse off. They will be inclined to resist the change (perhaps wisely), and management may need to use a range of political approaches to get things done. Change may require managers to combine their public performance with back-stage activity. Interpersonal skills and activities also need to be supported by appropriate institutions through which the change agents can exercise their skills.

Control

Some changes are introduced as an attempt by one group or department to gain more control over another. In that event change is not a neutral activity for the benefit of the organisation but a reflection of sectional interests. As such it may be contested by those who themselves want to retain or extend their control.

Major change projects are especially difficult to control – which may be one of the reasons why so many do not meet expectations. Measures need to be established for both the content and the process aspects of the change. When the change occurs in a volatile and uncertain environment monitoring and control are uniquely difficult. Post-project audits appear to be rare, and the opportunities of learning lessons on how to handle future change are thereby lost.

Despite the tight timescale the head of HR at the Environment Agency was able to implement the new structure on time. The account shows that she used, in varying degrees, all four approaches to change – from Gantt Charts to using her personal power to keep things moving – and several more besides. No one of the methods would have been sufficient to manage a complex and politically sensitive change. At the time of writing the national structure is working as the board had intended.

> **Q** **PART CASE QUESTIONS**
>
> ● Which model(s) of change did The Royal Bank of Scotland management use to implement its new policies? What evidence is there to support this conclusion?
> ● What are the differences and similarities between The Royal Bank of Scotland and the Environment Agency in terms of (a) the causes of change, and (b) the methods used to manage it?
> ● What aspects of the inner context at BP Amoco helped or hindered change?

11.9 Review questions

1 What types of change are likely to be the most difficult to introduce?

2 What are the implications for management of the systemic nature of major change?

3 Review the change that you identified in Activity 11.1 and compare its critical dimensions with those at The Royal Bank of Scotland or the Environment Agency.

4 Explain what is meant by the inner context of change, and compare at least two organisations in these terms.

5 How does the culture of an organisation affect change? Compare two examples, one where the prevailing culture helped change and one where it hindered it.

6 Outline the life cycle model of change and explain when it is most likely to be useful.

7 How does it differ from the 'emergent' perspective?

8 What are the distinctive characteristics of a participative approach?

9 What skills are used by those employing a political model?

10 Is resistance to change necessarily something to be overcome? How would you advise someone to resist a change to which he or she was opposed?

11 Evaluate an example of change management in view of the models in this chapter.

Further reading

Burnes, B. (2000), *Managing Change*, 3rd edn, Financial Times Prentice Hall. Long case studies supplement an up-to-date treatment of theory in the area.

Clark, J. (1996), *Managing Innovation and Change*, Sage, London. A study of change at Pirelli, the multinational tyres and cables group. By examining a major change in one division over several years it emphasises the long-term, evolutionary nature of change. Each chapter begins with a review of relevant theory that is then used to guide the analysis of events in the company.

Mabey, C. and Mayon-White, B. (eds) (1993), *Managing Change* (2nd edn), The Open University/Paul Chapman Publishing, London. Collection of readings, including some of the classic articles in the area of change management.

Lock, D. (1996), *Project Management*, (6th edn), Gower, Aldershot. A good source of information on conventional project management techniques.

Pfeffer, J. (1992a), *Managing with Power*, Harvard Business School Press, Boston, MA. A clearly written argument for the view that managers of all kinds should take power seriously, and understand how to use it to enhance their position and satisfaction.

Buchanan, D. and Badham, R. (1999), *Power, Politics and Organizational Change: Winning the turf game*, Sage, London. A modern approach to politics in organisations, offering a theoretical and practical guide, based on extensive primary research.

Annotated links, questions and resources can be found on
www.booksites.net/boddy

Part 5

LEADING

Introduction

Generating the effort and commitment to work towards objectives is central to managing any human activity. One person working alone, be it in private life or in business, has only him or herself to motivate. As an organisation grows management activities become, in varying degrees, separated from the core work activities. The problem of generating effort changes its nature: now one person, or one occupational group, has to secure the willing co-operation of other people and their commitment to the task. Those other people may be subordinates, peers or superiors whose support, and perhaps approval, needs to be generated and mobilised.

The quality of that commitment is as important as whether or not it is secured. Staff are often in direct contact with customers. They are aware of their unique and changing requirements, and have an immense effect on the view the customer forms of the organisation. Others are in creative roles, with a direct impact on the quality of the service delivered to the final customer, whether they are contributing to a core R&D project or a TV programme. Others need to work reliably and flexibly in order to meet changing external or internal customer needs.

Throughout a business, customers' expectations of service quality and efficiency translate into expectations of all those working in the business. Unwilling or grudging commitment damages the service offered and eventually the business itself. How does management secure the motivation it needs from others? Part Five offers several perspectives on the dilemma. Chapter 12 examines ideas on influencing others, while Chapter 13 presents a range of theories about what those others may want from work. Communication is central to most management functions and activities, and Chapter 14 examines this topic. Finally, as Chapter 8 showed, teams are an increasingly prominent aspect of organisations, and the motivation and commitment generated within them is often central to performance – and they are the subject of Chapter 15.

The Part Case is W.L. Gore and Associates, an organisation renowned for its use of teams.

W.L Gore and Associates in Europe

W.L. Gore and Associates is a remarkable example of a business organised around team principles. Since the company has grown from being a one-person business in 1965 to one with over 6,000 employees in over 40 plants around the world, can it still be a team? It depends on the creativity of its staff, as its business is based on innovation. Growth in size usually leads to more impersonal systems and controls: can this dilemma be managed? What if separate plants begin to develop competing products? Will that waste scarce development talent or is the greater risk that talent is demotivated by wider controls on research priorities? The plants have learnt to live with a great deal of self-management and followership, rather than leader-managers or leaders in the conventional sense. Is that a viable route still, or might leaders need to be appointed to ensure resources are used profitably?

These are some of the issues facing management in the European plants of this multinational high-technology company. Some of the background is set out below.

W.L. Gore and Associates is based on an invention made by the founder, William Gore. He discovered a way to make a fabric that was at the same time porous and waterproof – moisture could pass one way, but not the other. Initially used in outdoor clothing applications such as ski-wear and walking gear, many more applications have been developed by the company's research teams. These include industry (filtration bags for air-conditioning systems), medicine (porous membranes used in skin graft operations) and health and safety (firefighters' protective clothing). The business is at the high-technology end of any market, concentrating on inventing new uses for the basic technology. Because of their specialised nature most of the materials are manufactured in relatively low volumes for a very specific market.

The team emphasis is reported to have originated when, in the early 1970s, Bill Gore realised that he no longer knew everyone in the plant by name. Success had led to growth – and with it the dangers of anonymity. Believing that close and direct personal contact amongst people was essential to the success of this kind of innovative business, he immediately decided that no plant would have more than about 150 employees. Up to that number most people would be able to know each other personally.

Accordingly, as a plant grows towards that level, promising ventures are spun off into new plants. They in turn build up, and lead to further spin-offs: hence the 40 plants with a workforce of about 6,000. There are no job titles in the company – all employees are known as 'associates'. They are expected to join the company and then find where they can make the most contribution to the work of the plant they are in. Associates commit to a project, and work with the team developing that product or system. As it comes to completion they are responsible for finding another project where their skills can contribute.

Traditionally there was no formal leadership of projects, although leadership of different sorts was exercised by associates as required by the situation – some would provide technical leadership, others business leadership and so on. Pay is decided by a compensation committee made up of associates from several plants. The level of increase that an associate receives depends on a judgement of the contribution they have made to the work of their group in the previous six months. This judgement is based on the evaluations made by their colleagues in the group, on a 10-point rating scale. Each associate also has a more experienced sponsor who advises and guides them on where they may want, or be able, to make a contribution.

The company has several plants in Europe. An associate from the United Kingdom commented:

'Perhaps the concept of leadership has evolved slightly. Certainly in the UK the leader takes much more of a business focus and gives business direction, pulling together a group of individuals towards achieving a business objective. The sponsor then focuses on individual development. So any one person would normally expect to have a leader and also a sponsor. They would select the sponsor once they're in a position to be able to select someone able to give the appropriate guidance.

Leadership probably happens in three different ways. We still have the concept of natural leaders emerging through followership. There are then some areas of the business where leaders are imposed, and we probably find that more in this plant where we have a large production operation. We do have shift leaders and production leaders. That type of leader does tend to be more imposed. You also have the other side with perhaps the sales associates where they may decide for themselves that they've been working without a leader. They identify the need to have some focal point and the need to have a leader. They will get together and decide if there's somebody within the team who can take the role.

Decisions to take on additional staff are made on a consultative basis. At the moment it's very much project driven. So a group would be working on a specific project, and they'll look at the resources required for that project – and if they haven't got the resources a decision will be taken to go outside. What therefore tends to happen is that people are brought into the business with a specific project in mind. Not necessarily a job description, but a role description for that project. That would then settle that person into the business. Once that project has finished they'll then try to seek an alternative role in the business, in another project.

We have about 140 associates in this plant. The groups that people would fall into are research and development, where we have a group of engineers; then we have administration, sales, production and support. We also have a position called product specialist, and that person is typically someone with a technical background, who is perhaps working in sales. They develop very close links with our customers, and almost act as a lubricant between sales and manufacturing. They work very closely with our customers on current products, but also to identify customer requirements and move with them to research and develop new products. And we have a team of them in each plant. All of them take an industry sector. Say, for example, in the fabrics plant, we have a product specialist looking after the fire industry, one looking after police, one military, one ski.

They are groups, but they don't operate as a group within their functional area. They tend to operate on a project basis. So, for example, here in industrial filtration we are working on products for office automation technology – basically photocopiers – and we then assemble a team to develop that project. There'd be some production people, engineers, admin support, and they form a group around that project. Somebody will have seen a need, researched the product, brought together a team. They will see it through to manufacture and then, as it stabilises, it comes to a different team – the manufacturing and the ongoing sales. A distinction between R&D and steady state.

The focus is very much on R&D. The challenge we have is to get that working on a global basis, to get global teams. The challenge we have is that within our culture we don't want to create structures or processes that stifle creativity. So we don't want to say that in this area this is where you'll focus on this element of research. But it's finding ways of sharing that and stopping duplication.

Some leaders have the job of persuading people to make commitments – but done very informally, and very much on an individual persuasion basis. The sponsor would not be involved unless there was an element of personal development by joining the team, in which case the individual may have the dilemma between current and new commitment and may use the sponsor as a sounding board. The sponsor certainly wouldn't be involved in initiating it. It's done on a very ad hoc basis.

Freedom of choice is not total. People will be asked at some point to go on a project by the leader of the business group. So sometimes people are very forcibly asked to work on a project because they have a particular expertise. And it's expected that that skill will be used to assist the project.

Leaders of projects might be appointed by people recognised as having leadership within functions (chief chemical engineer). It could also be that each plant has an overall business leader. We have a business leader for industrial filtration and, if there was a particular skill needed on a project, he may make the decision to go and say to somebody that they need to work on that project.

The pay system could back that up, in that critical projects would attract bigger rewards. There is a negative element as well, in that the way the compensation process works is that people are put on to a compensation list – chemical engineers, research chemists or whatever – which typically has

10 people on it. Twice a year, everyone on that contribution list is asked to rank each other according to their contribution to the business. It was on a plant basis, but we are now working towards assessing the global contribution and the European contribution. The remuneration committee would collate all the information and come out with an overall ranking of the contributions within that particular group. That is used in determining the salaries. They rank each member in order of their perceived contribution to the group that six months.

However, from an HR [human resources] perspective I do have some concerns as it is open to being very subjective – what does contribution mean, and how do we determine contribution? I don't think there are any guidelines apart from the associates' contribution over the past year to the business, future potential, and their willingness to co-operate in other areas outwith their discipline. In the ideal world, if everybody is objective and thinks along the same basis, then that would be a very good system, but there are flaws in it. The principle is excellent, but there's the opportunity to do some more work to make it a more objective and robust system.

The compensation scheme could almost drive behaviour both positively and negatively because there's an element of visibility, of people being seen to be doing the right thing. It's part of the performance-related pay. If the overall salary increase is 5 per cent then the compensation committee will start off with 5 per cent and make decisions – this person 0, this 7 and so on. There are a number of associates on the committee, so the criteria tend to be applied evenly across the plant.'

The balance between procedures and guidelines, and human initiative

'We do have standard procedures and rules and regulations. The underpinning principle is to keep them to the minimum, and it's about questioning why we need them. If there's a business reason that that is the best way to deal with it then we're not afraid to put in a policies and procedures, for example ISO 9000. There is a mentality that people understand the need for processes when there's something tangible. So, in manufacturing, people accept that that is required. Less so in areas like HR,

where there is a reluctance to do anything that people would see as a limiting structure. So if people can readily see the need, we put in procedures; but when it's not tangible we are very questioning about whether it's required. We are very flexible in the way we introduce things. If it increases profits, protects health and safety, and if people can see the tangible results, then there really isn't too much of a problem. The buy-in is absolutely essential. Even on some fairly straightforward policies and procedures we very rarely impose anything without consulting and getting buy-in.'

How do you go about getting that buy-in?

'You go and speak to key people and influence people, and you make a judgement as to who is key to get this project through, trying to see where opposition might come from, and trying to deal with it before you actually impose the procedure. You don't need everyone to be fully committed – apart from those who actually have to do something. As long as they just keep quiet. Commitment in Gore is very much when you personally have to deliver something, so a commitment in Gore is when you commit to doing XYZ on a certain project. It's not in terms of 'you've got my support', it's 'I have to deliver for a certain project'. Buy-in is willingness to accept.'

Balance between people and institutions

'Our institutional processes are minimal. Our main focus is on people, and we try to ensure that is effective by this emphasis on commitment. So somebody starts a project, and it's so much ingrained into our culture that if you commit to do something then it's a sin not to see it through. So part of our culture enables us to be more successful through the people route than might be the case in a more traditional structure. We really have very few institutional structures. The one I mentioned is very recent and came about from a recognition that we wanted to start working towards global teams, and we're starting to try to create centres of excellence within plants. In order to do that we need to have some way of getting knowledge transferred between plants.

That really is a big issue for us at the moment. We just had a big international conference which looked at what sort of processes we have, and how we could introduce them without compromising the elements of our culture that have been so successful for us. For me that is a fascinating dilemma. We have massive growth plans, and our company has evolved slowly. We need to stop duplication of effort, and that's not something we've done in the past. Plants have grown because somebody's had a project which has taken off, and that team has developed the plant from that project. Given the commonality of the core technology, several plants could be developing in similar directions at the same time. At some point the duplication becomes wasteful. How do we control that in R&D without stifling people's creativity? The centre of excellence and economy of resources is raising the issue of some degree of global integration between teams as a top priority, and our growth plans – which could lead to duplication.'

Q PART CASE QUESTIONS

- How does management ensure that associates are motivated to work on projects that are important to the company's future prosperity?

- If you were a talented research scientist, what would be the attractions and rewards of working for Gore?

- Why do teams seem to work so well for Gore? What benefits do you think they bring both to the business and to the individuals? What if teams compete, rather than co-operate?

CHAPTER 12

Influence and power

OBJECTIVES

By the end of your work on this chapter you should be able to outline the concepts below in your own terms and:

1 Explain why the ability to influence is central to the management role

2 Compare personal and positional sources of power that people can use

3 Outline the trait, behavioural and contingency perspectives on leadership

4 Compare the styles identified by behavioural theorists and give examples of each

5 Compare situational perspectives with those stressing traits and behaviour

6 List the main contingencies in Vroom and Yetton's model

7 Outline the results of studies on the tactics of influence

8 Explain why a manager's position is a source of power to influence others

The company is now part of Compaq, but at the time of these events Digital Europe was the European manufacturing and distribution operation of Digital Equipment Corporation. Digital Europe had seven plants making different products within the company's range. The plants had a high degree of autonomy and often competed with each other for the 'charter' to make new products. At the same time they had to co-operate, as systems sold to customers were usually built with parts made by several of the European plants. Hence there is also competitive pressure to improve Europe-wide systems. A senior manager recalls one such attempt:

'I was asked to attend a meeting with a group of people interested in order fulfilment. They showed me some data about how long it took our competitors to process orders and how reliable their delivery promises were. It became clear that this was a major area of opportunity for our company.

I volunteered to pull together a group of people from our other facilities who understood order scheduling and who also had a vision of what it could be like. Between August and September we had two five-day meetings and came up with some ideas that I drafted into a formal document stating the problem and giving some indication of a solution. The next problem was how to enable that plan.

I then began a round of presentations to plant staffs in Europe and to our European management team, describing the problem and suggesting a way forward. The paper was well received but people were also a bit sceptical and wary. Major pan-European redesign work had been attempted in the past and had failed miserably. Europe-wide programmes, therefore, had a bad name.

Over the last year my part-time team have done a lot of work with their own staff to convince them of the need for investment in order fulfilment and scheduling. My European functional boss had also been working with the European management team to convince them of the need for major investment in order fulfilment systems. We agreed to do a presentation that looked at all our processes and systems in order fulfilment. The aim was to get the commitment and investment that we require from the managements of the separate plants.

We managed to gather our European staff team together in Ireland on 6 October for about six hours and we did our presentation. We clearly captured the interest, imagination and energy of the group, and very clearly they were going to try to find a way even though we have no formal budget to make a system happen. It was an excellent culmination of 15 months' work, though in many ways it was just the beginning.'

Q Case questions

- What other people was the manager at Digital Europe trying to influence?
- Which of them, if any, were his direct subordinates?
- What aspects of the company's history will affect his attempts at influence?

12.1 Introduction

This chapter introduces the following ideas:

- Influence
- Leading and managing
- Sources of power – legitimate, reward, coercive, referent and expertise
- Personal and positional sources of power
- Trait theories
- Behavioural theories
- Situational theories
- Positional power

The senior manager in the Digital Europe case is typical of many managers today. He has had an idea that he thinks will benefit the company, and is putting time and effort into winning the support of his colleagues. Other managers have different interests and priorities, and so will not automatically give their support. He needs to influence them to support his project by committing some of their resources to it.

All managers face this challenge – such as when Roy Gardner took over at Centrica (the company that owns British Gas). Many people had criticised the British Gas service, and he had to influence staff at all levels to give a higher priority to customer service. Bob Ayling at British Airways faced the same issues as he tried to change the way people worked, to reduce the company's costs in the face of competition from low cost airlines. He failed to win the confidence of the staff, and resigned. Ron Eddington took over and has the task of influencing staff to work enthusiastically to his new strategy of concentrating on business customers, rather than economy class passengers. The head of human resources at the Environment Agency (see Chapter 11) faced the challenge of influencing senior managers to accept a radical change in the direction and structure of the organisation.

> **MANAGEMENT IN PRACTICE** **Jorma Ollila of Nokia, and Bob Ayling of BA**
>
> Jorma Ollila is chief executive of Nokia, which in 2001 was the world's biggest supplier of mobile phones. He became chief executive in 1992 and led the transformation of the company from an undistinguished business into a world leader in the industry. In contrast, Bob Ayling resigned in March 2000 after four years as chief executive of British Airways. The precise reasons for his departure were unclear, but probably included the fact that profits and share price had fallen sharply. He inherited the world's most profitable airline, and in the year before he became chief executive BA made pre-tax profits of £585 million. In 2000 it was expected to make a loss of more than £200 million. When he took over the leadership in January 1996 BA's shares stood at 466p. When he left they were 293p.
>
> While commentators regard Ollila as one of the most successful leaders of the time, Ayling had failed. He was unable to influence staff, unions, customers and investors about the wisdom of his approach to the business.

Whatever their role in the organisation, managers can only get things done by influencing others. In terms of Figure 1.2, the functions of planning, organising, leading and controlling depend on securing the co-operation of other people. Some management issues can be dealt with using rational analysis, but as the issues become more complex the manager needs to influence other people to act in a particular way. People throughout an organisation do their jobs by influencing others, and their performance depends on how well they do so. The targets of influence will often be in more senior positions.

In that sense the work of the manager is not that of the careful analyst, working out precisely the best solution to the project. It is closer to that of an entrepreneur, determined to get things done in an often hostile, indifferent or political setting. Managers typically operate across established functional or departmental boundaries, and work with many different people who are pursuing their priorities and interests.

This chapter explores the topics shown in Figure 12.1. It begins by clarifying what influence means, its relation to management, and the power that people can use to influence others. This power comes both from the personal characteristics of leaders and from their position within the organisation. The chapter then presents four perspectives on the effectiveness or otherwise of different personal approaches to influencing others. These are the trait, behavioural, contingency and 'tactics' theories. The focus then turns to examine theories on how people can use their position within the organisation to influence others. The following chapters on motivation, communication and teams are also relevant to the influence process.

12.2 Managing and leading

People continually **influence** each other throughout any organisation. Research and commentary on influencing use the terms 'manager' and 'leader' (and their derivatives) interchangeably. There is no accepted or definitive distinction between them and this book does not seek to establish one. However, it is worth spending a few lines considering the meaning behind the terms.

Chapter 1 defined a manager as someone who gets things done with the support of others. Most commentators view an 'effective manager' as someone who 'gets things done' to ensure order and continuity. They maintain the steady state – keeping

Figure 12.1 A model of the influencing process

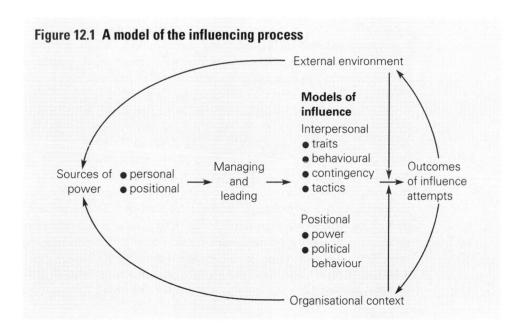

established systems in good shape and making incremental improvements. People generally use the term 'effective leader' to denote someone who brings innovation, who moves an activity out of trouble into success – who makes a measurable difference. They see opportunities for doing things differently, take the initiative to raise the issue and do something about it.

Leif Beck Fallesen, chief executive of *Borsen*

Borsen is a Danish business newspaper, equivalent to *The Financial Times*. During the early 1990s circulation and profitability declined. In 1996 the board appointed Leif Beck Fallesen as chief executive, with a brief to improve the position. The paper's circulation has grown by about 15 per cent a year since 1997, while that of similar papers has remained static or declined. The leadership actions he took included creating:

- regular features aimed at growing market segments (such as small businesses, family-owned businesses and younger readers);
- a joint venture providing business content to Danish Television;
- an innovative online version of the paper.

Source: Company presentation and other sources.

Peter Drucker (1985) writes of the leader's ability to generate unusual or exceptional commitment to a vision, and of **leadership** being 'the lifting of people's vision to a higher sight, the raising of their performance to a higher standard, the building of their personality beyond its normal limitations.' And Anita Roddick has said that: '[People] are looking for leadership that has vision ... You have to look at leadership through the eyes of the followers and you have to live the message. What I have learned is that people become motivated when you guide them to the source of their own power and when you make heroes out of employees who best personify what you want to see in the organisation' (1991, p.223).

Organisations need effective managers and effective leaders. Many people will perform both the steady state and innovation aspects in some degree, so there is no value in attempting a sharp distinction (John Adair quotes a Chinese proverb: 'What does it matter if the cat is black or white, as long as it catches mice' (1997, p.2)). Both need to influence others to put effort and commitment to the task. People such as Jorma Ollila of Nokia or Bob Ayling of BA could only succeed with the support of others.

The quality of leadership *throughout* an organisation influences its performance – whether in business, sport, or public organisations such as schools and universities. Anyone who wants to get something done needs to exercise leadership. The effectiveness of senior managers in influencing other people has the most visible effects on performance. They shape the overall direction of the business, moving it into new areas or changing the way it operates. Yet they depend on people lower down the organisation also being able and willing to exercise leadership – in the sense of bringing about change, moving an activity out of trouble into success and making a measurable difference – at their level. Effective leadership of a team shapes the work and success of the members and so contributes to the success of the organisation.

Managers (and leaders) often influence people who are equally powerful – as Lesley Macdonagh testifies. She is managing partner of Lovell's, an international law firm, and was the first woman to take the top management job at a leading City of London legal practice:

> 'The hardest things in management ... are complicated people issues. Sometimes you realise you can't solve everything. Our assets are the brains and personalities of some highly intelligent people, so there are a huge number of relationship issues. Most of these 250 people are very driven. If you get it right, the commitment is already sorted out. But you've got to take a lot of people with you a lot of the time.' (*Financial Times*, 15 February 2001, p.17)

So managing and leading requires people to influence colleagues on the same organisational level, those formally above them in the hierarchy and people outside the organisation. Figure 12.2 illustrates this.

How do managers ensure that others do what they want them to do? Largely by having a source of power and being able to use it to influence the behaviour of other people or groups.

12.3 Sources of power to influence others

Sources of power

What are the bases of one person's power over another? French and Raven's (1959) widely quoted classification identifies five sources of power:

- **Legitimate power** flows from the person's formal position in the organisation, and derives from the job that he or she holds. This position gives the job holder certain forms of power, for example to make capital expenditures, to offer overtime, to choose a supplier or to recruit staff.
- **Reward power** is the ability of someone to reward another. It is visible when one person complies with another person's request or instruction because they expect some reward in return. The reward itself can take many forms – a pay rise, time off or more interesting work.

Figure 12.2 Influencing in four directions

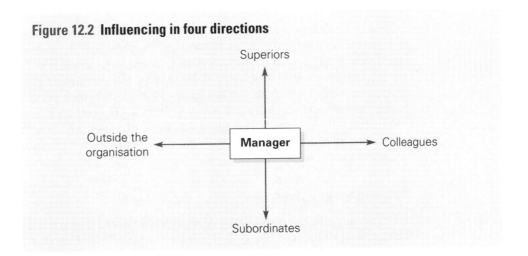

- **Coercive power** is the ability to obtain compliance through fear of punishment. It is the capacity to harm or restrict the actions of others, which they try to avoid. It may take the form of reprimands, demotions, loss of a job – or the threat of physical force. Aggressive language and a powerful physical presence are other forms of coercive power.
- **Referent power**, also called *charismatic* power, is visible when some characteristics of the manager are attractive to the subordinate. They want to identify with him or her, and this gives the manager power over them.
- **Expertise power** is visible when people acknowledge someone's specialised knowledge and are therefore willing to follow their suggestions. During a problem-solving activity it often becomes clear who knows most about particular aspects of the problem. The leadership of the group may temporarily move to that person. This knowledge and skill may be either *administrative* (how an organisation operates), or *technical* (how to do a task).

KEY IDEAS **Transformational leadership**

James Burns (1978) distinguished transactional from **transformational leaders**. Transactional leaders influence subordinates' behaviour by way of a bargain. The leader enables followers to reach their goals, while at the same time contributing to the goals of the organisation. If subordinates behave in the way desired by the leader they will receive rewards that they value.

Burns contrasted this approach with that of transformational leaders. They work in ways that lead subordinates to change their goals, needs and aspirations. Transformational leaders raise the consciousness of followers by appealing to higher ideals and moral values. They do this by displaying a number of identifiable behaviours, such as articulating 'transcendent goals, demonstration of self-confidence and confidence in others, setting a personal example for followers, showing high expectations of followers' performance, and the ability to communicate one's faith in one's goals' (Fiedler and House, 1994, p.112).

The degree to which a leader is transformational depends on the effect on his or her followers. Fiedler and House (1994) claim that empirical research supports the claims for the successes of charismatic leaders. Followers and superiors see them as more effective than transactional leaders.

Table 12.1 develops the French and Raven list, by showing that each type of power can have both a personal and a positional source. The most significant change to the French and Raven model is to show that referent (charismatic) power is not just personal but can also have a positional source (Hales, 1993). This happens when an organisation develops norms or beliefs that make up its culture, with which people want to identify. People can refer to the culture as a way of influencing how others behave.

Someone who has little access to these sources of power will have less influence than someone with much access. Managers continually defend their existing power sources, and try to gain new ones.

Perceptions of power

Power is only effective if the target of an influence attempt recognises the power source as legitimate and acceptable. If they dispute the knowledge base of a manager, or challenge their positional authority over a matter, the influence attempt is likely to fail.

Table 12.1 Personal and positional sources of power

Power resource	Personal	Positional
Coercive	Forcefulness, insistence, determination	Authority to give instructions, with the threat of sanctions or punishment available
Reward	Credit for previous or future favours in day-to-day exchanges	Authority to use organisational resources, including the support of senior people
Expertise		
Administrative	Experience of the business, who to contact, how to get things through the system	Authority to use or create organisational policies or rules
Technical	Skill or expertise relevant to the task	Authority to access expertise, information and ideas across the business
Referent	Individual beliefs, values, ideas, personal qualities	Authority to invoke norms and values of the organisational culture

Managers who are successful influencers ensure that their power sources are sustained, and take every opportunity to enhance them.

Marketing brand Me

People should manage their reputation like a brand. The most effective candidates (for promotion) do not leave their image to chance. They work at it, and massage its growth. They know that the best publicists they can have are their immediate staff. They are aware that team members talk about them more than anyone else. So they provide evidence to feed that grapevine ... Staff need stories about their leader.

Another way to manage your reputation is to manage your boss ... People keen to manage their reputation should find out what motivates the boss and try to satisfy those goals. If your boss likes punctuality and conscientiousness, turn up on time and work hard. If he or she needs reassurance, give it. If it is power, respond as someone who is less powerful. Why irritate a person who can influence your career path?

Source: John Hunt, 'Marketing brand Me', *Financial Times*, 22 December 2000.

FT

Responses to the use of power

People respond to influence attempts in three ways – resistance, compliance and internalisation. Table 12.2 describes the alternatives. Resistant staff will have no commitment to the work. They do what is required grudgingly, and without enthusiasm or imagination. While it may be possible to overcome resistance by using threats or coercion this may not be the most useful reaction in the longer term. Compliance too has limitations, especially if long-term success depends on further innovation. Only when staff are fully committed because they have internalised the influencer's goals, and see themselves as part of the creative process, is the influencing task complete.

Table 12.2 Three outcomes of influence attempts

Outcome	Description	Commentary
Internalisation	Target internally agrees with a decision or request and makes a great effort to meet it successfully	Usually the most successful outcome from the point of view of the influencer, especially on a difficult task
Compliance	Target willing to do what is asked, but is apathetic, unenthusiastic and makes minimal effort	For a complex task, an unsatisfactory outcome. For routine tasks it may be enough for the influencer to accomplish their goals
Resistance	Target is opposed to the request and actively tries to avoid carrying it out	Target may make excuses or try to dissuade the influencer from persisting. May also seek support from higher authority or undermine the influencer's efforts

Grudging compliance is unlikely to lead to satisfactory performance. The complexities of work processes often require people to work with imagination and flexibility. In service industries employee behaviour directly influences customer perceptions. Competition often requires that employees work responsibly and with concern for what they are doing. This is not likely to come if managers have used their power in ways that have secured only compliance, not the commitment that comes from internalisation. The following sections examine four theoretical models of the influencing process.

ACTIVITY 12.1

Identifying power sources

Try to identify at least one example of each of the personal and positional power sources. Examples could come from observing a manager in action (including people in your university or college) or from your reading of current business affairs.

Q Case questions 12.1

- In what ways did the actions of the manager at Digital Europe fit the definition of leadership?
- What role did creating a vision play in the manager's influence attempts?
- What lay behind the different degrees of enthusiasm that the plant managers showed for the plan?

12.4 Traits models

Early studies focused on the individual leader rather than the situation in which he or she worked. They tried to identify the **traits** that prominent leaders possessed, on the assumption that some people had certain attributes which made it more likely that they would be effective leaders. These attributes include both traits and **skills**.

Traits and skills combine heredity and learning, with some being more influenced by one than the other. For example, people's experiences and what they learn from them shape their values, whereas aspects of temperament such as energy levels or personal drive are inherited. The stimulus to early researchers on leadership was the belief that they could identify the traits and skills of effective leaders. They would then be able to use this knowledge to guide the selection of future leaders. Stogdill (1974) reviewed 163 trait studies published between 1949 and 1970. Table 12.3 presents his results.

Table 12.3 Traits and skills found most frequently to be associated with successful leaders

Traits	Skills
Adaptable to situations	Clever (intelligent)
Alert to social environment	Conceptually skilled
Ambitious and achievement oriented	Creative
Assertive	Diplomatic
Co-operative	Fluent in speaking
Decisive	Knowledgeable about group task
Dependable	Persuasive
Dominant (desire to influence others)	Socially skilled
Energetic	Well organised
Persistent	
Self-confident	
Tolerant of stress	
Willing to assume responsibility	

Source: Stogdill (1974).

The 2000 *Financial Times*/PricewaterhouseCoopers Annual Survey of the world's most respected companies continues this tradition of identifying the traits of effective leaders. Common traits included:

vision
ability to forecast trends
speed
decisiveness
courage
tenacity
optimism
enthusiasm

Table 12.4 indicates the characteristics that the senior managers who replied to the survey associated with the leaders of these companies.

Limitations

The major limitation of the traits model is the large number of factors that researchers have identified. Lists of desirable traits look like impossible ideals, which are rarely present in one person. A difficulty with this line of research is to take account of the intervening variables that affect whether a particular trait contributes to performance. Whatever traits Bob Ayling had that led to his appointment as CEO of British Airways were still there when he resigned. Other factors intervened to make his tenure less successful than those who appointed him had expected. Having certain traits is probably necessary for effective leadership, but will not be sufficient. Their relative importance is

Table 12.4 Traits of those leading some of the world's most respected companies, 2000

Leader	Company	Traits
Jack Welch	General Electric	'hard and soft qualities' 'understanding young people's way of thinking' 'willing to accept new ideas'
Chris Gent	Vodafone	'courage to make big moves'
Jurgen Schremp	DaimlerChrysler	'daring behaviour'
Michael Dell	Dell Computers	'listening to customers and employees'
Richard Branson	Virgin	'a maverick, encouraging people to do things differently'
John Browne	BP	'taking lead on environment and social responsibility'

Source: *Financial Times*, 15 December 2000.

likely to depend on other factors, including the situation in which the manager is operating. Thus the board of BP regarded Bob Horton as such a successful leader when he was running the North American operation that they appointed him as chairman and chief executive of the whole company in 1990. In 1992 they replaced him with David Simon. Traits that were valuable in North America seemed less suitable in the United Kingdom.

Contributions

Despite these limitations the traits model may help to explain why some people get to positions of great influence and others do not. Some items in Stogdill's list have been found to recur in many empirical studies linking traits and effectiveness, such as high energy levels, tolerance of stress, emotional maturity and at least a moderately high need for achievement (Yukl, 1998). Management selection practices reflect this belief, and the criteria often include supposedly relevant traits. As two of the foremost scholars of leadership concluded, 'There is no one ideal leader personality. However, effective leaders tend to have a high need to influence others, to achieve; and they tend to be bright, competent and socially adept, rather than stupid, incompetent and social disasters' (Fiedler and House, 1994, p.111).

ACTIVITY 12.2

Which traits do employers seek?

Collect some job advertisements and recruitment brochures. Make a list of the traits that the companies say they are looking for in those they recruit.

12.5 Behavioural models

Another set of theories sought to identify the behaviours or styles of effective leaders. What did effective managers do to influence subordinates that less effective managers did not? Scholars at the Universities of Michigan and Ohio State developed their models at about the same time. Their research identified two major categories of **behavioural style**: one was concerned with interpersonal relations, the other with accomplishing tasks. Subordinates judge their leaders on these two dimensions.

Ohio State University model

Researchers at Ohio State University developed questionnaires that subordinates used to describe the behaviour of their manager. The researchers who analysed the responses concluded that subordinates viewed their manager's behaviour on two dimensions, 'consideration' and 'initiating structure'.

A *considerate* style reflects concern for subordinates' well-being, status and comfort. Considerate leaders were those who tried to build a pleasant working environment, by listening to subordinates' problems, giving encouragement and treating subordinates with respect. Such leaders assume that subordinates want to work well and try to make it easier for them to do so. They place relatively little stress on their formal position and power. Typical behaviours of considerate leaders included:

- expressing appreciation for a job well done;
- not expecting more from subordinates than they can reasonably do;
- helping subordinates with their personal problems;
- being approachable and available for help;
- providing rewards for high performance.

An *initiating structure* style is one that emphasises defining and planning work, including the activities of subordinates. Leaders with this approach focused on getting the work done, ensuring that everything was properly planned and worked out. They asked subordinates to follow the procedures laid down, and made sure that they were working to full capacity. Typical behaviours of initiating structure leaders included:

- allocating subordinates to specific tasks;
- establishing standards of job performance;
- informing subordinates of the requirements of the job;
- scheduling work to be done by subordinates;
- encouraging the use of uniform procedures.

The results showed that leaders displayed distinctive patterns of scores on the two dimensions. Some were high on measures of initiating structure and low on consideration, while others were high on consideration and low on initiating structure. Some were high on both, others low on both.

Michigan University model

Researchers at the University of Michigan (Likert, 1961, 1967) conducted similar studies to those at Ohio at about the same time. They found that two types of behaviour distinguished effective from ineffective managers: task-oriented and relationship-oriented behaviour.

Task-oriented managers ensured that they worked on different tasks from their subordinates, concentrating especially on planning, co-ordinating and supplying a range of support activities. These were similar to the initiating structure activities identified at Ohio.

Relationship-oriented managers combined the task-oriented behaviour with a range of relationship-centred activities. They were more considerate, helpful and friendly to subordinates than less effective managers. They tended to engage in broad supervision rather than detailed observation of all activities. These behaviours were similar to what the Ohio group referred to as consideration.

Managerial grid model

Blake and Mouton (1964) developed the managerial grid model to extend and apply the Ohio State research. It identifies various combinations of concern for production (initiating structure) and people (consideration), as shown in Figure 12.3.

The vertical scale relates to concern for people, ranging from 1 (low concern) to 9 (high concern). The horizontal scale relates to concern for production, which also ranges from 1 (low concern) to 9 (high concern). At the lower left-hand corner (1,1) is the impoverished style: low concern for both people and production. The primary objective of such managers is to stay out of trouble. They merely pass instructions to subordinates, follow the established system, and make sure that no one can blame them if something goes wrong. They do only as much as is consistent with keeping their job.

At the upper left-hand corner (1,9) is the country club style: high concern for people and low concern for production. Managers who use this style try to create a secure and comfortable family atmosphere. They assume that their subordinates will respond productively. Thoughtful attention to the need for satisfying relationships leads to a friendly atmosphere and work tempo.

High concern for production and low concern for people is found in the lower right-hand corner (9,1). This is the produce or perish style. These managers do not consider subordinates' personal needs. All that matters is the achievement of the organisation's objectives. They use their formal authority to pressure subordinates into meeting production quotas. They believe that efficiency comes from arranging the work so that employees merely have to follow instructions.

In the centre (5,5) is the middle-of-the-road style. These managers seek to balance subordinates' needs and the organisation's productivity objectives. They obtain adequate performance by balancing the need to get the work done with reasonable attention to the interests of employees.

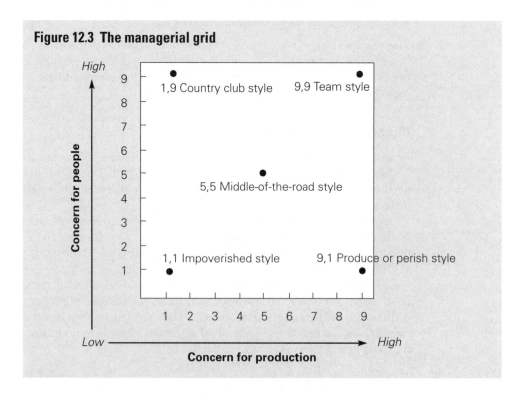

Figure 12.3 The managerial grid

In the upper right-hand corner (9,9) is the team style: high concern for both people and production. According to Blake and Mouton this leadership style is the most effective. Managers of this kind attempt to develop committed work groups and staff, to produce both high performance and high job satisfaction. The manager fosters performance by building relationships of trust and respect.

ACTIVITY 12.3

Applying the managerial grid

Reflect on two managers you have worked with, one effective and one ineffective from your point of view.

Which of the positions in the Blake and Mouton grid most closely describe their style? Note some of their typical behaviours.

What were they like to work for?

 Two leaders' styles

Jorma Ollila of Nokia

'He is extremely ambitious and extremely demanding. He gives authority to people to do things but he demands performance in return.' The main risk that Ollila sees is complacency. He talks of a 'daily, continuous fight against bureaucracy and against becoming an incumbent, stable institution. People easily move into their comfort zones and don't ask chilling enough questions of themselves, or question the environment they are in.'

Source: *Financial Times*, 8 December 2000. p.16.

Lesley Macdonagh of Lovell's

'My position is an elected one: I have been elected and re-elected three times. You've got to be convincing. But being adamant about the direction we should go is a card I would play only sparingly, so people are prepared to listen when I do feel something passionately. The only time I would get very resolute would be if I felt somebody was taking advantage of the firm, or not pulling their weight.'

Source: *Financial Times*, 15 February 2001, p.17.

Many trainers use the Blake and Mouton model with the aim of helping managers develop towards the '9,9' style. Implicit in the approach is the idea of flexibility. The '9,9' manager would be successful not by applying the same behaviour in every situation but by using task- or relationship-centred behaviours in a way that was appropriate to the situation at hand.

Others have questioned whether showing a high level of concern for both production and people is always the best approach. Sometimes a concern for production may be more important than concern for people – such as in a sudden crisis that requires swift action. Situational or contingency models offer a possible answer.

KEY IDEAS **Does style affect performance?**

Bass (1990) reviewed research to assess the effects of the leader's style on performance and found them inconclusive. In some cases subordinates were more satisfied with a structuring leader, while others failed to find any significant relationships. It is also possible that the direction of the cause/effect relationship is unclear. It is usual to assume that the relationship is from leader behaviour to subordinate behaviour. It may be that leaders behave in a considerate style to subordinates who are performing well.

12.6　Situational and contingency models

Situational models present the idea that managers influence others by adapting their style to the particular circumstances. This section presents three examples.

House's path–goal model

House argued that effective leaders are those who clarify their subordinates' path to the rewards available, and ensure that rewards which the subordinates value are available. They help subordinates to identify and learn behaviours that will help them complete the task and so secure the rewards for doing so. The model identifies four styles of leader behaviour and two 'contingencies' – the personal characteristics of subordinates and the work environment (House and Mitchell, 1974; House, 1996). The four styles are listed below:

1 *Directive*:
   - letting subordinates know what the leader expects;
   - giving specific guidance;
   - asking subordinates to follow rules and procedures;
   - scheduling and co-ordinating their work.

2 *Supportive*:
   - treating them as equals;
   - showing concern for their needs and welfare;
   - creating a friendly climate in the work unit.

3 *Achievement oriented*
   - setting challenging goals and targets;
   - seeking performance improvements;
   - emphasising excellence in performance;
   - showing confidence that subordinates will attain high standards.

4 *Participative*
   - consulting subordinates;
   - taking their opinions into account.

House suggested that the appropriate style would depend on the contingencies – the characteristics of the subordinate (skills, needs, motivations) and the work environment. For example, if an employee has little confidence or skill then the leader needs to provide coaching, training and other support. If the subordinate is one who likes clear direction then they will respond best to a leader who acts in that way. Highly skilled professionals will usually expect to work on their own initiative and would resent a directive style – they will be influenced more if the leader uses a participative or achievement-oriented style.

The work environment included the degree of task structure (such as whether it is routine or non-routine), the formal authority system (the extent to which rules and procedures guide activities) and the work group characteristics (the amount and quality of teamwork within the group). Figure 12.4 summarises the model.

The model predicts, for example, that a directive style would work best when the task is ambiguous and the subordinates lack flexibility – the leader absorbs uncertainty for the group and shows them how to achieve the task. A supportive style works well in highly repetitive tasks or those that are frustrating or physically unpleasant – the leader who joins in gains the respect of the subordinates. An achievement-oriented style works when the group faces non-repetitive ambiguous tasks, which will challenge their ability – so they need encouragement and pressure to raise their ambitions. The leader using this style urges subordinates to use their abilities to the full and encourages them by showing confidence in those abilities. A participative approach is likely to work best when the task is non-repetitive and the subordinate(s) are confident that they can do the work.

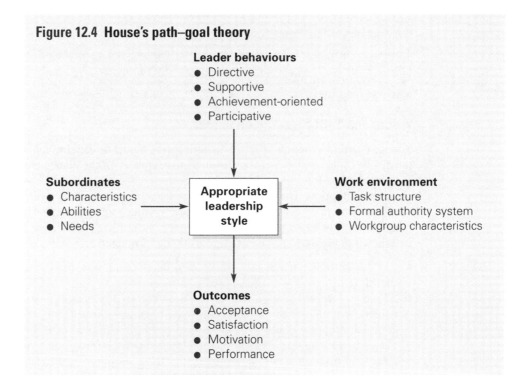

Figure 12.4 House's path–goal theory

MANAGEMENT IN PRACTICE **Roy Gardner, chief executive of Centrica**

By early 2001 the diversified group's share price had outperformed the FT-All share index by 130 per cent, since its demerger from (the original) British Gas in 1997. Roy Gardner has been chief executive for much of that time.

Each member of the senior executive team is expected to keep in touch by working at least one day a month alongside a gas service engineer, AA repairman, telephone sales staff or in another part of the business. Staff can also receive an unexpected call from the chief executive. One gas service engineer writing in the annual employee satisfaction survey criticised it as a waste of time.

'I got him in his van and told him to come round to talk to me in my office,' said Mr Gardner. 'We had a long chat. I learned a lot from him and he learned a lot from me.'

Source: *Financial Times*, 24 February 2001, p.18.

The path–goal model does not provide a formula for the best way to lead, and House stressed that it was in the early stages of development. Reviews of empirical work to test the theory (such as that by Indvik, 1986, who reviewed 48 empirical studies) have on balance supported the central proposition of the theory – that effective leaders select the style most appropriate to the situation and the subordinates. Contingency models indicate that participative leadership styles are not necessarily the most effective, and that, as Table 12.5 shows, there will be situations where a directive style is appropriate.

Table 12.5 Conditions favouring participative or directive styles

Participative style most likely to work when:	Directive style most likely to work when:
Subordinates' acceptance of the decision is important	Subordinates do not share the manager's objectives
the manager lacks information	time is critically short
the problem is unstructured	subordinates accept top-down decisions

Vroom and Yetton's decision model

The idea behind Vroom and Yetton's contingency model of decision making is to influence the quality and acceptability of decisions. This depends on the manager choosing how best to involve subordinates in making a decision – and being willing to change their style to match the situation. The model defines five leadership styles and seven characteristics of problems. The manager can use these characteristics to diagnose the situation. They can find the recommended way of reaching a decision on that problem by using the decision tree shown in Figure 12.5. The five leadership styles defined are:

- *AI (Autocratic)* You solve the problem yourself using information available to you at that time.
- *AII (Information-seeking)* You obtain the necessary information from your subordinate(s), then decide on the solution to the problem yourself. You may or may not tell your subordinates what the problem is in getting the information from them. The role played by your subordinates in making the decision is clearly one of providing the necessary information to you rather than generating or evaluating alternative solutions.
- *CI (Consulting)* You share the problem with relevant subordinates individually, getting their ideas and suggestions without bringing them together as a group. Then you make the decision that may or may not reflect your subordinates' influence.
- *CII (Negotiating)* You share the problem with your subordinates as a group, collectively obtaining their ideas and suggestions. Then *you* make the decision that may or may not reflect your subordinates' influence.
- *G (Delegating)* You share the problem with your subordinates as a group. Together you generate and evaluate alternatives and attempt to reach agreement (consensus) on a solution. Your role is much like that of a chairperson. You do not try to influence

the group to adopt 'your' solution, and you are willing to accept and implement any solution that has the support of the entire group.

The idea behind the model is that no style is in itself better than another. Some believe that consultative or delegating styles are inherently preferable to autocratic approaches, as being more in keeping with democratic principles. Vroom and Yetton argue otherwise. In some situations (such as when time is short or the manager has all the information needed for a minor decision) going through the process of consultation will waste time and add little value. In other situations, such as where the subordinates have

Figure 12.5 **Vroom and Yetton's decision tree**

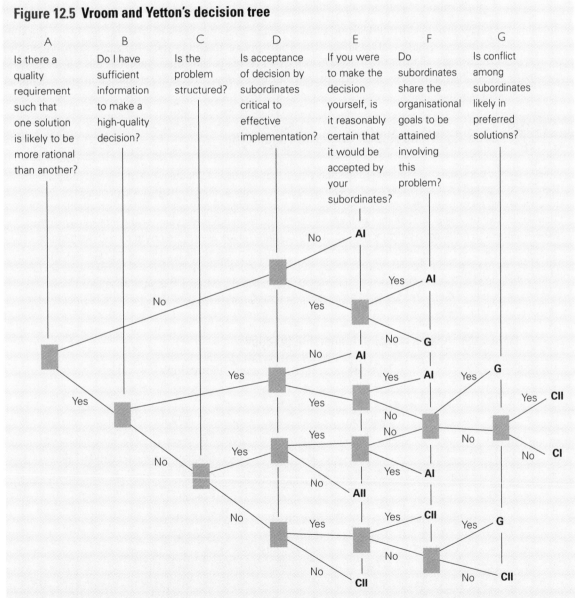

the relevant information, it is essential to consult them. The point of the model is to make managers more aware of the range of factors to take into account in using a particular decision-making style.

The problem criteria are expressed in seven diagnostic questions:

- Is one solution likely to be better than another?
- Does the manager have enough information to make a high quality decision?
- Is the problem structured?
- Is acceptance of the decision by subordinates critical to effective implementation?
- If the manager makes the decision alone, is it likely to be accepted by subordinates?
- Do subordinates share organisational goals?
- Is conflict likely amongst subordinates over preferred solutions?

The Vroom–Yetton decision model implies that managers need to be flexible in the style they adopt. The style should be appropriate to the situation rather than consistent amongst all situations. The problem with this is that managers may find it difficult to switch between styles, perhaps several times a day. Although the approach appears objec-

John Adair and Action Centered Leadership

Over 2 million people worldwide have taken part in the Action Centred Leadership approach pioneered by John Adair, recognised as an authority on leadership training. He proposes that people expect leaders to fulfil three obligations – to help them achieve the common task, to build and maintain the team and to enable individuals to satisfy their needs. These three obligations overlap and influence each other – if the task is achieved that will tend to sustain the group and meet individual needs. If there is a lack of skill or cohesion in the group it will not achieve the task and will be dissatisfying for the individual. So the three needs are represented by the overlapping circles in Figure 12.6 – almost a trademark for John Adair's work. To achieve these expectations the leader performs the eight functions shown in the figure – similar to those shown in Chapter 1.

Figure 12.6 Adair's model of leadership functions

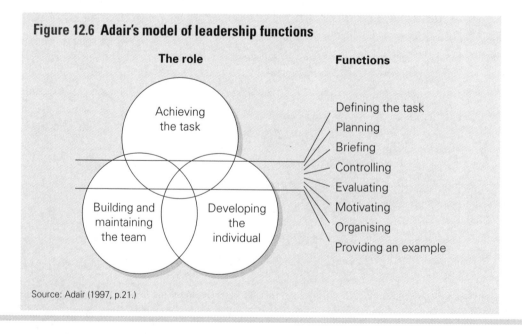

Source: Adair (1997, p.21.)

tive it still depends on the manager answering the questions. Requiring a simple yes or no answer to complex questions is too simple, and managers often want to say 'it all depends' – on other historical or contextual factors.

Nevertheless the model is used in management training to alert managers to the style they prefer to use and to the range of options available. It also prompts managers to consider systematically whether that preferred style is always appropriate. They may then handle situations more deliberately than if they relied only on their preferred style or intuition.

12.7 Tactics to influence others

Another approach to the study of influence has been to identify directly how managers tried to influence others. An early example of this was work by Kipnis *et al.* (1980), who identified a set of influencing tactics that managers used in dealing with subordinates, bosses and co-workers. Yukl and Falbe (1990) replicated this work in a wider empirical study, and refined the categories. Table 12.6 defines the Yukl and Falbe influence categories.

Table 12.6 Influence tactics and definitions

Tactic	Definition
Rational persuasion	The person uses logical arguments and factual evidence to persuade you that a proposal or request is viable and likely to result in the attainment of task objectives
Inspirational appeal	The person makes a request or proposal that arouses enthusiasm by appealing to your values, ideals and aspirations or by increasing your confidence that you can do it
Consultation	The person seeks your participation in planning a strategy, activity or change for which your support and assistance are desired, or the person is willing to modify a proposal to deal with your concerns and suggestions
Ingratiation	The person seeks to get you in a good mood or to think favourably of him or her before asking you to do something
Exchange	The person offers an exchange of favours, indicates a willingness to reciprocate at a later time, or promises you a share of the benefits if you help accomplish the task
Personal appeal	The person appeals to your feelings of loyalty and friendship towards him or her before asking you to do something
Coalition	The person seeks the aid of others to persuade you to do something, or uses the support of others as a reason for you to agree also
Legitimating	The person seeks to establish the legitimacy of a request by claiming the authority or right to make it or by verifying that it is consistent with organisational policies, rules, practices or traditions
Pressure	The person uses demands, threats or persistent reminders to influence you to do what he or she wants

Source: Based on Yukl and Falbe (1990).

The nine tactics cover a variety of behaviours that managers use as they try to influence others – whether subordinates, bosses or colleagues. Yukl and Tracey (1992) extended the work by examining which tactics managers used most frequently with different target groups. They concluded that managers were most likely to use:

- rational persuasion when trying to influence their boss;
- inspirational appeal and pressure when trying to influence subordinates; and
- exchange, personal appeal and legitimating tactics when influencing colleagues.

CASE STUDY   Digital Europe – the case continues

In many ways, system and process design is going through the very same as happens to some product design in its early days. An individual or a group of individuals needs to go out on a limb with an idea and be able to articulate that idea to a wider audience before they can get any interest and therefore any support and investment to go forward. In our company, where the products and the business plan change very quickly, it is enormously difficult to get people to focus on what is important rather than on what is urgent.

There are some interesting organisational and business discussions going on in each of these plants that have a direct bearing on this programme. We have seven sites, all at different stages of development. We have in some way to make sure that each of them is positioned, in terms of resources, energy and commitment, to support an integrated European programme.

The team member from Valbonne wrote to me two weeks ago indicating that he's now been asked to do another European programme. Therefore he will not be able to support this team. From my point of view that is totally unacceptable as his plant is a very big part of the order-fulfilment process. So without a representative from there, any solution that we devise will only be partially successful.

I have had to speak to the individual himself, who I know well from the past is making a very clear statement around availability. I understand the circumstances in Valbonne, having worked there for some time. I have therefore agreed that we will put together a plan to augment the materials and planning resource in Valbonne. I will take that plan to the manager in Valbonne and also to the European management team to try to provide the support required so that he can support both programmes.

Christmas holidays are looming, but prior to that I have to do an update on this programme to all my peers and my functional boss. They are obviously getting anxious about just exactly where we are. They are aware of some of the roadblocks that are causing me and the rest of team pain. So I am putting together a presentation that tries to be constructive about what is required to get the roadblocks out of the way and get us moving.

The European management team, from the conversations that I have had with them, is talking about some fairly unusual methods to drive this. For example, the concept of 'gold cards', which means that I can have the power to get whoever I want from wherever I want in Europe to drive the design for this system. Looks like we are in for a very interesting time within the first two to three weeks of January when we return to work.

Q Case questions 12.2

- Which of the sources of power in Table 12.1 has the manager at Digital Europe used?
- What has he done to increase his power and legitimacy in the eyes of those he is trying to influence?
- What other forms of authority has he been given?
- Which of the influence tactics in Table 12.6 did the manager at Digital Europe use?
- Is the pattern of use consistent with that found by Yukl and Tracey?

Whichever methods are used the outcome of an influence attempt will depend not only on the tactics used but on how well the influencer is able to meet the needs of the influencee, as discussed in Chapter 13.

12.8 Leaders and positional power

Earlier sections have centred on the personal skills of the manager and their ability to adapt to the situation. Managers can also use those sources of **power** that come from their position within the organisation. They can build and use their position to extend their power, and as Kanter (1979) observed, people are more likely to follow strong and influential managers than weak and isolated ones. She identifies four organisational factors that affect a manager's power:

- rules inherent in the job (fewer means more power);
- rewards for innovation (more means more power);
- external contact (more opportunities for this means more power);
- senior contact (more opportunities for this means more power).

The nature of the job and the pattern of contacts that come with it give the manager access to three 'lines of power':

- Supply: money and other resources that can be used to bestow status or rewards on others in return for their support.
- Information: being in the know, aware of what is happening, familiar with plans and opportunities that are in the making.
- Support: able to get senior or external backing for what he or she wants to do.

The more of these lines of power the manager has, the more that subordinates will co-operate. They do so because they believe that the manager has the power to engage in **political behaviour** and make things happen – they have 'clout' – weight or political influence in the organisation. A person's position in the organisation gives them access to one or more of the sources of power shown in Table 12.1.

Coercion

This is the ability to give instructions or threaten sanctions or penalties, derived from a person's formal position in the hierarchy. While this formal position appears to give someone in a particular position great coercive power over subordinates it is in practice usually an illusion. At best it is likely to produce compliant behaviour on the part of the subordinate, or may foster active resistance or more subtle attempts to undermine the manager's power.

Reward

This is the ability that position gives to use the financial and other resources of the organisation to bestow status or rewards on others in return for their support. Managers with large budgets and links into valuable networks of contacts have power. They can use their resources, or the promise of them, to generate effort. If they understand the rewards that others value they can use their position to satisfy them in return for the support they need. Managers who choose to be remote and isolated in back-room work will not have that power – and so will have little influence on people or events.

Expertise

Administrative expertise

This is the power that the holder of a position has to create organisation policies which support their influence attempts. Using their position skilfully they can create structures that help to sustain and increase their power – especially if they can also appoint loyal supporters, or those who are in their debt, to those positions. In this way they encourage others to act in the way they prefer – as Roy Gardner of Centrica did in persuading his staff to give more attention to customer service.

MANAGEMENT IN PRACTICE   **Structures and rewards at Centrica**

Centrica inherited severe customer relations problems when it demerged from British Gas, so restoring customer trust has been an important part of Roy Gardner's job. He has changed the structure of Centrica to influence other managers to give it priority as well. Customer service satisfaction targets were included in an executive bonus scheme covering its top 200 people. Also, a senior board executive was made responsible for all customer services.

Source: *Financial Times*, 24 February 2001, p.18.   **FT**

This idea was also central to Pettigrew's study of the evolution of ICI, one aspect of which is described in the next Key Ideas box. Kanter (1979) has also contributed to understanding in the area, and one implication of her ideas is that managers can increase their power by, paradoxically, delegating some of it to subordinates. By sharing power with subordinates managers can further increase their own power. As subordinates carry out tasks previously done by the manager, the manager has more time to build the external and senior contacts – which further boost his or her power. By delegating not only tasks but also a degree of power managers are able to enhance their own power.

The major benefit of delegation is that it reduces the manager's own workload. Relieved of the need to deal with the detail of a task the manager has more time to concentrate on major planning and creative work. More time can be spent on external matters, making contacts, keeping in touch with what is happening in the firm or the

---

KEY IDEAS   **Sir John Harvey-Jones's leadership at ICI**

In a classic study of ICI under Sir John Harvey-Jones, Pettigrew paid particular attention to the link between the leadership of the company and the change process. Sir John Harvey-Jones was clearly instrumental in initiating and implementing immense and fundamental change. Pettigrew's study shows that Harvey-Jones did not achieve this by a few dramatic acts or decisions. Rather it depended heavily on actions that he took over many years to change the structure of the organisation so that managers had more access to sources of power with which to influence others in the direction of radical change. For example, greater power was given to divisional directors to reward staff according to their performance.

This research led to the conclusion that studies of leadership should not focus only on the actions of individuals, important though they are. Rather they should view leadership as a continuous process taking place within a particular organisational context. The leader exerts influence by shaping that context and providing others with more positional power to initiate change.

Source: Pettigrew (1985, 1987).

industry. This builds the visibility and reputation of the manager's unit. A manager who fails to delegate, and who therefore looks inward rather than to the world outside, will become increasingly isolated from external events.

<table>
<tr><td>MANAGEMENT
IN PRACTICE</td><td>Too much internal focus</td></tr>
</table>

A department of a local authority consisted of a director, 2 senior officers, 3 officers and 14 staff. The director's style was to involve himself in operational matters, and he rarely found time to work with other senior managers. He normally met only with the senior officers within his department and rarely involved others in these discussions. He took the view that officers should not be involved in policy matters. He saw himself as the only competent person in the department and was comfortable in this operational role.

Staff consider themselves to be capable and professional. They expect to be involved more fully and are used to taking initiatives in both the routine and innovative aspects of the work. The fact that the director becomes involved in operational detail affects the officers in two ways. They are annoyed at the lack of trust this displays in their own abilities. They also suffer from the relatively low status of the department, caused by the director not being active externally and so lacking influence outside the department

Technical expertise

This is the power a person gains from holding a position that gives them access to information, of being in the know, aware of what is happening and of opportunities which are emerging. They can use their position, and the contacts that go with it, to build their image as a competent person. This credibility adds to their power to influence others. It is a contentious area, since people compete for access to information, and the power that goes with it – as the 'flowering of feudalism' feature indicates.

<table>
<tr><td>MANAGEMENT
IN PRACTICE</td><td>The flowering of feudalism</td></tr>
</table>

'Knowledge is power' has become such a managerial cliché that many at the top of big companies tend to forget that the principle can work both ways. Those lower down the management hierarchy also have an interest in husbanding information – and the power that goes with it. According to a recent survey of large European companies by the management consulting arm of KPMG, an accounting firm, the vast majority have found it impossible to establish pan-European management information systems for the simple reason that middle-ranking managers in different countries do not want those at headquarters to know what they are up to.

By 1993 few companies had succeeded in taking the first step by collecting information on their own far-flung European operations in a uniform way. After interviewing the chief executives or financial officers of 153 large European companies, KPMG found that only 8 per cent had established common information systems across their European subsidiaries. And this was not because of glitches with computers. 'Technically, of course, anything is possible with information systems these days,' observed the boss of a Danish tobacco firm. 'It is not the technical aspect that we find daunting; it's the time and energy we have to spend explaining it to people and persuading them to accept it.'

When they try to introduce the computers and procedures to gather such information, reported Alistair Stewart, who conducted the survey, European firms meet 'Ghandi-like' resistance from their subsidiaries. European HQs may be sending mixed signals to subsidiary managers: preaching autonomy and responsibility while trying to computerise all aspects of their business so that staff at headquarters can monitor their every move. 'People are reluctant to share their information,' complained the head of one French company, which manufactures industrial equipment. 'Managers in particular seem to think it gives them extra power.' Clever chaps.

Source: Based on an article in *The Economist*, 27 February 1993, © The Economist, London, 1993.

Referent

In terms of position, this is where managers can use their position to influence others by showing that what they propose is consistent with the accepted values and culture of the organisation. They invoke wider values in support of their proposal. The effectiveness of the influence attempt depends on the other people having a similar view of the culture to that of the influencer.

The more of these sources of power the manager has, the more others will co-operate. They do so because they believe that the manager has the power to make things happen. Such a manager has weight or political influence in the organisation, which encourages others to accede to their wishes.

12.9 Summary

Managing anything depends on understanding how to influence others to act in a particular way, consistent with the objectives of the task. The chapter has outlined the main conclusions and perspectives on the topic. The main contrast is between those that emphasise the benefits of developing a range of interpersonal skills and those which emphasise building and maintaining power, especially that which is based within an organisational position.

Content

Achieving objectives usually depends on the willing commitment of other people. Objectives that are seen as divisive or serving one interest will undermine that commitment. Conversely, working to develop common and agreed objectives may lead to staff seeing management's use of power as legitimate and acceptable. Transformational leadership methods use higher level objectives to gain fuller employee commitment. How management seeks to influence others affects people's reaction to being managed. Dominant use of power may ensure compliance, but such an approach is unlikely to produce the commitment required to meet innovative objectives.

Process

How management seeks to influence others began with a discussion of power and its sources. Situational approaches offer alternative ways of reaching decisions on plans. The form of action generated depends on accepting power as legitimate, and on employees being willing to accept a particular style. The contingency or situational approaches draw attention to the context in which management influences others, such as task, subordinates and external conditions. The chapter distinguished between personal and institutional sources. Kanter's argument for building power by sharing it was discussed. This led to an examination of how delegation can increase a manager's power by freeing time to build and use external contacts.

Control

One of the paradoxes of management is that managers who delegate control to others are able to enhance their power and control. A reluctance to delegate and share power reflects managers' (misguided, as not serving their long-term interests) attempts to retain control.

The manager at Digital Europe spent a great deal of time and effort influencing those above him in the hierarchy, and those over whom he had no direct control. The case illustrates that even with little formal power over the project at the start he was able to act in ways that gradually built a considerable resource of both personal and positional power.

> **Q** **PART CASE QUESTIONS**
>
> - How does W.L. Gore and Associates influence staff to work on vital projects?
> - How do research staff influence each other? Compare the way that project managers at Gore and the project managers at Digital Europe influence other members of the company.
> - How is W.L. Gore and Associates balancing personal and institutional sources of power and influence?

12.10 Review questions

1 Why is the ability to influence others so central to the management role?
2 Explain in your own words the main sources of power available to managers. Give examples of both personal and institutional forms of each.
3 What is meant by the phrase a '9,9 manager'?
4 What were the strengths and weaknesses of the behavioural approaches to leadership?
5 Discuss with someone how he or she made a particular decision. Compare this person's approach with one of the contingency approaches to leadership.
6 Evaluate the situational theory in the light of the evidence acquired in review question 5 and other considerations.
7 List the lines of power that Kanter identifies and give an example of each.

Further reading

Yukl, G.A. (1998), *Leadership in Organisations* (4th edn), Prentice Hall, Upper Saddle River, NJ. Combines a comprehensive review of academic research on all aspects of organisational leadership with clear guidance on the implications for practitioners.

Buchanan, D. and Badham, R. (1999), *Power, Politics and Organizational Change: Winning the turf game*, Sage, London. A modern approach to politics in organisations, offering a theoretical and practical guide, based on extensive primary research.

Roddick, A. (2000), *Business as Unusual*, Thorsons, London.

Branson, R. (1999), *Losing My Virginity*, Virgin Books, London.

Accounts of their approach to management by two charismatic leaders.

Adams, S. (1998), *The Dilbert Principle*, Boxtree, London. Light relief from your studies.

Annotated links, questions and resources can be found on
www.booksites.net/boddy

CHAPTER 13

Motivation

| AIM | *To examine theories of behaviour at work and to connect them with management practice.* |

By the end of your work on this chapter you should be able to outline the concepts below in your own terms and:

1 Outline the idea of the psychological contract

2 Compare behaviour modification theory with other theories of motivation

3 Compare and evaluate the theories of human need proposed by Maslow, Alderfer and McClelland

4 Compare the hygiene and motivation factors identified by Herzberg and use them to evaluate a person's job

5 Evaluate the usefulness of McGregor's Theory X and Theory Y

6 Compare the assumptions believed to be held by western managers and those in other cultures

7 Explain the expectancy and equity theories of motivation

8 Summarise the implications for management of work design theories

Management and motivation in the Benefits Agency

The Benefits Agency is responsible for delivering a range of UK state benefits to the public. Most Agency staff work in a network of local offices that are organised into district management units. The 159 districts are organised into 13 area units. Each area director is accountable to the Agency's top management team.

The Benefits Agency used to form part of the Department of Social Security (DSS), the largest organisation in the UK Civil Service. Traditionally, the Civil Service provided a secure place to work. Staff usually joined straight from school and were expected to follow precisely defined rules in order to ensure equality of treatment to all citizens. The work was routine, and the Service valued conformist behaviour: innovation was discouraged. The career path was predictable, jobs were secure, and a pension was guaranteed on retirement. The management structure was hierarchical; any unusual problem was referred up to the next level for decision.

In the early 1990s government policy brought radical change: the Benefits Agency would become a separate organisation within the Civil Service. It would conduct the same functions on behalf of government but would be managed differently.

A chief executive was appointed in 1991 on a three-year contract (which in itself sent out signals about the previous jobs for life culture). He defined a new vision: 'To provide the right money to the right person at the right time and the right place'. To deliver this more customer-centred service he gave district managers more control over their budget, thereby reducing control by senior managers at HQ. Management in some areas ignored the new freedoms and continued to manage in the old, hierarchical way.

The area, described in this study interpreted the freedoms as giving authority to make very wide changes. The management board of one such area defined their vision as: 'To be the leading provider of Social Security services in the UK'. District managers were encouraged to give more decision-making power to staff dealing with the public, and staff were encouraged to be innovative in their approach. A critical factor in achieving this vision was to have the right number of skilled and motivated staff.

Q Case questions

- What attracted staff to work in the Benefits Agency before these changes?
- How are they likely to have reacted to the changes introduced in 1991?

13.1 | Introduction

This chapter introduces the following ideas:

- Motivation
- Perception
- Psychological contract
- Existence needs
- Relatedness needs
- Growth needs
- Motivating factors
- Hygiene factors
- Subjective probability
- Job enrichment model

The problem for the Benefits Agency is that it cannot meet the expectations that people have unless it can retain and increase the **motivation** of its employees. Unmotivated employees will not provide good service, will make mistakes, and the reputation of the Agency will suffer. How will staff react to the changes prompted by the move away from a secure Civil Service status? Many staff joined the Agency or its predecessors because they valued the public service aspect of the work, and the secure and predictable employment that went with a Civil Service job. How they react will affect the success or otherwise of the changes that senior management is planning.

All businesses need enthusiastic and committed employees who work in a way that supports organisational goals. When Centrica attempted to improve customer satisfaction and trust (see Chapter 12) management depended on staff being motivated to deliver better service. Microsoft and Dell depend on their engineers being motivated to develop a constant flow of innovative products. Hospitals depend on medical and nursing staff being willing to work there, and to work in a way that provides good patient care.

Yet motivation arises within people – so work needs to meet their goals as well. People have different motivations, so that a reward that is attractive to one may be unimportant to another.

MANAGEMENT IN PRACTICE | **Terry Green of Debenhams**

'What is it you dream of when you you're young?' Terry Green, chief executive of Debenhams posed the question ... He is sitting in his shirt sleeves ... behind a massive desk in his rooftop office in London's West End.

'I'll tell you,' says Green, before I have a chance to answer. 'Having a flash car, a sexy girl-friend and a house in the country. And this,' he continues, pulling out a book of photos of his new home, a 10-bedroomed mansion set in 22 acres of countryside ... 'is my boyhood dream realised.'

If he has realised his dreams, will the hunger go? 'No,' he says, 'that's the brilliance of it.' Because since he took on [the new house] he's personally more in debt than he's ever been. He has to keep earning more money, making Debenhams a huge success, to pay off his mountainous mortgage.

Source: The Davidson Interview, *Management Today*, January 1999, p.40.

Money is evidently a major motivator for Terry Green (who no longer works for Debenhams) – as it is for many on very low incomes too. Others find deep satisfaction in the work itself – like Theresa Marshall, who is a classroom assistant in a city primary school:

> 'I've found my niche and couldn't be happier – it's no exaggeration to say that I absolutely love my job. My favourite part is helping the children with their reading skills and seeing the pleasure that they can get out of books.'

Some enjoy working with physical things or the challenge of designing an innovative product – while others enjoy working directly with other people.

With people having such diverse needs and interests, how can managers motivate people to work in ways that meet the manager's priorities? In small organisations the relationship between an owner-manager and a few employees is close and direct. Each can develop a good idea of what the other expects and adjust the pattern of work and the pattern of rewards to meet changing requirements. As the organisation grows the links become less personal. Motivation increasingly depends on more formal approaches, based on managers' theories of motivation – what they believe will influence employees. They make working assumptions about the likely response of employees to different inducements. For their part staff evaluate what is on offer and respond according to how well it meets their needs.

Figure 13.1 A model of motivation at work

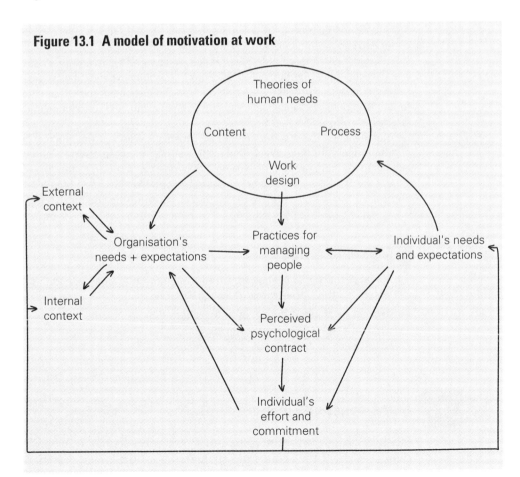

This chapter outlines and illustrates the main theories of human needs, as shown in Figure 13.1. The wider context influences the form of behaviour expected of people – who also have needs and expectations of the organisation. The next section examines the psychological contract that expresses these mutual expectations. It then presents three main theories about motivation at work – content, process and work design. Content theories help explain why people work, by identifying human needs that work may satisfy. Process theories help explain how people decide which action will satisfy their needs. Work design theories connect the content and process approaches to workplace practice.

CASE STUDY   The Benefits Agency – the case continues

Behaviour that had been valued was now a barrier to promotion. Staff who had hoped to gain promotion by playing to the rules now found they had little chance. Some became disillusioned but continued to deliver – at a reduced level of productivity. Some could not adapt, and left. Others applied their efforts to a new goal – that of resisting the changes.

Another group enthusiastically embraced this new culture where innovation, creativity and risk taking were valued. Districts introduced the 'one-stop' approach, so that one member of staff (rather than several) could deal with all the benefits that a person claimed. This led to the creation of multi-function teams, and to big changes in the way staff worked. Staff responded enthusiastically to these changes, even though pay awards were still strictly controlled and promotion opportunities had become fewer.

The mid 1990s brought further changes. A new chief executive was appointed in 1995. In line with the government's policy of controlling public expenditure the Agency's budget was reduced drastically in 1996. At the same time the National Audit Office, the body responsible for auditing public organisations, criticised the inaccuracy of benefit payments and the scope the system offered for fraud.

The new chief executive amended the Agency's vision to 'pay the right money to the right person at the right time every time'. The top management team became uneasy about the increased freedom of the area directors. Examples of a return to the older structure began to appear, such as the introduction of centrally controlled checking teams and increases in the number of mandatory management checks. Staff in the region reacted with dismay, and management again has the problem of how to create a skilled and motivated staff.

Q Case questions 13.1

● What rewards did management of the Benefits Agency use when it was operating as part of the Department of Social Security?

● How were these different after the change in approach?

● How did staff react to the changes?

13.2   Some constants in motivation

Much behaviour is routine, based on habit, precedent and unconscious scripts. This chapter is about the choices people make about the larger, precedent-setting choices about behaviour at work. For some people work is clearly an occasion for hard, enthusiastic and imaginative activity, and a source of rich satisfaction. They are motivated, in the sense that they put effort (arousal) into their work (direction and persistence). For others it is something that they do grudgingly – work does not arouse their enthusiasm, or does so for very short spells before they find something more interesting to do. Managers try to understand why such differences occur, and seek to encourage the former rather than the latter. Motivational theories can inform that consideration.

Targets of attempts to motivate

Who are managers trying to motivate? Theories of motivation originally concentrated on how managers can motivate subordinates, but managers need to influence many other people: colleagues, their own senior managers, or people in other organisations. They also try to influence consumers – marketing tactics also use theories of human motivation. In all of these cases managers are trying to understand human needs in the belief that doing so accurately makes it easier to influence what they do.

Those with a more critical perspective argue that 'workers need to be influenced to co-operate because of their essential alienation from the productive process' (Thompson and McHugh, 1995, p.304). In addition they suggest that management typically uses motivation theories to maintain the established power relations between employer and employee. Management often imposes schemes on a relatively passive workforce to make work more interesting. The latter accept these in the absence of realistic alternatives. Staff may even express greater satisfaction with a new arrangement as a way of coming to terms with the inherent stability of the power structure. As always in management, motivation people see motivation from many different perspectives: it is not a neutral or value-free topic.

Figure 13.2 illustrates a simple model of human motivation. We all have certain needs, such as for food, social contact or a sense of achievement, which motivates behaviours aimed at satisfying that need. If the action leads to an outcome that satisfies the need we experience a sense of reward. The feedback loop shows that we then decide whether the behaviour was appropriate and worth repeating.

Individuals do not act in isolation, but within a social context that includes the following:

- the job – how interesting, varied or responsible it is;
- the organisation – supervision, career and promotion prospects, pay systems;
- the environment – the chances of getting another job.

These contextual factors, some of which management can influence, affect the behaviours people choose to satisfy a need.

Figure 13.2 Human needs in context – the situational perspective

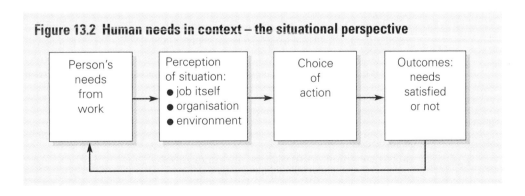

In using Figure 13.2 to organise the discussion, remember that:

● Needs can only be inferred: we can only make assumptions about which needs are important to someone.
● Needs will change, and people sometimes experience conflicts between them.
● The effect of satisfying a need on the strength of that need in future is uncertain.

Psychological contract

Managers have expectations of the people who work for them. At the same time employees have expectations of managers – not just on pay, but also on such things as fairness, trust and opportunities for self-development. This set of mutual expectations makes up the psychological contract.

ACTIVITY 13.1

Mutual expectations

Identify a time when you were working in an organisation, or think of your work as a student. Describe what the organisation expected of you.

What policies or practices did the organisation use to encourage these?

What did you expect of the organisation?

How well did the organisation meet your expectations?

What was the effect of that on your behaviour?

The **psychological contract** expresses the idea that each side has expectations of the other regarding what they will give and what they will receive in return. Employers offer rewards in the hope of receiving certain types and levels of performance. Employees contribute effort in the expectation of reward. Some elements in the contract are expressed in writing but most take a tacit, unwritten form. The current state of a psychological contract is the outcome of a continuing process of mutual adjustment between the parties. They have no legal status, and are in essence subjective and informal. They are also dynamic, as changes in the circumstances of both parties mean that they continually adjust the contract – people fill in the blanks along the way (Rousseau, 1995). This adjustment process is both inevitable and a source of difficulty, especially if the employer changes the contract in a way that makes employees feel worse off. As Kolb *et al.* (1991) remarked, 'a company staffed by "cheated" individuals who expect far more than they get is headed for trouble' (p.6).

Figure 13.3 shows the model that Guest and Conway (2001) use in their studies of how a sample of UK employees view the state of their psychological contract with their employer. They measured the current state of the psychological contract between respondents and their organisation by asking them for their **perceptions** of delivery of promises, fairness and trust. On the issue of delivery, the questionnaire asked respondents whether the company had kept its promise to provide the following:

● a reasonably secure job;
● fair pay for the work you do;
● a career;
● interesting work;
● fair treatment by managers and supervisors;
● help with problems outside work.

Figure 13.3 A conceptual framework of the psychological contract

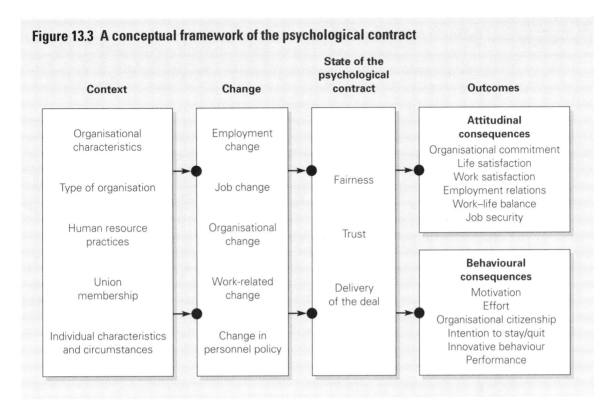

Table 13.1 summarises the results of the 1999 survey.

Table 13.1 Perceptions of fairness and trust in the psychological contract

% (n = 493)	A lot	Somewhat	Only a little	Not at all
In general, how much do you trust your organisation to keep its promises ... to you and other employees	33	50	14	3
To what extent do you trust management to look after your best interests?	27	48	18	7
	Yes definitely	Yes probably	No probably not	No definitely not
Do you feel you are fairly rewarded for the amount of effort you put into the job?	27	41	16	16

Source: Guest and Conway (2001, p.9),

The study also provided empirical support for the view that a positive psychological contract was a good predictor of work satisfaction and commitment. Those who felt they had been treated fairly were more satisfied than those who had not.

'Employees leave managers, not companies'

From the employee's point of view, there is clear evidence that good management rests squarely on four foundations. These are:

● having a manager who shows care, interest and concern for each of them;
● knowing what is expected of them;
● having a role that fits their abilities;
● receiving positive feedback and recognition regularly for work well done.

In a Gallup study of performance at unit level, covering more than 200,000 employees across a dozen or more industries, teams that rated managers highly on these four factors were more productive and more profitable. They also had lower staff turnover and higher customer satisfaction ratings.

Source: *People Management*, 17 February 2000, p.45.

At a time of great change in the business world there is always the danger that, however satisfied now, employees come to feel that their psychological contract has been broken. Technological changes and increased competition lead senior management to change employment policies and working conditions, or put staff under great pressure to meet demanding performance targets. The Benefits Agency is an example of this.

Q Case questions 13.2

● In the 1980s what were the main elements of the psychological contract between the DSS and its employees? List what each was expecting of the other.
● How did that change in the early 1990s?
● How did staff respond?
● Are there possible links between that response and later events in the organisation?
● Are there any lessons which that suggests?

The following section outlines an early theory of motivation, which some companies use to influence staff behaviour. Subsequent sections look at theories about the content of human needs at work.

13.3 Behaviour modification

Behaviour modification refers to a range of techniques that were developed to help treat various psychological conditions such as eating disorders or heavy smoking. They have also been used in organisational settings to deal with issues such as lateness or absenteeism. The techniques have developed from Skinner's (1971) theory that people are motivated by reinforcement. If they find that they are rewarded for doing something then they will tend to repeat that behaviour. If they experience something unpleasant as a result of a certain action then they will tend not to repeat it.

Hence behavioural modification techniques focus on specific observable behaviours rather than on attitudes and feelings. They try to identify what leads a person to act in a particular way and what reward he or she experiences as a result of the behaviour. If the influencer sees the behaviour as undesirable he or she may try to influence the person to change by affecting the rewards that are obtained.

To influence the person to change, the first steps help to pinpoint three relevant aspects of the situation:

- the specific behaviour that is undesirable (persistent lateness or carelessness, for example);
- the external events or cues (perhaps Monday, or a particular type of work) that consistently precede the behaviour and appear to trigger it;
- the pay-off that the person gets from the behaviour and which encourages him or her to repeat it (for example, avoids unpleasant work and is not disciplined).

The focus then shifts to:

- defining a desirable behaviour given the person's role and responsibilities;
- deciding how to change the cues so that desirable behaviour (for example, being on time) is more likely, and undesirable behaviour less so (such as by making the work more attractive or providing training that enables the person to do more interesting work);
- deciding how the present pay-off can be changed to encourage desirable behaviour and discourage the undesirable (such as by rewarding timely and effective performance with public recognition, increased status, promotion opportunities, and punishing the undesirable behaviour in some way).

Practitioners emphasise several principles used in the approach. The pay-offs (benefits) must be given only when the desired behaviour occurs. They must also be used as soon as possible after the behaviour, so that the link between behaviour and reward is evident. Desirable behaviour is likely to be repeated if reinforced by rewards. Reinforcement is more effective than punishment, as punishment only temporarily suppresses behaviour. Repeated reinforcement can lead to permanent change in behaviour in the desired direction.

 MANAGEMENT IN PRACTICE   **Attempting behaviour modification in a call centre**

'In our call centre staff are rewarded when behaviour delivers results in line with business requirements. Each month staff performance is reviewed against a number of objectives such as average call length, sales of each product and attention to detail. This is known as Effective Level Review and agents can move through levels of effectiveness ranging from 1 to 4, and gain an increase in salary after six months of successful reviews. Moving through effective levels means that they have performed well and can mean being given other tasks instead of answering the phone. The role can become mundane and repetitive so the opportunity to do other tasks is seen as a reward for good performance. Thus it reinforces acceptable behaviour.

Conversely staff who display behaviour that is not desirable cannot move through these levels and repeated failure to do so can lead to disciplinary action. This can be seen as punishment rather than behaviour modification. People can become resentful at having their performance graded every month, particularly in those areas where it is their line manager's perception of whether or not they have achieved the desired results.'

Source: Private communication from the call centre manager.

Above all, proponents of the approach stress the need to reward desirable behaviours rather than to treat them with indifference. These rewards can result either from individual action by a manager or through some more formal, institutionalised procedures. Advocates of the method believe that people behave to obtain what they want but do not have. It encourages management to look directly at what is likely to make a particular person act in a desirable way, and to ensure those rewards are available. For the behaviour to be sustained, the rewards must also be sustained.

In practice, management policy can:

- reinforce undesirable behaviours;
- fail to reinforce desirable behaviour;
- reinforce desirable behaviour.

A benefit claimed of the approach is that anyone can use it to establish norms of behaviour. As these are reinforced they become more habitual so that standards and precedents reflect a collective understanding. The method depends on identifying rewards that the person will value (or punishments they will try to avoid). Theories that attempt to understand these are known as content theories of motivation.

13.4 Content theories of motivation

Most writers on this topic have been attempting to identify the needs people have that are likely to influence their behaviour. For example, Frederick Taylor (see Chapter 2) believed that people worked for money. Employees would follow the strictly laid down methods if management rewarded their output with more money. The work of Frank Gilbreth helped to develop the systems for introducing such payment-by-results systems widely.

ACTIVITY 13.2

Was Taylor wrong?

Many managements believe that money is a powerful incentive. Find someone who works for an organisation where incentives or commissions make up a significant part of that person's pay and ask how that affects his or her behaviour, and whether there are any negative effects.

Chapter 2 described how writers such as Mary Parker Follett and Elton Mayo emphasised aspects of motivation other than money, especially the need for acceptance by other people. Evidence for this is when groups agree the level of output they will produce. If people value membership of the group more than the financial incentive they will conform to the group. Mayo drew attention to the social motivations of people at work, and advised management to foster these rather than counter them by individual incentives.

Abraham Maslow – a hierarchy of needs

Maslow was a clinical psychologist who developed a theory of human motivation to help him understand the needs of his patients. He stressed the clinical sources of the theory and that it lacked experimental verification. He also observed that Douglas McGregor (1960, see section 13.5) had applied the theory to industrial situations and had found it useful in ordering his data and observations.

Maslow proposed that individuals experience a range of needs, and will be motivated to fulfil whichever need is most powerful at the time (Maslow, 1970). What he termed the lower-order needs are dominant until they are at least partially satisfied. Then, Maslow predicted, normal individuals would turn their attention to satisfying the needs at the next level, and so on, so that the higher-order needs would gradually become dominant. He referred to these needs as being arranged in a hierarchy:

Self-actualisation
Esteem
Belongingness and love
Safety
Physiological

Physiological needs are the needs whose satisfaction is essential for survival – food and water particularly. Maslow proposed that if all the needs in the hierarchy are unsatisfied then the physiological needs will dominate. People will concentrate on activities that enable them to obtain the necessities of life. Until they have these they will not attempt to satisfy the higher needs.

Once the physiological needs were sufficiently gratified a new set of needs would emerge, which he termed *safety needs* – the search for 'security; stability; dependency; protection; freedom from fear, anxiety and chaos; need for structure, order, law, limits … and so on' (p.39). People concentrate on satisfying these needs, to the exclusion of other considerations. If this need is dominant for a person they can satisfy it by seeking a stable, regular job with secure working conditions and access to insurance for ill-health and retirement. They resent sudden or random changes in job prospects.

Belongingness needs would follow the satisfaction of safety needs:

> [If] both the physiological and the safety needs are fairly well gratified, there will emerge the love and affection and belongingness needs … now the person will feel keenly the absence of friends … and will hunger for affectionate relations with people in general. (p.43)

These needs include a place in the group or family, and at work they would include wanting to be part of a congenial team. People object when management changes work patterns or locations if this disrupts established working relationships. They welcome change that brings them closer to people they know and like.

Maslow observed that most people have *esteem needs* – self-respect and the respect of others. Self-respect is the need for a sense of achievement, competence, adequacy and confidence. People also seek the respect of others, what he called a desire for reputation in the eyes of other people – prestige, status, recognition, attention. They try to satisfy this need by taking on challenging or difficult tasks which will show that they are good at their job and can accomplish something worthwhile. If others recognise this they earn status and respect.

Lastly, Maslow used the term *self-actualisation needs* to refer to the desire for self-fulfilment and for realising potential. He pointed out that the specific form this takes will vary: 'At this level, individual differences are greatest. The clear emergence of these needs usually rests upon some prior satisfaction of the physiological, safety, love, and esteem needs' (pp.46–7). This implies that people seeking to satisfy self-actualisation needs will look for personal relevance in their work. They may value new responsibilities that help them realise their potential or discover unknown talents.

To illustrate Maslow's hierarchy with a practical example, a member of staff at the Benefits Agency summarised the ways in which the organisation had traditionally satisfied the different needs (Table 13.2).

Table 13.2 How the traditional system at the Benefits Agency enabled people to satisfy the needs identified by Maslow

Needs	How they were met
Physiological	Good working conditions Steady incremental salary
Safety	Attractive non-contributory pension Safe working conditions 'No redundancy' policy Payment for absence due to illness
Belongingness relationships	Sports and social clubs (local and national) Office parties/outings Permission for informal activities
Esteem	Regarded in society as a good job Grade prestige Promotion
Self-actualisation	Promotion opportunities (steady and fast track) Funding and time off for further education

Q Case questions 13.3

● Which needs were being met, and in what ways, under the new policy at the Benefits Agency?

Maslow did *not* claim that the hierarchy was a fixed or rigid scheme. His clinical experience suggested that most people with whom he had worked had these needs in about this order. He had also seen exceptions. There had been people for whom self-esteem was more important than love. For others creativeness took precedence, in that they did not seek self-actualisation once they had satisfied their basic needs, but in spite of these *not* being satisfied. Others had such permanently low aspirations that they experienced life at a very basic level.

Maslow also cautioned against the impression that as people satisfy one need completely another emerges. Rather he proposed that most normal people are partially satisfied and partially unsatisfied in their needs. This implied that a more accurate description of the hierarchy would be in terms of decreasing percentages of satisfaction at successive levels. So a person could think of himself as being, say, 85 per cent satisfied at the physiological level and 70 per cent at the safety level (the percentages are, of course, meaningless). Moreover, the emergence of a higher-level need was not a sudden event. Rather a person would gradually become aware that a higher need could now be attained.

MANAGEMENT IN PRACTICE   **A new manager at a nursing home**

In 1999 Jean Parker was appointed manager of a nursing home for the elderly. Recent reports by the Health Authority and Environmental Health inspectors had been so critical that they threatened to close the home. Jean recalls what she did in the first eight months:

'My task was to make sweeping changes, stabilise the workforce and improve the reputation of the home. I had no influence on pay, and low pay was one of the problems. To motivate staff I had to use other methods. Staff facilities were appalling – the dining areas were filthy, showers and some toilets were not working, there were no changing rooms and petty theft was rife. Given the lack of care and respect shown to staff it is little wonder that care given to residents was poor, and staff were demotivated. They turned up to work, carried out tasks and went home. There had been little communication between management and staff. My approach was to work alongside the staff, listen to their grievances, gain their trust and set out an action plan.

The first steps were easy. The staff room was cleaned and decorated, changing rooms and working showers and toilets were provided. Refreshments were provided at meal breaks. Police advice was sought to combat petty theft and lockers were installed in each area. The effect of these changes on staff commitment was astounding. They felt somebody cared for them and listened. In turn, quality of care improved and staff started to take pride in the home, and bring in ornaments and plants to brighten it.

I then started to hold monthly meetings to give management and staff an opportunity to discuss expectations. Policies and procedures were explained. Noticeboards displaying 'news and views' were put up. A monthly newsletter to residents and relations was issued. Staff took part enthusiastically in fund-raising activities to pay for outings and entertainment. This gave them the chance to get to know residents in a social setting, and was a break from routine. A training programme was introduced.

Some staff did not respond and tried to undermine my intentions. Persistent unreported absence was quickly followed by disciplinary action. By the end of the year absenteesim was at a more acceptable level, many working problems were alleviated, and the business started to recover.'

Source: Private communication and discussions with the manager.

In summary, Maslow believed that people are motivated to satisfy those needs that are important to them at that point in their life, and offered a description of those needs. The strength of a particular need would depend on the extent to which needs lower in the hierarchy had been met. In particular, he stressed the importance of the physiological needs, which he believed most people would seek to satisfy first, before the others became operative. Self-actualisation was fulfilled last and least often, although he had observed exceptions.

ACTIVITY 13.3

Working with the theories

Which of the needs identified by Maslow did Jean Parker's changes at the nursing home help staff to satisfy?

Do your studies and related activities on your course satisfy needs identified by Maslow?

What evidence can you gather from your colleagues on the relative importance to them of these needs?

How does Maslow's approach compare with Skinner's? Skinner believed that by providing positive reinforcement (or punishment) people would be motivated to act in a particular way. The rewards they obtained would satisfy their needs. Maslow took the slightly different position that people would seek to satisfy their needs by acting in a particular way. Both believe that to change behaviour it would be necessary to change the situation. Skinner emphasised that this would take the form of positive reinforcement to satisfy needs after an activity. Maslow implied that influencers should provide conditions that enable to people to satisfy their needs from the activity.

Clayton Alderfer – ERG theory

Doubtful about the empirical support for the hierarchy of motives proposed by Maslow, Alderfer developed another approach (Alderfer, 1972). His work both built on Maslow's ideas and presented an alternative to them. He developed and tested his theory in questionnaire and interview-based studies carried out in five organisations – a manufacturing firm, a bank, two colleges and a school. He aimed to identify the primary needs – those that an organism possesses by the nature of being the creature it is. Satisfaction refers to the internal state of someone who has obtained what he or she is seeking. Frustration is the opposite – when someone seeks something but does not find it.

Existence needs reflect a person's requirement for material and energy exchange with his or her environment. They therefore include all the material and physiological desires – hunger and thirst represent deficiencies in existence needs. Pay and benefits of various kinds represent ways of satisfying material requirements.

Relatedness needs involve relationships with significant other people – family members, colleagues, bosses, subordinates, team members, regular customers and so on. This includes groups and individuals. People satisfy their relatedness needs by sharing thoughts and feelings. Acceptance, confirmation and understanding are elements in this process of satisfying relatedness needs.

Growth needs are those that impel a person to be creative or to produce an effect on themselves and their environment. People satisfy these needs by engaging with problems that call upon them to use their skills fully or even require them to develop new ones. People experience a greater sense of completeness when they have satisfied their growth needs. That satisfaction depends on finding the opportunity to exercise talents to the full.

KEY IDEAS — Seven major propositions of Alderfer's theory

P1 The less that existence needs are satisfied, the more they will be desired.

P2 The less that relatedness needs are satisfied, the more existence needs will be desired.

P3 The more that existence needs are satisfied, the more relatedness needs will be desired.

P4 The less that relatedness needs are satisfied, the more they will be desired.

P5 The less that growth needs are satisfied, the more relatedness needs will be desired.

P6 The more that relatedness needs are satisfied, the more growth needs will be desired.

P7 The more that growth needs are satisfied, the more they will be desired.

Source: Alderfer (1972).

Alderfer showed how his formulation of needs compared with that put forward by Maslow. Figure 13.4 summarises his discussion of the point.

Alderfer proposed that his three categories of need are active in everyone, although in varying degrees of strength. There is no hierarchical relationship between the needs, but there are propositions relating lower-level need satisfaction to higher-level desires, and vice versa – see Key Ideas above.

The main difference from Maslow was that Alderfer did not find any evidence that the needs formed a hierarchy. He found that if higher needs are frustrated lower needs will become prominent again, even if they have already been satisfied.

Both theories are hard to test empirically – how do you establish operationally whether a person has satisfied a need? The value of the theories is that they integrate ear-

Figure 13.4 Comparison of Maslow and Alderfer's categories of needs

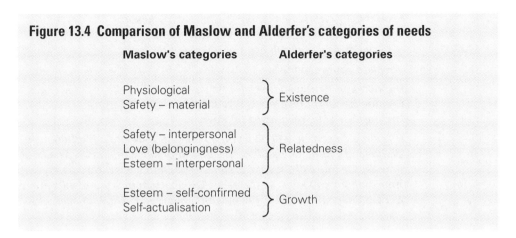

lier ideas that had concentrated on single needs and show the variety of needs which people have, some of which they seek to satisfy at work.

David McClelland

McClelland (1961) and his colleagues have examined how people think and react in a wide range of situations. This work led them to identify three categories of human need, which individuals possess in different amounts:

● need for affiliation – to develop and maintain interpersonal relationships;
● need for power – to be able to influence and control others and to shape events;
● need for achievement – to take personal responsibility and show successful task results.

McClelland used the Thematic Apperception Text to assess how significant these categories were to people. People taking part in the research were shown pictures with a neutral subject and asked to write a story about the picture. The researchers then coded the stories and claimed they could then estimate the relative importance to the person of the affiliation, power and achievement motives.

You can assess your scores on these motives by completing Activity 13.4.

ACTIVITY 13.4

Assessing your needs

From each of the four sets of statements below choose the one that is most like you.

1 (a) *I set myself difficult goals, which I attempt to reach.*
　(b) *I am happiest when I am with a group of people who enjoy life.*
　(c) *I like to organise the activities of a group or team.*

2 (a) *I only completely enjoy relaxation after the successful completion of exacting pieces of work.*
　(b) *I become attached to my friends.*
　(c) *I argue zealously against others for my point of view.*

3 (a) *I work hard until I am completely satisfied with the result I achieve.*
　(b) *I like to mix with a group of congenial people, talking about any subject that comes up.*
　(c) *I tend to influence others more than they influence me.*

4 (a) I enjoy working as much as I enjoy my leisure.
(b) I go out of my way to be with my friends.
(c) I am able to dominate a social situation.

Now add your responses as follows:

The number of (a) responses ( ) Achievement
The number of (b) responses ( ) Affiliation
The number of (c) responses ( ) Power

This simple exercise will give you an insight both into the differences between McClelland's three types of motive and into your preference. The larger your score in an area, the more likely your preference is in that area. Compare your answers with others whom you know in the class. Discuss whether the results are in line with what you would have expected, given what you already know of each other.

Source: Based on Jackson (1993).

Frederick Herzberg – two-factor theory

Herzberg (1959) developed his theory following interviews with 200 engineers and accountants about their experience of work. The researchers first asked them to recall a time when they had felt exceptionally good about their job. Further questions probed for the events that had preceded those feelings. The research team then asked respondents to recall a time when they had felt particularly bad about their work, and give the background. Analysis showed that when respondents recalled good times they frequently mentioned one or more of these factors:

- achievement;
- recognition;
- work itself;
- responsibility;
- advancement.

They mentioned these much less frequently when describing the bad times. When talking about the bad times they most frequently recalled these factors:

- company policy and administration;
- supervision;
- salary;
- interpersonal relations;
- working conditions.

They mentioned these much less frequently when describing the good times.

Herzberg concluded that the factors associated with satisfaction describe people's relationship to what they were doing. They included the nature of the task, responsibility carried or recognition received. He renamed these satisfiers '**motivators**', as they seemed to influence the individual to superior performance and effort. The second set, associated with dissatisfaction, related to conditions surrounding the work. He named these the '**hygiene**' or ('maintenance') **factors** as they served mainly to prevent dissatisfaction, not foster high performance. Figure 13.5 illustrates the results.

In summary, Herzberg concluded that the factors which produce job satisfaction are separate and distinct from those that lead to job dissatisfaction, hence the term 'two-factor' theory. He suggested that satisfaction and dissatisfaction are not opposites: they are separate dimensions influenced by different factors. The dissatisfiers (company

Figure 13.5 Herzberg's comparison of job satisfaction and job dissatisfaction scores

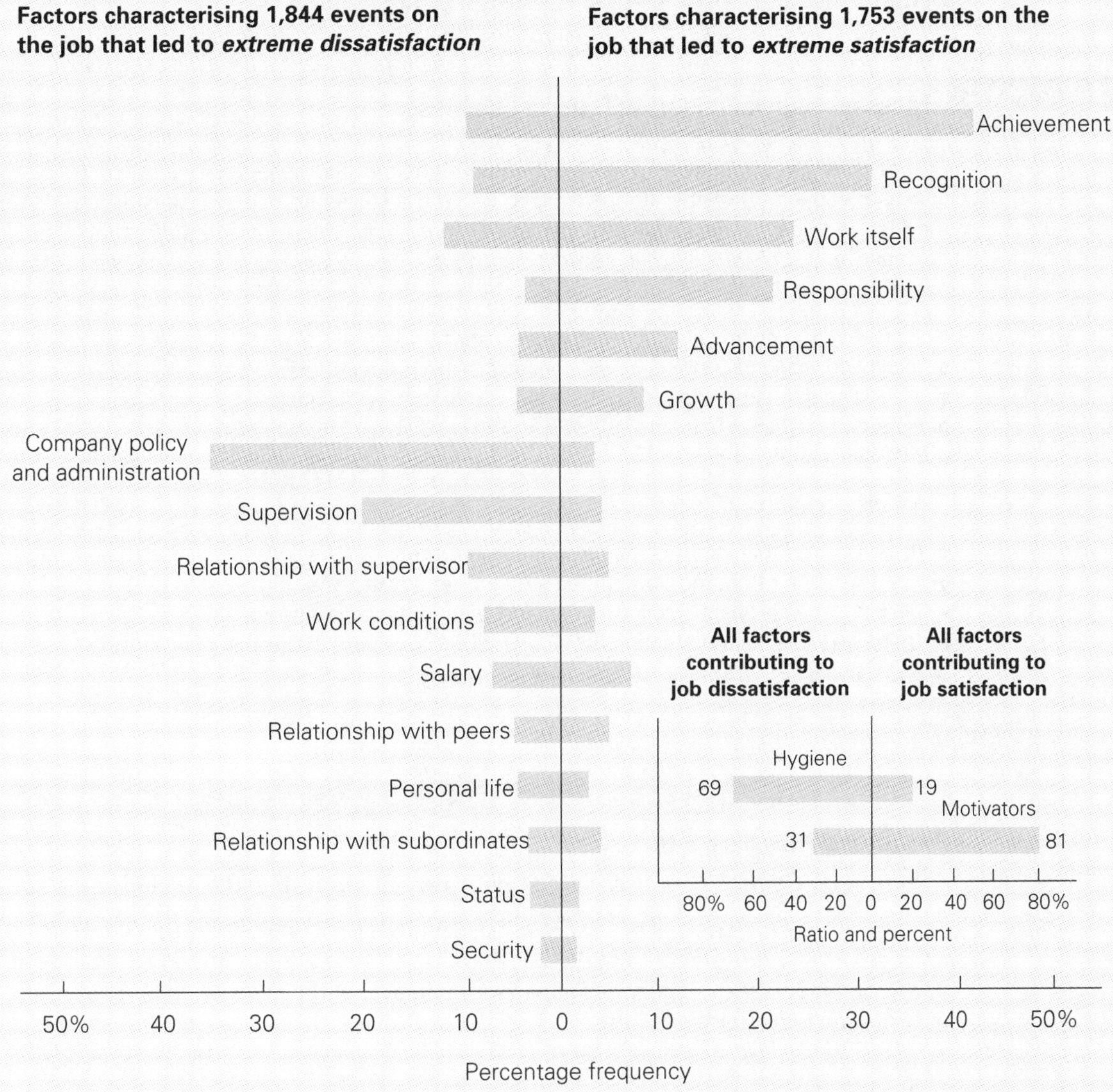

Factors characterising 1,844 events on the job that led to *extreme dissatisfaction*

Factors characterising 1,753 events on the job that led to *extreme satisfaction*

policy and administration, supervision, salary, interpersonal relations and working conditions) contribute little to job satisfaction. The factors that lead to job satisfaction (achievement, recognition, work itself, responsibility and advancement) contribute little to job dissatisfaction if they are absent.

Herzberg explained this by his observation that when respondents were feeling dissatisfied, this was because management had treated them unfairly. When they were satisfied it was because they were experiencing feelings of psychological growth and gaining a sense of self-actualisation. So the hygiene factors – an environment with fair policies – can prevent discontent and dissatisfaction but will not in itself contribute to psychological growth and hence satisfaction. Such positive feelings could only come, he argued, from the nature of the task itself, and the opportunities for growth that it offers. The Gamma Chemical story illustrates Herzberg's theory.

MANAGEMENT IN PRACTICE   **Focus on hygiene factors at Gamma Chemical**

Gamma Chemical purchased the site of another chemical company that had recently failed, and re-employed 30 of the 40 employees. While there was no overt dissatisfaction, during the first two years of ownership management found it hard to motivate staff. They showed no initiative or creativity, and no commitment to the new company or its goals. Yet the company had:

- increased the salaries of the re-employed staff;
- improved working conditions and provided better equipment;
- placed people in positions of equal status to their previous jobs;
- operated an 'Open Door' policy, with supervisors easily approachable;
- offered security of employment and a no-redundancy policy.

Other aspects of practice included:

- no structured training or development programmes;
- the small unit restricted opportunities for career advancement;
- people had little responsibility as management imposed decisions;
- there was no clear connection between individual work and company performance.

Source: Private communication and discussions with the manager.

ACTIVITY 13.5

Evaluating Herzberg's theory

Comment on Gamma Chemical's assumptions about motivating the re-engaged staff.

Evaluate the empirical base of Herzberg's research. What reservations do you have about the wider applicability of the theory?

Gather other evidence of changes in working practice, and decide whether it supports or contradicts Herzberg's theory.

There are many examples where management has redesigned people's jobs. Few if any were the result of knowing about Herzberg's theory, but their effects are often consistent with its predictions. Section 13.8 has more on this.

13.5   Management assumptions about people

Douglas McGregor

As a manager attempts to influence others he or she must make assumptions about how they will react to different incentives. These assumptions will guide the organisational arrangements they put in place. McGregor (1960) developed this idea in his book *The*

Human Side of Enterprise. In this he argued that 'every managerial act rests on assumptions, generalisations and hypotheses – that is to say, on theory' (p.6).

Such assumptions are often implicit and unconscious – but nevertheless shape managers' predictions that if they do a, then b will occur. The theories may or may not be adequate but it is impossible to reach a managerial decision, or take a managerial action, uninfluenced by them. 'The insistence on being "practical" really means "Let's accept *my* theoretical assumptions without argument or test"' (p.7).

McGregor went on to present two contrasting sets of assumptions underlying management policy and practice. *Theory X*, which he called the traditional view of direction and control, expresses the following assumptions:

- The average human being has an inherent dislike of work and will avoid it if at all possible.
- Because of this human characteristic, most people must be coerced, controlled, directed and/or threatened with punishment to get them to put forth adequate effort towards the achievement of organisational objectives.
- The average human being prefers to be directed, wishes to avoid responsibility, has relatively little ambition, wants security above all.

McGregor was critical of these assumptions. He believed that they led to a management strategy towards people which ignored the full range of possible human needs. Theory X assumptions concentrated on the lower-level needs that Maslow had identified. He believed that managers who accepted a Theory X view would fail to discover, let alone use, the potentialities of the average human being.

He then pointed out that accumulating knowledge about human behaviour made it possible to suggest a 'modest beginning for new theory about the management of human resources' (p.47). This he termed *Theory Y* – the integration of individual and organisational goals – which expressed a different set of assumptions:

- The expenditure of physical and mental effort in work is as natural as play or rest.
- External control and the threat of punishment are not the only means of bringing about effort towards organisational objectives. People will exercise self-direction and self-control in the service of objectives to which they are committed.
- Commitment to objectives is a function of the rewards associated with their achievement.
- The average human being learns, under proper conditions, not only to accept, but also to seek, responsibility.
- The capacity to exercise a relatively high degree of imagination, ingenuity and creativity in the solution of organisational problems is widely, not narrowly, distributed in the population.
- Under the conditions of modern industrial life the intellectual potentialities of the average human being are only partially utilised.

The contrasts between the two sets of assumptions are clear, as are the practical implications. Those who hold to Theory X believe that people dislike work, are lazy, unambitious, prefer to be directed and avoid responsibility. Work is secondary, so managers must coerce them with money or other extrinsic rewards. Common practices associated with a Theory X philosophy include time-recording systems, close supervision, quality checked by someone other than the person doing the work, narrowly defined jobs and precise job descriptions. The central principle of Theory X is that of external control, by systems, procedures or supervision.

The central principle of Theory Y is integration. It advocates 'the creation of conditions such that the members of the organisation can achieve their own goals *best* by directing their efforts towards the success of the enterprise' (p.49). Managers who hold to Theory Y believe that work is a natural activity that in the right conditions can provide great satisfaction – and see it as part of their job to create those conditions. They believe that people can accept responsibility, and apply imagination, ingenuity and creativity to organisational problems. McGregor argued that a problem of the modern organisation is that it does not tap the creative ability of its staff. To take advantage of these hidden assets managers should be more willing to provide employees with scope to use their talents. They should be less prescriptive and directive. They should create the conditions that integrate individual and organisational goals.

MANAGEMENT IN PRACTICE | **Motivating sales teams**

'I work as a sales manager for a medium-sized pharmaceutical company with a team of six. My role is to achieve maximum sales using the resources available. The company sets activity targets – "more calls mean more sales" is a favourite slogan. This produces a problem, as there are doctors who are readily available but who are unlikely to produce business: others are less available but have more potential. Do we follow the company strategy or do things the way our experience tells us will work better?

Management has structured the company on Theory X assumptions. We are told what we are expected to achieve, and how we are expected to achieve them. There are few opportunities for us to express a view. We meet the senior people about twice a year. The meetings usually have a rushed agenda, and seem to be a way of telling us what will happen rather than encouraging discussion on what should happen. They ask us to write two-monthly reports, but the points we raise seldom get a reply.

Another company in the industry is now taking a different approach. This involves each salesperson developing his or her business plan. They have considerably more autonomy to use their ideas. The trade-off is that the consequences of failure are more severe, and this will not suit everyone – it is a different psychological contract with which they are working. The curious thing is that that company had been very successful with an earlier approach, which was like ours. But the market is experiencing its biggest ever change, and shifting responsibility to salespeople who are in constant contact with customers has a considerable advantage.'

Source: Private communication and discussions with the manager.

ACTIVITY 13.6

Examples of Theory X and Theory Y

Write down the Theory X assumptions demonstrated in the first company in the motivating sales teams Management in Practice, and the Theory Y ones in the second.

Make a list of management practices that you have experienced which reflect the assumptions of Theory X and Theory Y respectively. What were their effects?

Can you identify someone who behaves in a way consistent with Theory X, and someone else who behaves according to Theory Y? Did this reflect the way they themselves were managed, or some other reason?

KEY
IDEAS **Lorsch and Morse, 'Beyond Theory Y '**

Although McGregor expressed the view that Theory Y assumptions were the most appropriate ones for effective management others have challenged this. They argue that Theory Y assumptions may be as inappropriate in some circumstances as Theory X assumptions are in others. Morse and Lorsch (1970) first raised this prospect following their comparative study of management practices in four companies.

Two were in routine operations, at which one was successful and one was not. The other two were in highly creative businesses, and again one was successful, the other not. They concluded that the successful company in the routine business used a consistent Theory X style. The successful company in the creative business used a consistent Theory Y style.

13.6 Individual and national differences

The patterns of needs differ significantly between people, and any attempt to understand motivation must take account of this. The relative importance of a need is likely to change over time as people's commitments and interests change. Young people or those with high-earning partners give security a low priority. People rate it more highly as they take on mortgage or family commitments. People also experience conflict between their needs. For example, a need for security because of family circumstances may challenge a need for recognition that could imply a risky job change or a move to another town.

People also vary in how they translate their needs into work behaviour. For example, one person with a high need for responsibility or advancement may satisfy it by seeking a transfer to a different department. Another may decide to move to a different type of work. How do people react when they fail to satisfy a need? Do they try harder or give up?

A final point of growing significance in the international business world is that the theories outlined were all developed in the United States. Do they apply to people working in other countries?

Hofstede (1989) articulated what he believed were the 'unspoken cultural assumptions' present in both Theory X and Theory Y. He writes:

in a comparative study of US values versus those dominant in ASEAN countries, I found the following common assumptions on the US side and underlying both X and Y:

1 Work is good for people.
2 People's capacities should be maximally utilised.
3 There are 'organisational objectives' that exist apart from people.
4 People in organisations behave as unattached individuals.

These assumptions reflect value positions in McGregor's US society; most would be accepted in other western countries. None of them, however, applies in ASEAN countries. Southeast Asian assumptions would be:

1 Work is a necessity but not a goal in itself.
2 People should find their rightful place in peace and harmony with their environment.
3 Absolute objectives exist only with God. In the world, persons in authority positions represent God so their objectives should be followed.
4 People behave as members of a family and/or group. Those who do not are rejected by society.

Because of these different culturally determined assumptions, McGregor's Theory X and Theory Y distinction becomes irrelevant in Southeast Asia. (p.5)

Hofstede's work that was presented in Chapter 4 showed marked differences in national cultures. These are likely to influence the relative importance that people in those countries attach to the various motivational factors. People in Anglo-Saxon countries tend to display a relatively high need for achievement, strong masculinity scores and low uncertainty avoidance. This is not the norm in other cultures. Harris and Moran (1991) also suggest that cultures emphasise different life goals, and contrast East Asian with western cultures. This implies people will attach different importance to motivational factors.

KEY IDEAS   **Prevailing cultural norms and beliefs**

East Asia	*Western*
Equity	Wealth
Group	Individual
Saving	Consumption
Extended family relations	Nuclear and mobile family
Highly disciplined and motivated	Decline in work ethic and hierarchy
Protocol, rank, status	Informality and personal competence
Avoid conflict	Conflict to be managed

Source: Harris and Moran (1991).

13.7 Process theories of motivation

Process theories try to explain why people choose one course of action towards satisfying a need rather than another. A person who needs a higher income could satisfy it by, say, moving to another company, applying for promotion or investing in training. What factors will influence their choice?

Expectancy theory

Vroom (1964) developed one attempt to answer that question with what he termed the expectancy theory of motivation. It focuses on the thinking processes people use to achieve rewards. Stuart Roberts is studying a degree course in Chemistry and has to submit a last assignment. He wants an A for the course, and so far has an average of B+. His motivation to put effort into the assignment will be affected by (a) his expectation that hard work will produce a good piece of work, and (b) his expectation that it will receive a grade of at least an A. If he believes he cannot do a good job, or that the grading system is unclear, then his motivation will be low.

The theory assumes that individuals:

- have different needs and so value outcomes differently;
- make conscious choices about which course of action to follow;
- choose between alternative actions based on the likelihood of an action resulting in an outcome they value.

There are, then, three main components in expectancy theory. First, the person's expectation (or **subjective probability**) that effort (E) will result in some level of performance (P):

$$(E \rightarrow P)$$

This will be affected by how clear they are about their roles, the training available, whether the necessary support will be provided and similar factors. If Stuart Roberts understands what the assignment requires and is confident in his ability to do a good job, his (E → P) expectancy will be high.

The second component is the person's expectation that performance will lead to a particular outcome (O):

$$(P \rightarrow O)$$

This will be affected by how confident the person is that achieving a target will produce a reward. This reflects factors such as the clarity of the organisation's appraisal and payment systems and previous experience of them. A clear grading system, which Stuart understands and knows that staff apply consistently, will mean he has a high (P → O) expectancy. If he has found the system unpredictable this expectancy would be lower.

The third component is the valence that the individual attaches to a particular outcome:

$$(V)$$

This term is best understood as the power of the outcome to motivate that individual – how keen Roberts is to get a good degree. It introduces the belief that people differ in the value they place on different kinds of reward. So the value of V varies between individuals, reflecting their unique pattern of motivational needs (as suggested by the content theories). Someone who values money and achievement would place a high valence on an outcome that was a promotion to a distant head office. He or she would try to work in a way which led to that. Such an outcome would be much less welcome (have a much lower valence) to a manager who values an established pattern of relationships or quality of life in the present location.

In summary:

$$F = (E \rightarrow P) \times (P \rightarrow O) \times V$$

in which F represents the force exerted, or degree of motivation a person has towards an activity. Two beliefs will influence that motivation, namely the expectation that:

- making the effort will lead to performance (E → P)
- that level of performance will lead to an outcome they value (P → O).

Adjusting these beliefs for valence – how desirable the outcome is to the person – gives a measure of their motivation. The beliefs that people hold reflect their personality and their experience of organisational practices, as shown in Figure 13.6.

The use of the multiplication sign in the equation signifies that both beliefs influence motivation. If a person believes that however hard they try they will be unable to perform to a required standard then they will not be motivated to do so (so E → P = 0). The same applies for (P → O). A low score in either of these two parts of the equation, or in V, will lead to low effort, regardless of beliefs about the other part.

A criticism of the theory is that it implies a high level of rational calculation, as people weigh the probabilities of various courses of action. It also implies that managers estimate what each employee values, and try to ensure that motivational practices meet them. Neither calculation is likely to be made that rationally, which may diminish the model's practical value.

Figure 13.6 Influence of organisational practices on subjective probabilities

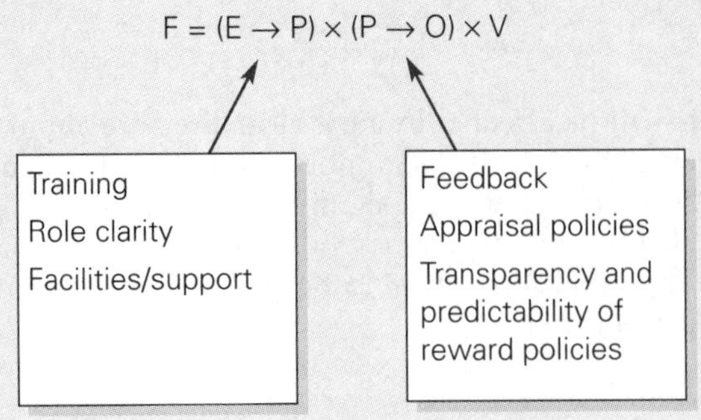

$$F = (E \rightarrow P) \times (P \rightarrow O) \times V$$

Training
Role clarity
Facilities/support

Feedback
Appraisal policies
Transparency and predictability of reward policies

However, the model is useful in recognising that people vary in their beliefs (or probabilities) about the components in the equation. It shows that managers can affect these beliefs by redesigning the factors in Figure 13.6. If people are unclear about their role, or receive weak feedback, the theory predicts that this will reduce their motivation.

MANAGEMENT IN PRACTICE   **Hindle Power**

In 2000 this family-owned engineering company employed 50 people, selling and servicing Perkins engines in the east of England. In 1996 Perkins told all its distributors that they would need to meet tougher customer service targets, or lose their contracts. Graham Hughes, Hindle's general manager, realised that long-term change would not occur unless people were trained to do their jobs better. Staff were given considerable scope in setting their own training needs. A new appraisal system was designed to help people clarify their career goals and request training to achieve them. The company's training manager Steve Widdrington believes the appraisal system encourages people to stretch themselves, rather than looking back and focusing on past results: 'People are taking more responsibility. I believe that works when you give staff the chance to develop.'

In 1996 the company was losing money on a turnover of £6 million. In 1999 it was profitable and hoped to turnover £15 million in 2000: 'Rarely has the link between training and the bottom line been so clear.'

Source: *People Management*, 3 February 2000, pp.52–3.

As at Hindle Power, managers can influence motivation by practical actions such as:

- establishing the rewards people value;
- identifying and communicating performance requirements;
- ensuring that reasonable effort can meet those requirements;
- providing facilities to support the person's effort;
- ensuring a clear link between performance and reward;
- providing feedback to staff on how well they are meeting performance requirements.

The theory links insights from the content theories of motivation with organisational practice.

Equity theory

Equity theory introduces the idea of fairness in comparison with others as an influence on a person's motivation (Vecchio, 1984). The argument is that people like to be treated fairly. They compare what they put into a job (effort, skill, knowledge, etc.) with the rewards they receive (pay, recognition, satisfaction, etc.). They express this as a ratio of their input to their reward. They also compare their ratio with the input-to-reward ratio of others whom they consider their equals. They expect management to reward others in the same way, so expect the ratios to be roughly equal. The formula below sums up the comparison:

$$\frac{\text{Input (A)}}{\text{Reward (A)}} : \frac{\text{Input (B)}}{\text{Reward (B)}}$$

Person A compares the ratio of her input to her reward to that of B. If the ratios are similar she will be satisfied with the treatment received. If she believes the ratio is lower than that of other people she will feel inequitably treated and be dissatisfied.

The theory also predicts that if people feel unfairly treated they will experience tension and dissatisfaction. They will try to reduce this by one or more of these means:

- reducing their inputs, by putting in less effort or withholding good ideas and suggestions;
- attempting to increase their outcomes, by pressing for increased pay or other benefits;
- attempting to decrease other people's outcomes by generating conflict or withholding information and help;
- changing the basis of their comparison, by making it against someone else where the inequity is less pronounced;
- increasing their evaluation of the other person's output so the ratios are in balance.

Q **Case questions 13.4**

- What evidence was there at the Benefits Agency of perceived inequity?
- How did people react?

As individuals differ, so will their way of reducing inequity. Some will try to rationalise the situation, suggesting that their efforts were greater or lesser than they originally thought them to be, or that the rewards are reasonable. For example, a person denied a promotion may decide that the previously desired job would not have been so advantageous after all. Members may put pressure on other members of the team whom they feel are not pulling their weight. Some may choose to do less, so bringing their ratio into line with that of other staff.

Clearly the focus and the components of the comparisons are highly subjective, although the theory has an intuitive appeal. There is plenty of anecdotal evidence of people comparing their own effort/reward ratio with that of other people or groups.

13.8 Motivation as a form of social influence

People value both extrinsic and intrinsic rewards. Extrinsic rewards are those that are separate from the performance of the task, such as pay, security and promotion possibilities. Intrinsic rewards are those that people receive from the performance of the task itself – the use of skills, a sense of achievement, work that is in itself satisfying to do. Recall that a central element in Frederick Taylor's doctrine of scientific management was the careful design of the 'one best way' of doing a piece of manual work. Experts carefully analysed how people did the job and identified the most efficient set of tasks, usually by breaking down the task into many small parts. Such work provided few if any intrinsic rewards – and Taylor's system concentrated on providing clear extrinsic rewards.

A problem with Taylor's approach was that jobs which are broken into small parts are boring to many people, making them dissatisfied, careless and frequently absent. As these limitations became clear managers looked for ways to make jobs more intrinsically rewarding – so that the work itself brought a reward of interest or challenge. The work of writers such as Maslow, Herzberg and McGregor prompted many experiments aimed at increasing the opportunities for people to satisfy their 'higher' needs at work. The idea was that staff would work more productively if management offered intrinsic rewards (motivators in Herzberg's terms) as well as extrinsic ones (Herzberg's hygiene factors). A series of research projects indicated the potential of this approach, and led to the development of the **job enrichment model**.

Job enrichment model

The job enrichment model formulated by Hackman and Oldham (1980) extended the work of earlier motivation theorists by proposing that managers could change specific job characteristics to motivate employees and promote job satisfaction. Doing so would enable staff to satisfy more of their higher-level needs and so lead to greater motivation and performance.

The model identifies three critical *psychological states* that must be present to achieve high motivation. If any are low, motivation will be low. The three states are:

- Experienced meaningfulness – the degree to which employees perceive their work as valuable and worthwhile. If workers regard a job as trivial and pointless, their motivation will be low.
- Experienced responsibility – how responsible people feel for the quantity and quality of work performed.
- Knowledge of results – the amount of feedback employees receive about how well they are doing the job. Those who do not receive feedback will care less about the quality of their performance.

These psychological states are influenced by five key *job characteristics* that contribute to experienced meaningfulness of work:

- Skill variety – the extent to which a job makes use of a range of skills and experience. A routine administrative job is low in variety, whereas that of a marketing or customer support assistant is likely to require a wide variety of analytical and interpersonal skills.
- Task identity – whether a job involves a complete operation, with a recognisable beginning and end. A nurse who organises and oversees all the treatments for a hospital patient has more task identity than one who provides a single treatment to many different patients.
- Task significance – how much the job matters to others in the organisation or to the wider society. People who can see that their job contributes directly to performance, or which is a major help to others, will feel they have a significant task.

- Autonomy – how much freedom and independence a person has in deciding how to go about doing the work. A sales agent in a call centre following a tightly scripted (and recorded) conversation with a potential customer has much less autonomy than a sales agent talking face to face to a customer.
- Feedback – the extent to which a person receives feedback on relevant dimensions of performance. Modern manufacturing systems can provide operators with very rapid information on quality, scrap, material use and costs. Operators can then receive a high level of feedback on the results of their work. Staff redesigning a product will have to wait much longer before they find out if their design meets customer needs.

The extent to which a job contains these elements can be calculated using a tested instrument, and then using the scores obtained to calculate the *motivating potential* score for the job. The model is presented schematically in Figure 13.7.

The model also shows how management (or staff) can increase the motivating potential of jobs by using five implementing concepts:

- *Combine tasks* Rather than divide the work up into small pieces, as Taylor recommended, staff can combine them so they use more skills and complete more of the

Figure 13.7 The job characteristics model

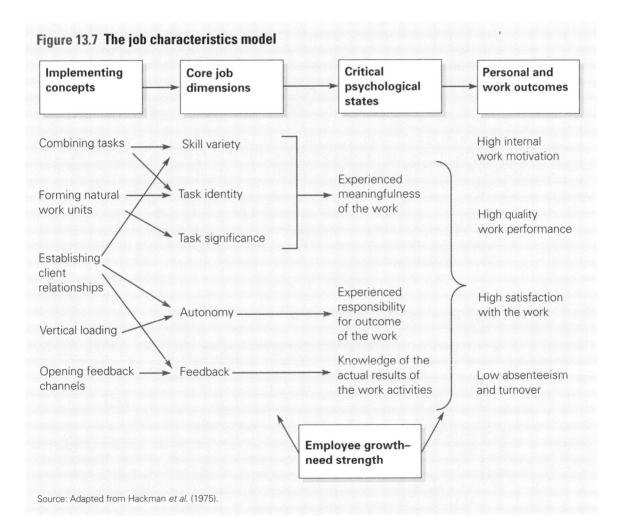

Source: Adapted from Hackman *et al.* (1975).

whole task. An order clerk could receive orders from a customer and arrange transport and invoicing instead of having these done by different people.

● *Form natural workgroups* In order to give more responsibility and enable sharing of skills, groups could be created that carry out a complete operation. Instead of a product passing down an assembly line, with each worker performing one operation, a group may assemble the whole product, sharing out the tasks amongst themselves.

● *Establish customer relations* This would bring home to employees the expectations of the people to whom their work goes, whether inside or outside the organisation, enabling them to see how their job fits into the larger picture. Instead of people doing part of the job for all customers they can look after all the requirements of some customers. They establish closer relationships and gain a better understanding of their customers' needs.

● *Vertical loading* This involves workers taking on some responsibilities of supervisors to solve problems and develop workable solutions, thus adding to their autonomy. Operators may be given responsibility for checking the quantity and quality of incoming materials and reporting any problems. They may use more discretion over the order in which they arrange a week's work.

● *Open feedback channels* This would ensure that people receive feedback on their performance from internal or external customers. Operators can attend meetings at which customers give their views on the service provided as a basis for improving performance and building client relationships. This is not only for problem areas – public recognition of achievement contributes to a positive psychological state and improved performance and satisfaction.

The last feature of the Hackman–Oldham model is growth–need strength, that is, the extent to which an individual desires personal challenges, accomplishment and learning on the job. Some employees may want jobs that satisfy only their lower-level needs but others want more from their job. Individuals with high needs for challenge, growth and creativity are more likely to respond positively to job enrichment programmes. If an individual's growth needs are low, attempts at job enrichment may cause resentment.

Since different individuals have different needs, they respond to the same job in different ways. A job that satisfies one may dissatisfy another. The job enrichment model takes this into account by showing that the strength of a person's need for growth moderates the relationship of job characteristics to performance and/or satisfaction.

Many managers, such as those at Gamma Chemical, have changed the kind of work they expect employees to do.

MANAGEMENT IN PRACTICE **Changing work at Gamma Chemical**

Some two years after taking control Gamma Chemical had made these changes to working arrangements:

● introduced a cross-training programme to improve job diversity and individual growth;
● created problem-solving teams from natural work units to give operators a sense of ownership and achievement;
● expected operators to make more decisions, increasing individual authority and accountability;
● an appraisal system that shows operators how their function affects company performance.

Management believed these changes had resulted in 20 per cent more output and 50 per cent less wastage.

Source: Private communication and discussions with the manager.

Managers have not usually introduced changes such as these to provide more interesting jobs for staff. They have usually been a response to more demanding business conditions and a need to cut costs and increase responsiveness. They can do this if more junior staff do a wider range of tasks, often beginning to work as a team that is jointly responsible for an area of work. Nevertheless the results of such changes often support what the theory predicts. Another approach is to give staff more responsibility for decisions, without referring to supervisors above them in the hierarchy. This is usually called empowerment.

13.9 Empowerment

People use the term 'empowerment' to refer to a wide range of practices that give more responsibility to less senior staff. Clutterbuck (1994) concluded that the common features of such approaches are that they are intended to help people to take more control of their job and working environment, and enhance the contributions they make as individuals and members of a team. They also provide opportunities for personal growth and self-fulfilment. Advocates of empowerment claim several advantages, including:

- Quicker responses to customer queries, since answers can be given or decisions made by staff over issues they previously had to refer to a more senior manager.
- Employees feel more satisfied as they are doing more responsible work and developing new skills.
- Employees welcome the chance to deal more intensely with customers.
- This in turn can encourage employees to come up with more practical ideas for service improvement than managers who are less directly involved with customers.
- The improved service builds customer loyalty and repeat business.

Such advantages in themselves are persuasive to managers and many have introduced programmes with the stated aim of empowering employees. Bowen and Lawler (1992) define empowerment in terms of the degree to which four ingredients of the organisation are shared with front-line employees:

- information about the organisation's performance;
- rewards based on the organisation's performance;
- knowledge that enables employees to understand and contribute to organisational performance;
- power to make decisions that influence organisational direction and performance.

They argue that the extent to which these are present distinguishes the degree of empowerment employees have. If they remain at the top of the organisation management still exercises fairly direct control. If they are pushed down the organisation so that front-line employees have more information and more power to make decisions, then this indicates that management is trying to adopt an empowering approach. The more that staff exercise self-control and self-direction, the more they are empowered.

Empowering nurses at Western General Hospital

A nurse manager at the Western General Hospital in a large city commented on the empowerment of nurses at the hospital, which had arisen from a variety of internal and external factors.

Many changes in the service stem from the 1989 White Paper *Working for Patients*, which aimed to make the health service more responsive to the needs of patients by delegating power and responsibility to local level. Other external factors have probably unintentionally contributed to empowerment as a means of motivation:

- a clinical grading review changed pay and grading structures and brought with it extra responsibilities;
- professional bodies have dictated changes in clinical practice, requiring nurses to extend the scope of their work and be more accountable for the care they deliver.

Nurses have recognised the benefits to patients if nurses were to carry out their work by patient allocation rather than by task allocation. This has developed into the 'named nurse' concept, which intriguingly incorporates four of the five core dimensions of the job characteristics model. The nurse assesses needs, plans, implements and evaluates the care of his or her patients, so having skill variety, task identity, task significance and autonomy. Perhaps even the feedback element is provided from the evaluation stage of each patient's care. In addition to the external factors, changes within the hospital had an effect:

- a layer has been removed from the nursing hierarchy;
- there have been staff changes at nurse manager level, and the new managers have a different style from their predecessors.

The empowerment approach fits with the organisation's unpredictable environment, the individualised service relationship and staff needs and characteristics. The recently appointed nurse managers are enthusiastic, and this has filtered down to staff. They are gradually becoming aware of the move from Theory X to Theory Y style of management. They appreciate that at last their skills and experience are being recognised and used.

Information flows more freely and openly. Decisions are made only after discussion with the staff who will be affected by the outcome. Nurses in the wards are aware of their allocated budgets and what they are spending. Recruitment of staff is now done by existing staff on the ward, where previously managers decided whom to appoint.

Source: Private communication from a senior nurse in the hospital.

Bowen and Lawler go on to suggest a model of levels of empowerment. At one extreme management takes a control orientation towards staff, while at the other extreme it takes an involvement orientation. Figure 13.8 summarises the range of options, and those embodying some degree of empowerment are described below:

- *Suggestion involvement* – staff are encouraged to submit ideas to improve ways of working and are rewarded for doing so. Control remains with management, which chooses whether or not to accept an idea.
- *Job involvement* – staff are able to develop and use more skills, have greater autonomy and receive more feedback. Supervisors' jobs change from direction to support.
- *High involvement* – occurs when organisations give their lowest-level employees a sense of involvement in the total organisation's performance. All of the four ingredients listed on page 413 are designed to support that condition.

Figure 13.8 Levels of empowerment

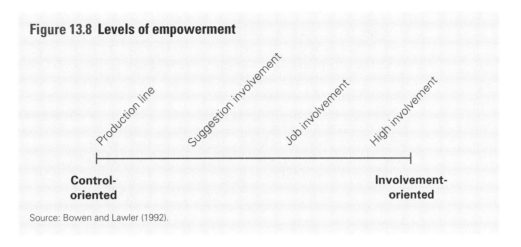

Source: Bowen and Lawler (1992).

As with the redesign of jobs, managers do not often empower people to enhance job satisfaction. It is often a response to external requirements, or a need to improve quality and reduce costs. A local authority made significant changes to the way it provided housing services, of which the most visible was a shift from a city-wide to a neighbourhood service. This was intended to provide a better and more responsive service to tenants. The change also allowed the authority to rearrange work so that staff performed duties previously done by other professions. At the same time, empowering more junior staff to take more decisions meant that fewer senior staff were required. To have presented the exercise as one in cost cutting would have provoked resistance. Presenting it as an exercise in tenant and staff empowerment helped to ensure acceptance.

The process is not without difficulties, which have included:

● the usual problems of introducing any significant change (see Chapter 11);
● resistance from some staff who value familiar ways, which give certainty and predictability to their working lives;
● resistance from middle managers who fear losing parts of their role (Ezzamel *et al.* 1994);
● the risks of losing control (Simons, 1995).

So, empowerment is a shifting balance, reflecting a variety of forces. As the term makes clear, it is also about power and is bound to be controversial. This may imply redistributing power from an over-concentration at the centre of the organisation. Alternatively, management may remove the constraints that prevent people using the power which they already have, for example through their knowledge of customers or processes.

3.10 Work and careers in a time of change

Major forces such as globalisation, deregulation, privatisation, developments in information technology, as well as changing lifestyles, have major implications for understanding motivation at work. These forces mean that the expectations of both organisations and people keep changing, implying that new kinds of psychological contract will be emerging.

The organisational world that McGregor and Herzberg observed was a place of large manufacturing organisations operating in relatively stable markets. Western organisations and values dominated the business world, natural resources seemed plentiful, and computers were novelties. In 1969 at least one major bank still kept customer records in handwritten books. Today the same company offers banking services on the Internet. Most employees were men, worked full time until retirement, and expected to stay with the same employer for many years – often for most of their career. All these features have changed, and will continue to do so.

Many organisations are operating in global markets and face severe competition, not only on price but also on quality, innovation, responsiveness. Most employees work in service occupations, where the quality of interpersonal interaction with the customer is an important part of the transaction. Information technology is having dramatic effects on the availability of information. This affects both organisational structures and what people delivering goods or services are expected to do. Another change is that many organisations employ other firms to provide functions that their own staff previously performed.

Many who joined the public sector find that their organisation has been sold to the private sector. This usually requires managers and staff to work in a radically different way if they want to keep their jobs. Those who remain in the public sector face new pressures (Flynn, 1997). They are more likely to face conflicts with members of the public who know their entitlements and are willing to argue for them. At the same time local and national governments require staff to work within tight budgets. They probably need to work more closely with private sector agencies that provide many services previously provided internally, and manage the shifting balance between central control and local autonomy. The psychological contract for many is very different from the ethos of public service prevailing when they joined. Then, many who joined the service may have been motivated by a sense of service to other people and of doing some good. This is quite different from being motivated by the prospect of making a profit and receiving some personal financial benefit.

CASE STUDY   The Benefits Agency – the case continues – further change

In 1998 another chief executive was appointed. The move towards tighter central control continued but lessons had been learnt. The Agency's senior management recognised that many improvements in service delivery had come from ideas generated by committed individuals with flair and imagination. There was no desire to lose this by going back to the strong command and control approach – but there had to be a balance between innovation and accountability. The Agency continued to encourage innovation but introduced a process to evaluate each idea against business objectives.

On 16 March 2000 the prime minister announced far-reaching reforms to the way the government provides services to people looking for work and claiming benefits. A new Agency, Jobcentre Plus, would be created to combine the Employment Service and those parts of the Benefits Agency dealing with people of working age. This agency will deliver a single, work-focused, integrated service to employers and benefit claimants – helping people into work and helping employers fill their vacancies.

Although the agency is new, the people working in it will transfer from the existing agencies. This means bringing together management and staff of two separate agencies. People who have been used to different cultures, values, personnel policies, pay and promotion structures and management styles will now be working together to create the new organisation. The need to establish common values has been identified by the chief executive of the new agency:

Both the Benefits Agency and the Employment Service have such values which they have introduced successfully over recent years. But Jobcentre Plus is a new organisation, with different objectives, and we need to build a new set of values to reflect its priorities and interests, and the aspirations of its staff and partners.

This is probably the biggest change that staff in both agencies have encountered. The problem for managers in trying to motivate staff in this changing climate is immense. Staff are uncertain of the future – will the nature of the work change, will new skills be required, will there be job losses, will the staff from one agency be more valued than the other, are all the previous values worth nothing?

Organisations are less likely to offer long-term or full-time careers. Competition is used to justify keeping staff costs low by minimising the number of regular jobs on offer and meeting extra demand by employing temporary or casual staff. Work is increasingly part time, done at what used to be regarded as unsociable hours. Standard procedures often structure the work processes tightly to fit the requirements of information systems that link all parts of the organisation. At the same time staff are expected to work together co-operatively in teams and build good relationships with customers. They must follow procedures, but also use their imagination and initiative as required to solve unusual problems.

People have different expectations of their organisations either because of wider social trends or in response to what organisations themselves are doing. As many women as men are in paid employment; both have to manage 'dual careers' in conjunction with family commitments, particularly the care of young children and elderly relatives.

MANAGEMENT IN PRACTICE How Littlewoods offers a work–life balance

Barry Gibson, Group Chief Executive of Littlewoods, a UK retail business:

Many employees have responsibilities for young children or elderly parents that conflict with responsibilities at work. Life is about much more than work ... Companies that support the work/life balance of their employees gain a committed and innovative workforce, which then provides a better service than their competitors. At Littlewoods we have found that the highest quality contributions have come from employees who feel they have real balance in their lives. We have worked hard to develop policies that are family friendly. Flexible working is a business reality for us. Sixty-two per cent of our employees work flexibly. Wherever it is operationally possible, people work part time, reduced hours, job share and work from home. It is essential to review your employees' needs regularly. Employee surveys provide good feedback. On the basis of our surveys we have introduced childcare information services in all of our business units, regular holiday play schemes for the children of employees in some areas, a pre- and post-school club and subsidised places at a nursery. But making such policies work in practice can only be achieved by regular top-level commitment. Our executive board formally discusses equal opportunities each quarter and twice a year we have a strategy committee to consider the issues.

Source: *Management Today*, October 1999, p.14.

More people are setting up their own business rather than work for an employer, although it is unclear whether this is from genuine preference or the lack of an alternative. It does mean that more employment is now in small organisations.

People differ in their commitment to work as a full-time career and expect very different things from an organisation. Work is central for many, but not for everyone, especially as the hours of work and the length of working life decline. Many do not expect self-fulfilment from their work. They seek it instead through a hobby, through social activities or perhaps by running a pressure group. New generations seek different things from life and from work, and many are less committed to conventional work patterns. Identifying the rewards that people seek from their work has always been a matter of intelligent guesswork and inference. It is likely to become more so as people come to expect more diverse rewards from fulfilling their side of the psychological contract.

Hiltrop (1995) reviewed the changes taking place in the psychological contract as both organisations and people change their expectations. Elements of the new contract include:

- Organisations are becoming more demanding places in which to work.
- The paternalism of earlier times, in which both sides expected a long-term career together, is gone.
- Roles and responsibilities are much more fluid and ambiguous.
- Increasingly, companies expect people to contribute their skills through specific, short-term tasks, not through long-term employment. In order to maintain their income people need to plan their development and careers, and build their reputation.
- Security, income and status derived from an employer are less available, implying people need to develop other sources of psychological reassurance.
- Opportunities to improve employability (by movement to another project) are more likely to be the reward for good work than promotion.
- People are increasingly paid on the basis of contribution rather than level or status.

Table 13.3 presents Hiltrop's summary of the main characteristics of the old and new psychological contracts.

Table 13.3 Changing psychological contracts

Characteristic	Old	New
Focus	Security	Employability
Format	Structured	Flexible
Duration	Permanent	Variable
Scope	Broad	Narrow
Underlying principle	Tradition	Market forces
Intended output	Loyalty and commitment	Value added
Employer's key responsibility	Fair pay for good work	High pay for high performance
Employee's key responsibility	Good performance in present job	Making a difference
Employer's key input	Stable income and career advancement	Opportunities for self-development
Employee's key input	Time and effort	Knowledge and skills

Source: Hiltrop (1995).

13.11 **Summary**

Management assumptions about other people have a fundamental effect on how they go about their role. The chapter has reviewed evidence that can guide management in the task of generating the commitment of others to behave in particular ways. Central to this is the idea of the psychological contract, representing both sides' perceptions of the fairness of the evolving relationship.

Content

The chapter showed that early approaches of Taylor and the scientific management approach assumed that people would do what was required in return for financial or other extrinsic rewards. This was a reasonable assumption in the context of the economic and social context in which these theories were developed. Later theories stressed the value of meeting people's social needs. Still later theories have shown the full complexity of people's needs and the fact that different needs will become dominant at different times, or as other needs are blocked. They have added the further complexity of not seeing the employee as an isolated individual but as someone with responsibilities and commitments outside work. This has encouraged more managements to devise approaches to motivation that are family friendly and promote work–life balance.

In many modern organisations management now tries to secure people's commitment to the goals of the organisation as a way of securing their willing and flexible co-operation. They seek to integrate individual and organisational needs so that people use their talents to benefit the organisation without constant direction by management. Research also suggests that jobs designed in a way that meets human needs are more likely to help meet organisational objectives than jobs which ignore human needs.

Process

As individual stakeholders in the organisation employees will have different and variable needs, and can to some degree exercise choice in how they react to influence attempts. The degree of choice will, however, be constrained by the relative power of the parties. There is evidence that many employees are able and willing to contribute more fully to the management activities of the enterprise. Managers with Theory Y assumptions will offer employees opportunities to take part in wider roles where they can learn to exercise more responsibility. Hence, greater involvement in decisions beyond the day to day may foster commitment by meeting higher-level needs for autonomy and decision taking. Unless management communicates with employees it cannot know their views and possible contributions.

Control

How management deals with control reflects their fundamental Theory X or Y assumptions – the former emphasising external control, the latter internal or self-control. The control process also affects the results of attempts at behaviour modification. The belief that people have in the probability of alternative outcomes is influenced by decisions by the control system – for example how managers use performance evaluation systems. High performance probably depends more on encouraging internal commitment from people than on imposing external control.

These dilemmas are still being worked out at the Benefits Agency. Some staff did not welcome the move from a stable Civil Service culture and left the agency – others took to the new approach with enthusiasm. That involved some risks to the organisation – if staff can use more initiative there is also a risk of inconsistency between claimants, which then leads to political questions at a higher level. Now the staff face a new change, and managers face a new set of motivational challenges.

> **Q PART QUESTIONS**
>
> - Which theories of human needs appear to be supported by the reported policies and attitudes at W.L. Gore and Associates?
> - What similarities and contrasts are there between the motivational practices at W.L. Gore and Associates and at the Benefits Agency?
> - In what ways are the associates at Gore empowered?

3.12 Review questions

1 Outline the idea of the psychological contract. What are you expecting (a) from a future employer in your career; (b) from an employer who provides you with part-time work while you are studying?

2 What are the three things that are pinpointed when using behaviour modification?

3 How does Maslow's theory of human needs relate to the ideas of (a) Frederick Taylor and (b) Elton Mayo and the human relations movement?

4 How does Alderfer's theory differ from Maslow's? What research lay behind the two theories?

5 How did you score on the McClelland test? How did your scores compare with those of your fellow students?

6 Explain the difference between Herzberg's hygiene and motivating factors. Give at least three examples of each.

7 Explain the difference between E $\rightarrow$ P and P $\rightarrow$ O in expectancy theory.

8 Outline the basic assumptions of Theories X and Y that Douglas McGregor used to characterise alternative ways in which managements view their workers. List three management practices associated with each.

9 What are the five job design elements that are expected to affect people's satisfaction with their work?

10 Give an example of an implementing concept associated with each element.

Further reading

Roethlisberger, F.J. and Dickson, W.J. (1939), *Management and the Worker*, Harvard University Press, Cambridge, MA.

Herzberg, F. (1959), *The Motivation to Work*, Wiley, New York.

McGregor, D. (1960), *The Human Side of Enterprise*, McGraw-Hill, New York.

Maslow, A. (1970), *Motivation and Personality* (2nd edn), Harper & Row, New York.

The original accounts of these influential works are unusually readable books showing organisations and research in action. Roethlisberger and Dickson's (1939) account of the Hawthorne experiments is long, but the others are short and accessible.

Clutterbuck, D. and Dearlove, D. (1996), *The Charity as a Business*, Directory of Social Change, London. For those interested in management in the voluntary sector and charities, this has chapters on motivation and leadership in such organisations.

Brown, R. (ed.) (1997), *The Changing Shape of Work*, Macmillan, London. A selection of papers on current trends and changes in the labour market.

Heil, G., Bennis, W. and stephens, D.C. (2000), *Douglas McGregor Revisited*, Wiley, New York. A review of McGregor's ideas, which the authors argue are more in tune with modern organisational needs than when he wrote *The Human Side of Enterprise* in 1960.

Annotated links, questions and resources can be found on
www.booksites.net/boddy

CHAPTER 14

Communication

AIM *To show how management can shape communication processes in ways that help or hinder organisational performance.*

OBJECTIVES

By the end of your work on this chapter you should be able to outline the concepts below in your own terms and:

1 Identify and illustrate each major link in the communication process

2 Explain the difference between informal and formal communication

3 Compare the advantages and disadvantages of spoken, written and non-verbal communication

4 Compare the suitability of different forms of interpersonal communication for different types of task

5 Use the concept of media richness to decide which communication medium to use for specified purposes

6 Compare the main features of a formal communication system

7 Describe how new technologies such as computer networks, video-conferencing and groupware are affecting organisational communication

8 Identify and describe the main barriers to communication in organisations

An ambulance service

This public organisation provides an accident and emergency (A&E) service at all times, and a daytime patient transfer service (PTS). This case deals with a major communication change introduced into the A&E service in 1995.

The system for handling an A&E call was typically as follows. When a member of the public dialled 999 to request an ambulance the call was transferred by the operator to the nearest ambulance service control room. A control assistant wrote down details of the incident, especially its location and the condition of the patient, and passed these to the control officer who reviewed the status of the available ambulances and decided which one should deal with the incident. The officer spoke by radio to the crew, who acknowledged the call and went to deal with the incident. The crew would usually update the control room as they arrived at and left the incident. This enabled the control officer to plan their schedule and to inform a hospital of the case being taken to them. When the crew had delivered the casualty to a hospital they informed the control room of their status and position.

The job of the control staff was very stressful, as they would be dealing with several emergency calls at any time with a fixed number of available ambulances. Callers were often distressed and frustrated at any delay in an ambulance reaching the scene.

As part of the drive to save money management decided to reduce the number of control rooms. These were expensive to operate and the plan was to use the money saved to provide additional crews and so meet the target that had been set for the time taken to respond to a call. Control staff now receive calls and despatch ambulances over a much wider area.

To make this possible the service invested in a computerised command and control system, linked to the ambulances by a new radio. The procedure now is that a control assistant receiving a call enters the data directly into the computer system. This incorporates a geographical information system containing all the physical features of the area. As it is directly linked by radio to the ambulances it also contains information about the present position and status of each vehicle. The system identifies immediately the most appropriate vehicle to despatch to the incident. That decision is conveyed electronically to a message box in the cab that the crew reads and acts upon. As they do the work they press codes on the message box to let the computer know the stage they have reached. Voice communication is unnecessary as the computer automatically updates the ambulance's position. Management hopes the new system will improve communication at all stages of the process, save money and enhance the service.

Q Case questions

- What external changes are affecting the management and staff of the service?
- How would you describe the previous communications system?
- What questions would you have about the possible effects of the new system on communications amongst staff?

14.1 Introduction

This chapter introduces the following ideas:

- Communication
- Communication process
- Encoding
- Channel
- Receiver
- Decoding
- Communication barriers
- Feedback
- Noise

Management at the ambulance service saw the need to improve radically the way communication took place between staff in the control rooms and the ambulance crews. They were under pressure to cut costs and improve service in a politically visible activity. They saw modern communications technology as a way of improving performance on all counts. The challenge will be to implement the system, and the associated changes, in a way that realises the potential benefits. The success of the communication project is of central importance to the service.

Most businesses experience communication problems of some sort, both between individuals or between members of separate functions. Companies such as W.L. Gore and Associates and Oticon want research teams to communicate ideas and results within and between research projects. Customer-service organisations such as Forté Hotels want staff to communicate ideas and suggestions – and to understand company policy. Management often underestimates the communication problems it faces. A manager with a major utility business recently wrote to the author:

> The majority of managers within [the business] consider themselves to be effective communicators. Staff have a different perspective, and a recent staff survey rated communications as being very poor, with information being top down, no form of two-way communications and managers only hearing what they want to hear.

Communication touches every management function, at all levels of the organisation. People need to communicate directly and personally with each other and also to take part in more formal and structured communication processes. Customer orders need to be communicated accurately to all the departments that will help to satisfy them – and then between departments as the task progresses. People communicate information in both directions through the vertical hierarchy, and horizontally between functions, departments and other organisations. Communication technologies support these processes, but in themselves do not solve communication problems. Dealing with a communication problem usually involves dealing with issues of culture, structure and power as well.

Q Case questions 14.1

- Which aspects of communication would you want management to improve first if you were (a) a member of the public, (b) an employee, (c) a senior manager of the ambulance service?
- The case focused on one aspect of communication within the service. What other forms of communication will also be taking place within the organisation?

This chapter explains the generic communication process that occurs as people try to transfer information and solve problems. It then examines aspects of interpersonal and organisational communication, before outlining the factors that hinder or help communication. A final section outlines some of the ways in which modern communication technologies can support that process.

14.2 Communication and management

Many activities succeed or fail because of the quality of the communication process. We base our understanding of the world on information and feelings that we receive and send.

Forté's Commitment to Excellence Programme

In 1999 Forté launched a pilot Commitment to Excellence Programme at 26 of its hotels, which the company claims has transformed communication between managers and staff. One junior employee commented that she was full of ideas, but until recently few members of staff, especially those in the 'back of house' jobs, would have dared to make any suggestions. There was a culture of fear, in which people were afraid to make decisions, or make mistakes. James Stewart is a regional general manager whose territory includes Burford Bridge, one of the hotels chosen to pilot the Commitment to Excellence Programme. He recalled that in the past there was 'no communication with head office, which was seen as being there not to help, but to find people out'.

The company's decision to launch Commitment to Excellence was as much about changing this culture as about improving customer care, although the two went hand in hand. As with most service providers, management had run customer care programmes before. These had helped, but had not got to the root of the company's problems. The extent of these became clear when Granada took over Forté in 1996. Tracy Robbins, worldwide customer service director, and Stephanie Monk, group human resources director for Granada, commissioned research by MORI (a market research consultancy) into customer and staff perceptions.

Interviews with more than 500 customers and 300 employees in seven countries revealed inconsistencies in service standards across and within the various Forté Hotel brands. There was often a stronger focus on accomplishing tasks than on looking after customers, while weaknesses in internal communication meant that hotels were not working effectively with head office. The research also drew attention to low staff morale: 'We knew that one of the key ways to improve staff satisfaction, which then clearly triggers customer satisfaction, was to address that [communication] issue.'

Source: Based on an article in *People Management*, 14 October 1999.

Figure 14.1 shows how communication is central to the management roles discussed in Chapter 1. People can only perform the functions of planning, organising, leading and controlling if they communicate information. Studies by Stewart (1967) and Mintzberg (1973) showed that formal and informal communication was central to the management job. This is most evident in the informational role – but equally managers cannot perform the interpersonal and decisional roles unless they communicate with other people. In the liasion role the manager receives emails, phone calls, holds conversations with people working on different aspects of a project. At the same time he or she is sending messages to those involved. Communication features in some way in every

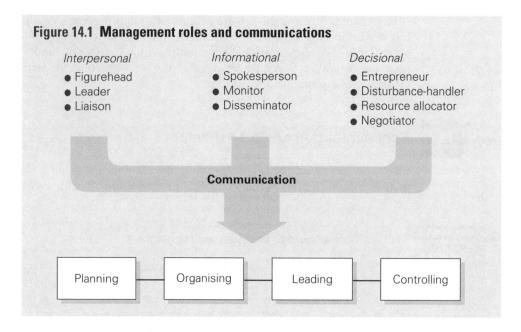

Figure 14.1 Management roles and communications

chapter – whether on influencing others, working in teams, giving marketing information to senior management or interpreting financial data. This chapter focuses on generic aspects of the process.

What is communication?

People co-ordinate their activities by communicating with each other. Speaking and writing are easy, but achieving mutual understanding is often difficult. People have different backgrounds, experiences and personal needs. These affect their ability to understand messages from those with different histories. It affects the meaning they attach to words or facial expressions. Management depends on conveying and interpreting messages clearly so that people can work together.

ACTIVITY 14.1

Collecting symbols and actions

The definition of communication refers to words, symbols and actions. Try to identify examples of symbols and actions that intentionally or unintentionally communicate a message to you. Some clues:

symbols: someone's style of dress or manner, or the appearance of the entrance to your college or university;

actions: someone taking time to offer directions to a visitor or looking bored during a meeting; interrupting someone.

The communication process

We communicate whenever we send a message to someone and as we think about what he or she says in return. It sounds a simple process, but is in practice subtle and complex, with great scope for sending and receiving the wrong message. Whenever someone makes a comment such as 'That's not what I meant' or 'I explained it clearly, and they still got it wrong' they are indicating a **communication** failure. We waste time when we misunderstand directions, or cause offence by saying something that the listener misinterprets.

We infer meaning from words and gestures and then from the person's reply to our message. We continually interpret their messages and create our own in turn. A manager and a colleague have a conversation. Each listens to the other's words, sees their gestures, reads the relevant documents or looks over the equipment to understand what the other means. When they achieve a mutual understanding about what they will do they have communicated effectively. To understand why communication problems occur we need a model of the steps in the process, as shown in Figure 14.2.

Figure 14.2 A model of the communication process

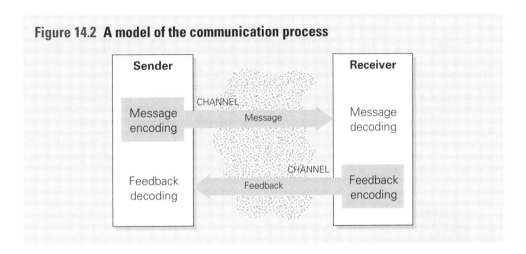

The communication process requires at least two people – a sender and a receiver. The *sender* initiates the communication when they try to transfer ideas, facts or feelings to the *receiver* – the person to whom they send the message. The sender **encodes** the idea they wish to convey into a message by using symbols such as words, actions or expressions. Deciding how to encode the message is an important choice. It depends in part on the purpose of the message. Is it to convey specific and unambiguous information? Is it

---

KEY IDEAS **Accurate encoding**

Hellriegel and Slocum (1988) suggest five principles for encoding a message accurately:

- **Relevancy** Make the message meaningful and significant, carefully selecting the words, symbols or gestures to be used.
- **Simplicity** Put the message in the simplest possible terms, reducing the number of words, symbols or gestures used.
- **Organisation** Organise the message as a series of points to facilitate understanding.

Complete each point in the message before proceeding to the next.

- **Repetition** Restate key points of the message at least twice. Repetition is particularly important in spoken communication because words may not be clearly heard or fully understood the first time.
- **Focus** Concentrate on the essential aspects of the message. Make the message clear and avoid unnecessary detail.

to raise an open and unfamiliar problem, and a request for creative ideas? Is it to pass on routine data, or to inspire people?

The **message** is the tangible expression of the sender's idea. This is sent through one or more **channels** – such as an email, a face-to-face meeting or a letter. The receiver **decodes** the symbols contained in the message, and tries to reconstruct the sender's original thought. Encoding and decoding are potential sources of communication failure as the sender and receiver have different knowledge, experience and interests. These act as filters (or '**noise**'), which interfere with the conversion of meaning to symbols and vice versa.

The final stage in the episode is when the receiver responds to the message by giving **feedback** to the sender. This turns one-way communication into two-way. Without feedback the sender cannot know if the receiver has the message or if they have inter-preted it as the sender intended. The flow of information between parties is continuous and reciprocal, each responding by giving feedback to the other. It is a two-way process, of which sending a message is only one part. Communication is only completed when the sender knows that the receiver has received and understood the message in the way intended.

Effective communicators understand the two-way aspect of communication, and posi-tively check for evidence of feedback. They do not rely on one-way methods, but ensure the receiver has the opportunity and encouragement to respond with feedback. Without some response – a nod, a question that implies understanding, a quick email acknowl-edgement – the sender does not know if he or she has communicated successfully.

'Assume that communication is going to fail, and then put time and effort into prevent-ing that.'

14.3 Effective communication

The model of communication in Figure 14.2 shows the steps that people need to take to communicate effectively. The process fails if either sender or receiver does not encode or decode the symbols of the message in the same way. Selecting the wrong communication channels can also lead to difficulty – for example sending a sensitive message that requires subtle interpretation as a written instruction with no chance for feedback.

Effective communication depends on using knowledge of four factors – perception, communication channels, non-verbal signals and listening.

ACTIVITY 14.2

Understanding communication practices

Think of an example where communication between two or more people failed. Note down why you think that happened, using the model in Figure 14.2.

More communication now takes place electronically: make a preliminary list of the advantages and disadvantages of that medium compared with face-to-face communication.

Q Case questions 14.2

- Use the model in Figure 14.2 to describe systematically the communication processes involved in dealing with an emergency call to the ambulance service (a) under the old system, (b) under the new system.
- Note on the model where the old system tended to interfere with the communication process.

Perception

When a receiver hears a message he or she tries to decode and interpret it. **Perception** is the process by which individuals make sense of their environment by organising and interpreting information. Perceptions of reality and its meaning influence what people say and do, not some objective or factual reality.

We receive a stream of information beyond our capacity to absorb, and a process called selective perception helps us to remain sane. We actively notice and attend to only a small fraction of the available information, filtering out what we do not need. Factors such as the strength of the signal or the reputation of the sender influence what we select.

Even when people observe a common piece of information they may interpret it, and react to it, in different ways. This perceptual organisation arranges incoming signals into patterns that give some meaning to the data – relating it to our interest in the topic, the status of the sender or the benefits of attending to it. Experience, social class, education or career plans influence this process of perceptual organisation, which leads people to interpret the same information in different ways. Effective communicators understand this, and are alert to the way it will affect how people react to a message.

A common form of perceptual organisation is known as stereotyping. 'They always complain' or 'You would expect people from marketing to say that' are signs that some-one is judging a message not by its content but by the group to which the sender belongs. An inaccurate stereotype means that we misinterpret the meaning because we are making inaccurate assumptions about the sender.

Perceptual differences are natural, but distort messages and interfere with communica-tion. Each person has their own personality and perceptual style, which affect how they interpret a message. Senders cannot assume that the **receiver** will attach the same mean-ing to a message as the sender intended.

Communication channels

Another factor in communication is which channel to choose – an email, a letter, a face-to-face meeting and so on. Channels have different capacities to convey information and this is known as their 'information richness'. Channel richness is the amount of informa-tion that can be transmitted during a communication episode. Lengel and Daft (1988) developed a contingency model using the idea of *media richness*. This is the capacity of a medium to convey information and promote learning. Figure 14.3 shows a range of media varying in richness from high to low.

The richness of a medium (or channel) depends on its ability to:

- handle many cues at the same time;
- support rapid two-way feedback; and
- establish a personal focus for the communication.

Face-to-face discussion is the richest medium, as both parties can pick up many infor-mation cues (concentration, eye contact, body movements, facial expression) in addition to the spoken words. This enables them to gain a deep understanding of the nuances of meaning.

Managers prefer to talk than to write. All studies of how they use their time show that most is spent in face-to-face contact with other people. They prefer oral communication because it is quick, spontaneous and enriched by non-verbal signals. It takes place in one-to-one conversation (face-to-face or on the telephone), through meetings of several people or when someone communicates to many people at a conference.

Figure 14.3 The Lengel–Daft contingency model of media selection

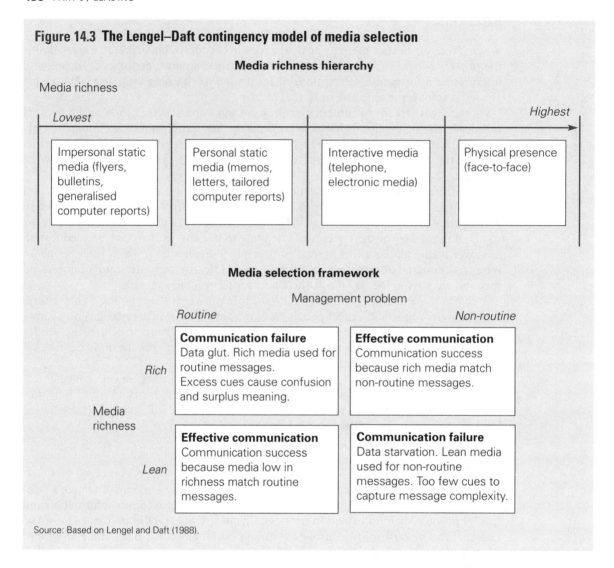

Source: Based on Lengel and Daft (1988).

Email and other forms of electronic communication increase transmission speed, but give no sense of personal contact. Misunderstandings can arise when the body language that adds meaning to words in a face-to-face conversation are missing – careless use of emails has been a source of tension between people. Newsletters and routine computer reports are lean media because they provide a single cue, are impersonal and do not encourage response.

Each channel has advantages and disadvantages. If the message is to go to many people and there is significant possibility of misunderstanding, some relatively structured written or electronic medium is likely to work best. If it is a question or problem upon which other people's opinions are needed then a face-to-face discussion will be more effective.

In a study of 95 executives in a petrochemical company Lengel and Daft (1988) found that the preferred medium depended on how routine the topic was: 'Managers used face-to-face [communication] 88 per cent of the time for non-routine communication. The reverse was true for written media. When they considered the topics routine and well understood, 68 per cent of the managers preferred … written modes' (p.227).

Communication during the CGU merger

When the Commercial Union and General Accident insurance companies merged in 1998 management used a variety of channels for different kinds of communication. As soon as the merger was agreed they wanted all staff to receive the same message very quickly. They told all branch managers to be in their office by 7am on the day of the announcement to receive a fax, which branch managers used to brief their staff (personal static media).

When the company sought the views of staff on the kind of organisation that the company should create to meet customer needs they arranged large gatherings of staff to debate these issues in small groups for several days (physical presence).

Source: Based on an article in *People Management*, 2 September 1999.

Remember also that the medium can become part of the message. A scrappy note or a badly presented essay tells the receiver a lot about the sender's intentions or attitude. Effective communicators ensure that the encoding and the medium transmit a consistent message.

Non-verbal communication

An important type of interpersonal communication is the non-verbal, which some people refer to as body language. Experts in the field (such as Argyle, 1988) claim that the actual words in a message have less impact on the sender than the accompanying non-verbal signals. These include the tone of voice, facial expression, posture and appearance, and provide most of the impact in face-to-face communication.

Sending non-verbal communications

Small changes in eye contact, such as raising eyebrows or a directed glance while making a statement, add to the meaning that the sender conveys. A stifled yawn, an eager nod, a thoughtful flicker of anxiety gives the sender a signal about the receiver's reaction. Gestures and body position give equally vivid messages – leaning forward attentively, moving about in the chair, hands moving nervously, gathering papers or looking at the clock. Whether intended or not, these send a signal to the receiver.

Receiving non-verbal communication

As with any interpersonal skill, some people are better at picking up clues from non-verbal behaviour than others. When listening to someone, especially over the telephone, the receiver will pick up more of the sender's meaning if he or she listens for what the sender does not say. This can either confirm the spoken message, or raise doubts about whether the speaker is telling the full story. The sender of a spoken message can benefit by noting the non-verbal responses to what he or she says. If they do not seem appropriate (raised eyebrows, or a hint of anxiety), the speaker should pause and take stock of the conversation. They should check that the receiver has received the intended message, and not misinterpreted it.

Giving non-verbal feedback

People give non-verbal feedback to others all the time, both intentionally and unintentionally. Positive non-verbal feedback helps to build relations within a team. A smile or wave from the manager to the staff members at least acknowledges that they exist.

Related to a task it indicates approval in an informal, rapid way that sustains the subordinates' confidence. Negative feedback can be correspondingly damaging. A boss who looks irritated by what the staff member sees as a reasonable enquiry is giving a negative signal. So too is one who looks bored or distracted during a presentation.

ACTIVITY 14.3

Evaluating communication methods

Think of a task you have done with a small group of people. It could be a voluntary or charity project, or a group assignment as part of your course. How did you communicate with each other? List all the methods used, and any advantages or disadvantages they had.

Q Case questions 14.3

- How has the balance shifted between verbal and electronic communication in the ambulance service?
- Identify where in the whole system each form has increased or decreased. What are the likely advantages and disadvantages from that change in pattern?

MANAGEMENT IN PRACTICE   Communication failure in a small Dutch company

The company was founded in 1881 and the present owner is one of the fourth generation of the family. The company trades and manufactures packaging machines and employs 16 people. Someone who has recently joined the company said:

'1997 was a difficult year. Five people left the company and took with them much knowledge and experience. The company really consists of one person – the owner. He does not delegate much and there is little communication between him and the rest of the organisation. The only part of the company that interests him is the game of selling machines. He describes the rest of his tasks as annoying. The result is that, for example:

1 When we sell a machine, Operations do not know exactly what Sales has promised a customer. The customer expects the machine they specified, but do not always get it.
2 There is lack of internal communication – people in the company do not know their precise responsibilities or who is responsible for which tasks.
3 There is no time planning for ordered machines. No one knows the delivery date that we have promised a customer.
4 There is no budget system for a machine project. When we sell a machine we do not know if we will make a profit or a loss.

All together, the company faces serious problems because of a lack of policy, management, information and communication.'

ACTIVITY 14.4

Assessing university communications

List the communications channels that your university or college uses to send you information about these aspects of your course:

- *changes to rooms, timetables, or dates;*
- *reading lists and other study materials;*
- *ideas and information intended to stimulate your thinking and to encourage discussion and debate;*
- *your performance so far and advice on what courses to take.*

Were the methods appropriate or not? What general lessons can you draw?

The art of listening

Communication experts stress the importance of listening. While the person sending the message is responsible for expressing the ideas they want to convey as accurately as they can, the receiver also has responsibilities for the success of the exchange. Listening involves the active skill of attending to what is said, and gaining as accurate a picture as possible of the meaning the sender wished to convey.

Many people are poor listeners. They concentrate not on what the speaker is saying but on what they will say as soon as there is a pause.

KEY IDEAS **Six practices for effective listening**

- **Stop talking**, especially that internal, mental, silent chatter. Let the speaker finish. Hear them out. It is tempting in a familiar situation to complete the speaker's sentence for them and work out a reply. This assumes that you know what they are going to say, when you should instead be listening to what they are actually saying.
- **Put the speaker at ease** by showing that you are listening. The good listener does not look over someone's shoulder or write while the speaker is talking. If you must take notes, explain what you are doing. Take care, because we all rely on the other person's facial expression while we are speaking to them. The speaker will be put off if you look away or concentrate on your notes instead of nodding reassuringly.

- Remember that your **aim is to understand** what the speaker is saying, not to win an argument.
- Be aware of your **personal prejudices** and make a conscious effort to stop them influencing your judgement.
- Be alert to **what the speaker is not saying** as well as what they are. Very often what is missing is more important than what is there.
- **Ask questions**. This shows that you have been listening and encourages the speaker to develop the points you have raised. It is an active process, never more important than when you are meeting someone for the first time – when your objective should be to say as little and learn as much as possible in the shortest time.

14.4 Communication structure and type of task

Different tasks require different forms of interpersonal communication. Figure 14.4 illustrates this. The figure shows two types of communication pattern within a group. In the centralised pattern information flows to and from the person or group at the centre. In the decentralised pattern more of the messages pass between those away from the centre. If the task requires communication between people in a group, but is relatively straightforward, the star pattern of communication will work adequately. An example

Figure 14.4 Communication structure and type of task

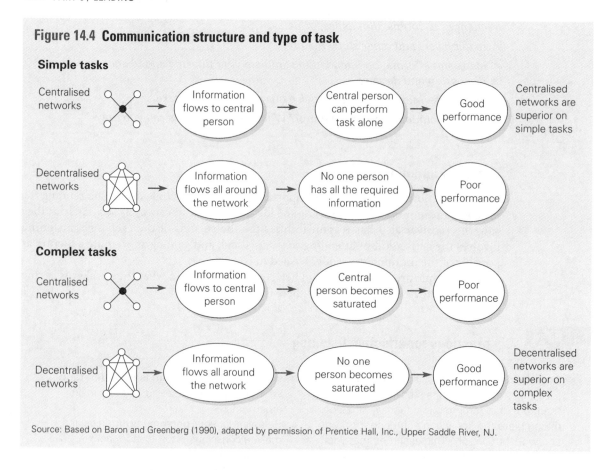

Source: Based on Baron and Greenberg (1990), adapted by permission of Prentice Hall, Inc., Upper Saddle River, NJ.

would be to prepare next year's staff budget for the library when there are to be no major changes. The person at the centre can give and receive familiar, structured information from section heads in an efficient way.

This centralised structure will obstruct performance if the task is uncertain, and when those away from the centre have information that will help the work. An example would be a team developing a new product rapidly in conjunction with suppliers and customers. Because of the novelty of the task, unfamiliar question or situations will arise. Group members can only deal with these by exchanging information amongst each other rapidly. That changes the situation for others who then have to change what they do in response to constantly changing circumstances. If all information has to pass through the centre, the centre will not be able to handle unexpected difficulties. That will lead to unacceptable delays while those away from the centre await a decision on their next move. So a web form of communication is more suitable, in which people communicate as required – amongst themselves and with the centre.

14.5 Organisational communication

As organisations grow they need to supplement informal communication methods with more formal arrangements. At first these are quite simple, such as a list of current orders and what stage they have reached. Then there may be a system for setting budgets for the different parts of the activity and for collecting information on what they cost. Later people probably develop some rules or guidelines about passing information to other departments so that they know about changes that affect them. These systems are the basis of the formal or institutionalised communication system. As Figure 14.5 shows, they pass information in downward, upward or horizontal directions.

Downward communication

Management uses downward communication to send messages to people below them in the hierarchy. They try to ensure co-ordination by issuing a plan and expect those lower in the hierarchy to follow it. Examples include information about the following:

- new policies, products or services;
- orders received, as a signal to relevant departments to start planning their part;
- budget changes or any changes in financial reporting and control systems;
- new systems and procedures;
- new appointments and reorganisations;
- changes to roles or job descriptions.

If the downward communication inhibits comments or responses the sender will be unclear how receivers reacted to the message. If downward communication is rare, so

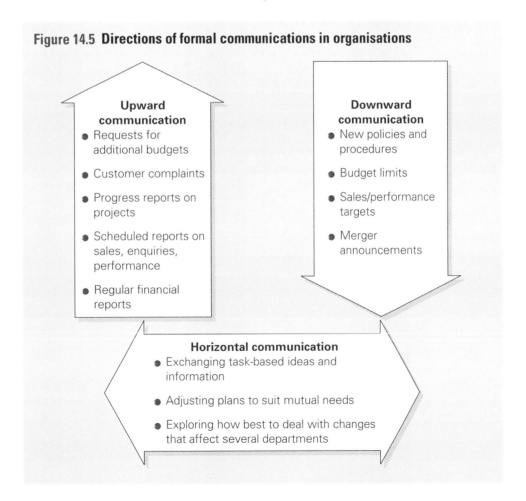

Figure 14.5 Directions of formal communications in organisations

Upward communication
- Requests for additional budgets
- Customer complaints
- Progress reports on projects
- Scheduled reports on sales, enquiries, performance
- Regular financial reports

Downward communication
- New policies and procedures
- Budget limits
- Sales/performance targets
- Merger announcements

Horizontal communication
- Exchanging task-based ideas and information
- Adjusting plans to suit mutual needs
- Exploring how best to deal with changes that affect several departments

that subordinates are unclear about policy or changes, it usually indicates that managers do not trust subordinates to understand the information or use it responsibly.

Team briefings

Team briefings are a popular way of passing information rapidly and consistently throughout the organisation – Blakstad and Cooper (1995) quote the results of a survey of 915 companies in which 57 per cent of respondents rated team briefings as the most common method of communicating with employees. Under this method senior management provides a standard message and format, and briefs the next level in the hierarchy. Those managers then brief their subordinates following the same standard format, and this process continues down the organisation. Team briefings are a way of communicating company issues to all staff through line managers. Addressing small groups with a common structure enables management to:

- deliver a consistent message;
- involve line managers personally in delivering the message;
- deliver the message to many people quickly;
- reduce the possible distortions by 'the grapevine'; and
- enable staff to ask questions.

MANAGEMENT IN PRACTICE   **Planning a team briefing**

Management needs to agree and follow the timing of a team briefing, otherwise some departments will hear before others and the grapevine will become active. The following steps help ensure an effective briefing:

Step1 What to communicate Senior management agrees what information to communicate to staff, then draws up a briefing outline.

Step 2 How it will be communicated The senior managers agree to hold individual team briefing sessions with the managers reporting to them on an agreed date.

Step 3 Delivering the message On the appointed day the senior managers gather their line managers, explain the purpose of the session, read through the brief and expand upon it as appropriate. The line managers receive a copy of the brief and are given time for questions and to make notes.

Step 4 Spreading the word to staff Each line manager conducts a team briefing – using the same briefing outline – to those reporting directly to them. This should take place within two to four hours. This process should continue until everyone in the organisation has attended a session.

Step 5 Feedback Line managers should provide brief comments to their senior managers using a standard format. This highlights problems raised by staff.

Upward communication

Upward communication refers to systematic methods of helping employees to pass on their views and ideas to management. Managers try to ensure co-ordination by encouraging feedback. In small organisations this is usually fairly easy. The owner-manager is likely to be in close touch with what employees are thinking. Information and ideas reach the boss quickly, and he or she can take them into account. However, it is wrong to assume that communication is necessarily good in small businesses. As the businesses grow the layers of the hierarchy can easily break the flow. Unless they create mechanisms to allow information to move upwards their boards, too, can act on incorrect information.

**MANAGEMENT
IN PRACTICE** **Hinckley and Rugby Building Society**

During the 1990s the new chief executive of this long-established building society introduced an open management style, together with a belief in giving employees a genuine part in running the organisation. One example of this philosophy in practice arose when the board recognised the need for a new computer system. It seemed natural to involve the workforce in every aspect of the project. There were only two suppliers with the necessary expertise and in many organisations the choice between them would have been made by senior operational managers or IT specialists. At the Hinckley and Rugby a working group including staff from all levels investigated the options and recommended its choice to the board. This willingness to listen to staff was characteristic of the new culture.

When the decision on the software was made all staff were informed through team briefings and via the first issue of *Summit News*, a newsletter that would be published monthly during the project. This set out who was going to be involved in the steering committee for the project, the planned timetable and the reasons for the change. The project involved intense communication between staff at all levels, and over half the employees were involved in some aspects of design and planning.

The new system went into operation very smoothly, and amongst the reasons for the success was the attention given to effective and sustained communications – the 'glue' of the process. Regular team briefings and a monthly newsletter kept people up to speed. With the society's open culture and so many people involved in the project informal communications also worked effectively, relaying first-hand information rather than rumour.

Source: Based on an article in *People Management*, 20 January 2000.

Employee opinion surveys

Some companies conduct regular surveys amongst their employees to gauge their attitudes and feelings towards company policy and practice. They may also seek views on current issues, or about possible changes in policy or practice. The surveys can be valuable both as a general indicator of attitudes and as a way of highlighting particular issues that need attention, such as a growing demand for childcare facilities.

**MANAGEMENT
IN PRACTICE** **Conducting an attitude survey**

Often, the most cost-effective source of advice is close at hand: the workforce. Employees at all levels are the key to improving performance; they really know how the business works. Tapping into their knowledge and expertise can provide the catalyst for change and ensure that the organisation is tackling the fundamental issues. Effective practices include:

- Define clear objectives for the survey.
- Brief everyone thoroughly beforehand.
- Always survey a complete and identifiable group from top to bottom.
- Plan time and facilities to enable the survey to be completed.
- Ensure absolute confidentiality.

- Consider the types of questions you want to ask. A mixture of open and closed questions will obtain views on the key issues as well as generate more 'off-the-wall' ideas.
- Structure the survey so that meaningful analysis of the data can be carried out.
- Plan how the results will be fed back to employees.
- Use the results to identify how performance can be improved and, where possible, implement these ideas quickly to show management commitment and support.

Source: Lesley Munro-Faure in *People Management*, 25 May 2000.

Suggestion schemes

These are devices by which companies encourage employees to suggest improvements to their job or other aspects of the organisation. Employees usually receive a cash reward if management accepts their idea.

ACTIVITY 14.5

Researching opinion surveys

Gather some evidence from a company about its experience of using employee opinion surveys or suggestion schemes. What are their purposes? Who designs them and interprets the results? What have the benefits been?

Formal appeal or grievance procedures

These set out the steps to be followed when an individual or group is in dispute with the company. For example, an employee who has been penalised by a supervisor for poor timekeeping may disagree with the facts as presented or with the penalty imposed. The grievance procedure states how the employee should set about pursuing a claim for a review of the case. Similar procedures now exist in colleges and universities, setting out how a student with a grievance about their assessment can appeal against their results to successively higher levels of the institution.

Horizontal communication

Horizontal communication crosses departmental or functional boundaries, usually connecting people at broadly similar levels within the organisation. Management seeks to ensure co-ordination by encouraging lateral interaction. As different parts of the organisation co-operate on projects to introduce new products or systems, people communicate frequently. They need to pass information to each other on the current state of affairs so that each distinct unit can be ready to contribute to the project as required.

MANAGEMENT IN PRACTICE   **Managing knowledge at Ebank**

Ebank is a large European bank that was created in the early 1990s by merging two separate banks. It has grown by acquiring other banks, and now operates in 70 countries. Separate divisions deal with different types of business, such as domestic, international and investment banking. In 1997 a major global client left the bank because it felt that it was not getting an integrated service across countries. Despite Ebank calling itself a 'global bank', the reality was very different. It was not integrated, each country and department operated independently and had its own systems and processes. There was little knowledge sharing across these internal boundaries. The vision from the top was to create a truly networked global bank.

Members of the corporate business strategy group wrote a paper recommending that Ebank develop a worldwide communication network connecting all the businesses, using intranet technology. An intranet is a website that only people within an organisation can access. The paper recognised that the true competitive advantage for the bank was not simply in financial transactions but in providing knowledge to customers. Thus the bank takes information from external sources, processes this using its internal knowledge of financial services, competitive forces, etc., and then sells this knowledge to customers. As an example, it may be able to advise a client (such as a large European supermarket chain) to buy a small supermarket chain in China based on its global knowledge. However, to be able to offer such advice the bank needs to integrate knowledge from a range of different departments and geographical locations. At the time this was simply not possible because staff did not share knowledge across such internal boundaries. So the vision was to develop a global communication system – a knowledge management system – to integrate the knowledge within the bank.

Source: Based on Newell (1999).

As management creates a structure for the organisation it influences how much horizontal communication will take place. In a hierarchical, mechanistic organisation (see Chapter 8) most information passes vertically between managers and subordinates. In organic structures, where managers delegate more decisions to lower levels, there is more horizontal communication. Instead of referring problems up the hierarchy to a common boss staff in the respective departments sort out problems themselves.

MANAGEMENT IN PRACTICE	**Communication policies in an electrical retailer**

The company grew rapidly during the late 1980s to become a major regional retailer of electrical goods. The two joint owners of the business were aware of the need for good communication and put in place several policies to reach high standards in this aspect of management practice. They put considerable effort into ensuring that:

- regional managers knew about new company policies in a rapidly changing business;
- shop staff also knew what was expected of them;
- all staff knew about forthcoming advertising campaigns, so that they could respond confidently to customer queries;
- all staff received comments on their performance.

They also:

- asked all staff for their views on the way the business was run;
- listened to staff complaints about, for example, gaps between advertising campaigns and deliveries of advertised goods to the shops;
- encouraged communication across departments within head office;
- arranged for manufacturers to make presentations to staff on new products.

14.6   Developments in communication technology

Information technology is radically changing many aspects of communication within and between organisations. To give just some examples: *email* makes it possible to send messages electronically and can be used for either one-to-one or one-to-many communications. *Video-conferencing* makes it possible for people who are physically remote to hold a meeting in which they can see all the others taking part. It can be used (with some difficulty) for interactive meetings of small groups or for a presentation by one person to a large group. The *intranet* – an internal version of the Internet – enables people within an organisation to access an internal website. This can be used to share company-specific information quickly and in the knowledge that everyone will receive identical information.

Q   Case questions 14.4

One issue that management needed to decide was how to deal with the system's recommendation on which ambulance should go to an incident. There are two possibilities: (a) the recommendation is sent directly as an electronic signal from the system to the crew, or (b) the recommendation is presented to the control officer who decides whether or not to accept it, and then sends the decision as an electronic signal to the crew. Both are technically possible. Which would you recommend and why?

ACTIVITY 14.6

Researching the benefits of new systems

Try to gather information on the practical use of at least one of these systems. Scan computer or professional journals for articles about the systems so that you are broadly familiar with them. Then try to discuss the system with someone who has some experience of using it in a working organisation. Ask that person about matters such as:

What are the advantages and disadvantages compared with (a) traditional communication devices, (b) the options realistically available in the particular situation for which it was used?

How has it affected the way people communicate with each other? Is it a satisfactory substitute for face-to-face, spoken communication?

MANAGEMENT IN PRACTICE   Using groupware at Price Waterhouse

In 1998 Price Waterhouse (now part of PricewaterhouseCoopers) was one of the world's leading accountancy and consultancy organisations; it employed almost 50,000 people in over 100 countries, including over 10,000 consultants. It had particular expertise in financial services, media, oil and gas, telecommunications and utilities. The company, founded 150 years ago, traditionally operated as a collection of national or regional groups, further divided into functions. These worked in relative isolation from colleagues, especially those in other countries.

In 1990 the company realised that clients (especially large multinationals) required it to handle bigger and more complex jobs. Staff would have to offer a wider range of experience – which was largely available in the collective but unorganised experience of the consultants. How could management gather and communicate this valuable information quickly? The solution was to install a groupware system incorporating database management, email, spreadsheets and other functions.

The system is built on a document database that enables staff to share information quickly worldwide. They use their PCs to communicate and work on the same electronic files. The company has invested heavily in knowledge databases, containing details on 'all the projects we've done in particular industries and topics. So I can find out from my desk where our knowledge base is. I can have a set of case studies on our client's desk in a few hours'. Other databases contain what the company has learned from those projects. Consultants on a project use the database as a source of ideas and information.

The system is central to communications between offices and consultants across time zones. This is essential in a global business and the system allows much easier internal communication, irrespective of location.

A senior manager in the company reflected on their experience with the groupware product:

'The ability to manage globally in a people-business depends on good communications. Our groupware has helped us to move as quickly as we have. We've been able to respond to opportunities partly because we had the systems in place. Virtually everyone in the practice is now a groupware user.'

14.7 Informal communication systems

Alongside the structural and technical complexity of any company's formal systems there is the grapevine. This is the spontaneous, informal system through which people pass information and gossip. It happens throughout the organisation and across all hierarchical levels. It is in action as people meet in the corridor, by the photocopier, at lunch, on the way home. The information that passes along the grapevine is usually well ahead of the information in the formal system. It is about who said what at a meeting, who has applied for another job, who has been summoned to explain their poor results to the directors or what orders the company has won.

The grapevine does not replace the formal system, but passes a different kind of information around – qualitative rather than quantitative, current ideas and proposals rather than agreed policies. As it is uncensored and reflects the views of people as a whole rather than of those in charge of the formal communications media, it probably gives a truer picture of the diversity of opinions within the company than the formal policies will. Nevertheless, the rumours and information on the grapevine might be wrong or incomplete. Those passing gossip and good stories of spectacular disasters in department X may also have their own interests and agendas. These may include promoting the interests of department Y. The grapevine is as likely to be a vehicle for political intrigue as any of the formal systems.

The grapevine can be a source of early information about what is happening elsewhere in the organisation. This allows those affected but not yet formally consulted to begin preparing their position. Put the other way round, someone preparing proposals or plans can be quite sure that information about them will be travelling round the grapevine sooner than they expect. Sometimes it is useful to deliberately let the matter slip out and begin circulating information to be able to gauge reaction before going too far with a plan.

14.8 Problems and barriers to communication

If communication was perfect the receiver would always understand the message as the sender intended. That rarely happens, as people interpret information from their own perspectives, and words fail to express feelings or emotions. Power games affect how people send and receive information, so we can never be sure that the message sent is the message received. Breakdowns and barriers can disrupt any communication chain.

Micro-barriers to communication

Some of the barriers to communication are at the interpersonal or 'micro' level. Micro-barriers are in the immediate situation and include the sender's message, mutual views of sender and receiver, choice of medium, and noise.

The sender's message

The subject, and how the sender views it, is as much part of the communication process as the message itself. A communicator who has badly misjudged a situation and is trying to communicate out-of-date, inaccurate, poorly argued or poorly presented information will not convince the receiver that the message is worth receiving.

Mutual views of sender and receiver

In planning to send a message the sender has (even if only implicitly) a view of the receiver. This shapes the form, nature and content of the communication. We talk differently to different people because we make allowances for what they can understand or for their known biases. The receiver also has a view of the sender which will shape the meaning and interpretation that he or she attaches to the message. If the two people are receptive and trusting communication will be easy. If they are antagonistic and suspicious it will be very difficult for the sender to communicate the message. The message received will be different from that intended.

Choice of medium

The medium we use greatly affects what we convey. Receivers prefer certain media and pay more attention to messages that come by a preferred route. Some dislike over-formal language, while others dislike using casual terms in written documents. Putting a message in writing may help understanding, but others may see it as a sign of distrust. Some communicate readily by email, others are reluctant to switch on their system.

Noise

Noise refers to anything that interferes with the intended flow of communication. Sometimes it may be physical interruptions or distractions, as when a video-conference breaks down for technical reasons. The term also includes multiple – sometimes conflicting – messages being sent and received at the same time. If our non-verbal signals or subsequent actions are inconsistent with the words we are using the receiver may see a different meaning in our message from what was intended.

Noise also refers to the inclusion in a message of distracting or minor information that diverts attention from the main business. Communication suffers from interruptions that distract both parties and prevent the concentration essential to good communication. The receiver's attention may be distracted by some completely separate matters.

Macro-barriers to communication

Macro-barriers concern the environment, the larger world in which communication takes place.

Information overload

Most people in organisations have too much information. They are trained to search for more and better information, and so place greater burdens on already overloaded communication systems. This leads to an increasing number of communications. Information systems such as email are adding to the problem, as the sender incurs no direct cost from adding more people to an electronic mailing list. Management is confronted by newspapers, specialist magazines, conferences, Internet communications, terrestrial, digital and satellite TV, special surveys and consultancy reports. The volume of public information becomes a barrier to its use.

Departmentalisation

Organisations are typically divided into separate units, focusing on their particular part of the total task. As explained in Chapter 10, this segmentation often leads to people focusing too much on their own corner and not enough on other players. This means departments forget that others will have an interest in what they are doing, or will be affected by it – and forget to communicate information until it is too late.

Information as currency

Information has great value. Those who possess it have something others do not have and may need or want. Sole ownership of information can also be used to boost or protect a person's status or the significance of his or her role. Chapter 12 showed that access to information and the means of communicating it to others is a source of power. People may hoard it rather than share it, and use it at the most opportune moment. Those with access to inside information have both prestige and power.

 A further look at Price Waterhouse

The manager also made the following comment, which illustrates how information can be seen as 'currency', and how the company dealt with it.

> 'We had to overcome a number of issues to encourage use because some of the consultant managers think they're competing with each other. The competition still exists in practice units. So we've 'incentivised' them to share. If they're not meeting the culture, not sharing, that's not going to help them. We have a peer recognition system and an upward appraisal system. So if a consultant thinks a manager is not applying the culture, that will show up. And the peer recognition system allows people who have been sharing and helping others to be acknowledged and rewarded. We apply peer recognition throughout the business. It also needs certain disciplines – people must see it as part of their job to maintain information and record details of their projects. It's part of how they manage a client.'

14.9 Communication from a critical perspective

Information is not neutral. People can use it to legitimise particular sets of values and to exclude discussion of others. Communication affects the distribution of power. Those with power can try to maintain it by managing what is communicated, encouraging some types of information or discussion and suppressing others. Habermas (1972) distinguished three types of knowledge that communication serves:

- *Prediction and control* Communication is used to understand the links between cause and effect, making it easier to predict and control events. Rational approaches to management emphasise using this kind of knowledge to serve the goals of the organisation. For this reason writers often refer to it as *instrumental rationality*. The knowledge can be of an uncontentious technical nature, or it can be used to influence employees to support organisational goals.
- *Mutual understanding* Communication enhances people's mutual understanding of each other. In organisations it helps people to share what the organisation means to them, how they are treated and how they experience the nature and meaning of their work.
- *Critical reflection* Communication enables people to reflect on the situation and challenge the goals pursued. Rather than focus on doing what is required in the name of instrumental rationality, communication provides the means of challenging what is being aimed for, questioning both means and goals.

Alvesson and Wilmott (1996) argue that most official company language uses terms that legitimise the idea of organisations as models of rationality and especially of instrumental rationality. Management typically encourages communication that supports instrumental rationality – a concern with means not ends. Arguments presented as supporting a rational analysis or solution often hide the self-interest of those presenting the information. Messages are labelled as containing 'rational' data and arguments and are used to support a particular course of action.

However, what is communicated as 'rational' may in fact be highly contentious or 'irrational'. Management may propose to concentrate production in larger factories on the rational grounds of lower costs. Opponents may argue that this ignores other costs such as extra traffic pollution or the effects on communities if plants are closed.

If these criteria are used the decision to concentrate production may be irrational. At the root of the issue is whether communication is used instrumentally to reach particular ends (low costs to one company) or to encourage critical reflection (the possibility that company goals could include avoiding pollution and supporting smaller communities). Alvesson and Wilmott argue that the prevailing management wisdom would be to belittle as unreal idealists those who attempted to challenge some of the goals of business organisations:

> Critical analysis subjects the rationality of such understandings and objectives to close scrutiny, arguing that the espoused rationality of conventional management theory and practice takes for granted the prevailing structure of power relations and is preoccupied with preserving the status quo. (Alvesson and Wilmott, 1996, p.51)

14.10 Summary

This chapter has outlined the main steps in the communication process and the points at which communication failure can so easily occur. It then discussed techniques of formal communication in both vertical and horizontal directions, showing how the form depends on the nature of the task and the wider organisational structure. It stressed that while effective interpersonal communication is vital, achieving this depends on more than interpersonal skills. It can be obstructed or distorted by macro- as well as micro-barriers.

Content

The quality of information available to managers in dealing with the content agenda reflects communication processes. To develop objectives and planning to achieve them they need useful information about external events and internal resources. This comes from many sources and needs to be received and accurately decoded. It could include non-verbal signals and the grapevine as well as more formal information sources. In generating action and motivation, ideas about the clarity of encoding and choosing the right medium are relevant. The more carefully these are considered the more likely it is that people will know what is expected of them. The quality of communication as people make proposals, express opinions, clarify ideas and get things done will affect performance. Management needs to create formal and informal systems to support communication required in the situation – such as lateral communication in changing environments, effective vertical or centralised systems in a stable environment.

Process

The process agenda is about how people work – including how the communication processes and institutions they create work. This affects how people try to influence others – which depends on understanding their needs and interests. This can only come from observing, listening and correctly interpreting what they say and do. Taking care to encode the meaning, choose the right medium and seek feedback is likely to support attempts to influence others as the message is more likely to be accurately interpreted and acted upon by individuals and teams. Stakeholders can be kept well informed through effective communication or they can be ignored. They may also be threatened by information and may distort it. Team briefings can help to ensure that all understand the objectives of the organisation. Information can be shared to encourage joint problem solving – or it can be suppressed and retained within a centralised communication system. Management styles that depend on input need to ensure that communication is not blocked.

Control

Information can also be used and sometimes distorted to control people, support particular interests and maintain an existing balance of power. As part of the control agenda managers monitor performance and communicate corrective action. Organisational learning depends on information flowing around the enterprise: communication barriers inhibit learning.

The project to introduce the new system at the ambulance service worked well, and was widely accepted as a great improvement on the old methods. One of the reasons for the success was the way in which great care was taken to match the new communication systems to the older ways of working – disruption was minimised. They also took care to use the communication technology to complement the personal communication skills of the staff, not to displace them. It was a good example of socio-technical design – the human and technological aspects of communication were planned together.

> **Q PART CASE QUESTIONS**
>
> ● What are the main methods of communication in W.L. Gore and Associates and which methods does management encourage?
> ● Use the Lengel–Daft model to explain why communication practices differ between Gore and the 'command and control' system in the ambulance service.
> ● How could a groupware product such as that used at Price Waterhouse help W.L. Gore and Associates?

14.11 Review questions

1 Draw a diagram of the communication process, showing each of the stages and elements. Then illustrate it with a communication episode you have experienced.

2 What is the difference between formal and informal communication?

3 What is non-verbal communication, and why is it important to effective communication?

4 What do you understand by the term 'media richness', and how does it affect the choice of communication method?

5 What is team briefing?

6 What are the weaknesses of technologically supported communications?

7 What is the meaning of the statement that information is a form of currency?

8 Explain and illustrate one micro-space and one macro-barrier to communication.

9 How does feedback help or hinder communication?

Further reading

Goffman, E. (1959), *The Presentation of Self in Everyday Life*, Doubleday, New York. A classic (and short) work that gives many insights into interpersonal communications.

Guirdham, M. (1995), *Interpersonal Skills at Work*, Prentice Hall International, Hemel Hempstead. To go deeper into some of the psychological aspects of communication, especially the non-verbal aspects.

Hargie, O.D.W. (1997), *Handbook of Communication Skills*, Routledge, London. A collection of papers covering all aspects of interpersonal communications skills, including non-verbal behaviour, explaining, listening, humour, and the selection interview.

Annotated links, questions and resources can be found on
www.booksites.net/boddy

CHAPTER 15

Teams

> **AIM** *To outline the significance of teams and how they develop.*

OBJECTIVES

By the end of your work on this chapter you should be able to outline the concepts below in your own terms and:

1 Explain possible reasons for differences in team performance

2 Explain why organisations use teams for a wide range of tasks

3 Summarise the views Mary Parker Follett and Rensis Likert on the benefits of teams

4 Describe types of team in organisations

5 Distinguish the stages of development through which groups pass

6 Explain Belbin's theory of team roles

7 Evaluate a team on three measures of effectiveness

8 Outline the organisational factors that influence team performance

9 Describe the meaning of 'groupthink', and give some examples of its symptoms

10 Use a theory to decide whether a team is always appropriate

Quintiles Transnational

Quintiles is a contract health organisation that undertakes a wide range of contract research services (such as testing or marketing) for the pharmaceutical industry. It has 70 offices in 25 countries, with the aim of helping clients bring new drugs to the market more quickly. Each customer project is managed by a team, drawn from the functional departments. These integrated teams work to strict deadlines by which they must complete their part of the research, and are directly accountable to the customer.

The company also uses teams to manage internal projects. For example, as part of a new initiative to develop a global distribution system for clinical trial material, management set up a team to review existing practices, facilities and regulations, and to make recommendations for change. The team had seven members – four functional directors, two research managers and a customer service manager.

The first meeting took the form of a brainstorming session over two days with social events and little formal agenda. At the end of the meeting action points were agreed and assigned. The meeting helped to develop the commitment of members, build a climate of trust and openness and develop relationships.

Team meetings continued every two months. In the interim period subgroups addressed their action items. One member found he could not meet his commitment to the team and resigned. The team had a very strong leader, who took the role of obtaining support for the initiative from senior management. He also kept close links with the team members, without taking over. The leader chose the team members carefully, avoiding people he believed would not be team players or who would have difficulty committing to the project. However, it became clear that team membership did not reflect the global nature of the project, as all initial members were European. Therefore team members were invited from the Americas and Asia Pacific regions as senior management support for the initiative increased.

Most communication was by video-conferencing and tele-conferencing, supported by email and shared databases. Despite this technological support it was agreed that a face-to-face meeting with the new members would be the best way to support team spirit. The team worked faster than initially hoped; the task challenged and energised the members and the leadership was strong but empowering.

Source: Private communication with a member of the team.

Q Case questions

- What actions did management take that helped to get the team off to a good start?
- Why do you think the team members found the task challenging and energising?

15.1 Introduction

This chapter introduces the following ideas:

- Group
- Team
- Formal and informal groups
- Content
- Structure
- Process
- Culture
- Preferred team roles
- Team-based rewards
- Observing
- Team Culture
- Groupthink
- High-performance team
- Pseudo-team
- Working group
- Supportive relationships

Quintiles is an organisation where management uses teams extensively to deliver its research service to customers. The people with the skills it needs for a particular project will be widely dispersed around the organisation but need to work together to meet customer needs. Teams are a way of bringing them together for the duration of a project – they then disperse and are re-formed to work on other projects. The company also uses teams for internal projects such as the one described in the case, where staff from a variety of functions and geographical areas work together on a part-time basis to deal with a pressing management problem.

People at work have always developed loyalties amongst small groups of fellow workers and there are well-documented examples of industries where work was formally organised in small, self-managing teams (Trist and Bamforth, 1951). This is now happening much more widely, with teams rather than individuals becoming the basic building block of many organisations. This is most evident in research-based organisations such as Microsoft (Cusumano, 1997), W.L. Gore and Associates or GlaxoSmithKline, where scientists or engineers from different disciplines come together to work on a common project and then disband when the work is complete. There are many cross-organisational teams – such as when Sun Microsystems and one of their major suppliers created a range of teams to manage the flow of components between the two businesses (Boddy *et al.*, 2000, and see Management in Practice on page 326). Teams can bring together people with different ideas and perspectives to solve difficult problems. Most economic and social problems require the contribution of several disciplines or organisations. Creating a team draws people from these areas together to work on the problem.

However, putting people together as a group does not in itself ensure either performance or satisfaction. Some teams, such as that at Quintiles, work to very high standards and levels of achievement. They are conspicuously successful and achieve more than was expected. Others fail, wasting both time and opportunity. The differences in performance – in meeting business goals or in satisfying members – reflect how the members managed the team.

Figure 15.1 A model of team performance

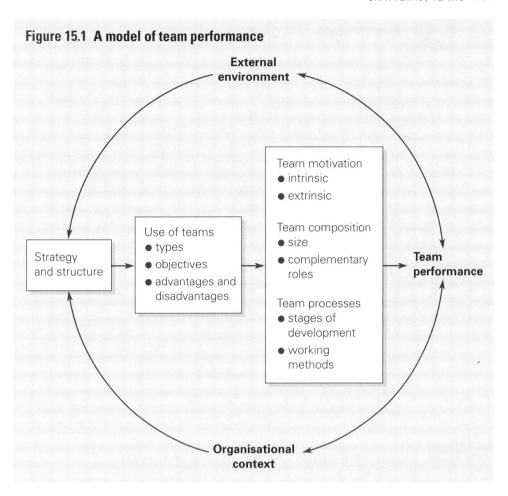

The diversity of backgrounds that makes a team worthwhile also makes it harder for the team to work. Creating a team (or 'group', 'section', 'task force' or 'working party') is only the start. Members then need to learn to work together collaboratively to reach a target. The greater the diversity, the greater the challenge it will be to make the team work.

This chapter examines the use of teams in organisations, and the management issues that they raise, as shown in Figure 15.1. The chapter begins by outlining why more organisations now use teams and introduces a way of evaluating how well a team performs. It then discusses the different types of teams and the stages through which an effective team must pass. This leads to a theory about the sources of team effectiveness, which forms the structure for the rest of the chapter – the motivation, composition and working methods of teams. For all their potential advantages teams have costs as well as benefits, and are not appropriate for all kinds of work. Deciding to invest in teams can follow a conscious decision rather than current fashion, so the chapter concludes with a way of reaching that decision in a particular situation.

15.2 Advantages of teams

There are both motivational and business reasons for the widespread use of teams.

Motivational reasons

The Hawthorne studies described in Chapter 2 showed that a supportive work group had more influence on performance than physical conditions. People have social needs that they seek to satisfy by being acknowledged and accepted by other people. This can be done on a person-to-person basis (mutual acknowledgement or courteous small-talk on the train), but most people also put some effort into being a member of several relatively permanent co-operative groups. These are an opportunity to express and receive ideas and to reshape their views by interacting with others. Acceptance by a group meets a widely held human need.

Follett and Barnard developed these ideas on the social nature of people and on the benefits of co-operative action. They saw the group as an intermediate institution between the solitary individual and the abstract society, and argued that it was through the institution of the group that people organised co-operative action. In 1926 Follett wrote:

> Early psychology was based on the study of the individual; early sociology was based on the study of society. But there is no such thing as the 'individual', there is no such thing as 'society'; there is only the group and the group-unit – the social individual. Social psychology must begin with an intensive study of the group, of the selective processes which go on within it, the differentiated reactions, the likenesses and the unlikenesses, and the spiritual energy which unites them. (Quoted in Graham, 1995, p.230)

<table>
<tr><td>

KEY IDEAS   **Mary Parker Follett and Japanese management**

According to Tokihiko Enomoto, Professor of Business Administration at Tokai University, Japan:

Follett's work has become part of our teaching on management, and is well known to quite a number of … managers in our government institutions and business organisations. Much of what Follett says about individuals and groups reflects to a substantial extent our Japanese view of the place of individuals in groups, and by extension their place in

society … She sees individuals not as independent selves going their separate ways, but as interdependent, interactive and interconnecting members of the groups to which they belong. This is something close to the Japanese ethos. We can fully agree with Follett when she writes that 'the vital relation of the individual to the world is through his groups'.

Source: Quoted in Graham (1995, pp.242–3).

</td></tr>
</table>

Likert developed this theme of the potential of groups as a basis for organising work. He observed that while effective managers used many of the traditional tools of scientific management they did not emphasise compliance by using hierarchical and economic pressures. Instead they encouraged participation by group members in all aspects of the job, including setting goals and budgets, controlling costs and organising work. Effective managers developed staff into a working team with high group loyalty. They used participation and other leadership practices to ensure that staff developed high levels of teamworking skill.

Why were these groups effective? Likert suggested the explanation lay in the *principle of supportive relationships*. He agreed with Maslow that people value receiving a positive response from others, as this helps to build and maintain their self-esteem. The relationships people experience within an organisation serve the same purpose, especially when they spend much of their time with their work group.

People value these **supportive relationships**, and Likert found that effective organisations had developed a system of interlocking groups with a high degree of group loyalty amongst the members. Their managements had deliberately built and linked such groups by ensuring people had overlapping membership of more than one group. He advocated that management should ensure that 'each person ... is a member of one or more functioning workgroups that have a high degree of group loyalty, effective skills of interaction and high performance goals' (Likert, 1961, p.104). Figure 15.2 shows the idea of supportive relationships.

These ideas continue to influence practice. Katzenbach and Smith (1993b) observed that members of a team who surmount problems together build trust and confidence in each other. They benefit from the buzz of being in a team, and of 'being part of something bigger than myself'.

Business reasons

As scientific or technical knowledge grows it becomes more fragmented between different professional groups. Solving many technical, production, social, health and other types of problem is therefore likely to involve several disciplines. Even if staff remain within their

Figure 15.2 Likert's principle of supporting relationships

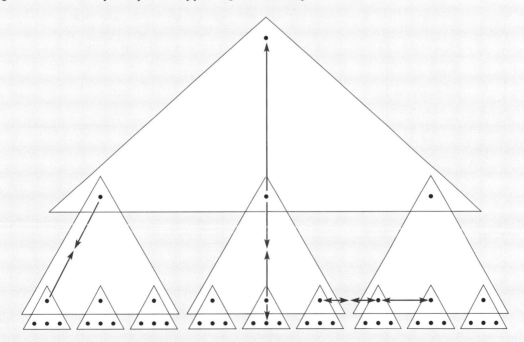

Note: The arrows indicate the linking pin-functions, both vertical and horizontal – as in cross-functional teams.
Source: Adapted from Likert (1967, p.50).

separate hierarchical structures management will often create multidisciplinary teams to work together in delivering a service or on resolving some common problem. Teams can bring complementary skills beyond those that any of the individual members could bring.

In the area of health care there is a long tradition that professional groups work independently and autonomously – and 'each has its own view of the patient, and its own view of the solution. Each profession has been given its own spectacles through which to view the world' (Soothill *et al.*, 1995, p.6). Yet there is growing interest in developing collaborative and teamworking practices between the various professions involved in delivering patient care. One reason has undoubtedly been the unnecessary suffering caused by different groups failing to pass on information. Others have been the need to improve the quality of care and make better use of resources. Many believe that these can best be achieved by encouraging independent professionals to work as teams. Teams can also reduce costs and blur expensive demarcation lines between professional staff.

> **MANAGEMENT IN PRACTICE** **Teamwork at a supermarket**
>
> As part of a major effort to change the culture in the Asda supermarket group, management has moved strongly towards a team structure. Each in-store bakery or fish department is a team effort, with a profit and loss account. Instead of an old-style weekly managers' meeting there are now twice-daily 'huddles'. Managers and their working teams in the stores meet to plan the next set of actions. As one said: 'In this business you've got to move quickly to invent the next thing: the team-based approach is one way of speeding things up.'
>
> Source: *Management Today*, December 1995, p.54.

Teams are also used when organisations need to make large improvements in performance quickly, or to enhance permanently their flexibility and responsiveness. They seem especially attractive where an organisation faces great uncertainty. Top management cannot have all the knowledge and information that is needed to specify in advance how an issue should be managed. Creating a group allows it to benefit from the insights and enthusiasm of people across the organisation – who are more likely to produce a solution than managers or professional staff working on their own. Creating a team with appropriate authority gets talent working on organisational problems much more quickly than hierarchical structures could. So teams are often seen by management as a way of using the talent and resources within the company more effectively than through more prescriptive, individual-centred styles.

Teams can also cut costs, as the Management in Practice feature shows.

> **MANAGEMENT IN PRACTICE** **Teams at Coats**
>
> In late 1998 Coats Ltd (a textile company) decided to introduce self-managed work teams into its manufacturing operations. This was a result of the need for improved quality and efficiency from the plant. The aim was to replace the traditional manufacturing set up with teams of highly trained employees fully capable of managing themselves and completing a whole piece of work. The members of each team would be able to perform a wide variety of tasks, have more decision-making power and access to more information. The teams would perform roles traditionally performed by supervisors such as scheduling, setting priorities and monitoring quality. A manager from the plant later commented:

'We started with some pilot groups, and after some initial difficulties over the composition of the groups they are working well. The performance of the teams has reached, and in some cases exceeded, expectations, especially in three key performance measures of machine efficiency, wastage and absence.

The role of individuals has also evolved as they became more at ease with the team set-up. They were more flexible, committed and also willing to act in different team roles. An attitude survey was carried out after six months and 85 per cent of staff said they preferred working in teams.'

Source: Communication from a manager in the plant.

They do not always work, however, and the Management in Practice example is a cautionary tale.

MANAGEMENT IN PRACTICE   **A community mental health team**

The management of a unit in the UK National Health Service decided to reduce radically the number of hospital places available. It would also increase the resources available for community care. As part of the change a resource centre was established in one area containing multi-disciplinary teams, each with about 30 staff. These teams would provide a round-the-clock service for the severely mentally ill in the community. The service was to be patient centred and would use a team approach with a flattened hierarchy and greater mutual accountability. A nurse became general manager. There were many team-building and similar activities.

Problems soon arose, and clear signals were given that many staff could not cope with the extra responsibility and shared decision making of empowerment. The job is difficult and sometimes dangerous, and one in which people's lives are at stake. Management changed the system to give a stronger role definition to each member of staff and a clearer structure of authority and management. It also recognised that, while teamworking may be an ideal to aim for, it has limitations. It needs to be supported by effective interteam functioning and by broader management structures.

Source: Communication from a manager in the service.

Q Case questions 15.1

- What were the business reasons that led Quintiles to use teams?
- What were the motivational reasons?

Why effective teams contribute to business performance

Many managers, especially in sectors facing severe competition, see teams as a way of reaching a new synthesis between high efficiency and high quality jobs (Wickens, 1995). Faced with complex problems, managers use teams to:

- provide a structure within which people with a wide range of technical skills and different perspectives can come together;
- provide a forum in which issues or problems can be raised and dealt with – rather than being left unattended;

- enable people to extend their roles, so possibly improving responsiveness and reducing costs;
- encourage acceptance and understanding by staff of a problem and the solution proposed;
- promote wider learning by encouraging reflection, and spreading lessons widely.

Gathering data on teams

Gather some original information on how at least two organisations have used teams to get work done, or where an organisation has abandoned teamwork. Use the questions below as a starting point for your enquiry. The data you collect may be useful in one of your tutorials, as well as adding to your knowledge of teams.

What is the main task of the organisation or department?

How are the staff in the area grouped into teams?

Use the definition (a 'real team' page 458, Table 15.1) to describe the team.

What type of team is it (use the ideas in section 15.5 as a guide)?

What do management and team members see as the advantages and disadvantages of teamworking in this situation?

Have there been any recent changes in the organisation of the teams, such as members taking on new tasks? If so, why?

15.3 Crowds, groups and teams

A group (or **team**) is not just any collection of people. A crowd in the street is not usually a group: they are there by chance, and will have little if any further contact. Are 150 students in a lecture theatre a team? What about the staff in a supermarket? In a take-away restaurant? In the same section of a factory? They are not a crowd: they have some things in common, and people may refer to them as a group. Compare them with five people designing some software for a bank, each of whom brings distinct professional skills to their collective discussions of the most suitable design, or with seven students working together on a group assignment. They have a **structure** to handle the whole process, work largely on their initiative, and move easily between all the tasks, helping each other as needed.

Crowds, groups and teams

Note down a few words that express the differences between the examples given. Do some sound more like a group than others?

One difference is in the extent to which they share a common purpose. Groups or teams aim to produce some outcome to which all members have contributed, and for which they share some collective responsibility. A second difference is in the extent to which members share ideas and activities to get the job done. Teams can add value to individual work by exchanging ideas, information and effort. There is some continuing interdependence, which leads to a sense of membership, and of being (temporarily) distinct from outsiders.

Teams or not?

Consider a Davis Cup tennis or Ryder Cup golf team, in which most of the action takes place between individual participants from either side. No significant co-ordination occurs between the members during each of the matches. In what ways would such teams meet the above definition?

Can you think of other examples of people who work largely on their own but are commonly referred to as a team?

In normal conversation people typically use the words 'group' and 'team' interchangeably – they mean the same thing. This book follows that common usage, but it is essential to be aware that the words can mean different things. Some work effectively

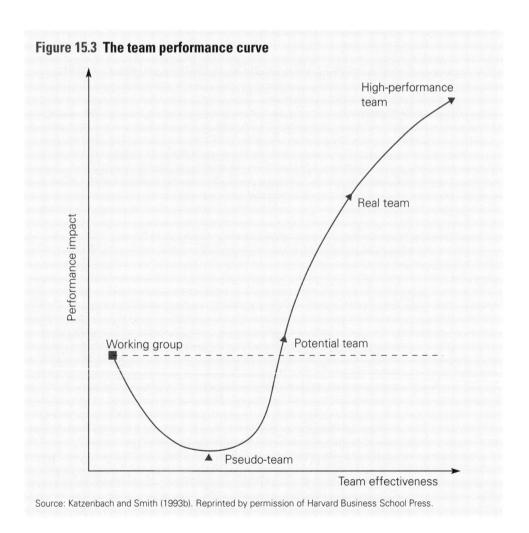

Figure 15.3 The team performance curve

High-performance team

Real team

Performance impact

Working group

Potential team

Pseudo-team

Team effectiveness

Source: Katzenbach and Smith (1993b). Reprinted by permission of Harvard Business School Press.

and others do not. Becoming an effective group or team costs time and effort. That cost is not necessary if the task could be done by well-motivated and co-operative individuals. It is worth taking a few sentences to clarify the meaning behind the terms.

Katzenbach and Smith (1993b) define a team as 'A small number of people with complementary skills who are committed to a common purpose, performance goals, and working approach for which they hold themselves mutually accountable' (p.45). A group of people that works together is not necessarily a team on this definition. The essential point is that groups (or teams) differ in what they produce.

Katzenbach and Smith (1993) use the 'team performance curve' shown in Figure 15.3 to make the point clear. While many groups call themselves teams most do not clarify their shared purpose or common approach, and so do not achieve as much as they could. They rely on the contributions and expertise of the individual members. Members engage in normal social courtesies and interactions, and perhaps exchange some task advice and information. But they are accountable for their work as individuals. In many situations such '**working groups**' (see Table 15.1) are all that is needed, provided individuals do their job competently. Teams use collective discussion, debate and decision to deliver 'collective work products' – something more than the sum of individual effort. Figure 15.3 shows this difference, with working groups delivering individual work products, while teams produce collective work products. Table 15.1 describes the five points on the curve.

Table 15.1 Description of the points on the team performance curve

Point	Description
Working group	There is no significant need to become a team. The focus is on individual effort. Members interact mainly to share information and best practices. They help each other to perform within their area of responsibility. There is no strong common purpose or joint work product for which they are all accountable
Pseudo-team	There are opportunities for collective performance, but members have not focused on trying to achieve it. No interest in shaping a common purpose or set of performance goals, though it may call itself a team. Time in meetings detracts from individual performance, without any joint benefits. Whole is less than potential sum of parts
Potential team	There are opportunities for collective performance, and members are trying to achieve this. They still need to develop clarity over purpose, goals or joint work products. They may require more discipline in working out a common approach or to establish collective accountability
Real team	A small number of people with complementary skills who are equally committed to a common purpose, performance goals and working approach for which they hold themselves mutually accountable
High-performance team	Meets all the tests of a real team, and in addition members are deeply committed to one another's personal growth and success

Source: Katzenbach and Smith (1993, pp. 90–2). Reprinted by permission of Harvard Business School Press.

Having, for the purpose of their argument, distinguished between working groups and teams, Katzenbach and Smith emphasise that they do not advocate particular labels. They recommend (and this author agrees) that people should use the terms with which they are comfortable. It is what groups and teams *do* that matter, not what they are called.

15.4 The basis of effective teams

The definition of a 'real team' suggests some of the tools that team members can use to assess their progress towards becoming an effective team, in the sense of meeting the expectations of those depending on the team.

Small number

Groups of more than about 12 people have great difficulty operating as a coherent team. It becomes harder for them to agree on a common purpose and the logistical problems of finding a place and time to work together increase. Most teams have between 2 and 10 people – with between 4 and 8 probably being the most common range. Larger groups usually divide into subgroups.

Complementary skills

Teams benefit from having members with three types of skill between them. First, there are *technical*, *functional* or *professional skills*, relevant to the subject of the group's work. A group implementing a networked computer system will require at least some members to have appropriate technical skills, while one developing a new strategy for a retailer will have strategic or business development skills.

Secondly, a team needs to include people with *problem-solving and decision-making skills*. These enable the team to approach a task systematically, using appropriate techniques of analysis. These include SWOT analysis, project management methods, cost/benefit analysis, diagramming techniques, and flowcharting.

Finally, a team needs people with adequate *interpersonal skills* to hold it together as a human institution. Members' attitudes and feelings towards each other and to the task change as work continues. The changing degree of commitment may generate irritation and conflict and someone needs to have the skill to manage these disagreements constructively.

Common purpose

Teams cannot work to a common purpose unless members spend time and effort clarifying that purpose. They need to express it in clear performance goals. These focus members' energy on activities that support their achievement. A common purpose helps communication between members, since they can interpret and understand their contributions more easily.

Common approach

Teams need to decide how they will work together to accomplish their common purpose. This includes deciding who does which jobs, what skills members need to develop, and how the group should make and modify decisions. The common approach includes supporting and integrating new or reticent members into the team. Working together on these tasks helps to promote the mutual trust and constructive conflict necessary to team success.

Mutual accountability

A team cannot work as one until its members willingly hold themselves to be collectively and mutually accountable for the results of the work. As members do real work together towards a common objective, commitment and trust usually follow. If one or more members are unwilling to accept this collective responsibility it will not become a fully effective team.

15.5   Types of team

Teams have to cope with different issues, depending on their type of work, formality, permanence and physical separation.

Type of work

Hackman (1990) distinguished seven types of team in terms of the functions they perform, and the risks and opportunities associated with each. Table 15.2 summarises these.

Table 15.2   Hackman's classification of team types and their associated risks and opportunities

Type	Risks	Opportunities
Top management teams – to set organisational directions	Underbounded; absence of organisational context	Self-designing; influence over key organisational conditions
Task forces – for a single unique project	Team and work both new	Clear purpose and deadline
Professional support groups – providing expert assistance	Dependency on others for work	Using and honing professional expertise
Performing groups – playing to audiences	Skimpy organisational supports	Play that is fuelled by competition and/or audiences
Human service teams – taking care of people	Emotional drain; struggle for control	Inherent significance of helping people
Customer service teams – selling products and services	Loss of involvement with parent organisation	Bridging between parent organisation and customers
Production teams – turning out the product	Retreat into technology; insulation from end users	Continuity of work; able to hone team design and product

Source: Hackman (1990)

> ### Q   Case questions 15.2
>
> ● What kinds of team do Quintiles use, in Hackman's typology?
> ● What other kinds of team from the list have you experienced?

Formality

Formal teams

Formal teams are created by the organisation as part of the business's basic structure. There are both vertical and horizontal teams, as shown in Figure 15.4.

Vertical teams consist of a manager and his or her subordinates within a single department or function. The manager and staff in the Treasury Department of a bank or the senior nurse, nursing staff and support staff in a unit of the Western General Hospital

Figure 15.4 Horizontal and vertical teams within an organisation

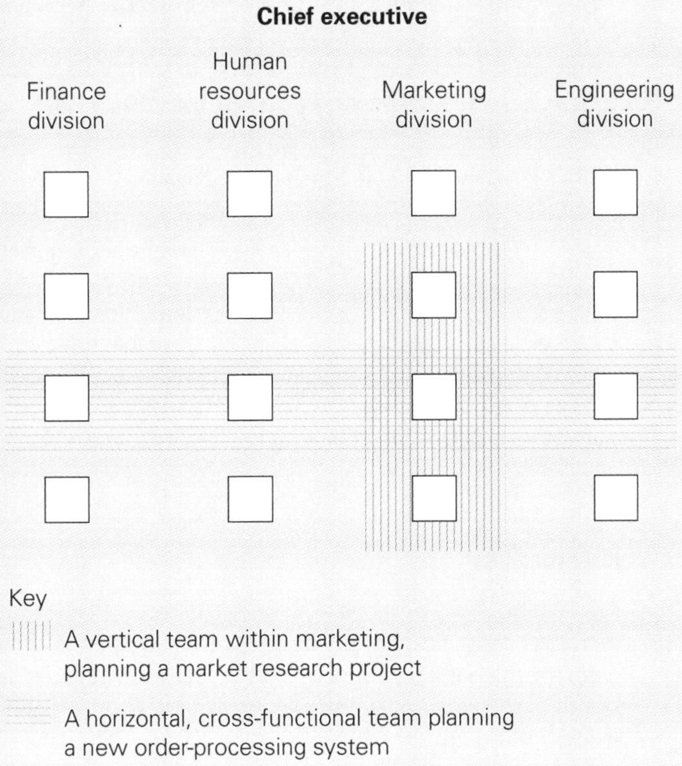

Key

| | | | | | A vertical team within marketing,
planning a market research project

A horizontal, cross-functional team planning
a new order-processing system

are formally constituted vertical teams. So is a team leader and his or her staff in the BT call centre in Bristol. In each case management created them to support broader goals by meeting the requirements in the earlier team definition.

Horizontal teams consist of staff from roughly the same level, but in various functional departments. The Quintiles team is an example, being brought together to deal with a specific problem to improve the delivery of test material. In Hackman's typology, task forces would be an example. They are often called cross-functional teams, frequently created to deal with a non-routine problem that requires several types of professional knowledge. Managers create them to take advantage of opportunities, such as to develop a new product or process.

Informal groups

Although not created by management, **informal groups** are a powerful feature of organisational life. They develop as the day-to-day activities bring people into contact with each other – and who then discover common interests or concerns. These may be unrelated to work – people find they share a common sporting or social interest with others in the organisation, and form a set of relationships with them through arranging outings or competitions. Informal groups form directly during work when people in different formal groups start exchanging information and ideas. Staff using a software package may begin to pass around problems or tips. Staff in separate departments dealing with a customer may start passing information to each other to avoid misunderstandings even though this is not part of the specified job. Informal groups may also develop in opposition to management – as when people believe they are being unfairly treated, and come together from across groups to express a common dissatisfaction with a management policy.

KEY IDEAS **Informal networks: the company behind the chart**

'If the formal organization is the skeleton of the company, the informal is the central nervous system. This drives the collective thought processes, actions and reactions of the business units. Designed to facilitate standard modes of production, management create the formal organization to handle easily anticipated problems. When unexpected problems arise, the informal organization becomes active. Its complex web of social ties form every time colleagues communicate and solidifies over time into surprisingly stable networks. Highly adaptive, informal networks move diagonally and elliptically, skipping entire functions to get work done.'

The authors argue that these informal networks can either foster or disrupt communication processes. They recommend that managers try to understand them in order to make use of their strengths, or even adjust aspects of the formal organisation to complement the informal.

Source: Krackhardt and Hanson (1993, p.104).

Permanence

Permanent teams give shape to the structure of an organisation even though individual members come and go. Functional or departmental teams are examples – they provide regular professional support (such as a legal group) or deliver customer services such as health care or concerts. Others are top teams responsible for the overall direction and strategy of the business.

Temporary teams are created to deal with a one-off project such as a new product, service or organisational structure. Hackman refers to these as task forces, which disband when the task is complete. Such teams face particular problems, which Boddy (2002) identified as:

- The next job they hope to be working on may distract them from completing the current, temporary, assignment.
- Varied technical skills: those less familiar with the technical aspects, perhaps because they come from a user department, will usually be reluctant to air their questions in the public forum.
- Other jobs to do, because in most cases they will only be part-time members of the project team.
- Political and possibly personal agendas, being there as representatives of a department or function rather than as individuals.

Physical separation

Modern communications technologies enable and encourage people to create teams in which the members are physically distant for most of the time, even though they are expected to deliver high quality collective outcome. Many of the teams in Quintiles are like this, including the one set up to create a new process for delivering materials across the world. Companies such as British Airways (at their headquarters near Heathrow airport) and most large consulting companies such as PricewaterhouseCoopers encourage staff to work from home or on clients' premises, reserving space in the office only as required (known as 'hot-desking'). They expect staff to communicate with other team members electronically or by telephone. While the method saves money it requires careful management to ensure the benefits of teamworking are retained. Practices include ensuring that some regular (or at least initial) face-to-face contact occurs, and that members resolve issues of roles, working methods and conflict management (Maruca, 1998).

15.6 Stages of group development

Putting people into a group does not mean they perform well immediately, as teams need to go through stages of growth. Some never perform well. Tuckman and Jensen (1977) developed a theory that groups can potentially pass through five fairly clearly defined stages of development. Figure 15.5 shows these.

Teams need to have the chance to grow up and to develop trust amongst the members. As the work makes progress people will learn about each other, and how they can work well together. The closer they get the easier it becomes to develop mutual trust.

Forming

Forming is the stage at which members choose, or are told, to join a team. Managers may select them for their functional and technical expertise or for some other skill. They

Figure 15.5 Stages of group development

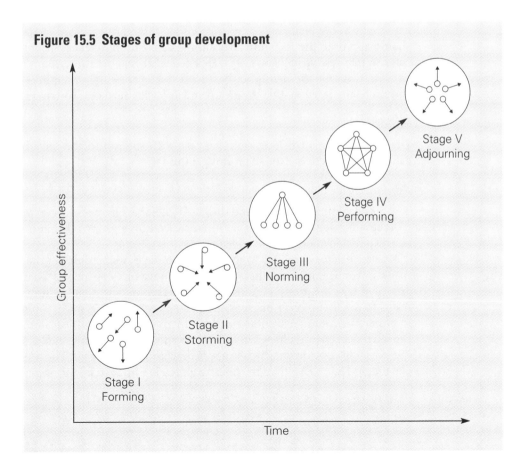

come together and begin to find out who the other members are, exchanging fairly superficial information about themselves, and beginning to offer ideas about what the group should do. People are trying to make an impression on the group and to establish their identity with the other members.

Storming

Conflicts may occur at the storming stage, so it can be an uncomfortable time for the group. As the group gets down to the actual work members begin to express differences of interest that they withheld or did not recognise at the forming stage. People realise that others want different things from the group, have other priorities and, perhaps, hidden agendas. Different personalities emerge, with contrasting attitudes towards the group and how it should work. Some may experience conflicts between the time they are spending with the group and other duties. As they work, differences in values and norms emerge. Some groups never pass this stage. Open conflict is not the only signal of problems. Members may believe the group is performing well – but may be deluding themselves. If the group does not confront disagreements it will remain at the forming or storming stage. It will do no significant work, and fall behind more successful teams. Eventual performance depends on someone doing or saying something that moves the group to the next stage.

Norming

Here the members are beginning to accommodate differences constructively and to establish adequate ways of working together. They develop a set of shared norms – expected ways of behaving – about how they should interact with each other, how they should approach the task, how they should deal with differences. People create or accept roles so that responsibilities are clear. The leader may set those roles formally or members may accept them implicitly during early meetings. Members may establish a common language to guide the group and allow members to work together effectively.

Performing

Here the group is working well, gets on with the job to the required standard and achieves its objectives. Not all groups get this far.

Adjourning

The group completes its task and disbands. Members may reflect on how the group performed and identify lessons for future tasks. Some groups disband because they are clearly not able to do the job, and agree to stop meeting.

A team that survives will go through these stages many times in the course of its life. As new members join, as others leave, as circumstances or the task change, new tensions arise that take the group back to an earlier stage. A new member implies that the team needs to revisit, however briefly, the forming and norming stages. This ensures the new member is brought psychologically into the team, and understands how they are expected to behave. A change in task or a conflict over priorities can take a group back to the storming stage, from which it needs to work forward again. The process will be more like that in Figure 15.6 than the linear progression implied by the original theory.

Figure 15.6 Modified model of the stages of group development

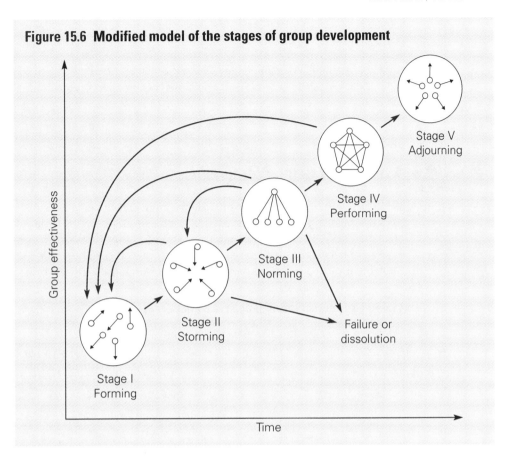

The evolution of a project team

A local authority created a project team to select and implement a computer-based housing management system. The chief executive appointed the assistant head of the information technology department as project leader, who then asked some members of the housing department to join the team. The director of the housing department allocated some project duties to his staff without reference to the project leader. The housing department believed the IT department was invading its territory. Both incidents caused relationship problems until managers clarified roles and expectations. To help gain the group's commitment the project leader explained the plan to the team. They discussed and agreed it in principle.

The group members pointed out that they could not work on the project as well as on their normal duties. They believed that working in their normal open-plan offices alongside other housing staff would distract them. The chief executive agreed to a limited amount of time off for the project, and allocated a separate room for those working on it. One member still refused to commit to timescales. The other members told him forcefully that they were equally busy but able to comply, implying his behaviour was affecting team performance. This was enough to persuade him to participate more fully. There was another early conflict when members of two functional groups put forward opposing system requirements and were reluctant to specify in writing what their joint requirements would be. The team, with the encouragement of the project leader, established some guidelines on the working practices they would use.

Members contacted suppliers and other sites that had installed similar systems to gather information about potential systems. The project leader noted that team members enjoyed these visits, and she used them as a motivator to encourage the completion of more boring but essential tasks such as systems documentation. Performance improved as the project continued. Each member had prepared a checklist for meetings with suppliers and users. As they learned how each other worked this process improved, with each evaluation increasing their effectiveness as a team. They completed document preparation, evaluation and recommendation on time and to the level of performance required. The group adjourned once they had implemented the project.

15.7 A model for team effectiveness

What models of team development can managers use to build a team that moves towards meeting one or more of these measures of success? Based on the work of Hackman (1990) Table 15.3 summarises three long-term measures of team effectiveness. These are necessarily subjective, and a team may succeed on some and fail on others. Judgement must also reflect the conditions in which the team is working.

Table 15.3 Criteria for evaluating team effectiveness

Criteria	Description
Has it met performance expectations?	Is the group completing the task managers gave to it – not only the project performance criteria, but also measures of cost and timeliness?
Have members experienced an effective team?	Is it enhancing their ability to work together as a group? Have they created such a winning team that it represents a valuable resource for future projects?
Have members developed transferable teamwork skills?	Are members developing teamwork skills that they will take to future projects? This indicates a team meeting the needs of the business and the team members.

Source: Based on Hackman (1990).

Based on research with 27 teams of different types (including 'task forces' – equivalent to project teams) Hackman proposed that to perform well a group must surmount three hurdles. The members must:

- be willing to exert sufficient effort to accomplish the task to an acceptable level;
- bring adequate knowledge and skill to the task;
- use group processes that are appropriate to the work and the setting.

These hurdles (see Figure 15.7) show how well a group is doing and where possible difficulties are arising.

To overcome each of these hurdles, Hackman argues that a team needs both internal and external support. The manager cannot rely on internal team practices (or personal enthusiasm) alone. He or she should also attend to wider organisational conditions such as the availability of **team-based rewards**. If both are in place it is more likely that the group will put in the effort, have the skill and use good team processes. Table 15.4 summarises these points.

Securing adequate effort is essentially a matter of motivation and so draws on the ideas in Chapter 13 – such as the intrinsic nature of the task and whether adequate extrinsic rewards are available. This chapter deals with the other two hurdles – team composition and team processes.

Figure 15.7 Hurdles in the way of team effectiveness

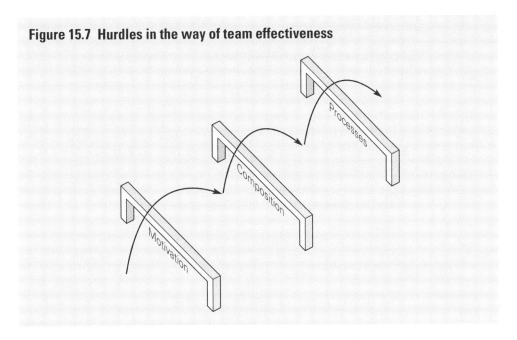

Table 15.4 Points of leverage for enhancing group performance

Requirements for effectiveness	Internal conditions	Organisational context
Effort (see Chapter 13)	Motivational structure of task	Remedying co-ordination problems and rewarding team commitment
Knowledge and skill	Team composition	Available education and training, including coaching and guidance
Performance strategies	Working processes that foster review and learning	Information system to support task and provide feedback on progress

Source: Based on Hackman (1990), p.13.

15.8 Team composition

In a mechanical sense, team composition includes questions of size and membership. Is it too large or too small? Is there an acceptable balance between part-time and full-time members? Do members have the right skills? Are they too similar in outlook, or so diverse that they are unlikely to agree a solution? Are all the relevant functions represented? These are important questions, but even more important is the question of whether members have the right skills and ways of working to form an effective team. Research by Uhl-Bien and Graen (1998), for example, led them to warn that 'Although cross-functional teams may be highly effective if implemented correctly (for instance, staffed with strong team players), if implemented incorrectly (staffed with independently focused self-managing professionals) they may .... harm organizational functioning' (p. 348).

As people work together in teams they behave in different ways. This is bound to happen, as a major benefit of creating teams is to bring together people with different perspectives, skills and interests. Members tend to take on a relatively distinctive role within the group. A group needs a balance of such roles, so a task for the project manager is to do what they can to shape the composition of the group to enhance perform-ance. Two ideas that project managers use are the distinction between task and maintenance roles and Belbin's research on team roles.

Task and maintenance roles

Some people focus on the project task, on getting the job done, on meeting deadlines. Others put most of their energies into keeping the peace, and ensuring the group stays together – they help to maintain the project team. Table 15.5 summarises the typical activities of people in the two roles.

Table 15.5 Summary of task and maintenance roles

Emphasis on task	Emphasis on maintenance
initiator	encourager
information seeker	compromiser
diagnoser	peacekeeper
opinion seeker	clarifier
evaluator	summariser
decision manager	standard setter

Teams need both roles, and skilful project managers try to ensure this happens.

Meredith Belbin – team roles

Belbin, of Oxford University, conducted a series of studies in which colleagues systemati-cally observed several hundred small groups while they performed a task. From these

---

KEY IDEAS   Belbin's research method

The research arose from the practice at the Henley School of Management of basing much of their training on work done by managers in teams. Groups of up to 10 managers worked on exercises or business simulations. The organisers had long observed that some teams achieved better financial results than others – irrespective of the abilities of the individual members as measured by standard personality and mental tests. The reasons for this were unclear. Why did some teams of individually able people perform less well than teams that appeared to contain less able people?

Belbin therefore undertook a study in which observers, drawn from the course members, used a standard procedure to record the types of contribution that members made. Team members voluntarily took the psychometric tests, and the researchers recorded quantifiable results of the team performance. The researchers formed teams of members with above-average mental abilities, and compared their performance with the other teams. The 'intelligent' teams usually performed less well. Of 25 such teams only 3 were winners, and the most common position was sixth in a league of eight. The explanation lay in the way such teams behaved during the task. Typically they spent much time in debate, arguing for their point of view to the exclusion of other opinions. These highly intelligent people were good at spotting flaws in other members' arguments. They then became so engrossed in these arguments that they neglected other tasks. Failure led to recrimination. The lesson was that behaviour (rather than measured intelligence) affected group performance.

Source: Belbin (1981).

observations he concluded that each person working in a group tends to behave in a way that corresponds closely to one of nine distinct roles. The balance of these roles in a group affects how well or badly it performs.

The researchers identified the types of behaviour that people displayed in teams – their preferred team roles. Some were creative, full of ideas and suggestions. Others were much more concerned with detail, ensuring that the team had dealt with all aspects of the situation and that quality was right. Others again spent most of their time keeping the group together. Table 15.6 lists the nine roles identified in Belbin (1993). Belbin and his colleagues observed that the composition of teams was crucial to their success, as members played a range of roles. Winning teams had members who fulfilled a balance of roles that was different from the less successful ones.

Table 15.6 Belbin's team roles

Role	Typical features
Implementer	Disciplined, reliable, conservative and efficient. Turns ideas into practical actions
Co-ordinator	Mature, confident, a good chairperson. Clarifies goals, promotes decision-making, delegates well
Shaper	Challenging, dynamic, thrives on pressure. Has the drive and courage to overcome obstacles – likes to win
Plant	Creative, imaginative, unorthodox – the' ideas' person who solves difficult problems
Resource investigator	Extrovert, enthusiastic, communicative – explores opportunities, develops contacts, a natural networker
Monitor-evaluator	Sober, strategic and discerning. Sees all options, judges accurately – the inspector
Teamworker	Co-operative, mild, perceptive and diplomatic. Listens, builds, averts friction, calms things – sensitive to people and situations
Completer	Painstaking, conscientious, anxious. Searches out errors and omissions. Delivers on time.
Specialist	Single-minded, self-starting, dedicated. Provides scarce knowledge and skill

Source: Based on Belbin (1981 and 1993).

Winning teams had an appropriate balance, such as:

- a capable chairman;
- a strong plant – a creative and clever source of ideas;
- at least one other clever person to act as a stimulus to the plant; and
- a monitor-evaluator – someone to find flaws in proposals before it was too late.

Ineffective teams usually had a severe imbalance, such as:

- a chairman with two dominant shapers – since the chairman will almost certainly not be allowed to take that role;
- two resource investigators and two plants – since no one listens or turns ideas into action; or
- a completer with monitor-evaluators and implementers – probably slow to progress, and stuck in detail.

Belbin did *not* suggest that all teams should have nine people, each with a different **preferred team role**. His point was that team composition should reflect the task:

The useful people to have in a team are those who possess strengths or characteristics that serve a need without duplicating those that are already there. Teams are a question of balance; what is needed is not well-balanced individuals but individuals who balance well with one another. In that way human frailties can be underpinned and strengths used to full advantage. (Belbin, 1981, p.77)

Trainers use the model widely to enable members to evaluate their own preferred roles. They also consider how the balance of roles within a team affects performance. Some managers use it when filling vacancies. A personnel director joined a new organisation and concluded that it employed few 'completer-finishers'. Management started initiatives and programmes but left them unfinished as they switched to something else. She resolved that in recruiting new staff she would try to bring at least one more 'completer-finisher' to the senior team.

However, there is little evidence that companies deliberately use the model when forming teams from existing staff. Managers typically form teams on criteria of technical expertise, departmental representation, or who is available. How the team processes will work is a secondary consideration. A team where members are capable and committed to the mission will ignore individual status or ego issues. People will be able and willing to cover roles if one seems to be lacking.

Whether widely used or not, there are some clear hints that a manager responsible for a team may find the work goes better if they put effort into securing the most suitable mix of members.

ACTIVITY 15.4

Team composition

This activity is intended to encourage you to reflect critically on this section about team composition.

Evaluate a team you have worked with using Belbin's team roles.

Which roles are well represented, and which are missing?

Has that affected the way the team has worked?

Which of the roles most closely matches your own preferred role?

What are the strengths and weaknesses of Belbin's model to the manager?

Have you any evidence of managers using it to help them manage teams? If so, in what way was it used, and with what effect?

15.9 Team processes

Teams need to decide the process that they will use to help them work together to accomplish their common purpose. This common approach includes some mechanical but vital aspects of planning meetings and identifying communication patterns.

Common approach

A primary outcome of an effective 'norming' stage is that members agree both the administrative and social aspects of working together. This includes deciding who does which jobs, what skills members need to develop, and how the group should make and modify decisions. In other words the group needs to agree the work required and how it will fit together. It needs to decide how to integrate the skills of the group and use them co-operatively to advance performance.

The common approach includes supporting and integrating new or reticent members into the team. It also includes practices of remembering and summarising group agreements and discussions. Working together on these tasks helps to promote the mutual trust and constructive conflict necessary to team success. Groups need to spend as much time on developing a common approach as they do on developing a shared purpose.

Team members need to control their meetings effectively – whether face to face or at a distance. That involves ensuring they are conducted in way that suits the purpose of the task, without participants feeling they are being manipulated. Table 15.7 is an example of the advice widely available to managers about effective and ineffective meetings.

Table 15.7 Five tips for more effective meetings

Meetings are likely to succeed if	Meetings are likely to fail if
they are scheduled well in advance	they are fixed at short notice (absentees)
they have an agenda, with relevant papers distributed in advance and invite additions at the start	they have no agenda or papers (no preparation, lack of focus, discussion longer)
they have a starting and finishing time and follow prearranged time limits on each item	they are of indefinite length (discussion drifts), time is lost and important items not dealt with (delay, and require a further meeting)
decisions and responsibilities for action recorded and circulated within 24 hours	decisions lack clarity (misunderstanding what was agreed, delay, reopening issues).
they keep subgroups or members of related teams informed of progress	the team is not aware of work going on in other teams that is relevant to its work

Content of communication

Group members depend on information and ideas from others to help them perform the group task; a further aspect of observation is to identify the kind of contribution that people make (Chapter 14 illustrated patterns of group communication), and whether this helps the group to manage the task. To study and learn how people behave in groups we need a precise and reliable way to describe events. There are many such models and you can develop one depending on the particular focus of interest. Table 15.8 illustrates one list of behaviours. The point is that if, for example, a group spends a lot of time proposing ideas and disagreeing with them it will not progress far. A more effective group will spend more time proposing and building, which of course implies developing better listening skills.

Table 15.8 Categories of communication within a group

Category	Explanation
Proposing	Putting forward a suggestion, idea or course of action
Supporting	Declaring agreement or support for an individual or their idea
Building	Developing or extending an idea or suggestion from someone else
Disagreeing	Criticising another person's statement
Giving information	Giving or clarifying facts, ideas or opinions
Seeking information	Seeking facts, ideas or opinions from others

Observing the team

Members can develop the skill of assessing how well a team is performing a task. There are many guides to help them do this, and anyone can develop their ability to **observe** groups by concentrating on this aspect rather than on the **content** of the immediate task. They work slightly apart from the team for a short time and keep a careful record of what members say or do. They also note how other members react, and how that affects the performance of the team. At the very least, members can reflect on these questions at the end of a task:

- What did people do or say that helped or hindered the group's performance?
- What went well during that task which we should try to repeat?
- What did not go well, which we could improve?

With practice, and of course in the reality of the workplace, skilled members of a team are able to observe what is happening at the same time as they work on the task itself. They can do this more easily and powerfully if they focus their observations on certain behaviour categories, such as those shown in Table 15.8 – but suited to the purpose of the observation.

15.10 The disadvantages of teams

For all the undoubted benefits of teams, they also have disadvantages and costs.

Take on their own purpose

Some groups take on a life of their own, and become too independent of the organisation that created them. As members learn to work together they generate enthusiasm and commitment – and become harder to control. The team may divert the project to meet goals that they value, rather than those of the sponsor. As experts in the particular issue they can exert great influence over management, by controlling or filtering the flow of information to the organisation as whole, so that their goals become increasingly hard to challenge. Their work becomes relatively isolated from other parts of the organisation, and they focus on what they see to be key issues.

Use too much time

The benefit of wider perspectives comes from discussion. This inevitably takes longer than if an individual made the decision. Time spent in discussion may encourage participation and acceptance – but only if the group manages this well. If discussion strays over unrelated issues, or goes over matters that they have already dealt with, the team loses time. This can also be an opportunity for members opposed to the project to prolong group discussion and to use the search for agreement as a blocking tactic. Some members will complain about the time spent. In fast-moving situations they may simply not be able to afford the time and so withdraw their support.

Allow an individual to dominate

Some teams allow one member to dominate. This may be the formal leader of the group in a hierarchical organisation, where people do not challenge those in a position of authority. It may be a technical expert who takes over, when others hesitate to show their lack of knowledge or to ask for explanations. In either case the group will not draw on the experience available, and it will probably be a dissatisfying and unproductive experience. It may produce a worse result, and be more costly, than if one person had dealt with the issue.

Succumb to groupthink

An influential analysis of how **groupthink** occurs was put forward by the social psychologist Irving Janis. His research began by studying some major and highly publicised failures of decision making, looking for some common theme that might explain why apparently able and intelligent people were able to make such bad decisions – such as President Kennedy's decision to have US forces invade Cuba in 1961. One common thread he observed was the inability of the groups involved to consider a range of alternatives rationally, or to see the likely consequences of the choice they made. Members were also keen to be seen as team players, and not to say things that might end their membership of the group. Janis termed this phenomenon 'groupthink', and defined it as:

> [Groupthink is] a mode of thinking that people engage in when they are deeply involved in a cohesive in-group, when the members' striving for unanimity overrides their motivation to realistically appraise alternative courses of action. (Janis, 1972, p.9)

He identified eight symptoms of groupthink, shown in Key Ideas.

KEY IDEAS **Irving Janis on the symptoms of groupthink**

Janis (1977) identified eight symptoms that give early warning of groupthink developing – and the more of them that are present, the more likely it is that the 'disease' will strike. The symptoms are:

- **Illusion of invulnerability** The belief that any decision they make will be successful.
- **Belief in the inherent morality of the group** Justifying a decision by reference to some higher value.
- **Rationalisation** Playing down the negative consequences or risks of a decision.
- **Stereotyping out-groups** Characterising opponents or doubters in unfavourable terms,

making it easier to dismiss even valid criticism from that source.
- **Self-censorship** Suppressing legitimate doubts in the interest of group loyalty.
- **Direct pressure** Strong expressions from other members (or the leader) that dissent to their favoured approach will be unwelcome.
- **Mindguards** Keeping uncomfortable facts or opinions out of the discussion.
- **Illusion of unanimity** Playing down any remaining doubts or questions, even if they become stronger or more persistent.

Source: Based on Janis (1977; 1982).

MANAGEMENT IN PRACTICE **Groupthink in medicine**

An experienced nurse observed three of the symptoms of groupthink in the work of senior doctors:

Illusion of invulnerability

A feeling of power and authority leads a group to see themselves as invulnerable. Traditionally the medical profession has been very powerful and this makes it very difficult for non-clinicians to question their actions or plans.

Belief in the inherent morality of the group

This happens when clinical staff use the term 'individual clinical judgement' as a justification for their actions. An example is when a business manager is trying to reduce drug costs and one consultant's practice is very different from his colleagues'. Consultants often reply that they are entitled to use their clinical judgement. This is never challenged by their colleagues, and it is often impossible to achieve change.

Self-censorship

Being a doctor is similar to being in a very exclusive club, and none of the members want to be excluded. Therefore doctors will usually support each other, particularly against management. They are also extremely unlikely to report each other for mistakes or poor performance. A government scheme to encourage 'whistle-blowing' was met with much derision in the ranks.

Source: Private communication.

ACTIVITY 15.5

Advantages and disadvantages of teams

This activity is intended to encourage you to reflect critically on the benefits or otherwise of teams.

Which of the advantages and disadvantages have you observed?

Does your experience suggest that teams have always performed well? What have been the reasons for any difficulties?

15.11 Are teams worth the investment?

Katzenbach and Smith (1993b) raise the question of whether teams as they have defined them are always necessary for effective performance. Individuals can handle many tasks as well as a group – and perhaps better. An example is where a task requires someone to use their expertise on a narrowly defined technical issue with no wider implications. For such purposes someone who is part of an effective working group can meet the performance required. There is no need to invest the extra effort needed for team performance. Indeed it could be counter-productive. Off-site team development activities can be exciting and motivating. If members then find that the task to be done involves little real interaction, beyond normal interpersonal co-operation, they will feel let down by the wasted effort.

In other projects the task clearly requires people to work together to create joint work products besides individual contributions. Then the risk and cost of creating a team will be worthwhile.

Critchley and Casey (1984), two British consultants specialising in developing teams at senior level, raised the same dilemma. Reviewing the many teams with which they had worked they concluded that teams were not always necessary, and may have represented an expensive solution to simple problems. They concluded that the expense of developing a high level of skill in teamworking is often unnecessary. The answer depended on the nature of the task being undertaken:

- *simple puzzles of a technical nature* could be done quite effectively by members working independently of each other, on the basis of their technical expertise, with a reasonable degree of polite social skills;
- *familiar tasks with moderate degrees of uncertainty* need some sharing of information and ideas, but the main requirement is reasonable co-operation between the people concerned using skills of negotiation and co-ordination;
- *a high degree of uncertainty and relatively unknown problems* requires high levels of information sharing and deep interpersonal skills to cope with the 'shared uncertainty'. Such tasks require a high level of team skills.

15.12 Summary

The chapter began by documenting the growing use of teams as a basic building block of organisational structure. While this is most pronounced amongst professional and scientific staff there is growing anecdotal evidence of wider use amongst manual workers.

Teams vary greatly in performance and the chapter introduced the team performance curve to provide a form of benchmark against which team members can assess their performance. It compared different types of teams and introduced the Tuckman and Jensen model of the stages through which a team must pass if it is to become effective.

That led to a theory about the sources of team effectiveness, highlighting that teams need to have members with motivation, appropriate skills and who have developed suitable working processes. Groups benefit if they develop a commonly understood structure and way of organising how they operate, together with norms for the way that members behave towards each other. Belbin's role models highlight the benefits of complementary skills. The ability of effective groups to generate action from members is well established.

Teams have costs as well as benefits, and these costs, such as groupthink, were examined. The last section introduced a way of judging whether a team is worth the effort. The more scope there is for joint work products the more it is worth investing in teams.

Content

As management faces new expectations about cost and quality many see teams as a way of using the talents and experience of the organisation more fully to meet these tougher objectives. The organising tasks that were traditionally performed by specialist groups of managers can be done by teams themselves. Many see organisations structured around teams as the way to improve performance and the quality of working life. Teams also meet important motivational needs – for social contact and to be part of a collective achievement. Teams are often becoming the basic vehicle through which management is performed. In that sense they reintegrate some management functions with direct work. Decisions on whether to invest in teams rather than working groups depend on wider strategy.

Process

Teams are a way of making sure that relevant stakeholders are visible and represented in management processes. Selecting membership, and indeed whether a team or a working group (Katzenbach and Smith) should do the work, is a potentially far-reaching management decision. Teams can develop lives of their own and set their own agendas. The structural links between the team and the rest of the organisation will affect communication between teams. Particular aspects of the team concept, such as team briefings, are used by management to try to ensure that a management message is passed rapidly thoughout the organisation.

Control

Creating teams, and reallocating functions to them, often threatens other stakeholders who may fear their power sources (personal or organisational resources and knowledge) will be eroded. Many self-managing teams take on responsibility for monitoring performance. The bases and methods of measurement may be jointly agreed between the team members and management. Groupthink may lead members of a team that is too cohesive to ignore or fail to recognise the need for corrective action. Teams can powerfully support organisational learning by passing ideas across functional boundaries.

At Quintiles management has successfully developed a team culture, to make the most of the skills and talents across the company. By using them so extensively in the normal way of working they make it easier to bring teams together on ad hoc projects such as that described in the case. That example is especially interesting as it shows how the team combined both traditional ways of team-building at the beginning with modern technology. Team members were sure that the face-to-face meetings were essential foundations to the effective use of the technology.

Q PART CASE QUESTIONS

● What are the benefits which W.L. Gore gains from its team-based organisation?

● What, if any, differences are there between Gore's approach and that used by Quintiles?

● What lessons about the benefits can you draw from the two examples?

15.13 Review questions

1 Why has the balance shifted recently in favour of teamwork? What are the main business and motivational reasons?

2 Katzenbach and Smith distinguish between working groups and real teams. Compare their argument, that real teams are often not necessary.

3 W.L. Gore and Associates is beginning to form more distant teams. What management issues raised are likely to arise in this form of team?

4 How many stages of development do teams go through? Compare, in terms of what happened at each stage and what was done to move to the next stage, two teams that have tried to develop.

5 List the main categories of behaviour that can be identified in observing a group.

6 Compare the meaning of the terms 'task' and 'maintenance' roles.

7 Evaluate Belbin's model of team roles. Which three or four roles are of most importance in an effective team? What is your preferred role?

8 Give examples of the external factors that affect group performance. Compare the model with your experience as a group member.

9 What are the potential disadvantages of teams?

Further reading

Belbin, R.M. (1993), *Team Roles at Work*, Butterworth/Heinemann, Oxford. An account of the experiments that led him to develop his model of team roles.

Hayes, N. (1997), *Successful Team Development*, International Thompson Business Press, London. A lively and well-referenced account of many of the issues covered here.

Hackman, J.R. (1990), *Groups that Work (and Those that Don't)*, Jossey-Bass, San Francisco, CA.

Katzenbach, J.R. and Smith, D.K. (1993b), *The Wisdom of Teams*, Harvard Business School Press, Boston, MA.

Both books contain many good examples of the use of teamwork in modern organisations.

Sandberg, A. (ed.) (1995), *Enriching Production*, Avebury, Aldershot. A very wide range of perspectives on the use of teams at Volvo, and of the wider forces that affected the fate of the Volvo experiments.

Annotated links, questions and resources can be found on
www.booksites.net/boddy

Part 6

CONTROLLING THE BUSINESS

Introduction

Any purposeful human activity needs some degree of control if it is to achieve what is intended. From time to time you check where you are in relation to your destination. The sooner you do this, the more confident you are that you are on track. Frequent checks ensure you take corrective action quickly to avoid wasting effort and resources.

An owner-manager can often exercise control by personal observation, reference to limited paperwork and then a decision about corrective action. As the organisation grows so does the complexity. It becomes increacingly difficult to know the current position as work goes on in many separate places at the same time. People in those separate places may differ about their precise objectives and targets.

To help them exercise control, management is able to use a range of sytems and techniques. Financial control is clearly of major interest – how does management try to keep the financial score while all around it everything is changing? Chapter 16 introduces the main issues in this area. Financial measures reflect what has been happening in the actual operations of the organisation. The more information management has about actual progress compared with intended performance, the easier it is to adjust, so Chapter 17 reviews the main concepts in operations management. Control depends on information. Developments in information technology are revolutionising this aspect of management. Technical developments make it possible to have much more informtion, much more quickly than ever before. These possibilities and the mangement issues raised in making effective use of new information systems are examined in Chapter 18.

The case is Kwik-Fit Holdings. A nationwide UK company (now owned by Ford), Kwik-Fit has grown rapidly since it was created in 1971. It operates in a competitive industry with low margins. Tight control of operating systems and costs have been central to its success. This has been greatly helped by the management decision to install innovative information systems that have supported its rapid growth.

Kwik-Fit Holdings

Until it was bought by Ford in 1999 Kwik-Fit was Europe's largest independent tyre and exhaust retailer. Tom Farmer had created the business in 1971, using the proceeds from the sale of an earlier company. Although now much bigger, the core business in 2001 was still the drive-in, 'while you wait' fitting of replacement tyres, exhausts, batteries, brakes and shock absorbers. The company also offered engine oil and filter change services and supplied and fitted child safety seats. In 1995 it had begun to sell motor insurance. The company had also entered the fleet market, offering the Kwik-Fit service to, for example, contract hire firms and large fleet operators.

Services were delivered to customers through roadside centres, each staffed by a manager and a team of fitters. A customer arriving at a centre was met by the manager or a fitter and stated his or her requirement. The fitter checked the fault, and that the parts were in stock. The fitter then gave the customer a written quotation of the cost and, if accepted, did the work immediately. The customer then paid and left.

The growing market

In 1991 the company estimated that it had 30 per cent of the market for replacement car exhausts and 12 per cent of that for replacement tyres. The aftercare market was rising long term, with growth in the number of cars. It was also competitive. Two groups owned by tyre companies each had over 400 depots and there were many local competitors. To build a dominant national position the company had to provide a standard of service that would, in the words of the Kwik-Fit slogan, achieve '100% delighted customers'. Factors thought to be valued by customers included convenience of location, cleanliness of premises, speed and quality of workmanship, price and availability of the parts required.

A critical and costly aspect of the business was to have enough spare parts on hand to cope with the range of cars requiring service. Each depot's stock reflected as accurately as possible the types of car likely to be driven in.

The administrative burden

Transactions generated administration – notably to account for the day's revenue, and to replenish stocks. In the early years the company used a manual administrative system. Records of transactions, receipts and stocks were kept on paper in boxes and files. There was a very small central management team, based in Edinburgh, and led by Tom Farmer. Kwik-Fit's structure was described by one insider as: 'a very flat structure, in as much as if we wanted to change something tomorrow we could do it – we haven't got a hierarchy that has to be gone through'. Farmer believed firmly in keeping the number of administrative staff as low as possible. With over 450 UK depots in 1991 it employed only about 90 staff at head office.

Organisation and style

The main operating company, Kwik-Fit (GB), was organised into five geographical divisions. Day-to-day management was in the hands of a management board between the main board and divisional management. Management throughout the company was expected to be in direct contact with market conditions facing the depot managers and staff. They were expected to support the depots, not to dominate them: 'We're not a big organisation – we're a collection of small businesses … in our company culture head office is seen as a support operation.'

Depots were grouped in partnerships, made up of three nearby outlets. A more senior manager, or partner, supervised two other depots as well as their own, and received a share of the profits each generated. This reflected the philosophy that staff should share in the success of the business.

These aspects of the structure were relevant to the operation of the computer network, and the scope it gave for central monitoring of the depots: 'The whole computer system is based around the depot manager as king. It doesn't restrict the manager in what he does, but he has to account for it.'

Farmer's philosophy was that, since continued success depended on the loyalty of customers, a high level of staff training was essential. All staff were trained to adhere to the Kwik-Fit Code of Practice, designed to ensure that every customer's vehicle received a high standard of service. Training also covered technical and product knowledge, depot management, sales methods and communications skills. In 1990 the company received a National Training Award in recognition of its commitment to training.

The network system

The first computer network system at Kwik-Fit was installed in 1982. It consisted of electronic point-of-sale terminals in each depot, linked to a mainframe computer at head office. A specially designed point-of-sale microcomputer, known as a Management Action Terminal (MAT), was installed in each depot. These were robustly designed for use by the managers and fitters.

The keyboard was clear and easy to use, each key being marked with a system function, such as 'cash sale' or 'stock delivery'. Pressing a key led the user through the process to be followed. Details of the stock held by the depot were stored in the MAT, and automatically updated as each transaction was processed.

During the day the MAT performed administrative tasks within the centre, such as issuing quotations in response to customer enquiries and producing invoices. For a few minutes each night the MAT became a terminal attached to the mainframe computer at head office. That computer automatically called each depot in turn. Each MAT responded by sending data about all transactions made during the day to the mainframe, such as sales, payments, stock received and transferred, and hours worked by staff.

These raw data were processed into management reports for internal use, and into instructions to suppliers and banks. The reports for head office use were printed out early the following day. The telephone link that brought the data in from each depot was also used to send information back, on such matters as price changes.

Stock levels were a critical feature of the business. These had to be sufficient for staff to meet service requests on demand, without the costs of excessive stocks making the operation uncompetitive. Stock control was previously done manually, with depots physically checking their stock and placing orders directly with suppliers. This was very time consuming, and a major aim of the system was to get better stock control:

'It's critical to the whole business that every depot has the right stock. You can't put the same stock in every garage, because the pattern is different between areas, depending on the cars people have. We needed to computerise because the information wasn't available sufficiently quickly. There was no method whereby any one person in head office, or at a given depot, could know what stock was in that depot.'

Previously stock had been controlled manually, with depots raising their own orders, and placing them with suppliers.

Outcomes

The EPOS system achieved the expected benefits – and many more. The system allowed automatic replenishment of stock. Sales were converted into orders that were automatically transmitted to four of the biggest suppliers overnight, giving a 48 hour cycle of delivery. By 1991 50 per cent of sales were being automatically reordered from suppliers through the computer, and 75 per cent of invoices were received and paid electronically.

'We run a very simple business. The only complexity in our business is size. MAT reinforces procedures in an easy way without being overburdensome. It removes from the equation a lot of the complexity that our size and geographical dispersal could create.'

The system also provided benefits that were not envisaged when the original specification was set. This was particularly true in the area of management information. The system had been designed to convert the existing (and effective) manual administration into an equally effective computerised one. Once that was implemented managers rapidly realised that they now had a great deal of information about the business which had previously been unavailable. The IT director responsible for implementing the system commented:

'We totally underestimated the potential for management information. When you switch an EPOS network on, you get flooded with mountains of data. It's live, current, happened yesterday – and you don't know what to do with it all. We totally underestimated that, and didn't realise just how useful the data would be in controlling the company.

We were producing tables and statistics that surprised a lot of people. "I didn't know that about the company" – but all of a sudden they had a tool that would let them find out.'

More generally, managers at head office now had much more information available to them about performance across the whole of the growing company. For example, the sales director could review the following day how any depot had performed, in as much or as little detail as required:

'It gives us prices, margin control, and all the necessary monitoring elements. All this information goes to the managers as well, because they need to know how they are doing as well. So if I call a depot, and ask the manager how he is doing, he could press the key on the machine and would be able to say what he sold today, and what he sold yesterday. And that information is important because their earnings depend on how well they are doing.'

The system also provided daily forecasts of sales and margins against budget for the current month. This allowed managers to see whether they were likely to be ahead of target or behind, and to take remedial action quickly.

Before the introduction of the system depot managers had a lot of autonomy. Although there were company price lists head office did not know what prices the depots actually charged. The information took weeks to reach them. Managers were also responsible for ordering their own stocks of parts, using their judgement about what was needed. The supplier delivered an order to the depot and was later paid by head office.

The area managers had to monitor what was going on in their depots – which in some cases was extremely difficult:

'With a manual system, some depots needed a lot of handholding. You couldn't leave them alone, because you always had to go back and do lots of checks on them – count the cash, make sure the stocks were there. Discounts were very difficult to monitor – we didn't have a clue what was going on.

Before computerisation it was uncontrollable. There was a price list, but we never knew if the depot was selling at that price or at half of it. There was no method of looking at sales and controlling sales of specific items, and particularly of controlling discounts, because there was no way to record them.'

The computer system significantly reduced the autonomy of the depot manager:

'Now there is a lot more control at head office. The depot can still do whatever it wants … the theory is that the point-of-sale system doesn't restrict the manager in what he does, but he has to account for it. The whole system is based around giving the depot manager freedom in running his business.'

The system enabled senior management to monitor what was going on in each depot – in effect a small business – and at the same time to provide them with support, by way of marketing, administration and a constantly balanced stock.

'I think it has enabled us to get the benefit of decentralised management, but with uniform procedures applied. And to be seen to be applied, and to be committed at the centre to intervene if there's a deviation.'

Senior managers were able to monitor compliance with depot procedures. If things were not being done in the correct way, such as unusual discounts or late banking, that would be visible at head office the following day. Depot managers came to realise that someone would be in touch with them very quickly and they did not repeat a mistake.

The system thus brought a sharper focus to the work of the depot manager:

'We have taken all of the essential elements of the Code of Practice over management procedures that were previously summarised on two sides of a plastic covered A4 sheet [known as the Management Summary] and we have encapsulated all of that within the MAT software. So now the MAT focuses the managers' attention on doing things exactly the way Kwik-Fit requires them to be done. That really was the breakthrough. It still allows a degree of discretion on the part of management, but any discretion has to be accompanied by a reason, and these reasons are carried forward into our central systems.'

Tom Farmer expressed the same point:

'Before we were computerised, to find out things that were wrong we had to check so much stuff – and we were always 8–10 weeks behind: and by then it wasn't much use speaking to the guy – it was too late to do anything about it. Whereas now we've got the information and can talk about things that happened yesterday.'

Similar views were expressed by another manager who saw it as bringing much tighter control:

'I would say there is less branch autonomy – it is more uniform. The guy will act to the same guidelines, wherever he is in the country – which again probably makes the company look a lot more professional – rather than each guy doing his own thing. It makes them more uniform. Head office have a greater command of the sales picture. They don't need to be in a depot to know how profitable it is – they can just tell from the information day by day.'

Tom Farmer commented on the process of striking the right balance of control in the business:

'We have gone through periods of centralising and decentralising. But with certain things like stock control, for example, we would never decentralise that. Whereas before it was left to every depot to look after their own stock, nowadays they have nothing to do with stock: that's entirely centralised, with automatic replenishment.

But there are other things, so we are not running a completely centralised operation. And one of the reasons is that you can't just run a centralised business – because you must make sure you don't lose the human element.'

Source: Based on a case in Boddy and Gunson (1996) and other information.

Q PART CASE QUESTIONS

- What are the main problems of control in a company of this sort?
- What information does management at different levels need in order to do its job well?
- How is the information system helping management to exercise control?

CHAPTER 16

Finance and budgetary control

> **AIM** *To show why organisations need finance, where it comes from, how its use should be controlled and why financial measures are critical indicators of performance.*

OBJECTIVES

By the end of your work on this chapter you should be able to outline the concepts below in your own terms and:

1 Understand the role of the finance function in management

2 Be able to interpret basic financial reports

3 Know the difference between profit and cash

4 Know what a simple financial plan contains and its purpose

5 Understand the importance of financial results to evaluate performance

6 Know the basic steps in calculating the financial consequences of a management decision

7 Be able to explain how budgets aim to ensure internal activities are directed at meeting external financial requirements

Siemens AG

Siemens began as a German company. Its corporate centre is in Munich, but it is now best described as an international company with various business activities spread across the world, particularly in the United States. Its main businesses are in electrical engineering and electronic activities.

The rapidly changing nature of its products, processes and markets requires that the company should have a strong commitment to research and development. In 2000 approximately 7 per cent of its sales revenue was spent on research and development (5.6 billion euros) and 75 per cent of its sales were derived from products and services that were less than five years old (48 per cent in 1980). To accomplish greater flexibility and responsiveness to changes in technology and markets the company has had to change its organisation and culture. During 1999 and 2000 Siemens completed an extensive reorganisation in order to concentrate on its core activities, those they believe will gain leading competitive positions in their markets. (The net gain from selling businesses it no longer required amounted to more than 4.5 billion euros.) Where appropriate Siemens will develop strategic alliances and joint ventures to strengthen competitiveness. The group maintains close contact with its customers in order to find solutions to their problems. In recent years the need to increase flexibility and responsiveness has required changes in organisation and working arrangements for employees. Fostering personal initiative, encouraging enterprise, more open management style, international experience as a requirement for appointments to key positions, commitment to training, flexible working hours and location such as tele-working from home are examples of changes taking place. Increased empowerment and encouragement of initiative also require a high degree of trust.

A summary of the Siemens AG financial report for year ended 30 September 2000 follows:

		Euros millions
Sales		78,396
Less Cost of sales		54,972
		23,424
Research and development	5,593	
Marketing and selling	10,402	
General administration	3,359	
Other items (gains)	(345)	19,009
Operating profit before tax		4,415
Income from investments in other companies		479
Interest and financial gains		395
		5,289
Less Taxation		(1,908)
Income after tax from continuing operations		3,381
Add Extraordinary gains		4,520
Net income		7,901

Q Case questions

- What was the company's profit in the year to 30 September 2000?
- What proportion of its sales revenue was spent on research and development?
- What questions does the information in the summary financial report raise for you?

16.1 Introduction

This chapter introduces the following ideas:

- Capital market
- Limited liability company
- Shareholder
- Cash flow statement
- Profit statement
- Balance sheet
- Assets
- Liabilities
- Fixed assets
- Current assets
- Shareholders' funds

In the financial year that ended in September 2000 Siemens made a profit of almost 8 billion euros from its activities during the year. This 'headline' figure is a very crude measure of the effectiveness with which the managers have run the company over the year. The problem for investors is how to assess this performance. How does it compare to other firms in similar businesses? Is it consistent with the stated targets of the company? Does the way it has been achieved bode well for the future, by, for example, investing in research and development that will bring returns in later years? They will also want to know how these broad summary figures relate to the work of managers and staff within the firm – are they motivated and organised in ways that encourage them to produce good returns in the future?

Similar questions arise about the annual report of any public firm – you can read commentaries on these every day in the financial pages of your newspaper. Investors and financial analysts continually evaluate a company's financial performance against its objectives and against comparable businesses. They try to judge its prospects, and how effectively managers are doing their jobs. The Part One Case presented information about The Body Shop. This is an interesting company, which has a strong sense of social responsibility. This is what the co-chairs said in the 2000 annual report: 'Campaigning for social and environmental change continues to be at the heart of The Body Shop. We are encouraged to see how the underlying values of this business are being maintained and nurtured.' The Body Shop can only pursue this and similar objectives so long as it continues as a business, and that requires that it should be profitable. Otherwise it will fail.

Chapter 1 described organisations as aiming to add value to the resources they used. It is crucial to the success of an organisation that it has the appropriate resources and that these are managed to achieve the results that stakeholders expect. Whatever the nature of the organisation or its line of business it will need financial resources to operate. It needs to manage these well if it is to prosper. Most companies depend on people in the external environment for the funds they need to grow the business. The main source of information for people outside the business who wish to asses its performance and prospects is the company's annual report to shareholders. This contains a great deal of financial and other data – but is more subjective than it at first appears. It is important to know how financial performance is measured, and the assumptions that people make in constructing the figures. It is also important to know how these financial measures relate to the performance of those working within the firm.

The chapter begins by explaining why companies need the capital market and how they communicate with it. A major link in that process is the annual report, so the chapter then explains important parts of that document. The chapter goes on to show how these figures are intended mainly for investors outside the organisation influence, and are themselves influenced by, processes of internal planning and control.

16.2 The pressures on companies to perform

Many people reading this book will be expecting to start a career that they hope will provide an income to support an attractive lifestyle. Few will be thinking about retirement or the need to support themselves after their working lives have ended. This may be a sombre subject to introduce, but it is fundamentally important to understanding the financial environment in which organisations operate. Governments are increasingly concerned about the ability of traditional public pension schemes to support people in their old age. They expect individuals to take more responsibility for their retirement.

ACTIVITY 16.1

Identifying shareholders

Find a copy of the annual report and accounts 2000 for Mothercare PLC. What can you discover about the shareholders in the company?

Pension funds and life assurance companies undertake to pay their investors an acceptable income when they retire. The funds can only do this if they invest contributions successfully, and investors naturally expect their premiums to be invested profitably by pension fund managers. These pension fund and life assurance companies compete with each other and the rewards for success, and consequent growth in contributions from investors, are high. There is pressure on the fund managers to perform well by identifying good investment opportunities, which is also in the investors' best interests as eventual pensioners. The fund managers will be looking for good investment opportunities in companies that are profitable and well managed.

This is where the discussion comes full circle, back to the investor. In order to attract money into its business to enable it to expand, management needs to demonstrate to the capital market that it is a profitable and successful business.

The fund managers in the **capital market** expect managements to operate their businesses profitably. So this pressure from the external capital market directly affects the organisation and all employees. There may be bad years or periods of low or negative profitability (losses) and the capital markets know that. But continual losses will eventually lead to failure. The business will simply run out of money and not be able to meet its financial obligations. So the pressures to perform that managers and employees feel originate outside the organisation. However, as future pensioners, dependent on the performance of fund managers, those pressures serve their long-term interests (Coggan, 1999).

Within an organisation it is unlikely that managers, apart from those at the top, will feel the direct pressure from outside. Yet, as the chapter shows, this external pressure does affect the expectations that top managers have of those below them. These expectations are gradually transmitted down the organisation, so that all staff experience them in some way, even if indirectly.

16.3 **The world outside the organisation**

Raising capital

If you have looked at the annual report of Mothercare PLC you will have discovered that life assurance companies and pension funds are major shareholders. Most reports do not show such detail, and it is often difficult to discover because the shares are not necessarily ultimately owned by the company named in the share register. They are just one of the many sources from which large organisations raise capital.

A large public company can raise money by issuing shares to people and institutions that respond to a share issue. The main benefit is to enable companies to finance large-scale activities. The shareholders appoint the directors who are ultimately responsible for managing the company. A shareholder is entitled to vote at general meetings in accordance with the number of shares owned. Once the shareholders have paid for their shares in full they cannot generally be required to pay more money into the company, even if it fails.

The affairs of companies are governed by company law, in some countries administered by a government body such as the Securities and Exchange Commission in the United States, and by the body governing the share market, such as the Stock Exchange in the United Kingdom and the Bourse in France. Before a company can invite the public to subscribe for shares it has to be registered with the national financial regulators and fulfil a number of requirements. The first step after registration in order to raise money is to issue a prospectus. Again there are many rules and legal matters that have to be satisfied. In essence, the prospectus explains the history of the company, what it plans to do as a business, and what it plans to do with the money raised.

If the business is small it will not invite the public to buy shares. The promoters will contribute their own money, most likely in sufficient amount to ensure that they have control (more than 50 per cent of the shares). The amount of capital available to the company in these circumstances will be limited by the money the founders can afford to contribute. They may go to a bank to seek finance, but the willingness of a bank to lend will also depend on the amount subscribed by the shareholders.

Banks, fund managers and investors at large will contribute only if they believe that there is a good, sound, well-managed business that is likely to make a profit. The investors have many investment opportunities. They will not invest in a company that will not reward them, as by investing they are taking a risk. The amount of return they expect will be related to the risk – the greater the risk the greater the required return.

ACTIVITY 16.2

Borrowing money

Find out the interest rate at which you could borrow money to (a) buy a car, (b) buy a house, (c) spend on your credit card. Can you explain what you discover?

A **limited liability company** gives a business access to large amounts of capital, but at the same time allows some protection to the **shareholders**, as they cannot be held liable for the debts of the business in the event of its financial failure. This is known as limited liability, and it means that investors can contribute capital knowing that their private and personal assets are not at risk. Of course they could lose all their investment in the shares. This is the risk they take, which is why they expect a higher return than they would receive if they put their money in a bank or in government securities, where the risk of default is virtually zero.

Because a company has access to capital in this form there has to be regulation. The Companies Act is the principal instrument of control, with the addition of the Stock Exchange for those listed as public companies within the United Kingdom. A most important requirement is to provide information about the performance of the business from time to time (Arnold *et al.*, 1995; Elliott and Elliott, 2001).

The most comprehensive information about the current affairs of a business is found in its annual report. Amongst other things it includes detailed financial information of three distinct types. There is a cash flow statement, a profit and loss statement and a balance sheet.

ACTIVITY 16.3

Reading an annual report

Obtain a copy of a company annual report and list the kinds of information that you find in it, for example financial, product, management. You will find some website references at the end of the chapter.

Cash flow statement

The easiest to understand of the three types of statement is the cash flow, as it states just that. It shows where cash has come from and how it has been spent. The following is a simplified summary of the **cash flow statement** for The Body Shop for the year ended 26 February 2000.

		£ millions
Net cash inflow from operating activities		31.4
Interest paid on loans, and dividends to shareholders		(1.5)
Payment of taxation		(9.6)
Investments (including property and equipment)		(13.8)
Acquisitions and disposals		(18.5)
Dividends to shareholders		(10.9)
Cash outflow from the above activities		(22.9)
Financing: short-term debt	6.6	
loans	7.8	14.4
Decrease in cash for the year		(8.5)

In the ordinary course of successful business it might be expected that the cash received from trading (selling products or services) should be greater than the cash spent to purchase components, supplies, labour, energy and all the other resources combined to make, promote, distribute and secure the sales. The cash surplus could then be reinvested to help finance expansion and some of it paid to the shareholders by way of dividend to recompense them for their investment. Their original contribution remains in the company, however, as part of the continuing capital base. In the case of The Body Shop there was a reduction of cash of £8.5 million after raising some loans, paying dividends and investing in some new **assets**.

The idea of a cash surplus as being the essential requirement from operations is appealing but unfortunately too simplistic. Taking as an example a motor vehicle manufacturer, a car has to be designed and tested, components sourced from suppliers, production lines prepared, cars distributed to dealers, and motoring journalists and publicity agents organised in preparation for a major launch promotion. All of this before any of the cars can be sold – so there will be very heavy cash outflows before cash starts to come in. This process may take a couple of years. In the pharmaceutical industry there is a large investment in continuing research and development that may take 10 years or longer before cash begins to flow back, and then only if the research is successful. Heavy investment in product development in the electronics industry has to be made before any products emerge.

Much the same thing occurs in new technology-based service companies such as ebay or lastminute.com. They, like all new dot.com companies, have to invest heavily in building their website and in advertising to make people aware that it exists before cash begins to flow in. It would be highly unlikely in these conditions for the business to show a cash surplus in periods when it is making such heavy investment. Indeed it may be necessary to raise additional capital from shareholders or banks to finance the investment in equipment and in training the people who will operate it.

ACTIVITY 16.4

Measuring R&D expenditure

Look at the annual report for Siemens, Solvay or any large manufacturing business and find out what it tells you about research and development. List the projects that the report mentions. What does the report say about the length of time before the projects will be profitable?

It would be impossible to draw sensible conclusions about the company's financial performance on the basis of cash flow alone. Not only is the annual surplus or deficit influenced by major investment, but other infrequent events, such as a major restructuring exercise following a new strategy, could also distort the impression.

The profit and loss statement

The **profit and loss** statement is designed to overcome the limitations of a cash flow statement, although cash has the important characteristic of complete objectivity. Cash flows can be observed, measured and verified. Subjectivity enters into the measurement of profit.

Here is a simplified summary of the profit statement for The Body Shop for the year ended 26 February 2000.

	£ millions
Sales of products	330.1
Cost of goods sold	(130.9)
Gross profit (or gross margin)	199.2
Operating expenses (shops, administration and distribution)	(166.2)
Operating profit	33.0
Restructuring costs	(2.7)
Payment of interest on loans	(1.5)
Taxation on profit	(10.4)
Profit after taxation	18.4
Dividends to shareholders	(7.5)
Profit retained in the business	10.9

The profit after taxation and the profit retained in the business are quite different from the cash surplus reported in the cash flow statement. This is because the profit statement is not based on cash but on business transactions that (a) may result in cash transactions in the future, or (b) reflect cash transactions from previous periods.

Sales may be credit sales that approved customers may pay for later. Cost of goods sold may include the purchase of goods that will be paid for in the next financial year. Operating expenses will include depreciation which, with other terms, is explained below.

Q Case questions 16.1

Refer to the summary profit statement of Siemens AG.

- Calculate the gross profit as a percentage of sales.
- Calculate the profit before tax as a percentage of sales.

ACTIVITY 16.5

Calculating and comparing profit

Look at the annual report of a company that interests you, probably in a similar line of business to Siemens.

Calculate the gross profit in a recent year as a percentage of sales.

Calculate the profit before tax as a percentage of sales.

How does the company compare on these measures against Siemens?

Is there a major difference in the items in the profit statements of the two companies?

Depreciation

Depreciation is a major cause of the difference between cash flow and profit. Think about the investments mentioned in relation to motor vehicle production. Apart from occasional modifications, the same basic model may be produced and sold for several years, perhaps as many as 10 for a small-volume producer. So the initial investment to develop the design and make the cars should be spread over the life of the investment and will be subtracted from sales revenue in each year. This process is called depreciation. The idea is simple, but there are several estimates required before the annual amount can be measured. Depreciation is based on the original cost of the investment, including set-up and training, less the expected scrap value at the end of its life. It may also be necessary to add the expected cost of decommissioning. Think about a nuclear power generator in this respect. Hence an estimation must be made of the life of the investment, the residual value and the initial cost, which itself is open to conjecture. To make matters worse there are at least four methods of spreading the cost over the lifespan. The simplest is to allocate an equal amount each year.

Credit

Most products are not sold for cash but on credit. In some cases the credit arrangement can spread over a long time. A retail store might offer generous credit terms in order to promote sales – 'nothing to pay for six months' or 'easy terms over nine months' are familiar promotional devices. Before the salesperson, or more probably the credit controller, will give credit, the customer's creditworthiness will be checked. However, even the most careful checkers cannot ensure that the customer may not become redundant or fall ill and not be able to work. As an example, suppose that the company's financial year ends on 31 December and that a customer is buying a personal computer at the end of October on nine months' credit of equal monthly payments. Should the company report the full value of the sale, the three instalments that the customer has paid, or nothing until the PC has been paid for in full? It is usual practice to report the full amount, as the business has a legal contract to force the customer to pay. The idea is fine, but experience shows that not all customers will pay in full. There will be bad debts. An estimate of doubtful debts has to be made before arriving at profit.

Warranty claims

If a problem arises with a product sold under warranty it will be replaced or fixed, but at a cost to the manufacturer. The cost of repairing under warranty has to be estimated because warranty claims may not be made within the same financial year as the sale.

These are simple examples of subjectivity in profit measurement. There are many more, but these suffice to illustrate the point that the measure of profit cannot be said to be accurate. It is an approximation. Nevertheless, it is the main indication of trading performance measured in financial terms. The question remains, how much does profit reflect good performance? To evaluate this, profit needs to be related to the amount of investment in the business.

16.4 Measuring periodic performance

Both the cash flow and the profit statements relate to a period of time – conventionally to a financial or trading year. It is usual for large organisations also to produce brief reports on their performance quarterly or half-yearly.

Just how much profit is desirable has to be considered in relation to the investment in a business. Therefore a measure of investment is needed with which to compare periodic profit. When you think that an investor (fund manager) could invest in risk-free government securities for a guaranteed minimum return known in advance, an investment in a risky company that did not offer at least the same expectation of reward would not be contemplated. So the return, or ratio of profit to investment, would be expected to be higher for a risky investment than for a risk-free opportunity. The rate of return required for a particular investment has to be assessed by comparing alternative investment opportunities and their rates of return.

Measuring the investment base

How can the investment base be measured? The obvious base is the amount of the initial investment. If you deposit money in a bank deposit account it will attract interest. At the end of the year you can measure the rate of return by expressing the interest earned for the year as a percentage of the initial investment. If you leave the interest in the account the following year the investment base would be increased by the amount of interest reinvested. The initial investment plus the interest you earned in the first year now becomes a part of the capital base as you chose not to withdraw it. The investment base can grow over time. Much the same happens in a business. Profit is generated, some is distributed as a cash dividend and the balance, usually the larger proportion, is retained in the business to finance expansion.

A simple measure of the capital base with which to compare profit appears to be the amount of capital originally contributed, plus profit that is retained and added each year to the base.

Another way to look at it, for companies listed on the Stock Exchange, is to relate the profit or earnings per share to the share price. This approach recognises that a successful business will grow and develop a good reputation and image that will reflect the results of good, professional management and reliable, high quality products and service. If you own shares in such a company you would expect the value of those shares to increase to reflect the success of the business, for example from customer loyalty, brand reputation and reliability, loyal relationships with suppliers of components and services and good design. You would only continue to hold the shares as long as the return based on the price at which you could sell the shares in the market is at least equal to that from an alternative investment with similar risk. This topic is revisited later in the chapter.

16.5 The balance sheet

The report that shows the capital base of a business is the **balance sheet**. The Body Shop balance sheet as at 26 February 2000 showed the following information.

		£ million
Property, plant and equipment (tangible **fixed assets**)		68.4
Investments		4.8
Goodwill (intangible assets)		31.5
Stocks of goods for resale	44.7	
Money owing from customers (debtors – UK or accounts receivable)	51.9	
Cash and bank accounts (**current assets**)	19.2	115.8
		£220.5
These resources were financed by shareholders (including retained profit)	121.4	
Money owing to suppliers, banks and tax	99.1	£220.5

The **balance sheet** reveals two separate but related aspects of the business. First it shows the total **assets** of the business. These include the physical resources such as property, buildings, machinery, computers, stocks (or inventories) of raw materials, work in progress and completed products, money owed by customers, and cash. The other dimension is the sources of the finance that have enabled the business to acquire its assets. Finance (or capital) comes from shareholders by way of contributions for shares when they are first issued together with retained profits from successful operations as previously explained. This is the shareholders' capital (or **shareholders' funds**). In addition there will usually be money borrowed from a bank and possibly from other sources as well. These are the liabilities of the organisation. The sum total of the shareholders' funds and **liabilities** will be equal in aggregate to the amount of assets. The former represents the source from which the finance has been raised. The latter shows the destination or the physical resources in which the capital has been invested.

The balance sheet of Siemens AG is presented as another example.

CASE STUDY
Siemens AG – the case continues

Group balance sheet as at 30 September 2000

Assets		Euros millions
Intangible (patents, licences, goodwill)		6,367
Property, plant and equipment at cost	35,660	
Less Accumulated depreciation	20,410	15,250
Investments		11,796
		33,413
Current assets		
Inventories	6,672	
Accounts receivable from customers and others	31,002	
Liquid assets (including cash)	8,168	45,842
		79,255
Shareholders' equity		
Issued shares and retained profit		25,640
Liabilities		
Pension fund and other commitments	26,468	
Loans	9,134	
Accounts payable and other short-term obligations	18,013	53,615
		79,255

The shareholders are the main risk takers and the profit is attributable to them, so the measure of the rate of return is profit after tax divided by shareholders' funds, commonly known as the *return on equity*. However, there are many imperfections in the measure, one of which is the fact that goodwill will not usually be included as an asset unless it appears following the purchase of another business. Brand names such as the title of a newspaper or the name of a consumer product may be valued by the directors and included as assets. This apparent inconsistency may be surprising. Accountants argue that newspaper mastheads, or brand names, could be sold separately from the business, whereas goodwill can only be sold with the business as a whole. Many companies only include brands if they have purchased them from another company or, in the case of goodwill, taken over another company for a price greater than the value of the tangible assets minus the liabilities (net worth). Further difficulties in measuring a rate of return arise from problems in measuring depreciation and, consequently, asset values, changes in price levels and share values.

Q Case questions 16.2

Refer to the summary financial information for Siemens AG. Calculate the rate of return (after tax) on equity (shareholders' funds).

Depreciation

The discussion of the profit statement explained that depreciation in particular was an expense item that was difficult to measure. It represents an attempt to estimate the proportion of the cost of using long-term assets that is attributable to a particular accounting period. Any of the cost that has not already been subtracted in the profit statements remains to be subtracted in the future.

MANAGEMENT IN PRACTICE	**Measuring depreciation at The Body Shop**

In The Body Shop annual report for 2000 the assets, plant and equipment were shown in note 12 as having cost £135.9 million. The depreciation for the year that was included in the profit statement as an item of expense (within the figure of £166.2 million) amounted to £13.4 million. When added to depreciation charged in earlier years, and allowing for the sale of some assets, the book value in the balance sheet as at 26 February 2000 was £68.4 million. This means that of the £135.9 million, there remains an amount of £68.4 million to be charged against sales revenue in future years. This remaining balance is the value that appears in the balance sheet for long-term assets (fixed or non-current assets).

If the value in the market – either buying price or selling price – is similar to the balance sheet figure, that is purely coincidental. The balance sheet figure is simply original cost minus the proportion so far depreciated.

The estimate of doubtful debts subtracted from customers' outstanding accounts (debtors or accounts receivable), estimated warranty claim costs, estimated pension fund liabilities, the value of goodwill, brands or other intangible assets are all highly subjective measures. Furthermore, the accounting policies may well differ between companies even though they are in the same industry. So the aggregate amount shown in the balance sheet for assets is not necessarily a reflection of market values.

ACTIVITY 16.6

Comparing accounting policies

Look at the annual reports for two or three companies in the same (or similar) industry and read the section called accounting policies. Make a list of practices that seem to be different.

Changes in price levels

There is a further complication to measuring performance, especially in periods of unstable prices. An asset is recorded at its original cost less depreciation. Suppose there are two companies involved in much the same business with similar assets, but one company purchased its equipment when prices were much lower than was the case for the second company. Although they may have similar physical assets the costs showing for one may be quite different from those for the other. Traditionally accountants do not make allowances for differences in price levels through time. Money amounts at different times are added together as though they represented the same values, which is clearly nonsense. Consequently, during a period of changing prices it is difficult to compare the rate of return on equity between companies based on the profit statement and balance sheet. These days most western economies this is not a problem, although the prices of some commodities, components and products will frequently change.

Share values

There is another way of approaching the question of performance measurement. If you were thinking of buying shares in the market through the Stock Exchange you would consider the likely future returns in relation to the price you would have to pay for the shares. You will therefore be comparing different investment opportunities and will attempt to choose the one that offers the best return for whatever degree of risk you are prepared to accept. The return you expect would be an estimate of future dividends plus the likely growth in the share price, and you would relate this to the price you would have to pay to buy the shares. If the potential investment offered a greater expected return than shares you already hold (assuming the same degree of risk) not only would you be interested in buying the new shares, but you would also be inclined to sell your existing shares to buy more new ones to increase your return. It would be rational for all investors in this position to behave in the same way. The consequence of this action should be clear. Selling pressure for the shares of one company would drive the price down to the point at which investors would be indifferent as to which company's shares they purchased as they would tend to offer the same expected return. This process, known as arbitraging, is likely to happen in a well-organised and efficient market (Ross et al., 2000).

So the measure of performance that shareholders are likely to adopt will not be directly related to the company's financial reports, but more to the financial markets. They will be comparing expected returns with the prices of securities (shares) in the market. This does not mean that financial reports from companies do not serve any useful purpose. They do, because they provide some of the information that helps the traders in shares to assess the likely returns from these companies in the future and, above all, provide information about past performance and recent financial position. While share prices in the market are directly influenced by buying and selling pressure, the expectations that give rise to those pressures come in part from the financial reports.

A company whose shares do not offer returns consistent with competitors' are likely to become takeover targets with bids from stronger, more efficient performers. Figure 16.1 shows the comparative changes in the share price for two companies in the banking business – Bank of Scotland and Halifax – at the time they were in the process of merging. The graph shows clearly how the share price for the Bank of Scotland has performed better than the Halifax. This may have enhanced the bargaining power of the Bank of Scotland.

Company directors have to watch share price movements. Unexpected movements might signal activity in the market that they ought to know about. For example, if a company is actively buying shares in the market and so pushing the price up this might indicate that a takeover bid is coming. If a shareholder is dumping shares, thus pushing the price down, has performance in the company fallen short of expectations? In both circumstances the directors need to find out what they can about the market activities in order to take defensive action.

Q Case questions 16.3

Look at the balance sheet for Siemens AG.

● Calculate the proportion of the finance for the company that is attributable to the shareholders, and the proportion attributable to the liabilities.

Figure 16.1 Pre-tax profits compared: Halifax/Bank of Scotland

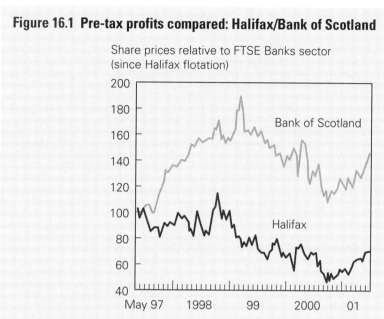

Share prices relative to FTSE Banks sector
(since Halifax flotation)

Source: *Financial Times*, 5/6 May 2001.

Comparing Siemens and The Body Shop

Look at the requirement for Case Question 16.3. Compute the same measure for The Body Shop. What strikes you about these measures? What do they tell you about these companies? Would it make a difference to your decision to buy shares in one and not the other? Can you explain why?

The directors and senior managers of a company cannot ignore what is going on in the markets outside their business. They operate in markets, some specific to their own activities, and some general – the capital and labour markets. Their performance is being evaluated all the time and they need to know what the markets (buyers and sellers) are thinking. Financial managers will be watching the share price. The external pressures that the market imposes have to be translated or converted into pressure for internal action. This is what financial management is about.

16.6 Internal control

Most managers and employees can do little themselves to influence the share price directly. Nevertheless much of what they do has financial implications and eventually all their decisions will indirectly affect the share price. So management needs systems and procedures to ensure that the financial consequences of decisions are understood and that the action proposed is acceptable. An organisation cannot wait until the accountant prepares a financial report at the end of the year to see if the operation has been profitable or not. It is too late to do anything. Profit does not just happen. It has to be planned (Horngren *et al.*, 2000). At least once a year management must prepare a financial plan, commonly known as a budget.

Preparing a budget

Prepare a simple cash budget for your own finances for next month. You will need to consider the cash you have available from savings in the past, how much cash you expect to receive during the month and what you plan to spend.

The budgeting process usually begins at the top level when the directors set a target or goal for the growth in shareholder value that will keep the business performing as well as, if not better than, its competitors. From this assessment they derive a profit target for the whole organisation. It may be expressed as a rate of return on invested capital (shareholders' funds) or as an absolute amount, but either way it will need to be translated into objectives that have meaning at lower operating levels within the business.

Controlling elements within an organisation

A large organisation will have a variety of products, markets and locations in which it operates. An international business may have virtually complete and independent operating divisions in a variety of locations, each expected to achieve a given rate of return.

In contrast, a smaller business may have just one location, but within it a range of functions such as purchasing, design, production, assembly, inspection, dispatch and accounts receivable. Each may be independently managed yet co-ordinated to ensure that they are all operating to achieve the required corporate objective. None of these divisions could be set a required rate of return or even a profit target because none of them has independent control over its activities. The volume of production will depend on sales, purchases will depend on production and accounts receivable on sales. However, each has control over certain aspects of the business. Purchasing must negotiate prices and specifications for supplies of material or components, but it has little control over volume. Based on the sales and production plan it will have a reasonable idea of volume, but it will be subject to change as the year progresses in light of actual sales and production. Similarly, the performance of the dispatch and shipping operation will depend on sales and customers' delivery requirements. They can base plans on the sales projections but, as with all plans in business, the actual activities will inevitably be different.

All parts of the organisation, then, have to be flexible and adaptable in response to market opportunities and customers' requirements. For this reason it is vital to establish and maintain good relationships with other organisations that the firm deals with. It is not unusual in smaller organisations to hear managers complain that the process of planning and budgeting is a waste of time because events always turn out differently. They certainly do, but this is no reason not to plan. As circumstances change plans should also change. Since the mechanics of budget preparation can be readily developed on fairly cheap desktop computers the tedium of budget revision involving numerous computations can easily be avoided by the use of suitable technology. So budgets should always be up to date and reflect contemporary operating and market conditions.

MANAGEMENT IN PRACTICE **Earnings per share at The Body Shop**

The earnings per share (profit after tax divided by the number of shares issued) for The Body Shop increased from a loss of 2.4 pence in 1999 to earnings of 9.6 pence in 2000. It cannot be known what plans the directors have for the future. The annual report does not include forecasts or plans. However, it can be seen from the chief executive's and operating reviews that the improvement in the rate of profit was probably attributable to major strategic changes.

Manufacturing was ended and sales in the United States were very strong. These plans will have been incorporated into the 1999/2000 budget. The achievable earnings per share will have been planned.

Without a plan there is no sense of direction or clarity of purpose at operating levels. The process of budget preparation in itself is a useful exercise: not only does it enable the various parts of an organisation to relate their activities to others, but also it is a valuable co-ordination device to help ensure that the various parts of the organisation are focused on the same objective. The starting point for planning at operational level is generally the sales plan in a profit-oriented organisation. In not-for-profit organisations it may be the desired level of service to its constituency, for example the number of units of blood to be collected by the transfusion service.

In all cases the capacity to achieve the desired volume will depend on the resources available – especially people, equipment and finance. If added resources are needed management can anticipate both what is required and when. For example, if more people are required they have to be recruited and trained so that they will be ready to contribute to productive activity at the appropriate time. If more cash is needed to pay for added supplies of raw materials it is important to have a financial plan to present to the bank manager well in advance of the time that a cash crisis begins to occur. Crises often arise because there has been insufficient care and attention with planning – and failure to update plans as circumstances change. Plans need to be changed as activity grows for the simple reason that growth requires added finance. Labour, supplies of materials and services will have to be paid for before cash begins to flow back from customers.

Q Case questions 16.4

You have read aspects of the annual report of Siemens. Now use your imagination to think through the process that might have been adopted in the construction of the budget for the year ended 30 September 2000. To help you, think about the following:

● Where did the process begin? How were the various elements brought together into a coherent plan?

● What steps were involved in arriving at an agreed budget?

Planning growth and improved performance

The length of the planning cycle depends on the kind of product or service. It may be no more than a couple of months or it could be much longer. Companies can fail as they grow simply because the rate of growth outpaces the ability to generate cash or because they have not anticipated the need for cash and made the necessary plans. Co-ordination of the various aspects has to be supervised centrally in the organisation to ensure that the overall objectives are achievable in the plan.

Much of the detail has to come from the operating units, especially performance targets related to work activity. It is here that there is likely to be a process of negotiation with central co-ordinators. Their activity is to improve productivity, whereas the objectives at the lower level may be to ensure that the performance targets do not put excessive pressures on employees. A process of genuine negotiation and co-operation may well lead to a budget that is acceptable both to operating divisions and to the central organisation. However, a budget cast in conditions of fear and apprehension can lead to attempts to create budget slack. This is exemplified by the readiness or otherwise of employees to introduce improved working methods. It is conceivable that more efficient working methods can be discovered through experience. Staff and management may choose not to disclose or introduce them at the earliest opportunity. Instead they may keep them in reserve to cushion the effects of a tight budget at some future time. Such behaviour is not in the best interests of the business as a whole, but it shows the way that budget preparation can lead to conflicts. The subject of participation in the process of budget preparation has been a topic for extensive research in recent years (Emmanuel *et al.*, 1991; Drury, 2000).

Typically a corporate budget will include:

- sales budget – showing expected revenue for each product in each market;
- materials budget – showing purchases for each component, from each supplier;
- labour budget – showing deployment of employees and staff to each activity;
- overhead budget – showing the consumption of resources that cannot be identified with particular products, e.g. advertising, directors' fees, energy;
- capital budget – showing planned spending on new equipment, buildings and acquisitions of other companies;
- research and development budget – showing planned spending on particular projects;
- cash budget – showing the cash receipts and payments;
- budget balance sheet.

Once the budget is negotiated and agreed it becomes an operating plan that reflects expectations about the conditions in which the organisation is operating. Each budget will be identified with a responsibility centre, i.e. with managers responsible for achieving the budget expectations. Sometimes alternative budgets are prepared for different purposes. For example, the performance targets incorporated for operating divisions may have been negotiated at a tighter level than past achievements with the objective of improving productivity. Although these targets may be achieved during the period of the budget the process may take some months. If the cash or profit forecast given to the bank is based on these targets it is likely that the cash or profit projections will not be achieved. So the cash budget may be based on looser performance. Similarly, a sales budget might reflect a higher sales level than that incorporated in the profit plan. The risk of having different budgets is the possibility that they will lose credibility within the organisation.

Performance measurement

Another favourite research topic has been the way in which budgets are used to judge performance. The behaviour of managers can be seriously influenced by the budget style in an organisation. If this is authoritarian and unthinking in manner, in which achieving the budget is the primary objective of management, it may lead to suboptimal performance. The pressure may be translated into action that is against long-term interests. For example, a salesperson might threaten customers with a price increase in the coming month to boost current sales and achieve a sales target.

In some organisations the immediate reaction to employees who fail to achieve budget is to presume that they are to blame. Any idea that the budget itself may be inappropriate or unachievable is not entertained. If this style is carried forward to performance evaluation it can be very destructive. In contrast, a budget can be prepared after discussion with those who know the area. It can then be used as a guide for judging performance after allowing for changing circumstances. This approach is more likely to achieve employee support.

Consistent failure to achieve budget should first lead to a review of the budget to ensure that the targets are fair and achievable. Only then should there be an attempt to take remedial action to improve an activity. The successful use of budgets depends on those affected, managers and staff alike, developing a sense of ownership towards them. As conditions change, the budget should be revised so that it continues to be credible.

A budget is, in essence, short term. Usually it is for no more than one year. Nevertheless it has to be set in a longer-term context and be consistent with the strategy for the future development of the organisation. Long-term investments in research and development, product and market development, new plant and equipment or even the acquisition of other businesses have to be included in the short-term budget and cash requirements in the cash budget.

If, in the longer term, a product is going to be phased out, it would be senseless to mount a major promotion campaign to strengthen its market position. It may make sense to promote it at a discount in stores in order to clear inventories. This further illustrates co-ordination, but, in particular, it shows a link between short-term action and longer-term strategy.

This conventional approach to budgeting is being challenged as businesses operate in rapidly changing conditions. More authority has to be delegated, with faster response times. So the emphasis is shifting towards value creation and benchmarking with other organisations rather than mere cost control.

16.7 Decision making

The one certainty in any organisation is that conditions will change. The budget cannot be revised every time minor changes occur or fresh opportunities arise. An organisation has to be flexible and responsive. Frequently opportunities arise that require prompt action – for example, a special order for a normal product or service, but to be sold at a low promotional price into a new market. In these circumstances the normal measurement of the average cost of producing and delivering the service may well be an inappropriate starting point for computing potential profit. Many of the costs will not change as a result of accepting this opportunity: there will be no further research and development, no requirement to increase productive capacity (assuming that capacity is available) and, possibly, no added labour cost. In these conditions consideration need only be given to the costs that will increase directly as a result of choosing to accept this order: delivery, materials or additional resources consumed that will have to be paid for. Depreciation can be ignored and, in the very short term, so too can the labour cost since the employees will already have been paid for their time.

Let us suppose that Osram has an opportunity to make and sell electric light bulbs to a retailer. The bulbs will be packaged especially for the retailer and not identified with Osram. How will the costs be estimated?

- Is there enough manufacturing capacity without having to reduce normal production? If so, there is no need to take account of any additional capital costs.
- Are additional employees required or will existing employees have to work longer? If so, the extra costs will be attributable to this order; otherwise there are no added labour costs.

- Materials will be required according to the retailer's specification.
- Are there packaging costs? In this case there may be design and printing costs as well as costs of packaging material. The set-up costs will have to be included.
- Will the retailer collect the bulbs, or do they need to be delivered? Will there be added costs, or will existing transport arrangements be adequate?

The important issue is to identify costs that are directly traceable and attributable to this opportunity. The normal average cost of producing light bulbs may be irrelevant, since that includes research and development, capital equipment costs and administrative overheads which will not necessarily increase with this order.

Undoubtedly the retailer is looking for a special price, lower than that which Osram might normally charge. If this price exceeds the identified cost it may be an attractive opportunity. The critical issue for Osram to decide is whether or not this might damage its own long-term market position. Against this is the threat that the retailer will probably also be negotiating with a competitor to supply the light bulbs.

Suppose that the normal selling price is 80 cents and that the usual cost is made up (per unit) as follows:

	cents
Labour	10
Materials	20
Packaging	5
Delivery	3
Overheads	25
	63
Contribution to profit	17
	80

The retailer wants to buy lamps at a price of 60 cents. If we establish that Osram's overheads will not increase, that labour costs will be 8 cents, materials 20 cents and packaging 10 cents, then the appropriate cost per unit will be 38 cents. If additional delivery is 100 per journey for up to 10,000 light bulbs and the design and set-up costs for printing the packaging is 10,000 and the order is for 100,000 bulbs, is it acceptable to sell at 60 cents?

		cents
Unit costs:	labour	8
	material	20
	packaging	10
		38
		$
Cost for 100,000		38,000
Delivery cost		1,000
Design, set-up		10,000
Relevant cost		49,000
Revenue		60,000
Contribution to profit		$11,000

This appears to be an acceptable sales opportunity as long as it does not erode Osram's normal market and as long as the existing customers do not expect the normal price to be lowered.

It is the job of the cost or management accountant to process financial information quickly in order to assist managers to take decisions of the kind described above. It is not usual for the information to be directly available from the financial records. The accountant will have to find out the alternative courses of action, extract the appropriate financial data from the system, process it and report in a coherent and understandable way to those responsible for taking the decision. Accountants are more likely to be useful if they understand the processes of service or product delivery. They also need to appreciate that they are providing a service to other managers.

Routine information for managers

Another aspect of internal financial measurement is more routine. Unlike the system of financial reporting for the organisation as a whole, which is geared to the needs of the capital market, internal information has to be related to the needs of the managers. They will be interested in financial measurements related to their own area of responsibility. For example, a marketing manager will need information about groups of products, brands, customers, regions or marketing areas. In research and development, costs accumulating for each project might be compared with research progress to date. This approach runs right through the value chain, recognising that value can be added from research, development, design, through to distribution and customer service. It is not just the manufacturing process or service delivery process that adds value and requires measurement.

As organisations develop stronger alliances and co-operative arrangements, at both the strategic and operational levels, the role of the accountant is expanded beyond the limits of the organisation within which he or she works. Co-operation in the supply chain can result in improved performance for both organisations involved. To achieve benefits of cost reduction and/or improved profitability through quality improvement there has to be an open relationship and trust between the organisations. Accountants play a role in this co-operation by advising on the financial consequences for both organisations (Atkinson *et al.*, 2001).

16.8 International aspects of financial reporting

Internal financial analysis and control processes are generally designed to meet the needs of management and are not constrained by legal requirements. The principles and methods are universally applicable, although in some locations cultural factors and custom may mean that accountants go about their tasks in a different manner.

External financial reporting is rather different. In the English-speaking world financial reports appear to be similar, terminology aside. Nonetheless, across the western world the system of double-entry book-keeping is at the foundation of all financial record-keeping systems. Within the United Kingdom, the limits to acceptable methods of reporting are governed by the Companies Acts and the Accounting Standards Board, which produces accounting standards.

Different legal systems, industry financing, taxation systems, structure of the accounting profession, language and traditions mean that financial reporting varies from one country to another. France, Germany, Portugal, Spain and Japan have historically required compliance with a rigid framework for financial reporting (Alexander and Nobes, 2001).

> ### Q Case questions 16.5
>
> Look at the summary of significant accounting policies in the annual report for any company. Do these help you to understand the report? Can you explain why?

In eastern Europe accountants were regarded merely as book-keepers. There was no need to produce financial statements for public consumption since the system was centrally controlled. Political changes accompanied by privatisation have created a need for a different system more akin to those in the English-speaking world.

Not surprisingly, the system in the United States has much in common with the UK system, but there are also important fundamental differences. The US system has been much more regulated through the Securities and Exchange Commission, at least in so far as large public companies are concerned. Accounting standards are established by the Financial Accounting Standards Board. Its requirements have tended towards a more conservative approach than in many countries. For example, it generally requires all research and development costs to be subtracted from revenue as incurred and not carried forward in the balance sheet to be offset against future gains.

The differences in detail make it difficult to compare the financial performance of companies in different countries. Given the increasing integration of business and the international nature of capital markets these differences are not helpful for investors or anyone else who is interested in evaluating the performance of companies in financial terms. This was why, in 1973, the International Accounting Standards Committee (IASC) was formed with the purpose of developing accounting standards that could be applied worldwide. By 1994, 80 countries were represented on the IASC. Some countries have adopted the international accounting standards directly (e.g. Malaysia), some adapt to suit local conditions (e.g. Singapore) and others develop their own standards independently, but adapt them to conform to the IASC requirements (e.g. United Kingdom). The international standards have been bland because they have had to reflect a consensus, and therefore a variety of accounting treatments may be possible. Early in 2001, the IASC board was revamped with the intention of strengthening the international standards. Pressure has come from capital markets to enhance comparability to make financial reports more understandable. As time passes it is to be expected that the standards will be revised and improved to promote international conformity. Within the European Union aspects of company law have been, and continue to be harmonised. This helps to promote compatibility, but cultural differences persist. The Commission is keen to see uniformity in accounting. Possibly the development of a strengthened IASC will provide the vehicle for this.

MANAGEMENT IN PRACTICE **ABB earnings hit by accounting switch**

In early 2001 the shares of ABB fell sharply when the company disclosed that under new US accounting rules its 2000 net income from continuing operations of $881 million was 27 per cent less than under old rules.

ABB, which has switched to US accounting rules to satisfy the requirements for a planned New York Stock Exchange listing, had warned analysts that the new rules would depress its stated earnings and reduce its profit margins.

However, the scale of the reduction, combined with weak revenue growth and a more than one-third fall in cash flow, surprised analysts. ABB's shares, which had fallen by more than 20 per cent in the last year, closed 8.5 per cent lower.

The confusion over the accounting changes have complicated the assessment of a group in the midst of a big reorganisation in a bid to accelerate its rate of growth, which remains well below that of its rivals, such as Germany's Siemens.

Source: Based on material in *Financial Times*, 15 February 2001.

Whatever happens to the development of standards possibly the most pressing need for accountants is to value intangibles. Modern service companies including dot.coms often have few or no significant tangible assets. They may have a very sophisticated workforce, which is where the value of the business resides. You will not routinely find these items in the balance sheet, and sometimes when they are reported the values are excessive.

ACTIVITY 16.9

Anticipating changes

Look at the 2000 annual report for Siemens. Will the financial reporting processes change in 2001 when US Generally Accepted Accounting Principles are applied?

16.9 Summary

Managing the financial resources of an organisation is fundamental to its success, but no more so than other aspects of management. Without a good product and a receptive market the best financial management in the world cannot create a profitable company. Conversely, an otherwise successful company can soon fail without proper financial information to assist decision making and control.

Content

Management needs funds, along with other resources, to help achieve the objectives of the business. It also needs to decide which of many opportunities facing the business it should invest in. Shareholders expect management to invest in projects and gradually develop a strategy that adds to shareholder value. To do this management depends on adequate financial information if it is to make the right strategic choices. The budgeting process can help to give focus and direction to the plans that management makes to achieve objectives. It also helps to co-ordinate the activities of different functions and departments by giving them a common framework and plan within which to work. The finance function offers a system for assessing the financial consequences of decisions in a relatively objective way – though there are also many uncertainties in financial information. The levels at which budgets are set have effects on motivation – impossible budgets or very slack ones have little beneficial effect. Those that are challenging but achievable have a positive effect on commitment.

Process

Organisations normally have a regular cycle of budgeting activity, conducted between those at the centre and those in the operating units. This is to ensure that the separate parts work towards the overall objectives. This process may challenge local interests and may be contentious. Hence budgets are typically set through a process of negotiation, with varying degrees of participation by line managers in the process. In some companies line managers are heavily involved in decisions about budgets, in others the budgets are imposed from the centre in an authoritarian way. These alternative styles affect the degree to which employees and managers accept ownership of the budgets. Management is also required to communicate financial information about the company to actual and prospective shareholders.

Control

Owners and shareholders, and the capital market generally, exercise significant control over managers. This is institutionalised in legislation such as the Companies Acts and by the *Regulations of the Stock Exchange.* The capital markets' reaction to reports of financial performance affect the ability of the company to raise capital. Management will experience this pressure from outside. As it begins to change policy and practice to satisfy these external interests internal arrangements will also be affected. Financial information also helps to measure management performance internally – as when actual expenditure can be compared with the budget. Routine financial information is also used to help control the management of projects, to ensure that what is spent corresponds to what has been agreed.

16.10 Review questions

1 Why do companies have to make a profit? Check the website for Marks & Spencer plc. What do the directors have to say about profit and recent performance?

2 How is profit measured?

3 Explain why profit is different from cash. Look up any company report on http://www.carol.co.uk and see if you can explain the main difference between profit and cash for the company.

4 What does a balance sheet tell us about an organisation? What can you discover about the activities of Solvay from the balance sheet? http://www.solvay.com/business/

5 Can you explain how the external pressures on a company to generate a profit are translated into internal planning systems?

6 What is the purpose of a budget?

7 How does a budget operate as a control mechanism?

8 Explain why the financial information prepared for external purposes is not necessarily appropriate for managers.

9 Explain the notion of contribution to the profit of a business. What do the directors of Marks & Spencer or Solvay have to say in the 2000 annual report about sources of profit?

10 What are international standards of accounting? Explain how they differ from requirements in your country.

Q PART CASE QUESTIONS

- How do you expect that Kwik-Fit's investment in IT systems will have affected specific items in (a) the profit and loss statement, and (b) the balance sheet?
- How will the systems have helped the internal control of decision making? With what financial consequences, explicitly?
- What can you discover from the financial press about the movement in the company's share price over the past year and the reasons for this? Is there any evidence of it affecting internal management policy and practice?

Further reading

Coggan, P. (1999), *The Money Machine*, Penguin, Harmondsworth. A useful introduction to the mechanisms that management can use to raise capital and the expectations they have to satisfy.

Alexander, D. and Nobes, C. (2001), *International Introduction to Financial Accounting*, Financial Times Prentice Hall, Harlow. Provides a European perspective on the topic.

Horngren, C.T., Foster, G. and Datar, S.M. (2000), *Cost Accounting* (10th edn), Financial Times Prentice Hall, Harlow. A standard text that covers all areas of the topic in great detail.

You should also write to one or two prominent companies that interest you and obtain a copy of their annual reports for the last two years. You may also access these on the appropriate websites. As well as illustrating the financial issues covered in this chapter they usually provide a lot of information that relates to other chapters.

Annotated links, questions and resources can be found on
www.booksites.net/boddy

CHAPTER 17

Managing operations and quality

AIM *To set the operations function in its historical context and show how it supports business performance.*

OBJECTIVES

At the end of your work on this chapter you should be able to outline the concepts below in your own terms and:

1 Understand how the operations function can support perfomance in manufacturing and service organisations

2 Describe five types of transformation and their physical layout

3 Compare the process approach to operations with the functional approach

4 Compare operations approaches and select those best suited to a context

5 Recognise the need to manage operations across an extended supply chain

6 Explain how the idea of 'order winners' and 'order qualifiers' links operations to the strategic process of meeting customer needs profitably

Benetton

There are many aspects to the success of Benetton. One of these is undoubtedly its unusual operations management system.

With a radical approach to knitted goods, the Benettons in effect created a knitted pullover as a seasonal fashion good rather than a garment for comfort intended for years of service. Their bold colours brought a youthful image and created a need for dedicated retail outlets working to a closely defined and controlled specification. As a two-person business there was little need for systems. Giuliano designed and produced while Luciano sold. Their early success encouraged them to buy new machines and recruit local staff to produce a small range of goods in greater volume.

Where production was in Benetton factories, employees' suggestions for improvement were encouraged and acted upon while, early on, the company used subcontractors as producers. Initially these were outworkers to whom part-made garments would be delivered in their homes for completion and later collected. Larger groups of such workers formed a subcontractor network around the main Benetton factories. These grew up at a time when Benetton could not raise its own capital to build capacity internally. Instead, Luciano devised a partnership agreement with them such that, in return for providing a steady stream of work, the suppliers would invest in fixed assets. They had to promise to work only for Benetton, however.

The nature of the relationship with the retailers also impacts on Benetton's operations systems. The retail outlets are separate businesses (that do not pay royalties to their parent company) which are expected to pay cash on delivery to earn a 10 per cent discount.

The product line has increased each year with new garments and materials being used, but the essence of the Benetton system remains in operation terms dependent on a large number of independent entrepreneur suppliers working very closely in partnership with Benetton, growing and developing with them.

Benetton thus demonstrates many of the characteristics of the Japanese auto companies in their supply system relationships: tiers of subcontractors collaborate to make their supply chains effective against Benetton's competitors. All of this is done without compromising the core of the Benetton belief system that customers deserve choice, variety, value for money and a guaranteed level of quality and service.

Source: Based on *Building the Benetton System*, European Case Clearing House, No. 390-042-1.

Q Case questions

- What business practices has Benetton introduced that seem unusual to you?
- What particular issues do you think may arise in managing an organisation with so many independent suppliers and shop owners?
- What contrasts and similarities are there between Benetton and The Body Shop from a management point of view?

17.1 Introduction

This chapter introduces the following ideas:

- Craft production
- Factory production
- Scientific management
- Inventory
- Economic order quantity (EOQ)
- Material requirements planning
- Systems approach
- Input and output
- Transformation
- Feedback
- Line layout
- Cell layout
- Functional layout
- Concentric layout
- Innovation
- Cost reduction
- Total quality management
- Business process
- Demand and supply leadtime
- Supply chain
- Just-in-time
- Partnering relationship
- Order winners
- Order qualifiers

This chapter sets the operations function in its historical context and shows how this function supports other manufacturing or service activities. It then considers the current state of development of the management approaches inside the function and the increasingly cross-boundary aspects being demonstrated in the best organisations. The boundaries being crossed include those between departments of the same organisation. The role of the operations function often incorporates the management of the whole integrated supply chain. This begins with the supplier of raw material and ends with the delivery of the product or service to the customer. Thus the function has a major strategic dimension where it can hinder or help the achievement of corporate goals.

The first section outlines the main historical events, people and techniques. These have shaped our understanding of what we mean by operations and quality and how they support business activities. The chapter then describes five types of operations system, and the advantages of each. It outlines how operations contributes to quality in both manufacturing and services, and how the discipline extends beyond one organisation into other stages of the supply chain. It concludes by showing the link to marketing, and thus to the strategic position of operations in management.

17.2 Historical development

Craft production

The operations activity has existed for as long as there have been intelligent beings working with tools to transform base material into something different and desirable. In this regard, management created the specialism earlier than marketing, information systems and human resources. These latter depend more on size and complexity to justify separate status. Nevertheless, in some European cultures, management saw the purpose of operations as being to provide whatever the rest of the business wanted. They often did (in some fashion), but often this was due mainly to the abilities of the people in the function, not to a coherent approach.

This chapter looks at how the evolutionary process has changed the nature of the need that the operations function has to fill. It also examines how some organisations are paying more attention to designing and operating this transformation function. Their intention is to benefit customers and providers alike.

ACTIVITY 17.1

Visiting a craftworker

Visit a craft fair and talk to one or two of the craftworkers about the way they work, how they sell, if they design to order or according only to their ideas, and how they organise the production of goods and the supply of materials.

From the beginnings of trade, **craft producers** have embodied their ideas and skills in a product or service, and usually some elements of both. Craft producers do everything themselves. With or without customer involvement they design, source materials, make, display, sell, perhaps service and do the accounts. Once they generate income they reinvest and often train apprentices to continue the skills.

Craft producers conduct each stage of the complete product lifecycle. Their output is unique and very variable. Sometimes batch production is possible – for example, the limited edition of 500 prints from an original piece of artwork, each signed by its creator.

The range of skills employed by a craftworker is a microcosm of the operations function. The flexibility that craft producers can achieve, and their ability to modify ideas to suit customer requirements, are now sought by large producers. Craftworkers also gain a personal satisfaction from completing the whole set of tasks that is often absent in factories.

Factory production

Factory production made it possible to increase the supply of goods to rapidly growing populations. It broke down the integrated nature of the craftworker's approach. Management realised that dividing work into smaller units allowed workers to concentrate on developing a narrow range of specialised skills. The division of labour was between different tasks and between the thinking and doing tasks of manager and worker. This division began the evolution towards narrow, functionally defined boundaries with jealously guarded 'patches of turf'. These would become the focus of territorial wars across the organisation.

Visit a factory

Many large manufacturers offer visiting facilities. Try to visit several to see if you can understand the way that they work.

Dividing tasks into simple and repetitive sequences allowed managers to employ a wider range of people in the factory and so enabled them to increase production.

Managers found that they needed two other techniques to enable high volume production – standardisation and interchangeability. If several people are producing sets of parts that must fit together at some stage they must work to a standard specification. Moreover, each part must be completely interchangeable with its equivalent produced by someone else. This was not an issue for the craftworker as he or she could only work on one product at a time, and they had the skill to shape the parts to ensure a good fit.

Management in the developing factory system wanted to avoid this 'fitting' effort, so they designed both processes and machines to be regular and repeatable. This also influenced the nature of capital investment. At first, factory owners used this mainly to provide motive power for essentially human-based machines – they invested largely to supplement human muscle power. By removing variable human effort and increasing machine power the machines themselves worked more precisely, so it became easier to make interchangeable parts.

Q **Case questions 17.1**

● Is Benetton a craft or a factory system?

● Review the information about the system Benetton uses and list the advantages and disadvantages.

Twentieth-century developments

The aim of Frederick Taylor (1917) and the Gilbreths (1911, 1914) in creating a '**scientific**' approach to management was to move away from methods that were very variable and dependent on individual abilities and motivation (see Chapter 2). Some western commentators have devalued Taylor's approaches to work measurement. Yet people who are performing a sequence of related activities need to know how long to allow for each stage and what resources they need. The method study approaches that the Gilbreths pioneered as they searched for the 'one best way of working' have a great deal to offer. What has changed is that management often expects operating staff themselves to look for improved ways of working. This is part of the continuous improvement effort.

A disadvantage of the scientific school was the concentration on finely subdivided tasks that a worker would repeat thousands of times in a working life. This process was deskilling and dehumanising – it permitted no variation or individuality.

This reached its peak with Henry Ford's automobile assembly plants. Ford brought high levels of interchangeability to moving production lines, highly 'scientific' management and vertical integration along the lines of supply (Ford, 1922). That is to say, Ford owned all the stages of production from raw materials through to final distribution to customers. In the 1920s his system could transform iron ore into a finished car in 81 hours, of which only about 5 hours were manufacturing and assembly. It was economically very efficient and reduced the real cost of producing a car over many years of continuous improvement. Over an 18-year period the retail price of the Model T Ford decreased from just over $3,000 to less than $900. Ford's was a single model system, but General Motors later offered more varied products. They used different organisational principles, and created severe competition for Ford.

At the height of Ford's capability one of the many visitors was Taichi Ohno. who was the production engineer at the fledgling Toyota car company in Japan. While some of the Ford system impressed Ohno he learnt more from US supermarkets. He noted in particular how stores satisfied the needs of customers with minimal shelf space in the store. As customers took products away staff restocked the shelves. This is the logic behind what many observers regard as the world's best manufacturing company. It was also an early example of the two-way technology transfer (of managerial technologies) between west and east.

It was around this time that engineers developed a statistical approach to control quality. The method used control charts and sampling plans. Control charts tried to prevent people creating defects. Sampling plans ensured that any defects did not pass beyond the sampling stage. This statistical process control was instrumental in supporting production effort in the Second World War. It was also during that war that a different applied mathematical approach began its development. Operational research, or management science, attempted to create mathematical models of management situations. Staff could then manipulate these models to develop optimum results that management could use to inform their decisions. The assumptions needed to make some problems feasible for mathematical models were sometimes too great for managers to regard them as suitable surrogates for the real world. Nevertheless some of the approaches still offer utility to practising managers. A prime example is critical path analysis, which helps people to manage complex projects.

It was during the 1960s that availability of relatively cheap computing power encouraged people to develop techniques for managing production and **inventory**, known as material requirements planning (MRP) systems (Orlicky, 1975). These aimed to manage the production activity by controlling every part at every stage, and seemed to offer the complete computer integration of the manufacturing process. The reality was often less than ideal. Nevertheless it caused managers in the western world to look to computers to solve the problems of managing increasingly complex production systems.

Management in resource-starved Japan followed a different approach. Ford's model of mass production had not made sense to Toyota. Ohno began to build a system that used the supermarket model of simplicity and customer-driven operations. This approach did not need computers, but did need dedicated and capable people working together.

ACTIVITY 17.3

Visit Burger King

Visit a Burger King or similar fast-food outlet and try to discover the material inventories that are used. What non-material inventories will there be?

Consider a hospital accident and emergency unit. What inventories are normally stored in such units?

Systems thinking and models

Any operation can be represented as a **system** that takes inputs of various kinds and transforms them into some kind of desired output. Inputs may include materials, equip-

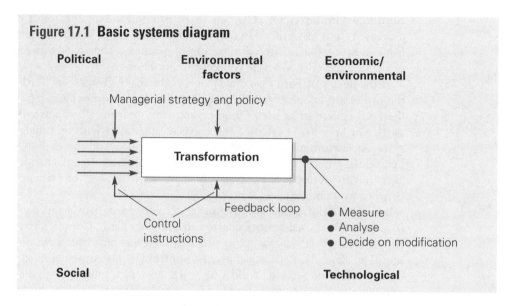

Figure 17.1 Basic systems diagram

ment, finance and people. Outputs include products, services, reputation and waste. The aim of systems thinking is to use an abstract view of the total system and then to operate each subsystem according to the defined 'best way' for the complete system. This can be drawn as a simple systems diagram. A control mechanism is included to ensure that the outputs expected are delivered and that they meet customers' needs. A feedback control loop measures, analyses and modifies the inputs, as shown in Figure 17.1.

The transformation stage can take many forms, only one of which is production. Service-oriented types are more numerous, although the history of the subject concentrates on production.

Q Case questions 17.2

- Draw a systems diagram that represents the Benetton production system.
- What are the main sources of feedback?
- How critical are they to input activities?

Table 17.1 lists the transformation types. Operations systems need to deal with two distinguishing features. The first is whether the system results in a tangible 'product' that can be stored. If not, either someone consumes the output immediately or the system has wasted the capability. If nobody occupies a hotel room or an airline seat it creates no output. The companies cannot store the capacity and have lost for ever the opportunity to sell it. A car, on the other hand, embodies its value in a less time-dependent form.

The second distinguishing feature is that in a pure service transformation (such as a visit to the hairdresser) the customer must be present throughout the transformation and largely defines the details of the transformation. In product production both design and transformation can be done without contact with the customer. In service businesses the people with whom the customer interacts *are* the service. In practice some service businesses are becoming more like factories, especially in back-office areas that have no contact with customers. An example is the cheque-processing activity in banks,

Table 17.1 Transformation types

Transformation	System	Variations
Physical	Production	Additive, e.g. automobile assembly Subtractive, e.g. oil refining
Locational	Transportation	Goods, people
Attitudinal	Education Entertainment	Statutory or voluntary Escapist or informative
Physiological	Health care, fitness	Remedial/preventive
Presentational	Fashion	Clothes, hair, cosmetics

which nowadays usually perform all such routine work in its dedicated processing facilities. Conversely, many factories are trying to become closer to their customers to satisfy needs more precisely.

The objectives of operations managers are to select and manage the best mix of resources and transformation process to meet customer requirements. They must also do this in a way that permits the organisation to make an acceptable financial return on its investments. The customer requirements will cover aspects of product or service design, delivery, reliability, speed and quality. All must be at an acceptable cost.

KEY IDEAS — **Characteristics differentiating operational systems**

- **Output volume**.
- **Nature of processing** (continuous or intermittent).
- **Outputs are continuous or discrete** (e.g. electricity or cars).
- **Specificity to actual customer requirements** (degree to which the output and the flexibility of the system's response is specific to or specified by the customer).
- **Physical layout** of transformation equipment.

Volume ranges from unique items, such as a dam or fine art picture, through multiple copies or batches of similar items through to mass production. The latter can be continuous (cement) or discrete (video recorders). Figure 17.2 shows these systems with examples of each. It lists across the top the physical layouts that tend to match each type.

Line layout is specified by the sequence of activities needed to perform a given transformation. It is relatively fixed but may have similar processes scattered through the line as and when needed. It will tend to have specially designed process equipment and use people with a limited range of skills.

Cell layout permits more variety by creating multiple cells (which look like small line layouts) dedicated to producing families of output types. Within the cell people have several skills and move between jobs as required to keep the flow of transformation steady. The people are likely to have a wider range of skills and more decision-making authority.

Both of these types focus on the transformed materials or customer. The aim is to keep them flowing through the system without delay. If necessary, operators use parts of the transformation system at less than the theoretical capacity to keep the process moving.

In the **functional layout** the thinking is different. Here the system tries to keep the elements of the transformation process fully used and able to produce the required variety of output. Similar physical processes are located together, and the materials and/or customers visit these areas as required by the product or service design. This produces a

Figure 17.2 Forms of operations system

Volume	Line	Cell	Layout Functional	Concentric	Examples
High	MASS (Rigid)				Ford model T (discrete) Cement (continuous) General Motors Electricity supply
		MASS (Flexible)			Toyota
			BATCH		90 per cent of organisations
Low				UNIQUE	Civil engineering Bespoke tailor

Low   **Flexibility**   High

very tangled flow round these locations, often involving extensive queuing time between the different processing stages. This system needs high levels of inventory while the operating staff perform highly specialised tasks. It is a common way of organising manufacturing and service operations.

In a **concentric layout** people focus activity on an area where something – such as a dam or a ship – is being assembled. The process is one of bringing the resources together in the required sequence and time to create a unique output. People have extensive skills. Integration is complex, so staff often use the critical path analysis technique to plan activities.

It is important to realise that these stereotypes are simply that. They are labels that bring certain assumptions with them so that using the label paints a mental picture as a form of shorthand in discussions. In practice organisations can often display a number of these stereotypes under one roof. For example, a restaurant might have a functionally organised kitchen producing batches of meals for parties of diners. The waiter is a pure service person interacting to create a uniquely specified meal for a single diner. If there is a buffet or carvery area this may be in a line with customers moving along and being part of the transformation process.

ACTIVITY 17.4

Defining transformation types

Define the transformation type and possible layout form of the following: (a) university matriculation or enrolment process, (b) a motorway fast-food servery, (c) a hospital accident and emergency unit, (d) a Benetton customer sales and service area.

One of the dangers of diagrams such as Figure 17.2 is that they may imply that there are limited choices. Certainly there is a tendency to fit these categories together. The idea of the trade-off suggests that people can design systems to do certain things well – but they will then do other things less well (Skinner, 1969). When this is true, that original decision is very important, especially since the time and cost to make major changes of system structure will be significant. Nevertheless it may be possible to reduce these trade-offs in some way. If customer satisfaction is improved then this will be an important aspect of competitive advantage. This is what the best organisations try to do. They challenge the assumptions underlying the trade-offs and continually strive to do more with less while ensuring continuing and expanding customer support.

17.3   The operations function and its contribution

The operations function has been set in its historical context and some models have been provided of the balance between market need and supply capability. The chapter now examines how the operations function can support the rest of the business.

In what follows it is assumed that management has made decisions on product or service design. Ideally it will have discussed the options with the operations function – but the marketing and design staff play the major role in that. The operations function can help ensure that people implement design decisions in a way that adds value to the business. The main contributions are in the areas of innovation, quality, delivery and cost.

Innovation

In products, the impetus for change comes from two sources. Market pull occurs when customers make new demands or when competitors try to change the strategic balance in some way. Such innovations are low risk. It is likely that there will be a demand for the new product. Since the product is based on what is known and understood it should be easy to estimate costs. The danger is that such innovations are too incremental – while safe, they do not advance quickly enough to gain a competitive advantage.

CASE STUDY   Benetton – the case continues – innovations

One famous innovation took place in 1972, at a time when the colours were still simple, i.e. one colour per garment and no complicated patterns. Traditionally, wool is dyed its final colour when it is still a yarn, i.e. a long time before being used in a garment and a long time ahead of actual customer demand. By designing a process to dye the completed garment Benetton incurred some increased production costs but greatly reduced the cost of carrying the inventory of coloured garments formerly needed to react to customers' demands. Instead, the decision about colour was moved much closer to customers' buying decision, thus removing much risk and complexity. It also meant that stocks that were selling well could be replenished, while stocks of less popular goods could be minimised.

As the company grew it continued to rely on a network of subcontractors – often created by internal groups being encouraged to become independent contractors to Benetton. By 1987 only 5 per cent of final garment sewing assembly was done internally by Benetton.

Source: Based on *Building the Benetton System*, European Case Clearing House, No. 390-042-1.

Technology push is the other main force for innovation. Here an expert with an idea proposes a new and often dramatic innovation. The danger is that no customer has yet requested this item, and many will not be able to express a need for it. Such innovations are high risk. There are no forecasts of market demand and no historical data for cost estimates. Many innovations of this type fail. Those that succeed, however, can change companies, industries and societies, as the Benetton case demonstrates. Only think of the photocopier, jet engine, scanning electron microscope to realise the importance of major breakthrough innovations. In reality management needs to consider both possibilities. It can seek incremental innovation continuously while the essentially intermittent nature of a breakthrough needs a different management approach.

Technology is more likely to stimulate process innovation. Even here multiple small changes can create wide competitive gaps if continued over a long period.

Organisations need innovation in both products and in processes – and not just those in the production area. Many office systems and most service businesses repay a serious effort to redesign them in more effective ways. Telephone-based insurance companies have dramatically increased their market share by innovations in the way they deliver the service. Banking is going in the same direction. Inditex shows the role of innovation in fashion retailing reaching new heights with Zara's attempts to remove 'seasons' from the business.

MANAGEMENT IN PRACTICE	**Inditex group**

This fast-growing group of fashion-related companies has Zara, Pull and Bear, Massimo Dutti, Berschka and Stradivarious in its list. It is active in 33 countries with 1,137 stores in 2001. Over 200 designers help meet the aim to be close to their customers and do away with seasons in fashions. They now introduce 20,000 new items a year – and to do this they need to be even more responsive than Benetton.

Source: *Forbes Global,* 28 May 2001, pp.24–5, 28–9; and www.inditex.com/izara.htm

Quality

In craft production the **quality** of output is crucial, for without it customers may not pay and will certainly not return. Craftspeople also tend to have pride in their work and continuously strive to improve their mastery of the craft. During the evolution of the factory system this ideal suffered as management subdivided the work process. Management separated quality approval from production. Even quality control charts were tools for quality inspectors not production workers.

During the 1950s the Americans sent a number of their statisticians to Japan to help rebuild their productive capability. The Japanese learned from Joseph Juran (Juran, 1974), W.E. Deming (Deming, 1988), Armand Feigenbaum (Feigenbaum, 1993), and applied the lessons widely and conscientiously. They also recognised the fundamental truth of craft production – that the person who performs the transformation is the best person to ensure quality is correct at the moment of its performance. History has thus come full circle, with individuals taking pride in doing quality work and striving to make regular improvements.

Another realisation is that quality and customer satisfaction are responsibilities for all in the business and not simply the producer at the end of the chain. Each customer throughout the chain must receive top quality performance. This is a message top management must believe in and then act on accordingly.

Principles of total quality management (TQM)

- **Philosophy**: waste reduction through continuous improvement.
- **Leadership**: committed and visible from top to bottom of the organisation.
- **Measurement**: costs involved in quality failures – the cost of quality.

- **Scope**: everyone, everywhere across whole supply chain.
- **Methods**: use simple control and improvement techniques implemented by teams.

The underpinning philosophy of TQM is that not having perfect quality wastes resources. Some of these wastes are obvious – scrapped material through equipment failure – but other wastes come through bad systems or poor communications and may be more difficult to find and measure. The philosophy advocates that a constant effort to remove waste pays dividends. Progressive, small improvements repay mightily from both customer satisfaction and revenue viewpoints. They reduce costs as the system uses resources more effectively. Leadership of a visible and tangible type is needed to keep the efforts going. It also avoids a tendency to consider delivery of any product as more important than the delivery of the correct product. Crosby introduced the idea that 'quality is free': it is getting it wrong that costs money (Crosby, 1979).

In contrast to the scientific management approach, modern writers propose that quality should not be separated from production. Everyone has to take responsibility for his or her proportion of the quality effort. This includes those people outside the organisation who nevertheless contribute towards the total quality of the supply chain. The whole supply chain must function as a total quality system. Methods used include simple descriptive statistics, brainstorming techniques and simple statistical process controls (Oakland, 1994). The people performing the transformation are the ones trained and encouraged to use these tools and they will often display the results in their work area to spur further improvement. In this they will work as a team, calling on different people to support them as required.

Company teams can take part in Quality Award schemes. The Deming prize in Japan set the tone, with the winners enjoying high prestige. In the United States, the Baldrige Quality Award has set a pattern of very wide-ranging definitions of quality, and this has influenced the equivalent European Quality Awards (see the EFQM website **www.efqm.org**). At a more local level various national standards for quality are often demanded of organisations to qualify as approved providers of goods or services (see **www.iso.ch**). The key is not the award but the thought processes of all the people in the organisation and their commitment to the total quality ideals.

Sources of quality cost

- **Prevention** – getting the systems right.
- **Appraisal** – measuring how the systems are performing.
- **Internal failure** – faults found during checks inside the operation.
- **External failure** – faults found by users – the worst kind.

Quality is never completely free because of the investment in prevention. It is clear, however, that switching proportionately more resources into prevention cuts other costs such that the total reduces.

Elida Faberge – Best Factory Award, 2000

Unilever's Elida Faberge plant in Leeds won the *Management Today* Factory of the Year award, and the judges rated it one of the best factories they had ever seen. The factory produces 300 million aerosols a year for demanding customers such as Sainsbury, Tesco, Boots and Carrefour. The factory is complex, producing 30 brands in many variants and sizes.

'What makes the factory so good? The best operative-based total productive maintenance that the judges had ever seen, clearly specified procedures, problem-recording charts, perspex-sided maintenance trolleys with colour-coded lubricants and cleaners, glass inserts let into machinery so that belt-drives, etc. could be inspected without removing covers ... and many more. The best human resource management initiatives for another: "Every single person on site is paid not according to their trade union's ability to negotiate with me, but according to their achievement of personal objectives," says Gary Calvely, works director.'

Source: *Management Today*, November 2000, p.110.

Thinking about quality at the design stage brings important benefit. Choices here should incorporate ideas and information from as many insiders, customers and suppliers as is sensible. Such processes capture the prevention and 'right first time' ideals and create opportunities to save cost and time. Waste minimisation is the goal. Waste is any use of resources that does not add value for the customer. Note that customers are not the only stakeholders. Management may be able to justify an activity not directly related to the requirements of a direct customer. Environmental considerations fall into this category, as do those based on legislation. A counter view from John Seddon (*The Observer*, 19 November 2000):

Seddon argues that the rush for the international ISO standard for quality has missed the point by over emphasizing the command and control approach at the expense of 'thinking and feeling' or the 'what and why' of quality. He argues that the standard has forced organizations to concentrate on the procedures rather than on service and to do so in an overly bureaucratic way.

Many western organisations have been trying to catch up with best Japanese experience and practice in understanding and applying the lessons of quality control. They will have active measurement and improvement programmes in place, but many will not yet be paying the same attention to delivery.

Dell Computing

By redesigning their whole supply chain Dell have made a virtue out of speed and response to customers in a way that repays Dell by efficient use of money. Customers buy online and pay for their product in advance. Dell also tries to manage the elective choices customers make by offering discounts for inventory that is moving too slowly. Their operational control system is such that a customer can call into Dell to check progress in the manufacture of their order. By then Dell has the use of their money and some time later will pay their suppliers' bills for the materials they have provided. This system is so responsive that Dell is able to change its pricing structure daily to take advantage of material price fluctuations and to price aggressively for certain markets in ways that their less flexible competitors find difficult to match.

Source: *Financial Times*, 20 June 2001.

FT

ACTIVITY 17.5

Defining quality

Define what quality means in the following: (a) a fast-food hamburger restaurant, (b) a five-star hotel, (c) an executive automobile, (d) a travel agency, (e) the products sold by Benetton, (f) the service provided by Benetton sales staff.

Delivery

Each link in the chain of supply from raw material to final consumer is formed between an individual or group acting as a customer to a supplier. The customer is in turn the supplier to another. Thus the next customer along the chain immediately feels any failure in quality, unless large amounts of inventory hide the failure. This is a direct benefit of reducing inventory: it exposes quality problems so that people can deal with them permanently.

CASE STUDY

Benetton – the case continues – innovations

The fashion cycle for the important spring/summer season begins in February with selection of around 500 items. During May–July small samples are produced to allow retailers a chance to place orders for the season seven months ahead. As the first orders roll in production plans are made and subcontractors informed. The shop owners are then obliged to buy the goods produced as Benetton does not accept any returned goods unsold at the end of the season. Most of the shop orders are delivered between November and the following May as the Basic collection in readiness for the new season. The balance of the orders fall into two categories: 'Flash' consists of reactions to new trends or competitor offerings while 'Reassortment' allows for individual choice of produce mix in a particular store, and possibly for those late-dyed popular colours.

Thus the operations system has to cope with fairly stable production runs of the 'standard order' for 80–90 per cent and 'specials' on a much faster response time for the late variations.

Source: Based on *Building the Benetton System*, European Case Clearing House, No. 390-042-1.

As with quality, so with **delivery**. Any failure to supply the customer when expected causes the wastes of delay, remedial action and extra effort. The first step in delivery performance is total reliability. Every downstream customer is dependent on every upstream supplier fulfilling his or her delivery promise, otherwise there is more waste. Every chain needs reliability, but sometimes it also needs speedy delivery. Speed is crucial when a company is bringing a new product to the market. It wants to make sales to early adopters before competitors can produce alternatives that will drive the price down. In competitive situations speed of response may be the distinguishing factor that wins the order. Figure 17.3 captures the relative timescales on the supply and demand side.

Figure 17.3 illustrates a manufactured product for which the customer is prepared to wait some time between placing and receiving the order – the **demand leadtime**. In some markets, such as retailing, this time is zero. That is, supply has to be instantaneous (off the shelf) or the buyer goes elsewhere or selects another product. In most manufacturing situations the addition of all the supply-side activities that constitute the **supply leadtime** far exceeds the demand leadtime. The critical fact is that all of the investment

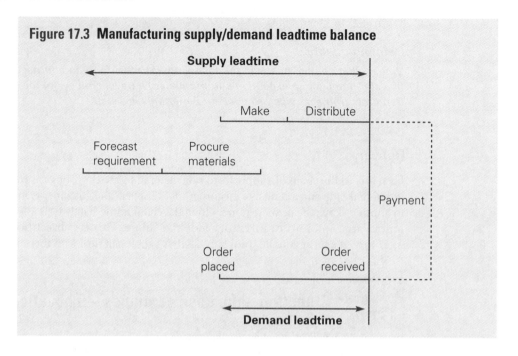

Figure 17.3 Manufacturing supply/demand leadtime balance

tied up in decisions to the left of the order placement point are at risk. In these areas there is no guarantee that a customer will place an order. So there is continual pressure to reduce the time needed on the supply side of the balance. Ideally the supply total would be less than the demand total. That would guarantee sales success, but only markets producing customised products to order are like this.

In service businesses the situation is different since the customer must be present during the service (see Figure 17.4). The service processing time will extend through the need to provide capacity (people and equipment) plus any consumable materials needed for the service. Generally there is likely to be a closer balance. Here, however, the customer perception of what is an acceptable service time can produce difficulties for the supply system if the system cannot match expectations effectively.

One of the most effective ways to reduce the supply leadtime in any linked supply chain is to consider the flow of materials through to the final customer as the real challenge. The task then is to synchronise all of the tributary flows into the main stream to

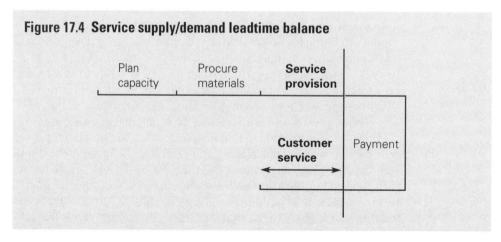

Figure 17.4 Service supply/demand leadtime balance

maximise the main flow and minimise waste. Such synchronisation calls for co-ordinated effort in scheduling deliveries from internal and external suppliers according to an integrated master plan and reinforces the need for absolute control of quality and delivery performance.

ACTIVITY 17.6

Consider the leadtime for a dress

Consider the total supply leadtime for a bridal dress made from Chinese silk. List and guess the timescales for the different stages of production and supply up to the final garment being made for the bride.

Cost

There is no disputing the need for the real **cost** of a transformation process to reduce with time. If organisations continually innovate to improve their systems and remove waste, and given that the learning effect of operating the systems also reduces waste and time taken, then cost should decrease. There is, however, a preferred sequence. An organisation must first build a solid base of quality performance and reinforce it with careful control over delivery. Doing these things correctly will lead to lower cost. If, on the other hand, the organisation tries to reduce costs and simply take resources away, this is likely to lower overall quality and delivery performance.

Cost is also an internal factor that customers do not always need to know. What they need to understand is what pricing possibilities the organisation can offer as a result of its performance on cost reduction. It is also important that an organisation does not concentrate solely on the direct money aspect of the business transaction since many of the factors that go towards creating a satisfied customer will not necessarily be reflected in the unit price quoted for the good or service. The operations function has an important role to play as part of the supply chain team that delivers the goods and/or services in the most effective manner.

Synchronisation and flow

The operations area now needs to be considered as part of the much wider idea of the supply chain. The essence of the argument about delivery reliability is the need to ensure that all of the wastes in the chain are removed. Information needs to flow efficiently from the consumer to the producers at all points upstream. Materials should flow continuously downstream to satisfy all the intermediate customer requirements before passing from the chain to the final consumer. The concept of flow is a useful one. It is implied in the concept that Michael Porter describes as a value chain. Here the horizontal flow consists of the five stages of inbound logistics, transformation, outbound logistics, sales and service, and the generation of a financial margin (see Chapter 6). Porter extends the value system idea to include the output from one organisation's value chain being the input to another one. It is then similar to the supply chain model described above (Porter, 1980b).

The key part of this concept is that final consumers want to receive their chosen goods as they require them without hindrance or problem. So organisations need to make the flow as smooth, speedy and consistent as possible. Anything interfering with this smooth flow is a waste, causing customer dissatisfaction. Speed of flow also brings financial benefits: the quicker the flow becomes a sale, the quicker the company can recover the investment incurred in supply.

Q Case questions 17.3

Consider the supply leadtime for the Benetton Basic collection and for the Flash or Reassortment goods. What is the demand leadtime for each of these categories?

This concept lies behind the just-in-time system of production where the total quality management and synchronised flow approaches are coupled with a cross-trained and committed workforce to produce very effectively (Schonberger, 1983). The synchronisation is not internal to just one organisation, and so managements try to establish a complete supply chain working collaboratively on this basis.

MANAGEMENT IN PRACTICE Nissan Motor Manufacturing Company

The suppliers of colour co-ordinated seats for Nissan cars are located close to the main factory and are connected electronically to the workflow on the Nissan line. When cars leave the paint oven and are accepted as ready for assembly this is the signal for the particular colour of car seat to be produced and matched to the flow on the car line. The complete seat assembly with all electronic equipment, positions adjusters, etc. must then be produced and delivered direct to the point of use on the Nissan line in less than 30 minutes. It must be in a condition such that the Nissan workers need only position it into the car and fix it to its mountings with complete confidence that everything about the seat is completely correct.

To make synchronisation possible management has to attack the problem that led to a functional focus. This is the traditional view that the best way to make a financial return on a piece of equipment is to keep it producing. The new thinking is that the equipment has to support the flow and no more. Thus, if the output is already sufficient then the process should stop and not build inventory for which there is no immediate demand. Management also needs to attack the thought that if it is expensive to change over from one production run to another it should do this less often; in other words it should produce large quantities before changing. This builds those costly inventories again. A better approach is to reduce the costs of changing, so that the pressure for large production runs is no longer there. Management can then approach the just-in-time ideal of making a little of everything every day. When this is achieved, the system can produce to customer order with no delays and no inventory.

MANAGEMENT IN PRACTICE Bottling and packaging

During work with a bottling company and a supplier of high quality printed cartons the extent of potential cost reductions became clearer the wider the investigation spread. Initially the buyer was trying to reduce its costs of buying the cartons by around 5 per cent per year over a three-year period. This was worth around £242,000 per year. However, the opportunities for real cost reduction in product design over the same period were £1 million; in ordering procedures they were £135,000; in production they were worth £153,000; and in planning they were worth £14,000. Many of these potential savings required action across many functions in both companies and were not as easy to obtain as a demand for a price reduction, but the impact on the business was clearly much bigger.

Source: www.scmg.co.uk

The bottling and packaging example shows that the impact of a decision does not fall in only one organisation. There needed to be a mechanism by which all the interested parties come together to decide a course of action that will be an effective solution for all.

This form of system awareness is important when possible cost reductions in the supply system are considered. Each organisation or unit has an interest in supporting both the immediate and the final customer. Each also has to look good in terms of its own current performance. The difficulty is that sometimes the best supply chain solution means that one part operates less efficiently (from a local perspective) to improve overall chain performance.

KEY IDEAS   **Conflicting performance targets**

The classic description of the problem of each part trying to maximise its own performance relates to the ideal specifications for the production area and the sales area. The manufacturing stereotype is a preference for long runs of a standard product. The sales stereotype is a preference for providing unique products that meet particular customer requirements. There has to be a balance. It is possible for an organisation to become bankrupt satisfying customer requirements that it is not designed to satisfy, so the maxim cannot be 'customer satisfaction at all costs' since some costs are unacceptable.

Thus cost reduction is a continuing necessity but needs to be done with care. Suppliers can reduce some costs without any impact on the customer simply by doing things more smartly. One waste worth challenging is the amount of material held in the various categories of stock. By re-examining where to hold protection stocks and eliminating all others a supplier can make large savings at no risk to customer service.

Q   **Case questions 17.4**

Examine the points in the Benetton supply chain where inventory is stored and identify why it is likely to be held there.

The major leverage point for cost reduction is, however, at the initial design stage. Staff make decisions here that incur costs later. By thinking through both quality and operational logistics issues at this stage people can avoid creating unnecessary costs at the source.

17.4   **The business process view**

The concept of flow as horizontal through the organisation is opposed to the vertical orientation of traditional organisational principles based around functions. This is in accord with a greater focus on customers and their satisfaction. The functional structure reflects the same thought patterns that lead to the functional layout discussed earlier. Both optimise internally regardless of the effect on the customer.

To escape from this mindset organisations are trying to restructure their activities around basic business processes that all organisations will use to meet their customers' requirements. By defining these in generic terms they hope to create new insights. The essence of flow also means removing the waste from the interfaces between the traditional functions. Since organisations are unique there are no universal definitions of these core processes. They will vary between organisations, but it is possible to identify some relatively common ones.

MANAGEMENT IN PRACTICE   **Direct Line Insurance**

Re-engineering business processes have been critical for this company, which redefined the insurance business in the United Kingdom. Most other providers were then forced to copy this model just to remain in the same marketplace.

Each of Direct Line's products is designed with the same basic philosophy: to offer consumers *clear, straightforward, good value* alternatives to products that are sold through traditional distribution channels. This is especially so where those channels involve a 'middleman' that can be cut out to reduce costs.

As the company conducts the vast majority of its business using the telephone, customer service is at the core of the Direct Line proposition. It introduced new levels of service to the financial services sector, putting customer needs and considerations first in everything that it does.

To ensure that standards are maintained the company provides all staff with extensive customer care training and re-engineers sales processes to cut out complicated forms and jargon. In one of its first revolutionary moves Direct Line removed the need for 'cover notes' by arranging for all documents such as policy and insurance certificates to be laser printed immediately and forwarded by first-class post to customers – usually in time for the following day.

Innovative technology helps Direct Line keep down costs that, in turn, helps to reduce premiums. For example, most Direct Line products are paid for using credit cards or direct debits so that all payments are processed electronically. This keeps staffing levels and overheads to a minimum. Automated call handling systems also ensure that the company's 15 million customer calls each year are quickly and effortlessly rerouted between Direct Line's six different city centres to ensure the minimum wait for an available operator.

Source: www.directline.com

Create and capture customers' intent to buy the product or service

This process recognises the two sources of innovation – technology push or market pull – and uses either or both to define new product or service packages to bring to the customer market. Defined as a business process this will cover activities often associated in the past with marketing, product design, prototype production, trial marketing, and product advertising and launch. The creative process is intended to bring together all of the interests associated with a forward look at customers. The aim is to fully define their requirements. In the case of truly innovative ideas the intention is to specify the product or service in a way that determines what the operations systems have to do to support these new market requirements.

Customer order fulfilment

Having created the intention to buy, this process does everything necessary to deliver the product or service to the customer. It aims to do this in such a way that the transaction satisfies both the customer and the supply system.

The process starts with capturing a customer order. From here it will cover all of the planning stages that allocate resources to produce and deliver the order. It also recognises the need to source resources from other suppliers in the chain. Thus the traditional functions of sales processing and forecasting, production planning and control, manufacture or service provision and resource procurement (buying) can all be included. So too can those concerned with the physical movement of materials and ensuring people are available to do the work. The flows in this process are clearly two way: from customers to supply system about demand, and from supply system to customers with the order. The flow returns again with money to pay for the exchange. There are many interfaces between activities in this business process often acting in very short timescales, and clearly this is one of the major (direct) value-adding sets of activities in the organisation.

MANAGEMENT IN PRACTICE **An e-business portal**

General Motors, Ford and DaimlerChrysler in the USA have joined together with Renault-Nissan and PSA Peugeot-Citroën to provide one marketplace for all of their suppliers. This is intended to handle all commercial transactions between these major automotive customers and their global suppliers and is intended to becomes the 'one stop shop' for all business transactions.

Suppliers are not yet convinced, since all they have seen so far is pressure to reduce costs or lose the business. Such portals are being established in all sectors of business but many are expected to disappear as the dot.com boom fades in 2001 and 2002.

Source: Public information. For more information, see **www.covisint.com**

Depending on the nature of the demand (a forecast or a firm customer order) the planning process can be aimed either at building inventory or at meeting the customer order. Speed is not always necessary, although delivery reliability is. In building for inventory, management strikes a balance between the costs of making a large and economical batch now and the costs of holding stocks of finished goods. If it produces too much for immediate requirements it has to store and care for the product until it is sold. The economic order quantity can be calculated by making assumptions about actual cost patterns. Management can then establish and manage stockholding policies.

Computerised planning approaches are appropriate when demand is known or can be calculated. Every order for a family car will generate an order for five wheels. Planners then add to this how long they believe it will take to produce or purchase the wheels. They can then decide when they need to place an order for the earlier parts of the supply system.

The just-in-time approach omits the computer calculations. It replaces them with a simple 'pull' signal sent when a customer removes some material from the end of the previous stage of the supply chain. This action sends a replenishment signal (a *kanban*) upstream telling the supplier to produce replacement parts. The signal can then ripple its way upstream and, ideally, the supply chain then operates quickly and with a much reduced level of inventory compared with both of the other ways described.

Pure service operations concentrate on scheduling service staff to ensure that they are available to deal with the customers as they arrive.

Cash handling and reporting

Transactions to transfer the ownership of goods or to pay for services must be properly accounted for. It is also necessary to create an audit trail to establish that the activities have been done legally. This process also provides the funds with which the organisation pays its own bills. More businesses fail through mismanaging their cash flow than fail for lack of customers. This is another reason to look for speed through the business processes in order to convert customer interest into cash.

MANAGEMENT IN PRACTICE   **Cash handling process in supermarkets**

Supermarkets have a very profitable cash handling process. They receive cash or credit transfers almost instantaneously but pay their suppliers as long as 30 days from the date of the invoice. Meanwhile they can earn interest on both sets of money in the short-term financial marketplace. It is perhaps not surprising that the larger retail chains are providing their own banking opportunities for their customers. In some ways they have been behaving as banks for years. At the same time they have been highly efficient at converting shelf space to sales with minimum in-store inventory.

New ways of working eliminate many paper-based and costly transaction-processing activities. They use simplified techniques and place greater responsibility on the suppliers to do what they have contracted to do without the customer checking. In the car wheel example, all cars leaving the assembler's premises must have five wheels. Rather than arrange a transaction for each delivery of wheels common practice now is to record the number of cars leaving the system (which is done anyway). The system multiplies that number by five and regularly pays the supplier for that number of wheels. As an alternative, for low-value items all purchasers can be issued with the equivalent of a plastic bank card so that orders can be sent in, deliveries made and a fully detailed statement sent to the purchasing organisation at the end of the month for one payment.

These are well-established examples of what has come to be called electronic or e-commerce. The speed of web-based electronic communications allows for more efficient markets to be established. Whole industries are trying to move in this direction.

Maintaining service

In many product areas management has come to realise that it is much cheaper to retain a customer than to find a new one (a common estimate of the ratio is 1:10). This has caused them to re-examine the nature of the customer relationship and to support valued customers well beyond any contractual or warranty requirement. In service areas the degree of direct involvement with the client or customer changes the nature of the considerations again. The arguments about customer retention are even more important in this environment and often there will be a need to keep in regular contact (special newsletters, magazines, offers) to try to keep the relationship going.

In all cases current customers have great value in evaluating new product or service ideas at the trial market stage. They also help secure new customers through recommendations and contact names. This will be the case particularly where the price for a single transaction is not the most important factor in the buying decision.

17.5 Interfaces with other functions – partnering in the supply chain

In traditionally structured organisations the operations function has many interfaces as it contributes to nearly all crucial decisions relating to business performance. In some of these the operations function will be in a distinctly subordinate position, in others more to the fore. The aim should be to meet business requirements by satisfying the customer at the end of the chain. To do this all parts of the organisation need to understand each other's strengths and weaknesses. They then need to build a system that recognises the first and improves on the second. The new way of looking at the needs of the business in terms of the business processes recognises explicitly the need to manage across boundaries. Most commonly, change teams focus on processes that cross department functions. Some also review processes that cross the boundaries between organisations into (upstream) suppliers or (downstream) to the customers.

The argument here is that certain parts of the chain are experts at their portion of the total task. Those at other stages should allow them to perform those tasks without interference from customers telling them what to do. Those in the chain need to manage the relationships so that the chain as a whole meets the needs of the final customer. So the tasks are now about influence, information and co-ordination between independent but co-operating organisations. This is a different form of management from that which exercises command and control within an isolated business. It is also about encouraging, recognising and implementing innovation from all in the chain to the chain's competitive advantage and the ultimate customers' delight.

When separate organisations use this approach they often refer to it as **partnering** (Macbeth and Ferguson, 1994). The logic applies to all management activities that cross boundaries, not only those with different ownership. The essence is to recognise complementary capabilities, look for ways to co-ordinate informational and logistical flows and to invest for the long term in a jointly planned way.

KEY IDEAS — Principles of co-operative supply chain management

- **Philosophy**: sharing information to reduce waste, increase value add and generate joint competitiveness.
- **Leadership**: led by the experts wherever they are.
- **Measurement**: reducing real costs demonstrated by measurement of both parties' behaviour.
- **Scope**: cascaded from each buyer supplier link to the extended network of interacting organisations.
- **Methods**: joint benchmarking and joint improvement teams.

Q Case questions 17.5

- What would a partnering approach imply for Benetton's management?
- What benefits might the company obtain from such a practice?
- What benefits might its suppliers and shop owners obtain?
- What could be the obstacles?

This recognises that internal competition is no longer the only way to demonstrate value for money. Rather it is about demonstrating that by removing the wastes from the chain the whole chain becomes more competitive than other chains. Working together increases the chances of success and of obtaining the rewards of success. It is not a comfortable or easy option since the pressures to stay expert in each area are intense. The need to innovate constantly to reduce waste further and to enhance the offer to the final consumers is unrelenting. In addition, the need to fully support the partner organisation creates its own dynamic pressure.

In order to make this a reality partners must be chosen carefully. The parties then need to create joint teams to address, in a planned manner, areas where improvements can be made that benefit both sides. They also need to measure and reward joint performance in new and creative ways (Supply Chain Management Group, 1995, and see www.scmg.co.uk). In all of this they aim to apply the essential operations management practices that have been described across all aspects of the joint organisations. Companies have to be best in class in three areas: inside each of the partner organisations and in the areas of explicitly joint responsibility.

The future orientation of the partnering process means that each has a responsibility to scan its field of expertise and interest. The customer organisation has to keep sight of developments in its own marketplace. It has to get close to its customers and watch its competitors' movements. It must also watch for new entrants with developments that threaten the whole chain. The supplier should scan its environment in a similar way. In particular, it should look for new technologies that might improve service to the immediate and ultimate customer. In this view organisations, departments and individual people are both customers of and suppliers to others. While the roles may take a different importance at different times the responsibility to manage proactively in both directions is not diminished.

17.6 Strategic position of operations

Section 17.5 has demonstrated a new realisation of the importance of the operations function in an integrated approach to managing the supply system in support of the customer. The key questions relate to the capabilities that the system needs currently and which should be developed for future requirements. A related issue is the selection of those complementary suppliers who can provide the other aspects of the product or service, and finally the choice of market segments in which to compete. This latter decision might be still more influenced by factors associated with financial returns and market positioning. The broad nature of the operations activity means that making these decisions without reference to the ability of the system to respond and change will in turn make it difficult to achieve the objectives.

Customer demands in the markets usually change faster than production systems. These latter are made up of investments in hardware, software and people – not all of which can be changed rapidly. There needs to be an iterative process involving all interested parties deciding what the company must do well to succeed in the market. The concepts of order winners and order qualifiers can help to frame the discussion and bridge the language gap between the marketing and the operations staff (Hill, 2000).

An **order winner** is some feature or combination of features of the product and service that positively differentiates it from those of competitors and makes customers want to buy it in preference to those others. Ideally it is something that is unique which competitors cannot replicate. An **order qualifier** is the ticket to the game. It is a feature that is a necessary but not a sufficient requirement for purchase. Customers will not consider you without it. Qualifiers get the seller into the race but do not guarantee that it will win the prize. Some qualifiers are so critical that any deviation from the expected standard means instant disqualification. Customers will ignore otherwise attractive features if the seller does not meet this basic requirement.

These concepts are useful in opening up the debate between marketing and operations personnel since they can be defined in terms that both can understand. The operations staff can convert them into system specifications for process design once the parties agree them. It is also possible to rein in the wilder flights of fancy from marketers who see a new opportunity that the operations system has no prospect of satisfying in a sensible time. It is better to recognise this and to modify the target market than to risk everything to make a total change of operating system.

Of course, such order winners and qualifiers are dynamic. They change as customers become more demanding and as competitors become more proficient.

> **MANAGEMENT IN PRACTICE**   **Japanese colour television production**
>
> When the Japanese producers of colour televisions first entered the European market they created the order winner of quality and produced at such an improved level that they captured a large market share. The European producers took up this competitive challenge and attempted to match the quality standards. Quality then became a qualifier and the Japanese moved the order winner to price. In doing so they further improved their competitive position. The Europeans had failed to understand and implement cost-efficient ways of ensuring quality, so they were unable to compete as they were spending more than the Japanese merely to reach the qualifying levels of quality. They were certainly not able to reduce their production costs enough to compete on price as well.
>
> Source: Various industry reports.

Thus the discussion of order winners and qualifiers needs to be a regular part of the chain process. Often it is a service-related feature that distinguishes qualified products. It is these aspects that are most likely to occur at the boundaries between traditional organisations. An integrated view of the whole supply chain helps management to improve them.

> **ACTIVITY 17.7**
>
> ***Defining order winners and qualifiers***
>
> *Define the order winners and qualifiers for the following: (a) a music, food and drink club catering for students; (b) a personal computer.*
>
> *Highlight those features most likely to change and comment on the implications for the operations system design needed to support them.*
>
> *How might new communication technologies (for example, the Internet) affect the supply chain for food shopping?*

17.7 Summary

The chapter has traced the evolution of the operations function, as part of the development of wider ideas about organisations and their management. Initially the discipline reflected the scientific management principle of separating functions, but operations now stresses the value of integrating functions such as design and quality into the responsibilities of those doing the work. The chapter described different types of transformation and the features of manufacturing or service activity for which managers need to design operating process. The area now pays particular attention to designing organisations around horizontal processes rather than vertical hierarchies, as a better way of focusing on customer needs. This principle extends beyond the organisation to link several independent organisations into a single supply chain, focused on customer needs. That interaction between customer needs and operational systems marks out the strategic contribution of the operations function to management.

Content

Having set objectives and strategies management is able to use ideas from the operations area in planning how to achieve them. Operations exists to develop systems that satisfy customers. Operations managers try to select the best mix of resources and types of transformation process to meet customer needs. Their particular contribution is in the areas of innovation, quality, delivery and cost. They also aim to secure a smooth flow through successive processes and to contribute towards worthwhile cost reductions. The current emphasis is to challenge conventional functional structures in favour of structures based on business processes. The perspective also emphasises the possibilities of working closely across organisational boundaries with partners. These may be at earlier and later points in the value chain.

Process

There are stakeholders in functional areas and attempts to reorganise around business processes may threaten their interests. In contrast to early management practice, which sought to divide the responsibilities of managers and workers, operations stresses that management cannot divide responsibility for functions such as customer satisfaction and quality. Those at all stages in the supply chain are responsible and so should take part in decisions on those matters that affect them. Operations seeks to understand the links in the supply chain and to manage them in a more integrated way. To do this it creates mechanisms to bring the parties together to agree a solution that is most effective for all. It promotes system awareness rather than narrow functional concentration.

Control

Reducing waste in manufacturing or service processes depends on control. Systems theory emphasises the significance of feedback loops to measure, analyse and modify inputs. The earlier someone exercises control, the cheaper it is to find and rectify problem areas. The discipline offers many techniques of control, such as critical path analysis and statistical process control. Control systems indicated the failures of functional organisations and led to the current emphasis on business processes.

The Benetton case has shown how that company successfully innovated, both in the customer needs it sought to satisfy and the operating system through which it achieved that. A small business had great flexibility and few systems – an approach that it tried to retain as the business grew. It achieved growth by building a wide network of related organisations with which it worked very closely, giving it the flexibility to innovate in design and to respond to changing fashion. The dynamism of the operations function is illustrated by the emergence of even more flexible fashion groups such as Inditex.

Q PART CASE QUESTIONS

● What were the main operational problems that Kwik-Fit management had to deal with as the company grew?

● What similarities and differences are there between Kwik-Fit's retail operation and that of Benetton?

● What are the major business processes in Kwik-Fit that are crucial to satisfying customer requirements?

17.8 Review questions

1 Describe systems concepts as they apply to an operating system.

2 What are the major categories of operations system and their associated physical layout types?

3 Why is control over quality at source so important?

4 Why is delivery reliability more important than delivery speed?

5 Describe and discuss the importance of the demand/supply balance.

6 In what ways is the business processes approach different from traditional approaches?

7 List and discuss the main features of a partnering approach to business relationships. (See the SCMG website for ideas.)

8 Discuss the concepts of order winners and order qualifiers.

Further reading

Bicheno J. (1998), *The Quality 60: A guide for service and manufacturing*, Picsie Books, Buckingham. A simply presented collection of many of the quality approaches you are likely to need.

Brown, S. (1996), *Strategic Manufacturing for Competitive Advantage*, Prentice Hall International, Hemel Hempstead. Provides much detail about operations management in a product environment and offers extra material about many of the concepts covered in this chapter.

Womack, J.P. and Jones, D. (1996), *Lean Thinking*, Simon and Schuster, NY. Develops the theme established in *The Machine that Changed the World* by Womack *et al.* (1990), which first comprehensively described the Toyota production system as clearly superior to other car assemblers' systems by means of a benchmarking study. It sets JIT, TQM and supply chain thinking in an integrated framework. The latest book uses a number of case examples.

Heller R. (2001), 'Inside Zara', *Forbes Global*, 28 May 2001, pp.24–5, 28–9. Comments on the development of this fashion brand and the company founder behind it.

Hughes J., Ralf, M. and Michels, B. (1998), *Transform Your Supply Chain: Releasing value in business*, International Thomson Publishing, London. A variety of useful examples and models to set the supply chain in a modern context.

Wheatley, M. (2000), 'Best Factories 2000', *Management Today*, November, pp.109–30. This reports an annual awards process to find the best factories in the United Kingdom. It provides excellent examples of the issues discussed in this chapter and will be updated in *Management Today* at around the same time each year.

Kay, J. (1993), *Foundations of Corporate Success*, OUP, Oxford. A highly rated text on strategy but, interestingly, emphasises a number of key capabilities that are related to operations and the supply chain view as described here.

Krajewski, L.J. and Ritzman, L.P. (2002), *Operations Management: Strategy and analysis* (6th edn), Prentice Hall, London. This is a US textbook that provides a wealth of extra materials including useful website exercises.

Annotated links, questions and resources can be found on
www.booksites.net/boddy

CHAPTER 18

Managing information systems

AIM *To examine why managers need information and how they can use technology to make the most of this resource.*

OBJECTIVES

By the end of your work on this chapter you should be able to outline the concepts below in your own terms and:

1 Explain the difference between data and information

2 Show how information is critical to management performance

3 Explain the role of information systems in organisations

4 Describe different forms of information system

5 Explain the elements of a computer-based information system

6 Understand how information systems affect the functions and roles of management

7 Explain how the Internet enables radical changes in organisations and their management

Manufacturing website of Boeing's Wing Responsibility Center

In 1995 Boeing Commercial Airplanes (BCA), a division of The Boeing Company, created responsibility centres. Management did this to focus attention on major segments of the aircraft by having all of the functional areas required to design, build and service the product in one organisation. Wings and tail sections constitute such a segment, and make up the Wing Responsibility Center (WRC).

That centre is accountable for all aspects of designing, producing and supporting wing and tail sections. In doing so the WRC is also responsible for the quality, cost and delivery of these products, as well as the safety and morale of its employees. The centre operates plants in Seattle, Washington and Toronto. To help the centre meet production targets management established a WRC website as part of the larger Boeing intranet.

The original purpose of the website was to give a comprehensive view of the factory status each day. It would also provide the primary means of communication between the vice-president and his management team. Enhancements to the site enabled all levels of management, employees and internal suppliers to see the same information. The company also expected that sharing information in this way would reduce travel between the WRC locations and allow employees from the Toronto plant to participate in meetings held in the Seattle area. As a result of this site the days of chart-lined visibility rooms and staff attending meetings with large computer printouts are dwindling.

The site opened in the autumn of 1996 as a set of static pages. The web team completely redesigned the site in the following months in response to customer requests. Much of the site is now interactive and by 1999 contained 3,000 pages. 800 staff used it each day.

One part of the website shows, for example, how many wings the company delivered in a given week, the number of engineering releases, and current staff. This gives an immediate and detailed picture of the manufacturing organisation's health. It summarises critical performance measures to show trends quickly. Staff can drill down to obtain more detail on items that concern them.

Another part of the website records machine set-up, run and lost time, to measure asset capacity, efficiency, availability and quality. This enables managers to compare available capacity with that required to meet customer demand. This has helped the company to use capacity more efficiently and reduced capital expenditure.

Source: Based on Fowler et al. (2000).

Q Case questions

- What is the input and the output of the system?
- What are the objectives of this system?
- What are the likely advantages of such systems?

18.1 Introduction

This chapter introduces the following ideas:

- Data
- Database
- Information
- Information system
- Information systems management
- Operational system
- Monitoring system
- Decision support system
- Knowledge system
- Organisational system
- Inter-organisational system
- Intranet
- Extranet
- Sociotechnical approach
- Internet

Managers at Boeing WRC first created their website to help them give them a clearer picture of what was happening within the factory. The plants handle many projects at the same time, each of which requires a different combination of the manufacturing facilities. Planning the most efficient use of those physical and human resources was hampered by the lack of accurate information about the current status of each task. Management hoped that the website would help them to plan, organise, lead and control these diverse resources more effectively. Since then they have extended the system to perform other functions, taking account of technical developments and rising expectations from users.

This pattern of relatively simple systems evolving into more complex ones, with wide management implications, is common. The Part Case shows how Kwik-Fit introduced their first electronic point-of-sale system with the limited, though important, aim of reducing the administrative burden on the growing business. As management realised the full potential of the system they moved quickly to use this new tool to change the way they managed the business. More recently they have used the same technology as the basis for a new line of business in motor insurance. Banks were early users of computer-based information systems, offering a more efficient way of processing huge volumes of routine transactions. They still perform that function – but have also enabled banks and other providers of financial services to offer a wider range of services through many new distribution channels. More radical applications of the available technology have come from completely new dot.com companies. Most of those that started during the Internet boom of the late 1990s have failed or will soon do so. Nevertheless, start-ups like ebay.com or lastminute.com have shown that in the right circumstances managers with the right skills can build a new business around the technology of modern information systems.

Managers in any business can only carry out their role effectively if they receive accurate and timely information. Computer-based information systems make internal processes more efficient. They can integrate business functions and create electronic links with suppliers and customers. Technological developments make it possible for managers to have more information about their business, and about external developments, than they have ever had. Such information (on internal developments, competitors, markets and so on) is critically important to the strategy and competitiveness of many organisations The challenge managers face is to ensure that their organisation uses, rather than squanders, the potential of such systems to enhance their performance. So while the design of information systems depends on the skills of information systems (IS) experts, management rarely leaves this whole field to them. It is a management task to ensure that the IS staff focus their skills on developing systems that serve the needs of the business.

This responsibility has become more widespread in recent years as information technology has moved from the background to the foreground of organisations. In many it is the basis of their business, which means that all managers take an active role in the information systems of the organisation. The functionality, possibilities and value of information systems are greater than ever before.

The chapter begins by outlining the development of information systems, and the role of information in organisations. It describes the components of computer-based information systems: hardware, software, networks, telecommunications and data. It shows how managers use computer-based information systems for an ever-widening range of operational tasks. More significantly, it shows how such systems also enable changes in the way that managers perform their functions and roles. The chapter also shows that the benefits of such investments depend as much on human as on technological factors. Finally it shows how the Internet, a special example of an information system, makes possible far-reaching changes in organisations and their management.

18.2 The evolution of information systems

Between 1965 and 1975 organisations concentrated on automating those functions where they could make large efficiency gains. Typical targets were those that processed many routine transactions, such as payrolls, inventory and financial transactions. Department managers often delegated responsibility for information management to their information systems department. These became very skilled at running large, routine and usually centralised systems. The IS function also became influential, and line managers were rarely involved in discussions of IS strategy and development. The technologies had little effect on smaller organisations. The objective of most applications was to process routine transactions more efficiently.

In the following decade automated systems spread widely. Technical developments made smaller systems possible and more attractive to managers in other parts of the organisation such as planning, manufacturing and distribution. More departments discovered the possibilities of computer-based information systems and their managers became familiar with issues of budgeting for hardware, requesting support, defining requirements and setting priorities – alongside established IS departments. Suppliers developed systems that were suitable for smaller organisations.

Since the mid-1980s the information systems environment has continued to change significantly. Technical developments have brought information systems to the foreground of corporate policy. Systems that for decades have supported the business functions of finance, manufacture and distribution continue to develop and employ more modern technology. In addition, computer-based systems have extended to serve many other business functions. Software suppliers have expanded product lines to support functions as diverse as production forecasting, supplier rating and project management. Information technology often supports managers and professional staff directly. Non-technical staff or small business owners now depend heavily on computer-based information.

Examples of such new developments are:

- the emergence of fast, relatively cheap and portable computer power;
- the ability to link these into networks (local and in a wider environment);
- the use of the Internet to link computer systems with those in other organisations;
- using information technologies for communication – such as email and video-conferencing;
- creating integrated databases that staff can use in different applications throughout the organisation, for example in customer relationship management (CRM).

The rise of the Internet since the mid-1990s has further stimulated these developments. It challenges many traditional organisations to innovate their processes and change their operations. But it also enables completely new 'dot.com' firms to enter the marketplace with totally new ways of doing business, and to challenge established players. Figure 18.1 shows the widening role of information systems for many organisations. The early stages featured single, unconnected systems for separate business functions. In stages 3 and 4 managers are linking systems together and using them to make radical changes to previously separate processes. In stage 5 they are using common information systems based on the Internet to move information between organisations and often having direct electronic links with their customers.

18.3 The role of information in organisations

The chapter case shows an information system using an **intranet**. It has characteristics that are common to many information systems:

- the fit between the strategy and structure of the organisation (setting up integrated responsibility centres) and the creation of the information system;
- the links between the parts of the system and the many functions it performs, such as showing factory capacity, enabling communications and showing performance trends;
- the gradual development and adaptability of the system to changing information needs;
- the sharing of the same (consistent set of) data by many people and departments.

The next section outlines some concepts and terms.

What is information?

Organisations store and process large amounts of data, which they may or may not convert into information (Martin *et al.*, 1994). **Data** refers to recorded descriptions of things, events, activities and transactions. A **database** consists of stored data items organised for retrieval. **Information** is data that has been processed so that it has meaning and value for the recipient (Turban *et al.*, 1999). This means that information is subjective: what one person perceives as information another may see as data. It depends on their interests and role. People can also use information to create knowledge – the expertise, understanding and experience that comes from learning. Figure 18.2 shows this relation between data, information and the information system that tramsforms the one to the other.

Figure 18.1 **The widening effects of information systems in organisations**

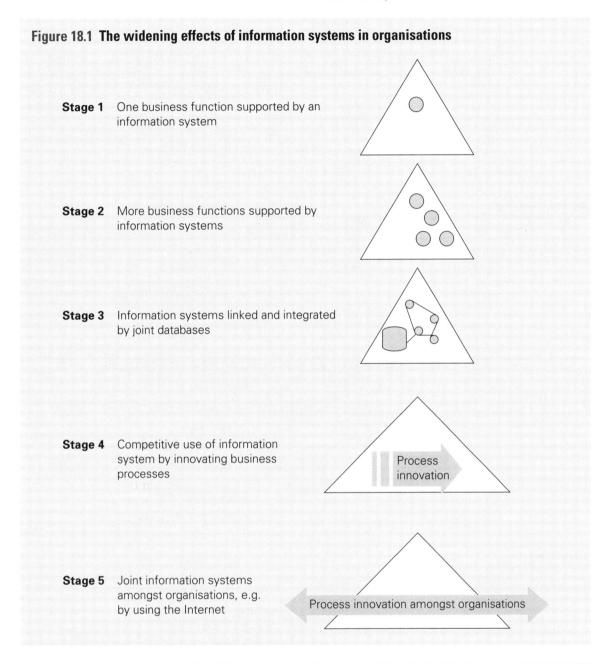

Stage 1   One business function supported by an information system

Stage 2   More business functions supported by information systems

Stage 3   Information systems linked and integrated by joint databases

Stage 4   Competitive use of information system by innovating business processes

Process innovation

Stage 5   Joint information systems amongst organisations, e.g. by using the Internet

Process innovation amongst organisations

Figure 18.2 **Producing information from data**

Data

Raw, unanalysed facts, figures and events

Data transformation

Through people, procedures, hardware, software, paper, etc.

Information

Useful and relevant knowledge

Historically people recorded data on paper, transformed it into information and presented it on paper. Now they are more likely to use some form of computer-based information system to record, transform, store and present information. An **information system** is a set of people, procedures and resources that collects and transforms data into information and disseminates this information. Figure 18.3 shows the elements of a computer-based information system. The significance of the figure is that it shows the breadth of the term 'information system'. It is not just a technical matter of hardware and software. Including people and procedures within the topic brings in many organisational issues. These are as important as the technical ones to the successful management of an information system.

> **MANAGEMENT**
> **IN PRACTICE**

A computer-based student record system

This description of part of the information system in a university illustrates each of the elements in Figure 18.3. The system requires people (e.g. clerical staff) to enter data (name and other information about students and their results) following certain procedures. For example there is a rule that only employees may enter data on student results into the system. The rules do not permit students to do this. Another rule is that a student cannot graduate unless the system confirms that the student has paid their fees and library fines.

Figure 18.3 The elements of a computer-based information system

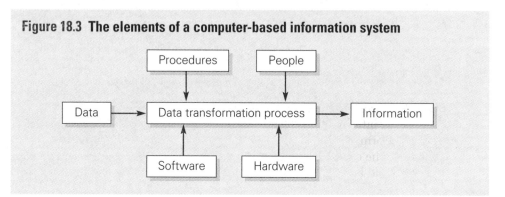

> **KEY**
> **IDEAS**

Quality of information

The quality of information depends on four criteria:

1 **Reliability** (accuracy). If a railway timetable changes by only 10 per cent, most people will see the old timetable as highly unreliable. If only a small part of the information provided in a document is inaccurate people will see the quality of the whole source as low and treat it with suspicion.

2 **Timeliness**. Information is only useful if it is available in time. A manager who needs to keep expenditure within a set budget requires cost information frequently enough to be able to act on any unfavourable trends. If the information arrives in three months it will be too late.

3 **Quantity**. Most managers suffer information overload, in the sense that they are not able to use and digest all the information they receive as a basis for action – there is simply too much. This may suggest that the data has not be processed to a format or level of detail suitable for managerial action.

4 **Relevance**. This depends on a person's tasks and responsibilities. A manager with daily responsibility for production wants a daily report about output, cost, scrap, etc. of each machine. A senior manager wants more aggregated data such as overall production costs, and the balance between capacity and likely future demand.

The hardware consists of the computers and peripherals such as printers, monitors and keyboards. This runs the student record system, using software to manipulate the data in a particular way and to print out the results for each student. Another procedure sends results to each student. For the students this is information. The staff in the department and the faculty want to be able to compare the pass rates of all the courses – so the results system then becomes an element of the university's management information.

Information systems management includes the planning, acquisition, development and use of information systems such as this. One aim of information management is to ensure that information meets certain quality standards, affecting its value to managers.

Gathering information

Consider the information used in an organisation that you know, or can find out about.

Give a specific example of a piece of information that is used regularly by (a) a senior manager, (b) a departmental manager.

What information do you need regularly from your bank or from your university? What information does it provide that is relevant to you?

Since organisations are open systems (see Chapter 2) interacting with their environment, those managing them depend on exchanging information with that environment. Figure 18.4 shows an open systems model with the information flows emphasised. Materials and other resources are inputs to the material transformation process, which turns them into an output of goods and services that flows back to the environment. The information system gathers data about the internal transformation process and from the environment (demand, competitor action, customer opinions, etc.) and feeds the resulting information to those managing at different levels of the organisation. They use this information to manage the material transformation process.

The data that is the basis of this system is of many kinds and from many sources. It could be the manager's informal system (such as a conversation with a colleague) or it could be a formal company system that collects internal data about matters such as productivity, quality, inventory or staff turnover, or external data about suppliers'

Figure 18.4 Information systems in organisations

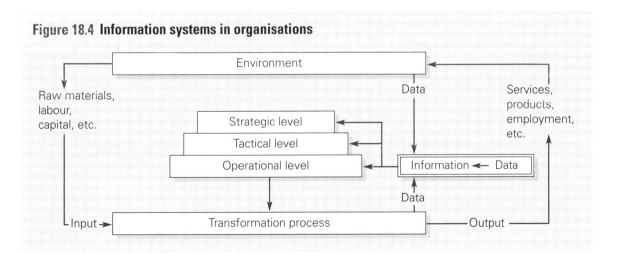

performance, customer preferences, market share and economic trends. At the Boeing WRC the website includes information about the number of wings delivered, engineering releases and staffing levels.

Applying the open systems model

Apply the open systems model in Figure 18.4 to an organisation that you know.

What are the inputs and outputs?

Describe the transformation process.

What information do managers at various levels need to help them manage the business?

Information systems traditionally provided information about products and services to managers and other staff. Modern systems sometimes do more than that, in the sense that they directly perform a process (such as automatically ordering new inventory) or deliver the actual product (such as a digital book or piece of music over the Internet).

18.4 Elements of computer-based information systems

Figure 18.5 shows the main elements of a computer-based information system – hardware, software, networks, telecommunications and data. While these elements are in themselves technical products each of them raises management issues. Managers do not need to be familiar with the technical questions – they do need to be aware of the management ones.

Figure 18.5 Elements of a computer system

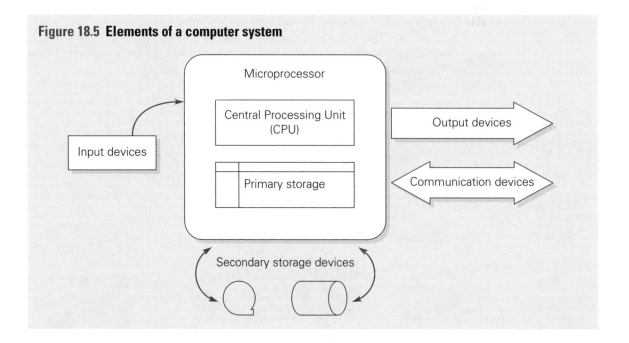

Hardware

Hardware refers to the physical components within a computer system. They consist of:

- *input devices* (such as keyboard, mouse, joystick, scanner, touch screen, camera, microphone, sensor);
- *central processing unit* (manipulates data and controls the computer system);
- *storage devices* (such as the primary (internal) storage, and secondary storage such as the magnetic disk, magnetic tape and the optical disk);
- *output devices* (such as printers, plotters, monitors, voice output); and
- *communication devices* (to link the computer with computer networks).

There are different kinds of computers, such as mainframes, minicomputers, personal computers and server computers. Mainframes are very large computers with massive memory and very rapid processing power, used in large businesses and governments. Users work with passive terminals or work stations to enter data and receive information from the mainframe. A mini computer is a mid-range computer often used in factories and middle-sized companies. Personal computers can sit on a desktop or be carried from room to room (portable desktops, laptops, notebooks and palmtops). A network to link PCs enables users to share files, software, printers and other network resources. A network also requires server computers – specifically optimised for network use – with large memory and disk storage capacity. Laudon and Laudon (2000) and Turban *et al.* (2001) examine these points in more detail.

Developments in computer hardware raise several issues for managers. One is that they often need to decide whether to use the latest available hardware to benefit the business. They receive attractive promotional literature about many technical developments, but it is not always obvious that the benefits will justify the investment. Technical advances make it possible to alter working styles. Portable computers and mobile phones enable employees to remain connected to the office (Turban *et al.*, 2001). While the technology may promise potential benefits it is a management question whether people will be able and willing to change the way they work, and whether it is worth the disruption.

Software

Software is a set of instructions written in a specialised language that controls the operation of the computer. *System software* is a set of programs that manage the resources of the computer, such as the central processor, communication links and peripheral devices. Windows, Unix and Linux are examples of system software. *Application software* (of most relevance to management) enables users to apply the computer to specific tasks, such as email, word processing, spreadsheets or browsing the Web. A common management issue, as with hardware, is whether to invest in the latest version. Related to that is the issue of whether to use custom-made software or to buy a standard package.

Telecommunications

This is the communication of information by electronic means over distance. In the past this meant voice transmission over the telephone. Today a great deal of telecommunication is digital data transmission, using computers, software and devices such as modems and cables to transmit data from one location to another. Since the beginning of the 1990s many more companies provide telecommunication services in competition with the established telecom firms. These changes have stimulated the creation of a worldwide digital telecommunications network, which enables businesses and the general public to obtain and distribute information and reduces barriers of time and place.

The death of distance

In time ... it will be no more expensive to telephone someone on the other side of the world than to talk to someone in the house across the street ...The death of distance as a determinant of the cost of communicating will probably be the single most important factor shaping society in the first half of the next century. Technological change has the power to revolutionize the way people live, and this one will be no exception. It will alter, in ways that are only dimly imaginable, decisions about where people work and what kind of work they do, concepts of national borders and sovereignty, and patterns of international trade. Its effects may well be as pervasive as those of electricity, which led in time to the creation of the skyscraper cities of Manhattan and New York, and transformed labour productivity in the home.

Source: Cairncross (1997, p.1).

The Boeing intranet is an example of people using telecommunications to pass information between locations within a company, enabling separate functions to work more easily together. Management issues with respect to telecommunications include whether to use the falling costs and increasing speed of telecommunications to expand the business or to support the existing business more effectively. They also face the potential threat that the company will face competition from unexpected quarters, as distance provides less protection.

Data

Managing data effectively is increasingly important for many businesses. The Boeing website is one example of a company that has put a great deal of effort into making data available to everyone involved to support more effective working. Databases are collections of data organised to service many applications at the same time and using the same integrated set of data. Database design is increasingly important for storing data that is relevant to business objectives. Distributed databases are stored and updated in more than one location, yet the data remains consistent. A database that is designed around major business subjects such as customers, vendors or activities is called a data warehouse.

Customer relationship management systems

CRM systems collect and integrate information about customers – such as their buying patterns, personal characteristics, income bracket, demographics and lifestyle (Peppard, 2000). Companies use such data to strengthen the ties with their more profitable customers and to attract other customers by special offers or promotions carefully targeted to suit their individual circumstances. For example, when a customer calls their insurer to ask about their car insurance, the agent gets an immediate overview on the computer of all the policies that customer has. The system also suggests some questions. So when the agent has answered the car insurance question they can then say, 'You also have a fire insurance policy – do you think it still provides sufficient cover for you?'

18.5 Type and scope of information systems

Information systems range from very informal, through paper based, to highly auto-mated computer-based systems.

Human information systems

These are informal information systems. Everyone uses sense organs to receive impulses from the environment; the brain interprets these impulses that lead to decisions on how to respond. From this perspective, everyone is an information system. For managers, this means observing events in the organisation and in the environment and using this infor-mation to help manage their area of responsibility. Direct observations by managers and discussions with other people are effective ways of collecting information. Studying is also a human information process. The study material is data, but the student has to transform that data and present it as information which is relevant to tutorial discus-sions and examination questions.

Paper-based information systems

People still use many paper-based systems as they are cheap to implement and easy to understand. Paper systems have some virtues and the genuinely paperless office is rare. Companies often define their procedures on paper, and staff are confident with informa-tion on paper. They can file a hard (paper) copy and use it easily for audit purposes. Staff often use paper systems when traceability is important and responsibility is high. Consider an insurance company in which senior directors must still write and sign cheques of high value. The format of paper information systems is often a piece of A4 paper with printed instructions or boxes to complete. It may be a label attached to a part being routed through a shop floor with instructions on what work to do. A manual, paper-based attendance list kept by a lecturer is another example, as is an address book or diary.

ACTIVITY 18.3

Evaluating paper systems

Identify two formal but paper-based information systems that you use, or which affect you. What are the advantages and disadvantages of a paper-based system?

Computer-based information systems

Most information systems beyond the smallest now use electronic means to collect data and to provide information. Electronic devices often collect the initial data, such as the barcodes and scanners that capture product details in shops. Thereafter electronic sys-tems process, manipulate, distribute and record the data. The systems can provide paper output if required at various stages – such as a till receipt for the customer or a sales report for managers. Table 18.1 lists some examples of electronic systems.

Table 18.1 Examples and descriptions of computer-based information systems

Sector	Example	Description
Retailing	EPOS terminals	Provide faster customer checkout, identify customer preferences and improve inventory control. This control is linked with the computer systems of the suppliers
Financial services	Automated teller machines, telephone banking	Support 24-hour a day banking services. Telephone banking enables customers to make transactions from their home. Online and Internet banking
Travel	Computer-based reservation systems	Provide up-to-date information to agents that makes it possible to advise travellers better and to alter prices depending on circumstances
Manufacturing	Computer-aided design and manufacturing	Linking design and manufacturing improves the time to market significantly. Better logistics by computer-based material requirements planning. Electronic data interchange with suppliers and customers

ACTIVITY 18.4

Evaluating computer-based systems

List three computer-based information systems you use or that affect you. What are the objectives of these systems? Could you process that information without using computers?

What advantages and disadvantages have you experienced with these systems? Are computer-based systems always better?

Scope of computer-based information systems

Computer-based information systems vary in the reach of their operation and this affects their influence on management and organisations.

Individual

Many people use word-processing systems, spreadsheet programs and database systems to manage their work. It is also possible to download data from company-wide systems for use on individual tasks. The main advantage of such systems is that the user is deciding what to use the system for and is able to control the way they work. The disadvantage is that the quality of the software varies greatly. The data extracted from the corporate database quickly becomes out of date and the systems may not link easily with the systems of other users. Two examples: *secretaries or professional staff use individual word-processing and office systems; schedulers using stand-alone scheduling systems.*

Local or departmental

If separate units or departments in companies have a distinct task to perform, it may be worthwhile having their own information systems. Management often creates these as separate systems, though many are now being integrated into the systems network of the whole company. An example: *a department of a university uses a system that provides information about courses and assessments on the local departmental network which students can access.*

Organisational

Organisational systems integrate departments, and people throughout the organisation use them. An example: *in hospitals many units use centralised patient data to retrieve or update information about a patient. Such systems make it easier for staff from various departments to treat a patient in a consistent way.* If the hospital is to implement such a system successfully it needs to discourage the continued use of stand-alone systems – such as a list of one doctor's patients held on a spreadsheet that he or she considers to be the definitive list, but which will not contain data that other doctors have.

Inter-organisational systems

Many systems now link organisations electronically by using the Internet, which makes it easier to set up **inter-organisational systems** and introduce new ways of managing transactions between companies. An example: *in 1998 IBM announced that, by the end of 1999, 95 per cent of its transactions with suppliers (of whom there are many thousands around the world) would be conducted over the Internet. This enables much faster and more efficient ordering, automatic invoicing, faster payments and substantial savings in clerical costs.*

KEY IDEAS **Five functions of information systems**

Markus (1984) distinguished five functions that information systems can perform, as follows:

1 **Operational** These process routine transactions in an efficient, reliable and uniform way. Management uses them widely for activities such as payroll calculations, order entry and invoicing.
2 **Monitoring** These check the performance of a system at regular intervals. The factor being monitored can be financial, quality, departmental output or personal performance. Being attentive to changes or trends gives the business an advantage. It can act promptly to change a plan to suit new conditions.
3 **Decision support** These can help managers to calculate the consequences of different alternatives, and so make better decisions. This

happens for instance by simulation and what-if analysis. A decision support system incorporates both data and models to help a decision maker solve a problem.
4 **Knowledge (or expert**) These help people to make decisions by incorporating human knowledge into the system. A knowledge engineer tries to learn how the experts make decisions and incorporates that into the knowledge base of the system.
5 **Communication** People design communication systems to overcome barriers of time and distance. They make it easier to pass information around and between organisations. Electronic mail is an early example, and the Internet and related technologies are also examples.

ACTIVITY 18.5

Collecting examples of applications

The media regularly report new applications of computer software. Collect examples over the next week of new inter-organisational systems. Identify what they are likely to mean for the way people will work and manage in organisations adopting such systems. Compare notes with others and decide which of the systems you have found is likely to be of greatest organisational significance over the next two years.

18.6 Information systems and operational work

Early computer systems were **operational** ones in the sense that management introduced them to process routine transactions. This is still a major function as they rationalise and standardise transactions in an efficient, reliable and uniform way. Common examples are payroll and order entry systems. Some examples:

> When a student informs the administration that they have a new address they expect the change to apply quickly and to all the files of the university. The university would use a transaction processing system. Banks and other financial institutions rely on operational systems to process millions of transactions (such as cheques and other payment instructions) daily in an efficient, reliable and uniform way.

Such operational systems are often inter-organisational. In retailing, such applications help retailers to control the amount of stock and manage the whole supply chain much better:

> The attraction of EPOS systems is that they instantly record each sale, using a laser scanner that reads the bar code on the product. The retailers no longer waits for a periodic stock-take to find out what they need to reorder. The shops have a direct link to the computers of the firm's main suppliers.

Many Internet-based systems that deliver digital goods such as software or news are also operational systems.

18.7 Information systems and management functions

Chapter 1 presented the management job as being the pursuit of objectives through the functions of planning, organising, leading and controlling the use of resources. Whatever their level, managers perform these four related functions in a fluid, interactive way, and through their relations with other people. Modern computer-based information systems have considerable implications for how people perform each of these functions.

Planning

This deals with the overall direction of the work to be done. It includes forecasting future trends, assessing actual and potential resources and developing objectives and targets for the business. Chapter 6 introduced Porter's five forces, widely used as a tool for identifying the competitive forces affecting a business. Figure 18.6 shows that modern information systems can alter each of these forces. Information systems are a source of competitive advantage if a company can use them to strengthen one or more of these forces. They can equally represent a competitive threat if other organisations use them more effectively.

Table 18.2 illustrates some of the many possibilities.

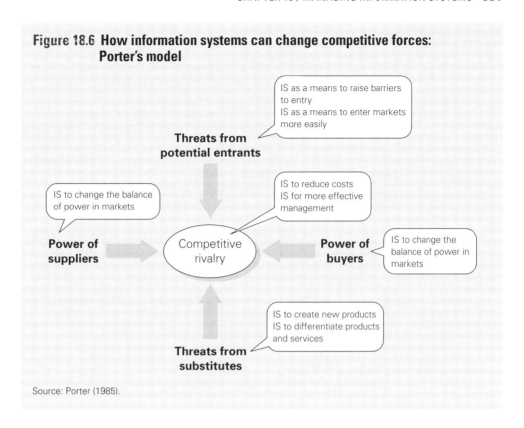

Figure 18.6 How information systems can change competitive forces: Porter's model

Source: Porter (1985).

Table 18.2 Using information systems to affect the five forces

Porter's five forces		Examples of information systems support
Threat of potential entrants	Raise entry barriers	Electronic links with customers makes it more costly for them to move to competitors. Supermarkets use electronic links to banks and suppliers, and so gain a cost advantage over small retailers
	Entering markets more easily	Bertelsmann, a German media group, entered book retailing by setting up an online store. Virgin offers financial services by using online systems
Threat of substitutes	Creating new products	Telephone banking (a threat to branch banking) has only been possible with modern information systems
	Differentiating their products	Using database technology and CRM systems to identify precise customer needs and then create unique offers and incentives
Bargaining power of suppliers	Increasing power of suppliers	Airlines use yield management systems to track actual reservations against capacity on each flight, and then adjust prices for the remaining seats to maximise revenue
	Decreasing power of suppliers	Auto companies have set up electronic marketplaces that suppliers must use, and which allow the customers (such as Ford or General Motors) to compare prices offered more easily, and identify new suppliers
Bargaining power of buyers		Buyers in many industries and sectors can use the Internet to access more suppliers, and to compare prices for standard commodities
Intensity of rivalry	Using IS to reduce costs	Enterprise Resource Planning systems make it possible to make radical changes in manufacturing systems leading to greater consistency in planning and lower costs
	More effective management	Information systems provide more detailed information on trading patterns – enabling them to make better-informed pricing and other decisions

easyJet

The low cost airline has a strategy that includes a sharp focus on customer needs, using technology wherever possible and adapting processes to suit market conditions. When it began to operate it took reservations on the telephone, so paid no commissions to travel agents. The company's emphasis on technology meant that as the Internet became available it rapidly adapted their business model to offer on-line reservations. EasyJet took its first online reservation in April 1998. By April 2001 over 85 per cent of reservations were made online – probably the highest proportion of total sales for any established business. Its success in using the Internet has led it to launch a further range of online services, such as easyRent (car rental) and, in 2001, easyMoney (financial services).

Managers also use information systems to support their chosen strategy – such as a differentiation or cost leadership. Information systems can support a cost leadership strategy when companies substitute robotics for labour; use stock control systems to reduce inventory costs; use online order entry to reduce order processing costs; and reduce downtime and scrap by systems that automatically identify a machine fault about to occur.

A differentiation strategy tries to create uniqueness in the eyes of the customer. Managers can support this by, for example, using the flexibility of computer-aided manufacturing and inventory control systems to meet customers' unique requirements economically. CRM systems can have similar effects in differentiating one company's services from others.

Organising

This is the activity of moving abstract plans closer to reality, by deciding how to allocate time and effort. It is about creating a structure to divide and co-ordinate work. Information systems make possible new forms of structure. Computer-based systems can remove routine tasks in functions such as purchasing or finance. Staff can then spend more time with suppliers or customers, concentrating on forward planning and ways to improve efficiency.

Computer-based systems allow organisations to centralise some functions and decentralise others. Telephone sales can be centralised to single call centres. This is currently proving massively successful with banks and other services. This centralisation reduces the cost of sales and allows the companies to compete with new entrants.

Finco

Finco was established in 1998 as a joint venture between a major oil company and a consulting business. The purpose was to centralise and harmonise the oil company's transaction processing activities in a single location. This was based on the idea that advanced computer and communications systems would enable the company to ensure consistent processes, and very large cost savings across the European operation. Finco was established in the United Kingdom, and drew work from the 18 existing national operating companies.

Other companies have used the power of information systems to decentralise aspects of their operations. While Kwik-Fit initially used the EPOS system to centralise the business, it then moved on to decentralise more power to the newly created geographic divisions – supported by the same information system.

Others businesses use expert systems to help people make decisions by incorporating human knowledge into the system. A knowledge engineer works with one or more experts in the domain under study to build a **knowledge system**. He or she tries to learn how the experts make decisions, and incorporates this into that part of the software known as the knowledge base.

MANAGEMENT IN PRACTICE   ## Examples of expert systems

ABN-AMRO Bank uses a knowledge system to analyse proposed bank loans. The system incorporates the experience of experts in the field and enables loan decisions to be processed automatically at head ofice rather than by staff in the branches.

The Amsterdam Medical Centre, a large Dutch hospital, uses an expert system that enables people with relatively little experience to deal with emergency calls. The system proposes the questions they should ask, interprets the answers given, and recommends a plan of action.

Aegon, a Dutch insurer, uses a knowledge system to process applications, which enables agents to make insurance contracts with clients without involving the insurer.

Many systems of this sort do not replace the experts, but support them in making their decisions (Balachandra, 2000; Flores and Pearce, 2000). The system makes suggestions to the human experts, but does not take over their jobs. In this context Hirschheim and Klein (1989) distinguished between 'systems for experts' (these are supportive to the human experts) and 'expert systems' (which replace people who are expert in a certain field).

Leading

This is the activity of generating effort and commitment towards meeting objectives. It includes influencing and motivating other people to work in support of the plans. Most computer-based information systems have significant effects on the organisation. They can change the tasks and the skill levels required for them. In a hospital, the emergency room receives telephone calls that require some action. This room could be staffed by a two-person team of a nurse and a doctor. Alternatively an operator with less medical knowledge can use an expert system that prompts the operator to ask questions. The operator enters the responses and the system suggests the most appropriate action. This allows medical staff to be employed in other areas.

Research into many computer-based information systems (Boddy and Gunson, 1996) shows that some managers use them in a way that reduces the intrinsic quality of work (see Chapter 13), others use them to enhance it. This has little to do with the nature of the technology itself, but with how managers choose to design and implement it.

<table>
<tr><td>MANAGEMENT
IN PRACTICE</td><td>Computer systems in an ambulance service</td></tr>
</table>

The organisation transports patients to and from hospitals for routine treatment at a clinic. The Patient Transport Service work involves ambulance crews transporting patients between their homes and clinics within a hospital. The manual procedures that the service used to plan drivers' routes were flexible but labour intensive. To reduce costs the service had invested heavily in computer systems, including a route-planning system.

Planning officers received orders and keyed them into a computer that stored them until the day before the appointment. It then sorted them by area and allocated them to an available ambulance crew. The list was then printed, checked for feasibility and issued to the crew. Two years after implementing the system a control manager said:

> 'The basic system has not changed but we have made some changes in how we use it. We used to tell the crew how to do the run: what we do now is put all the patients in a geographic area on to a log sheet, with their appointment times. We have devolved responsibility to the crew members to decide how best they should schedule that journey to meet the appointments. Initially we told them in much more detail, manually intervening with the computer data. But it was very labour intensive, and we did not see the traffic jams. We hand out the work in the morning, and we only want to hear if the crews are having operational problems.
>
> The planning officer's role has developed into a liaison role with the hospitals, building up a relationship with them. The planner becomes a crucial personality, not just a worker. Someone coming into the job now could take two years to build up those working relationships. The machine does the routine bits. At first the planning officer did that: now we have pushed it down.'

Source: Based on a case in Boddy and Gunson (1996).

Business becomes more dependent on skilled and committed people as technology increases. Since the business world is dynamic and uncertain there will be changes, errors and uncertainty to cope with. Staff need to be able and willing to use their initiative to deal with that, to exploit the hidden potential of the system, and generally to contribute imaginatively to the work. That can best be achieved by paying attention to how their jobs change with the introduction of the new system. Chapter 13 includes the theoretical basis for this, in terms of the work design model. The Chem-Tec case in Chapter 1 showed how the manager there is using a new information system to increase the responsibility and motivation of his staff. This is also enabling him to redefine the way he performs his leadership role.

Controlling

Computer-based **monitoring systems** can check the performance of an operation at regular intervals. The factor being monitored can be financial, quality, departmental output or personal performance. Being attentive to changes or trends gives the business an advantage as it can act promptly to change a plan to suit new conditions.

Universities in the Netherlands use student trail systems that monitor the academic progress of students. These systems link to the national institution that provides scholarships. This information enables the institution to stop or reduce the scholarship when results are below the required standard.

Information systems allow management at head office to control subsidiaries or branch offices much more tightly. Head office can gather information much more frequently and measure branch performance almost as it happens rather than by weekly or monthly reports. It is a matter of management judgement whether that is a wise or unwise move.

MANAGEMENT IN PRACTICE   **Knowing where to draw the line**

A multinational with manufacturing plants around the world decided to install an office automation system at its head office in Europe. When equipment and software suppliers were asked to submit proposals they all emphasised that their system would allow management to obtain financial and other performance information from their operating units much more rapidly than before. At the time, the information was provided monthly in a very summary form, and quarterly in more detail.

Senior management considered that one of the reasons for the company's success was that subsidiaries had been allowed to operate with considerable autonomy. It believed that if local managers knew that their performance was being monitored on a weekly or monthly basis they would be more concerned about ensuring that the most recent figures looked good than about developing the business in the way they believed best. Consequently senior management declined to include tighter subsidiary monitoring systems in its automation plans.

18.8   Information systems and the process of management

Chapter 1 also introduced Henry Mintzberg's (1973) analysis of the roles of management as consisting of interpersonal, informational and decisional. How do computer-based information systems affect these roles?

Interpersonal roles

Interpersonal roles arise directly from a manager's formal authority and status, and involve relationships with other people both in and out of the organisation. Information systems can affect the leader role, which defines the manager's relationship with other staff, including motivating, communicating and development. The way they introduce and relate information systems to the work of employees has major influence on the commitment, as shown by the Chem-Tec example. If information systems take away the routine aspects of work they then allow managers to spend more time on interpersonal contacts – the Kwik-Fit case illustrates this. Conversely there is also anecdotal evidence that some managers can use the technology as a substitute for personal contact, thus becoming more distant from staff and colleagues.

Informational roles

Information systems by definition support the monitor role by providing access to much greater sources of information than were previously accessible. Intranets and extranets make it much easier to communicate consistent information quickly, so reducing the scope for error and misunderstanding. Modern information systems bring with them the danger of providing managers with too much information, beyond their capacity to absorb.

Decisional roles

In the entrepreneurial role the manager initiates change within the organisation. They see opportunities or problems and create projects to deal with them. Developments in information systems offer many opportunities for them to exercise this role, either within the business or as part of a new venture. The resource allocator role involves choosing amongst competing demands for money, equipment, personnel, and other demands on a manager's time. **Decision support systems** (DSS) can help managers to calculate the consequences of different alternatives, and so make better decisions. This happens for instance by simulation and what-if analysis. A DSS incorporates both data and models to help a decision maker solve a problem. Some businesses use decision support systems to calculate the expected financial consequences of alternative investments.

18.9 Implementing systems

Implementing information systems is not just a technical activity of developing or buying a package that provides the information needed. Information systems have social, technical, organisational, economical and political dimensions. Many systems fail to realise their potential because managers have given insufficient attention to these aspects.

KEY IDEAS — Reasons for failed systems

An article in *Forbes Magazine* described a number of failed systems development projects. The main reasons for these failures were:

- User needs were not fully understood.
- User requirements were made secondary or even disregarded in favour of technical enthusiasm for the latest or most exciting, but inappropriate, method.
- Business changes during the development period were not reflected in the system by the implementation date.

- The time and money needed to develop and implement systems were underestimated. This caused overspending, partial implementation and dissatisfied users.
- During implementation politics and conflicts emerged as departments protected old systems.

Source: *Forbes Magazine*, 29 August 1994.

Many authors suggest that organisational culture, interest groups, the user community and the structure have a major influence on systems development (Keen, 1981; Markus, 1983; Markus and Robey, 1983; Noble and Newman, 1993; Boddy and Gunson, 1996). This is consistent with the idea in Chapter 1 that managers work within a context, made up of the eight factors shown in Figure 1.3. Changing an information system involves a change in technology – but will also involve changes in several other of the elements shown – such as structure, power or culture (Markus and Keil, 1994). Boddy and Gunson (1996) found that managers who took account of these factors were likely to have successful projects, by establishing a coherence between the elements in Figure 1.3. The issues to be managed in implementing an information system are exactly the same as those to be handled in any of the change projects that Chapter 11 examined.

These extensive organisational consequences imply that the process of introducing information systems is especially important. Mumford and Weir (1979) argued that in many system development projects there is an overemphasis on the technical side, leading to neglect of the human side. To balance this, they developed the Ethics method. Ethics is an acronym for Effective technical and human implementation of computer-based systems. The assumptions of this method are as follows:

● Many kinds of computer technology are sufficiently flexible to allow for the design of systems that take into account the need of employees for satisfying work. Therefore designers should work on both the technical and the human parts of a system with this objective in view.
● That even in situations where designers have produced a technical system it is still possible to redesign jobs in a way that will make them more satisfying.

The method follows two tracks: the technical track and the human track. Each side is worked on independently and brought together in a later stage. This method is intended to ensure that developers give enough time and attention to both dimensions. Figure 18.7 shows the Ethics approach.

The approach leads not only to working systems (from a technical perspective) but also to more attractive systems from a human point of view, enhancing motivation and job satisfaction. It develops the idea of organisations as **sociotechnical systems** that were discussed in Chapter 2.

These principles have been developed from research into many kinds of information system – and are likely to be just as true of attempts to implement information systems based on Internet technology.

Figure 18.7 Ethics approach to system development

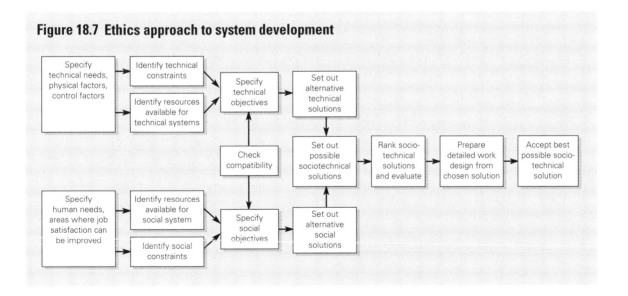

18.10 The role of the Internet

The significance of the Internet for everyone who works in organisations can scarcely be overstated. Although the hyperbole surrounding the dot.com mania of the late 1990s has subsided with the bankruptcy of many of the businesses created at the time, the Internet is, and will remain, a major focus of management action. It affects all aspects of organisational activity, enables new forms of organisation to arise, and opens up many new ideas for the management of organisations.

The **Internet**, a linkage of many small computer networks throughout the world, works because there are agreed rules about how computers exchange information. Specific drivers and search engines facilitate information exchange over the Internet. This now includes graphics, audio and video transmission and interactive communication. The Internet assists business processes, business transactions and communications. An important improvement in the attributes of the Internet has been the development of the World Wide Web (Lawrence *et al.*, 2000), which allows users to connect documents and access locations with a web address.

The management importance lies in applying Internet technologies to support business processes, communications and transactions. This includes selling a product or service to the customer (whether a retail consumer or another business) over the Internet. It also includes the more important application in which managers use the Internet to integrate an organisation's processes from its suppliers through to its customers.

Another relevant term is the **intranet**. This refers to a private computer network, operating within an organisation. It uses Internet standards and protocols and is protected by various forms of security. Intranets operate as separate networks within the Internet. The opposite is an **extranet**, that is, a closed collaborative network that uses the Internet to link businesses with specified suppliers, customers or other trading partners. Extranets usually link to business intranets where information is accessible through a password system.

The simplest Internet applications provide information, enabling customers to view product or other information on a company website; conversely suppliers use their website to show customers what they can offer. Internet marketplaces are developing in which groups of suppliers in the same industry operate a collective website, making it easier for potential customers to compare terms through a single portal. The next stage is to use the Internet for interaction. Customers enter information and questions about (for example) offers and prices. The system then uses the customer information, such as preferred dates and times of travel, to show availability and costs.

A third use is for transactions, when customers buy goods and services through a supplier's website. Conversely a supplier who sees a purchasing requirement from a business (perhaps expressed as a purchase order on the website) can agree electronically to meet the order. The whole transaction, from accessing information through ordering, delivery (in some cases) and payment, can take place electronically.

MANAGEMENT IN PRACTICE — Novotel

The hotel group Novotel has the strategic objective of putting the customer first, and is determined to relate every action to satisfying their needs. It has for many years used information systems to support this strategy. As the Internet became available managers analysed how best to use it to support their strategy. They identified several possible applications. In setting priorities the main factor was the impact on satisfying existing customers and attracting new ones. Novotel decided to give priority to having a presence on the Internet, an easily accessible website, online reservation system and useful information for customers.

Finally a company achieves integration when it links its own information systems and (within limits) links them in turn to customers and suppliers and transforms into an e-business. Dell Computing is a familiar example amongst many others. As customers decide the configuration of their computer and place an order this information moves to the systems that control Dell's internal processes, and those of its suppliers. Figure 18.8 shows these stages. Established companies such as IBM use all of these stages.

Internet applications at IBM

IBM aims to become the premier e-business company in the information technology industry, and also to be recognised as a leading Internet business regardless of industry. As well as providing goods and services to other Internet firms, the company uses the Internet for its own activities, as shown below:

- *Information* – the company website gives information about the company, including products, employment opportunities and financial performance.
- *Interaction* – prospective online purchasers can select options and configurations for their chosen machine and receive information on price and delivery. The company places current purchase orders for suppliers on a secure Internet website – to which suppliers respond.
- *Transaction* – customers can order their computer or other products online; suppliers can accept orders and send invoices online.
- *Integration* – the production planning system takes customer orders and automatically translates those into the components required in the following period. This passes electronically to a buyer, who in turn releases it to the Extranet site. Contracted suppliers

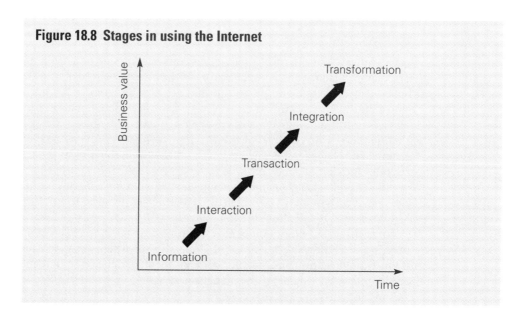

Figure 18.8 Stages in using the Internet

access this, and indicate their acceptance or otherwise. After delivering the physical goods the supplier converts the original electronic purchase order into an electronic invoice, which passes to IBM for electronic payment.

Source: Interviews with company managers and public documents.

Other companies use the Internet to create and orchestrate active customer communities. Examples include Kraft (www.kraftfoods.com), Intel (www.intel.com), Apple (www.apple.com) and Harley Davidson (www.harley-davidson.com). These communities enable the companies to become close to their customers, and to learn how best to improve product or service much more quickly than is possible through conventional market research techniques.

Wide Internet access has generated a huge increase in businesses offering new services. These include electronic auctions, search engines, electronic retailers, electronic hubs (Dutta and Segev, 1999; Timmers, 2000; Kaplan, 2000) and Internet providers.

MANAGEMENT IN PRACTICE | **Chemdex**

David Perry is founding chief executive of Chemdex. He reinvented the supply chains of many chemical and pharmaceutical companies (mainly in the field of life sciences) by bringing together the many fragmented buyers and sellers in this field on the Internet.

This market is worth about $15 billion a year in the United States, with more than 1,500 suppliers and even the largest company with only a 15 per cent share. In the past prices for identical products could vary by as much as 200 per cent.

Perry set up an e-marketplace, which makes it far easier for buyers to make their purchasing decisions. The market is more transparent so that transaction costs are lower. Buyers enter their requirements on the Chemdex website. The system suggests those suppliers that can meet this demand, including information about prices and delivery conditions. The buyers make their choice and the transaction takes place.

Chemdex receives a small part of every transaction. In January 1998 it had three suppliers: by 2000 it had more than 500 suppliers selling more than 1.5 million products. Its revenue was more than $150 million (**www.chemdex.com**).

Source: *The Economist*, 6 November 1999.

The Internet is evidently challenging many established ways of doing business. People can communicate quickly and cheaply without regard to distance. Companies can do business with people and organisations that were previously beyond reach. Combined with political changes this is creating a wider, often global, market for many goods and services. Although some commentaries probably exaggerate the scale and speed of change there is no doubt that the Internet facilitates radical change in the economic system. The challenge for managers is to make profitable use of these possibilities. This includes looking beyond technology – which receives most attention – to some wider organisational issues. A manager who played a major role in guiding Internet-based changes at his company commented: 'The Internet is not a technology challenge. It's a people challenge – all about getting structures, attitudes and skills aligned'.

Experience from other companies confirms that these are essential elements in transforming a traditional business into one that prospers on the Internet. Boddy and Boonstra (2000) brought together some of the experience of companies doing business on the Internet to highlight the management issues they had had to deal with. The overriding conclusion was to confirm the range of organisational issues, besides technological ones, that companies which have taken the lead in this area have managed.

Successful implementation required constant adjustments to the organisational infra-structure – precisely the range of factors in the organisational context with which this book began.

The Internet opens up choices for managers over how they adapt the organisation. To make a success of this opportunity requires them to recreate the context in which they manage their relationships with other people in and around the organisation. Creating a coherent context encourages people to make a success of the Internet project. Creating that same coherent context will enable managers to make a success of any other aspect of organisational innovation.

18.11 Summary

The chapter began by highlighting the importance of information to managers in all organisations, and how computer-based systems have spread from the background to the foreground of organisations. Some, such as the dot.com companies, depend entirely on using computer-based information systems and would not exist without the Internet. The chapter drew attention to the forms of information systems (human, paper, com-puter based) and the range from individual to inter-organisational systems. While the earliest information systems dealt with operating systems (a vital function still in most systems) they now contribute to a wider range of activities. The chapter illustrated the range of those activities by showing how information systems affect all aspects of the functions and roles of management.

Securing a useful benefit from investing in information systems depends on managing the context in which the change takes place – exactly the same approach as set out in Chapter 11. Research on implementation has also shown that the way managers imple-ment an IS project affects how readily people will take up the system. The chapter concluded by showing the scale of the changes that the Internet is bringing to organisa-tions and their management.

Content

Management depends on accurate and timely information about internal and external events to perform its role effectively. Information helps ensure that organisations add value to the resources they use. Developments in computer-based information systems are having considerable effects on the functions of management. IS affects the planning function as it is a way of altering each of the five forces in the Porter model of competi-tive advantage.

IS affects the organising function as it can be used to centralise or decentralise struc-tures and to alter the horizontal dimension of the structure by enabling closer relations between distinct departments. The same is true of the links between separate organisa-tions, which can work more closely with the aid of modern IS. How work is designed in conjunction with the technology affects how managers shape their leadership role. Staff motivation is affected by the way technological developments and human aspects inter-act. Management choices – for example about the use of complementary, sociotechnical models – affect these outcomes.

Process

Information systems also affect the roles of management. They affect the pattern of interpersonal contact – and can be used to increase or decrease this, depending on how they are implemented. They evidently affect the informational role, by vastly increasing the ability of managers to gather and disseminate information – thus leading to the dangers of information overload. Several applications directly affect the decisional role, by providing technical support to the analysis of alternative scenarios.

The effects of such systems also depend on process in the sense of how managers handle the change. Implementing IS depends on changing several elements in the context of managing, not those related only to technology. They are often ignored, but research has shown the benefits of design and implementation processes that enable users to contribute to their shape – especially if they are widely dispersed in the innovating organisation and in other organisations with which it does business. The chapter recalled the Ethics method, a process that enables the joint design of human and technical elements of the context.

Wider flows of information enable more people and interests to be involved in decision making, especially through technologies such as groupware and video-conferencing. Other factors, such as the existing culture and distribution of power, constrain whether what is technologically possible is actually used.

Control

Information technologies can significantly increase the ability of those in power to control others. Systems design is not a neutral activity but is shaped by those providing the resources, who will tend to preserve rather than disrupt existing power relations. The performance of subsidiaries, divisions, branches and individuals can be much more closely monitored with modern information systems. However, action on this information by those at the centre can be constrained by other considerations. These include awareness of the benefits of local autonomy and responsiveness that would be damaged by heavy-handed control from the centre. The systems can also be designed in a way that enables people to enhance their control over operations. They can be designed to feed more useful performance information to operators and teams so that they are better able to use their skills to manage the situation responsibly.

In implementing the intranet at the Boeing WRC management has made both structural and technological changes in support of the broader competitive strategy. The system appears to be helping them to control widely dispersed functions, by gathering and disseminating large quantities of information to all employees. It is also notable that management did not implement the whole system at one time. A relatively simple system was installed first, and as technical developments and user expectations grew they added further functions: this iterative process of implementation is a common feature of large advanced systems. It also shows how large, well-established businesses can make good use of Internet technology. As the last section of the chapter indicated, this has, and will continue to have, profound implications for organisations and their management.

Q PART CASE QUESTIONS

- What information is most important to managers at different levels within Kwik-Fit, and how does the MAT system provide this?
- How has Kwik-Fit been able to use the MAT system to support the strategic development of the business?
- How has the system changed the role of the depot managers?

18.12 Review questions

1 Give some examples of data and of information that you have at this moment. Use these to explain the difference between the two.

2 What information do you lack that harms your work or study performance? How could this information be generated?

3 Give examples of the use of information systems in a business you know. How are they helping or hindering the managers in performing their tasks? Compare the needs of senior and lower-level managers if possible.

4 What are the advantages of human and paper-based information systems over computer-based ones, and vice versa?

5 What are the four criteria that define the value of information?

6 Give examples of how an information system can affect at least two of the forces in Porter's model, and so affect the competitiveness of a business.

7 Describe how an IS can support either a cost leadership or a differentiation strategy, with an example of each.

8 How do information systems affect the other functions of management – such as leading or controlling?

9 How do they affect the roles of management as set out by Mintzberg?

10 How are companies in an industry of your choice (e.g. finance, music, news, manufacturing) using the Internet, and how is this affecting the structure of the industry and the power of the different players?

Further reading

Applegate, L.M., McFarlan, F.W. and McKenney, J.L. (2000), *Corporate Information Systems Management: Text and cases* (5th ed), Irwin, Chicago, IL. Provides a broad perspective on the management implications of the rise of information systems. The book is organised around a management audit of the information services activity.

Laudon, K.C. and Laudon, J.P. (2000), *Management Information Systems: Organization and technology in the networked enterprise*, Prentice Hall, Harlow. This text, written from a management perspective, focuses on the opportunities and pitfalls of computer and communications technologies.

Earl, M.J. (1998), *Information Management: The organizational dimension*, Oxford University Press, Oxford. A useful non-technical book that looks at ways of exploiting information systems strategically. It emphasises the relation between corporate strategy and IS strategy.

Timmers, P. (2000), *Electronic Commerce: Strategies and models for business to business trading*, Wiley, Chichester. This introduces the strategic aspects of e-commerce and e-business and illustrates this by many examples from a variety of industries. Timmers explains how the Internet enables the reinvention of value chains and the reconsideration of a company's business model.

Kalakota, R. and Robinson, M. (1999), *E-business: Roadmap for success*, Addison Wesley, Harlow. Shows how companies can build strategies that are strongly based on the opportunities which the Internet offers.

Annotated links, questions and resources can be found on
www.booksites.net/boddy

References

Academy of Management (1996), Human Resources Division, *News*, Summer.

Acker, J. and Van Houton, D.R. (1992), 'Differential recruitment and control: the sex structuring of organizations', in A.J. Mills and P. Tancred (eds), *Gendering Organizational Analysis*, Sage, London.

Ackroyd, S. and Thompson, P. (1999), *Organizational Misbehaviour*, Sage, London.

Adair, J. (1997), *Leadership Skills*, Chartered Institute of Personnnel and Development, London.

Adams, K. (1996), 'Respecting the difference: international competences for managers', *Competency*, vol. 4, no. 1, pp.24–30.

Adams, S. (1998), *The Dilbert Principle*, Boxtree, London.

Alderfer, C. (1972), *Existence, Relatedness and Growth: Human needs in organizational Settings*, Free Press, New York.

Alexander, D. and Nobes, C. (2001), *International Introduction to Financial Accounting*, Financial Times Prentice Hall, Harlow.

Al-Faleh, M. (1987), 'Cultural influences on Arab management development', *Journal of Management Development*, vol. 6, no. 3, pp.19–33.

Alvesson, M. and Wilmott, H. (1996), *Making Sense of Management*, Sage, London.

Andersen, T.J. (2000), 'Strategic planning, autonomous actions and corporate performance', *Long Range Planning*, vol. 33, pp.184-200.

Ansoff, H.I. (1965), *Corporate Strategy*, Penguin, London.

Applegate, L.M., McFarlan, F.W. and McKenney, J.L. (2000), *Corporate Information Systems Management: Text and case studies* (5th edn), Irwin, Chicago, IL.

Argenti, J. (1997), 'Stakeholders: the case against', *Long Range Planning*, vol. 30, no. 3, pp.442–5.

Argyle, M. (1988), *Bodily Communication*, Methuen, London.

Arnold, J., Hope, T., Southworth, A. and Kirkham, L. (1995), *Financial Accounting* (2nd edn), Financial Times/Prentice Hall, Hemel Hempstead.

Ashkenas, R. (1995), *The Boundaryless Organisation: Breaking the chains of organisation structure*, Jossey-Bass, San Francisco, CA.

Atkinson, A., Banker, R.D., Kaplan, R.S. and Young, S.M. (2001), *Management Accounting* (3rd edn), Financial Times Prentice Hall, Harlow.

Babbage, C. (1835), *On the Economy of Machinery and Manufactures*, Charles Knight, London. Reprinted in 1986 by Augustus Kelly, Fairfield, NJ.

Bain, P. and Taylor, P. (2000), 'Entrapped by the electronic panopticon? Worker resistance in the call centre', *New Technology, Work and Employment*, vol. 15, no. 1, pp.2–18.

Baker, M. (1991), *The Marketing Book*, Butterworth/Heinemann, Oxford.

Balachandra, R. (2000), 'An expert system for new product development', *Industrial Management and Data Systems*, vol. 100, no. 7, pp.317–28.

Ballé, L. and Gottschalk, A. (1994), 'Negotiating with other Europeans', *Management Extra*, Association of MBAs, London.

Barham, K. and Heimer, C. (1998), *ABB: The dancing giant*, Financial Times Management, London.

Barham, K. and Wills, S. (1992), *Management Across Frontiers: The competences of successful international managers*, Ashridge Management Research Group/Foundation for Management Education, Berkhamsted.

Barnard, C. (1938), *The Functions of the Executive*, Harvard University Press, Cambridge, MA.

Bass, B.M. (1990), *Handbook of Leadership: A survey of theory and research*, Free Press, New York.

Beardwell, L. and Holden, L. (2001), *Human Resource Management: A contemporary approach* (3rd edn), Prentice Hall, Harlow.

Beaumont, P.B. (1996), 'Trade unions and HRM' in B. Towers (ed.), *A Handbook of Human Resource Management* (2nd edn), Blackwell, Oxford.

Becker, B., Huselid, M.A. and Urich, D. (2001), *The HR Scorecard*, Harvard Business School Press, Boston, MA.

Beer, M. (1985), 'Note on performance appraisal', in M. Beer, and B. Spector, (eds) (1985), *Readings in Human Resource Management*, Free Press, New York.

Belbin, R.M. (1981), *Management Teams: Why they succeed or fail*, Butterworth/Heinemann, Oxford.

Belbin, R.M. (1993), *Team Roles at Work*, Butterworth/Heinemann, Oxford.

Bendell, T., Boulter, L. and Kelly, J. (1993), *Benchmarking for Competitive Advantage*, Pitman, London.

Bennett, R. (1997), *European Business*, Pitman, London.

Bennis, W.G. (1969), *Organization Development: Its nature, origins and prospects*, Addison-Wesley, Reading, MA.

Bicheno J. (1998), *The Quality 60: A guide for service and manufacturing*, Picsie Books, Buckingham.

Biggs, L. (1996), *The Rational Factory*, The Johns Hopkins University Press, Baltimore, MD.

Birsh, D. and Fielder, J.H. (eds) (1994), *The Ford Pinto Case: A Study in applied ethics, business and technology*, Albany State University of New York Press, NY.

Bjorn-Andersen, N. and Turner, J. (1994), 'Creating the twenty-first century organization: the metamorphosis of Oticon', in R. Baskerville *et al.*, *Transforming Organizations with Information Technology*, Elsevier Science/North-Holland, Amsterdam.

Blake, R.R. and Mouton, J.S. (1964), *The Managerial Grid*, Gulf Publishing, Houston, TX.

Blakstad, M. and Cooper, A. (1995), *The Communicating Organisation*, Institute of Personnel and Development, London.

Blau, P.M. (1970), 'A formal theory of differentiation in organizations', *American Sociological Review*, vol. 35, no. 2, pp.201–18.

Blyton, P. and Turnbull, P. (1994), *Reassessing Human Resource Management*, Sage, London.

Boddy, D. (2002), *Managing Projects: Building and leading the team*, Financial Times Prentice Hall, Harlow.

Boddy, D. and Buchanan, D. (1992), *Take the Lead: Interpersonal skills for project managers*, Prentice Hall, Hemel Hempstead.

Boddy, D. and Gunson, N. (1996), *Organizations in the Network Age*, Routledge, London.

Boddy, D. and Boonstra, A. (2000), 'Doing business on the Internet, managing the organizational issues', *Journal of General Management*, vol. 26, no. 1, pp.18–35.

Boddy, D., Macbeth, D.K. and Wagner, B. (2000), 'Implementing collaboration between organisations: an empirical study of supply chain partnering', *Journal of Management Studies*, vol. 37, no. 7, pp. 1003–17.

Boddy, D and Macbeth, D.K. (2000), 'Prescriptions for managing change: a survey of their effects in projects to implement collaborative working between organisations', *International Journal of Project Management*, vol. 18, no. 5, pp.297–306.

Boddy, D., Boonstra, A. and Kennedy, G. (2002), *Information Systems: An organisational perspective*, Financial Times Prentice Hall, Harlow.

Bowen, D.E. and Lawler, E.E. (1992), 'The empowerment of service workers: what, why, how and when?' *Sloan Management Review*, Spring vol. 33, no. 3, pp.31–9.

Bowen, D.E., Ledford, G.E. and Nathan, B.R. (1996), 'Hiring for the organization, not the job', in J. Billsberry, (ed.), *The Effective Manager: Perspectives and illustrations*, Sage, London.

Bowman, E.H. (1973), 'Corporate social responsibility and the investor', *Journal of Contemporary Business*, Winter, pp.21–43.

Branson, R. (1999), *Losing My Virginity*, Virgin Books, London.

Brech, E.F.L. (1957), *Organization: The framework of management*, Longmans Green, London.

Brewster, C. (1994), 'European HRM: reflection of, or challenge to, the American concept?' in P. Kirkbride (ed.), *Human Resource Management in Europe, Routledge*, London.

Brown, R. (ed.) (1997), *The Changing Shape of Work*, Macmillan, London.

Brown, S. (1996), *Strategic Manufacturing for Competitive Advantage*, Prentice Hall International, Hemel Hempstead.

Buchanan, D.A. (2001), *The Lived Experience of Strategic Change: A hospital case study*, Leicester Business School Occasional Paper 64.

Buchanan, D.A. and Boddy, D. (1992), *The Expertise of the Change Agent*, Prentice Hall International, Hemel Hempstead.

Buchanan, D.A. and Badham, R. (1999), *Power, Politics and Organaizational Change: Winning the turf game*, Sage, London.

Burnes, B. (1996), *Managing Change*, Pitman, London.

Burns, J.M. (1978), *Leadership*, Harper & Row, New York.

Burns, T. (1961), 'Micropolitics: mechanisms of organizational change', *Administrative Science Quarterly*, vol. 6, pp.257–81.

Burns, T. and Stalker, G.M. (1961), *The Management of Innovation*, Tavistock, London.

Butt, J. (ed.) (1971), *Robert Owen: Prince of cotton spinners*, David & Charles, Newton Abbott.

Cairncross, F. (1997), *The Death of Distance*, Orion, London.

Campbell, A. (1997), 'Stakeholders: the case in favour', *Long Range Planning*, vol. 30, no. 3, pp.446–9.

Cannon, T. (1994), *Corporate Social Responsibility*, Pitman, London.

Cannon, T., (1996), *Basic Marketing: Principles and practice* (4th edn), Cassell, London.

Carlson, S. (1951), *Executive Behaviour*, Stromberg Aktiebolag, Stockholm.

Carr, A.Z. (1968), 'Is business bluffing ethical?' *Harvard Business Review*, Jan./Feb. pp.143–53.

Catterick, P. (1995), *Business Planning for Housing*, Chartered Institute of Housing, Coventry.

Chaffey, D. (ed.) (1999), *Business Information Systems*, Financial Times Pitman, London.

Champy, J. and Nohria, N. (1996), *Fast Forward*, Harvard Business School Press, Cambridge, MA.

Chandler, A.D. (1962), *Strategy and Structure*, MIT Press, Cambridge, MA.

Cherns, A. (1987), 'The principles of sociotechnical design revisited', *Human Relations*, vol. 40, no. 3, pp.153–62.

Child, J. (1972), 'Organizational structure, environment and performance: the role of strategic choice', *Sociology*, vol. 6, pp.1–22.

Child, J. (1984), *Organisation: A guide to problems and practice* (2nd edn), Harper & Row, London.

Chow, I. (1994), 'An opinion survey of performance appraisal practices in Hong Kong and the People's Republic of China', *Asia Pacific Journal of Human Resources*, vol. 32, pp.62–79.

Chrysalides, G.A.D. and Kale, J.H. (1993), *An Introduction to Business Ethics*, Chapman & Hall, London.

Clutterbuck, D. (1994), *The Power of Empowerment*, Kogan Page, London.

Clutterbuck, D. and Dearlove, D. (1996), *The Charity as a Business*, Directory of Social Change, London.

Coggan, P. (1999), *The Money Machine*, Penguin, London.

Coombs, R. and Hull, R. (1994), 'The best or the worst of both worlds: BPR, cost reduction, and the strategic management of IT', paper presented to the OASIG Seminar on Organizational Change, London, September.

Corfield, R. (1999), *Successful Interview Skills*, Kogan Page, London.

Cravens, D.W. (1991), *Strategic Marketing* (3rd edn), Irwin, Chicago, IL.

Critchley, W. and Casey, D. (1984), 'Second thoughts on team building', *Management Education and Development*, vol. 15, no. 2, pp.163–75.

Crosby, P. (1979), *Quality is Free*, McGraw-Hill, New York.

Cully, M., O'Reilly, A., Millward, N., Woodland, S., Dix, G. and Bryson, A. (1999), *Britain at Work: As depicted by the 1998 Workplace Employee Relations Survey (WERS)*, Routledge, London.

Cusumano, M. (1997), 'How Microsoft makes large teams work like small teams', *Sloan Management Review*, vol. 39, no. 1 (Fall), pp. 9–20.

Cusumano, M.A. and Nobeoka, K. (1988), *Thinking Beyond Lean*, The Free Press, New York.

Daft, R.L. (1999), *Management* (4th edn), The Dryden Press, Forth Worth, TX.

Daniels, J.D. and Radebaugh, L.H. (1998), *International Business* (8th edn), Addison-Wesley, Reading, MA.

Davies, P.W.F. (ed.) (1997), *Current Issues in Business Ethics*, Routledge, London.

Davis, K. (1960), 'Can business afford to ignore social repsonsibilities?' *California Management Review*, vol. 2, no. 3, pp.70–6.

Davis, K. (1971), *Business, Society and Environment: Social power and social response*, McGraw-Hill, New York.

Davis, K. (1975), 'Five propositions for social responsibility', *Business Horizons*, June, pp.19–24.

Deal, T.E. and Kennedy, A.A. (1982), *Corporate Culture: The rites and rituals of corporate life*, Addison-Wesley, Reading, MA.

Deming, W.E. (1988), *Out of the Crisis*, Cambridge University Press, Cambridge.

Dent, C.M. (1997), *The European Economy: The global context*, Routledge, London.

Department of Trade and Industry (1996), *The Rewards of Success: Flexible pay systems in Britain*, DTI, London.

De Wit, B. and Meyer, R. (1998), *Strategy: Process, content and context, an international perspective*, International Thomson Business, London.

Dibb, S., Simkin, L., Pride, W.M. and Ferrell, O.C. (1997), *Marketing: Concepts and strategies* (4th edn), Houghton-Mifflin, New York.

Dicken, P. (1992), *Global Shift: The internationalisation of economic activity*, PCP, London.

Dobson, P. and Starkey, K. (1993), *The Strategic Management Blueprint*, Blackwell, Oxford.

Donaldson, L. (1995), *Contingency Theory*, Dartmouth, Aldershot.

Donaldson, L. (1996), *For Positive Organization Theory*, Sage, London.

Drucker, P. (1981), 'What is business ethics?' *The Public Interest*, Spring, pp. 18–36.

Drucker, P.F. (1985), *Innovation and Entrepreneurship*, Heinemann, London.

Drucker, P.F. (1999), *Innovation and Entrepreneurship* (2nd edn), Butterworth-Heinemann, Oxford.

Drummond, H. (1996), *Escalation in Decision-Making*, Oxford University Press, Oxford.

Drury, C. (2000), *Cost and Management Accounting* (5th edn), Business Press, London.

Dutta, S. and Segev, A. (1999), 'Business transformation on the Internet', *European Management Journal*, vol. 17, no. 5, pp 466–76.

Earl, M.J. (1998), *Information Management: The organizational dimension*. Oxford University Press, Oxford.

Economist Intelligence Unit (1992), *Making Quality Work: Lessons from Europe's leading companies*, Economist Intelligence Unit, London.

Egan, G. (1993), *Adding Value*, Jossey-Bass, San Francisco, CA.

Elliott, B. and Elliott, J. (2001), *Financial Accounting and Reporting* (5th edn), Financial Times Prentice Hall, Harlow.

Emmanuel, L., Otley, D. and Merchant, K. (1991), *Accounting for Management Control*, Chapman & Hall, London.

Engel, J., Kollatt, D. and Blackwell, R. (1978), *Consumer Behaviour*, Dryden Press, Boston, MA.

Ezzamel, M., Lilley, S. and Wilmott, H. (1994), 'The "new organization" and the "new managerial work"', *European Management Journal*, vol. 12, no. 4, pp.454–61.

Fayol, H. (1949), *General and Industrial Management*, Pitman, London.

Feigenbaum, A.V. (1993), *Total Quality Control*, McGraw-Hill, New York.

Fiedler, F.E. and House, R.J. (1994), 'Leadership theory and research: a report of progress', in C.L. Cooper and I.T. Robertson (eds), *Key Reviews of Managerial Psychology*, Wiley, Chichester.

Fletcher, C. (1996), 'Appraisal: an idea whose time has gone?' in J. Billsberry (ed.), *The Effective Manager: Perspectives and illustrations*, Sage, London.

Flores, B.E. and Pearce, S.L. (2000), 'The use of an expert system in the M3-competition', *International Journal of Forecasting*, vol. 16, no. 4, pp. 485–93.

Flynn, N. (1997), *Public Sector Management* (3rd edn), Prentice Hall International, Hemel Hempstead.

Follett, M.P. (1920), *The New State: Group organization, the solution of popular government*, Longmans Green, London.

Fombrun, C., Tichy, N.M. and Devanna, M.A. (1984), *Strategic Human Resource Management*, Wiley, New York.

Ford, H. (1922), *My Life and Work*, Heinemann, London.

Fowler, S.L., Novack, A.M.J. and Stillings, M.J. (2000), 'The evolution of a manufacturing website', *Computer Networks*, vol. 33, pp. 365–76.

Frederick, W.C., Post, J.E. and Davis, K. (1992), *Business and Society*, McGraw-Hill, New York.

French, J. and Raven, B. (1959), 'The bases of social power', in D. Cartwright (ed.), *Studies in Social Power*, Institute for Social Research, Ann Arbor, MI.

Friedman, M. (1970), 'The social responsibility of business is to increase its profits', *New York Times*, 14 September.

Gabrial, Y. (1988), *Working Lives in Catering*, Routledge, London.

Gallagher, M. (1992), *Women and Men in Broadcasting: Prospects for equality*, Commission of the European Communities, Brussels.

German, C. (1995), 'It all comes out in the wash', *The Independent*, 21 January.

Gerwin, D. (1979), 'Relationships between structure and technology at the organizational and job levels', *Journal of Management Studies*, vol. 16, no. 1, pp.70–9.

Ghauri, P.N. and Prasad, S.B. (eds) (1995), *International Management: A reader*, Dryden Press, London.

Ghoshal, S., Gardner, A., Hansen, R., Marchant, L., Ronte, H. and Thambiah, I. (1996), *Lufthansa: The challenge of globalisation*, Case 396-142-1, European Case Clearing House, Cranfield.

Gilbreth, F.B. (1911), *Motion Study*, Van Nostrand, New York.

Gilbreth, L.M. (1914), *The Psychology of Management*, Sturgis & Walton, New York.

Gillespie, R. (1991), *Manufacturing Knowledge: A history of the Hawthorne experiments*, Cambridge University Press, Cambridge.

Glaister, K.W. (1991), 'Virgin Atlantic Airways', in C. Clark-Hill and K. Glaister, *Cases in Strategic Management*, Pitman, London.

Glaister, K. W. and Falshaw, J.R. (1999), 'Strategic planning: still going strong?' *Long Range Planning*, vol. 32, no. 1, pp.107–16.

Glass, N. (1996), 'Chaos, non-linear systems and day-to-day management', *European Management Journal*, vol. 14, no. 1, pp.98–106.

Goffman, E. (1959), *The Presentation of Self in Everyday Life*, Doubleday, New York.

Goldratt, E. and Cox, J. (1989), *The Goal*, Gower, Aldershot.

Goold, M. (1997) 'Institutional advantage: a way into strategic management in not-for-profit organizations', *Long Range Planning*, vol. 30, no. 2, pp.291–3.

Graham, P. (1995), *Mary Parker Follett: Prophet of management*, Harvard Business School Press, Boston, MA.

Greenwood, R.G., Bolton, A.A. and Greenwood, R.A. (1983), 'Hawthorne a half century Later: relay assembly participants remember', *Journal of Management*, vol. 9, Fall/Winter, pp.217–31.

Greer, C.R. (2001), *Strategic Human Resource Management*, Prentice Hall, New Jersey.

Groonroos, C. (2000), *Service Management and Marketing: A customer relationship management approach* (2nd edn), Wiley, Chichester.

Grundy, F. (1996), *Women and Computers*, Intellect Books, Exeter.

Guest, D. E. (1987), 'Human resource management and industrial relations', *Journal of Management Studies*, vol. 24, no. 5, pp.502–21.

Guest, D. (1988), 'Human resource management: a new opportunity for psychologists or another passing fad?' *The Occupational Psychologist*, February.

Guest, D.E. and Conway, N. (2001), *Organisational Change and the Psychological Contract: An analysis of the 1999 CIPD Survey*, Chartered Institute of Personnel and Development, London.

Guirdham, M. (1995), *Interpersonal Skills at Work*, Prentice Hall International, Hemel Hempstead.

Habermas, J. (1972), *Knowledge and Human Interests*, Heinemann, London.

Hackman, J. R. (1990), *Groups that Work (and Those that Don't)*, Jossey-Bass, San Francisco, CA.

Hackman, J.R. and Oldham, G.R. (1980), *Work Redesign*, Addison-Wesley, Reading, MA.

Hage, J. and Aiken, M. (1967), 'Program change and organizational properties: a comparative analysis', *American Journal of Sociology*, vol. 72, pp.503–19.

Hagman, E. (2000), Keynote address to Arthur Anderson European Business and Environment Network Annual Conference, 15 September.

Hales, C. (1993), *Managing through Organization*, Routledge, London.

Hall, W. (1995), *Managing Cultures*, Wiley, Chichester.

Hamel, G. and Prahalad, C.K. (1994), *Competing for the Future*, Harvard Business School Press, Boston, MA.

Handy, C. (1988), *Understanding Voluntary Organizations*, Penguin, Harmondsworth.

Handy, C. (1993), *Understanding Organizations* (4th edn), Penguin, Harmondsworth.

Hargie, O.D.W. (1997), *Handbook of Communication Skills*, Routledge, London.

Harris, N. (1999), *European Business* (2nd edn), Macmillan Business, Basingstoke.

Harris, P.R. and Moran, R. (1991), *Managing Cultural Differences*, Gulf Publishing, Houston, TX.

Hartley, R.F. (1993), *Business Ethics: Violations of the public trust*, Wiley, New York.

Hartley, J., Bennington, J. and Binns, P. (1997), 'Researching the roles of internal change agents in the management of organizational change', *British Journal of Management*, vol. 8, no. 1, pp.61–74.

Harvey, B. (ed.) (1994), *Business Ethics: A European approach*, Prentice Hall International, Hemel Hempstead.

Hayes, N. (1997), *Successful Team Development*, International Thompson Business Press, London.

Heffcutt, A.I. and Arthur, W. (1994), 'Hunter and Hunter (1984) revisited: interview validity for entry-level jobs', *Journal of Applied Psychology*, vol. 79, no. 2, pp.184–90.

Heil, G., Bennis, W. and Stephens, D.C. (2000), *Douglas McGregor, Revisited*, Wiley, New York.

Heller R. (2001), 'Inside Zara', *Forbes Global*, 28 May, pp. 24–5, 28–9.

Hellriegel, D. and Slocum, J.W. (1988), *Management* (5th edn), Addison-Wesley, Reading, MA.

Hellriegel, D., Jackson, S.E. and Slocum, J.W. (2002), *Management: A competency-based approach*, South Western College Publishing, Cincinatti, OH.

Herzberg, F. (1959), *The Motivation to Work*, Wiley, New York.

Herzberg, F. (1987), 'One more time: how do you motivate employees?' *Harvard Business Review*, vol. 65, Sept./Oct.

Hill, C.W.L. and Pickering, J.F. (1986), 'Divisionalization, decentralization and performance of large United Kingdom companies', *Journal of Management Studies*, vol. 23, no. 1, pp.26–50.

Hill, T. (2000), *Operations Management: Strategic context and managerial analysis*, Macmillan, Basingstoke.

Hiltrop, J.M. (1995), 'The changing psychological contract: the human resources challenge of the 1990s', *European Management Journal*, vol. 13, no. 3, pp.288–94.

Hirschheim, R. and Klein, H.K. (1989), 'Four paradigms of information systems development', *Communications of the ACM*, vol. 32, no. 10, pp.1199–214.

Hofstede, G. (1980), *Culture's Consequences: International differences in work-related values*, Sage, Beverley Hills, CA.

Hofstede, G. (1989), 'Organizing for cultural diversity', *European Management Journal*, vol. 7, no. 4, pp.390–7.

Hofstede, G. (1991), *Cultures and Organizations: Software of the mind*, McGraw-Hill, London.

Hogwood, B.W. and Gunn, L.A. (1984), *Policy Analysis for the Real World*, Oxford University Press, Oxford.

Honderich, T. (ed.) (1995), *Ethical Reasoning: The Oxford Companion to Philosophy*, Oxford University Press, Oxford.

Hopfenbeck, W. (1993), *The Green Management Revolution*, Prentice Hall International, Hemel Hempstead.

Horngren, C.T., Foster, G. and Datar, S.M. (2000), *Cost Accounting* (10th edn), Prentice Hall, Upper Saddle River, NJ.

House, R.J. (1996), 'Path–goal theory of leadership: lessons, legacy and a reformulation', *Leadership Quarterly*, vol. 7, pp.323–52.

House, R.J. and Mitchell, T.R. (1974), 'Path–goal theory of leadership', *Contemporary Business*, vol. 3, no. 2, pp.81–98.

Howard, J.A. and Sheth, J.N. (1969), *The Theory of Buyer Behaviour*, Wiley, New York.

Hughes J., Ralf, M. and Michels, B. (2000), *Transform Your Supply Chain: Releasing value in business*, International Thomson, London.

Huselick, M.A. (1995), 'The impact of human resource management practices on turnover, productivity and corporate financial performance', *Academy of Management Journal*, vol. 38, no. 3.

Ichniowski C., Kochan, T.A., Levine, D., Olson, C. and Strauss, G. (1996), 'What works at work: overview and assessment', *Industrial Relations*, vol. 35, no. 3, pp.299–333.

Indvik, J. (1986), 'Path–goal theory of leadership: a meta-analysis', *Proceedings of the American Academy of Management Meeting*, pp.189–92.

IDS (1997), *Pay and Conditions in Call Centres*, Incomes Data Services, London.

Institute of Management (1995a), Report of the Taylor Working Party, Institute of Management, Corby.

Institute of Management (1995b), *Finding the Time: A survey of managers' attitudes to using and managing time*, Institute of Management, London.

IPD (1996), *The IPD Guide on Team Rewards*, Institute for Personnel and Development, London.

IPD (1999), *Organisational development: whose responsibility?* Institute for Personnel and Development, London.

IRS (1994), 'Improving Performance? A survey of appraisal arrangements', *Employment Trends*, 556, pp. 5–14, Industrial Relations Services, London.

IRS (1997), 'The state of selection: an IRS survey', *Employee Development Bulletin*, 51, pp.5–8, Industrial Relations Services, London.

IRS (1999), 'New ways to perform appraisal', *Employment Trends*, 676, pp.7–16, Industrial Relations Services, London.

Jackall, R. (1988), *Moral Mazes: The world of corporate managers*, Oxford University Press, Oxford.

Jackson, T. (1993), *Organizational Behaviour in International Management*, Butterworth/Heinemann, Oxford.

Janis, I.L. (1972), *Victim of Groupthink*, Houghton-Mifflin, Boston, MA.

Janis, I.L. (1977), *Decision Making: A psychological analysis of conflict, choice and commitment*, The Free Press, New York.

Jennings, D. (2000), 'PowerGen: the development of corporate planning in a privatized utility', *Long Range Planning*, vol. 33, pp.201–19.

Jobber, D. (2001), *Principles and Practices of Marketing* (3rd edn), McGraw-Hill, London.

Johnson, G. and Scholes, K. (1997), *Exploring Corporate Strategy* (4th edn), Prentice Hall, Hemel Hempstead.

Johnson, G. and Scholes, K. (1999), *Exploring Corporate Strategy* (5th edn), Prentice Hall, Harlow.

Johnson, G. and Scholes, K. (eds) (2000), *Exploring Public Sector Strategy*, Prentice Hall, Harlow.

Johnston, R.A., Kast, F.E. and Rosenweig, J.E. (eds) (1967), 'People and systems', in *The Theory and Management of Systems*, McGraw-Hill, New York.

Juran, J. (1974), *Quality Control Handbook*, McGraw-Hill, New York.

Kakabadse, A. (1993), 'The success levers for Europe: the Cranfield executive competences survey', *Journal of Management Development*, vol. 12, no. 8, pp.12–17.

Kalakota, R. and Robinson, M. (1999), *E-business: Roadmap for success*, Addison Wesley, Reading, MA.

Kanter, R.M. (1979), 'Power failure in management circuits', *Harvard Business Review*, vol. 57, July/Aug. pp.65–75.

Kanter, R.M. (1983), *The Change Masters*, Unwin, London.

Kaplan, S. (2000), 'E-hubs: The new B2B marketplaces', *Harvard Business Review*, vol. 78, no. 3, pp.97–113.

Katzenbach, J.R. and Smith, D.K. (1993a), 'The discipline of teams', *Harvard Business Review*, Mar./Apr., pp.111–20.

Katzenbach, J.R. and Smith, D.K. (1993b), *The Wisdom of Teams*, Harvard Business School Press, Boston, MA.

Kay, J. (1993), *Foundations for Corporate Success: How business strategies add value*, Oxford University Press, Oxford.

Kay, J. (1996), *The Business of Economics*, Oxford University Press, Oxford.

Keen, P. (1981), 'Information systems and organization change', in E. Rhodes and D. Weild (eds), *Implementing New Technologies*, Blackwell/Open University Press, Oxford.

Kipnis, D., Schmidt, S.M. and Wilkinson, I. (1980), 'Intra-organizational influence tactics: explorations in getting one's way', *Journal of Applied Psychology*, vol. 65, pp.440–52.

Knights, D. and Murray, F. (1994), *Managers Divided: Organizational politics and information technology management*, Wiley, Chichester.

Kochan, T.A. (1992), *Principles for a Post-New Deal Employment Policy*, Sloan School of Management, MIT, Working Paper 5.

Kolb, D., Rubin, E. and Osland, J. (1991), *Organizational Psychology*, Prentice Hall, Englewood Cliffs, NJ.

Kotler, P. (1997), *Marketing Management: Analysis, planning, implementation, and control* (9th edn), Prentice Hall International, Hemel Hempstead.

Kotler, P. and Armstrong, G. (1997), *Marketing: An introduction* (4th edn), Prentice Hall International, Hemel Hempstead.

Kotler, P., Armstrong, G., Saunders, J. and Wong, V. (1996), *Principles of Marketing* (European edn), Prentice Hall International, Hemel Hempstead.

Kotter, J.P. (1982), *The General Managers*, Free Press, New York.

Kotter, J.P. and Heskett, J. (1992), *Corporate Culture and Performance*, Free Press, New York.

Kotter, J.P. and Schlesinger, L.A. (1979), 'Choosing strategies for change', *Harvard Business Review*, March/April.

Krackhardt, D. and Hanson, J.R. (1993), 'Informal networks: the company behind the chart', *Harvard Business Review*, July/Aug., pp.104–11.

Krajewski, L.J. and Ritzman, L.P. (2002), *Operations Management: Strategy and Analysis* (6th edn), Financial Times Prentice Hall, Harlow.

Lancaster, G. and Messingham, L. (1993), *Essentials of Marketing* (2nd edn), McGraw-Hill, New York.

Laudon, K.C. and Laudon, J.P. (2000), *Management Information Systems: Organization and technology in the networked enterprise*, Prentice Hall,Upper Saddle River, NJ.

Laurent, A. (1983), 'The cultural diversity of western conceptions of management', *International Studies of Management and Organization*, vol. 13, nos 1/2, pp.75–96.

Lawler, J.J., Jain, H.C., Ratnam, C.S.V. and Atmiyanandana V. (1995), 'Human resource management in developing economies: a comparison of India and Thailand', *International Journal of Human Resource Management*, vol. 6, no. 2, pp.320–46.

Lawrence, P. and Lorsch, J.W. (1967), *Organization and Environment*, Harvard Business School Press, Boston, MA.

Lawrence, E., Corbitt, B., Fisher, J. Lawrence, J. and Tidwell, A. (2000), *Internet Commerce, Digital Models for Business*, Wiley, Brisbane.

Lawson, P. (2000), 'Performance-related pay', in R. Thorpe, and G. Homan (eds), *Strategic Reward Systems*, Prentice Hall, Harlow.

Leach, S. (1996), *Mission Statements and Strategic Visions: Symbol or substance*, Local Government Management Board, London.

Leavitt, H.J. (1965), 'Applied organizational change in industry: structural, technological and humanistic approaches', in J.G. March (ed.), *Handbook of Organizations*, Rand McNally, Chicago, IL.

Legge, K. (1978), *Power, Innovation and Problem Solving in Personnel Management*, McGraw-Hill, London.

Legge, K. (1995), *Human Resource Management: Rhetorics and realities*, Macmillan, London.

Lengel, R.H. and Daft, R.L. (1988), 'The selection of communication media as an executive skill', *Academy of Management Executive*, vol. 11, no. 3, pp.225–32.

Levene, Y. (2001), 'Few set out on road to ethics', *The Guardian*, 14 April.

Levitt, T. (1958), 'The dangers of social responsibility', *Harvard Business Review*, Sept./Oct., pp.27–36.

Levitt, T. (1960), 'Marketing myopia', *Harvard Business Review*, July/Aug., pp.45–56.

Lewin, K. (1947), 'Frontiers in group dynamics', *Human Relations*, vol. 1, pp.5–41.

Likert, R. (1961), *New Patterns of Management*, McGraw-Hill, New York.

Likert, R. (1967), *The Human Organization: Its management and value*, McGraw-Hill, New York.

Lindblom, C.E. (1959), 'The science of muddling through', *Public Administration Review*, vol. 19, no. 2, pp.79–88.

Lock, D. (1996), *Project Management* (6th edn), Gower, Aldershot.

Lodge, D. (1989), *Nice Work*, Penguin, London.

Lorsch, J.W. (1986), 'Managing culture: the invisible barrier to strategic change', *California Management Review*, vol. 28, no. 2.

Lowe, T.R. (1986), 'Eight ways to ruin a performance review', *Personnel Journal*, January.

Lucas, H.C. (1996), *The T-form Organization: Using technology to design organizations for the 21st century*, Jossey-Bass, San Francisco, CA.

Luthans, F. (1988), 'Successful vs effective real managers', *Academy of Management Executive*, vol. 11, no. 2, pp.127–32.

Mabey, C. and Mayon-White, B. (eds) (1993), *Managing Change* (2nd edn), The Open University/Paul Chapman Publishing, London.

Macbeth, D.K. and Ferguson, N. (1994), *Partnership Sourcing: An integrated supply chain approach*, Financial Times Pitman, London.

Manz, C.C. and Sims, H.P. (1993), *Business Without Bosses: How self-managing teams are building high-performing companies*, Wiley, New York.

Markus, M.L. (1983), 'Power, politics and MIS implementation', *Communications of the ACM*, vol. 26, no. 6, pp.430–44.

Markus, M.L. and Robey, D. (1983), 'The organizational validity of management information systems', *Human Relations*, vol. 36, no. 3, pp.203–26.

Markus, M.L. and Keil, M. (1994), 'If we build it, they will come: designing information systems that people want to use', *Sloan Management Review*, Summer, pp.11–25.

Marshall, J. (1984), *Women Managers: Travellers in a male world*, Wiley, Chichester.

Martin, E.W., Hoffer, J.A., DeHayes, D.W. and Perkins, W.C. (1994), *Managing Information Technology: What managers need to know*, Macmillan, New York.

Martin J. (1992), *Cultures in Three Organizations: Three perspectives*, Oxford University Press, London.

Martinko, M.J. and Gardner, W.L. (1990), 'Structured observation of managerial work: a replication and synthesis', *Journal of Management Studies*, vol. 27, no. 3, pp.329–57.

Maruca, R.F. (1998), 'How do you manage an off-site team?' *Harvard Business Review*, vol. 76, no. 4, pp.22–35.

Maslow, A. (1970), *Motivation and Personality* (2nd edn), Harper & Row, New York.

Mayer, M. and Whittington, R. (1996), 'The survival of the European holding company: institutional choice and contingency', in R. Whitley and P.H. Kristensen (eds), *The Changing European Firm*, Routledge, London.

Mayo, E. (1949), *The Social Problems of an Industrial Civilization*, Routledge and Kegan Paul, London.

McClelland, D. (1961), *The Achieving Society*, Van Nostrand Reinhold, Princeton, NJ.

McGregor, D. (1960), *The Human Side of Enterprise*, McGraw-Hill, New York.

Michaels, E.G. (1982), 'Marketing muscle', *Business Horizons* May/June, pp.63–74.

Middlemist, R.D. and Hitt, M.A. (1988), *Organizational Behavior: Managerial strategies for performance*, West Publishing, St Paul, MN, p.462.

Mill, J. (1994), 'No pain, no gain', *Computing*, 3 February, pp.26–7.

Mintel (1999), *The Green Consumer Report*, Mintel Publications, London.

Mintzberg, H. (1973), *The Nature of Managerial Work*, Harper & Row, New York.

Mintzberg, H. (1979), *The Structuring of Organizations*, Prentice Hall, Englewood Cliffs, NJ.

Mintzberg, H. (1983), 'The case for corporate social responsibility', *Journal of Business Strategy*, vol. 4, no. 2, pp.3–15.

Mintzberg, H. (1989), *Mintzberg on Management*, The Free Press, New York.

Mintzberg, H. (1994a), *The Rise and Fall of Strategic Planning*, Prentice Hall International, Hemel Hempstead.

Mintzberg, H. (1994b), 'Rethinking strategic planning. Part I: Pitfalls and fallacies', *Long Range Planning*, vol. 27, no. 3, pp.12–21.

Monbiot, G. (2000), *The Captive State*, Macmillan, Basingstoke.

Moncrieff, J. and Smallwood, J. (1996), 'Strategic management: ideas for the new millennium', *Financial Times*, 19 July.

Moore, J.I. (2001), *Writers on Strategy and Strategic Management* (2nd edn), Penguin, London.

Morgan, G. (1997), *Images of Organization*, Sage, London.

Morse, J. and Lorsch, J. (1970), 'Beyond Theory Y', *Harvard Business Review*, vol. 48, May/June, pp.61–8.

Moutinho, L. (1995), *Cases in Marketing Management*, Addison-Wesley, Wokingham.

Mumford, E. and Weir, M. (1979), *Computer Systems in Work Design: The Ethics method*, Associated Business Press, London.

Nash, L. (1990), *Good Intentions Aside*, Harvard Business School Press, Boston, MA.

Newell, S. (1999), 'Ebank: a failed knowledge management initiative', in H. Scarbrough and J. Swan (eds) *Case Studies in Knowledge Management*, Institute for Personnel and Development, London.

Noble, F. and Newman, M. (1993), 'Integrated system, autonomous departments: organizational invalidity and stem change in a university', *Journal of Management Studies*, vol. 30, no. 2, pp.195–219.

Nugent, N. and O'Donnell, R. (1994), *The European Business Environment*, Macmillan, Basingstoke.

Oakland, J. (1994), *Total Quality Management*, Butterworth/Heinemann, Oxford.

OECD (1993), *Private Pay for Public Work: Performance related pay for public sector managers*, OECD, Paris.

Ogbonna, E. and Harris, L.C. (1998), 'Organizational culture: it's not what you think', *Journal of General Management*, vol. 23, no. 3, pp.35–48.

Orlicky, J. (1975), *Material Requirements Planning*, McGraw-Hill, New York.

Parker, D. and Stacey, R. (1994), *Chaos, Management and Economics: The implications of non-linear thinking*, Hobart Paper 125, Institute of Economic Affairs, London.

Pascale, R.T. (1984), 'Perspectives on strategy: the real story behind Honda's success', *California Management Review*, vol. 26, part 3, Spring, pp.47–72.

Pascale, R. (1990), *Managing on the Edge*, Penguin, London.

Peppard, J. (2000), 'Customer relationship management in financial services', *European Management Journal*, vol. 18, no. 3, pp.312–27.

Peters, T.J. (1987), *Thriving on Chaos: Handbook for a management revolution*, Alfred A. Knopf, New York.

Peters, T.J. and Waterman, D.H. (1982), *In Search of Excellence*, Harper & Row, London.

Pettigrew, A. (1985), *The Awakening Giant: Continuity and change in Imperial Chemical Industries*, Blackwell, Oxford.

Pettigrew, A. (1987), 'Context and action in the transformation of the firm', *Journal of Management Studies*, vol. 24, no. 6, pp.649–70.

Pfeffer, J. (1992a), *Managing with Power*, Harvard Business School Press, Boston, MA.

Pfeffer, J. (1992b), 'Understanding power in organizations', *California Management Review*, vol. 34, no. 2, pp.29–50.

Pfeffer, J. (1994), *Competitive Advantage Through People*, Harvard Business School Press, Cambridge, MA.

Pinto, J. (1998), 'Understanding the role of politics in successful project management', *International Journal of Project Management*, vol. 18, no. 2, pp.85–91.

Podmore, D. and Spencer, A. (1986), 'Gender in the labour process: the case of women and men lawyers', in D. Knights and H. Willmott (eds), *Gender and the Labour Process*, Gower, Aldershot.

Porter, M.E. (1980a), *Competitive Strategy*, Free Press, New York.

Porter, M. (1980b), *Competitive Advantage*, Free Press, New York.

Porter, M.E. (1985), *Competitive Advantage: Creating and sustaining superior performance*, Free Press, New York.

Porter, M.E. (1990), *The Competitive Advantage of Nations*, Free Press, New York.

Porter, M.E. (1994), 'Competitive strategy revisited: a view from the 1990s', in P. Barker Duffy (ed.), *The Relevance of a Decade*, Harvard Business School Press, Boston, MA.

Pridham, H. (2001), 'Better returns from adopting higher principles', *The Guardian*, 25 January.

Pugh, D.S. (ed.) (1990), *Organisation Theory: Selected readings* (3rd edn), Penguin, Harmondsworth.

Pugh, D.S. and Hickson, D.J. (1976), *Organization Structure in its Context: The Aston Programme I*, Gower, Aldershot.

Purcell (2000), 'Pay per view', *People Management*, 3 February.

Quinn, J.B. (1980), *Strategies for Change: Logical incrementalism*, Irwin, Homewood, IL.

Quinn, R.E., Faerman, S.R., Thompson, M.P. and McGrath, M.R. (1996), *Becoming a Master Manager* (2nd edn), Wiley, New York.

Recardo, R. (1991), 'The what, why and how of change management', *Manufacturing Systems*, May, pp.52–8.

Redman, T. and Wilkinson, A. (2001), *Contemporary Human Resource Management: Texts and cases*, Prentice Hall, Harlow.

Reed, D. (1999), *Call Centres: The next generation*, Informa Retail and Consumer, London.

Reed, D. (2000), *Is e-cruitment Working? A new report on maximising the effectiveness of Internet recruitment*, Reed Executive, London.

Ritzer, G. (1993), *The McDonaldization of Society*, Pine Forge Press, London.

Robbins, S.P. (2000), *Managing Today!* Prentice Hall, Englewood Cliffs, NJ.

Robertson, I. (1996), 'Personnel selection and assessment', in P. Warr (ed.), *Psychology at Work* (4th edn), Penguin, Harmondsworth.

Robin, D.P. and Reidenbach, R.E. (1987), 'Social responsibility, ethics and marketing strategy: closing the gap between concept and application', *Journal of Marketing*, vol. 51, Jan., pp.44–58.

Roddick, A. (1991), *Body and Soul*, Ebury Press, London.

Roddick, A. (2000), *Business as Unusual*, Thorsons, London.

Roethlisberger, F.J. and Dickson, W.J. (1939), *Management and the Worker*, Harvard University Press, Cambridge, MA.

Ross, S.A., Westerfield, R.W. and Jordan, B.D. (2000), *Fundamentals of Corporate Finance* (5th edn), Irwin, Homewood, IL.

Rousseau, D.H. (1995), *Psychological Contracts in Organisation*, Sage, London.

Sandberg, A. (ed.) (1995), *Enriching Production*, Avebury, Aldershot.

SAUS (1993), *Good Business: Cases in corporate social responsibility*, New Consumer/SAUS, Bristol.

Schein, E.H. (1985), *Organizational Culture and Leadership*, Jossey-Bass, San Francisco, CA.

Schonberger, (1983), *Japanese Manufacturing Techniques*, Free Press, New York.

Scottish Executive (2000), 1998-based household projections for Scotland, Statistical Bulletin Housing Series HSG/2000/4.

Shaw, W.H. (1991), *Business Ethics*, Wadsworth, Belmomt, CA.

Simons, R. (1995), 'Control in an age of empowerment', *Harvard Business Review*, Mar./Apr., pp.80–8.

Skinner, B.F. (1971), *Contingencies of Reinforcement*, Appleton-Century-Crofts, East Norwalk, CT.

Skinner, W. (1969), 'Manufacturing: the missing link in corporate strategy', *Harvard Business Review*, May/June.

Smith, A. (1776), *The Wealth of Nations*, ed. with an introduction by Andrew Skinner (1974), Penguin, Harmondsworth.

Smith, N.C. (1990), *Morality and the Market*, Routledge, London.

Smith, P.B. (1992), 'Organizational behaviour and national cultures', *British Journal of Management*, vol. 3, pp.39–51.

Smith, R.J. (1994), *Strategic Management and Planning in the Public Sector*, Longman/Civil Service College, Harlow.

Snape, E., Thompson, D., Ka-ching, Y.F. and Redman, T. (1998), 'Performance Appraisal and culture: practice and attitudes in Hong Kong and Great Britain', *International Journal of Human Resource Management*, vol. 9, no. 5, pp.841–61.

Sonnentag, S. (1994), 'Team leading in software development: a comparison between women and men', in A. Adams, J. Emms, E. Green and J. Owen (eds), *Women, Work and Computerisation* (A-57), Elsevier/North-Holland, Amsterdam.

Soothill, K., Mackay, L. and Webb, C. (eds) (1995), *Interprofessional Relations in Health Care*, Edward Arnold, London.

Sparrow, P. and Hiltrop, J. (1994), *European Human Resource Management in Transition*, Prentice Hall International, Hemel Hempstead.

Spriegel, W.R. and Myers, C.E. (eds) (1953), *The Writings of the Gilbreths*, Irwin, Homewood, IL.

Stacey, R. (1994), *Managing the Unknowable*, Jossey Bass, San Francisco, CA.

Stamp, P. and Robarts, S. (1986), *Positive Action: Changing the Workplace for Women*, National Council for Civil Liberties, London.

Stark, A. (1993), 'What's the matter with the business ethics?' *Harvard Business Review*, May/June, pp.36–48.

Steiger, T. and Reskin, B.F. (1990), 'Baking and baking off: deskilling and the changing sex makeup of bakers', in B.F. Reskin and P.A. Roos (eds), *Job Queues, Gender Queues*, Temple University Press, Philadelphia, PA.

Steinbock, D. (2001), *The Nokia Revolution*, American Management Association, New York, NY.

Stewart, R. (1967), *Managers and their Jobs*, Macmillan, London.

Stogdill, R.M. (1974), *Handbook of Leadership: A survey of the literature*, Free Press, New York.

Stone, C. (1990), 'Why shouldn't corporations be socially responsible?' in W.M. Hoffman, and J.M. Moore (eds), *Business Ethics: Readings and cases in corporate morality*, McGraw-Hill, New York.

Stonham, P. (1996), 'Whatever happened at Barings?' *European Management Journal*, vol. 14, no. 2, pp.167–75 and no. 3, pp.269–78.

Storey, J. (1992), *Developments in the Management of Human Resources*, Blackwell, Oxford.

Storey, J. (ed.) (1995), *Human Resource Management: A critical text*, Routledge, London.

Supply Chain Management Group (1995), *The Supply Chain Improvement Process and the Relationship Positioning Tool*, SCMG Ltd, University of Glasgow, Glasgow.

Suutari, V. (1996), 'Leadership ideologies among European managers: a comparative study in a multinational company', *Scandinavian Journal of Management*, vol. 12, no. 4, pp.389–409.

Tayeb, M.H. (1996), *The Management of a Multicultural Workforce*, Wiley, Chichester.

Taylor, B. (1997), 'The return of strategic planning: once more with feeling', *Long Range Planning*, vol. 30, no. 3, pp.334–44.

Taylor, F.W. (1917), *The Principles of Scientific Management*, Harper, New York.

Taylor, W. (1991), 'The logic of global business: an interview with ABB's Percy Barnevik', *Harvard Business Review*, Mar./Apr., pp.90–105.

Thomas, A.B. (1993), *Controversies in Management*, Routledge, London.

Thompson, J.D. (1967), *Organizations in Action*, McGraw-Hill, New York.

Thompson, P. and McHugh, D. (1995), *Work Organisations: A critical introduction* Macmillan, Basingstoke.

Thurley, K. and Wirdenius, H. (1989), *Towards European Management*, Pitman, London.

Timmers, P. (2000), *Electronic Commerce: Strategies and models for business to business trading*, Wiley, Chichester.

Towers Perrin (1999), *Euro Rewards 2000: Rewards, challenges and changes*, Towers Perrin, London.

Treanor, J. (2001), 'Power to the people in Co-op Bank's ethics poll', *The Guardian*, 17 April.

Trevino, L.K. and Nelson, K.A. (1999), *Managing Business Ethics*, Wiley, Chichester

Trist, E.L. and Bamforth, K.W. (1951), 'Some social and psychological consequences of the Longwall Method of coal getting', *Human Relations*, vol. 4, no. 1, pp.3–38.

Tuckman, B. and Jensen, N. (1977), 'Stages of small group development revisited', *Group and Organizational Studies*, vol. 2, pp.419–27.

Turban, E., McLean, E. and Wetherbe, J. (1999), *Information Technology for Management*, Wiley, Chichester.

Turban, E., Rainer, R.K. and Potter, R.E. (2001), *Introduction to Information Technology*, Wiley, Chichester.

Tyson, S. and Fell, A. (1985), *Evaluating the Personnel Function*, Hutchinson, London.

Uhl-Bien, M. and Graen, G.B. (1998), 'Individual self-management: analysis of professionals' self-managing activities in functional and cross-functional teams', *Academy of Management Journal*, vol. 41, no. 3, pp.340–50.

Vallance, E. (1996), *Business Ethics at Work*, Cambridge University Press, Cambridge.

Vecchio, R.P. (1984), 'Models of psychological inequity', *Organizational Behavior and Human Performance*, vol. 34, pp.266–82.

Venkatraman, N. and Henderson J.C. (1998), 'Real strategies for virtual organising', *Sloan Management Review*, vol. 40, no. 1, pp. 33–47.

Votaw, D. (1973), 'The nature of social responsibility', in D. Votaw and S.P. Sethi (eds), *The Corporate Dilemma:*

Traditional values and contemporary problems, Prentice Hall, Englewood Cliffs, NJ.

Vroom, V.H. (1964), *Work and Motivation*, Wiley, New York.

Vroom, V.H. and Yetton, P.W. (1973), *Leadership and Decision-making*, University of Pittsburgh Press, Pittsburgh, PA.

Walsham, G. (1993), *Interpreting Information Systems in Organisations*, Wiley, Chichester.

Wastell, D.G., White, P. and Kawalek, P. (1994), 'A methodology for business process redesign: experience and issues', *Journal of Strategic Information Systems*, vol. 3, no. 1, pp.23–40.

Watson, T.J. (1994), *In Search of Management*, Routledge, London.

Weber, M. (1947), *The Theory of Social and Economic Organization*, Free Press, Glencoe, IL.

West, M. and Allen, N. (1997), 'Selecting for teamwork', in Anderson, N. and P. Herviot (eds.), *International Handbook of Selection and Assessment*, Wiley, Chichester.

Wheatley, M. (2000), 'Best Factories 2000', *Management Today*, November, pp.109–30.

Whipp, R., Rosenfeld, R. and Pettigrew, A. (1988), 'Understanding strategic change processes: some preliminary British findings'. in A. Pettigrew (ed.), *The Management of Strategic Change*, Blackwell, Oxford.

Whitley, R. (1996), 'The social construction of economic actors', in R. Whitley and P.H. Kristensen (eds), *The Changing European Firm*, Routledge, London.

Wickens, P.D. (1995), *The Ascendant Organisation*, Macmillan, Basingstoke.

Williams, K., Haslam, C. and Williams, J. (1992), 'Ford vs Fordism: the beginnings of mass production?' *Work, Employment and Society*, vol. 6, no. 4, pp.517–55.

Wilson, F. (1995), *Organizational Behaviour and Gender*, McGraw-Hill, London.

Wilson, F. (1996), 'Research note. Organizational theory: blind and deaf to gender?' *Organization Studies*, vol. 17, no. 5, pp.825–42.

Wisniewski, M. (2001) 'Measuring up to the best: a manager's guide to benchmarking', in G. Johnson and K. Scholes (eds.), *Exploring Public Sector Strategy*, Prentice Hall, Harlow.

Womack, J.P. and Jones, D.P. (1996), *Lean Thinking*, Simon & Schuster, New York.

Womack, J.P., Jones, D.P. and Roos, J. (1990), *The Machine that Changed the World*, Macmillan, Basingstoke.

Wood, S. (1999), 'Human resource management and performance', *International Journal of Management Review*, vol. 1, no. 4, pp.367–413.

Woodward, J. (1958), *Management and Technology*, HMSO, London.

Woodward, J. (1965), *Industrial Organization: Theory and practice*, Oxford University Press, Oxford (2nd edn 1980).

Woodward, J. (1980), *Industrial Organization: Theory and practice* (2nd edn), Oxford University Press, Oxford.

Woodward, J. (1997), *Construction Project Management*, Thomas Telford Publications, London.

Yukl, G.A. (1998), *Leadership in Organisations* (4th edn), Prentice Hall, Upper Saddle River, NJ.

Yukl, G. and Falbe, C.M. (1990), 'Influence tactics in upward, downward and lateral influence attempts', *Journal of Applied Psychology*, vol. 75, pp.132–40.

Yukl, G. and Tracey, J.B. (1992), 'Consequences of influence tactics used with subordinates, peers and the boss', *Journal of Applied Psychology*, vol. 77, no. 4, pp.525–35.

Zeithaml, V.A. and Bitner, M.J. (2000), *Services Marketing: Integrating customer focus across the firm*, Irwin/McGraw-Hill, Boston, MA.

Glossary

Administrative management is the use of institutions and order rather than relying on personal qualities to get things done.

Applied ethics is the application of moral philosophy to actual problems, including those in management.

Assessment centres are multi-exercise programmes designed to identify the recruitment and promotion potential of personnel.

Assets are the property, plant and equipment, vehicles, stocks of goods for trading, money owed by customers and cash: in other words, the physical resources of the business.

Authority refers to the rights inherent in a position to give instructions and to expect others to follow those instructions.

Balance sheet shows the financial position of a company at a particular time. It shows the physical resources (assets) of the business and, to match that, the sources from which finance has been raised both from shareholders and from borrowing.

Behaviour models of leadership attempt to identify the behaviours that effective managers use to influence subordinates.

Behaviour modification is a general label for attempts to change behaviour by using appropriate and timely reinforcement.

Benchmarking is a process of comparing organisational performance and practices with others (preferably leaders) in the same or different industries.

Bureaucracy is a system in which people are expected to follow precisely defined rules and procedures rather than to use personal judgement.

The **business process** view puts satisfying customer's requirements at the heart of a design process to develop a supply system that will operate without waste. The orientation is towards speed of response and two-way flow of information and other resources.

The **capital market** comprises all the individuals and institutions that have money to invest, including banks, life assurance companies and pension funds and, as users of capital, business organisations, individuals and governments.

Cash flow statement shows the sources from which cash has been generated and how it has been spent during a period of time.

A **cell layout** creates multiple cells dedicated to producing families of output types.

Centralisation is when a relatively large number of decisions are taken by management at the top of the organisation.

A **channel** is the medium of communication between a sender and a receiver.

Coercive power is the ability to obtain compliance through fear of punishment.

Collectivism pertains to societies in which people, from birth onwards, are integrated into strong, cohesive groups.

Communication is the exchange of ideas, opinions and information through written or spoken words, symbols or actions.

Competence (1) Competence concerns the actions and behaviours identified by change agents as contributing in their experience to the perceived effectiveness of change implementation.
(2) Competences are those behaviours required for satisfactory ('threshold competence') or excellent ('superior competence') performance in a job.

Competitive advantage 'arises from discovering and implementing ways of competing that are unique and distinctive from those of rivals, and that can be sustained over time' (Porter, 1994).

A **competitive environment** is the industry-specific environment comprising the organisation's customers, suppliers and competitors.

Competitive or business strategy 'is concerned with the firm's position relative to its competitors in the markets which it has chosen' (Kay, 1996).

Concentric layout occurs in, for example, shipbuilding where the product is so large that it remains static while labour and materials come to the centre to assemble the ship.

Consumer-centred organisation is focused upon and structured around the identification and satisfaction of the demands of its consumers.

Consumers are individuals, households, organisations, institutions, resellers and governments that purchase the products offered by other organisations.

Content is the specific substantive task that the group is undertaking.

Contingency approaches to organisational structure are those based on the idea that the performance of an organisation depends on having a structure that is appropriate to its environment.

Corporate social responsibility is the awareness, acceptance and management of the implications and effects of all corporate decision making.

Corporate strategy 'is concerned with the firm's choice of business, markets and activities' (Kay, 1996), and thus it defines the overall scope and direction of the business.

Cost expresses in money units the effect of activating or consuming resources. It is an internal control process of the producing organisation and is not visible to outside parties.

Counterimplementation refers to attempts to block change without displaying overt opposition.

Craft production refers to a system in which the craft producers do everything. With or without customer invovlement they design, source materials, make, display, sell, perhaps service and do the accounts.

A **critical perspective** is one which evaluates an institution or practice in terms of its contribution to human autonomy, responsibility, democracy and ecologically sustainable activity.

Critical success factors are those aspects of a strategy that *must* be achieved to successfully meet objectives and, if possible, to secure competitive advantage.

Current assest can be expected to be cash or to be converted to cash within a year.

Data are raw, unanalysed facts, figures and events.

A **database** consists of items of data stored in a way that enables them to be organised and retrieved in many ways.

Decentralisation is when a relatively large number of decisions are taken lower down the organisation in particular operating units.

A **decision support system** is a computer-based system, almost interactive, designed to assist managers in making decisions.

Decoding is the interpretation of a message into a form with meaning.

Delegation occurs when one person gives another the authority to undertake specific activities or decisions.

Delivery relates to the achievement of all promises made by any supplier to a customer.

Demand leadtime is the elapsed time that a customer is prepared to allow between placing an order for a product or service and actually receiving it; in certain situations this time is effectively zero.

Deontology is the application of established general rules or moral laws to a decision.

Determinism is the view that an organisation's structure is determined by its environment.

Differentiation (1) Consists of offering a product or service that is perceived as unique or distinctive on a basis other than price.

(2) The state of segmentation of the organisation into subsystems, each of which tends to develop particular attributes in response to the particular demands posed by its relevant external environment.

Egoism is the practice of evaluating a decision against the criterion of whether it serves a person's self-interest.

Emergent models of change emphasise that in uncertain conditions it is likely that the results of a project will be affected by unknown factors, and that planning has only a limited effect on the outcome.

Encoding is translating information into symbols for communication.

Enlightened self-interest is the practice of acting in a way that is costly or inconvenient at present, but which is believed to be in one's best interest in the long term.

Ethical audits are the practice of systematically reviewing the extent to which an organisation's actions are consistent with its stated ethical intentions.

Ethical consumers are those who take ethical issues into account in deciding what to purchase.

Ethical investors are people who only invest in business that meet specified criteria of ethical behaviour.

Ethical relativism is the principle that ethical judgements cannot be made independently of the culture in which they are made.

Existence needs reflect a person's requirement for material and energy.

Expertise power is evident when a person's knowledge of the topic enables them to influence decisions.

External fit is when there is a close and consistent relationship between an organisation's competitive strategy and its HRM strategy.

An **extranet** is a version of the Internet that is restricted to specified people in specified companies – such as major customers or suppliers.

Factory production broke down the integrated nature of the craftworker's approach and made it possible to increase the supply of goods by dividing tasks into simple and repetitve sequences.

Feedback occurs as the receiver expresses his or her reaction to the sender's message.

Femininity pertains to societies in which social gender roles overlap.

Five forces analysis is a technique for identifying and listing those aspects of the five forces most relevant to the profitability of an organisation at that time.

Fixed assets are the physical properties that the company possesses – such as land, buildings, production equipment and vehicles – and which are likely to have a useful life or more than one year. There may also be intangible assets such as patent rights or copyrights.

Formal structure is the official guidelines, documents or procedures setting out how the organisation's activities are divided and co-ordinated.

Formal team is one that management has deliberately created to perform specific tasks to help meet organisational goals.

Formalisation is the practice of using written or electronic documents to direct and control employees.

Functional managers are responsible for the performance of a common area of technical or professional work.

A **functional layout** groups similar physical processes together and brings materials and/or customers to these areas.

The **general environment** (sometimes known as the macro-environment) includes economic, political, social and technological factors that generally affect all organisations.

General managers are responsible for the performance of a distinct unit of the organisation.

Globalisation is a more advanced form of internationalisation that implies a degree of functional integration between internationally dispersed economic activities.

Groupthink is 'a mode of thinking that people engage in when they are deeply involved in a cohesive in-group, when the members' striving for unanimity overrides their motivation to realistically appraise alternative courses of action' (Janis, 1972).

Growth needs are those which impel people to be creative or to produce an effect on themselves or their environment.

High-context cultures are those in which information is implicit and can only be fully understood by those with shared experiences in the culture.

A **high-performance team** is one that meets all the requirements of a real team, but in addition shows commitment to the personal growth of members and performs beyond expectations.

Horizontal specialisation is the degree to which tasks are divided among separate people or departments.

Human resource management is the effective use of human resources in order to enhance organisational performance.

Hygiene factors (or maintenance factors) are those aspects surrounding the task which can prevent discontent and dissatisfaction but will not in themselves contribute to psychological growth and hence motivation.

Individualism pertains to societies in which the ties between individuals are loose.

Influence is the process by which one party attempts to modify the behaviour of others by mobilising power resources.

An **informal group** is one that emerges when people come together and interact regularly.

Informal structure is the undocumented relationships between members of the organisation that inevitably emerge as people adapt systems to new conditions and satisfy personal and group needs.

Information is useful knowledge derived from data.

An **information system** is a set of people, procedures and resources that collects and transforms data into information and disseminates this information.

Information systems management is the planning, acquisition, development and use of these systems.

Innovation covers incremental and/or step (breakthrough) changes in products and/or processes which change function, form, performance or resource use in an advantageous way.

Institutional advantage 'is when a not-for-profit body performs its tasks more effectively than other comparable organisations' (Goold, 1997).

Integration is the process of achieving unity of effort amongst the various subsystems in the accomplishment of the organisation's task.

International management is the practice of managing business operations in more than one country.

Internal fit is when the various components of the HRM strategy support each other and consistently encourage certain attitudes and behaviour.

Internationalisation is the increasing geographical dispersion of economic activities across national borders.

The **Internet** is a web of hundreds of thousands of computer networks linked together by telephone lines through which data can be carried.

An **inter-organisational system** is a computer system that enables data and information to pass between organisations, such as electronic orders or invoices.

An **intranet** is a version of the Internet that only specified people within an organisation can use.

Inventory consists of materials and part or finished goods that are held in anticipation of need by customers along a chain of supply from raw materials through to final consumption (and recycling?).

Job analysis is the process of determining the characteristics of an area of work according to a prescribed set of dimensions.

A **job enrichment model** represents the idea that managers can change specific job characteristics to promote job satisfaction and so motivate employees.

A **knowledge system** is a system that incorporates the decision-making logic of a human expert.

Leadership is 'the lifting of people's vision to a higher sight, the raising of their performance to a higher standard, the building of their personality beyond its normal limitations' (Drucker, 1985).

Legitimate power flows from the person's formal position, which gives them authority over defined matters.

Liabilities of a business as reported in the balance sheet are the debts and financial obligations of the business to all those people and institutions that are not shareholders, e.g. a bank, suppliers.

Life cycle models of change are those that view change as an activity which follows a logical, orderly sequence of activities that can be planned in advance.

A **limited liability** company has an identity and existence in its own right as distinct from its owners (shareholders in Europe, stockholders in North America). A shareholder has an ownership right in the company in which the shares are held.

Line layout is completely specified by the sequence of activities needed to perform a givem transformation.

Line managers are responsible for the performance of activities that are directly involved in meeting customers' needs.

Low-context cultures are those where people are more psychologically distant so that information needs to be explicit if members are to understand it.

Management is the activity of getting things done with the aid of people and other resources.

Management as a general human activity occurs whenever people take responsibility for an activity and consciously try to shape its progress and outcome.

Management as a specialist occupation develops when activities previously embedded in the work itself become the responsibility not of the employee but of owners or their agents.

A **manager** is someone who gets things done with the aid of other people.

Market segmentation is the process of dividing markets comprising the heterogeneous needs of many consumers into smaller parts or segments comprising the homogeneous needs of smaller groups of consumers.

Marketing is a management process that identifies, anticipates and supplies consumer requirements efficiently and effectively.

The **marketing environment** consists of the actors and forces outside marketing that affect the marketing manager's ability to develop and maintain successful relationships with its target consumers.

A **marketing information system** is the systematic processes and systems for the effective and efficient collection, analysis and distribution of marketing information.

The **marketing mix** is the mix of decisions about product features, prices, communications and distribution of products used by the marketing manager to position products competitively within the minds of consumers.

Marketing orientation is an organisational orientation that believes success is most effectively achieved by satisfying consumer demands.

Masculinity pertains to societies in which social gender roles are clearly distinct.

A **mechanistic organisation** means there is a high degree of task specialisation, people's responsibility and authority are closely defined and decision making is centralised.

The **message** is what the sender communicates.

A **metaphor** is an image used to signify the essential characteristics of a phenomenon.

A **model** represents a complex phenomenon by identifying the major elements and relationships.

A **monitoring system** is a computer-based system that processes data to provide information about the performance of a business process.

Motivating factors are those aspects of the work itself that Herzberg found influenced people to superior performance and effort.

Motivation refers to the forces either within or external to a person that arouse enthusiasm and commitment to pursue a certain course of action.

Noise is anything that confuses, diminishes or interferes with communication.

Non-linear systems are those in which small changes are amplified through many interactions with other variables so that the eventual effect is unpredictable.

Observing is the activity of concentrating on how a team works rather than taking part in the activity itself.

An **open system** is one that interacts with its environment.

Operational research attempts to solve complex problems by developing mathematical models to analyse the many variables.

Operational strategies are those deployed by the different functions of the organisation, such as manufacturing, marketing, finance and human resource management, and which contribute to the achievement of corporate strategy.

An **operational system** is a computer application that processes transactions in an orderly and efficient way to provide a desired output.

An **order qualifier** is a necessary but not sufficient requirement to be considered by a customer.

An **order winner** is some feature or combination of features of the product or service that positively differentiates it from thoses of competitors and make customers want to buy it in preference to those others.

An **organic organisation** is one where people are expected to work together and to use their initiative to solve problems; job descriptions and rules are few and imprecise.

Organisation consists of people trying to influence others to achieve certain objectives that create wealth or well-being through a variety of processes, technologies, structures and cultures.

An **organisation chart** shows the main departments and senior positions in an organisation and the reporting relations between them.

Organisation culture is the collection of relatively uniform and enduring values, beliefs, customs and practices that are uniquely shared by an organisation's members and which are transmitted from one generation of employees to the next.

Organisation structure 'The structure of an organisation [is] the sum total of the ways in which it divides its labour into distinct tasks and then achieves co-ordination among them' (Mintzberg, 1989).

An **organisational capability** is an activity that an organisation can perform better than its competitors.

An **organisational system** is a computer system that enables data and information to pass between units of an organisation.

Outer context of change relates to environmental factors, such as competitor behaviour, customer demands or other factors in the external environment.

Participative models of change are those that recommend change managers to consult widely and deeply with those affected and to secure their willing consent to the changes proposed.

Partnering describes a business relationship based on taking a long-term view that the partners wish to work together according to a mutually acceptable vision in ways which enhance all customers' satisfaction. The partners also seek to develop the relationship so that each will benefit in recognised business performance areas.

Perception is the active psychological process in which stimuli are selected and organised into meaningful patterns.

Performance appraisal is a systematic review of a person's work and achievements over a recent period, usually leading to plans for the future.

Performance-related pay refers to payment systems in which a percentage of pay depends on the assessed performance of individuals, groups or the organisation as a whole.

Person culture is one in which activity is strongly influenced by the wishes of the individuals who are part of the organisation.

PEST analysis is a technique for identifying and listing the political-legal, economic, socio-cultural and technological factors in the general environment most relevant to an organisation at that time.

Philanthropy is the practice of contributing personal wealth to charitable or similar causes.

Political behaviour is 'the practical domain of power in action, worked out through the use of techniques of influence and other (more or less extreme) tactics' (Buchanan and Badham, 1999).

Political models of change emphasise that change is likely to affect the interests of stakeholders unevenly and that those who see themselves losing will resist the change despite the rationality of the arguments or invitations to participate.

Power concerns 'the capacity of individuals to exert their will over others' (Buchanan and Badham, 1999).

A **power culture** is one in which people's activities are strongly influenced by a dominant central figure.

Power distance is the extent to which the less powerful members of organisations within a country expect and accept that power is distributed unevenly.

Preferred team roles are the types of behaviour that people display relatively frequently when they are part of a team.

A **process** is the way people interact with each other in performing a task, such as how they make decisions.

Product is a generic term used to identify both tangible goods and intangible services.

The **product life cycle** suggests that products pass through the stages of introduction, growth, maturity and decline.

A **project manager** is someone who is responsible for managing a project, usually intended to implement a change in some aspects of organisational working.

Product position is the position in which consumers place a product relative to that of an alternative supplier.

Profit and loss statement reflects the benefits derived from the trading activities of the business during a period of time.

A **pseudo-team** is a collection of individuals who could perform more effectively but have shown no interest in developing the necessary skills and methods.

A **psychological contract** is the set of understandings people have regarding the commitments made between themselves and their organisation.

The **quality** of a product or service is the (often imprecise) perception of a customer that what has been provided is at least what was expected for the price he or she paid.

A **receiver** is the person whose senses perceive the sender's message.

Referent power (or charismatic power) arises when subordinates want to identify with the leader, on account of some personal characteristics of the leader.

Relatedness needs involve a desire for relationships with significant other people.

Relationship marketing is an approach that focuses on developing a series of transactions with consumers.

Responsibility refers to a person attempting to meet the expectations others have of them.

Reward power is the ability of someone to reward another through possessing resources the other values.

A **role** is the sum of the expectations that other people have of a person occupying a position.

Role culture is one in which people's activities are strongly influenced by clear and detailed job descriptions and other formal signals as to what is expected of them.

Scenario planning is an attempt to build plausible views of a small number of different possible futures for an organisation operating in conditions of high uncertainty.

Scientific management The school of management called 'scientific' attempted to create a science of factory production.

Selection tests are formal, often psychologically based methods of assessing candidates' likely suitability for a job.

Shareholders are the principal risk takers in a company. They contribute the long-term capital for which they expect to be rewarded in the form of dividends – a distribution from the profit of the business.

Shareholders' funds are the capital contributed by the shareholders plus profits that have not been distributed to the shareholders.

Situational models of leadership attempt to identify the contextual factors that affect when one style will be more effective than another.

Skill refers to a person's ability to perform various types of cognitive or behavioural activity effectively.

The **social contract** consists of the mutual obligations that society and business recognise they have to each other.

A **sociotechnical approach** is a systems development strategy that attempts to improve simultaneously the performance of the organisation and the quality of the working life of the workers.

A **sociotechnical system** is one in which outcomes depend on the interaction of both the technical and social subsystems.

A **span of control** is the number of subordinates reporting directly to the person above them in the hierarchy.

Staff managers are responsible for the performance of functions that provide support to line managers.

Stakeholder mapping is a means of identifying the expectations and power of different stakeholders.

Stakeholders are individuals, groups or other organisations with an interest in what the organisation does.

A **strategic business unit** consists of a number of closely related products for which costs are not shared with other businesses and for which it is meaningful to formulate a separate strategy.

Strategic management is an organisation-wide task involving both the development and implementation of strategy. It demands the ability to steer the organisation as a whole through strategic change under conditions of complexity and uncertainty.

Strategy is concerned with deciding what business an organisation should be in, where it wants to be, and how it is going to get there.

Structural choice approaches emphasise the scope management has for deciding the form of structure, irrespective of external conditions.

Structure is the regularity in the way a unit or group is organised, such as the roles that are specified.

Subjective probability (in expectancy theory) is a person's estimate of the likelihood that a certain level of effort (E) will produce a level of performance (P) which will then lead to an expected outcome (O).

Subsystems are the separate but related parts that make up the total system.

Succession planning is the use of a deliberate process to ensure that staff are developed who are able to replace senior management as required.

Supply leadtime is the total elapsed time between the decision to obtain the basic input resources to the final delivery of the product or service to the customer.

A **SWOT analysis** is a way of summarising the organisation's main strengths and weaknesses relative to the significant opportunities and threats in the external environment.

A **system** is a set of interrelated parts designed to achieve a purpose.

A **system boundary** separates the system from its environment.

A **system of supportive relationships** refers to the interactions and experiences that build a person's sense of personal worth.

The **systems approach** looks at the different parts of an interacting set of activities as a whole and considers the best way for the whole to function.

A **target market** is the segment of the market selected by the organisation as the focus of its activities.

A **task culture** is one in which the focus of activity is towards completing a task or project using whatever means are appropriate.

A **team** is 'a small number of people with complementary skills who are committed to a common purpose, performance goals, and approach for which they hold themselves mutually accountable' (Katzenbach and Smith, 1993b).

Team-based rewards are 'payments or non-financial incentives provided to members of a formally established team and linked to the performance of the group' (IPD, 1996).

Teleology is the practice of evaluating a decision against the criterion of whether the outcome achieves the original goal.

Traits are a variety of individual attributes, including aspects of personality, temperament, needs, motives and values.

Transactional marketing is an approach that focuses upon one-off exchanges with consumers.

Transformational leaders raise the consciousness of followers by appealing to higher ideals and moral values.

Uncertainty avoidance is the extent to which members of a culture feel threatened by uncertain or unknown situations.

Utilitarianism is the practice of evaluating a decision against the criterion of its consequences for the majority of people.

Validity occurs when there is a statistically significant relationship between a predictor (such as a selection test score) and subsequent measures of on-the-job performance.

Value is added to resources when they are transformed into goods or services that are worth more than their original cost plus the cost of transformation.

A **value chain** 'divides a firm into the discrete activities it performs in designing, producing, marketing and distributing its product. It is the basic tool for diagnosing competitive advantage and finding ways to enhance it' (Porter, 1985).

A **value for money service** is one that is provided economically, efficiently and effectively.

Vertical specialisation refers to the extent to which responsibilities at different levels are defined.

Virtual organisations are those that deliver goods and services but have few, if any, of the physical features of conventional businesses.

A **working group** is a collection of individuals who work mainly on their own but interact socially and share information and best practices.

Index

Entries in **bold** are defined in the Glossary.